D1222895

Ray Bradbury

Ray Bradbury

The Life of Fiction

Jonathan R. Eller

William F. Touponce

THE KENT STATE UNIVERSITY PRESS

KENT & LONDON

© 2004 by The Kent State University Press, Kent, Ohio 44242

ALL RIGHTS RESERVED

Library of Congress Catalog Card Number 2003021206

ISBN 0–87338-779-1

Manufactured in the United States of America

08   07   06   05   04   5   4   3   2   1

Library of Congress Cataloging-in-Publication Data

Eller, Jonathan R., 1952–

Ray Bradbury : the life of fiction / Jonathan R. Eller, William F. Touponce.

p. cm.

ISBN 0-87338-779-1 (alk. paper)

1. Bradbury, Ray, 1920– 2. Science fiction, American—History and criticism.

3. Authors, American—20th century—Biography. 4. Science fiction—Authorship.

I. Touponce, William F. II. Title.

PS3503.R167Z66 2004

813'.54—dc22

2003021206

British Library Cataloging-in-Publication data are available.

To Donn Albright
Who showed us
This attic where the meadow greens.

To Marguerite McClure Bradbury
In Memoriam

I mean come *on*, all you smartass literary cynics who make points off other men's careers, can you ever *really* forget that thing that called to the foghorn from the sea? Can you really forget Uncle Einar? Can you put out of your mind all the black folk leaving for Mars, years before the black folk started telling you they wanted out? Can you forget Parkhill in "—And the Moon Be Still as Bright" doing target practice in one of the dead Martian cities, "shooting out the crystal windows and blowing the tops off the fragile towers"? There aren't many guys in our game who've given us so many treasurable memories.

    —Harlan Ellison, *Again, Dangerous Visions*

It's the same in all the arts: as technology advances, humor declines. The limits and definitions of art disappear, then the art is forced to satirize itself too earnestly, and the visual arts become literary, and that, my friends, is the very first sign of cultural degeneracy.

    —James Crumley, *The Last Good Kiss*

I have suggested how for Shakespeare any derangement of social classes seems always to imply a derangement of the senses in madness or dream, some elaborate joke about the nature of reality. This great joke is the matter of the book which we acknowledge as the ancestor of the modern novel, *Don Quixote*; and indeed no great novel exists which does not have the joke at its very heart.

    —Lionel Trilling, "Art and Fortune"

And even when the long twilight and the weariness of death come, you will not set in our sky, you advocate of life. New stars you have let us see, and new wonders of the night; verily, laughter itself you have spread over us like a colorful tent. Henceforth, children's laughter will well forth from all coffins; henceforth a strong wind will come triumphantly to all weariness of death: of this you yourself are our surety and soothsayer.

    —Nietzsche, *Thus Spoke Zarathustra*

It was the mask engaged your mind,
And after set your heart to beat,
Not what's behind.

    —W. B. Yeats, "The Mask"

Contents

Foreword: Ray, Ray, and Ray

WILLIAM F. NOLAN

Ray Bradbury's fiction exploded into my life in the mid-1940s, when I was a Missouri teenager in Kansas City. Reading "The Jar" in *Weird Tales* was a stunning experience. Who *was* this guy? What had I been missing? I began buying a copy of each new publication that carried a Bradbury story and was soon prowling used-magazine shops (they had them in those days) for any back issues containing his byline. No one else wrote like Ray Bradbury. He was unique.

Moving to California, I met Ray in the summer of 1950, shortly after publication of *The Martian Chronicles.* We soon became friends. He encouraged me to pursue a writing career and, in a wonderfully uplifting letter from Ireland, he solved the story ending of what became my first professional sale in 1954.

Among the seventy-plus books of mine, three of them deal with Bradbury: *Ray Bradbury Review, The Ray Bradbury Companion,* and *The Bradbury Chronicles.* In addition to these, over the past half century I have written a sizable number of shorter items about Ray (profiles, articles, introductions, reviews, bibliographies, and story headings). At last count the total had reached sixty-five (some thirty-eight of which are listed in the appendix to this book).

Have I exhausted my subject? Not at all. Why? Because there are so *many* Bradburys to write about.

There is Bradbury the poet (who saw his first piece of verse in print at age fifteen), Bradbury the artist and painter (who has executed the dust jackets for several of his books), Bradbury the designer (providing creative input on projects from Disneyland to Epcot), Bradbury the playwright (with new dramas staged each year), Bradbury the public speaker (with lectures delivered to public audiences, libraries, business groups, universities, and high schools across the nation), Bradbury the film and television scriptwriter (with a multitude of credits from

Moby Dick to the *Ray Bradbury Theater*), Bradbury the critic (with multimedia book reviews), and Bradbury the essayist (with pertinent messages for the space age).

This book celebrates Bradbury the "fictioneer"—the creative powerhouse whose massive output of stories has inspired literally thousands of other writers over the past six decades. I think it is safe to say that no other modern author, with the possible exception of Ernest Hemingway, has exerted a wider literary influence.

As clear proof of his presence in the field of education over the past half century, more than one hundred of his stories have been selected for a multitude of school textbooks. The most-often reprinted titles include "There Will Come Soft Rains" and "All Summer in a Day," each of which has achieved over seventy textbook appearances since the mid-1950s.

In the pages that follow, Jonathan Eller and William Touponce trace, dissect, analyze, and list all of Bradbury's fiction, from short stories to full-length novels. The effort involved in this remarkable undertaking boggles the mind.

Late in 1973 I completed *The Ray Bradbury Companion* (published in 1975), containing what was up to then the most comprehensive printed record of Ray's work extant. I listed his poems, essays, articles, reviews, published speeches, stage works, radio/television/film projects, and printed letters—and, of course, his stories and novels. My total for his fictional works by late 1973 ran to just under 300. More than 100 others have been printed in the decades since. They are all fully catalogued here by Eller and Touponce—some 400 published stories and another 230-plus titles of (as yet) unprinted works.

My friend, Donn Albright (to whom this book is rightfully dedicated)—that indefatigable Bradbury bibliographer whose stunning, all-inclusive collection of works by and about Ray runs into the many thousands—has carefully sifted through every Bradbury file drawer containing Ray's typed manuscripts. In the course of his Herculean task, Donn has uncovered a truly impressive number of early tales from the 1940s and 1950s that Bradbury never mailed to his agent. ("I didn't want to crowd the market back then," he stated, "so I just put away a lot of stories once I'd finished them. Then Donn, God bless him, dug them all out, one by one, and I had my children back!")

As a result, Bradbury's recent collections (*Quicker Than the Eye, Driving Blind,* and *One More for the Road*) contain a mix of old and new stories, many of them "rescued" by Albright from Ray's buried file folders. Thus far, more than thirty of these early Albright-discovered tales have been printed in Bradbury collections, with many more to come.

Fiction is never created out of a vacuum. All professional writers have read, admired, and been influenced by a host of others. The influences on Bradbury's fiction can be classified into several groups.

First—during his earliest years—he was inspired by Charles Dickens, Edgar Allan Poe, H. G. Wells, Jules Verne, L. Frank Baum, and Edgar Rice Burroughs.

Then—as he moved from amateur to professional—he became deeply involved in the world of science fiction, writing fan letters to *Astounding, Thrilling Wonder Stories, Fantastic Adventures,* and *Amazing Stories.* During this science fiction period, he was aided and encouraged by several then-current genre writers: Leigh Brackett, Edmond Hamilton, Henry Kuttner, Jack Williamson, and Robert A. Heinlein. (And Ray has also acknowledged the strong influence of Theodore Sturgeon.)

When he began selling his science fiction, he quit reading in the genre, turning to such mainstream literary masters as Hemingway, John Steinbeck, Thomas Wolfe, F. Scott Fitzgerald, Franz Kafka, Shirley Jackson, John Collier, Jessamyn West, and John Cheever. Along the way he was introduced to the crime novels of Dashiell Hammett, Raymond Chandler, and Ross Macdonald.

During the 1950s—when he was hired to write the script for *Moby Dick*—he became a disciple of Herman Melville, William Shakespeare, and George Bernard Shaw. In recent years—as a playwright—Bradbury's stage works strongly reflect these classic influences.

I have mentioned only his major sources of inspiration, but there were others who shaped Bradbury's thinking—essayists (such as Loren Eiseley) as well as a host of philosophers and poets. In fact, decades ago, Ray all but abandoned the reading of fiction in favor of verse, plays, and essays.

In tracing the progression of Bradbury's work, we can discern the influence of all these writers. In his stories and poems, Ray has paid open tribute to several of them: Nathaniel Hawthorne, Hemingway, Wolfe, Verne, Dickens, Poe, Melville, Shaw, Fitzgerald, and Emily Dickinson.

This study lists eighty-seven Bradbury books and pamphlets (novels, collections, single-story volumes, and such) containing fiction in which Ray's stories are cycled and recycled. The reader is guided through the complex creative history of each fictional work. Drawing from hitherto unavailable correspondence, the authors trace the often-lengthy interaction between Bradbury and his agents, editors, friends, and publishers in shaping the stories and novels from manuscript to printed text.

These pages provide detailed textual and thematic analysis for all of Ray's major fictional works. If—in this writer's opinion—the criticism is tipped too heavily in favor of a Nietzschean interpretation (Bradbury claims never to have read Nietzsche), Eller and Touponce have every right to interpret Bradbury's work as they see it. Their judgment is obviously based on an in-depth reading of the Bradbury canon, and their critical conclusions are of unquestioned value. Without doubt, future scholars will be compelled to take into full account the groundbreaking analysis revealed in this carefully considered study.

The book is in no way a Bradbury biography, yet many biographical facts emerge via the history of Ray's work, echoing the book's title, *The Life of Fiction*.

Of particular interest and value, the authors include a detailed examination of two unfinished Bradbury novels, *The Masks* and *Summer Morning, Summer Night*. The former supports their ongoing "carnivalization" theory—that all of Bradbury's work fall into the category of "masks, myths, and metaphors" and are rooted in the carnival aspects of life. They show us that the carnival has formed—both literally and symbolically—the centerpiece of Bradbury's work. Citing the bold theatricality of Ray's fiction, and using *The Masks* as their starting point, Eller and Touponce expand this theory with each succeeding chapter.

The notion of carnivalization is itself well founded in the history of Bradbury criticism, of which I have made several surveys. Bradbury himself acknowledged this source for his work when he declared that "the carnival . . . along with magicians and magic . . . has shaped much of my thinking and my existence." *The Masks*, as the authors of this study tell us, "is infused with carnival ideas and concepts."

In Ray Bradbury's world, what he terms "the intolerable truths of life" must be masked in order for us to confront them. ("The dramatic play of masking/unmasking is at the heart of Bradbury's major fiction.") One mask, when removed, uncovers another and—with that one removed—reveals yet another in Bradbury's metaphorical prose.

In the case of *Summer Morning, Summer Night* (initially projected as a sequel to *Dandelion Wine*), Eller and Touponce explore the author's intention to dramatize a war between youth and age in which the passage of time itself is seen as a deadly adversary.

Of course, Ray's fictional children ultimately discover that time cannot be stopped and that their battle is hopeless. In truth, Ray himself never wanted to grow up, and this unfinished novel is testimony to the fact that the child in Bradbury is enemy to the man.

The Life of Fiction is enhanced by an impressive variety of graphic charts, tables, and manuscript pages that supplement and clarify the main text. The appendixes alone—an amazing job of research and compilation—are worth the price of the book. In them, all of Bradbury's over four hundred fictional items are listed, showing their progression through first printings, reprints, anthology and textbook appearances, and media adaptations (radio, films, television, and stage).

A full decade of painstaking effort is represented in the pages that follow. This book will take you on a compelling journey through Bradbury Country.

It is a trip you will never forget.

Preface and Acknowledgments

The Life of Fiction represents the first attempt to bring textual criticism to bear in an in-depth study of Ray Bradbury's authorship. In terms of their textuality, Bradbury's books usually have something to hide, especially with regards to the early origins of many of his stories. Often too they mask many stages of revision. Bradbury's authorship—where the warp and woof of his works is always stories in process—seriously needs such a study. Indeed, his authorship has been intimately involved with the play of textuality throughout his career. In his own mind his stories often live on in different intertextual and thematic relationships than those established when they were first published or collected. Behind the woven pattern of his published books there is much documentary evidence indicating the fluidity of his authorship and themes over the years. Books can also hide what comes after the first edition, and this can be just as misleading in Bradbury's case, where multiple versions of *The Martian Chronicles* remain in print, and where multiple versions of his most important stories slip into successive story collections. It is essential to clarify these textual processes and reveal the pattern of his work in ways not seen before. When we compare variations as they appear across successive publications of his stories and books, hidden pathways begin to appear, and we can discern the fundamental process of creativity that is Bradbury's focus as a writer. The first goal of this book is to make these textual pathways visible to Bradbury's readers.

Our second goal is to illuminate another kind of textual transformation: Bradbury's movement from the margins to the mainstream of American literary culture. Textual analysis illuminates this path as well, for the decisions he makes about texts reveal much about his developing vision of himself as a writer. Bradbury's numerous intertextual references both to popular culture—in such forms as carnivals, circuses, and magic shows—and literary culture (Shakespeare, among a host of others) have profoundly influenced his growing sense of himself as a "serious" author. Indeed, he claims that no author has written more tributes to other literary authors than himself. Bradbury's intertextuality is rich and manifold, drawing on and transforming texts from both areas of culture. The global processes at work in his writings are surveyed in the introduction. We believe we have found a textual and cultural process—"carnivalization"—to be at the heart of Bradbury's authorship. This examination invokes current cultural interpretations of genre (Mikhail Bakhtin) and of authorship and influence (Freudian-based critiques) to explore Bradbury's involved use of genre writing in each succeeding chapter. We argue that Bradbury has "carnivalized" genres in ways that are uniquely personal to him.

Mainstream literary criticism has tended to situate the fantasy genre (which in our view includes science fiction) at the margins of literary creativity, but in his aesthetic Bradbury insists that fantasy is central to our cultural health. This is indeed the "argument" at the heart of his fiction. As Bradbury tells us, fantasy is that intangible source of unconscious fears and desires that fuels our dreams, our phobias, and therefore our creativity as manifested in fictions. He insists that we must not forget the persistent presence of fantasy in our lives nor be misled by specifically formal groupings of his works that situate him merely as a writer of fantasy, horror, and science fiction (that is, merely an entertainer, a writer of "nonserious" fiction). Bradbury heartily embraces the role of entertainer in his authorship, but we aim to show also how his multifarious use of carnivalization helped him deal with his fears, create unique fictions of his own, and in the process unmask the high seriousness of official culture, becoming a famous "author" while remaining suspicious of—or indeed hostile to—the notion of "Author" as a category of high culture outside the play of the textuality. We hope thereby to raise the discussion of Bradbury's writings to a new level of understanding and significance.

As an author of fantasy, Bradbury insists that without fictions life would become unbearable, a conviction he shares with the late romantics and the philosopher Friedrich Nietzsche. But by a process of cultural osmosis that we will explore in depth in later chapters, psychoanalysis in the early twentieth century took over the very themes of the fantastic. In evolving as a science fiction–fantasy writer in midcentury, Bradbury could hardly avoid such themes. Indeed, in nearly all of his major fiction, we can discern a struggle with psychoanalytic culture as a kind of "internalized Gothic" and a carnivalization of that culture. We wish to stress that we are not writing a psychobiography of Bradbury (though this book lays much of the groundwork for such a reading). For the most part we have chosen not to explore how Bradbury's writings reveal the unconscious depths of his life but to show how Bradbury *lived by his fictions* and to relate his creations to a certain set of cultural thematics operative in American popular and literary culture during his formative years (the 1940s and 1950s) yet still active in his novels and short fiction of the 1980s and 1990s.

After an introduction exploring the origins of Bradbury's authorship, *The Life of Fiction* explores in six extensive chapters how Bradbury's carnivalization of genres evolves in his major novels and short-story cycles as he transforms original stories and story groups into book-length fiction and as he continues to reshape and repackage these books through successive editions—often bringing what was once "marginal" into the mainstream of literary success. In each of the six chapters devoted to a major work or series of works, we seek to explore every version of a text, not just the one found in book form. Such in-depth analyses seek to define an adventure in authorship, telling in detail how Bradbury overcame his limitations as a short-story writer and engaged major narrative forms such as the novel. The chapters are organized so that Bradbury's authorship is first introduced in terms of publishing history; much of the complex history of his relationships with publishers and editors is presented here for the first time. The chapter then goes on to study his authorship from within the narrative world in terms of authorial position with regards to characters, ideas and themes, and readers. The category of text used in these analyses tends, of course, to undermine a distinction that has long divided studies of authorship: that of the separation between extrinsic and intrinsic meanings. We seek to investigate the text as a "methodological field" in which many voices interact. We do not assume that the author is the sole producer of literary meaning, but nonetheless we seek to show how Bradbury has reinvented himself at each stage of his career, strengthening and deepening his "final" authority to control the meaning of his authorship.

From the beginning of his career, Bradbury's publishers and agents pressured him to produce novels (that is, to engage with major form). But this proved very hard for him to do. As a young writer he especially feared committing himself to the labor and time of producing a novel, which might in the end prove to be of no great significance. He felt that his creativity expressed itself best in the short-story form, which was relatively easier and quicker for him to create spontaneously and to revise later. He felt that if he worked hard enough on the short story, he would eventually achieve a reputation. As a result Bradbury today is one of the world's most anthologized authors and is primarily thought of as a short-story writer with a characteristic "poetic" style.[1] When we examine Bradbury's unpublished work, however, we find that the field of his texts is strewn with plans for unfinished novels (*The Masks, Where Ignorant Armies Clash by Night,* and *Summer Morning, Summer Night* being those we discuss in detail, but see Appendix B for a complete list of titles). In the background he was always struggling with major form and with important ideas that were "in the culture," that is, Freudianism, nihilism, and the crisis of values. This background in novelistic projects is something we are pleased to document here. Readers of this study will understand how much hidden history and effort Bradbury intended to mask by calling such works as *The Martian Chronicles* and *Dandelion Wine* "accidental" novels.

We have not attempted to provide in-depth analyses of each book by Bradbury, however. Such a lengthy task would quickly become unwieldy and in the end is really quite unnecessary to our focus here. Although each book by Bradbury is its own model and has its own intrinsic interest, we believe that we have uncovered in six chapters the most important and common textual processes and themes involved in all of his fiction, processes and themes that are still operating in his most recent fiction. We have investigated fully only those works that exhibit carnivalization on every level of the text (character, plot, themes, style, implied author and implied reader, and such). Each reader has favorite stories by Bradbury, and some of ours are not even discussed. Chapter 7 does, however, investigate Bradbury's fantasy and science-fiction story collections, which are carnivalized to varying degrees. A final chapter surveys his other novelistic projects in terms of metaphors, myths, and masks. We conclude in this chapter that Bradbury writes from a carnival sense of life that is visible to varying degrees in all of his fiction.

Bradbury's stories constantly evolve, often intricately, into radio plays, stage plays, teleplays, and even (in the hands of other artists) into graphic or comic adaptations. A story may grow into a novella or novel. Two separate stories may later merge into one, or a single story may be split into two distinct chapters of a novel. Groups of stories may become a unified collection or may be bridged into novel form. Novels may become stage plays, teleplays, screenplays, musicals, and even opera. The story-by-story appendix to this book provides a master chronology of all of Bradbury's published stories. Reprintings in magazines, in Bradbury's own story collections and novels, and in anthologies are documented here as well as adaptations of his stories for radio, television, stage, film, and graphic (comic) presentation.

Although it proceeds chronologically through his major writings, this study assumes a certain amount of familiarity with Bradbury's life and career. We do not reproduce basic information—beyond what is pragmatically necessary—because it is readily available in introductory studies of Bradbury (some of which are mentioned in our secondary bibliography) and has long been widely distributed in reference volumes. We have endeavored to read Bradbury in a new and different way than has previously been attempted, suggesting that his real achievement lies in his creative struggle with major forms such as the novel and the short-story cycle. Unpublished manuscripts, correspondence, and interviews cited throughout the book shed new light on the publishing history of the stories and pave the way to a better understanding of Bradbury's approach to his craft. We have also included facsimiles from manuscript pages, which dramatize the ongoing textual process of authorship. We hope thereby to involve our readers in this fascinating life of fiction.

Finally, the title of our book—*Ray Bradbury: The Life of Fiction*—is intended to be read in a double sense. As we have mentioned, it is Bradbury's firm belief as a writer that life without fictions is unbearable. We believe that his writings have much to tell us about the need for the fantastic in culture, and this book is to a large extent an investigation into the ways in which such writings affirm the life of the author. But there is an equally important sense in which we mean the phrase "the life of fiction" to be taken—the complicated and fascinating life of Bradbury's texts themselves, much of it previously hidden from view. Therefore, we have not written a conventional "life in fiction" work about Bradbury, seeking to relate his works to his private life, but instead have undertaken the more difficult and, we think, significant task of discovering the ways in which textual criticism and textual thematics can combine to illuminate the major writings of one of America's most popular authors.

In a very real sense, this book is the product of hundreds of conversations we have had about Bradbury over the past decade in a variety of circumstances, both electronic (in its final stages the book was mounted on a university server) and face-to-face. Before we ever wrote a line about Bradbury, we had talked about him many times, appreciating our different yet complementary approaches to his work. "Wouldn't it be an exciting challenge," we thought, "to combine our efforts in a study of Bradbury's career?" Soon we began to focus on the notion of authorship as central to our concerns. A storyline emerged of how Bradbury's works defined that terrain as both popular and literary, and we began to see it in great detail. The book that you have before you reflects our conversational approach to understanding Bradbury's authorship in the presentation of each of its chapters. Before we began writing, our general practice was to discuss thoroughly what the chapter would reveal about Bradbury's authorship from our different perspectives and then to comment on each other's discoveries.

But in the actual writing of the book, we had different responsibilities. A division of labor had to be put in place in order to produce such a large volume, for the book that we were originally contemplating quickly became much larger and more complex than anything either of us had written before. In general, Jonathan Eller wrote the textual histories that open each chapter, and William Touponce wrote the thematic sections, revising, reconceptualizing, and greatly expanding his 1989 guide to Bradbury. He also wrote the introduction and the conclusion. Eller was responsible for all of the appendix backmatter documenting Bradbury's published and unpublished fiction, for chapter 7 on the story collections, the many charts and graphs that grace our study, and the global editing of the manuscript. The basic structure underlying "Bradbury's Fiction Year by Year" developed from Eller's 1992 *Bulletin of Bibliography* finding list; research for his 1995 source study of *The Martian Chronicles* provided a point of departure for the textual narrative of chapter 2. Passages from Eller's 2001 introduction to the limited edition of *Dark Carnival* were revised and included in chapter 1. But by far the greatest part of *The Life of Fiction* provides a fresh look at Bradbury's authorship based on new critical connections and studies of Bradbury's largely unevaluated manuscripts and correspondence.

A study of this kind owes a great deal to those who have made these unpublished materials available to us, and our greatest debt is owed to Ray Bradbury himself. His thoughtful and encouraging correspondence with both authors spans the better part of two decades, and his willingness to reflect on his life of fiction through long hours of taped interviews from 1998 through 2002 provided key insights into his aesthetic and biographical milestones. Bradbury also allowed us to document his life of fiction through close study of his manuscripts and letters, and his kind permission to cite and quote from these materials (in his possession and in various archives) provided the narrative backbone for the textual sections of this book. We are also grateful to those writers, editors, and friends close to Bradbury who provided detailed interviews, including fellow writer William F. Nolan. Professor Donn Albright, the legendary science fiction editor and collector Forrest J. Ackerman, and Bradbury's longtime editors at Knopf, Nancy Nicholas and Managing Editor Kathy Hourigan. We are also grateful to Elizabeth Albright and Jason Marchi for their work in recording some of the primary interviews with Ray Bradbury as indicated in the bibliography to this volume.

A significant portion of the manuscripts examined in the preparation of this book are located in archives across the country. We are grateful to the late Professor Emeritus Willis McNelly of California State University, Fullerton, for his decades of work in Bradbury studies and his indispensable help in arranging proxy access to the early manuscripts of "The Fireman" and *Fahrenheit 451;* we are also grateful to Sharon Perry, university archivist and special collections librarian at California State Fullerton's Pollak Library, and Kathy Morris, for providing access and research copies of these manuscripts. Onsite examination of Bradbury's papers in the UCLA Research Library, which includes Bradbury's typesetting copy of *The Martian Chronicles* and *A Medicine for Melancholy*, was only possible through the able assistance of Special Collections Research Librarians Charlotte Brown and Cindy Newsome. We are also grateful to the UCLA

Special Collections Department for allowing access to Bradbury's unpublished Oral History Program interview. An equal debt of gratitude is owed to Research Librarian Tara Wenger of the Harry Ransom Humanities Research Center, University of Texas, Austin, for coordinating proxy access to the Bradbury holdings of the Alfred A. Knopf publisher's deposit, and to our own colleague at Indiana University, Dr. Albert C. Lewis, for acting as proxy researcher onsite at Austin.

Access to many important letters from Ray Bradbury to Doubleday editor Walter Bradbury and to editor-critic Anthony Boucher (William Anthony White) was granted by the Lilly Rare Book and Manuscript Library, Indiana University, Bloomington. We are grateful to Curator of Manuscripts Saundra Taylor for providing permissions and to Francis Lapka for coordinating research copies from these collections. Joel Silver, curator of books, has gone the extra mile to provide access to the Lilly's excellent collection of Bradbury first editions. We are grateful to Bradbury's agent of more than half a century, Don Congdon, for permission to cite and quote from his letters and for permission to access his agency deposits at Columbia University. Jason Marchi of McGraw-Hill-Dushkin, who has done yeoman service recording Eller and Albright interviews with Bradbury in 2001 and 2002, has also surveyed the Columbia University holdings of Bradbury correspondence in the Don Congdon Associates and Harold Matson Agency deposits of the Butler Library on our behalf. Delays in gaining access to the Butler Library deposits limited our results, but we are grateful for the assistance of Columbia librarian Bernard Crystal during the last stages of research. Randy Kryn, one of the early activists for the preservation of Bradbury's hometown records in Waukegan, Illinois, contributed material from his own work with the Waukegan Initiative and provided our first look at the Bradbury letters located in the August Derleth Papers of the Wisconsin Historical Society. We also acknowledge the help of archives reference assistant Alexis Ernst-Treutel and Kimberly O'Brien, who served as our proxy researcher in the Wisconsin archives.

Special thanks are due to Michael Scott and William Stuckey of Indiana University's Integrated Technology Support Staff, who designed and maintained dedicated computer-server space for this project; their expertise and advice made it possible for us to write and revise this book in the absence of any other support from our university. We have also benefited from access to "October's Friend," the unpublished finding list for the Donn Albright Collection prepared by Albright and Jim Welsh. Selective readings by Randy Kryn and Bob O'Malley provided important feedback during the later stages of revision, and a full reading of the first complete draft by William F. Nolan was of great help as we made the final structural adjustments to the critical and textual narratives. Nolan's close association with Bradbury's career has been invaluable to us, and we are truly honored by his support through a decade of interviews and advice that has now culminated in his foreword to this volume. We are also honored to have the support of the late Marguerite Bradbury, who graciously contributed advice and interviews that provided a uniquely personal perspective on her husband's career. Alexandra Bradbury's encouragement, as well as her tireless work with her father's manuscripts and correspondence, has made our own work much easier. Over the years Patrick Kachurka has coordinated complicated transportation and interview schedules with great skill, and we are grateful for the personal and professional support he provides the Bradbury family. And we would like to thank our own families for encouraging us through a decade of individual and collaborative scholarship.

The magnitude of this project is reflected in the wide range of individuals who have provided support along the way, but one person has been indispensable at every stage of work. As individual scholars, our various Bradbury projects always led to Donn Albright—and often through the advice of Bradbury himself. Donn has provided a clear path through the complex creative tapestry of Bradbury's published and unpublished work in all media, and we were able to build on his years of research as we began the search for patterns of authorship in Bradbury's fiction. His unmatched collection of Bradbury publications has provided a single point of research that most scholars can only dream of finding, and his close involvement with the writer's later career is only matched by his acquired knowledge of Bradbury's entire creative life. We have had the great benefit of his wide-angle view of popular American culture and Bradbury's place in it. *The Life of Fiction* is dedicated to Donn Albright, for it could not have been written without his guidance and support.

Metaphors, Myths, and Masks

Origins of Authorship in the Texts of Ray Bradbury

We must be entertainers—carnival people, circus people, playwrights, poets, tellers of tales in the streets of Baghdad, we're all of the same family that exists throughout history to explain ourselves to one another.
—Ray Bradbury

When Bradbury's *Something Wicked This Way Comes* was released as a film in 1983, science fiction editor Judy Del Rey suggested to an interviewer, perhaps facetiously, that defining science fiction could be achieved by simply saying three names, Isaac Asimov, Robert A. Heinlein, and Arthur C. Clarke: "One could almost add Bradbury. The four of them established touchstones for those who are to come."[1] Defining science fiction by invoking the category of influential authors is a refreshing, if naive, proposition, and one that has a certain amount of charm when one considers the abundance of mutually conflicting interpretations of the genre. By evoking the "author function," Judy Del Rey neatly sidestepped the whole issue of genre. But her gesture of hesitation about Bradbury being one of the founding fathers of American science fiction is symptomatic of Bradbury's decentered status in the world of publishing. One could *almost*—the qualifier is strategically placed—add Ray Bradbury in this canonical list of authors, the four of them then serving to establish in the Golden Age of American science fiction (the 1940s and 1950s) all the thematic touchstones for writers who were to come. Del Rey's hesitation is due to a well-known circumstance of Bradbury's writings. Unlike Asimov, Heinlein, or Clarke, his literary reputation has transcended the narrow world of science fiction. Early in his career, in fact, he came to represent to the popular imagination what was best (that is, literary) about the genre. In the 1960s Orville Prescott called him "the uncrowned king of science-fiction writers." As late as 1988 the covers of his Bantam paperback reprints still proclaimed the epithet, "The World's Greatest Living Science Fiction Writer."

The question of Bradbury's contested relationship to the science fiction field is something addressed in detail in later chapters. Actually, it is our view that Bradbury is primarily a fantasist, a mythmaker, and a writer of moral fables. We situate science fiction broadly within the field of fantastic literature. But we can state here unequivocally that if Bradbury ever personally thought of himself as the king of science fiction, which seems doubtful, he would certainly have been willing to be dethroned. Everything that he has ever said about his involvement in the field indicates that he never saw his relationship to fellow authors as hierarchical in the least. Although in his career he acquired a certain authority, Bradbury was not telling anyone else how to write. When he left the field behind, however, other writers were not happy to see him represent their field to outsiders, and some bitterness about his popularity and his role as a spokesman for science fiction ensued as time went on and the field developed new concerns (see the discussion of *The Stories of Ray Bradbury* in chap. 7).

In academic discourses about science fiction, Bradbury has not fared much better. Although often recognized as a pivotal writer in the acceptance of the genre by the mainstream, usually he is given a marginal position in the field, far from the center of the science fiction galaxy, and praised for his elegiac little planet of poetic reverie but not for much else.[2] *Science Fiction Studies,* the most aggressively theoretical journal in the field, has never published a major article on Bradbury. Usually, he is mentioned as a point of comparison with other "real" science fiction writers who are perceived as having the right stuff. Systematic genre criticism, when it discusses Bradbury at all, tends to drum him solemnly out of the science fiction corps for alleged inconsistencies of thought. From their point of view, Bradbury is the source of error, the one who goes wrong in the use of scientific and rationalistic science fiction conventions. For these thinkers it is either their system, with its unified and exclusive reason, or nothing, non-meaning. The scandal is, of course, that each theorist's system contradicts the other's, and as a result the field of genre study has (as yet) no general agreement about the definition of science fiction or of fantasy. It does not seem to have occurred to anyone that there might be dimensions of meaning in Bradbury that are not systematic but that nonetheless manifest a high degree of coherence. It is never considered that a genre such as science fiction might manifest an *open* structure of dialogue, or that an author could embrace a plurality of points of view and voices in interaction, or that he himself could be a whole solar system of different planets.[3]

In terms of his early authorship, this is how Bradbury defined the genre: "Over and above everything the writer in this field has a sense of being confronted by dozens of paths that move among the thousand mirrors of a carnival maze, seeing his society imaged and re-imaged and distorted by the light thrown back at him."[4] In this study, drawing on theoretical insights about the nature of genre as a dialogic interaction of voices, we argue that Bradbury sees his relationship to science fiction—and other genres a well—as a process of carnivalization. We hope thereby to raise the discussion of Bradbury's relationship to genre to a new level of understanding. The process of carnivalization by its very nature does not set up hierarchies and lasting canons of literature in a field of literary endeavor. On the contrary, it tends to undermine outworn conventions, introduce novelty, and thereby renew the field. Bradbury reminds us that a genre is a realm of possibilities, a potential with "dozens of paths" that move among thousands of mirrors. For Bradbury, science fiction could never be a closed monologic system of thought. For him, science fiction was the apotheosis of continuous change and intellectual freedom.

Of course the influence of carnival on Bradbury was a commonplace of the criticism about him from the very beginning of his career. For instance, in studying Bradbury's themes, Henry Kuttner pointed out that in Bradbury's stories there is always "the equivalent of a carnival" or a "carnival concept" operating in them. To strengthen his assertion, Kuttner deliberately picked a then-recent science fiction story to analyze instead of a fantasy or a horror story ("A Little Journey," *Galaxy*, August 1951). From our perspective, he was very astute in pointing out the ambivalence of carnival themes in Bradbury, as have been other critics who have linked carnival to the author's thematics.[5] But instead of "carnival concept," we prefer the term "carnivalization." First coined by the Russian critic Mikhail Bakhtin to designate the transposition of carnival images and themes into literature, the term has gained currency in contemporary literary and cultural studies.[6] Beyond this simple definition, Bakhtin saw carnival as a form of life and carnivalization as a dialogic process of literary meaning deeply implicated in the ideological clashes of its day. We believe that this is how Bradbury conceives of it too. Quite apart from generic concerns, Bradbury's works manifest a preoccupation with desire and the unconscious (Freud) as well as the modern crisis of values (Nietzsche) and provide critiques—through carnivalization—of those notions.

We believe that our attempt to study carnivalization as the central focus of Bradbury's fiction is well founded in the history of Bradbury criticism, but we hope to take this important cultural and literary process far beyond the point of previous criticism, which has tended to be impressionistic and limited. What we seek to provide is a broad historical and cultural context of carnival in which to study his major fiction. We should mention at the outset, however, that carnival in this study is not narrowly confined, as it has been in most previous Bradbury criticism, just to narratives that overtly represent the world of carnival. Indeed, some realist-based stories such as "The Last Circus" (1980) may not manifest carnivalization to any great degree at all, while others that do not take place in a carnival setting may manifest intensive explorations of its ability to unsettle preconceived notions about what it is possible to do in a genre. The carnivalization of literature was a complex historical process, as the carnival itself was, and developed over centuries. Beyond the brief definition given above, we will not explore at present how many aspects of carnival—that period of festivity and merriment undermining authority that first got its name in the Middle Ages—were transposed into literature, by what means, or to what effect. We should also mention, though, that at the very least it involved various "reduced" forms of carnival laughter, including parody, jokes, satire, hyperbole, and masks of authorship such as the clown, the rogue, and the fool, as well as the celebration of the grotesque body.

Historically, the central act of carnival was the ritual crowning-decrowning of the carnival king (see the discussion of the narrative poem "Christ, Old Student in a New School," given as a brief example of carnivalization, below). But this ritual act, the one most often transposed into literature according to Bakhtin, has symbolic dimensions beyond that of the literal: "Carnival celebrates the shift itself [crowning-decrowning], the very process of replaceability, and not the precise item that is replaced. Carnival is, so to speak, functional and not substantive. It absolutizes nothing, but rather proclaims the joyful relativity of everything." This statement neatly suggests carnival's ambivalent relationship to fixed ideas: it subjects them to a process of destruction and rebirth when they become too serious or one sided. It is interesting to note that Bakhtin uses almost the same metaphor as Bradbury to describe the function of literary carnival perspectives of parody and decrowning: "it was like an entire system of crooked mirrors, elongating, diminishing, distorting in various directions and to various degrees."[7] Suffice it to say that Bradbury carnivalizes each genre in which he writes, the specifics of which are contained in each of the following chapters. (In the first chapter, for instance, we discuss Bradbury's own reflections on his carnival themes both during and after he produced his first book, *Dark Carnival*.) As this study progresses, the reader can expect the definition of carnivalization to broaden and deepen considerably to include such notions as the relationship between author and hero and author and genre.

Although we are suspicious of authorial rhetoric claiming uniqueness—many others, fellow authors, friends, publishers, and editors, have affected the meaning and shape of Bradbury's authorship, to say nothing of the thematic history of the genres in which he chose to write—we do agree with Bradbury (and certain of his critics) about the importance of understanding carnival as perhaps *the* central and unique aspect of his authorship throughout his career. Indeed, our position is that the creative processes behind Bradbury's books can be most productively understood in the ramifying context of his developing career, as best we can reconstruct it, by examining this fascinating process of the carnivalization of genres.[8] It is the very life of fiction to which the title refers. That is why the following discussion proceeds from that of textual criticism (including Bradbury's relations with his publishers and editors) to that of the "finalized" thematics of a published book. Authorship and thematics are thus two sides of the same coin.

Perhaps at this point a brief discussion is necessary too of how we intend the word "thematics" to function in this study. Although the importance of themes for literary study and interpretation is generally recognized, no one has produced a total theory of how themes operate in a literary work. Indeed, theorists acknowledge that literary thematics touches upon the most complex and murkiest problem of all literary theory: how to speak about what literature speaks about. But the Russian formalists, in particular Boris Tomashevsky, who coined the word "thematics," made the useful distinction that theme has at least two functions: to create interest and arouse sympathy in the reader and to lend the work coherence. Tzvetan Todorov, who produced the first systematic study of the themes of the fantastic, warns us that there are two symmetrical dangers involved in the study of themes. The first is the tendency to reduce literature to pure content; one could study themes, but they would no longer have anything literary about them. The second, converse danger would reduce literature to pure "form," denying the pertinence of themes for literary analysis.[9]

We hope to avoid the dangers of both these extremes. We hold that a literary work does signify on all of its many levels, from the sentence to the larger narrative and its system of motifs. Theme in this study indicates the meeting place of the semantic levels of a literary work with formal structuring qualities such as prose rhythm, style, and narrative. It is the semantic dimensions of a work (what is being said in a piece) dispersed by and through its formal elements, including those involving intertextual relationships with other works (that is, allusion, citation, and others). Our analyses distinguish several varieties and levels of thematics in dialogue with each other and with these formal elements, moving outward from the personal to society and culture at large and to the general interest of the theme, which is determined by the historical conditions prevailing when the work appeared (and in some instances reappeared) in the context of contemporary cultural thought. Textual thematics—our main concern—lies between these two levels and indicates the study of themes as they are transformed by the authorial processes of revision and reshaping that characterizes most of Bradbury's output as a writer of fiction.

Beyond outlining the meaning of such terms as carnivalization and thematics, the main purpose of this introduction is to explore Bradbury's notion of authorship. (We will have more to say about the role of various cultural "gatekeepers"—publishers and editors—in Bradbury's career.) In doing so, one must study the Bradburyan process of authorship under the broad rubrics of metaphor, myth, and mask. Each helps us organize the many processes, both textual and thematic, involved in carnivalization and key them specifically to Bradbury's concerns as an author. They are, in fact, derived from Bradbury's own usages in various essays, prefaces, and stories and not from Bakhtin's or Tomashevsky's theories. For that reason, although they certainly have a history beyond Bradbury as critical terms, they do not constitute for us a "metalanguage" in which we could hope to master all of the meanings at play in his texts. By using them we do not stand "outside" Bradbury's texts. Nonetheless, they are key terms that help us unlock those meanings. In what follows we have assumed that these terms can be understood as having generally much the same meaning in all phases of Bradbury's career, though his textual use of what metaphor, myth, and mask designate in his writings clearly broadened and became increasingly complex as his career developed.

We will deal first with statements Bradbury has made about the role of metaphor in his own creative life before going on to discuss his pronouncements about the cultural value of myth (or fantasy in general). Metaphor has many functions in his texts, but its primary aesthetic function is to establish a sense of intimacy with otherness. Shared with the reader, metaphor represents a kind of privileged glimpse into the workings of Bradbury's imagination. Myth is, of course, a narrative category. Bradbury's myths are life-affirming fictions and represent the shaping of metaphors into a coherent story. Sometimes the myths he uses already belong to the general context of society shaped by American history (for example, the frontier myth in *The Martian Chronicles*) or to religion, as do the myths of Christ and Apollo, which Bradbury combines in his own unique way in a long cantata poem included in one of his fiction collections ("Christus Apollo," *I Sing the Body Electric!*).

A study of Bradbury's poetry can provide important insights into his process of mythmaking and masking. Bradbury regularly includes poetry in his reflections on the nature of authorship and writing (especially in *Zen and the Art of Writing*), and he has included poems in his story collections. Harlan Ellison, one of the field's leading writers and anthologists, thought Bradbury's poetry "dangerous" enough to include in one of his *Dangerous Visions* anthologies ("Christ, Old Student in a New School"). Therefore, we will briefly assess what the poems tell us about Bradbury's deliberate fashioning of an authorial myth. Mask is the dimension of character and personality in the creative process, and here too Bradbury's poetry can be revealing. His late-romantic view of identity is evident in his understanding of how a literary self must be fashioned out of a dialogue between "Self" and imagined "Other." We discuss metaphor, myth, and mask in the context of both published and unpublished writings. All three terms help us understand Bradbury's style, his distinctive voice, but mask is the most important to him as the central theme of carnival and thus receives the most attention.

It is also important to note that metaphor, myth, and mask are not intended to be taken as terms exclusive of one another; indeed, they inhabit somewhat overlapping semantic territories in our analyses and are kept in constant dialogue. The fact is that, in the fluid symbolic field of Bradbury's texts investigated here, a metaphor can transform into a mask and vice versa. This fluidity of terms reflects the ongoing or open quality of Bradbury's texts, his carnivalization of genres, and we do not want them to become a rigid system.

Metaphor

Broadly speaking, Bradbury regards his fictions as (largely unconscious) interpretations of his life. Metaphor is the primary process constituting these interpretations. We know, however, that there is some authorial history to the notion of metaphor in his writings. Even as a child, Bradbury regarded the world as full of magical objects that allowed for transfers of meaning: "Lord, I didn't even know what a metaphor was. But, hell, I collected 'em anyway.... Metaphors, symbols, bright objects for jackdaws like me to seize and make nests of."[10] He found metaphors everywhere in popular culture, especially in radio, film, and comic strips, later in more-mainstream American Gothic–romantic writers such as Edgar Allan Poe, Nathaniel Hawthorne, and Herman Melville. Eventually, he came to extend metaphor to embrace the hyperbolic process of carnivalization, piling one upon another in such works as *Something Wicked This Way Comes*, the detective novels, and *From the Dust Returned*. Bradbury's publishers and editors through the 1950s generally wanted him to cut back on this rampant overgrowth of metaphor in his texts, but by the time he began to write *Something Wicked*, he had both the stature and an editor who acceded to and indeed encouraged such excesses as essential to the Bradbury style.

At age eighteen, Bradbury was strongly influenced by Dorothea Brande's *Becoming a Writer* (1934), which emphasizes the unconscious as "the great home of form" and stresses the importance of feeding the unconscious mind with art works it loves. In seeking to become a writer himself, Bradbury adopted many practices from this book so that he could allow his unconscious mind to express itself freely without the curbing restrictions of the intellect. It was Brande who brought to Bradbury's attention the process of writing down early morning daydreams, where the writer transforms "inactive reverie" into "written reverie," and of the importance of recovering the child's "innocence of eye" in establishing oneself as an original artist. Brande's view of the unconscious was unquestionably romantic (and Freudian: the young writer is constantly being given advice on how to outwit the id and make it work for him), believing as she did that every writer's unconscious may be found to have "a type-story of its own." (We have indicated elsewhere how Bradbury's stories are governed by the types of literary reverie.)[11]

Bradbury tells us that in his early twenties he floundered into a word-association process that helped him find topics to write about each morning: "I would then take up arms against the word, or for it, and bring an assortment of characters to weigh the word and show me its meaning in my own life." In this manner he composed his well-known story "The Veldt" (*The Illustrated Man*) by suspending a whole fantasy from the word "playroom." For Bradbury, it seems that loved objects in the unconscious are never lost but are always already interpretations, or "metaphors within metaphors within metaphors," part of a mobile and constantly transforming "inner theater": "In the years since [my childhood,] I have learned to watch those metaphors drift in my subconscious in the relaxed hour before dawn, instructing me for my day's occupations. In that early morning theater, trapped between my ears, the old images of hunchback, phantom, dinosaur, world's fairs, red planets, and apemen perambulate as they wish. I do not own them. They control and bid me jump to run and trap them with my typewriter before they sleep."[12]

For Bradbury, the unconscious must be approached with the "wise passiveness" of William Wordsworth or the Zen Buddhists. But although the sense of the theatricality of the unconscious is strong in his work, his conception of it is not, evidently, the Freudian theater of the return of the repressed. For Bradbury, the unconscious is not so much the place of repression or castration, or lack, but of *flows* of desire. The writer's conscious sense of self-identity comes much later in the process of desiring: "At last he [the writer] will begin to see himself. At night the very phosphorescence of his insides will throw shadows long on the wall. At last the surge, the agreeable blending of work, not thinking and relaxation will be like the blood in one's body, flowing because it has to flow, moving because it must move, from the heart."[13]

Bradbury goes on in this same essay to define plot as "human desire let run." In short, he trusts his unconscious implicitly as the source of his creative endeavors. He suggests that the young writer absorb as many influences as possible into the unconscious until the mind "explodes" in an overflow of affect. It is not surprising then that Bradbury—whose major fictional efforts involve struggles with Freud, psychoanalysis, and strong "pessimist" fathers such as Schopenhauer and "dread" Nietzsche[14]—needed to find the strength to overcome such dark thinkers. He found it in the "joyful wisdom" of the doctrine of art as a mask, a lie necessary for life, but especially in the philosophy of life represented by carnival.

One further thing, then, to be aware of at the outset is the matter of how Bradbury's themes are bound to metaphoric means of expression, that is, style. His works have often been called richly lyrical or romantic. Christopher Isherwood, in reviewing *The Martian Chronicles*'s debut as *The Silver Locusts* in England, referred to Bradbury as a "poet-philosopher." A review of *The Golden Apples of the Sun* earned him the dubious accolade of "Poet of the Pulps." We ourselves, following Bradbury's lead, have stressed the crucial role of metaphor in his thematics. But these are oversimplifications. Actually, Bradbury's prose alternates, even on the basic level of description, between two stylistic poles, which for the sake of indicating the most significant influences on his writing, we will identify with Ernest Hemingway and Thomas Wolfe.[15] Two passages from *The Martian Chronicles* are good examples. Both have as an underlying theme the encounter with the strange Martian landscape and the threat it represents to the memories and lives of the Earthmen who come to colonize the planet. The first passage is taken from late in the book, when the invasion has more or less been called back by the outbreak of atomic war on Earth. One man remains alone on the deserted planet: "Whenever the wind came through the sky, he and his small family would sit in the stone hut and warm their hands over a wood fire. The wind would stir the canal waters and almost blow the stars out of the sky, but Mr. Hathaway would sit contented and talk to his wife, and his wife would reply, and he would speak to his two daughters and his son about the old days on Earth, and they would all answer neatly."[16]

As in Hemingway, there is a mistrust of abstractions. The voice of the chronicler tries to eschew metaphor for a kind of naive truth-telling economy and understatement. Furthermore, the themes of this discourse, which condenses time repeatedly spent in waiting out the yearly Martian dust storms, are themselves elementally simple: earth, air, fire, and water. The themes are linked together as contiguities with the connective "and." Except for one bit of fantastic exaggeration about the force of the wind on this alien planet, the voice seems to be reporting the bare truth, moving from detail to detail and from cause to effect. It approaches realistic verisimilitude. We are not asked explicitly to interpret the situation by converting it into a total metaphor. But in the conversation of Hathaway and his "family" (we later find out that they are robots built by him), there is a subtle contrast set up between the present situation on Mars and the old days on Earth. Meaning is just barely shifted in the direction of a search for equivalences between the two planets, with the wind bringing the threat of forgetfulness, so that we can subliminally feel that the landscape is somehow symbolic.

The second passage is from a bridge chapter in the approximate center of the book, with the theme of the invasion in full swing: "The rockets set the bony meadows afire, turned rock to lava, turned wood to charcoal, transmitted water to steam, made sand and silica into green glass which lay like shattered mirrors reflecting the invasion, all about. The rockets came like drums, beating in the night. The rockets came like locusts, swarming and settling in blooms of rosy smoke. And from the rockets ran men with hammers in their hands to beat the strange world into a shape that was familiar to the eye, to bludgeon away all the strangeness, their mouths fringed with nails so they resembled steel-toothed carnivores."[17]

The thematic elements (and above all, fire) are present again but transformed and metamorphosed by the carnivalizing activity of the rockets, which leave behind mirrors that reflect or even parody the invasion. That they are later shattered may serve to indicate the relative nature of our knowledge about the invasion and the many points of view or interpretations we must necessarily have of it, unlike the "naive" stance of the chronicler in the first passage. Once again the topics of discourse are few: the rockets, the landscape, and the men. But the syntax relating these topics is more complicated, especially in the last sentence (of which we have only reproduced half). Furthermore, there is a submerged biblical analogy with the mention of the locusts (or perhaps it is more likely that Bradbury wants us to think of the experience of the Mormons in Utah). We are, then, encouraged to interpret the invasion metaphorically according to a submerged analogy with one of the religious groups that settled the American West, except that the values are inverted. *We* are bringing the locusts to Mars. As in some passages of Thomas Wolfe, the voice is lyrically rhapsodic, but not without a touch of the comic in referring to the men as "steel-toothed carnivores." In contrast to the previous passage, where all the items are drawn from the same general context or environment, here we have things that do not belong to the landscape at all (locusts, carnivores). Meaning is generated primarily by resemblance or similarity, though, of course, we have the presence of cause and effect in the action of the rockets as well.

In any one passage of Bradbury's writings, either the metaphoric pole or the metonymic pole (the pole of contiguities, to use the term of the linguist Roman Jacobson) will dominate and determine how the reader assembles the meaning of the text, though the communication of meaning is, of course, impossible without the cooperation of both poles.[18] In the larger context of a novel or a short story, it is the alternation between these two stylistic modes that produces the tension, pacing of narrative interest, and poetic suggestion—the "magic" of the Bradbury style. In effect, they are cultural and stylistic masks that Bradbury wears when he wants to suggest the "literary" qualities of Hemingway or Wolfe and thereby win his own place among his chosen precursors.

Bradbury, then, can certainly write sparingly and without metaphor, but most often he does not, tending toward the pole of metaphor and similarities. In reading metaphor, critics from Aristotle on down to I. A. Richards have always assumed that one begins with some literal ground or concept that is then clothed in figurative language. It is then the critic's job to "unmask" the metaphor and return it to its literal meaning (William Blake's sunflower counts the "steps of the sun," that is, the hours of the day). But at its most extended reaches in such novels as *Something Wicked This Way Comes* and *From the Dust Returned*, Bradbury's practice defeats such conceptual analysis and evades any mere literal ground of meaning. He seems to start with metaphor, which is then revealed to be only another metaphor, and so on indefinitely. In fact, his carnivalized use of metaphor is closer to masquerade and metamorphosis than to the illustration of philosophical ideas (though these can be found as well, to be sure). For Bradbury, to express oneself metaphorically is to become metamorphosed and transposed, thus becoming comparable to the other. For literary carnival to happen, the same must partake of the other. Through metaphor Bradbury explores the major thematic networks of the fantastic: themes of the self—including metamorphosis—and themes of the other (the interplay of these in Bradbury's texts more fully discussed in later chapters).[19] Self and other meet in the last passage quoted above, where the rocketship-locusts transform the Martian landscape, but the emphasis is on the attempt to beat the strange into familiar shapes. Still, the language deploys some of the hyperbolic exaggeration associated with carnival: the men resemble "steel-toothed carnivores."

Myth

But why is fantasy necessary for life? Why the need for interpretations, for fictions? To answer this question, we have first to take a look at certain statements Bradbury has made of a programmatic nature about fantasy.

In 1968 Bradbury wrote an article summarizing his views on the nature of fantasy that was in itself a carnivalesque fantasy—an unproduced television scenario about Halloween. In this scenario Bradbury and the Phantom of the Opera sit in an otherwise empty theater and comment on all the famous horror and fantasy films of the past—*The Mummy, Dracula, Frankenstein, King Kong,* and others—as autumn leaves are blown in magically from the street and into a projector where they are cast as images across "the velvet abyss" onto a ghostly screen. This fantasy-theatrical scenario gives Bradbury a framework within which to vent his spleen about what he takes to be the literalness of the modern horror film, which seems to spare us nothing in its search for the true and terrible image (one thinks of the recent controversies surrounding the "splatterpunk" horror movement, for which the literalness and not the suggestion of horror is paramount). For Bradbury, fantasy must have a system of symbolic meanings, and he offers us many convincing reasons why the detour through the metaphorical realm of appearances is a necessary part of the historical development of modern fantasy, including, in his view, myths, folk tales, religions, and personal myths. Since the article is not readily available, selective quotes provide a sense of the developing argument and its highly metaphorical style, skipping over for the moment the obvious element of carnival staging and theatricality in the text itself. Bradbury begins by noting that his scenario has never been produced because it is too "serious" for television producers in its declared love of the old horror films and their value for culture. He finds the terror of such films "strangely life-enhancing." Toward the end he asks several rhetorical questions about the origins of myth and religion in the fear of death:

What were we doing? Naming the unnamable. Why? Because man by his very nature must describe. The names change from generation to generation, but the need to name goes on. We were picturing the unpicturable. For, consider, does death have a size, shape, color, breadth, width? No, it is "deep" beyond infinity and "far" beyond eternity. It is forever incapsulated in the skull we carry, a symbol to itself, behind our masking face.

Our religions, our tribal as well as personal myths, tried to find symbols then for the vacuum, the void, the elevator shaft down which we must all journey and no stops evermore again. We had to know. We had to lie, and accept the lie of labels and names, even while we knew we lied, for we had work to do, cities to build, children to rear, much to love and know. Thus we gave gifts of names to ward off the night some little while, to give us time to think on other things. . . .

These are the stuffs of dreams that went to make the best old horror films. How rarely today do we bother to act out the most solvent, the most creative and therefore our most curative dreams.

We have fallen into the hands of the scientists, the reality people, the data collectors. . . .

I do not for a moment demean their function. They are the vital necessaries without which we would remain ignorant. . . .

The horror film began to kill itself off when it began to explain itself.

Fantasy, like the butterfly, cannot stand handling. Touch the wing the merest touch, brush some of that powder with finger tips and the poor thing won't fly again. You cannot explain a dream. The dream exists. It is. It cleanses itself. It is the mountain spring that, traveling dark distances underground, purifies itself. We do not know all the reasons. We will never know. But the modern horror film, by merely cutting a man's skull bone to show us the transistorized Grand Guignol stage, all miniaturized in the frontal lobes, bypasses the dream to capture and kill with facts, or things that appear as facts. . . .

What are we saying here? Let me recapitulate. The basic facts of man's life upon earth are these: You will love. You will not be loved. People will treat you well. People will treat you badly. You will grow old. You will die. We *know* this.

You cannot tell a man that death and age are after him again and again all his lifetime without freezing his mind ahead of the reality. *He must be told these truths by indirection* [emphasis added]. You must not hit him with lightning. You must polarize the lightning through transformers, which are the arts, then tell him to grab hold of the one-cent Electrocute Yourself for a Penny Machine. His hair may stand up, his heart beat swiftly as he juices his veins. But the truth, thus fed, will make him free. . . .

Fact without interpretation is but a glimpse of the elephants' bone yard. . . .

A new generation will scramble the sick bones of this one. And the health and strength of that generation will be built on the old ability to fantasize. To fantasize is to remain sane. . . .

There is a scene in one of my *Martian Chronicles* where rocket men come to Mars, sense there the fleeing spirits of all our best fantasy writers. Hid deep in the Martian hills, victims of the computer-data-fact-collecting age, the shades of Dickens and his Christmas Ghosts, Poe's falling House of Usher, Baum's Emerald City of Oz wait to be summoned back by a greater age of tolerance. A new age that will take raw fact in one hand and transcending intuition in the other. Only with a grasp on each rein can man move forward in space and time.

To these ["intellectuals" who despise fantasy and "commercial fools" who debase it,] I say: Give us back our small fears to help us cure the large. We cannot destroy the large death, the one that takes us all. We need a tiny one to be crushed in our hand to give us confidence. The complete and utter truth, completely known, is madness. Do not kick us off the cliff and send us screaming down to that. For God's sake, give us our morsel of poisoned popcorn to munch in the cinema dark.[20]

Anyone familiar with modern cultural criticism will have no difficulty in recognizing the thematic oppositions at play in these statements. One cluster of ideas can be grouped around the idea of "culture-values-creativity," which Bradbury favors, and the other around "intellectual knowledge-morality-reason," which he considers a secondary role. Scientific reason and instrumental reason, while they clearly have an important part to play in our increasingly technological lives, are in themselves powerless to create new values. At best they can only transmit, routinize, and normalize values. In a worst-case scenario, such as that depicted in *The Martian Chronicles,* they have become agents of domination. Indeed, the "truth" revealed by scientific reason seems, when completely known, to lead only to madness and the negation of all values (nihilism). Myths are what animate a culture, and these are created by artists who are close to the abysses of non-meaning but who are strong enough to create saving fictions. Not only popular art such as the horror film but all art, then, is fundamentally discordant with the truth. Art exists to mask the intolerable facts of life, to reveal them in a manageable form.

These notions about the need for art and creativity entered our culture at a specific point in the history of modernism with the philosopher Friedrich Nietzsche, who is often held responsible these days for the malaise of "cultural relativism."[21] Bradbury has paid tribute elsewhere to Nietzsche in a poem that could well stand as his *ars poetica* ("We Have Our Arts So We Won't Die of Truth," *Zen in the Art of Writing*). Nowadays he openly cites Nietzsche as a source for his philosophizing: "Don't confuse me with facts if they're going to paralyze me! I'm reminded of Nietzsche's old saying 'We have art that we do not die of the truth.'"[22] But Bradbury is no weak version of an "anything goes" relativist. On the contrary, he goes much further than this to assert what the entertainer-artist—the horror-film director—must take care to do: cure us of our fears while evoking them. He even has the nerve to suggest that classic horror films such as *Franken-stein* and *Dracula* might be a *source of spiritual values!* Clearly, he is concerned here about a tradition of the mythical horror film that he felt was in danger of being debased and vulgarized by a different kind of horror film that offered facts and not interpretations. This concern about the vulgar debasement of horror is at the heart of his recent novel *A Graveyard for Lunatics,* in which an "impossible" horror film is being produced by a studio bent on showing people very directly what scares them, with Bradbury as the reluctant screenwriter (see chap. 6).

Conscious of himself as a doubled figure, an artist-entertainer, Bradbury in such essays as "Death Warmed Over" was performing postmodern carnivaliza-tions of such oppositions in our culture at a time long before it became fashionable in academia.[23] He addresses both audiences, the "intellectuals" who would analyze the creative dream and the "commercial fools" who would debase it. It would not be difficult to see, with the full text before us, how Bradbury's own television scenario, presented thematically here, is self-deconstructing. One narrative voice (the thematic one we have brought into the foreground) tells us the "truth" about fantasy, while another voice, Bradbury the stage manager of a television scenario, tells us that literal truth will kill us and therefore must be framed as an illusion. Bradbury's own rhetoric shows him to be aware of this text's status as a fiction and therefore of its own "authority" to make assertions, no matter how deeply felt, about the nature of reality. In short, it mirrors itself while naming the abyss again, as indeed Bradbury says all naming or interpreting does. The ogre Death is deconstructed—removed from its literal meaning—at the very beginning by as simple a textual device as putting its supposed meaning in quotes. Thematically, the voice laying bare to us the "truth" about fantasy wants primarily to speak in innocent metaphors; it even tells us somewhat disingenuously that the dream cannot be explained. It is a natural force, a mountain stream or a natural object like a butterfly. But we know that metaphorical naming is anything but natural. It is a specifically human magic, one of the ways in which man has mastered his fear of the chaotic abyss and the total loss of meaning it threatens. Knowing that metaphors and myths are lies, however, makes no difference. The recognition of the falsity or error of dreams, the not taking them to be real, is constitutive of their importance. They leave the dreamer free; they give him free space for the upsurge of his power and cultural activity—building cities and raising children, as Bradbury phrases it.

Through the art of carnivalization, horror is transformed into the sublime and the absurd rendered comic (Bradbury's poison popcorn and the Electrocute Yourself for a Penny Machine are pop-culture examples of the latter). We are rescued by the essential theatricality of art, the terror and horror of existence having been "polarized" and filtered by art. What is more, in a beautifully resonant metaphor that is very much his own, Bradbury tells us that man forever encapsulates the natural symbol of the unpicturable abyss in his own skull, a "symbol to itself," thereby indicating the nonmimetic character of fantastic art. Bradbury's text aspires to be both an intellectual inquiry into the origins of fantastic art and a work of popular art itself. And the artist, we sense, is expected to wear many convincing masks while he entertains us—these are the signs of his vitality. Otherwise, we bypass the dream to capture and kill with facts, or things that *appear* as facts. (Bradbury is careful to add the qualification; perhaps there are no such things as facts, for Dionysian insight reveals the illusory nature of all "reality.") In Bradbury's philosophical thematics, the truth is something that has to be masked.[24] Our very faces are masks that hide the truth, and yet in those faces, however grotesque and frightening they may become, we sense something that is worth more than the truth.

Perhaps the most significant affinity that Bradbury shares with Nietzsche is the metaphorical and psychological manner in which he diagnoses the sickness and health of our present civilization, predicting that the next generation will scramble the sick bones of this one. We might say that for Bradbury literal truth is death. The way to cultural health and to the revitalization of worn-out literary conventions is not by being more literal but by creating metaphors of metaphors, new interpretations. Without the ability to fantasize in the name of life, culture loses the healthy natural power of its creativity. Nietzsche would say that new myths have to be born continually out of the Dionysian womb. Myths give us the ability to name the abyss. Only a culture ringed and defined by such stories is complete and unified. Bradbury's use of the myth of the American frontier in his Martian stories is one major instance of this sort of rejuvenation of old myths. Thus, the task that Bradbury has set for the fantastic is very close to what Nietzsche said was his own in investigating tragic art: "to see science under the optics [perspective] of the artist, but art under the optics of life."[25]

A complete survey of all the myths constructed (and deconstructed) by Bradbury's fiction is beyond the scope of this study, but we can at least discuss personal and religious myths. Childhood itself is certainly among the most important personal myths, containing multiple variations. As others have noted, children are Bradbury's most interesting characters, for they frequently wear masks in front of adults that hide strange and even lethal worlds of fantasy.[26] The future children in "The Veldt," for example, use the machinery of their nursery to create a real African world in which lions come to devour their parents, who are threatening to shut down the nursery and this separate world of fantasy. Even Bradbury's Martian children react to the news of the American invasion by clapping golden expressionless masks on their faces ("The Earthmen," *The Martian Chronicles*). But because there are so many different representations of children in Bradbury's stories, ranging from whimsical irony to total horror and repugnance (for example, "Hail and Farewell," *The Golden Apples of the Sun;* "All Summer in a Day," *A Medicine for Melancholy;* and "The Playground," collected in some editions of *Fahrenheit 451*), we are made aware of just how much ambivalence is built into this myth. We are inclined to think that Bradbury's children are at their best when they oppose adult norms and conventions in stories based on carnival, for example, *The Halloween Tree*. Bradbury's unpublished Ur-novel, *Summer Morning, Summer Night* (discussed for the first time in chap. 4), was in fact based on a carnivalized war between young and old.

A related personal myth of childhood crops up in Bradbury's repeated insistence, to the total disbelief of just about everybody, that he has total recall from the moment of birth. It is rather hard to believe in an individual who claims never to have had a writer's block, or repressions; who consequently has no screen memories functioning; and to whom all past experience is readily available to consciousness. But versions of this assertion in Bradbury's prefaces and introductions are too numerous to list. The issue tends to come up whenever he discusses the circumstances of his childhood in relation to his authorship or the question of where he gets his ideas. It is a theme in his autobiographical poems as well, especially one poem entitled, appropriately enough, "Remembrance."[27]

According to Wayne L. Johnson, this poem "touches on the heart of the Bradbury experience" because of the way in which it plays with the paradoxes of time.[28] Supposedly, it represents real events that happened near a ravine in Waukegan, Illinois (Bradbury's hometown), some forty years earlier. In the dramatic situation of the poem, the speaker, Bradbury himself, returns to Waukegan and finds a message left by himself as a child and addressed to the man he would one day be (and also hidden from his older brother, Skip, who figures in the poem). The note, written on a piece of paper and hidden in a tree, becomes, according to Johnson, a "magical device" that allows its seeker to complete a circle in time and encounter his past self in a new and disquieting way, for the child says to the man, "I remember you."

If we consider the poem's theatricality and rhetoric, however, and not just its theme, what we find first is an attempt to reactivate a Dionysian feeling for the abyss that seems to be lacking in Bradbury the older man: "Fools! I thought. O boys of this new year, / Why don't you know the Abyss waits you here?" But this willful attempt to call past feelings about the ravine—one of the most important recurring themes in Bradbury, representing a place of contact with the wildness of the Dionysian experience—into presence gives way to another milder mood of sweet recall. The speaker comes upon the oak tree he climbed when twelve years old and remembers being too frightened of the height to climb down; his older and more athletic brother had to rescue him. After climbing the tree, he remembers placing a piece of paper "On which I'd written some old secret thing and *forgot* [emphasis added]." To his surprise, the paper is still there after all those years, and a feeling of the strangeness of this miraculous world is restored to him.

On an emotional level the poem is successful, at least for its speaker, but what inhabits the poem is the logical paradox. Its effect depends not so much on remembrance as it does on forgetting—or perhaps on a kind of cryptomnesia—for logically it cannot work both ways; either Bradbury has total recall or he does not (unless, of course, he wrote the message as a secret hidden from himself, if such a thing were possible). And if he does have total recall, why did he not remember what he had written on the paper? Why does it have to be staged as a scene of uncanny unveiling at the end of the poem? It would seem that if Bradbury cannot have the youthful *frisson* of a glimpse into the terrors of the abyss, then he will have the uncanny and knowing child as father to the man. In short, the poem seems to point toward a Lacanian logic of unconscious signification in which we receive our own lost message from the "Other" (Bradbury's earlier self) in an inverted form. But blithely unaware of its narrative and logical contradictions, this late romantic poem will simply deny any loss of reality.

Another aspect of a personal myth in Bradbury may be that of religion, which, since the Apollo lunar missions, has coalesced as his insistent theme that mankind will only achieve immortality and defeat death when it reaches out for the stars and leaves Earth behind. Death himself delivers this very message to Tom Skelton, the boy protagonist of Bradbury's children's novel, *The Halloween Tree.* In that context, however, it appears somewhat out of place since Death is otherwise an agent of demythologization, speaking in a manner reminiscent of Bradbury himself in "Death Warmed Over." Instead of being unmasked, this theme is bodied forth fully clothed in a long poem, "Christus Apollo," in which Bradbury pleads with man in exalted quasi-biblical language to venture forth toward the stars and grasp his destiny, thereby becoming "the Savior's Savior." In a long section of apparently open questions near the beginning of the poem, Bradbury wonders whether Christ exists on other worlds and if so in what form, in what manner the narrative of salvation is played out, and indeed whether creatures on other worlds need salvation. His answer is:

It must be so.
For in this time of Christmas
In the long Day totaling up to Eight,
We see the light, we know the dark;
And creatures lifted, born, thrust free of so much night
No matter what their world or time or circumstance
Must love the light,
So, children of all lost unnumbered suns
Must fear the dark
Which mingles in a shadowing-forth on air.
And swarms the blood.
No matter what the color, shape, or size
Of beings who keep souls like breathing coals
In long midnights,
They *must* need saving of themselves.
So on far worlds in snowfalls deep and clear
Imagine how the rounding out of some dark year
Might celebrate with birthing one miraculous child![29]

It has to be admitted that we can read this passage with its repeated emphasis on *must* as either romantic desperation or as the triumph of a poet who has created a supreme fiction in which he is completely capable of believing. Because the poem does present a sustaining religious myth—that of Christ reborn in different forms elsewhere in the universe—we are inclined to the latter view. Briefly, Christ is the Dionysian aspect of this religious fantasy, an impulse that "wanders in the Universe / A flesh of stars, / He takes on creature shapes / To suit the mildest elements," while man in this age of technology appears as an Apollonian who dares cast about "And clothe himself in steel / And borrow fire / And himself in the great glass of the careless Void admire."[30]

God in Bradbury's vision is radically immanent in creation but needs man to understand and see himself, to grow. Man is already half a god, the builder of rockets that will one day put an end to death by allowing him to inhabit other planets. On these new worlds we will be allowed "To birth ourselves anew / And love rebirth." In the conquest of space as myth, mankind's light and dark impulses will achieve a balanced tension in a life that knows no end. Ultimately, though, it is the mutual incitement of these two impulses that determines the origin as well a the goals of man, why "Apollo's missions move, and Christus seek." Although Bradbury was raised as a Baptist, this poem is quite outside the bounds of Christian orthodoxy, being, in fact, a vision of man saving the universe by disseminating his "holy seed" in the vast abyss. In this poem Bradbury is the voice of God sending man forth to reconquer Eden by being fruitful and multiplying.

In 1977 Bradbury summarized his views on God and religion in an article, "The God in Science Fiction." Looking back over his career and remembering all of the stories he had written on the subject, he reflects, "the Life-Force moves in the Universe, changing, and Christ moves also, symbolizing that Force, putting off old masks to put on new." In Bradbury's religious myth God certainly masks himself but voices the lament "My universe needs seeing, / That's Man's eternal task: / What's the use of being / If God is but a mask?" It is the task of mankind to "rise behind God's masking," to see through (literally) the masks of God. Being is perhaps the key word here, for it is not the *being* of God that Bradbury's myths ultimately affirm, but the radical *becoming* of man through the creation and shattering of masks.[31]

Given his view of fantasy that requires the multiplication of all kinds of masks, it seems doubtful that Bradbury in his religious myths is arguing for a spiritual realm whose objects, contents, and values would transcend the sensory (that is, aesthetic) sphere. On the contrary, God manifests himself as the hunger for new forms of life in *this* world. Just the opposite is true for the orthodox Christian, however. For him, the mere prolongation of human life is never the "greatest good." Life—and therefore human society and history—is in this view important because it is a stage on which the "kingdom of God" must emerge. Furthermore, in Christian ethics, whenever the preservation and advancement of life conflict with the realization of values that exist in the kingdom of God, life becomes futile and is to be rejected. To Nietzsche this otherworldly attitude was manifested historically as a sickness in man, as one of the most virulent stages of nihilism. To Bradbury also man can be trapped into negating life through an aspiration to heavenly ideals. Perhaps this is the ultimate irony of his famous story "Mars Is Heaven!" There the Martians appropriate the Earthmen's ideals of heaven, goodness, and family values, projecting them telepathically to deceive and murder them. It is unfortunate that Bradbury changed the title to "The Third Expedition" when he revised the story for inclusion in *The Martian Chronicles,* thereby lessening the irony of the tale in the process of integrating it into the larger *Chronicles* concept.

Bradbury also reverses the orthodox view of the Christ figure and his role in the salvation process in a poem called "Christ, Old Student in a New School," collected in Harlan Ellison's *Again, Dangerous Visions.* It is one of his longer poems, and this allows the theme of carnivalization to fully develop. Although the word "carnival" is never mentioned, the semantic play of this text is a concise example of what carnivalization seeks to achieve with its laughter at static hierarchies of meaning. In order to defamiliarize the process of salvation, in which man has lost hope, Christ himself is taken down from the cross and mankind put in his place. It seems that Christ, so long prayed to, has himself forgotten the prayer he made to the Father to undo "this dreadful work / this antic agony of fun." With man crucified, mankind begins to realize that "The slave and master in one skin / Is all your history." In other words, man realizes some way out of the violent dialectic of recognitions that Georg F. W. Hegel and Karl Marx say necessarily structures human history. The way out is through the recognition that man is a fool (a variation on the "wise fool" and the "tragic clown" of Russian carnivalized literature).[32]

The laughter liberated from this moment sets man free from the cross and transforms Christ as well, for he now receives communion from us: "Now Man puts to the lips and tongue of Christ / His last Salvation crumb, / The wafer of his all-accepting smile, / His gusting laugh, the joy and swift enjoyment of his image: / Fool." Christ is united to mankind once again, though not in a hierarchical, gloomy, and serious way that places him above mankind. As both enter the openness of language and life in the gay relativity of "the marketplace," all such hierarchies are abolished, and mankind must wear its wits "which means their laughter / as their crown."[33] Thus, mankind recognizes itself in the image of Christ the Fool in a process of decrowning-crowning that is liberating through the acceptance of carnival ambivalence. We are all fools both "guilty and guile-less" in our interactions with others. The poem ends with Bradbury hoping to subject all of mankind's one-sided ideologies "in every school" to the new school of carnival ambivalence. This would seem to include Freud and Nietzsche (who never understood the value of the Incarnation in redeeming this world) them-selves. They will have no final authority in his writings. They too must be sub-jected to the "new school" of carnivalization so that humanity can "give birth to new beginnings," reach its destiny among the stars, and live forever.

Like religious myth, technology must be subordinated to a humanizing vision. In itself technology for Bradbury is merely the embodiment of technique, a de-cision procedure, what science has already thought, its ideas.[34] Technological thinking is dangerous not when it creates some monstrous accident like a super plague or a reactor meltdown (which, if the experimenters were responsible, they should be technically competent to prevent) but when it becomes totalizing and forces humankind to confront existential problems with merely technical thinking. Bradbury argues that technique by itself cannot determine a philoso-phy, and he is surely right. His overtly anti-technological stories are almost never of the type where science finds an answer to the problems it has created (the Isaac Asimov robot stories, for instance).

Fahrenheit 451, for example, presents us with many ostensibly utopian machines that have made life easier or save lives, but they do not make the peo-ple of this future society any happier—quite the opposite, in fact. When Mildred, the wife of the protagonist of the story, attempts suicide by taking an overdose of sleeping pills, society provides two impersonal "operators" who come to rescue her. But in a cleverly staged scene during which they eventually replace all of her blood with that of a stranger's (a gruesome-enough revitalization of the blood-less and abstract philosophical theme of alienation) and pump out her stomach with a kind of vacuum cleaner mounted with an electronic eye, we are made acutely aware of the individual's dependence on a bureaucratized state where knowledge of what to do on such occasions is the property of the "helping pro-fessions," those outside experts who intervene in family problems. The irony of the scene consists in the fact that the rescuers are not even doctors but "handy-men." Suicide has become so common in their society that it required the crea-tion of a new machine and a new profession to deal specifically with the problem.

At the same time as we are working out for ourselves the depths of irony in this story in which no one is really getting at the actual existential problems behind Mildred's suicide (though, of course, the operators are efficient, practical, and helpful, if somewhat bored with it all), the narrator asks us a question about the machine and the real powers of its eye: "Did it drink of the darkness? Did it suck out all the poisons accumulated with the years?" We must imagine through this critical questioning of technology how time has stopped flowing toward the future for Mildred, how it has gathered in a liquid melancholy (Bachelard's *l'eau lourde*) that cannot be sucked away by the machine, indeed that the "eye" of the machine cannot even see. Unlike the equipment and its operators, we must give a full human response on the level of cognition and imagination.[35]

To survive in our science-fictional culture, humankind must build what Bradbury calls "empathy machines" (in "Cry the Cosmos") or "compensating machines" (in "I Sing the Body Electric!" see chap. 7). And the artist must play a central role in the designing of such machines. Bradbury regards Jules Verne as an example of this sort of artist and introduces him as one of his own precursors.[36] He compares Melville's mad Captain Ahab to Verne's Captain Nemo. According to Bradbury, technology in Verne's fantasy allows Nemo to transcend Ahab's fate. By building his submarine, the captain "becomes" a whale and dwells in the very sea that Ahab fears. Bradbury returned to this theme in a poem called "N" (In *They Have Not Seen the Stars*). In it Bradbury as a twelve-year-old boy dreams of resurrecting the frozen body of Captain Nemo, which has lain in his submarine, the *Nautilus*, locked beneath the Arctic ice. The compatibility between Verne and childhood, as Bradbury shows us in this poem, is not due to a banal mystique of adventure but to a desire to enclose oneself in a finite and blissful world. On a deeper level than the obvious theme of travel, the *Nautilus* is an emblem of enclosure, of a safe technological appropriation of the world. True, Bradbury travels around the world with Nemo on various and sundry adventures, but he is always "snug and warm" in the belly of the White Whale–submarine.

Fully half of the poem is, in fact, given over to inhabiting the vessel. Bradbury implicitly unveils his relationship to a "healthful" form of romanticism, for Verne did not seek to enlarge the world by romantic ways of escape from it or by mystical plans to reach the infinite, rather he found a more humanized way to inhabit the world we already possess. Melville's mad Ahab, put in one of Verne's stories, would seem a relic from an extinct romantic age, a prey to remorse and spleen who would only serve to show, by striking contrast, the health of the true owners of the world. Bradbury sympathizes with Ahab's madness and understands it (as a form of the spirit of revenge; Nemo in Verne's story is also motivated by revenge, though not at nature), yet for him it is self-destructive. At play in the text is the word "nothing" and others related with Nemo's name, but this is hardly the apprehension felt by Ishmael that the White Whale may symbolize nothing, the total loss of meaning. And just to make his moral position clear, Bradbury affirms unequivocally, "I think, old Nemo, I do love your madness most." Ultimately, then, Bradbury rejects a complete aesthetic involvement with the White Whale as representing the threat of chaos, of nonmeaning, for the French spirit of conscious reverie. With such "good reading" embracing childhood and reverie,

Nemo will never die—and neither will Bradbury, it is implied—as the poet proclaims at the end.[37]

Masks

We have characterized Bradbury above as a romantic because his authorship reflects (in varying degrees) the desperate attempt to overcome the problems that resulted from the nineteenth-century romantic crisis in Western culture. According to art historian Arnold Hauser, ever since the romantic period, art has become a quest for a home that the artist believes he possessed in his childhood and that assumes in his eyes the character of a paradise lost—he can only surmise—through his own fault. Romantic art is based, therefore, on a loss of reality and is produced as a substitute that tries both to deny and to replace that loss. What is more, the practice of art not only is a compensation for real life but also seems incompatible with its enjoyment, a realization that leads to "romantic disillusionment" and the problem of nihilism. Hauser summarizes succinctly the ambivalence of the romantic artist: "The romantic reaction to the artist's emancipation from reality is, however, ambivalent: it produces a feeling of triumph as well as of nostalgia, a sense of freedom and independence as well as a yearning after normal, natural, spontaneous life, a desire to live out life simply and directly. The artist's sense of guilt is, therefore, not the origin of his renunciation of life, as has been assumed, but rather a result of his flight from life." Hauser's essay also explores the romantic character of psychoanalytical theory. Indeed, he argues persuasively that psychoanalysis came into being as an answer to the problem of a civilization in which, "as a result of the romantic crisis, an individual's life and his work became two separate provinces, and in which a cleft has been opened between his private self and public performance." Hauser demonstrates that for Freud, art is linked to neurosis, for both art and neurosis equally reject reality, both are failures in adaptation to the social order. In Freudian theory as in romanticism, there is no artistic creation without the feeling of a loss or a wrong, without the experience of being tricked out of life.[38]

The romantic position on authorship—always teetering on the brink of disillusionment—can be seen in Bradbury's most ambitious fictional use of masks, a planned seventy-thousand-word novel that he began late in 1945 after a visit to Mexico to collect masks for the Los Angeles County Museum. He continued to develop it in episodes, outlines, and even an unproduced radio play through the fall of 1949. The surviving manuscript materials include a folder titled in ink by Bradbury as "*The Masks:* Short Novel—Begun 1945–1946." A thirty-page run of typescript composes an outline for the entire book, beginning with a half-dozen opening episodes that gradually shorten into a series of paragraphs describing (in outline form) highlights from the rest of the plan for the novel. Forty more pages (typed on the same lightweight-wove unwatermarked paper) contain non-sequential episodes and fragmentary scenes, representing an earlier stage of work. A final run of pages (on this same paper) contains two short versions of a radio play that is likely an even earlier form of the project.[39]

The seventy typescript pages of novel material appear to date from the 1947–1949 period; an abstract (typed on the same paper) is filed with a draft and a carbon of Bradbury's unsuccessful October 1949 application for a Guggenheim Fellowship in support of the *Masks* project. Progress seems to have been tortuously slow; Bradbury once noted that he compiled this relatively small body of text and notes "slowly and certainly over the previous two years." What appears to be a parallel draft of this abstract contains a somewhat fuller articulation of his plan for the novel:

> My novel THE MASKS would concern itself with the life of one man who through the use of a large collection of masks that he had purchased or had manufactured, or carved himself, reveals the inner lives of his closest friends. Confronting people on the street, in businesses, or in his parlor, with representations of themselves, he reveals to them the parts they are playing in the world. He examines, with his Masks, the process whereby people shape their personalities not to their heart's desire, but to the expectancies of their friends and the demands of business and society. Through his Masks he hopes to prove that each person is in reality many persons, assuming identities which are the most convenient and profitable in life. He proves that life is a rehearsal, a fitting-on, a discarding of roles and parts, for some the Mask fits well and happily, for others it is a burden, it smothers, and only through the wit and mimicry of the Man and His Masks, can they find their way to their true selves.[40]

What Bradbury's hero, William Latting, hopes to prove is that "faces are only faces and masks are only masks, and we must be careful which mask or which face we wear to the great Ball, the great Dance" (allusions to *The Phantom of the Opera*). The opening episodes of the thirty-page text-synopsis offer a glimpse of the full range of Latting's ability to mask. After taking rooms in a working-class neighborhood, he viciously reflects the whining petulance of his suspicious landlady back on herself, then charms her the next morning with the mask of an old lover. He plays off masks of his society friends against each other. And in an interview with a young girl, Latting reveals that he has a mask for church "pure as the purest bone ivory, and it is aesthetic, really passionless," with its eyes turned up to the skies and incense smoking out of the top. The girl finds this very amusing and clever.

Subsequent episodes in the finished text-synopsis offer ever-changing variations on love in human relationships. Loved by one woman, he proves that her feelings are as changeable as the mask he wears. Simply by substituting one mask for another, he causes her to lose interest. He wins another woman (the socialite Lisabeta Simms) by shaping his clay mask into mocking faces of the girl's other suitors. She is promiscuous (Bradbury calls her a whore in one plan for the work), and Latting discovers that she has never loved before, has gone from one man to another never satisfied. But in Latting she has at last found the one who is every man, the man with the masks, the man who is Variety itself. The masks then satisfy her promiscuity. But Latting soon tires of this conquest and causes her to lose interest by a simple expedient, wearing one blue Grecian mask all of the time until he becomes "One Man" constantly. The affair ends. Latting then has affairs with four different women but believes they only love the mask, not him, so they cannot accuse him of polyandry. Another woman, Annette, loves him only because he is *one* man. Nevertheless, Latting becomes more and more bitter as his experiments continue. People come to him for advice and he offers them vicious caricatures of themselves. Some learn, but others are enraged and hurt.

Besides its ironic exploration of love relationships, the incomplete novel also features a trial. As Latting's masked intrusions into the lives of others mount up, he is charged with disturbing the peace. Although it is clearly not against the law to wear a mask in public, many people find encountering the "Man in the Mask" unnerving and disturbing. The synopsis only touches on the trial itself, but the larger forty-page body of working papers includes a fairly lengthy version of the proceedings. In court Bradbury's hero wears a plain mask covered with malleable clay. As the prosecuting attorney cries out against him, Latting puts a quick hand to the mask and forms features that mock both the prosecutor and the judge. The audience finds this amusing until Latting mocks them as well. The trial ends in disorder and anger; everyone hates Latting. He is sentenced for contempt of court, but against his orders his lawyer enters a plea of insanity, and he is remanded to the custody of a psychologist who turns out to be a police psychiatrist: "You know what that means. A seedy, conceited, loud-mouthed ignoramus who had read a digested copy of Freud, been kicked out of college psychiatrics, learned the rest from those little nickel blue-books and a copy of *Esquire.*" (Bradbury may be mocking here his own alter ego as a writer of detective fiction.) During the psychiatric interview he puts on a pink mask (over the gray one) with a shining smile whose light overcomes his questioners objections to his wearing masks. He also tells them a convenient lie that in itself is a mask: the reason why he wears the mask is that he is a veteran horribly disfigured by the Korean War (the story is set in 1952). Wearing masks is thus part of his planned self-rehabilitation.

Bradbury wastes no time raising the whole issue of masks and artistic endeavor. In one of the opening episodes, Latting talks with a young writer, Mr. Smith, who has come to find out what his perpetual masquerade is all about. No one has seen Latting's face since he was eighteen ("I sometimes wonder if I ever had a face," he says). He wears masks even when he sleeps and makes love—an ironic mask is provided for that. Latting reveals to Smith that he has gotten the masks all over the world. Some of them he had especially carved "by men of good hate, who wore masks during a period of great anger and hatred." As for himself, he says he is a "chaos inside." He is whatever mask he wears; he can mimic voices of both men and women absolutely convincingly. In the next episode, quoting from T. S. Eliot, Latting says, "I am a Hollow Man, one of the great hollow men of this age." He expresses a sadness that real human expressions cannot be held permanently; they fade into sadness.

We eventually learn that Latting has masks made in Mexico by a certain Senor Cerda. Bradbury's handwritten notes on the manuscript reveal that *cerda* means "swine" in Spanish: "He changes Latting to Everyone. Circe (the whore) changed men to cerda (swine)." Latting first sends sketches done in charcoal pencil to Cerda, who then carves the design. Through metaphor—a process that always simultaneously reveals and masks Bradbury's mind—the author asks the reader to imagine the process of the mask being carved, the precision needed to fit Latting's face perfectly, and moments when Latting is "filled to a sexual bursting with his need of a face." Cerda plays a game with his client, telling him that he is working on a new mask Latting cannot imagine, cannot know. Cerda's surprise masks are different from the sexual clasping of the masks he designs for Latting, which necessarily have to be reflections of Latting's desire. Thinking about them sends Latting off into new metaphorical channels of thought: "The surprise masks were cold, like an instrument, a flute, a trumpet, to be played, to be tested with voiceless gestures, moods, attitudes, subtleties. It was a tickling, a delight, a surprise, it was like a match lit in darkness discovering a mirror, a face, a new thrill."

A later working title for the novel was "The Mask beneath the Mask beneath the Mask," and indeed Latting has developed nests of up to six masks, reasoning, "We carry a nest of masks within us constantly." Life and encounters with others he describes as the "shelling and slaking off of our skins and images." Latting is later suspected of murder, but the inference to the reader is that he is killing something inside himself—masks are finally seen as weapons against his own soul and faith. Bradbury had planned a great deal of negative disillusionment for his hero. When Latting realizes that facial expressions cover up "our great inner foulness," he becomes deeply psychopathic. In the ending that concludes the synoptic outline of the novel, his friend Smith sends him a mask made in Mexico from a photograph of what Latting looked like at seventeen. On seeing it, he horrifyingly realizes all that he has lost—trust, faith, goodness—and kills himself. When the clay mask at last is removed, we discover that Latting's actual face is flawlessly good—there was no reason for him to hide. Smith has the masks and his friend cremated together.

Whatever else Bradbury may have intended, the end of this unfinished novel (at this time) is permeated with the problem of romantic disillusionment. Latting's sense of guilt at his separation from life (represented as a conflict between his libidinal and destructive impulses) reveals the ambivalence of his artistic endeavors with masking. Apparently unable to construct a supreme fiction he could believe, Latting is thrown ultimately into anxiety, despair, and nihilism. Although initially elated with the power of his artistic freedom, artistic creation becomes in the end an instrument of self-punishment. Bradbury consistently claims that he is each and every one of his characters (and Latting is no exception), but as author he had to find a way to overcome nihilism and make his art an affirmation of life. Even before he abandoned work on this novel, Bradbury wrote the now classic stories that comprise *The Martian Chronicles*, which presents us with the spectacle of masked Martians who are mature enough to accept philosophically their fate at the hands of Earthmen. Viewed in the light of *The Masks*, *The Martian Chronicles* (and in particular the characterization of Spender, the authorial mask of "—And the Moon Be Still as Bright") is manifestly an attempt to overcome romantic disillusionment. Recently, the more overtly autobiographical works looking back on this early period in Bradbury's career still are structured by the ambivalent play of masks, especially *A Graveyard for Lunatics*, in which forgiving others their need for masks becomes a way out of despair.

The Masks is very important to our understanding of Bradbury's authorship and themes for several reasons. First, although it was clearly a dead end for him aesthetically because it was too self-conscious an approach to authorship—henceforth, he would think of himself as a writer of short stories that he would shape into cycles and novelistic texts such as *The Martian Chronicles* (1950)—the thematics of masks became the heart of his social criticism. Second, masks structure the whole psychological thematics of Halloween in such novels as *Something Wicked This Way Comes* and *The Halloween Tree* (which we will explore in later chapters). In *The Masks* Bradbury intended Latting's masks to function as devices that exposed the "safe little identities" of friends and strangers to irony, scorn, and ridicule, all of which got Latting in a good deal of trouble, thus separating him from life (romantic disillusionment) instead of having the intended therapeutic effect of liberation and the deepening understanding of how we create a self out of the demands of others. Incidentally, the process the character hoped to enact by wearing masks bears some similarities to Jungian depth analysis and archetypal conceptions of the psyche in which the individual can become hardened and rigidified by identifying too closely with the persona, or social mask (exactly what has happened to Montag at the beginning of *Fahrenheit 451*). For the subject in Jungian analysis, discovery of the real self begins with the understanding of the limiting role of the persona. By 1950 Bradbury was well aware of both Freudian and Jungian approaches to writing characters.[41]

At any rate, in *The Martian Chronicles*, Bradbury's acknowledged masterpiece, masks play an important role and function both psychologically and as social criticism. If we look at the textually evolving thematics of that collection, we find that Bradbury added the masking of the Martians as another thematic layer during its complex revisions. In the pulp versions of these stories, there is hardly any mention of Bradbury's Martians being masked; the exception is "The Off Season," where Martians who are dying from human diseases come down from the hills to deed vast tracts of the planet to one of the colonists. We cannot detail every instance of these additions here—they are mostly in the early part of the book—but in general Bradbury has, in fact, taken the function of this masking device to another level of understanding. Unlike the Earthmen who invade the planet, the Martians, although telepathic and prone to mental illness, are psychologically healthy enough to wear masks if they choose to and emotionally balanced enough not to become rigidly identified with them, to wear them as a form of play. They have embraced the Dionysian "joyful wisdom" about the nature of the ego-persona and can affirm their lives: "The little town was full of people drifting in and out of doors, saying hello to one another, wearing golden masks and blue masks and crimson masks for pleasant variety, masks with silver lips and bronze eyebrows, masks that smiled or masks that frowned, according to the owners' dispositions."[42]

Bradbury's very different use of this motif in his earlier *Masks* manuscript offers a contrast that is key to understanding *The Martian Chronicles* as a work of social criticism. As he developed his masked Martians in some of the individual tales of 1948–1949, and as he wove the masking motif even more pervasively into the larger fabric of the *Chronicles* during the summer and fall of 1949, Bradbury moved beyond romantic disillusionment to a knowing affirmation of personality as fiction. In the process he reversed the role of the mask wearer from lonely social outcast to (albeit alien) everyman. Once he had done this, there was no future for Bradbury as a writer in pursuing *The Masks* manuscript as his first published novel.

There is some evidence that Bradbury made one final attempt to turn this bleak tale toward a positive resolution. Both versions of the short abstract apparently drafted for the October 1949 Guggenheim application were probably prepared just after Bradbury had completed his mask-laden revisions for the *Chronicles*, and these documents clearly begin to move away from the tragic ending outlined in the synopsis. The more fully developed of the two abstracts offers the best glimpse of this changing vision: "Through this novel, I hope [to] contribute something o[f] worth in the field of social satire, I hope to examine as many professions as come within the reach of my man with the Masks, I hope to turn a sharp light upon civilization today, where it has been, and where it is going." There are, in fact, nearly a dozen pages of typed fragments that reveal a much more upbeat beginning and ending for the novel, and these pages are leaves of a much finer watermarked onion-skin paper more characteristic of what Bradbury would use to prepare submitted typescripts for *The Martian Chronicles* and his subsequent Doubleday titles. Here we find the title "The Mask beneath the Mask beneath the Mask" as well as a forty-one-chapter outline that includes ten from the earlier storylines followed by a run of nearly thirty professional character "types" as chapter subjects. Several openings follow, along with what purports to be a suggested ending keyed to page 250 of an unknown typescript of the novel. In this last version of the ending, the protagonist finally unmasks himself and goes off with his lawyer-confidant to have a night on the town. It is unclear (in both Bradbury's files and in his recollections) if this final version, set in 1952, ever existed. But it is clear that the dark premise of the original novel was not successfully transformed into a sustained work of social satire. Of Bradbury's first two attempts at novel-length fiction, only parts of *Summer Morning, Summer Night*—the basis for *Dandelion Wine*—would ever reach print.

The Masks is also very important for understanding Bradbury's authorship in relation to the play of carnival masks that permeates his writings, especially his later novels. According to Mikhail Bakhtin, whose book on the role of medieval folk culture in the writings of François Rabelais has been so influential in cultural studies of modern forms of carnival, masks and unmasking are at the heart of the experience of carnival, "the most complex theme of folk culture." Originally an expression of "gay relativity," of the joy of change and rebirth, and a complete rejection of conformity to oneself (insofar as it is defined by one's role in serious, "official" culture), the play of masking and unmasking became limited in its romantic form: "In its Romantic form the mask is torn away from the oneness of the folk carnival concept. It is stripped of its original richness and acquires other meanings alien to its primitive nature: now the mask hides something, keeps a secret, deceives. . . . The Romantic mask loses almost entirely its regenerating and renewing element and acquires a somber hue. A terrible vacuum, a nothingness lurks behind it. But an inexhaustible and many-colored life can always be descried behind the mask of folk grotesque."[43] Our argument is that Bradbury (re)discovered this source of inexhaustible life through his experiment with *The Masks*, which is almost entirely late romantic in inspiration. But even in modern life, as Bakhtin observes, the romantic mask is never just an object among other objects, it retains "a particle of some other world." That other world, of course, found expression in *The Martian Chronicles* (shown in detail in chap. 2). Other central carnival themes, such as the grotesque body and laughter, are also evident in Bradbury's writings throughout his career and are examined in later chapters.

A discussion of the role that literary masks derived from carnival figures— particularly the rogue, the clown, and the fool—have played in the history of the novel as argued by Bakhtin is necessary at this point. According to him, in con- trast with the epic, drama, and lyric, the novel has no essentially fixed authorial position. It needs to be invented for each text and is always, in general, a highly complex and problematical affair (this is certainly affirmed by Bradbury's cre- ative struggles with *The Masks*). For the novel, authorship is not just one issue among others, it is a formal and generic concern as well. And it is precisely here, Bakhtin says, that the masks of the clown and the fool, transformed in various ways in different historical periods, came to the aid of the novelist:

> In the struggle against conventions, and against the inadequacy of all avail- able life-slots to fit an authentic human being, these masks [the rogue, the clown, and the fool] take on an extraordinary significance. They grant the right *not* to understand, the right to confuse, to tease, to hyperbolize life; the right to parody others while talking, the right not to be taken literally, not "to be oneself"; the right to live life in the chronotope of the entr'acte, the chronotope of theatrical space, the right to act life as a comedy and to treat others as actors, the right to rip off masks, the right to rage at others with a primeval (almost cultic) rage—and finally, the right to betray to the public a personal life, down to its most private and prurient secrets.[44]

Bakhtin is here alluding to the "chronotope" of carnival (which he also calls the "Rabelaisian chronotope") that represents the fantastic, grotesque allegori- zation of the human being. Every genre has its own specific chronotope, or way of organizing space and time thematically. The chronotope of carnival is designed to bring abstract clock time into the realm of lived time (a concept more fully explored in chaps. 4 and 5). The difficulty in using such "allegorical" figures, how- ever, lies in the fact that they tend to separate the author from connectedness with others. Indeed, that is their very function, to be in life but not of it: "Essen- tial to these three figures is a distinctive feature that is as well a privilege—the right to be 'other' in this world, the right not to make common cause with any single one of the existing categories that life makes available; none of these categories quite suits them, they see the underside and the falseness of every situation. Therefore they can exploit any situation they choose, *but only as a mask* [emphasis added]."[45]

Here is the heart of a seeming paradox. These popular masks provide what Bakhtin calls a certain "outsidedness" to the author; they cannot be defined and finalized by others in the narrative world either. Yet because they are masks, they tend to separate the author from life and to have no essential identity in themselves (this could seemingly lead, of course, to the problem of nihilism as it does in *The Masks*). But the paradox is, in our view, only an apparent one. These figures, when transposed into literature, are as Bakhtin says, "heroes of a life process that is imperishable and forever renewing itself, forever contemporary."[46] They are images of carnival freedom and can assume any destiny. It is this use of masks—freely assumed and not defined or imposed from above by others—that Bradbury wants to achieve *while remaining connected with life*, indeed, *while increasing connectedness with others and with life.* This is the very life of fiction Bradbury has pursued in his writings from *Dark Carnival* onward. It is at the heart of both *Something Wicked This Way Comes*, which we argue is the epicenter of his writings, as well as his most recent novel, *Let's All Kill Constance!* in which a movie actress seeks to kill off all of her past roles and masks in order to discover a new life beyond them. In this last novel, as in both of the two previous detective novels, Bradbury as hero wears the mask of "the fool who knows" as he seeks to unravel the fearful mysteries posed by the narrative with the help of humor and laughter, in the process helping others affirm their lives, no matter how desperate they may seem.

Bakhtin argues convincingly that the romantic use of masks is largely a failure in attempting to reincarnate the life of carnival in literature. This is because the masks of real carnival do not hide anything behind themselves. Collectively, everyone in carnival knows what the masks are designed to do: mock at official serious culture. Everyone knows whom the masks represent. Thus, they are for the most part comic and parodic and not intended to produce fear. Bradbury did not entirely leave behind him these early preoccupations with romantic or Freudian masks; rather he increasingly tended to assume the mask of the fool to defeat and mock the things that terrified him in life (which he also demands to be masked). Over the years Bradbury has explored almost every possible aesthetic variation on the use of carnival masks, from those that are imposed by others on the hero (*Fahrenheit 451*) to those that are self-imposed (the detective novels), from the near abject ("Pillar of Fire") to the Nietzschean sublime (the noble Martians of *The Martian Chronicles*). We examine Bradbury's authorial position, his complex use of the interplay of various types of masks, in the thematics section of each of the following chapters.

Interestingly, Bradbury's manuscript of *The Masks* at one point contains his own sketches of masks-faces drawn in pencil (see fig. 1). Here we can observe the discourse of Bradbury's text turning into a figured body and offer our own interpretation of that transformation. The part of the chapter briefly outlined verbally on this illustrated page contains the direct expression of a Freudian incestuous wish as a woman comes to Latting, asking him to wear the mask of her father so that she can desire him (not only Latting but also, we assume, her father). It does not take much effort on the reader's part to give a classic Freudian symbolic interpretation to the "little gift in a tissue-wrapped box" that she offers Latting, and, indeed, schematic images of the female body with genitalia appear in the lower right-hand corner of the page, apparently derived from a series of half-formed masks directly above them.

Our attention is primarily focused, however, on the large male figure in the center of the page who looks terribly oppressed and worried, with darkened bags under his eyes. An hourglass appears on his chest where his heart should be so that we know he is preoccupied with the passage of (abstract) time. This figure strikes us at first as Bradbury's wry parody of a psychoanalyst caught up in the transference worries of the fifty-minute hour. He does not appear to notice the carnival taking shape around him, which has a different chronotope (or organization of time and space), one that gives concrete significance to the body as the source of creativity. But the laughter of carnival is deeply ambivalent; it could also be a figuration of the author, Bradbury himself, through his hero, Latting, anxious about the progress of his novel and wishing to have more access to women. Bradbury had not yet met his future wife, Marguerite McClure, when he began this project, and the Oedipal woman is fantasized by the discourse as just one of many attracted to Latting-Bradbury's artistic masks.

It is possible to discern in Bradbury's sketch nearly all of the important elements, albeit in a literary and reduced form, of carnival according to Bakhtin. The central theme of masking and unmasking we have commented on already. The mere presence of so many masks means that stable social identities are in question. There are also several reduced forms of laughter present: mocking parody, and especially caricature, that creates the grotesque body. Throughout *The Masks*, Bradbury is mocking the imposition of social masks structured by unconscious desire and the romantic problems that these yearnings create: the woman's desires are spoken of as "quite horrible" and "perverted." The paradox is that Latting has to wear the mask of the father (the *nom du père*, the "Name/No of the Father" in Lacanian terms) in order to be wanted by this woman. No positive resolution to her desires is possible within any culture. Perhaps this is another reason why the mask is so distorted and heavily circled.

It is important to understand, though, that however Freudian the text may

There is a young woman who comes to me, do you know why? It is quite horrible, quite perverted, I shudder to speak it out to you, but it is true, so I must tell you. She has always loved her father. But society prevents her from doing so. So, she came to me, yes came to me and brought a little gift in a tissue-wrapped box. And she handed it to me and said,

"Do you know my father, William Sanders?" And I said "Yes." And she said, "Open this box." And I opened it and there was a mask of her father. "Put it on," she said. I put it on. "Now," she said, sitting down. "You may hold my hand."

But that is only one of the many women.

Figure 1. The Oedipus complex and the multiplication of masks. A draft of an episode in Bradbury's "40 pages of unassimilated notes" for *The Masks* (1947–49) includes his own sketches of masks and faces. A more fully developed treatment of this episode survives within his "30 pages of completed text and synopsis" prepared for his unsuccessful October 1949 application for a Guggenheim Fellowship. From the Albright Collection, courtesy of Donn Albright and Ray Bradbury.

be in inspiration, images of Freudian desire mentioned in the text have been carnivalized by the grotesque body taking shape around the central figure, especially the images of the clowns just to the right of the man's head. The clown and the fool, Bakhtin claims, are the world's primordial laughers, and they laugh not just at others but also at themselves. Important too are the multiplication of masks—so necessary a requirement in Bradbury's developing carnivalesque thematics—that goes beyond the mere structuring effect of Oedipal desires and invokes both laughter and the carnival. In the grotesque world of carnival, the id is "uncrowned" (it no longer has any authority over us) and is converted into a "funny monster" that can be laughed at.[47] In short, this page prefigures many of the techniques Bradbury would later use in carnivalizing the genres of horror, science fiction, and fantasy: laughter (in its reduced forms of parody, caricature, and mock seriousness), the grotesque body (seen as a liberation from imposed social limits), and the play of masking and unmasking. It is a dramatic moment that shows us in a vivid way how Bradbury was living his fiction at this early time in his career and may well reflect his characteristic way of dealing with his own "unconscious" fears.

Although we are not attempting to "biographize" Bradbury's fiction by reducing his works to events in his life—on the contrary, we are trying to show how Bradbury *lived by his fictions*—nonetheless, it is important to understand that the presence of so many forms of carnivalesque textuality in the body of his writings necessarily points to Bradbury's real experiences with carnival. We will analyze many forms of the carnivalization of genre in detail in later chapters. Here it is important to note that carnival seems to have had a determining influence on Bradbury's authorship and that he experienced carnival culture in a deeply ambivalent manner.

Early in his life (1931–32) he was inspired by magicians and characters he met in the traveling sideshows and carnivals that visited Waukegan, Illinois. This childhood experience was apparently quite transforming, and Bradbury has written about it in interviews and correspondence, most recently in the afterword to this volume. Indeed, in Bradbury's reminiscences two of these figures (Blackstone the Magician and Mr. Electrico) are credited as being responsible for awakening his desire to live forever by creating his own special magic. Recently, in the 1999 afterword to the Avon edition of *Something Wicked This Way Comes*, "Carnivals, Near and Far," Bradbury explicitly linked his origins as a writer to an emotional experience he had with Mr. Electrico when he was twelve years old. The boy was "electrocuted" by this man (an ascetic-looking defrocked Presbyterian minister turned carny who electrocuted himself and other people in an electric chair) and told to "live forever." Bradbury was not a spectator at this carnival but a participant, and this ambivalent participation—he was being told to live forever while being electrocuted—is indeed at the heart of the carnival experience according to Bakhtin. The carnival is both death and life, it unmasks any pretensions to permanence while pointing the way toward rebirth. Birth is fraught with death, and death with new birth.

But during the 1945 trip to Mexico in which he experienced the Day of the Dead, Bradbury became terrified and wounded (he writes of it almost as a kind of trauma), especially after visiting the mummies in the catacombs of Guanajuato. This ambivalent relationship to carnival culture was clearly intolerable to the young author and needed to be worked out in *The Masks* and in a series of stories, beginning with "The Next in Line." That story was published in 1947 and collected as the last entry of *Dark Carnival*. (Incidentally, in the approximate center of that collection is a story called "Interim," which deals with the topic of pregnant death, another prominent theme in carnival-influenced writing according to Bakhtin.)

Bradbury's most recent novels are prolonged imaginative encounters with death and madness, limit concepts of romanticism, or indeed of psychoanalysis. Bradbury has fictionalized himself and the encounter with psychoanalysis in these two novels to such an extent that it is often difficult to know where fiction ends and reality begins. For instance, in the autobiographical detective-fantasy *Death Is a Lonely Business*, Death himself is a "Lonely" (A. L. Shrank) who has been murdering people. To survive, the narrator (Bradbury) must endow his own creative dreams with life by writing about the murders—in the form of detective stories influenced by Freudian theory that he actually *was* writing and publishing at the time—and thereby avoid becoming a Lonely himself. In this book Freud and the "truth" of the unconscious are caricatured in the figure of A. L. Shrank. Of course, Freud himself was fully aware of the analogies between psychoanalytic investigation and detective work; he admired Arthur Conan Doyle and his creation, Sherlock Holmes, for instance. By the end of this novel, Bradbury defeats both death and Shrank, whose business, psychoanalysis, is revealed as not only a business concerning Lonelies but also the business *of* a Lonely. Paradoxically, Death is figured in this novel as literal truth.

A conventional study of author and works, seeking the "truth" of the work in the author's life, would then find this doubled act of autobiography-fiction difficult to read. Is death (A. L. Shrank) literal or a metaphor for the death of the creative imagination (or in some uncanny way both)? Similarly, the sequel *A Graveyard for Lunatics* explores, from Bradbury the screenwriter's point of view, the madness of literal representation—film being largely without the possibility of metaphor—through the construction of an "impossible" horror film. At times the narration of this novel becomes so clogged with metaphors that it becomes difficult to follow the literal story.[48] To a psychobiographer—a role we decline to play here—this book would represent a real challenge, for the purpose of psychological biography is to reveal the literal man behind the metaphorical mask.[49]

Because of his awareness of masks, Bradbury's texts are modern despite their evident nostalgia. As previously mentioned, Latting, the hero of *The Masks*, refers to himself as a "hollow man," defining himself in reference to one of the classic poems of modernism. Bradbury's stories deal with such modern problems as the overcoming of nihilism (for example, *Fahrenheit 451*). His magic is to believe in his own fictions as such, and his power as an artist is to persuade us to do the same. Writer Brian Aldiss says precisely this in discussing the effect of Bradbury's work on early 1950s science fiction readers tired of the same old props and conventions. To them, Bradbury seemed like a magician, and Aldiss records how enchanting Bradbury's early books were at the time and "how much we needed them." He continues: "Bradbury is of the house of Poe. The sickness of which he writes takes the form of glowing rosy-cheeked health. It is when he makes functional use of this, contrasting sickness and health in one story, that he is at his most persuasive."[50] Indeed, we shall argue later that this thematic interplay of sickness and health is at the heart of Bradbury's cultural criticism.

Although he is sometimes called an epigone of Poe by critics who have only read his early books, Bradbury is not of the house of Poe on his fantasy side, nor is he of Jules Verne on his science fiction side, since in reading these (self-chosen) precursors, he inevitably transforms their writings into masks of himself anyway. Furthermore, Bradbury continually revises his relationship to his influences at different stages of his career. For instance, the transformation of Verne into a benign precursor is manifest in an imaginary interview with him. Here, Bradbury has Verne, the founder of science fiction (though Bradbury hastens to add that Verne did not use such a prosaic term for it), grant him a poetic license to romanticize the space age: "Lie to us, writers; we'll make it true." He also has Verne's voice make clear the connection between romanticism and science in Bradbury's writings: "All science begins with romance, dwindles naturally to facts, and when the facts turn brittle and dry, the process of refertilization, of re-romanticizing reality, begins, as it must always begin, since there is so much we do not, nor will ever, know."[51] Similar things happen to Poe's influence. In Bradbury's early political fantasy, and most obviously in such stories as "Usher II" (*The Martian Chronicles*) and "The Exiles" (*The Illustrated Man*), Poe is very much a reactive figure full of rage against the forces of repression and censorship, one whom Bradbury needed to ward off the anxiety and frustration of being a fantasy writer in an America that was rejecting fantasy. But *Death Is a Lonely Business* completely transforms his earlier relationship with Poe and makes him appear to be, while still admired, a figure of pessimism and despondency who needs to be overcome.

In his poetry Bradbury seems clearly aware of the sources of his creativity in the identification with a mask and with the doubling of the self that such identification entails. Two poems included in *Zen in the Art of Writing* sum up the need for masks. The first poem, "The Other Me," relates to the uncanniness of the creative process, the doubling of the self:

> I do not write—
> The other me
> Demands emergence constantly. . . .
> His task
> To tell me who I am behind the mask.
> He Phantom is, and I facade
> That hides the opera he writes with God.[52]

One should note that this other creative self—in this case the Phantom of the Opera (whom Bradbury saw and identified with as a child)—is himself also masked. Bradbury too is simultaneously a facade, hiding the workings of this other self, who coauthors with God, and the one who will tell him who he is, that is, his literary self.

The other poem, "We Have Our Arts So We Won't Die of Truth," could certainly stand as Bradbury's *ars poetica*, a poem whose title comes from Nietzsche (section 822 of *The Will to Power*). It ends with a litany to those whom Bradbury regards as true artists:

> Milton does more than drunk God can
> To justify Man's way toward Man.
> And maundered Melville takes as task
> To find the mask beneath the mask.
> And homily by Emily D. shows the dust-bin Man's anomaly.
> And Shakespeare poisons up Death's dart
> And of gravedigging hones an art.
> And Poe divining tides of blood
> Builds Ark of bone to sail the flood.
> Death, then, is painful wisdom tooth;
> With Art as forceps, pull that Truth,
> And plumb the abyss where it was
> Hid deep in dark and Time and Cause.
> Though Monarch Worm devours our heart,
> With Yorick's mouth cry "Thanks!" to Art.[53]

It would seem that every great precursor of Bradbury needs a mask, an evasion of the direct communication of the horrible truth about the chaos of life. Art is a medical instrument, the forceps, that extracts painful "truth" (that is, "wisdom" teeth) from the body. Art is fundamentally discordant with truth, and each artist Bradbury mentions deepens our understanding of the need for masks. In fact, rhetorically, literal meaning in this poem *is* death, against which the poem tropes itself: Melville is maundered,[54] Poe builds an ark of bone, Hamlet "goes mad," and Bradbury speaks through the—presumably toothless—skull of the jester in that play, Yorick, giving thanks to grotesque art, one of the supreme beauties of Shakespeare's theater, according to romantic critics such as Victor Hugo.[55]

Bradbury's poem constructs an entire lineage of artists down from Shakespeare who have looked into the chaos of the abyss and created art. Interestingly, it is God himself who is intoxicated and requires Milton's Apollonian art to justify his ways to man. Among the Americans are Melville, Poe, and Emily Dickinson (the last two seen as Bradbury's literary parents in another poem, "Out of Dickinson by Poe"),[56] each with different masks. Melville's mad Ahab, of course, proclaims that one must "strike through the mask" at the inscrutable reality behind appearances, for him the White Whale (lines whose Shakespearean qualities Bradbury especially sought to preserve in his screenplay for the John Huston film). For Nietzsche, Hamlet was a prime example of the Dionysian character, one who has gained a terrible knowledge that inhibits action: "Action requires the veils of illusion: that is the doctrine of Hamlet." Bradbury's poem voices Nietzsche's words not through the mouth of Hamlet but through the skull of Yorick, who was a fellow of infinite jest. This should serve as a warning about taking Bradbury's Nietzschean themes—and ourselves—too seriously.[57] Although he clearly wants to be among the company of such literary giants, we may discover in him nothing but a jesting mask beneath the mask.

Bradbury's affinities (we do not say influences, for Bradbury claims never to have read Nietzsche directly) with the thematics of Nietzsche's cultural criticism will engage us throughout this study. It is important to note at the outset, however, that in many respects Bradbury differs from the atheist Nietzsche, who considered the will to power a force greater than the will to life. The philosopher used this principle to explain not only man's domination and exploitation of other men but also his capacity to destroy himself. As he tells us at the end of *The Genealogy of Morals,* man would rather will the void than be will-less. It seems to us that, lacking this principle, Bradbury's moral view of the universe may seem "somewhat Teddy-bearish."[58] As a writer of moral fables, he only occasionally looks at how much blood and cruelty lie at the bottom of all human ideals. Although he is clearly at odds with the notion of original sin and Christian guilt and wants to transvalue these notions, Bradbury does not seem to feel that Christianity as a whole is a conspiracy of the weak against the strong. Nor does Bradbury seem to share Nietzsche's radical relativism (which states that there are no facts, only interpretations). He holds that science does uncover a world of facts, even if these facts are powerless to create new values.

Nonetheless, Bradbury seems to share with Nietzsche a high regard for artists as the creators of new values and a concern about overcoming the problems of modernity—nihilism and the crisis of values, in particular—through art and laughter. Like Nietzsche, he wants to overcome the spirit of revenge (in the form of a Gothic past of sin and guilt) and the spirit of gravity, which weighs down all things toward a center of meaning that negates the life of this world. Beyond laughter, Bradbury has different, though related, philosophical and artistic answers to these problems. Where Nietzsche sought to overcome the crisis of modernity by preparing the way for a future culture based on the aristocratic superman (who is the meaning of the Earth) and the eternal return of things as they are, disdaining almost every libertarian and democratic ideal, Bradbury's heroes are often the commoners of the future. Faced with the collapse of religious faith, the death of God, and the vast distances of space, they too must rediscover in their own individual ways the value and the meaning of the world as a principle toward which to be loyal.[59] Although critical of the leveling trends of mass democracies, Bradbury's writings are far from being elitist. On the contrary, they celebrate the popular life of the body in carnival, which is the undoing of all social hierarchies. It is important to remember that the finest wine Bradbury asks readers to imagine is dandelion wine, made from a common flower whose life-enhancing meanings are available to everyone.

There is no question anymore of an "innocent" reading of Bradbury. Everyone reads his works with certain ideological views about his authorship, even those who think they have no theory while viewing him as a "mere entertainer." In our view, these are the most blinded readings because they set up a view of culture depending on hierarchies of meaning ("high" culture versus "low") that Bradbury's writings, considered in their entirety, seek to undermine. Some readers of this book, perhaps most, will resist seeing Bradbury as anything other than a writer of popular fiction. All we can do is present our own critical presuppositions as straightforwardly as possible, alerting the reader to how they function in our critical discourse about Bradbury. We have tried to introduce and clarify critical terms as we go along. This study invokes recent critical understandings about the notion of authorship, about the relationship between an author and his precursors, and the problem of literary genres. Bradbury has been publishing now for over a half century and has virtually become his own influence in the fantasy genre. We are convinced if he is ever going to be taken seriously as more than a mere entertainer, these detours through the mirror maze of contemporary literary theory are necessary. Certainly, Bradbury's fantasy works struggle darkly with some of the same psychic territory Freud explored—delusion and dream, reverie and desire, self-deceptions, fantasies, fears and obsessions, revenge, guilt, and self-punishment—but he seems to have arrived at a post-Gothic affirmation of life. How specifically was this accomplished? That is the question at the center of this study.

Early in his career Bradbury discovered the aesthetic use of masks. The following chapters show that the thematic interplay of masking and unmasking became the heart of Bradbury's carnivalization of genres, which seeks to overcome romantic disillusionment and the pain, anguish, and guilt associated with the internalized Gothic. Actually, for most writers of the fantastic in the latter half of the twentieth century—not just for Bradbury—Freud represents some considerable anxiety of influence, to borrow a term from Harold Bloom. In fact, Tom Shippey, in his introduction to *The Oxford Book of Fantasy Stories*, points out, "one evident fact about modern fantasy is that its authors are perfectly capable of working out Freudian interpretations themselves, and in composing deliberate transformations of traditional structures." Shippey's remarks suggest that Freud himself is implicated in modern fantasy in ways resembling an unconscious complex. Consciously or unconsciously, modern fantasy now *includes* Freud.[60]

What we find compelling about Bradbury's authorship is the way in which he has dealt with the cultural influence of Freud—and other thinkers such as Nietzsche who were "in the culture" during his formative years—through his semi-autobiographical fictions in order to "write dammed fine books and be loved," as he says in his final confrontation with A. L. Shrank. For Bradbury does more than just respond to these thinkers, he carnivalizes them and their ideas. They are not allowed any final authority in his writings. A more detailed account of the uses of the fantastic after Freud is in the discussion of Bradbury's *The October Country*.[61] Further exploration of Bradbury's Nietzschean masks in *The Martian Chronicles* is provided by chapter 2. Our reading of his mystery novels, *Death Is a Lonely Business* and *A Graveyard for Lunatics*, further investigates how Bradbury handles the threat of the death of the author as represented by "pessimist" thinkers such as Freud as well as the threat of madness and obsession that Hollywood film—where the movie screen becomes a captivating mirror— poses to his aesthetic of fantasy.

Among Bradbury's unpublished novels and stories, we also find evidence that he struggled with the dominant ideas of modern culture. *The Masks* deals with the realm of psychoanalysis and was crucial in shaping Bradbury's later aesthetic of fantasy. At around the same time as he was working on that, he was also dealing with the problem of nihilism in culture. Figure 2 reproduces a page from *Where Ignorant Armies Clash by Night*, in which the modern crisis of values

"So," said the old man to the child, "if the scheme of
things is purposeless and meaningless, then the lives of men
are purposeless and meaningless, too. Everything is futile,
all effort is in the ene worthless. A man may, of course, still
pursue disconnected ends, money, fame, art, science, and may
gain pleasure from them. But his life is hollow at the center.
Hence, the dissatisfied, disillusioned, restless, spirit of
modern man. Hence the Death as a value. If Life has no Value,
then give Death a Value. Peace. Peace from worrying, peace
from wondering. Death is positive and restful. It is the
only value we can be SURe, be certain of. There, fore kkk
let our word be OF ALL THINGS, NEVER TO HAVE BEEN BORN IS BEST.
And isn't that right?

   "Yes," said the boy.

   "If you can't fight the meaningless with a religion,
then slide along down the chute with it into oblivion. Make
a religion of Meaninglessness. Make a sect of cruelty. Let
man for the first time revoke the natual laws of survival and
self-preservation. Self preservation? For what, For purposeless
life' No, no! Man now wades further and further out into the
black deep tarpit of Death. Son he will slide from view. Then
the animals will come. The whole thing will start again, from
Faith to Faithlessness, from Meaning to Meaninglessness. Do
you see, my son?"

   "Yes."

   "And this man, this gre t William Donne, is our god, and
we his deciples, revolting against meaninglessness, dying proud
and true to our values, cynical as they may seem."

Figure 2. Cycles of nihilism. The "wise" old man of the dystopian novel *Where Ignorant Armies Clash by Night* explains that the crisis of values tends to go in cycles of increasing intensity and justifies the "religion of Meaninglessness" set up to break cycle. In every dystopian novel there is a figure who explains the rationale of the society to the utopian traveler. The irony emerging from this passage is that the hero, William Donne, is disillusioned with his role as a god. Bradbury never merged the fragments of this novel into a sustained narrative, but he would begin again with another disillusioned hero in "The Fireman" and *Fahrenheit 451*. From the Albright Collection, courtesy of Donn Albright and Ray Bradbury.

is seemingly "overcome" by a reversal of values in which the instinct for self-preservation is negated. The future society that Bradbury depicts has attempted to protect itself from the threat of nihilism (in this case the radical repudiation of value, meaning, and desirability) by creating a civil religion of death. The main features of this faith are being explained by the wise old man of this dystopian novel to a child. Note in particular the idea that nihilism tends to run in culturally intensifying cycles, an idea also prominent in Nietzsche's analysis of nihilism.[62] At the center of this religion are "democratic" rituals of murder and the debasement of high art (that is, book burning), presided over by the "Great Killers" or "Assassins" such as William Donne, popular figures very much like famous entertainers. The novel deals with nihilism ironically by having the assassin himself undergo a crisis of values in which he no longer believes in the meaning of his calling. This unfinished novel later became, after a considerable process of textual transformation detailed in chapter 3, Bradbury's most celebrated book, *Fahrenheit 451*. Both stories deal with the pathos that impels us to seek new values. The hero of *Where Ignorant Armies Clash* only briefly glimpses his way out and ends by committing state-mandated suicide. The hero of *Fahrenheit 451*, Montag, undergoes a similar crisis of values but discovers a way out of the cycles of nihilism though a rediscovery of the meaning of the earth, the notion that this world is far more valuable than previously believed.

This study, while not a biography that simply treats his heroes as versions of himself, does deal with Bradbury's evolving notion of authorship. The center of this is his struggle with the internalized Gothic that Freud's influence represents in our literary culture as well as his struggle with the modern crisis of values. An author is someone who constantly has to reinvent himself through his fiction, often in a struggle with influential precursors. In his introduction to *Modern Fantasy Writers*, Harold Bloom argues that the act of writing is itself a crucial act of living, offering us his conviction that "the life of the author is not merely a metaphor or a fiction, as is 'the Death of the Author,' but it always does contain metaphorical or fictive elements."[63] Our hope is that this study reveals something of the complex interplay between the real Bradbury and his fictive life as an author. We have made extensive use of Bradbury's unpublished manuscripts and his correspondence with his agents and editors to provide information about how they influenced him in the shaping of his stories and how he described his creative ideas and methods to these trusted colleagues. Each chapter opens with an in-depth textual history revealing how Bradbury's literary meanings are the result of a long and often difficult historical process of struggle and self-discovery.

Another compelling aspect of Bradbury's authorship is that, along this path of serious self-discovery, he seems often to have found amusing ways to carnivalize his story ideas for publishing outlets beyond the mainstream. For instance, another unpublished story related to *Where Ignorant Armies Clash by Night* is "Of All Things—Never to Have Been Born Is Best," which creates a parodic travesty of the cycle of tragic nihilism depicted in that novel. The story takes place on "a planet of wild values" whose landscape of "little white chess cities" set beside dry sea bottoms and lit by "unbelievable" red dawns and sunsets suggests the Mars of *The Martian Chronicles*. The mist that surrounds these "fog people" is symbolic of the confused state of values in their culture. William Richard, the unhappy descendant of one of the Greatest Killers, is repeatedly urged to commit a ritual slaying by an old man who believes that "There is nothing better than Nothing-ness" and who claims that it would be an honor to be killed by him. Richard abuses him comically throughout their dialogue by viciously attacking various parts of the old man's body, protesting after each outrage that he still feels nothing. Although the old man finally falls down dead, Richard apparently demurs on the final killing because he is still undergoing a crisis of values and belief in his calling. In the end we learn that the old name of this planet is Earth, but no one cares about that. In this story, which was probably intended for publication in a pulp sci-fi magazine instead of a mainstream publisher, Bradbury creates a twist ending or joke on the more serious notion of a search for earthly meaning.[64]

The very nature of Bradbury's development as a writer—from pulp magazines through massive revision and carnivalization of themes to mainstream book forms that exist on the borderlines of the serious and nonserious—requires literary and textual criticism, publishing history, and a modified form of analytical bibliog-raphy. Such methodological tools are used throughout this study, especially in chapter 2 on *The Martian Chronicles*, where they help reveal how Bradbury trans-formed his pulp fiction stories into those possessing "literary" qualities. Here we investigate Bradbury's compositional process itself by examining the stylistic changes he made to the pulp versions of these stories. His methods of writing, his strategies for revision and sequencing, and his involvement with various drafts of his stories are documented by various facsimiles of pages from Bradbury's manuscripts. The reader will also find various tables and charts that summarize the stages of Bradbury's career or show the evolution of the contents of his story collections. These are designed to enable the reader to grasp at a glance often complicated authorial decisions and selection processes that are covered in detail in the textual histories. Readers can use the charts and tables (together with the appendixes) to pursue their own investigations of Bradbury's career in publishing.

But sometimes these provide information that is not discussed in detail. For instance, table 1 organizes information about Bradbury's early publication ven-ues and indicates the first signs of the startling transformation of his authorship that was to mark his rapid entry into the American mainstream. We do not dis-cuss Bradbury's early career in specific detail in the main body of the text, but

Table 1. Bradbury's progression from amateur fanzines to pulps to major-market "slick" magazines can be traced over the first dozen years of his career through the frequency of publication in each venue. The numerals indicate the number of stories published in a periodical in a given year; numerals in parenthesis indicate second (reprint) magazine appearances. See appendix A for a full listing of stories, year-by-year. See William F. Nolan's *Ray Bradbury Review* (1952) for the first listing to distinguish between Bradbury's pulp and slick publications.

The Early Years: Bradbury's Magazine Story Publications by Market and Title

Year	Amateur Science Fiction Fanzines	Weird and Horror Pulps	Detective Pulps	Science Fiction and Fantasy Pulps	Major Market Periodicals
1938	*Imagination!* 1 *Mikros* 1				
1939	*D'Journal* 2 *Futuria Fantasia* 2 *Science Fiction Fan* 1				
1940	*The Damn Thing* 2 *Fantasite* 1 *Futuria Fantasia* 2 *Polaris* 2 *Spaceways* 1				*Script* (humorous short) 1
1941	*The Damn Thing* 2 *Snide* 1			*Super Science Stories* 1 (co-authored)	*Script* (humorous short) 2
1942		*Weird Tales* 1		*Astounding SF* 1 *Super Science* (Canada) (1)	
1943	*Captain Future* 1 (co-authored)	*Weird Tales* 4 *Weird Tales* (Canada) (5)		*Astonishing Stories* 1 *Astounding SF* 2 *Astounding SF* (UK) (1)	

Table 1. (continued)

The Early Years: Bradbury's Magazine Story Publications by Market and Title

Year	Amateur Science Fiction Fanzines	Weird and Horror Pulps	Detective Pulps	Science Fiction and Fantasy Pulps	Major Market Periodicals
				Famous Fantastic Mys. 1 *Super Science* (Canada) (1) *Thrilling Wonder Stories* 2	
1944		*Weird Tales* 6 *Weird Tales* (Canada) (4)	*Detective Tales* 4 *Dime Mystery* 1 *Flynn's Detective Fiction* 1 *New Detective* 1 *New Detective* (Can.) (1) *Strange Detective Mysteries* (Canada) (1)	*Amazing Stories* 2 *Planet Stories* 3 *Super Science* (Canada) 1	
1945		*Weird Tales* 4 *Weird Tales* (Canada) (7)	*Detective Tales* 1 *Detective Tales* (Can.) (1) *Dime Mystery* 3 *New Detective* 1 *Strange Detective Mysteries* (Canada) (3)		*American Mercury* 1 *Mademoiselle* 1 *Script* 1
1946		*Strange Tales* (UK) (1) *Weird Tales* 4 *Weird Tales* (Canada) (3)	*Dime Mystery* 1 *New Detective* 1 *Rex Stout's Mystery Magazine* (1)	*Amazing Stories* 2 *Planet Stories* 4, including 1 co-authored novella *Thrilling Wonder Stories* 1	*Californian* 2 *Charm* 1 *Colliers* 1 *Mademoiselle* 1 *Story Digest* (1)

Table 1. (*continued*)

The Early Years: Bradbury's Magazine Story Publications by Market and Title

Year	Amateur Science Fiction Fanzines	Weird and Horror Pulps	Detective Pulps	Science Fiction and Fantasy Pulps	Major Market Periodicals
1947		*Weird Tales* 2 *Weird Tales* (Canada) (3)	*Dime Mystery* 1	*Avon Fantasy Reader* (1) *Fantastic Adventures* 1 *Planet Stories* 2 *Thrilling Wonder Stories* 1	*Epoch* 1 *Harper's* 1 *Mademoiselle* 1 *New Yorker* 1 *Touchstone* 1
1948		*Weird Tales* 3 *Weird Tales* (Canada) (3)	*Dime Mystery* 1 *Detective Book* 1	*Avon Fantasy Reader* (1) *Famous Fantastic Mys.* 1 *Planet Stories* 3 *Startling Stories* 1 *Thrilling Wonder Stories* 6	*Charm* 1 *MacLean's* (Canada) 1 *Script* 1
1949				*Avon Fantasy Reader* (1) *Planet Stories* (1) *Planet Stories* (Canada) (1) *Startling Stories* 2 *Super Science Stories* 3 *Super Science Stories* (1) *Super Science* (UK) (1) *Thrilling Wonder Stories* 5	*Argosy* (UK) (3) *Arkham Sampler* 3 *Charm* 1 *MacLean's* (Canada) 1 *Seventeen* 1

that information is available in tabular form. Most of his publications during this period are in fan or pulp magazines, but after the war things began to change—his apprentice years were giving way to years of consistently good writing in an office he set up in the garage his father shared with his employer, California Power and Light. Bradbury soon began to place more and more stories in major American magazines, and by 1947 he was actively, though unsuccessfully, marketing his novel *Summer Morning, Summer Night* (a decade later Bradbury would transform the best episodes of this manuscript into *Dandelion Wine*) and a number of story-collection concepts to major publishing houses. But Bradbury held back all his *Masks* chapters and chapter concepts from publishers—only the primitive masks on the dust jacket of *Dark Carnival* provide any indication of his deepening fascination with carnival aspects of the creative process. Largely unknown manuscripts such as these have an important role to play in the unfolding discussion of Bradbury's authorship that forms the bulk of this study. His literary agents and publishers, whom we will now briefly mention, played an equally important role.

The hallmarks of Bradbury's creative genius in the carnivalization of genres is perhaps most evident in his relationships with those individuals in his life who most clearly understood and supported his sense of authorship. Frequently, he had some difficulty in placing his stories in the more formula-ridden genre-market magazines, which did not always understand how he used carnival themes in his writing. During the war years, he found an excellent advisor and agent in Julius Schwartz, who marketed Bradbury's unique brand of pulp fiction through the full range of science fiction, weird, fantasy, and detective magazines. By the end of World War II, Bradbury was working closely with Arkham House publisher August Derleth on what would become *Dark Carnival*, his first collection of stories. As discussed in chapter 1, Bradbury's talent matured incredibly fast during these years, and he found himself leaving both his first agent and his first editor behind even as he continued to work on projects with them. By 1945 Bradbury was sending his stories to major-market magazines on his own, and to the delight of both author and agent, placing them in the slicks with increasing regularity. The next year Derleth found that he could not keep up with Bradbury's changes in the proofs of *Dark Carnival*, for the young author worked feverishly to capture his new maturity in what had been intended initially as a showcase for his successful early career as a writer of weird tales. Bradbury would also no longer need the mentorship of his good friends and fellow writers Leigh Brackett and Hank Kuttner, though he would remain a close friend to each of the science fiction writers who encouraged him and occasionally helped him through blocks in his early pulp stories. His unique style and deeply felt, often autobiographical subjects quickly matured into a lifetime of Bradbury originals.

Two abiding influences came into his life during the early postwar years.

Bradbury has often expressed in his personal as well as professional correspondence the significant influence of his wife, Marguerite McClure Bradbury, and Don Congdon, his agent since 1947. Maggie Bradbury's wide-ranging education in languages and literature always complemented Bradbury's own passion for reading, and Congdon's combination of business sense and discerning literary tastes made him Bradbury's chief advisor and sounding board in all his various creative ventures. Carnival has no spectators—everyone participates—and Bradbury has always drawn his editors (as well as many of his publishers) into the process of launching and marketing his books. By 1949 he had signed with Doubleday's Walter Bradbury, and by the time his editor moved on a decade later, they had worked together on *The Martian Chronicles, The Illustrated Man, The Golden Apples of the Sun, Dandelion Wine,* and *A Medicine for Melancholy.* During those years, only two significant titles went elsewhere, as Ian Ballantine lured Bradbury away briefly to publish *Fahrenheit 451* and *The October Country,* an updated collection of weird tales based in large part on the *Dark Carnival* collection.

After the departure of Walt Bradbury, dissatisfaction over Doubleday's failure to promote him as a major-market author led Ray Bradbury to Simon and Schuster in 1960. Chapters 4 and 5 document the circumstances that led Doubleday to release Bradbury from his contract for *Farewell Summer,* a novel previewed by *Dandelion Wine* but never published in its own right. Bradbury would do no more original work for Doubleday, but he returned in the early 1960s to produce the largely derivative but immensely popular young-reader collections *R Is for Rocket* and *S Is for Space.* His first sustained full-length novel, *Something Wicked This Way Comes,* was produced with crucial support from both Congdon and his Simon and Schuster editor, Bob Gottlieb, who would also edit *The Machineries of Joy* and bring back *Fahrenheit 451* in a hardbound edition to observe the release of director François Truffaut's critically acclaimed film version. Gottlieb soon became the top executive at Knopf, and in 1968 Bradbury also signed on, thus beginning a twenty-three-year publishing association with three Knopf editors. Between them, Gottlieb, Nancy Nicholas, and Kathy Hourigan worked closely with Bradbury on three major story collections (*I Sing the Body Electric! Long after Midnight,* and *The Toynbee Convector*), *The Halloween Tree,* three volumes of verse, and the two detective novels that confirmed Bradbury's ability to consolidate his reputation as a master of both short and long fiction—*Death Is a Lonely Business* and *A Graveyard for Lunatics.*

Bradbury's enduring availability through libraries and through the carefully marketed Bantam and Ballantine paperback editions of his books has provided the foundation for his own lifelong efforts to stay on top of the carnival procession called publishing. In 1991 Lou Aronica made it possible for Bradbury to come to Avon and establish a line of both hardbound and quality trade paperbound editions, in effect guaranteeing that the Bradbury canon would always be in print. Under the capable editorship of Jennifer Brehl, Bradbury has weathered the transition of Avon within the larger Morrow and HarperCollins publishing umbrellas. In nearly every chapter we will also discuss Bradbury's close working relationship with Rupert Hart-Davis, who published and sustained British editions of all the major Bradbury titles well into the 1970s. Corgi, Bantam's British imprint, carried his British paperback popularity through the same period, but both of these publishers gave way to Grafton, Granada, and eventually the same HarperCollins empire that now oversees much of the Bradbury canon on both sides of the Atlantic.

Over the last quarter century, Bradbury has also worked closely with friends beyond the walls of his publishing houses. Such extended relationships have always been an indicator of the intensity with which Bradbury revised his work before releasing it for publication. The three middle chapters of this study, chronicling the textual and thematic histories of *Fahrenheit 451*, *Dandelion Wine*, and *Something Wicked This Way Comes*, also reveal an author who worked best with an agent and a single sponsoring editor at the publisher. In the mid-1950s Don Congdon was able to persuade Bradbury not to send close friend and literary critic Gilbert Highet manuscripts to read, for this would only extend the tortuous process of revision. Decades later, as Bradbury brought a more effective and fully carnivalized writing process to bear on his longer fiction, it became easier for him to bring other trusted readers into the mix. In chapters 6 and 7 we describe how fellow writers William F. Nolan and Sid Stebel have at times become part of the carnival procession and how the manuscript discoveries of Nolan and principal bibliographer Donn Albright inspired Bradbury to revisit the best of his unpublished early fiction as he conceived all of his later story collections.

Nolan is, in fact, the prime example of a colleague who influenced Bradbury's thinking about fantasy, and he has done so as both a bibliographer and a fellow writer. Nolan's pioneering *Ray Bradbury Review* includes significant early insights into the carnival life of Bradbury's fiction by Henry Kuttner and Bradbury himself. Decades later, Nolan would author the first comprehensive essay on Bradbury's carnivalized process of authorship. Along the way, Nolan would also help Bradbury reflect on his own multiple-author fantasy anthologies and all of his own story collections during the second half of his career. In his introduction to *The Circus of Dr. Lao and Other Improbable Stories* (1956), for instance, in which he thanks Nolan for his help "all down the line," Bradbury draws upon the essays of Lionel Trilling in order to show how fantasy disrupts the laws of the physical world (adhered to by science fiction) in order to bring change to the heart and mind. Citing Trilling's definition of romance, Bradbury defines fantasy as "a synonym for the will in its creative aspect, especially in its aspect of moral creativeness, as it subjects itself to criticism and conceives for itself new states of being." Fantasy must move beyond the physical facts of life to encounter new realities in "the beautiful circuit of thought and desire."[65]

In a manner reminiscent of Bakhtin's thinking about carnival, Bradbury off-sets Charles Finney's fantasy circus (in the title story of the Bradbury anthology) against the sphere of official culture, against those "still in the temple, political gymnasium, or school," where the body is seen as completed, finished, and under its classical aspects, equally removed from the womb as from the grave. The romantic vision, however, sees the world and the body through a "grotesquely warped lens"—the parallel with Bakhtin's notion of "grotesque realism" in carnival is striking—that emphasizes its unfinished character and often sees it in the throes of death or the birth of new life. Furthermore, considered as a text, Finney's circus (and the other stories Bradbury selected for inclusion in the volume) embraces its own ambivalence and destruction, inviting, if readers desire them, "critical assaults which may burn Dr. Lao's miraculous show to earth. No matter; others, happening by, will raise its tents again." In the carnival, as Bakhtin observes, there are no "footlights." We simply cannot be spectators. We are deeply implicated in the life and death of the carnival and its play of masking and unmasking life and death. Bradbury insists that we live by creating and that we create "by alternating wonder and criticism followed by new states of wonder."[66]

To Bradbury, awareness of the will in its beautiful circuit of thought and desire is the peculiar property of fantasy, which itself alternates wonder with carnivalesque criticism. Above all, fantasy shows us that intellectual structures themselves are not to be adhered to indefinitely: "Man should not live to keep any single political or philosophical architecture, neat, clean, and impregnable; rather such frameworks should exist for *use,* to be razed and burnt, once their time is past [emphasis added]." Here is a kernel of knowledge about Bradbury's use of Nietzschean and carnivalesque philosophical themes: only what is necessary to affirm one's life—the life of fiction—must be kept and maintained, only to be further transformed.[67]

In terms of textual history and textual thematics, the story of Bradbury's authorship will emerge from the pages that follow. Metaphors, myths, and masks are the global structures by which he constructs the various versions of himself that the reader will encounter in the main chapters of this study. It is a story that involves us in the textual life of his fiction, for the manuscript and correspondence record leads us through an "unmasking" of Bradbury's books to find the author in process behind the published work of art. In many of the chapters that follow (especially those on *The Martian Chronicles* and *Fahrenheit 451*), we have taken special care to present facsimile illustrations that recapture the creative evolution of Bradbury's manuscripts so that readers too can become participants in this story of authorship.[68]

1

Out of the House of Arkham

Dark Carnival and The October Country

Dark Carnival, Bradbury's first book, showcases his unique approach to weird fiction, an approach that focuses more on the hopes and fears of his own childhood and hardly at all on the traditional plot conventions of the genre. Despite its title, which describes Bradbury's intention for the collection as a whole, this first book is not an integrated literary carnival. But its very conception shows a gathering of past achievements joined with an openness to reshaping and recontextualizing the individual stories within a new and larger whole; such an ongoing creative process is the essence of carnivalization in literature. He would soon achieve a fully integrated literary carnival through the bridges and revised story-chapters of *The Martian Chronicles.* But Bradbury began his lifelong process of placing his stories in new contexts with *Dark Carnival,* and the process of creating that collection spanned his transition from the niche-market pulps to the mainstream magazines. Many of these tales could have succeeded in a wider market, and indeed four of the collected stories—"The Homecoming," "The Cistern," "The Man Upstairs," and "The Next in Line"—were purchased by major market magazines while *Dark Carnival* was still at press. Even those that appeared in the pulps have had an enduring popularity. "The Lake," "The Crowd," and "The Small Assassin" have rich reprint histories, and Bradbury would eventually rework them all in the 1980s for *The Ray Bradbury Theater.* "The Night" and "The Man Upstairs" represent two of the earliest Green Town stories and would eventually become part of the larger fabric of fiction from which *Dandelion Wine* would take shape. In "The Homecoming," "The Traveler," and "Uncle Einar," Bradbury created the first of the vampire "family" stories that, after more than fifty years of development, finally became a fully novelized story cycle, *From the Dust Returned.*

The pieces selected for *Dark Carnival* represent the beginning of a tremendous range of storylines radiating far beyond Bradbury's pulp fiction years, and not surprisingly he revised most of the magazine originals as he developed this first collection. *Dark Carnival* also marks the beginning of Bradbury's lifelong impulse to revise and modify the contents of entire volumes; in fact, his first book would prove to be a perpetual work-in-progress. Even before the collection reached print, Bradbury was already transforming the contents into a more literary, less vulgar carnival collection that showed more of where he was going and less of where he had been. He moved stories in and out of the volume for months before he felt right about the American edition, only to face abridgment of the English edition due to continuing postwar paper shortages. Over the next fifteen years, *Dark Carnival* would form the basis for *The October Country* in the United States (1955) and England (1956), as well as an English two-volume conflation of both collections published in paperback as *The October Country* (abridged, 1961) and *The Small Assassin* (1962). In 2001 Bradbury authorized a limited edition expanded to include four of the *Weird Tales* stories he had originally left out in 1947. He revised most of these stories at least once and over the years has reprinted them often as separates in magazines and anthologies. Yet the stories at the heart of these successive variations were all written between 1943 and 1946; even before its publication in the spring of 1947, Bradbury's first book represented a backward glance at a kind of story he would rarely write again. Nevertheless, his weird tales provided the first opportunity for Bradbury to publish book-length fiction, and here a significant textual history begins.

Bradbury's Texts

By 1946 Bradbury had gone as far as he could with weird fiction, but his impressive three-year run in that field, along with simultaneous success as a writer of detective fiction, earned him a solid reputation with an ever-widening circle of magazine editors. Much of the time he still lived with his parents and older brother, having moved with them from Los Angeles out to the slowly declining working neighborhoods of Venice Beach, California, in 1941. He sold newspapers at a downtown Los Angeles newsstand until the end of 1942, when he was able to make a living, of sorts, from his story sales to the pulps. During the war years, he maintained a day office in a cheap apartment on Figuroa Street, within the diverse Filipino, Mexican, and Chinese neighborhoods that would provide material for later stories and novels. Bradbury took his mail there and occasionally lived in this section of town. He also worked from a home office in his father's garage, next to the humming powerhouse of the local electric utility, transforming metaphors and personal experiences into a wider range of fantasy and science fiction stories that were selling more and more frequently to the mainstream quality magazines. It was here, in spring 1946, that Bradbury reworked the contents of *Dark Carnival* to make it more than a showcase of his initial success as a very unusual writer of weird tales. His transitional view of the project reflected the rapid changes in his own career during these years, and his desire to rework and reprint stories from the collection sometimes clashed with the editorial wishes of his friend and first publisher, Arkham House founder August Derleth.

Bradbury was not yet a professional writer when he began to correspond with Derleth. In 1939 Derleth and his partner, Donald Wandrei, established Arkham House to publish the complete work (and eventually the correspondence) of H. P. Lovecraft. Derleth handled all editorial and business matters from his home in Sauk City, Wisconsin; in November 1939 his first Lovecraft volume, *The Outsider and Others*, elicited an enthusiastic fan letter from then nineteen-year-old Bradbury.[1] The contact developed further, for Bradbury had access to letters Lovecraft had written to Adolph de Castro and offered to copy them for the Arkham House letters project. Bradbury sent the copies and in turn asked Derleth for stories to include in issues of his amateur fanzine, *Futuria Fantasia*. Derleth was financing Arkham House with equity loans and sales of his own stories and so was unable to supply Bradbury with any material for his shoestring publication.[2] But their shared tastes in weird fiction extended to music, poetry, and even newspaper comics, and a long-distance friendship was established. Derleth's personal interest grew into genuine admiration in 1942, when Bradbury began to place stories in *Weird Tales*, the most enduring and best known of the American fantasy pulps.

Bradbury's relationship with *Weird Tales* began the same year he wrote to Derleth and developed just as slowly. He had met longtime *Weird Tales* editor Farnsworth Wright in 1939 during his summer pilgrimage to the first world science-fiction convention in New York.[3] His efforts to interest Wright and a number of other science fiction and fantasy pulp editors in his earliest stories were not successful, but he made useful contacts and returned home to Los Angeles and the fruitful influence of the fans and writers of the Science Fiction League. He prospered under the encouragement of such writers as Robert Heinlein and Henry Kuttner, who was also a good friend of Derleth. Kuttner began to work with Bradbury's manuscripts in late 1938 and continued to do so even after his move to New York the following year. In 1942 he suggested a more effective conclusion for Bradbury's story "The Candle," and this conventional horror tale was accepted by Farnsworth Wright's successor, Dorothy McIlwraith, for the November issue of *Weird Tales*.[4]

But by the time "The Candle" appeared, Bradbury had already grown out of the weird formula and discovered a creative approach that would dominate the early pulp-fiction years of his career. A decade later he pinpointed the moment of transition. "My first story for *Weird Tales* was an unsuccessful narrative THE CANDLE, using familiar plot, stock characters, and a predictable climax. The same can be said of my first stories for *Planet* and *Thrilling Wonder Stories*. It was only when I learned to write from my own experience and asked myself 'What have *you* got that is *new* to give to the field?' that my stories began to shape themselves with some degree of originality." What he had to give was indeed new and original, as he recalled in a later unpublished interview. "After that first sale, I began to find myself, and I began to write the more unusual type of weird story based on my own encounters with life. I realize, now, that I knew absolutely nothing about human character: I knew nothing of life. I was naive, to the point of distraction, about most things; but I did know one thing very well. I knew my own nightmares and terrors and fears about the world."[5]

Bradbury's subsequent submissions were often very different from the usual *Weird Tales* fare, but McIlwraith was willing to stretch the traditional criteria to get Bradbury's unique style and talent into her magazine on a regular basis. Derleth, who had contributed stories to *Weird Tales* since the mid-1920s, quickly realized that his young friend's unique talent was fast becoming a strong new presence in the field. He and Bradbury both placed stories in the March 1943 *Weird Tales*, and Bradbury would appear in the May, July, and November issues as well. In 1944 Bradbury stories appeared in all six bimonthly issues, and he placed thirteen more tales in science fiction, fantasy, and detective pulps. McIlwraith and Montgomery Buchanan, who made the initial recommendations on submissions to *Weird Tales*, wanted more stories, but by this time they were reluctant to take any more of Bradbury's examinations of childhood fears. In September he described his reaction to Derleth: "Weird warns me not to write any more child fantasies, and this saddens me because I have ten or more of them finished or half-finished. And I hate to write about vampires, darn it."[6] Bradbury placed many of his subsequent childhood terrors with other pulps and would soon develop his own very special kind of vampire story for other markets as well. Meanwhile, Derleth found the entire range of Bradbury's weird fiction exceptional, and by the end of the year, he asked for a selection of stories to consider for *Who Knocks?* an anthology of weirds he was beginning to put together for Rinehart. The selections made quite an impression on Derleth, and in early January 1945 he made an offer to publish a collection of Bradbury's "off trail" weirds if the young author would come up with a unifying concept.[7] This proposal showed just how much he thought of Bradbury's talent—by this time Derleth was reaching beyond the Lovecraft canon to publish the work of friends who were established writers in the weird field, but the firm's tight budget left little money to gamble on a new writer.

Derleth's offer has not been located, but Bradbury's response indicates that other Arkham projects had priority: "I want to thank you for your suggestion that some time in the next two years Arkham House might try an anthology of Bradbury stories." Derleth may also have wanted to see more production before offering a contract, for Bradbury added, "I certainly hope to continue turning out stories of the calibre necessary to make such a volume possible." His hope would become fact—he published thirteen stories in 1945, including five in *Weird Tales*, and finally two in "slick" tabloid magazines with national circulations. Bradbury was entering his first period of sustained sales, yet he was already looking back with an eye to revise stories for his first collection: "Some of my early stories, if ever reprinted, would need quite a bit of rewriting to re-shape them into my present way of thinking and producing." He immediately offered an overall structure and topical concept that he had been developing on his own for some time: "For over a year now I've been working and planning an entire volume of short stories concerning children in fantasy and weird settings . . . this volume to be titled A CHILDS [*sic*] GARDEN OF TERROR. I hoped to eventually submit the completed book to a publisher in 1946 or 1947, depending on the development and quality of each yarn" (ellipses Bradbury's).[8]

A page-long typed paragraph from an apparently incomplete introduction still survives, along with a typed table of contents. Thirteen stories are listed, and eight would eventually appear in *Dark Carnival*. These documents are undated but were prepared no later than the fall of 1944; in November he offered the concept to his friend Jack Snow at NBC radio as a reading anthology, but network concerns over possible PTA responses made that offer a nonstarter (Snow himself was unable to place his own Oz stories on the air for the same reason).[9] Bradbury's tentative introduction to the collection reveals the motivation behind the concept: "A CHILD'S GARDEN OF TERROR is based on my fears of death and of growing old, and of my loving and longing for childhood. When these fears are so bound up in a writer's personality, it makes it very easy for him to write his stories." But the opening is fragmentary and unfocused, and Bradbury's garden of terror was never fully cultivated in this form. A letter from Derleth requesting a tentative list of contents and suggesting a broad rather than a narrow unifying theme crossed Bradbury's January 29 letter in the mail. Two days later Bradbury broadened his initial concept accordingly: "Your letter also completely changed my ideas about a title for such a book, if and when we were able to agree on its various facets. A CHILD'S GARDEN OF TERROR is an unsuitable title, because it would restrict the contents. Such stories as THE SCYTHE, THE JAR, and THERE WAS AN OLD WOMAN simply wouldn't fit under such a title. Therefore I'll give myself over to the task of worrying out a shorter, more all-inclusive title. The CHILD'S GARDEN OF TERROR can be laid aside until much later, until I am able to struggle through and finish all my child stories."[10] Although they never became a collection in their own right, these children's stories would prove to be central to some of Bradbury's most significant lifelong projects. The 1944 story-collection concept provided stories for *Dark Carnival* and *The October Country*, including Bradbury's own unique stories of a hybrid family of vampires that would evolve a half-century later into the novel *From the Dust Returned*. The *Child's Garden* quickly evolved into outlines for two of his nostalgic masterpieces—a dark carnival novel that in 1962 would become *Something Wicked This Way Comes* and a novel of a small-town battle of wills between young boys and old men. This latter project, under various titles, remains an unpublished novel, but he transformed its most nostalgic elements into the timeless classic *Dandelion Wine* in 1957.

Bradbury soon shaped some of these childhood stories and others into a new context that fit the offer he had received from Derleth, who soon suggested that the young author develop subheadings to group stories with like themes or subjects. This carnivalizing process opened up the stories to new interpretations, and perhaps not at all surprisingly, Bradbury would turn to an overarching metaphor from his own childhood loves to define the collection. In March 1945 he suggested *Dark Carnival* as the new collection's title and described two titled sections: "One section could do well under the title A CHILD'S GARDEN OF TERROR. Another, concerning circuses and their inhabitants, a series of such tales which I am now planning, would go well under the main title heading DARK CARNIVAL. I'm writing the *story* DARK CARNIVAL now and will submit it to Weird in a few weeks. Some time in the next few months I'll send the partial list."[11]

Bradbury's draft of this letter also includes a detailed proposal for a jacket illustration of a surreal carnival dominated by a grotesque carousel.[12] A preliminary version of the table of contents offered to Derleth survives, containing four untitled groupings of five stories each (fig. 3). Most of the childhood terrors are listed in a single grouping, but only two carnival tales remain, and only one ("The Jar") would make it into the published collection. An unknown story, "Carnival," appears directly above "The Jar" in the list. It may be the original title story "Dark Carnival" that Bradbury described in his March 1945 draft proposal; if so, it would become "The Black Ferris" (1948), one of the last stories Bradbury would publish in *Weird Tales*. It is also possible that "Carnival" evolved into "The Illustrated Man"—the very same outline includes "The Tattooed Man" as an alternate title for the book. From the beginning, the carnival concept seems to have been bigger than the volume could accommodate, for Bradbury would eventually develop both stories into books. The tattooed man became both title and linking device for *The Illustrated Man* (1951), and "The Black Ferris" would

```
DARK CARNIVAL
    1.                          2.
  THE BABY                    THE EMISSARY

  THE CROWD                   THE LAKE

  THE SCYTHE                  THE NIGHT

  THE POEMS                   THE MAN UPSTAIRS

  THE OLD WOMAN               THE PEOPLE OUT THERE

    3.                          4.

  SKELETON                    THE DUCKER

  THE TOMBSTONE               CHRYSALIS

  CARNIVAL                    THE WATCHERS

  THE JAR                     THE MOKIE THING

  THE WIND                    THE LLUBLE.




THE DARK CARACEL

FOUR AND TWENTY


DARK CARNIVAL

THE TATTOOED MAN


DARK CARNIVAL. . . cover design showing merry-go-round with weird
                   blue and grey and black monsters rotating,
                   also huge banners showing weird monsters in side-
                   show. . .on the shore of a lake, perhaps. . .
```

Figure 3. Bradbury's revised outline for a collection of weird tales incorporates August Derleth's suggestion for contents divided into five-story segments. By early March 1945 Bradbury had settled on the *Dark Carnival* title, which appears at the top of the outline and again at the bottom, after a short list of possibilities. Twelve of the twenty stories listed here eventually appeared in the collection: "The Baby" (as "The Small Assassin"), "The Crowd," "The Scythe," "The Old Woman" (as "There Was an Old Woman"), "The Emissary," "The Lake," "The Night," "The Man Upstairs," "Skeleton," "The Tombstone," "The Jar," and "The Wind." The identifiable stories in group 2 appear to be the "Child's Garden of Terror" grouping described in Bradbury's draft letter of March 8, 1945. He eventually abandoned the idea of grouping stories within the volume. From the Albright Collection, courtesy of Donn Albright and Ray Bradbury.

become an unpublished screenplay before growing into the novel *Something Wicked This Way Comes* (1962).

Despite the lack of a carnival grouping of stories, his new title remained—the metaphor was powerful enough to absorb changes in content, and Bradbury knew it. "I think that the mood of [the] cover and the apt title—DARK (suggesting strange, outre and blasphemous things) CARNIVAL (suggesting a procession, a celebration, a series of activities) would sell the book well."[13] His willingness to move from the "Child's Garden" concept into the "Dark Carnival" concept, and to experiment with contents at every stage of development, provides the first evidence of his lifelong tendency to move stories in and out of book-length projects in ways that often blurred the distinction between story collection and novel. The textual history of *Dark Carnival*, largely unstudied today, reveals the pattern for revision that Bradbury would bring to all his major book titles of the 1950s.

In the end he eliminated internal divisions completely and eventually settled on a bookend structure that placed his two best stories at the beginning and the end of the collection. But these two stories—"The Homecoming" and "The Next in Line"—were not even ready for serial sales yet. Much work remained before the contents were stabilized, and this task would be complicated by two factors: the continuing explosion of acceptances for Bradbury stories, and the fact that more and more of these acceptances were coming from mainstream magazines. He tacitly acknowledged this transition by dedicating *Dark Carnival* to Grant Beach, a close friend who convinced Bradbury to submit his stories to major "slick" magazines as early as 1945. Beach's advice quickly paid off—during a single week in August 1945, Bradbury received three major magazine acceptances (all three works were broader-market fantasies that would appear in later story collections). The money paid for the pair's eight-week trip to Mexico later that fall.[14] These events signaled the beginning of his break with the pulps, but the darker experiences of the trip would find their way into perhaps the best *Dark Carnival* selection, "The Next in Line." And the excursion would have a decisive influence on Bradbury's visual concept of the dust jacket—his idea for a carousel-centered carnival scene would be discarded in favor of a photographic collage of primitive masks collected during his Mexican odyssey.

During the summer of 1945, Derleth had seen enough progress to go ahead with negotiations for *Dark Carnival*. In August Bradbury provided a three-tier list of titles he wanted to see in the collection: seven tales that Derleth had already seen and approved, seven more that were submitted and awaiting approval, and a final group of seven that Bradbury was still writing. This last group included only one story that would appear in a pulp ("Dark Carnival," published as "The Black Ferris"). Another story in this yet-unpublished group was "Powerhouse," which would earn Bradbury his second O. Henry Prize Story award in 1948. With this list, Bradbury began to alter the concept of the collection from a survey of his best weird tales to a record of his movement away from the pulps and into the mainstream of American periodicals. And now that this transition had landed him in the book market, he would have to negotiate for himself. Julius Schwartz was now an executive with All-American Comics and on his way to a pioneering role in the silver-age development of the hugely popular DC Comics group. He only represented Bradbury in his negotiations with pulp magazine editors and advised his client to secure a full-time agent to represent him in major-market magazine and book negotiations. Schwartz knew that Derleth would want half the income from reprint sales of individual stories and advised against it; he also sensed that Bradbury would soon draw book and media offers for his work and felt that Derleth might not offer the best terms for a rising talent.[15]

Bradbury's growing need for an agent who could negotiate editorial flexibility began to surface as he entered final contract negotiations with Derleth. By the end of August, *Dark Carnival* was on the Arkham House list of titles for fall 1946 release, with manuscript submission scheduled for February 1946. In early December 1945 Derleth prepared a first-book contract and sent it out to Bradbury for signature. Mindful of Schwartz's advice and of his own changing conception of the collection, Bradbury wanted assurance that he had some freedom to market his stories after the collection was published. In a surviving draft of his request for clarification, Bradbury initially agreed to enclose the signed contract, but in the final letter he decided to send the contract only after Derleth clarified this clause: "It is further agreed that the profits arising from any publication of said work, during the period covered by this agreement, in other than book form shall be divided equally between the PUBLISHERS and said AUTHOR."[16]

Derleth explained that Arkham House would control reprint negotiations and take half of the payments on the reprint of any of the stories from the time that the book was set in galleys until six months after *Dark Carnival* went out of print. This was a standard agreement based on Derleth's own experiences as an author with larger publishing houses such as Scribner's, Pellegrini and Cudahy, and Rinehart. The terms of the contract would create friction at times with some of his authors, but it was not unusual for a publisher to request a share of second serial and anthology profits for the contents of story collections, which are almost always a tough marketing venture from the publisher's point of view. Bradbury assumed correctly that the 50-50 split on subsidiary rights applied to anthology and magazine reprints but not to initial magazine sales prior to publication of *Dark Carnival*. The young author was riding a wave of creativity that led him to push for any contractual flexibility he could get, an impulse most evident in the evolving table of contents. He continued to move older or less successful stories out of the collection, replacing them with newer, better weird tales that had not yet appeared in magazines. For his part, Derleth was willing to use the publicity generated by Bradbury's newer major-market stories, but he was not at all interested in adding them to what he still considered a selection of Bradbury's best weird tales.[17]

He did, however, allow Bradbury to work on his own to turn his idea of masks into a printable dust-jacket illustration. This new concept became all the more important as Bradbury moved his "Dark Carnival" story completely out of the collection, for he was now seeing it as the beginning of a different novel-length project that would eventually become *Something Wicked This Way Comes*. The carnival-carousel jacket idea was further exploded late in 1945 with the coincidental appearance of the Arthur Hawkins carousel design on the jacket of Henry Robinson's popular new novel *The Perfect Round*. In December Bradbury gathered some of the Mexican Indian masks from his recent trip and began work with noted California photographer George Barrows to create a suitable photographic collage. Barrows was known for the covers and illustrations he had photographed for various literary magazines, and he had received critical attention from Ansel Adams. By March 1946 Derleth had selected one of two covers that Bradbury had designed with Barrows and added his own editorial touch—angry red letters for the title and byline.[18] Bradbury was pleased with the overall effect; it allowed him to retain the *Dark Carnival* title, for the masks emerged out of an image of a carousel horse in motion. But the collage and its origins also allowed him to visually raise the collection out of the vulgar low carnival of the pulps and into a more literary carnival that looked forward to all that the future promised; the self-conscious, artistic masks replaced the low-carnival artifacts of the carousel and other midway rides. Bradbury had carefully chosen a recognized artist to create this effect rather than any of his beloved pulp illustrators, and he was careful to give Barrows equal space on the back jacket flap for his own biographical note.

In March 1946 Bradbury was still working on four new stories and was granted an extension to mid-April for submission. Derleth was already getting advance orders for a book that was far from finished.[19] But by now the collection was beginning to take shape. Bradbury had locked in "The Homecoming" as the opening story and was nearly done with "The Next in Line," the long story he would use to close the book. He was willing to drop three of the pulps (including "The Watchers" and "The Poems") to fit in this new tale but held off for the time being. By April he was hard at work on major rewrites of "The Crowd" and "The Wind," and Derleth had no choice but to extend the deadline again. In early June Bradbury submitted a twenty-nine-story typescript to match Derleth's earlier advertisements for the contents of the book, but the submission included seven new titles that had not been on earlier outlines of contents. Meanwhile,

Bradbury continued to send the newer unpublished stories out to the mainstream slick magazines. In this way he was able to secure major periodical sales for "The Homecoming," "The Man Upstairs," "Cistern," and "The Next in Line."[20]

These sales all came prior to book publication and caused no major problems between author and editor. Derleth was a conscientious and straightforward publisher, but his tendency to be a stickler on details soon led to minor disagreements. During June 1946, he patiently worked with Bradbury on the copyright statements for the volume. This would prove to be an area of conflict between Bradbury and his successive editors for decades to come, but Derleth did more than most to present the publisher's position in an objective way. Bradbury insisted that the copyright statements refer to the original pulp publications as little as possible—he was convinced that any references to such origins for the collection would make a negative impression on reviewers and critics. His solution was to combine the copyright citations for each magazine publisher, thus reducing the number of *Weird Tales* citations from fifteen to one providing only the years that the stories appeared in that magazine. This was a very reasonable request, but his further suggestion touched on the real issue—he asked Derleth to look into securing full releases from *Weird Tales* so they could eliminate all references to the magazine on the copyright page.

Derleth realized that many of Bradbury's pulp stories were quality tales suitable for a wider audience; in the end he acquiesced and gave the minimal legal statements on the copyright page. But he clearly had not accepted the fact that Bradbury was moving out of the genre for good and took issue with the author's view that *Weird Tales* had confined his talent in any way. From Derleth's perspective, the magazine's editors had gone out of their way to publish Bradbury's off-trail weirds because they found him to be a strong new talent, and they should not be bought out of the copyright credits. Even the agreed-upon minimal copyright reference to the magazine was risky; Derleth felt that the general copyright statements Bradbury wanted could jeopardize the copyright protection on the individual tales.

Bradbury's three-page reply laid out in no uncertain terms his willingness to leave those stories unprotected if necessary to secure his departure from his early roots in the pulps. And he offered a strong counterpoint to Derleth's observation that *Weird Tales* had provided adequate creative space for Bradbury: "Well, that may be true, but the pressure was there all of the time to turn me into a hack. And it was an unfair pressure, because I had no money, and the temptation was great." He held nothing against his editors, but they wanted him to be an entertainer, and he was becoming more than that. He was quite willing to cut off his creative connection to the low carnival life of the entertainer, and this is evident in his final metaphor on the subject: "In closing, then, I hope you'll let me take the responsibility for the castrated copyright page, for in the event of any literary pilfering, it shall be I, not you, who will some time later be heard crying in a high, eunuch's soprano."[21]

His declared intention to marginalize the vulgar aspects of his dark carnival led to major structural changes that extended the carnivalization process into a more literary context (table 2). Through revisions to old stories and the submission of new ones, Bradbury was able to use the evolving *Dark Carnival* collection to signify that a literary author had arrived—the book was no longer just a record of his promising pulp origins. Throughout most of 1946, he would continue to rewrite stories, add new ones, and discard those older and less mature, in the process giving the collection a tremendous new range in tone. Bradbury's September trip to New York delayed galley revisions, and release was rescheduled for April 1947. But from his perspective, that long cross-country bus excursion was worth the delay, for he accomplished a number of literary objectives along the way. Bradbury stopped in the Midwest to reconnect with hometown friends and relatives in Waukegan and to pave the way for local media and bookstore publicity when the book was released. He also made a brief detour to Sauk City, Wisconsin, for his first face-to-face visit with August Derleth. But there was little time to discuss business, for Bradbury had to get to New York for scheduled meetings with a number of magazine editors and book publishers. In 1939 he had ventured only to the pulp editorial offices; this time he made a wide swing through the major-market-magazine editorial offices as well and secured a verbal commitment from Simon and Schuster to publish *The Blue Remembered Hills*, a novel that was already growing out of some of the Child's Garden stories and his Green Town memories of Waukegan. The manuscript, soon retitled *Summer Morning, Summer Night*, would not come together for some years; more than a decade later Doubleday, not Simon and Schuster, would publish a part of it as *Dandelion Wine*. But his warm reception at Simon and Schuster in 1946 was largely due to his new friendship with one of the editors, Don Congdon, who was about to strike out on his own as a literary agent.[22]

Finally, in late November, he began a final stage of transformation involving six stories that still did not meet his increasingly literary expectations for the book. Bradbury solved his longstanding problems with "The Poems" by pulling it out of galleys and replacing it with a new story, "The Coffin." In early March 1947 he still wanted to excise entire paragraphs from "The Crowd," "The Watchers," "Trip to Cranamockett," and "The Man Upstairs," and he also wanted to rephrase dialogue in "There Was an Old Woman." But these late changes proved to be more of an issue for Derleth than the copyright business. He was on a tight budget and did not anticipate the degree of revision that Bradbury had already brought to the galleys, especially after the round of revisions the author had completed prior to submission nine months earlier. He was still marketing *Dark Carnival*

Table 2. The evolution of *Dark Carnival* from *A Child's Garden of Terror* (1944) through the limited edition of 2001 shows a continual process of reconfiguration. Bradbury had little control over the abridgment of the U.K. first edition, but all other stages show a continual process of revision and rearrangement. Note that the title story, "Dark Carnival," disappears from the published forms; it would become the nucleus of *Something Wicked This Way Comes*. The stories first grouped as *A Child's Garden of Terror* supplied some of the contents for *Dark Carnival* as well as plot elements for *Dandelion Wine* and the unpublished Illinois novel, *Farewell Summer* (formerly *Summer Morning, Summer Night*). Only one page of the submission list has been located; stories after "The Handler" are inferred from comments in Bradbury's letter of transmission dated June 2, 1946 to Arkham House.

Dark Carnival: Evolution of the Contents

A Child's Garden of Terror [1944]	Dark Carnival Section Outline [March 1945]	Dark Carnival Outline 3 August 1945	Submitted Manuscript 2 June 1946	Galleys and Proofs November 1946–March 1947	Dark Carnival 1st Edition May 1947	Dark Carnival English Edition 1948	Dark Carnival Limited Edition 2001
The Lake	**1**	**Approved:**	The Emissary	The Homecoming (revised)	The Homecoming	The Homecoming	The Homecoming
The Night	The Baby	Skeleton	The Man Upstairs	Skeleton	Skeleton	Skeleton	Skeleton
The Sickness (Fever Dream)	The Crowd	The Tombstone	Reunion	The Jar	The Jar	The Jar	The Jar
The Sea Shell	The Scythe	The Jar	The Lake	The Lake	The Lake	The Lake	The Lake
The Ducker	The Poems	The Dead Man	There Was an Old Woman	The Maiden	The Maiden	—	The Maiden
The Man Upstairs	The Old Woman (There Was an Old Woman)	The Lake	The Small Assassin	The Tombstone	The Tombstone	The Tombstone	The Tombstone
The Colored Windows		The Scythe	The Night	The Smiling People	The Smiling People	The Smiling People	The Smiling People
The Baby (The Small Assassin)	**2**	There Was an Old Woman	The Scythe	The Emissary	The Emissary	The Emissary	The Emissary
I Got Something You Ain't Got	The Emissary	The Watchers	The Room of the World (Jack-in-the-Box)	The Traveler	The Traveler	The Traveler	The Traveler
The Reunion	The Lake	**Submitted:**	The Jar	The Small Assassin	The Small Assassin	The Small Assassin	The Small Assassin
The Emissary	The Night	The Baby	The Poems	The Crowd (revised)	The Crowd	The Crowd	The Crowd
	The Man Upstairs	The Man Upstairs	The Tombstone	Reunion	Reunion	—	Reunion
	The People Out There	The Night	The Watchers	The Handler	The Handler	The Handler	The Handler
		The Homecoming	The Masks	The Coffin	The Coffin	—	The Coffin
		The Traveler		Interim	Interim	—	Interim
					Jack-in-the-Box	—	Jack-in-the-Box

Table 2. (*continued*)

Dark Carnival: Evolution of the Contents

A Child's Garden of Terror [1944]	Dark Carnival Section Outline [March 1945]	Dark Carnival Outline 3 August 1945	Submitted Manuscript 2 June 1946	Galleys and Proofs November 1946–March 1947	Dark Carnival 1st Edition May 1947	Dark Carnival English Edition 1948	Dark Carnival Limited Edition 2001
The Room of the World (Jack-in-the-Box)	**3**	The Emissary	Skeleton	Jack-in-the-Box	The Scythe	—	The Scythe
Let's Play Poison!	Skeleton	And Then—The Silence	The Dead Man	The Scythe	Let's Play "Poison"	Let's Play "Poison"	Let's Play 'Poison'
	The Tombstone	**In Progress:**	The Homecoming	Let's Play "Poison"	Uncle Einar	Uncle Einar	Uncle Einar
	Carnival (The Black Ferris)	Meeting at Cranamockett	The Traveler	Uncle Einar	The Wind	The Wind	The Wind
	The Jar	Uncle Einar's Wings	The Wind	The Wind	The Night	The Night	The Night
	The Wind	Dark Carnival (The Black Ferris)	The Crowd	The Night (revised)	There Was an Old Woman	There Was an Old Woman	There Was an Old Woman
	4	The Tattood Man	Dark Carnival (The Black Ferris)	There Was an Old Woman (revised)	The Dead Man	The Dead Man	The Dead Man
	The Ducker	The Siamese Twins (Corpse Carnival)	And Then—	Trip to Cranamockett (heavily revised)	The Man Upstairs	The Man Upstairs	The Man Upstairs
	Chrysalis	The Power House	The Silence	The Dead Man	The Night Sets		The Night Sets
	The Watchers	Room of the World (Jack-in-the-Box)	The Handler	The Man Upstairs	Cistern	Cistern	Cistern
	The Mokie Thing		Interim	The Watchers (heavily revised)	The Next in Line	The Next in Line	The Next in Line
	(unknown)		The Maiden	The Night Sets			The Sea Shell
	The Lluble		Let's Play "Poison"	Cistern			Bang! You're Dead!
	(unknown)		Uncle Einar	The Next in Line			The Poems
			(Trip to Cranamockett)				The Watchers
			Cistern				
			The Next in Line				

as an anthology of what Bradbury had done in the pulps and resisted Bradbury's sense of the collection as a representation of what he was becoming. When Bradbury offered to help defray the cost of resetting, Derleth pointed out that he had already allowed more changes in the galleys of *Dark Carnival* than he had done for the first thirty Arkham House titles combined. He also made it clear that no money remained for wider market advertising—the periodic notices in *Weird Tales* were all he could afford. Bradbury understood but offered his own perspective as a writer who was constantly writing new stories for the future while still, in stolen moments of reflection, revising the stories of his past to make them a living part of that very same future: "My only defense is that in the time of rewriting a book for publication, a writer becomes so blind to his work, so exhausted of critical faculty, that he lets a lot of things slip through that only months later become perfectly obvious. When he sees these things in print he moans quietly and his fingers itch for a blue pencil. God knows I do not want to appear a 'purist' but neither do I wish to be called a fool by people who might point out to me grievous errors in writing on certain stories I should have corrected but did not."[23]

Bradbury received page proofs on March 12 and, as promised, cut whole paragraphs from "The Watchers" and the volume's fourth vampire-family story, "Trip to Cranamockett." Again he offered to share the costs but suggested that it would be even better if these two pieces could be removed entirely. He also made minor revisions in proof pages to "The Homecoming," "The Crowd," "There Was an Old Woman," and "The Night." Derleth finally acquiesced somewhat to Bradbury's more literary vision for this carnival of stories and dropped the two problem tales entirely. The page proofs were repaginated from page 240 on as the collection was reduced from twenty-nine to twenty-seven titles, and the very minor final revisions to the other four tales were accepted. But Derleth had long since stopped Bradbury from making major revisions to other stories that were already quite good. This is undoubtedly the case for three of the major-market sales that Bradbury closed after volume submission. In fact, these three stories—"The Homecoming," "The Man Upstairs," and "Cistern"—have long presented a major textual mystery for Bradbury scholars. All three magazine issues *predate* book publication, but a comparison of magazine versions against book versions reveals that all three magazine texts represent a *later* stage of revision. Derleth's tightening control over revisions, along with Bradbury's accelerating movement into the mainstream magazine market, forced Bradbury to leave the *Dark Carnival* texts of these stories in proof and move ahead on his own with revised magazine versions.

Bradbury had submitted "The Homecoming" to *Mademoiselle* about the same time he submitted the book manuscript to Derleth, but it languished without a reader for months. Bradbury was not surprised—he was beginning to send his remaining weirds to the major magazines that were publishing his fantasies—but the story was saved by a most unlikely chain of events. Truman Capote, who was then an editorial apprentice with *Mademoiselle,* was at loose ends one day in the late winter of 1946 and found the story on the floor of the fiction editor's office. He read it, loved it, and recommended it to Rita Smith, his editor. Soon Bradbury found himself working closely with the magazine's staff as his story became the centerpiece of a ghoulish October 1946 issue complete with a Charles Addams illustration.[24] Bradbury knew the original longer version was already good and did not want to risk more trouble with Derleth in trying to get the revised story, now titled simply "Homecoming," into *Dark Carnival;* he opted instead to make only small revisions in the page proofs.

The same pattern followed for the other major-magazine stories published before the book was released. When *Weird Tales* turned down "The Man Upstairs," Bradbury sent it out to *Harper's* and placed it in the March 1947 issue. He remembers making no changes between his initial submission to *Weird Tales* and his subsequent submission to *Harper's,* but collation shows that Bradbury made a major revising pass later, probably after acceptance. The *Harper's* text not only contains a number of minor editorial stylings but also includes substantive revisions by Bradbury, including a resequencing of the boy-protagonist's early encounters with the mysterious "man upstairs." He carried many of his *Harper's* revisions over to the *Dark Carnival* galleys but waived them as he got a clearer picture of the tight printing budget; he would save his big revisions for the older, weaker stories.[25]

Finally, Bradbury followed up his great "Homecoming" success by submitting "Cistern" to *Mademoiselle* well after it had been set in type for *Dark Carnival.* It appeared in the May 1947 issue as "The Cistern" and bears evidence of the same kind of editorial copyediting and authorial revision that is evident in "Homecoming" and "The Man Upstairs." Bradbury's most significant revision involves the latent sexual fantasies of the younger sister. (These changes, and what they reveal about Bradbury's maturing aesthetic, are discussed below.) In terms of the history of the text, this rather late magazine sale created the final delay to book publication. Since *Mademoiselle* could not place "The Cistern" any earlier than the May 1947 issue, Derleth had to hold release until the first serial rights had been exercised. But he was able to send review copies out in April, and Bradbury supplied a reviewer list that went far beyond the normal range for an Arkham House book in an effort to reach more-mainstream fantasy critics.

All of this activity ran parallel to the actual preparation of the volume, which continued at a slow but steady pace. Advance announcements for *Dark Carnival* had appeared as early as the spring 1946 Arkham House catalog, but the aforementioned changes in content, revisions in proof, and Derleth's limited range of advertising minimized the market effect of the changes in content. The volume was deposited for copyright on May 10, 1947; Derleth now controlled reprint rights to the volume and held a 50 percent interest in individual story reprintings, but he was completely unwilling for Bradbury to take an active role in marketing. Derleth was used to working with authors, mostly old friends, who were not marketable beyond the weird genre, and he expected to control all aspects of residuals with the help of his own agent, longtime friend and retired pulp author Otis Adelbert Kline. But Bradbury was no longer his to control and, in fact, never really was. He had been moving into mainstream publications since 1945, had placed a story in *Best American Short Stories of 1946,* and by 1947 had heard a number of his stories presented on the major radio networks. "Homecoming" won an O. Henry Award and a place in *Prize Stories of 1947.* Ironically, his reputation as a rising star was not unlike that of Derleth a decade earlier, before he took on the burden of Arkham House and the time-consuming risks of small-market publishing. Derleth was not uncomfortable with Bradbury's success and was actually proud of his achievements. But he was not eager to share decision making with Bradbury or with his new agent, Don Congdon.

Congdon had left Simon and Schuster to become a fulltime agent, and since late 1946 he had been working with Bradbury on the retrospective Illinois novel as it developed from *The Blue Remembered Hills* into a full manuscript as *Summer Morning, Summer Night.* Shortly after the release of *Dark Carnival,* Congdon joined Harold Matson Associates and officially became Bradbury's major-market agent. But conflict between Bradbury's two advisors began—even before *Dark Carnival* was out—over British publication. Derleth planned to use Kline's agency in the usual way to secure an overseas publisher. While this work was in progress, an *Atlantic* editor recommended the title to London publisher Hamish Hamilton, who queried both Bradbury and Derleth. Bradbury, naturally enough, discussed the news with Congdon, who offered advice on financial terms. When he passed these suggestions on to Derleth, Bradbury found that Kline was already closing a deal with Hamilton for the British edition.[26] Bradbury's own connections in the major-magazine world had set up the negotiations, and there was certainly nothing wrong with consulting his new agent for advice, but Derleth focused on procedural issues and took both author and agent to task in his next letter:

> I must say I sympathize with you in your desire to make the most of your fine ability, and so on, but you must learn to let your publishers handle your work. I have to say that it is fine and easy of Mr. Congdon of Simon & Schuster to suggest terms for DARK CARNIVAL; they are NOT the publishers of the book, and if they would have published it on any terms—I, knowing what the short story market is, will eat a copy, page by page. The

terms we got are advantageous enough, far better than we have had on any other Arkham House book thus far. Congdon is right when he says that Hamilton is a good, reliable publisher; I told you that same thing, as you know.[27]

Derleth may have been reluctant to network with anyone in Bradbury's new world, but he did secure favorable publishing terms from Bradbury's first British publisher. Kline Associates closed on an agreement with Hamilton for a four-hundred-dollar advance and royalty rights. Derleth took 10 percent for Arkham House, and Kline another 10 percent for the agency. Derleth relayed this information to Bradbury in his May 8 letter, written the day that Hamilton agreed to terms. Derleth also noted that most British publishers offered two hundred dollars outright (no royalty rights) and that American publishers often took as much as 50 percent of foreign rights. These comparisons are open to debate, but there is little doubt that Hamish Hamilton was a good publisher for the young author. Hamilton was half-Scottish and half-American and had, in fact, managed the London office of the American publisher Harper's until striking out on his own in 1931. His publishing interests were Anglo-American from the beginning, and his listings always featured fiction among the major categories.[28]

Dark Carnival was scheduled for U.K. release in 1948. This was the last year that the British government would enforce wartime paper rationing, which since 1940 had restricted British publishers to as little as 60 percent of prewar consumption. Under these limits, Hamilton would only be able to publish an abridged form of the collection; consequently, seven pieces were deleted to form a twenty-story collection, printed in small type on lightweight paper. The three least substantial sketchlike stories were omitted: the single-page "The Maiden" and the two-page "Interim" and "The Night Sets." Only two of the better stories were dropped—"The Coffin" and "Jack-in-the-Box"—but these were not yet fully developed; Bradbury would subsequently revise both significantly for republication in *The October Country*. "Reunion" and "The Scythe" were also casualties of postwar English austerity. Two fires (one in Hamilton's office and another at his printer's) further delayed publication, but *Dark Carnival* finally reached the British book market in November 1948.[29]

Bradbury's longstanding ambivalence over *Dark Carnival* surfaced again in early 1949 when he received his copies of the English edition. His comments to Derleth are quite revealing: "A peculiar thing has happened—for the first time in two years I am able to reread DC. Now that it is in a fresh new type on new paper I am able to go through the book once more, a thing which I found unbearable up until this week. I suppose my inability to do so before this time is the result of my long seige [*sic*] of rewriting and proofing the stories two years ago."

His deeper sense of frustration with the apprentice years of writing that these stories represented was also softened as he read the new edition. "I mean to express my surprise and amazement more than anything, because, regardless of reviews, my growing opinion in the last 24 months was that my book was quite shoddy. Perhaps this new type-face has hypnotized me, perhaps I'm only fooling myself." He enjoyed most aspects of the abridged British edition, regretting only that he had cut "The Scythe" along with the less substantial tales.[30]

The delays in British publication (and a corresponding delay in transmitting Bradbury's share of the advance) were compensated by Hamilton's willingness to publish a specialized story collection in Britain's bleak postwar publishing environment and to give personal attention to the young American author. In August 1949 he wrote to Bradbury with sales figures and noted that the forty copies sent to English critics had netted twelve reviews (seven were favorable). The book had sold over 1,250 copies in the first ten months, more than six times Derleth's 1947 estimate of one-to-two hundred. Bradbury was delighted, but Hamilton had a different perspective: "this is not good from the publisher's point of view as we should have had to sell almost twice this number to come home on the book." The British edition eventually sold out, but Hamilton, who did not care for backlisted titles, never reprinted *Dark Carnival.* He agreed to read *The Martian Chronicles* but did not come to terms for that book or any other. Bradbury characteristically maintained long friendships with his principal editors and publishers, and Hamish Hamilton was no exception; but he would turn to Rupert Hart-Davis for British editions of his subsequent books, including *The October Country.*[31]

Dark Carnival would also be the last title August Derleth would publish for Bradbury. His first book was never reprinted in America (except for the new Gauntlet limited edition); the single printing—slightly more than three thousand copies—makes *Dark Carnival* the rarest of his domestic trade-fiction titles.[32] Bradbury's subsequent success with *The Martian Chronicles* and *The Illustrated Man* (under his 1949 Doubleday contract) translated into increased sales for *Dark Carnival* as well; by early 1951 only about eight hundred copies remained in stock. Despite this brief boost, sales of the American edition were predictably slow, reflecting the nature of the niche market for horror and weird tales that Bradbury had already left behind. Arkham House had very little presence in the general marketplace, and the specialized nature of its books led Derleth to rely heavily on catalog mailings to loyal subscribers and a handful of independent bookstores. Understandably, Bradbury's collection of weird tales generated few notices and only two significant reviews—one from Anthony Boucher in San Francisco and one by Will Cuppy in the *New York Herald Tribune.*[33] Cuppy considered Bradbury "something special, perhaps the first of the high-pressured weirdists suitable for general consumption." He predicted that Bradbury would gradually move away from the weird and "up in the general direction of the John Collier bracket." Both Cuppy and Boucher were aware of Bradbury's major-market stories, and Boucher had tracked Bradbury from his earliest appearance in *Weird Tales:* "For years I have been prowling newsstands and buying any magazine with a Ray Bradbury story; to me he is the most fascinating and individual talent to appear in the fantasy field for a long time." Boucher, who within a year would found *The Magazine of Fantasy and Science Fiction*, already considered Bradbury a major-market talent: "He's not only a fantasy writer; he is also a writer, period, and there's no telling what may come of this still very young man." Boucher's review was little more than a notice, but he made every word count toward distancing Bradbury from the weird collection and its limited range of readers.

As Bradbury moved further into the mainstream magazine market, additional critical recognition (including a second O. Henry Award in 1948 for "Powerhouse") began to change his relationship with Derleth in ways that neither man could afford to ignore. Derleth had been a supportive publisher and a good friend, but Bradbury had simply outgrown the professional side of the relationship. He was now writing for a much broader audience; furthermore, Derleth's control of all reprint rights to the *Dark Carnival* stories complicated Bradbury's marketability and effectively excluded his own literary agent, Don Congdon, from negotiating new sales for some of his most successful early stories. Derleth continued to place some of these pieces in his own multiple-author anthologies and pay the usual rate he gave all his writers for pulp fiction reprints, but Bradbury had outgrown the pay scale of a pulp writer. He needed Derleth to actively pursue the secondary reprint market, where the best of his older stories were always in demand. Both men would share equally in the profit by the very nature of the contract Derleth held him to, but Derleth wanted to control all negotiations for such subsidiary rights and firmly refused to let Bradbury or Congdon initiate any contacts. They often did anyway, and surviving correspondence shows continual arguments over Bradbury's right to initiate a deal without Derleth's clearance in advance.[34]

Bradbury was not yet experienced with book publishing, and he was perhaps overeager to reprint materials while his first collection was still settling into the marketplace. His eagerness intensified after he married in the fall of 1947. On a personal level, Derleth was always understanding; when the English advance on *Dark Carnival* was delayed, he went so far as to make an early royalty advance from U.S. sales to help out the newlyweds. At least once he passed the full reprint fee for a story on through to Bradbury. But professionally he was frankly surprised that a writer of Bradbury's talents and growing success should bother with reprints at all: "I could understand your insistence on negotiating about [rights to stories which] are in our hands clearly if it were your only work, or the only work of which you are capable; but the fact is you are going on to so much more important work that the dabbling with DC . . . is totally inexplicable. And repeatedly annoying." So Derleth held to the letter of the contract and insisted that all reprint deals be initiated by Arkham House or Kline Associates. For his part, Bradbury always followed the spirit of the contract—working within the existing fee structure—but balked at the loss of opportunity that Derleth was perpetuating. The honesty and sincerity of both men is evident in the way they kept their personal relationship separate from business; Bradbury was always grateful for Derleth's personal friendship and considerations, and they remained friends for life. But the two men were immutable on the issue of control, and by April 1948 Derleth summed it up this way: "I assure you I will be delighted when we have sold out our edition of DARK CARNIVAL, and rights have reverted to you."[35]

Even with the boost of Bradbury's growing commercial success, it would be a long time before the niche market for weird tales could exhaust the first edition stock. Bradbury adopted a simple strategy—he bought the final few hundred copies in increments during 1953 and 1954. Derleth understood Bradbury's strategy and the reasons behind it and knew Bradbury's departure was inevitable. His letter of May 9, 1953, includes a release of all book reprint rights as well as some characteristic advice about the publishing game intended to help Bradbury market a new edition with a larger press.

In June 1954 Derleth removed *Dark Carnival* from his catalog and stock list, retaining only the magazine and anthology reprint rights to the stories of Bradbury's first collection. As Bradbury began to reshape and retitle his early work for a new edition with another publisher, Derleth could only hope that Bradbury might someday return—just for a moment—to the fiction niche where he started: "I wish we had a good Bradbury title on our list, but I know how impossible that is, what with your current arrangements with agents and other publishers. But some day, perhaps, you may turn out an offtrail fantasy in the 15,000 to 25,000 word length for which no other market may turn up, and then perhaps we'll be able to do a ltd. edition of it." That wish was never fulfilled, and in fact, Derleth knew he could never compete with the wider market that Bradbury and Congdon could command by the 1950s.[36] Bradbury did indeed transform his weirds a second time for a new and broader readership, replacing some stories with new ones and resequencing the whole in a collection titled *The October Country*.

Bradbury's major recasting of the book concept for *The October Country* does not diminish the importance of earlier revisions made while *Dark Carnival* was still at press. Sixteen of the twenty-seven stories appeared in pulps prior to book publication, and a word-by-word comparison of the magazine texts with the *Dark Carnival* texts reveals that all were revised to some degree. "The Handler" was the last story published in the pulps prior to book release; as one would expect, it was merely corrected for *Dark Carnival,* with only two minor revisions by Bradbury. Eleven others were lightly revised for the book: "Skeleton," "The Jar," "The Lake," "The Tombstone," "The Smiling People," "The Small Assassin," "The Crowd," "Reunion," "Let's Play 'Poison,'" "The Night," and "The Dead Man." For these stories, Bradbury reworked descriptions and tightened up dialogue but made few changes to plot or character. Occasionally, one sees the birth of a new metaphor in revisions, the best example of which is found in "The Crowd."

The plot of this story is typical of the best Bradbury "weirds." His point of departure is a seemingly innocent puzzle of everyday life that suddenly reveals a darker side. The protagonist Spallner describes the situation to his friend Morgan this way in the pulp version: "there's a universal law about accidents. *Crowds gather.* They *always* gather. And people, just like you and I, have wondered from time to time, from time immemorial, why they gathered so quickly. *I* know the answer."[37] This observation is prompted by an auto crash in the street below. For the *Dark Carnival* version, Bradbury would, in fact, transform the crowd approaching the accident into an equal and opposite reaction to the explosion of a car crash, a bizarre inversion of the universal laws of physics:[38]

A great bond of ice closed in on Spallner as he stood there, looking at his watch, at the small second hand. One, two, three, four, five seconds—people running—eight, nine, ten, eleven, twelve—from all over people came running—fifteen, sixteen, seventeen seconds and more people and more cars and more blowing of horns. Spallner shook uncontrollably. He couldn't stop shaking. He was afraid.

The crowd gathered so fast.

Spallner walked to the window. He was very cold and as he stood there, he looked at his watch, at the small minute hand. One two three four five seconds—people running—eight nine ten eleven twelve—from all over, people came running—fifteen sixteen seventeen eighteen seconds—more people, more cars, more horns blowing. Curiously distant, Spallner looked upon the scene as an explosion in reverse, the fragments of the detonation sucked back to the point of impulsion. Nineteen, twenty, twenty-one seconds and the crowd was all there. Spallner made a gesture down at them, wordless.

The crowd had gathered so *fast.*

In revision, Bradbury deleted the clichéd opening metaphor and reshaped the entire paragraph around a striking new metaphor of imploding energy that is hard to forget. In the process he also understates Spallner's reaction in a way that actually heightens the sense of terror. Spallner's fear, and the shaking manifestation of being afraid, is now left completely unstated, yet the reader still feels it.

Occasionally, Bradbury heightened the shock effect of a description for *Dark Carnival*. In "The Smiling People" the homicidal introvert Mr. Greppin turns his noisy and vulgar relatives into silent, smiling people by slitting their throats and seating them around the dinner table. In revision, Bradbury adds one final shock to his description of Greppin's smiling aunt.[39]

Her bosom was hidden in a salad of fluffy linen. Beneath the table her stick legs in high-button shoes went up into a pipe of dress.	Her bosom was hidden in a salad of fluffy linen. The breasts had not been exhumed for years; either for love or child-suckling. They were mummies wrapped in cerements and put away for all time. Beneath the table her stick legs in high button shoes went up into a sexless pipe of dress.

The mummified breasts and sexless dress suggest that the aunt has been dead in a very real sense for many years before Mr. Greppin actually kills her, and this clinical observation heightens the horror of the situation to a level that did not seem possible in the pulp version.

Such a level of substantive revision is uncommon in the eleven lightly revised stories, but it does occur in three more heavily revised tales. "The Traveler," "The Scythe," and "There Was an Old Woman" contain significant revisions in descriptions and dialogue but no changes to the basic structure. Revisions to "The Scythe" are worth mentioning, for they help verify a known but unstudied collaboration between Bradbury and his good friend Leigh Brackett. She had more of an influence on his early work than either Heinlein or Kuttner, for they read each other's manuscripts almost weekly throughout the early 1940s. When Bradbury had trouble starting his idea for this story, the more experienced Brackett wrote the first five or six hundred words (he would later pay her back by writing the second half of her novella "Lorelei of the Red Mist").[40] In her opening, an itinerant farmer takes over the farm of a mysterious reaper who has died and left his work to the next farmer who comes along. Bradbury continued her opening by developing the newcomer's growing realization that this strange field of wheat is sown with the souls of the world and his parallel realization that the irresistible scythe is the tool of the grim reaper himself. But Bradbury's bridge into the main story is rather unevenly and incompletely developed for the original *Weird Tales* version; as he revised this story for *Dark Carnival*, he completely restructured the bridge between Brackett's opening and the main story, in the process developing a clearer description of the strange properties of both the wheat field and the scythe. He also provided more motivation for the new farmer's wife, whose desire to remain within the seeming security of the strange farmstead further entraps her husband in the role of grim reaper.

Less extensive changes to descriptions and dialogue continue in the *Dark Carnival* version of "The Scythe" and can be found throughout the *Dark Carnival* versions of "The Traveler" and "There Was an Old Woman," but Bradbury made no structural changes to any of these three pulp tales. Yet there are significant structural revisions to "The Man Upstairs," one of the three stories that Bradbury revised for a major magazine while the *Dark Carnival* text continued through proofs essentially unchanged. Douglas, the boy-protagonist of the story, is the same character that Bradbury would develop in all the *Summer Morning, Summer Night* stories selectively chronicled in *Dandelion Wine* a decade later. In this gruesome forerunner to the *Dandelion Wine* grouping, Douglas discovers that his grandparents' newest boarder sleeps by day and is a vampirelike killing machine by night. A careful reader of the *Dark Carnival* text will find that version somewhat disjointed. For the *Harper's* magazine revisions, Bradbury interchanged and reconnected the middle half of the story to create a much more effective flow of events. Since the restructuring is extensive, the two versions are best compared in outline form.

Original text: *Dark Carnival*	Revised text: *Harper's*
1. Grandma opens and guts a chicken for dinner.	1. Grandma opens and guts a chicken for dinner.
2. The mysterious man arrives and rents the room upstairs.	2. The mysterious man arrives and rents the room upstairs.
3. Douglas dislikes him and notes his odd behavior.	3. Douglas dislikes him and notes his odd behavior.
4. Douglas peers at the world through grandma's multicolored window in the morning.	12. We learn that the man "works" nights and sleeps soundly upstairs by day.
5. The man upstairs wants to know what he is doing.	6. Douglas hates what the man upstairs has done to the room.
6. Douglas hates what the man upstairs has done to the room.	4. Douglas peers at the world through grandma's multi-colored window in the morning.
7. The man returns from "work" in the morning.	7. The man returns from "work" in the morning.
8. Douglas looks through the multicolored window and sees strange things inside the man.	

9. The man sees Douglas, enters the house, and confronts him.
10. While Douglas plays in his sandbox, the window is mysteriously broken.
11. Douglas is wrongly punished but saves some fragments of glass.
12. We learn that the man "works" nights and sleeps soundly upstairs by day.
13. Douglas enters the room to disturb him but does not succeed.
14. Grandpa comes home and Douglas asks what humans are like inside.
15. Grandpa presides as the boarders eat dinner.
16. The next morning the boarder returns to sleep.
17. Douglas examines him with the glass fragments.
18. He sees things inside the man that are not human.
19. He goes to the kitchen and gets grandma's chicken knife.
20. He vivisects the man upstairs while he sleeps.
21. Douglas gets his piggy bank and returns to the man upstairs.
22. He shows grandpa the results.
23. The authorities come and find Douglas's silver pocket change inside the man-vampire's chest.

8. Douglas looks through the multicolored window and sees strange things inside the man.
9. The man sees Douglas, enters the house, and confronts him.
5. The man upstairs wants to know what he is doing.
10. While Douglas plays in his sandbox, the window is mysteriously broken.
11. Douglas is wrongly punished but saves some fragments of glass.
14. Grandpa comes home and Douglas asks what humans are like inside.
15. Grandpa presides as the boarders eat dinner.
16. The next morning the boarder returns to sleep.
13. Douglas enters the room to disturb him but does not succeed.
17. Douglas examines him with the glass fragments.
18. He sees things inside the man that are not human.
19. He goes to the kitchen and gets grandma's chicken knife.
20. He vivisects the man upstairs while he sleeps.
21. Douglas gets his piggy bank and returns to the man upstairs.
22. He shows grandpa the results.
23. The authorities come and find Douglas's silver pocket change inside the man-vampire's chest.

By restructuring the middle half of the story, Bradbury is able to present the events through a much more continuous (and much less confusing) sequence of revelations. For instance, the events at the multicolored window happen in an uninterrupted sequence of action that effectively sets up Douglas's motivation to explore the mystery of the man upstairs. In the same way, Douglas's discoveries in the vampire's room are chillingly continuous and lead directly to the vivisection and the vampire-killing silver "bullet" of pocket change.

Only one pulp story, "The Wind," was completely rewritten for *Dark Carnival*. This was one of the earliest published works included in the collection, and Bradbury's rewrite almost certainly predates his June 1946 submission to Derleth. In the revision Bradbury shifted the dominant point of view from the victim of the relentless wind to his friend who lives some miles away. In the 1943 *Weird Tales* version, the reader watches the wind slowly demolish the house of the explorer, who has guessed the secret intelligence of the earth's major wind currents. His frantic phone calls to his friend are merely periodic interruptions that provide expository dialogue for the reader. In rewriting the story for *Dark Carnival*, Bradbury centers the action at the home of the friend, who must deal with a wife and visitors who are wholly indifferent to the explorer's predicament. Each desperate phone call heightens his concern and increases his disgust with his selfish wife and oblivious dinner guests. In this way Bradbury builds a story within a story and uses the neighbor's slowly rising internal tension to control the tempo of the narrative. At the same time, he reveals less of the monster—as the phone line goes dead, we can only imagine how the wind destroys the one who knows too much.

Along with the revised group of sixteen previously published pulp stories and the three destined for major market slick magazines, Bradbury also submitted eight new unpublished stories. No manuscripts have been located for the eight, and there is no way of telling how much revision went into these stories. The most remarkable of these tales, "The Next in Line," is the longest story in the book. Unlike all the others, it does not grow out of a childhood terror but rather out of his fall 1945 trip to Mexico with Grant Beach. The characterizations clearly have their sources in the adult world of experience and place the story among the very best selected for *Dark Carnival*. In fact, "The Next in Line" was actually slated for publication in Marshall Field's new major-market magazine *USA* later in 1947. Although that magazine was unexpectedly cancelled before the first issue, "The Next in Line," like his *Mademoiselle* and *Harper's* stories, is a major-magazine sale, and the depth of character found in it provides a preview of the best work Bradbury would produce in his better-known story collections of the 1950s and 1960s.

In 1955 these twenty-seven stories were once again the focus of Bradbury's creative genius as he found an opportunity to present an updated version of the

Dark Carnival selections against the backdrop of a new land of shadows—*The October Country*. But the opportunity would not come from his new editors at Doubleday. In 1949 Bradbury began a long-term relationship with Doubleday that, by 1953, had earned an international audience through his first three titles—*The Martian Chronicles, The Illustrated Man,* and *The Golden Apples of the Sun*. As soon as Derleth released reprint rights to *Dark Carnival,* he contacted his Doubleday editor, Walter Bradbury (no relation), and proposed a new and restructured edition. In May 1953 editor Bradbury declined, advising that it was best to get on to new work, citing the illusive "Illinois" book that had been promised but not delivered since the beginning of the Bradbury-Bradbury relationship four years earlier: "I have always urged you to look to the future instead of the past not only in the matter of writing new material, but also in the matter of your general psychology about your writing. I have attempted to dissuade you from turning back—turning back to worry about what you did yesterday and the day before, to re-evaluate it, [to] re-work it, to re-publish it with corrections, to look over your shoulder instead of looking ahead."[41]

It would take four more years for the two Bradburys to carve *Dandelion Wine* out of the *Summer Morning, Summer Night* manuscript that held all the various Illinois tales. In the meantime author Bradbury would turn to screenwriting for a year (John Huston's *Moby Dick* production) and then complete the full transition of *Dark Carnival* into *The October Country*. To do this he would turn to Ian Ballantine, who had first encountered Bradbury while at Bantam, a house he had founded in 1945 with the backing of a consortium of hardback publishers. Bantam picked up the paperback contracts on all three of Bradbury's Doubleday hardbacks and had provided mass-market advertising and sales volume for them. But in 1952, less than a year after publishing the paperback edition of the *Martian Chronicles,* Ballantine and his wife, Betty, founded a house under their own name that could offer authors limited hardback publishing as part of a mass-market-paperback deal. This innovative concept meant that authors could get bookstore trade, quality review attention, and mass-market sales with a single publisher, and the economy of production would mean increased royalties as well. One of their first major successes was, in fact, a brand new Bradbury collection, for Don Congdon was quick to realize the inherent advantages of the new Ballantine concept for his client. In early 1953, when Doubleday was not interested in yet another story collection to follow *The Golden Apples of the Sun,* Congdon suggested that Bradbury try Ballantine. Stanley Kauffmann, who left Bantam with Ballantine, worked with Bradbury to streamline the collection and showcase the longest of the four remaining stories—"Fahrenheit 451"—as the title novella. The result was Bradbury's most enduring title of the 1950s, and it is not surprising that Bradbury would turn to the Ballantines once again to craft a new version of *Dark Carnival*. For his part, Walt Bradbury did not try to interfere; he knew the idea was marketable but closed his May 6 letter with this appeal: "Of course I understand that someone else may re-publish DARK CARNIVAL and there is nothing I can do about it. It will probably make money. In that respect my position is a poor one for a publisher, but as I see it[,] it is a good one for an editor. And all I can do is to play them as I see them. I hope you understand."[42]

Now clear to act, Bradbury wasted no time in presenting his proposal to Ian Ballantine, who was eager to secure another book from the rapidly rising young author.[43] *Fahrenheit 451* was still in revision when Ballantine and Kauffmann agreed to take on the *Dark Carnival* project. By mid-May 1953, Bradbury had a contract and a fifteen-hundred-dollar advance. But *Fahrenheit* took priority until midsummer, when both the manuscript and the now-classic fireman illustrations by Joe Mugnaini were at press. Bradbury sent Ballantine and Kauffmann a concept of the new collection in August, but a grueling nine-month trip to Ireland and England for the *Moby Dick* project slowed work considerably. In March 1954 Kauffmann and Ballantine sent Don Congdon a suggested list of twelve *Dark Carnival* stories to carry over into the new concept and added four more as possible alternatives. They also indicated a desire for new and uncollected Bradbury stories. In April, Kauffmann wrote Bradbury directly to make a further recommendation that six new stories—all left over from the *Fahrenheit 451* deletions—be added to the March list of the sixteen best *Dark Carnival* stories. The new titles were "The Watchful Poker Chip of H. Matisse," "The Calliope," "The Dwarf," "Touched with Fire," "The Mice," and "The Wonderful Death of Dudley Stone."

The Ballantine editors were not demanding about the selections; by October Bradbury (now back in the States) agreed to carry forward ten of their sixteen *Dark Carnival* suggestions and added five of his own *Dark Carnival* favorites that the editors had passed over (fig. 4). To these fifteen, Ballantine hoped to add the six new Bradbury stories, but "The Calliope" and "The Mice" were still being shopped in the magazine market. He offered the other four from the original *Fahrenheit 451* contents, all of which had already appeared in magazines earlier in the year. To these four he added a fifth story, "The Dragon," to round out the new concept as a twenty-title collection, agreeing to rework the older stories prior to final submission.

In mid-December, thinking he had persuaded Bradbury to swap out one of the old stories for another new one, Kauffmann took the opportunity to make a fateful suggestion: "We have been talking—as we do almost every day—about DARK CARNIVAL, and it struck me that since almost one-third of the book will be material that did not appear in the first DARK CARNIVAL, and since the other two-thirds have been reworked, you might well want to give the book another title. . . . Does this idea appeal to you? If so, do you have any ideas for a new title?"[44]

Bradbury quickly came up with a concept that extended the territory of the collection from the confines of a dark carnival to an entire landscape of the strange and wonderful and a climate of the imagination. On the first day of the new year, he drafted a two-page sketch of the "October Country" concept, revealed through a dialogue between a grandfather and his grandson. The final paragraph framed this autobiographical memory as the source of inspiration for both *Dark Carnival* and its new incarnation as *The October Country* (fig. 5). Later he would narrow the sketch to a single magical definition of strangeness, which begins every commercial edition of the book. The explanation that originally closed the sketch became a cover note that, along with a new dedication, thanked August Derleth for all he had done for Bradbury in his early years as a writer.

And there were, in fact, new stories to go with the new title; one of his best new weirds, "The Dwarf," was the result of an evening out at Ocean Park's mirror maze and other attractions with Leigh Brackett and Edmund Hamilton.[45] Between November 1954 and January 1955, Bradbury sent Ballantine the five promised new stories along with reworked typescripts of fourteen *Dark Carnival* selections, apparently deleting "The Emissary" from this group of older stories. But "The Dragon" fell through, possibly because of a magazine deal with *Esquire* and a reprint agreement with his good friend Anthony Boucher, who found that story ideal for *Fantasy and Science Fiction*. Bradbury left Ballantine with only the four new pieces, nothing unpublished, but did send in a reworking of "The Emissary" to bring the collection back up to nineteen stories. And the entire concept had the added magic of some of Joe Mugnaini's most compelling line art. The cover, developed by Mugnaini from drawings by Bradbury himself, is quite likely the most familiar image of a haunted house in late-twentieth-century American pop culture.

The older *Dark Carnival* stories were carefully rearranged by Bradbury to create an entirely new progression that opens and closes with two of the new ones—"The Dwarf" and "The Wonderful Death of Dudley Stone." These two works frame the collection as meditations or self-reflections on the nature of authorship, in both the popular genres and "serious fiction," by an author now eight years beyond his first success in the book market. "The Dwarf" reflects on cultural aspects of Bradbury's early career as a struggling writer of detective or weird fiction. Its Freudian themes are analyzed in depth later, but here we may note that because "The Dwarf" is set in a sideshow at an amusement park, it undoubtedly mirrors the marginal cultural situation of writers in such genres. "The Wonderful Death of Dudley Stone," however, deals much more ironically, and even humorously, with the situation of a "literary" writer who, in the typical modernist fashion, has chosen the death of the author to cope with his literary success. Clearly, in closing the collection with this story, Bradbury was signaling

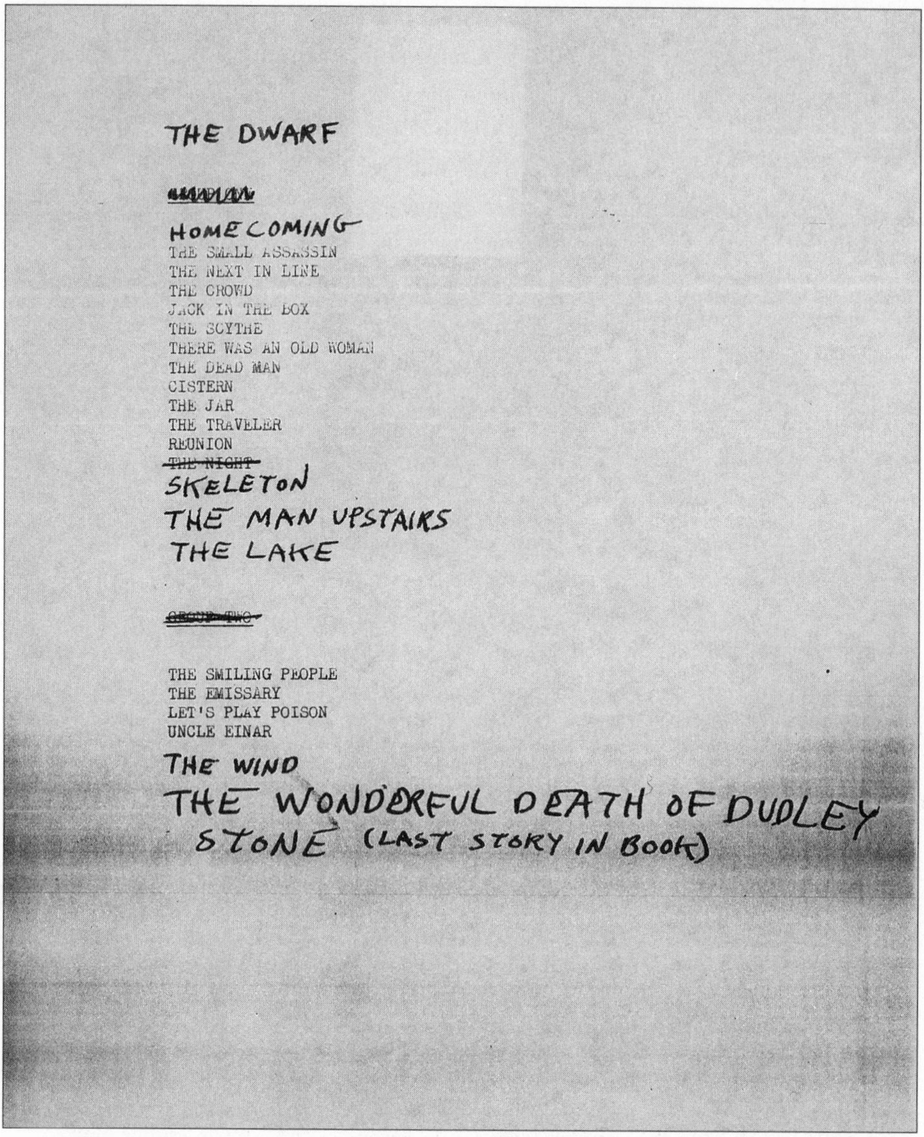

THE DWARF

~~THE MAN~~

HOMECOMING
THE SMALL ASSASSIN
THE NEXT IN LINE
THE CROWD
JACK IN THE BOX
THE SCYTHE
THERE WAS AN OLD WOMAN
THE DEAD MAN
CISTERN
THE JAR
THE TRAVELER
REUNION
~~THE NIGHT~~
SKELETON
THE MAN UPSTAIRS
THE LAKE

~~GROUP TWO~~

THE SMILING PEOPLE
THE EMISSARY
LET'S PLAY POISON
UNCLE EINAR

THE WIND
THE WONDERFUL DEATH OF DUDLEY
STONE (LAST STORY IN BOOK)

Figure 4. Bradbury's working copy (left) of the list of *Dark Carnival* stories recommended by Ballantine editors for the "new" edition probably dates from the summer of 1954. Here he has deleted "The Night," which would soon appear as a chapter in *Dandelion Wine*, and has added five of his own *Dark Carnival* favorites. Above and below this list, Bradbury has added two of his newer uncollected stories to open and close the volume. The October 1954 listing (right) is nearly complete—only "The Dragon" would be deleted while the new collection took its final form as *The October Country*. But the story sequence would continue to shift as Bradbury revised and reworked the older tales—his ink marks suggest that three of the most heavily revised stories—"The Emissary," "Jack-in-the-Box," and "Uncle Einar"—were not yet ready; in fact, they would not be submitted until early in the new year. From the Albright Collection, courtesy of Donn Albright and Ray Bradbury.

CONTENTS

- Homecoming
- The Dwarf
- Skeleton
- The Jar
- The Lake
- The Watchful Poker-Chip of H. Matisse
- The Emissary
- Touched With Fire
- The Small Assassin
- The Crowd
- Jack-In-The-Box
- The Scythe
- Uncle Einar
- The Wind
- The Man Upstairs
- There Was An Old Woman
- Cistern
- The Next in Line
- THE DRAGON
- The Wonderful Death of Dudley Stone

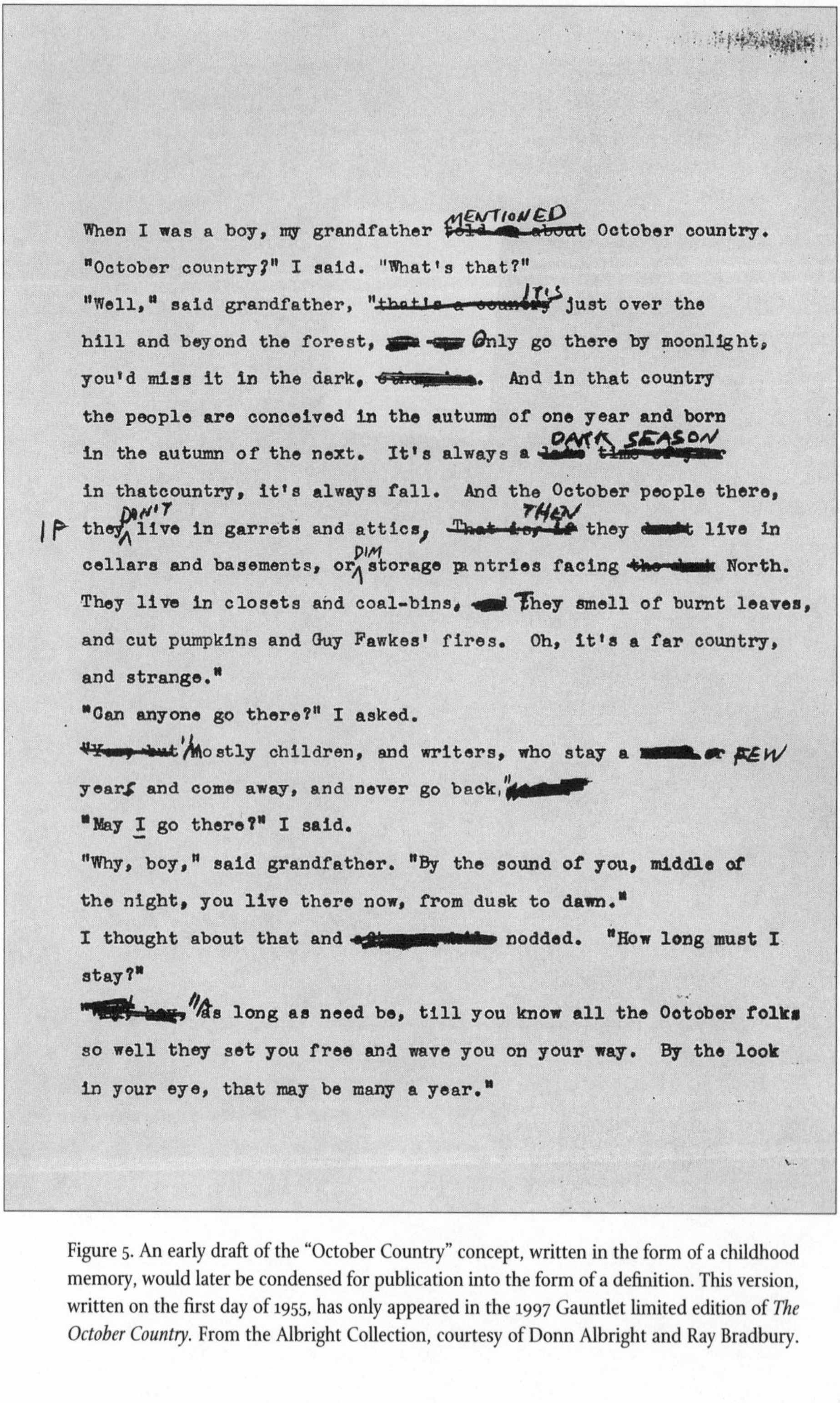

When I was a boy, my grandfather ~~told me about~~ ^{MENTIONED} October country.

"October country?" I said. "What's that?"

"Well," said grandfather, "~~that's a country~~ ^{IT'S} just over the hill and beyond the forest, ~~you can~~ Only go there by moonlight, you'd miss it in the dark, ~~sunshine~~. And in that country the people are conceived in the autumn of one year and born in the autumn of the next. It's always a ~~late time~~ ^{DARK SEASON} in thatcountry, it's always fall. And the October people there, ^{DON'T} they˄live in garrets and attics, ~~That boy is~~ ^{THEN} they ~~don't~~ live in cellars and basements, or˄^{DIM} storage pantries facing ~~the dark~~ North. They live in closets and coal-bins, ~~and~~ ~~T~~hey smell of burnt leaves, and cut pumpkins and Guy Fawkes' fires. Oh, it's a far country, and strange."

"Can anyone go there?" I asked.

~~"You, but~~' Mostly children, and writers, who stay a ~~week or~~ FEW year~~s~~ and come away, and never go back,~~'~~

"May I go there?" I said.

"Why, boy," said grandfather. "By the sound of you, middle of the night, you live there now, from dusk to dawn."

I thought about that and ~~after a while~~ nodded. "How long must I stay?"

~~"Why boy,~~" As long as need be, till you know all the October folks so well they set you free and wave you on your way. By the look in your eye, that may be many a year."

Figure 5. An early draft of the "October Country" concept, written in the form of a childhood memory, would later be condensed for publication into the form of a definition. This version, written on the first day of 1955, has only appeared in the 1997 Gauntlet limited edition of *The October Country*. From the Albright Collection, courtesy of Donn Albright and Ray Bradbury.

I thought about that for awhile and said, "I'm not afraid."

"~~Of course you're not,~~ *"NO."* " said grandfather. "Because you tell
me all about your jaunts and meetings with the autumn tribes.
Tell others, too, any way you want. You might as well enjoy
what just comes natural. Sing from the Gothic belfry, son,
and listen for the brooms whispering in the closet long after
midnight. Not many can tell what they say. But you got a gift
for tongues. What did you hear last night, Doug, what did you
hear last night?"

"Well!" said I, warming to it, "~~not long~~ *JUST* after midnight---"

And that's how it began. First, ~~khfkfkgkfkfkfkhhk~~ thinking
it. Then, talking it. And, at last, writing it.
My visits to October country, which started when I was five
and drew my first skeleton in green chalk, and ended when
I wrote FINIS to my first book DARK CARNIVAL, were frequent
and fascinating. It was a long journey, gladly taken, for in
coming to know the October people, they helped me find my
way from attic and cellar, run half a lifetime across strange
burying-grounds, to emerge on a street where, if people from
some fresher season were not exactly engaged in normal commerce,
rockets were at least rushing at the sky. I do not think I will
return to that unseasonable land. Now, others, reading the 15
stories, here included, from DARKC ARNIVAL, must make the circuit.
Your report on conditions there, will always be welcome. Some
say that the view is still good, most of the way. But since I
can't go home again, you must carry my best wishes to all you find
there. Bon voyage, bon appetite!   R.B. January 1st, 1955

his arrival as a literary author, doing so with more than a touch of irony since the story deals with the anxiety of influence. It is framed within the narrative of "Mr. Douglas" (Bradbury's middle name), who has gone in search of Dudley Stone, a fictitious literary giant of the 1920s who has not written a word in over a quarter century. Stone tells Douglas that his seclusion resulted from a jealous writer's attempt to murder him at the height of his career. The great author disarms his potential assailant by destroying his new work, his magnum opus, promising never to write again and thus convincing his rival that he is essentially dead. Dudley Stone's "death" is wonderful because he is reborn into a new life, free of the need to sell his genius to make a living. In between these two reflections on authorship, Bradbury's reconfigured collection contains a progression of other stories (old and new) with thematics of surreal body horror and unease.

With the addition of "The Emissary," fifteen of the *Dark Carnival* stories were carried over into *The October Country*, and they have remained in print as part of that collection—at home and abroad—ever since. But a close comparison of the two books reveals textual differences that go far beyond *The October Country*'s new table of contents. Bradbury made a few stylistic changes to all fifteen of the older tales, but his commitment to rework this material led him to depart radically from the *Dark Carnival* texts in six cases. During the winter of 1954–1955, as he sent successive groups of revised stories to Ballantine, Bradbury completely rewrote three of the stories original to *Dark Carnival*—"The Emissary," "Jack-in-the-Box," and "Uncle Einar." These were, in fact, among the last stories that he sent on to Ballantine as he rounded out the collection, and the rewriting is apparent in nearly every paragraph.[46] In all three cases the earlier versions found in *Dark Carnival* were not inferior, but none had been through the usual revising process of magazine publication back in 1947—they were among the eight new stories first published in that collection.

In three other cases Bradbury did not work from the *Dark Carnival* texts at all. *The October Country* includes the 1946–1947 magazine versions of "The Man Upstairs," "[The] Homecoming," and "[The] Cistern," the three stories that Bradbury revised for major slick magazines while earlier versions—longer but certainly no less polished—continued through proofs for *Dark Carnival*. For these three stories, the magazine texts represented a more mature version than the *Dark Carnival* texts. Only one major variation in the periodical editions was problematic—space constraints apparently forced either Bradbury or the *Mademoiselle* editors to cut a 250-word passage near the end of "Homecoming." The text is significant, for it involves a reconciliation between the boy protagonist and his telepathic sister. But even here Bradbury did not restore the *Dark Carnival* text—he rewrote a shorter, more effective version of the missing passage for *The October Country*.

Table 3. Except for the Ballantine American paperback, all *OC* editions lack Bradbury's third light revision to "The Homecoming," as well as his restored reconciliation scene; all American editions (again, with the exception of the Ballantine paperback) contain two pages of transposed text in "The Homecoming." The revised *DC* text of "The Night" was later rewritten into an untitled episode of *Dandelion Wine* (1957). Stories omitted from a collection are so indicated. Story order is that of *DC*; stories new to *OC* conclude the list. The 2001 limited edition of *DC* was set from the 1947 edition (see table 2).

Evolution of the Texts: *Dark Carnival (DC), The October Country (OC),* and *The Small Assassin (SA)*

Original Title (and subsequent title)	First Publication (and version published)	DC American 1947	DC English 1948 abridged	OC American 1955 all bindings	OC English 1956	OC English 1961 abridged paper	SA English 1962 paper
"The Homecoming" ("Homecoming")	*Mademoiselle* Oct. 1946 1st major revision	Original text and title	Original text and title	2d / 3d light revisions	2d light revision	2d light revision	*omitted*
"Skeleton"	*Weird Tales* Sept. 1945 original	1st light revision	1st light revision	2d light revision	2d light revision	2d light revision	*omitted*
"The Jar"	*Weird Tales* Nov. 1944 original	1st light revision	1st light revision	2d light revision	2d light revision	2d light revision	*omitted*
"The Lake"	*Weird Tales* May 1944 original	1st light revision	1st light revision	2d light revision	2d light revision	*omitted*	2d light revision
"The Maiden"	*DC* original	original	*omitted*	*omitted*	*omitted*	*omitted*	*omitted*
"The Tombstone"	*Weird Tales* Mar. 1945 original	1st light revision	1st light revision	*omitted*	*omitted*	*omitted*	1st light revision
"The Smiling People"	*Weird Tales* May 1946 original	1st light revision	1st light revision	*omitted*	*omitted*	*omitted*	1st light revision
"The Emissary"	*DC* original	original	original	1st full rewriting	1st full rewriting	1st full rewriting	*omitted*
"The Traveler" ("The Traveller")	*Weird Tales* Mar. 1946 original	1st major revision	1st major revision	*omitted*	*omitted*	1st major revision	*omitted*

Table 3. (*continued*)

Evolution of the Texts: *Dark Carnival (DC), The October Country (OC)*, and *The Small Assassin (SA)*

Original Title (and subsequent title)	First Publication (and version published)	DC American 1947	DC English 1948 abridged	OC American 1955 all bindings	OC English 1956	OC English 1961 abridged paper	SA English 1962 paper
"The Small Assassin"	Dime Mystery Nov. 1946 original	1st light revision	1st light revision	2d light revision	2d light revision	*omitted*	2d light revision
"The Crowd"	Weird Tales May 1943 original	1st light revision	1st light revision	2d light revision	2d light revision	*omitted*	2d light revision
"Reunion"	Weird Tales Mar. 1944 original	1st light revision	*omitted*	*omitted*	*omitted*	*omitted*	*omitted*
"The Handler"	Weird Tales Jan. 1947 corrected original	uncorrected original	uncorrected original	*omitted*	*omitted*	*omitted*	uncorrected original
"The Coffin"	DC original	original	*omitted*	*omitted*	*omitted*	*omitted*	*omitted*
"Interim"	DC original	original	*omitted*	*omitted*	*omitted*	*omitted*	*omitted*
"Jack-in-the-Box"	DC original	original	*omitted*	1st major revision	1st major revision	*omitted*	1st major revision
"The Scythe"	Weird Tales July 1943 original	1st major revision	*omitted*	2d (light) revision	2d (light) revision	2d (light) revision	*omitted*
"Let's Play 'Poison'"	Weird Tales Nov. 1946 original	1st light revision	1st light revision	*omitted*	*omitted*	*omitted*	1st light revision
"Uncle Einar"	DC original	original	original	1st major revision	1st major revision	1st major revision	*omitted*
"The Wind"	Weird Tales Mar. 1943 original	1st full rewriting	1st full rewriting	2d (light revision)	2d (light revision)	2d (light revision)	*omitted*
"The Night"	Weird Tales July 1946 original	1st light revision	1st light revision	*omitted*	*omitted*	*omitted*	1st light revision

Table 3. (continued)

Evolution of the Texts: *Dark Carnival* (DC), *The October Country* (OC), and *The Small Assassin* (SA)

Original Title (and subsequent title)	First Publication (and version published)	DC American 1947	DC English 1948 abridged	OC American 1955 all bindings	OC English 1956	OC English 1961 abridged paper	SA English 1962 paper
"There Was an Old Woman"	*Weird Tales* July 1944 original	1st major revision	1st major revision	2d (light) revision	2d (light) revision	2d (light) revision	*omitted*
"The Dead Man"	*Weird Tales* July 1945 original	1st light revision	1st light revision	*omitted*	*omitted*	*omitted*	1st light revision
"The Man Upstairs"	*Harper's* Mar. 1947 1st major revision	original	original	1st major revision	1st major revision	*omitted*	1st major revision
"The Night Sets"	*DC* original	original	*omitted*	*omitted*	*omitted*	*omitted*	*omitted*
"Cistern" ("The Cistern")	*Mademoiselle* May 1947 1st major revision	original text and title	original text and title	1st major revision	1st major revision	*omitted*	1st major revision
"The Next in Line"	*DC* original	original	original	1st light revision	1st light revision	*omitted*	1st light revision
"The Dwarf"	*Fantastic* Jan.–Feb. 1954	—	—	1st light revision	1st light revision	1st light revision	*omitted*
"The Watchful Poker Chip" (of H. Matisse)	*Beyond* Mar 1954	—	—	1st light revision	1st light revision	1st light revision	*omitted*
"Shopping for Death" ("Touched with Fire")	*Maclean's* (Canada) June 1, 1954	—	—	1st light revision	1st light revision	1st light revision	*omitted*
"The Wonderful Death of Dudley Stone"	*Charm* July 1954	—	—	1st light revision	1st light revision	1st light revision	*omitted*

The hardcover was released, appropriately enough, in October 1955, with the mass-market paperback (printed from the same plates) released by Ballantine in 1956. Bradbury enjoyed very favorable terms on both editions and was given a better hardbound format and materials than Ballantine generally provided. The transformed and newly illustrated collection earned brisk sales and generally favorable reviews. A few critics, including Anthony Boucher, wondered why Bradbury was revisiting a land of the past. The noted Princeton literary critic Carlos Baker, writing in the *New York Times,* savaged Bradbury for this apparent regression, but reactions (including one from a Yale professor) led Baker to contact chief *Times* reviewer Francis Brown for room to print a letter moderating his views.[47]

But the true test of reader awareness would come in England. Rupert Hart-Davis, who had enthusiastically published all three of Bradbury's Doubleday titles there, had not been involved with the earlier Hamilton edition of *Dark Carnival.* He was careful with specialized fiction and persuaded Bradbury to replace *The Martian Chronicles* with his rocket metaphor, silver locusts, as the English title. But Hart-Davis was enthralled by the Mugnaini illustrations and intrigued by the reworking of the book's concept. He agreed to terms and published the British hardback in 1956. But Corgi, Bradbury's London paperback publisher for all three of his Doubleday science fiction and fantasy volumes to that point, was reluctant to purchase the paperback rights for a horror collection, and there was no British paperback edition of any kind for five years.

Ace of London finally purchased the paperback option, but the result was as strange as anything in the book itself. Ace published an abridged edition in 1961, deleting seven of the nineteen *October Country* stories and adding "The Traveller" from the British edition of *Dark Carnival.* The next year Ace acquired Four Square Books and brought out the seven deleted stories, along with the remaining six stories from the British abridgement of *Dark Carnival,* and titled the companion volume *The Small Assassin.* By purchasing both books a reader could have all the weirds found in the British hardback editions of both *Dark Carnival* and *The October Country.* But there were no publisher's notes to explain any of this at all.

The complex publication history of these tales provides many opportunities for error to creep into the art. The most destructive of these is also the most pernicious, and it involves, unfortunately, one of the best tales—"Homecoming," *Mademoiselle's* revised version of *Dark Carnival's* "The Homecoming" and published eight months *before* the book reached the market. The brief but significant deletion in the concluding pages of the revised magazine version, described above, was still missing when *The October Country* went to press in 1955 with yet a second series of revisions by Bradbury. A major typesetting error was also introduced at that point—the Ballantine hardback contains a two-page transposition of text that cuts through two entire scenes and makes the middle of the story completely unintelligible. Bradbury corrected this transposition error, provided a new version of the closing reconciliation between Timothy and his sister, and made a third series of revisions for the paperbound edition in early 1956.[48] The Ballantine paperback remains the most reliable text and represents Bradbury's settled intention for the story, but it is by no means the only version on the shelves of libraries and bookstores. The Ballantine hardback was never corrected; unfortunately, it is the source of three recent editions of *The October Country*—a new Ballantine trade paperback (1996), the Gauntlet limited edition (1997), and the Avon hardback (1999). All British editions, as well as Knopf's 1970 edition, were set from uncorrected proofs of the paperback; they include Bradbury's revision and the restored reconciliation, but they all contain the egregious transposition. The Knopf edition is long out of print, and the British texts are not available in America. If the old mass-market Ballantine paperback ever slips out of print, then "Homecoming" will only be available in a transposed form that lacks both the third layer of revision and the important reconciliation between brother and sister that brings full closure to the events of this most remarkable tale.

A fourth and heavily rewritten version of "Homecoming" holds a pivotal place in one of Bradbury's newest books, a closely knit cycle of stories about this same eerie family titled *From the Dust Returned* (fall 2001). By providing a new setting typescript, Bradbury has finally escaped the fifty-year cycle of error, but in the process he has, of course, transformed this story and several others from the original *Dark Carnival* grouping into yet another distinct work of fiction. The weave includes "The Traveler," "Uncle Einar," and two more vampire-family stories drafted in the 1940s and reworked years later for publication as standalone pieces, "The April Witch" (1952) and "West of October" (1988). "Trip to Cranamockett," the lost vampire story deleted from the page proofs of *Dark Carnival*, also finally found a home in this late-career novel. (Chapter 8 provides a fuller discussion of Bradbury's final transformation of these tales.)

Bradbury's first book transcended the pulp themes of the individual stories as he brought a carnivalized authorial intention to the structure of the entire volume. His intention for the contents changed throughout the publishing process as he transformed what was to be a focused look back at his pulp origins into a collection with tremendous range and tone that also looked ahead to what he would become as an author. In the final arrangement of contents, Bradbury closed with "The Next in Line," a subtle masterpiece of anxiety and unease in a complicated marital relationship. It was a far cry from the juicy terrors of his earlier weird tales, and he would try to give many such works a new life in two major waves of revision that ran even into the page proof stages of publication. For *The October Country*, he would transform this collection yet again with a new title and new stories that demonstrated what he could do with this genre as a recognized master of short fiction. This second stage of carnivalization completed the transformation of Bradbury's collected weird tales from the low-carnival entertainments of the early pulps into a far more literary carnival that looked to both his past and future career. Bradbury structured *The October Country* with new opening and closing stories that show in startling contrasts the insights he had gained into the nature of (his) authorship: through carnivalization, an author can either resituate past achievements in an ever expanding context of creativity or rest on the success of the past—and die. In Bradbury's life of fiction, carnivalization provided the only sure way to reaffirm the life of the author.

Thematics

In a very real sense, Bradbury's sojourn into weird fiction was an accident. We now know that his entry into the field was a direct result of his initial inability to sell high-quality science fiction. As he told Anthony Boucher, editor of *The Magazine of Fantasy and Science Fiction:*

> In fact *Dark Carnival*, to me, is an irony. I never intended writing in the weird field. I didn't much care for it, it had been run into the ground. All of my finest submissions, from 1936 through 1941, were s-f, and very bad. I got so many rejections that I decided to try a few weird stories. Thus, my entry into the weird field was an accident. And once I got going and seeing my way clear in the field, I began having fun, writing what I thought were "variations or reversals on old themes." Later, in 1946, I knew that I had come to the end of the trail. I knew that I could go on writing weird stories and selling them to *Weird Tales*, but I also knew from that year on they would not be good weird stories, for my vein was run dry and I would have to *force* to keep going. Only then did I turn my full force around and point it at s-f, where I had originally intended to go.[49]

But however accidental his entry into the genre was, early critics of Bradbury took him seriously and tried to discern in his weird fiction a largely unconscious symbolism and certain obsessive themes. And as a young author, Bradbury responded with wit and charm to their criticisms. For instance, Boucher pointed to a preoccupation with the theme of return: "The earliest published Bradbury stories were derivative and unimportant. The first in which his individuality began to manifest itself (particularly those in *Weird Tales* starting in 1942) were dominated by the theme of return—not quite to the womb, but to an unrealistically recalled golden childhood, a desire to escape from the gray burdens of adult life."[50]

Bradbury has acknowledged that he was repeating "the psychological aura of loneliness" in many of these early stories. "Again and again the unconscious theme [of separateness or loneliness] recurs in my stories, their psychology is of a piece."[51] Much later in his career, Bradbury would title one of his retrospective novels *Death Is a Lonely Business*, thereby creating a work that is a reflection on his authorial anxieties and aesthetic projects during this period of his life (especially his involvement with detective fiction). Bradbury did not want to end up resembling one of his own characters, a "Lonely," but rather to become a writer famous for his fine stories, loved by his readers, and able to live on in their imaginations.

In an essay written in 1951, Bradbury himself pointed out that his childhood fascination with carnivals, magic, and Halloween masks was something that carried over into his life as a writer. In fact, he reminds his critics that his most intense early desire was to be a stage magician. That he became quite aware of the play of Freudian themes in his fiction at this point of his career is revealed in a letter written to Anthony Boucher several years earlier. In responding to Boucher's favorable review of *Dark Carnival*, Bradbury referred to earlier conversations along this line: "I recall with some vividness your talk with Leigh Brackett some years ago, which Leigh duly reported to me, in which you said what a good writer Bradbury was, and what a hell of a big back-to-the-womb complex he had. I have taken this little slogan along with me to banquets, where I shock maiden lady writers by adding my own tag-line to it: 'Yes, but I wish Boucher would tell me whose womb I was heading back to!'"[52]

Remarks such as these (and others contained in William F. Nolan's *Ray Bradbury Review*) indicate that Bradbury at the time of *Dark Carnival* was clearly a post-Freudian writer of the fantastic able to joke with his critics about his own compulsion to repeat a "return-to-the-womb" fantasy in his writings. But Boucher's later qualification—it is not quite a "return-to-the-womb" fantasy that he now locates in Bradbury's fiction but a much more generalized theme of return to origins—indicates that the critic may have been modifying his views in response to Bradbury's awareness of what he had said. We do not know exactly which story Boucher was referring to when he mentioned the "return-to-the-womb" fantasy; Bradbury implicitly used the womb as an ambivalent background source in both "The Small Assassin" and "The Jar," full-length weirds well known to Boucher and Brackett. But the most explicit use of such a fantasy in Bradbury's early writing is "Interim," a short–short story published in *Weird Tales* in July 1947 and collected and placed in the approximate center of *Dark Carnival*. The pulp-magazine version contains the caption, "For after all are not the secrets of life and death inextricably woven together?" This points, through its metaphor of weaving, to the nature of textuality and how it contains thematic opposites in ambivalent tension.

The story text is also framed by spooky Halloween images of long rootlike hands emerging from a grave in the heading and by a footer depicting the grotesque image of a laughing twisted tree with its arms in the air, as if in celebration.

In this carnivalesque atmosphere the story unfolds. We quickly find out that it is about a graveyard. The tale is set in the dark just before dawn, and what takes place happens at a point of time between life and death, an interim. Bradbury describes the coffins in the graveyard explicitly as each being "a womb for silent, stiffened contents, each deep, each separate." But each individual coffin begins to link with every other one by means of a "code," a beat that is tapped out, which eventually becomes a great heart beating under the earth. Gradually, this heart beats out a name and speaks of Mrs. Lattimore, a pretty woman who was buried a year ago just before the planned birth of her child. Then the voice declares that she will be having her child today. With this revelation the lids of the coffins or wombs are battered "in questioning hysteria" (*hystera* being the Greek word for womb, and *hysterikos* meaning "suffering from the womb"; hysteria was once thought to be caused by uterine disturbances, even in Freud's day). These suffering wombs want to know what the child will look like and why it is being born. No answer is given, but the baby, whose image is left up to the reader's imagination, is born at daybreak from its "earth-moist box."

Bradbury is here giving voice to a theme that has deep roots in the culture of carnival, the theme of pregnant death, which is incarnated in the grotesque body. As Bakhtin describes it, "Life is shown in its two-fold contradictory process; it is the epitome of incompleteness . . . ; it is not a closed, completed unit; it is unfinished, outgrows itself, transgresses its own limits." This, he adds, is a body in which there is no longer one body, nor are there as yet two: "Two heartbeats are heard; one is the mother's, which is slowed down." Bradbury takes special care in the style of this story to bring out the double heartbeats, separating the units of his text by the slowing of the mother's heartbeat and the quickening of the child's. In literary terms this is a cosmic reverie of earth—all the coffins or wombs are united into one body that is the ever unfinished, ever creating body of the earth. Of course, the story is meant to be transgressive and disturbing to our modern and rational sensibilities, which tend to separate death from the rest of the life of the world. After he became more of an established author and wanted to leave behind his pulp origins, Bradbury chose not to include "Interim" in *The October Country*. When asked recently about its origins in his personal life, he only replied laughingly that the author of the story was sick: "That's a sick story by a sick author, and I don't want to know him. Ha-ha." Nevertheless, many images of the grotesque carnival body do survive in *The October Country*.[53]

But in an early retrospective essay "Magic, Magicians, Carnival, and Fantasy," Bradbury specifically addresses the influence of carnival on his authorship, going over in some detail the incident with Mr. Electrico that formed his relationship of deep ambivalence to that popular-festive form of life. Looking forward to what he might develop next, Bradbury writes: "somewhere along the line, you'll bump into Mr. Electrico, or someone much like him. No matter what I do I don't think I'll ever get that blue electricity out of my veins. . . . .When they pin me down for an autopsy some day, I wouldn't be at all surprised if they found carnival serpentine and an ever-flowering magical rose-bush in my chest."[54] In this passage Bradbury is looking forward jokingly to his "autopsy" by literary critics or literary biographers, anticipating that they will find in his body (the body of his writings) images from the carnival and from the world of magic. Serpentine is a long, colored paper ribbon that is unrolled and thrown into the air during times of rejoicing, especially during carnival. Here he uses it as a metaphor for his guts or intestines, the essence of his life. The rose bush alludes to the world of magic and signifies ongoing life. Through ambivalent carnival images, the death of the author is anticipated as a celebration of his life. Bradbury's writings are thus deeply carnivalized, especially in relation to Freud. Mr. Electrico, Bradbury's "father" in the real carnival of 1932, will make his appearance in the fictional carnival of *Something Wicked This Way Comes*, where he curses instead of blesses.

Regardless, Bradbury always claims to write spontaneously and originally from deep sources in his unconscious life in a way associated with romanticism and literary reverie, or even surrealism, and to discover things about himself only much later through the writings of others. Yet this position becomes increasingly difficult to sustain in the light of his work in detective fiction, which involves ratiocination and characters who are "psychoanalytically" motivated, and in the light of the many revisions he put these early stories through.

Written in 1942, though not published until May 1944 in *Weird Tales*, Bradbury considers "The Lake" to be his first quality story. A brief reading of it indicates the origins of Bradbury's aesthetic in nostalgia for a lost childhood and shows how he was concerned with such aesthetic issues in his revisions. He has provided two different accounts of the origins of this story in his childhood. In one essay he indicates that the story goes back to when he was seven and "my blonde cousin almost drowned." But in a later interview he indicates that in writing the story, he came upon "the recollection of a girl I knew [not very well] who drowned when I was eight or nine"; Bradbury mentions being at the beach when he heard the news of the drowning. In both accounts the image that seems to trigger the creative reverie is the "long golden hair" of the drowned girl, which is an important detail in the story.[55]

The opening paragraph, which immediately sets the story in motion, is essentially unchanged in Bradbury's *Dark Carnival* revisions (c. 1946), but it is considerably different (and much improved aesthetically) in *The October Country* version (1955), which embodies the theme of return with a description of a wave that shuts the child protagonist off from the adult world, thus establishing him in a "moment of green silence."[56]

They cut the sky down to my size and threw it over the Michigan Lake, put some kids yelling on yellow sand with bouncing balls, a gull or two, a criticizing parent, and me breaking out of a wet wave, and finding this world bleary and moist.

The wave shut me off from the world, from the birds in the sky, the children on the beach, my mother on the shore. There was a moment of green silence. Then the wave gave me back to the sky, the sand, the children yelling. I came out of the lake and the world was waiting for me, having hardly moved since I went away.

It is this moment of separation from the adult world that the boy craves in order to develop a fantasy of his lost drowned love. He later wades out into the water to establish just such a moment (even though he has been told by his mother not to do so—in all versions the water is seen metaphorically as a magician that saws him in half). In the pulp and *Dark Carnival* versions, however, the opening references are to his "breaking out of a wet wave, and finding this world bleary and moist." There is much more potential for readerly reverie in *The October Country* version, which is, of course, a self-consciously revised version. The opening passage now actually redoubles the theme of nostalgia as a painful return to origins and is told much more from a child's perspective. This is interesting in itself, and somewhat daring aesthetically, for we do not normally associate the complex emotion of nostalgia with childhood. Adults may be nostalgic about their childhoods and lost loves, but children generally are not. The nostalgic child and the theme of return are present in all versions but artfully redoubled and intensified in the last.

A careful collation of the story in its three versions reveals that, besides rewriting the opening paragraph, which effectively establishes the reader in the dreamlike magical substance of water and initiates us through bodily sensation into the theme of the return to lost love, Bradbury systematically removed all "factual" references that might form an intellectual block to the reader in responding to his story as a reverie. The stages of revision point toward an aesthetic intent that was realized more fully in later versions. For instance, both the *Weird Tales* and *Dark Carnival* versions open at Lake Michigan with adults "cutting the sky down" to the child's size. Bradbury actually says "*the* Michigan Lake" (emphasis added), thereby describing Lake Michigan in a childlike way rather than meaning a little place called "Michigan Lake." Waukegan, Illinois, where Bradbury was born, fronts a short stretch of the oceanic-sized western shore of Lake Michigan. So it is not only a real place, it is a vast body of water that, even as a passing reference, dwarfs the human dimension of the story.

Reverie requires that the element (in this case water) not be hostile or threatening to the imagination, rather that it be intimate. Having adults (the "They" in the earliest versions) do the work of making the lake intimate and available to the child's imagination—and in the process cutting it down to size—is also not conducive to reverie. Bradbury removed these problems and activated the reader's reverie by having the child *already* immersed in the water of his dreams in the revised version.

In *The October Country* the location is not specified, leaving it up to the reader to construct his own version of the lake out of imagination and associative memory. Furthermore, in talking about the psychology of loneliness in children, the earliest published version in *Weird Tales* makes the comment that, due to the presence of adults, the only place children can be alone is in their minds— an idea expressed in the same way in all three versions—but adds "that's why children imagine such fantastic things," a judgment that clearly intellectualizes and is inimical to building the state of reverie in the reader. This sentence was removed from the *Dark Carnival* version. Also removed is the explanation that in building the sand castle the young boy is creating "a sort of symbol," a phrase that tends to mark out his activity as intellectual, not emotive or imaginative.

As Bradbury revised the story, he also excised from later versions grosser suggestions about the state of a body that had been in the water for ten years in a state of decay, for this would clearly destroy reverie. In the *Dark Carnival* version, for example, the lifeguard refers to the fact of sexual difference by saying that the only way he knows the body in the sack he carries is a girl's is because she still wears a locket. Here, as an object reverie, the locket works on a intellectual level to suggest ideas of remembrance, keepsakes and such. But in *The October Country*, Bradbury wisely removed this passage and has the narrator recognize Tally purely by means of her long, golden, and perfectly preserved hair (a typical content of lockets). The sexual references are not appropriate to the kind of lost love Bradbury wants to suggest in all three versions, one that comes "before all significance of body and morals." The final version is the one that most perfectly evokes the ideal of a love untouched by time or death. The body that we are to imagine here is identified with the natural elements in reverie, one that is "no more bad than wind and sea and sand lying side by side forever."

One of the fullest expressions given to water reverie in Bradbury's early writings is in "Cistern," which also underwent revisions that remove overtly Freudian meanings and sexual references.[57] For instance, going back to the mother's womb is explicitly mentioned in the earliest version (as the comparison below reveals). But the sequence of revision to this story is more problematic than the sequence recovered for "The Lake"—the earliest version is, in fact, that for *Dark Carnival*, which appeared *after* the story had been revised for publication in *Mademoiselle; The October Country* version is identical to the *Mademoiselle* version. An extended aesthetic reading of *The October Country* version of "Cistern" is beyond the scope of this study (but can be found in *Ray Bradbury and the Poetics of Reverie)*. Here, the story indicates again how Bradbury revised with a view toward creating readerly reverie.

The theme of separateness and loneliness is very much in evidence as the reader follows the reveries of Anna about her lost lover, Frank, who has died before the story opens. As she sits by the window during a rainstorm talking to her sister, Anna narrates a cosmic reverie in which she and her lover meet in a cistern beneath the city and go on a journey out to sea. The entire story is structured by Anna's image of flowing water, which projects reciprocal masculine and feminine aspects of the psyche in a Jungian manner. In her daydream Anna is quite happy (because she imagines herself and her lover as already dead, so nothing can interrupt their pleasure). But in the *Dark Carnival* version, there is an undercurrent of sexual frustration that surfaces to disrupt the continuous pleasure of the reverie. It finally erupts near the end of the story when Anna identifies to her sister who the unnamed lovers in her fantasy are. As seen in the following comparison, Bradbury modified the initial outburst in his revisions.[58]

"Cistern" *Dark Carnival* (1947)	"The Cistern" *Mademoiselle* (1947); *The October Country* (1955)
"The man is Frank, that's who he is! And *I'm* the woman!"	"The man is Frank, that's who he is! And *I'm* the woman!"
"Anna!"	"Anna!"
"Yes, it's Frank, down there!"	"Yes, it's Frank, down there!"
"But Frank's been gone for years, and certainly not down there, Anna!"	"But Frank's been gone for years, and certainly not down there, Anna!"
Now, Anna was talking to nobody, and to everybody, to Juliet, to the window, the wall, the street. "Poor Frank," she cried. "I know that's where he went. He couldn't stay anywhere in the world. His mother spoiled him for all the world! So he saw the cistern and saw how	Now, Anna was talking to nobody, and to everybody, to Juliet, to the window, the wall, the street. "Poor Frank," she cried. "I know that's where he went. He couldn't stay anywhere in the world. His mother spoiled him for all the world! So he saw the cistern and saw how

secret and fine it was, and how it went down to the ocean and everywhere in the world, and it was like going back to his mother's womb where it was nice and secret and nobody criticized. Oh, poor Frank. And poor Anna, poor me, with only a sister. God, Julie, how'd we get this way and why didn't I take Frank when he was here! But if I'd have held onto him he'd have been revolted and so would I, and Frank would have been shocked and frightened and run off like a little boy, and I'd have hated him if he had touched me. Christ, Julie, what good are we!"

"Stop it, this minute, do you hear, this minute!"

secret and fine it was. Oh, poor Frank. And poor Anna, poor me, with only a sister. Oh, Julie, why didn't I hold onto Frank when he was here? Why didn't I fight to win him from his mother?"

"Stop it, this minute, do you hear, this minute!"

In the *Dark Carnival* version, this initial outburst of repressed sexual frustration continues. Anna imagines Frank looking at her in the bathtub in a scene that stages a very active and voyeuristic male gaze:

> "It's rained three days, and all the time I sat here, and thought. And when I got the idea of Frank, down there, I knew it was the place for him, and when I turned on the faucet in the kitchen I heard him calling from deep in the cistern, up the long metal piping, calling and calling. And when I bathed this morning he looked out from the little grille in the tube and saw me. I soaped myself to hide myself! I saw his eye shining behind the grille!"
> "A soap bubble," said Juliet frantically.
> "No, an eye."
> "A drop of water."
> "No, Frank's eye!"
> "A piece of metal, a nut or a bolt."
> "Frank's lovely, seeing eye!"
> "Anna!"[59]

The Frank the reader encounters earlier in the story—during the reverie of the cistern—is only moved, like Anna, by the tidal waters. But this scene represents Frank as more frightening (prompting Anna to try to hide her naked body with soap) and clearly indicates psychoanalytic meanings, for she imagines herself as the object of the look of the desiring male Other, that would destroy reverie. The bathing scene is completely excised in the *Mademoiselle* and *October Country* versions.

The rationale for revision is not hard to understand if one recalls that psychoanalysis was dubbed "the talking cure" by one of Freud's "hysterical" woman patients. Simply put, the purpose of language in the psychoanalytic session is to get the analysand to assume her unconscious desires in speech (*la parole pleine*, as Lacan phrases it). This was seen by Freud as a liberating effect, a lifting of repression. But in Bradbury's original version, the voicing of the real persons behind the reverie has the opposite effect, it is bitter and disillusioning. The later version does not back away from the frustration, but neither does it allow one to so easily reduce Anna's beautiful dream to the mere effect of sexual frustration. It is fantasizing itself, so fragile to maintain, that seems liberating.

From the point of view of literary reverie then, "Cistern" is clearly more developed than "The Lake" in the sense that it develops an almost "anti-psychoanalytic" aesthetic stance by using reverie to combat the reduction of the imagination to the brutal "facts" about our sexual lives. (Frank was too attached to his mother ever to love another woman, it seems.) Anna remains a prodigious dreamer, and her reverie cannot be reduced so easily to an underlying return-to-the-womb fantasy. But certainly "The Lake" manifests literary qualities that could have placed it in the slicks as well had the timing been right. They are both stories Bradbury could be proud of, signs of an author just beginning to develop his powers of fantasy and imagination to transform life.

As discussed earlier, editors close to Bradbury tried more than once to keep him from turning back to past work. Walter Bradbury's warning against reworking *Dark Carnival* clearly shows his own conviction that the health of his friend's "general psychology" about writing depended on looking ahead to new work. Nevertheless, the "variations or reversals on old themes," which Ray Bradbury had described to Anthony Boucher as his point of departure for his original weird tales, eventually led him to develop *The October Country* from its origins in *Dark Carnival* as a way to reflect on the nature of his own authorship. With this new volume it became even more apparent how Bradbury followed through on the initial creative spark in writing the best of his weird tales: he played his reversals and variations on old themes of the fantastic largely by bringing his stories into dialogue with the general text of Freud, for these stories explore the territory of psychosis, hysteria, delirium, neurosis, hypochondria, the death wish, the unconscious—the very vocabulary of psychoanalysis. But the remark made by Mr. Harris, the protagonist of the story "Skeleton" who is deliriously obsessed with protecting his internal organs from an attack by his own bones, could well serve as an epigraph for the entire volume: "How is it we never question our bodies and our being?"[60] It was Freud who first demonstrated, in his *Studies on Hysteria* (1895), that the body is the site where the symptoms of the unconscious can be read. In reading *The October Country*, one seems to discover one's body for the first time as the site of the fantastic, an unfamiliar and frightening territory full of surreal frescoes. (Bradbury evokes the paintings of Salvador Dali and Pablo Picasso as equivalents to this experience.) The grotesque body, which ordinary vision obscures or even represses, is, in fact, the theme and landscape of the book, a hidden carnival that unifies an otherwise disparate collection of stories.

The fantasized body is also the means by which *The October Country* represents its psychological themes of unconscious desire. An analysis showing how each story uses the symptomatic body is beyond the scope of this study, but a brief indication of what each story is about is in order before analyzing "The Dwarf," which opens the collection, in some detail. In "The Next in Line," the body is a kind of mummified clay sculpted by Death into grotesque and horrifying shapes—images based on Bradbury's own visit to the cavern of the mummies of Guanajuato, Mexico—that are symbolic of the protagonist's morbid obsession with her own death. In "The Watchful Poker Chip of Henri Matisse," an average and ordinary man slowly adds artificial parts to his body, making himself into a work of art celebrated by the avant-garde. "The Jar" is a carnival sideshow–related story in which the body is an amorphous pale thing from the wet swamps that provokes each character to project his own—sometimes-murderous—fantasy.

In "The Lake" the body of a girl who drowned long ago washes up on shore still possessed of its golden hair. The adult narrator, who was present when the girl drowned, realizes that he will love her forever. The other woman in the story, the narrator's wife, now seems very strange to him. This story evokes the Freudian notion that our earliest love objects are the strongest and that they are never truly abandoned, though they may be submerged; we can only find substitutes for them in adult life. "Emissary" deals with a sick boy who learns to read the body of his dog for signs of the outside autumn world. In "Touched with Fire" a grotesquely fat woman (called Mrs. Death-Wish) is driven by a heat wave into provoking her own murder. "The Small Assassin" (analyzed in more detail in the chapter on detective fiction) deals with the ambivalence of a pregnancy. A woman gives birth to a baby whose body is so well developed that it can kill his parents in revenge for bringing him into the world. In "The Crowd" the desire to look at what happens to a body in a car accident involves us in the paranoia of crowds.

"Jack-in-the-Box" records with imagistic precision the (phallic) onset of puberty, which is frightening to a boy who has always inhabited a protected "Garden World" and house dominated only by the presence of his dead father, whose place he is seemingly destined to take. Even his mother, masked at times as his teacher, participates in the "Law of the Father," which governs this world. This is one text in *The October Country* that clearly invokes psychoanalytic structures. Indeed, "Jack-in-the-Box" generates its sense of the fantastic around the question of whether or not the boy protagonist will be governed by the Law and Name of the Father, taking his place with the mother in the Symbolic order (language and the symbolic function), or whether he will break out of his captivity in some fashion. But the mother-teacher mysteriously dies before the boy reaches such a decision, and like a jack-in-the-box, he springs outside of the house into a fantastic world—our real world—that he has been told is death. This and other stories like it show that the general text of psychoanalysis—as interpreted by the Lacanian orders of the Imaginary (capture of the self by mirror images), the Symbolic, and the Real—is frequently implicated by Bradbury's fantasy.

In "The Scythe" the mother's body is a wheat field that her son is compelled to cut down, killing her. "Uncle Einar" is about a morose man with vast tarpaulin wings who learns joy by turning his body into a kite for children. In "The Wind" a supernatural malevolent wind wants to incorporate the protagonist into its huge body. "The Man Upstairs" deals humorously with the biological facts of sexual difference when a young boy eviscerates the fantastic body of a vampire-like creature living in his grandmother's boarding house. "There Was an Old Woman" tells how an elderly woman, by sheer force of will, wards off death and the efforts of morticians to autopsy her body. In "The Cistern" a frustrated old maid projects the fantasized body of her lover and herself into a cistern during a rainstorm. In "The Homecoming" a young witchlike girl inhabits the bodies of others, and a boy born normal into a family of supernatural freaks dreams of flying and drinking blood just like them. Finally, "The Wonderful Death of Dudley Stone" constructs a playful mystery story that explores the ambivalence of authorship—and the death of the author—by evoking a writer who is content to disappear into the body of his writings.

As to why the themes of psychoanalysis should be the themes of a beginning fantasist, there are ample historical reasons. Tzvetan Todorov presents some of the most compelling in *The Fantastic*, a study of the genre largely confined to the nineteenth century. He demonstrates that in the twentieth century psychoanalysis has replaced—and thereby made useless—the literature of the fantastic. Todorov argues that there is no need today to resort to the devil to speak of an excessive sexual desire nor reason to resort to vampires to designate the attraction exerted by corpses. Psychoanalysis and the literature that is directly or indirectly inspired by it deal with these matters in undisguised terms: "The themes of fantastic literature have become, literally, the very themes of the psychological investigations of the last fifty years."[61]

The October Country can be read as an attempt to reverse this situation and find innovative ways to write the fantastic after Freud. Freud's ideas have been so widely disseminated that it need not be a question of direct influence. One can speak about a kind of *general text* of Freud that exists in the cultural imagination. But Bradbury used Freud extensively to motivate characterization in his detective fiction published at the same time as his weird fiction. Bradbury's fantasy also engages psychoanalytic structures—especially Oedipal structures—in such books as *Something Wicked This Way Comes*. And he confronts Freud again with the character of A. L. Shrank in *Death Is a Lonely Business*.

What in fact often occurs in Bradbury is that psychoanalysis finds itself standing before the court of fantasy, its notion of authority unmasked and exposed as a fiction. This is the central semantic process referred to herein as carnivalization, whether the story explicitly mentions carnival or not. Two stories in particular, "The Small Assassin" and "The Wonderful Death of Dudley Stone," are structured by the Freudian logic of ambivalence, a word prominent in both texts, one that comes to the English language from the pen of Freud himself. No fantasy writer *before* Freud could have used it, and ambivalence became a central thematic focus of the internalized Gothic in Bradbury's early writings. "The Wonderful Death of Dudley Stone" provides the reader with a mystery story dealing with the problem of literary fame, fortune, and influence, always fertile ground for the psychoanalytic critic interested in a writer's anxieties. (Since it was originally published as detective fiction, a discussion of "The Small Assassin" will come in a later chapter.) Usually, Bradbury's strategy is to include a psychoanalytic explanation of seemingly fantastic events in the story—for example, a small child whose mother thinks it can murder, or a famous writer who was seemingly murdered by a jealous epigone, but who is somehow still mysteriously alive—and then to show that the accepted rational explanation is insufficient or downright wrong.

Both of these stories, taken together with "Jack-in-the-Box," would be a bit too long for analysis here, but "The Dwarf," which opens the collection (not part of *Dark Carnival* but originally published in *Fantastic*, 1954), is brief and interesting enough to be treated as a sort of parable about the fantasy writer's ambivalent relationship to reality. In the classical Freudian view of this relationship, the artist is a kind of neurotic who cannot confront the frustrations of reality directly. Rather, he has a strong impulse to fantasize about himself in daydreams centering on that exalted personage Freud calls "his Majesty the Ego."[62] If one also happens to have artistic talent, however, the writer can disguise the obviously egotistical character of these adventurous daydreams, or substitute gratifications, by using the formal properties of art. If readers respond in turn to these disguised wishes with their own, the author may become successful, winning a place of fame and fortune in the real world by a circuitous route.

The dwarf mentioned in the title of Bradbury's story is a writer of pulp detective fiction. Bradbury himself was initially a writer of such fiction, and as a matter of fact, his "Douser" stories, published in *Detective Tales* in 1944, form a kind of mirror to this story (especially "Half-Pint Homicide," where the miniature detective Bradbury—whose own family nickname was "Shorty"—created stands for the reality principle). Known to the denizens of the seedy hotel he inhabits as Mr. Big, the dwarf lives near the Venice Amusement Pier (Douser's locus of operations, too). As the story opens, the dwarf's tales have not won him much recognition, but another character, Aimee, at least thinks she understands his psyche. The dwarf comes every night to a cheap seaside carnival show, after the crowds have dispersed, to see himself in the mirror maze, specifically the "thin" mirror that makes him appear normal. Ordinarily, a mirror maze is an attraction because it offers grotesquely carnivalized images of the body. One takes pleasure in seeing one's body image momentarily distorted and then returned to normalcy, knowing it is an illusion limited by the mirror's frame. But Mr. Big's body is already distorted in reality. He is described as a "dark-eyed, dark-haired, ugly man who has been locked in a winepress, squeezed and wadded down and down, fold on fold, agony on agony, until a bleached, outraged mass is left."[63] If the mirror distorts reality into grotesque fantasy for most people, it corrects a distorted reality for Mr. Big. The mirror maze will become the object that (de)constructs the paradoxes of narcissism explored by this story.

Two other characters are involved in "The Dwarf," and they represent opposite attitudes toward the human need for fantasy. The owner of the mirror maze, Ralph, is completely cynical about human nature. When asked why people want to ride the roller coaster, he replies that people want to die, and the roller coaster is the handiest thing to dying there is. But Ralph is something of a voyeur, for he spies on his customers. He takes his neighbor Aimee, who runs the hoop circus and whom he has been trying to seduce, back behind a partition, from where they can see Mr. Big dance and pirouette and wink before the thin mirror. But instead of laughing, as Ralph expects, Aimee feels sorry for the dwarf. And when she finds out to her surprise that Mr. Big is indeed an author, she reads a passage from one of his stories that she especially admires to Frank, who jealously responds by asking her why Mr. Big is not, then, rich and famous. This leads Aimee to speculate that perhaps Mr. Big needs something to boost his ego, to give him the courage to try and sell his stories to quality magazines. She considers what effect having a private mirror all for himself might have on Mr. Big: "A mirror for your room where you can hide away with the big reflection of yourself, shining, and write stories and stories, never going out into the world unless you had to."[64]

Aimee wonders whether this all-of-a-piece illusion would help his writing or hurt it, and this is the story's connection with the Freudian aesthetic of fantasy.

The mirror under such conditions would be an ideal place where narcissistic and pleasurable representations of the ego could be indulged in without shame or disguise, no public need for the softening of fantasy being required. But the stories Mr. Big currently writes, from which we are given a sampling when Aimee reads to Ralph, are ones that have a murderous dwarf as antihero, a victim of his parents having raised him in a doll's house until their death, never telling him of the real world outside in which he will be a freak: "Only now [after their death] do I see the magnificent size of my parents' psychosis."[65] When his parents die, the protagonist has to face a "landslide of reality" as he is cast out into society. The dwarf in Mr. Big's story suffers then from a loss of illusion, not a loss of reality. Would the ideal mirror that Aimee is thinking of destroy Mr. Big's need for such fictional disguises or increase them? This is an unanswerable question set within a frame mirroring an abyss. Are Mr. Big's stories really disguises masking his true self, or are they closer to actual displays of narcissism—are they mirrors of his existence—since most readers do not, in fact, know that the author is a dwarf? The story deconstructs, through repetition and reversal, the central notions of the Freudian theory of art that links authorial fantasy and substitute gratifications back to the reality principle and fame in the social world. How can one distinguish fiction from reality in the mirror maze?

While the story poses these questions, it provides no adequate means to answer them. Soon, out of malicious jealousy of the dwarf's stories, which Aimee has read and interpreted to him, Ralph meanly switches the thin mirror with one that makes even normal-sized people seem frightfully small. Needless to say, this is a horrible humiliation to the dwarf, who can only scream when he sees himself crushed and wadded down even further in it; his body becomes unimaginably fantastic. But fiction seems to reflect reality at the end when the dwarf runs off with a gun stolen from the shooting gallery to become the murderer about whom he has written. Our last glimpse of the mirror maze is paradoxically a "true" reflection of Ralph grotesquely distorted in one of his own mirrors, "a horrid ugly little man with a pale squashed face under an ancient straw hat."[66] This carnivalized image expresses the "truth" about him. Ralph, who cruelly destroys other people's illusions about themselves, is shown to himself as he really is, captured by the illusions of his own mirror maze.

"The Wonderful Death of Dudley Stone," which closes *The October Country*, reflects not on the struggle of a marginal West Coast writer, but on the ambivalence of success in the eastern literary establishment, which has always subjected the writer to the power of literary and critical reviews that upheld a Freudian reading of powerful unconscious precursors in a tradition of what Harold Bloom has called the anxiety of influence. Where "The Dwarf" presents us with a diminutive character, "The Wonderful Death of Dudley Stone" makes its eponymous hero almost a giant, looking down on the narrator "like Michelangelo's God creating Adam with a mighty touch."[67] Having had a full measure of success as a literary lion, Dudley Stone in midcareer now has to deal not only with literary critics but also with a doppelgänger, John Oatis Kendall, who bears an "amazing ambivalence" toward Stone because he feels overshadowed by him.

What is significant about this story in cultural terms is that Stone, at the same time, has to deal with his *own* ambivalence toward success in the eastern literary establishment. And he does this by becoming his own critic. He gets "free of it all"—the love-hate logic of ambivalent influence—by weighing the value of literary success against his life and trusting in his subliminal estimate of his future as a writer. His subconscious tells him that the two books John Oatis Kendall would have destroyed were very bad: "They would have killed me deader than Oatis possibly could." In this sense Stone is already dead as an author, but by affirming his life in destroying his new books—a carnivalesque gesture—he has the pleasure of seeing his critics panting and waiting in vain for his next masterpiece after his public renunciation of writing. "And then I had the pleasure of seeing myself compared to all the greats when I announced my departure from the literary scene. Few authors in recent history have bowed out to such publicity. It was a lovely funeral. I looked, as they say, natural. And the echoes lingered. 'His *next* book!' the critics cried, 'would have been *it!* A masterpiece!' I had them panting, waiting. Little did they know." This last phrase is almost mocking, implying that the critics have little knowledge of the author's struggles (or perhaps that they themselves are "little").[68]

Always a West Coast writer, Bradbury now has the last laugh on the eastern literary establishment, which was so dependent on Freudian modes of reading. Stone frees himself from such readings of his works (represented by John Oatis Kendall, who is suffering from the anxiety of influence) and from the critics, who would read him as a powerful father figure, indeed almost a god himself. In the end the critics are waiting and dependent on him for his next book. By becoming his own critic, Bradbury has moved the anxiety of influence from authors onto critics themselves. But even before this story became the critical capstone of *The October Country*, Bradbury himself became a full-blown critic of culture by expanding the notion of carnival into the sphere of postwar political and social life through the publication of *The Martian Chronicles* and *Fahrenheit 451*.

2

Martian Carnivals

The Martian Chronicles (The Silver Locusts)

In the history of American science fiction, *The Martian Chronicles* is often discussed as a pivotal event in the field's growing respectability. Most accounts note that the book was reviewed by a critical community that extended well beyond the science fiction publishing "ghetto," including two prominent reviews by Christopher Isherwood. While the book was published as science fiction and was ostensibly about the colonization of the planet Mars, mainstream readers found in it a serious exploration of the social and political problems of postwar American culture (that is, fears about nuclear war, racism, and censorship). Bradbury's style was also praised for its literary and poetic qualities.[1] The cultural matrix of the United States was clearly shifting toward the growing realization that most people now lived in a "science fictional" culture anyway, and with this realization came new fears and anxieties about the future. Because it dealt with these themes and issues, *The Martian Chronicles* was the first science fiction book to find two distinct reading audiences. It could, with fairness, be said then that after the publication of *The Martian Chronicles* in May 1950, science fiction was still seen as different from mainstream literature but no longer separate from it. The permanent barriers fell.

With regards to Bradbury's authorship, the book's publication and reception was a pivotal event as well. Bradbury began to feel that he had "arrived" as a mainstream author.

> I still didn't know what I had until I went to Chicago in the late Spring of 1950, on my way to New York. CHRONICLES had just been published and advance copies had arrived in Chicago ahead of me. I was supposed to meet two friends for lunch in Chicago, and went to meet them at the top steps

of the Art Institute. I saw a crowd of people there at the top, and thought: there must be a tour going through. It wasn't a tour. It was the first readers of CHRONICLES who had come, all 20 of them, with my friends to welcome me to the Windy City. On that midafternoon in Spring of 1950, I felt my first great love and acceptance, and my heart wept with the good knowledge.[2]

By May 1953, three years after this event, Bradbury had become an unofficial spokesman to the mainstream about science fiction as a literary field, publishing in *The Nation* an account of what the field meant to him. It was in this article that he began to reflect on the carnivalized qualities of science fiction in terms that linked it to such Renaissance writers as François Rabelais, in whose texts ideas are treated with an open seriousness so they could be laughed at and, if need be, reinvented in "continually renewed and renewable concepts."[3]

How did Bradbury achieve such a dramatic cultural feat of carnivalization, moving from a subculture to the mainstream? What is it exactly about *The Martian Chronicles* in its text and themes that made it such a pivotal work?

Bradbury's Texts

Exactly three years passed between the release of *Dark Carnival* (May 1947) and Bradbury's second book, the breakthrough story-cycle-cum-novel published in America as *The Martian Chronicles* (May 1950) and later in England as *The Silver Locusts*. During this period, Bradbury's new author-agent partnership with Don Congdon continued to pay off as Congdon placed more and more Bradbury stories in both the intermediate- and big-circulation slick magazines. Congdon also negotiated overseas serial rights for many stories and secured anthology and radio adaptations that continued to gain name recognition for his client. Yet they were unable to get the major-market magazines to take a significant number of the quality science fiction stories that Bradbury had been producing in quantity since the final years of the war. Most of these—including more than forty Martian stories—were written in his parent's garage in Venice, California, adjacent to a powerhouse that inspired him with its constant hum of creative energy. Most too were written prior to his September 1947 marriage. Many found their way into the pulps, but even Congdon, who became his literary agent that same summer, was unable to place more than a couple of the Martian stories in major-market magazines.[4] Three of them saw their first publication in *Chronicles;* others, with plots more tangential to the concept of Martian colonization developed in the *Chronicles* weave, would appear individually in magazines and Bradbury story collections for the next twenty-five years (see app. A).

Until the summer of 1949 Bradbury and Congdon had no better luck marketing book concepts, Martian or otherwise. The success of "Homecoming" as the centerpiece of the October 1946 issue of *Mademoiselle* with the accompanying Charles Addams illustration led Bradbury to propose an entire collection of vampire tales illustrated by Addams. Many were already written, and Congdon was able to generate a great deal of interest from William Morrow. Editors there went so far as to plan an illustrated collection of a half-dozen Bradbury vampire stories set in white type on black paper, but Addams's fees were too high to risk on a story collection by a relatively new author.[5] In early 1949 Bradbury put together a larger and broader collection, and Congdon submitted a typescript compilation to Farrar, Straus. The response was negative and suggested a bias against pulp authors. This Bradbury could accept, but the letter also indicated that the reviewers at Farrar, Straus were extending this label to stories in the proposed collection that had appeared in the quality magazines as well as other quality stories he had either not yet placed or had placed in the pulps during his apprentice years. The rebuff became a catalyst for action; when Norman Corwin suggested that Bradbury go to New York with typescripts in hand, he quickly made arrangements to make the publishing rounds with Congdon during June 1949.

By this time, Bradbury had a number of working outlines for other story collections as well as a few novels. His earliest extended concept, the never-published *Masks*, had given way to an extension of the title metaphor of the 1947 *Dark Carnival* collection; a nineteen-chapter contents page, titled "DARK CARNIVAL, a novel of 70,000 words," survives today in Bradbury's papers. This project would evolve into *Something Wicked This Way Comes* nearly fifteen years later. But in 1948 and 1949 only one novel manuscript was actually taking shape, the nostalgic and autobiographical *Summer Morning, Summer Night*, from which would emerge *Dandelion Wine* a decade later. Bradbury had also generated at least ten often-overlapping outlines for story collections under a half-dozen or more titles. In June 1949 Bradbury boarded the bus to New York intent on marketing the *Summer Morning, Summer Night* manuscript and at least one of the story collections. His surviving working outlines support his own recollections that a dinner meeting in New York with Doubleday editor Walter Bradbury provided the spark that led him to shape some of these stories into the unified fable or chronicle that first established Ray Bradbury's international reputation in science fiction and fantasy.

Critics have assumed from this often-published account that the title for *The Martian Chronicles* was born during that same fateful evening, but surviving manuscripts reveal that it predates the crucial events of June 1949. Four typed contents listings for story collections with this title survive; one is dated in ink by Bradbury "Sept., 1948," and the contents listed in the others suggest that all were prepared during that period (see table 4). The first undated list includes nine stories under the title "The Martian Chronicles, a book of short stories" and contains a story-by-story word count suggesting that this is the earliest outline of the group. Another contains two short-story collections and is annotated in ink by Bradbury as "Planned Books to be Published Later." A general science-fiction collection, tentatively titled "R Is for Rocket," is to the left of a collection actually titled "The Martian Chronicles." Both collections list twenty-one titles, but only "Chronicles" includes an estimated word count for each tale. A third undated list, annotated in Bradbury's hand as "Planned Books of Short Stories," includes "The Martian Chronicles" (twenty stories), a shorter general science-fiction collection titled "Pillar of Fire" (fifteen stories), and a collection of the major-market stories titled "Power House" (fourteen stories), which, like many of the others, were written while Bradbury worked next door to the humming electric dynamo in Venice Beach. Only some of the pieces are actually listed under each collection, but the number of stories appears after each collection's title. Although stories are sometimes grouped by theme or similarity of plot, there is no evidence that *Chronicles* as first formulated was anything more than a story collection in any of these outlines.

The mixture of finished and working story titles contained in the undated listings seem to precede a more detailed outline that Bradbury has initialed and dated, in ink, "Sept. 1948." In this form *The Martian Chronicles* collection consists of thirteen stories, most of which are carried forward from the two major situations (contact and colonial abandonment) grouped in the undated outlines. But here as in two of the undated listings, the stories are not in chronological order and, in fact, nearly reverse the chronological progression of contact, exploitation, and retreat found in the final book concept. Even so, Bradbury revised the word count for each story and for the first time provided an estimated length (61,500 words) for the entire collection. His handwritten drawing for a dust jacket appears in the upper right corner of the page and includes instructions for black lettering on a red background. Beneath the *Chronicles* listing is a thirteen-story collection titled "The Bronze Faces." Most of these works are identifiable and support Bradbury's own holograph notation that it was to be a volume of "weird stories."

But by December 1948 Bradbury had collapsed the best from all these proposed collections into a more general collection titled "The Illustrated Man" (see table 4). A surviving draft title page and attached table of contents bears the date December 8, 1948, and the annotation "carbon manuscript of completed book." There are twenty-one stories pulled from all of the earlier listings of that year and an additional story added on March 19, 1949. This is almost certainly the collection that Bradbury and Congdon had offered to Farrar, Straus early in

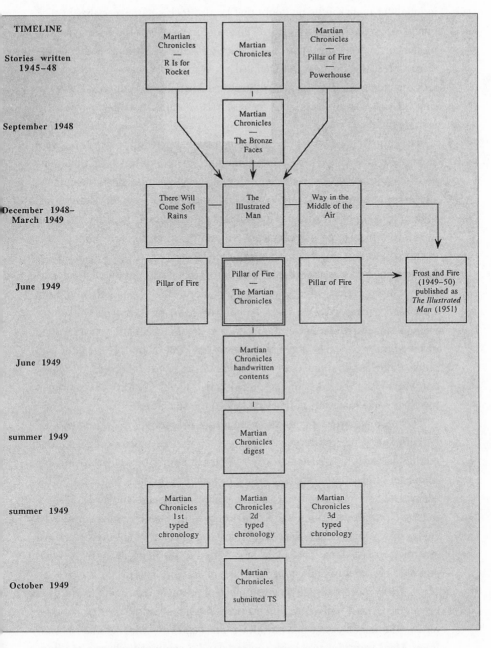

Table 4. A timeline of Bradbury's surviving story-collection outlines as they developed into *The Martian Chronicles*. Many stories from the *Illustrated Man / Pillar of Fire* nest became *Frost and Fire*, a collection finally published as *The Illustrated Man* (1951).

1949, and it was probably still on the market when Bradbury went to New York in June. But there can be no doubt that he also took a more specialized collection of science fiction stories titled "Pillar of Fire"—one of three surviving listings of this collection contains notes made immediately after his fateful dinner discussion with Congdon and Doubleday's Walter Bradbury. All of these listings (including the more general "Illustrated Man" listing) contained seven or eight of the Martian tales, and these stories would take center stage as the evening unfolded.

Earlier in the week Bradbury and Congdon had offered the *Summer Morning, Summer Night* novel and at least one of the story collections to several publishing houses. The three-way conversation with Walter Bradbury initially focused on the advantage of novels over story collections, especially for a writer who was just beginning to establish himself in mainstream publications. Doubleday was about to launch a pioneering line of science fiction titles, and this was no doubt the main reason that Congdon and writer Bradbury had corralled editor Bradbury for the evening. It was clear that Ray Bradbury's fantasy and science fiction material and his marvelous stylistic talents were tailor-made for this series, but from a publisher's perspective the young author was clearly marketing his work in the wrong format. In his reminiscent introduction to the fortieth-anniversary edition of *The Martian Chronicles*, Ray Bradbury recalled Walt Bradbury's breakthrough observation: "What about all those Martian stories you've published in the past four years? Isn't there a common thread buried there? Couldn't you sew them together, make some sort of tapestry, half-cousin to a novel?"

This probing series of questions reminded Ray Bradbury of his first encounter with Sherwood Anderson's *Winesburg, Ohio* in 1944 and the long-discarded outline he had prepared for a cycle of Martian stories of settlers resembling Anderson's isolated grotesques. Nothing had come of this idea, and certainly the characters of his subsequent Martian stories bore little resemblance to Anderson's, but the dinner conversation had led Bradbury to the sudden realization that he could create a unified fable that would transcend the "story collection" genre just as Anderson had done. That night he returned to his room in the YMCA and selected the stories to pull out of the "Pillar of Fire" outlines for the reconceived "Chronicles" concept. Bradbury spent much of the night reformulating the project on his portable typewriter, and the proposals he submitted the next day (one for *The Martian Chronicles* and one, titled "Frost and Fire," that became *The Illustrated Man*) won him two book contracts and a combined advance of fifteen hundred dollars from Doubleday. As Bradbury recalled a dozen years later, the book was outlined within a day: "Sure enough, just from memory, without having the stories on hand, the next day I put together the structure of the *Martian Chronicles*."[6] That Bradbury could do all this from memory is consistent with his commitment to be a storywriter above all else and his conviction that the novel and other sustained forms of fiction, for him, would take care of themselves over time:

[W]hen you work in the novel *per se,* you focus your attention and your talents on just one thing. You don't give your mind the free play it should have, and you sort of bind it down and constrict it. . . . I would much rather collect over a period of ten years a vast body of short stories, five hundred, six hundred or seven hundred short stories or fragments thereof, and at some later date magnetize them, hold up a central theme, and see which stories cluster to it automatically. The process does happen quickly, as I pointed out with the *Martian Chronicles.* Bang! In two or three short hours, I sat down and wrote the whole outline that was dictated to me by the short stories that I had already done. I didn't have to think about it: it was an emotional process again.[7]

The idea of allowing stories to attract or cluster to form a larger whole underlines Bradbury's consistent view that genre labels mean very little in the act of creative writing. He has referred to *The Martian Chronicles* as a novel only in the sense that each story reflects the same authorial vision: "even though these stories were written separately, they do represent my philosophy at the time. It's pretty hard to read one and not recognize the sort of person I am and see that the tone is the same all the way through."[8] He is more at ease using Walter Bradbury's "half-cousin to a novel," and in the 1997 edition he calls *Chronicles* a "book-of-stories-pretending-to-be-a-novel." In Bradbury's case, where the notion of text rather than genre provides the focus for the writer's creative vision, the surviving textual evidence is essential to a critical understanding of the author's evolving vision. Unfortunately, the textual history of *Chronicles* has been buried— in long-lost pulp and slick magazine issues, in manuscript archives, and in un-collated variant editions—for more than half a century. This history begins in earnest with the results of a long night's work in New York.

The initial worksheet survives from that night's work—Bradbury's handwritten selection arrows for nine Martian stories are embedded in one of the "Pillar of Fire" typed outlines. The arrows radiate from his marginal notation, "use in new book on Mars? Martian Chronicles?" Bradbury's handwritten inscription in the lower right margin pinpoints the moment of insight: "June 1949. Y.M.C.A. N.Y.C." A draft title page styled as advertising copy also survives and contains the following summary: "A novel comprising 15 short stories concerning the first landing settlements on Mars." This first reference to the book as a novel is followed by a "sampler" list of eight stories and was probably compiled directly from the accumulated lists of collections at hand. The sampling offered in the announcement includes "Martian Homecoming," apparently the interim title for the pulp classic "Mars Is Heaven!" (that would eventually become "The Third Expedition"), as well as two titles ("The Stranger" and "The Man") that would not appear in any subsequent content listings.

But a surviving handwritten list of contents probably represents the first chronological working out of the concept for the book. It shows fourteen (and possibly fifteen) stories progressing through exploration, settlement, and eventual abandonment of the Martian frontier (see fig. 6). The four stories of first contact are here labeled sequentially, but the remainder of the listing is somewhat tentative; there is no running word count for the individual stories, but a breakdown of the overall length given at the top of the page (54,000) indicates that the interlined chapters 7, 10, and 11 were added later along with the usage, for the first time, of the term "chapter" in connection with a listing of *Chronicles* contents.

The most revealing record of that night's work survives in the form of three pages from a four-page typed story-by-story digest of *Chronicles* (fig. 6). This fair-copy typescript is the result of further and more detailed outlining after Bradbury returned from New York. For the first time one can see the stories behind the listings and understand just how Bradbury saw them cohering at this early stage of development, literally hours after Walter Bradbury triggered the idea in the author's mind. The sixteen titles listed are called chapters, and the summaries open up a full chronology of the book's storyline. During the summer, Bradbury sent his Doubleday editor a full set of his Martian stories in typescript as a preliminary (and probably unsequenced) master of working materials. There were more than two-dozen stories to work from, and at various times through the end of 1949, many were considered for the collection.[9]

Three undated working chronologies postdate the summary outline and show how Bradbury continued to move existing stories in and out of the book concept through the summer of 1949. All are typed on Bradbury's typewriter; their contents (along with those of all listings resulting from the New York trip) are charted in table 5. The first is very close to the digest sequence and almost certainly dates to the New York trip or shortly thereafter. It contains seventeen chapters, and again the opening section of contact and exploration remains largely unchanged from the New York sequence laid out in the digest outline and the earlier handwritten list of titles. But the middle and closing chapters are not as stable at this point; as table 5 shows, midbook stories of settlement move in and out, and the later stories of the consequences of war back on Earth continue to change position.

The second undated chronology includes twenty-one titles. Most of the changes appear in the still-developing midsection of the book, which at this stage remained far from complete. But chapter numbers have been replaced with a provisional run of the date prefixes for each chapter that Bradbury would adopt for every edition of *The Martian Chronicles*. Six (and possibly seven) of the eleven short bridging chapters now appear. Two of these, "The Settling In" and "Threat of War on Earth," are working titles for two bridges ("The Settlers" and "The Luggage Store") that mark the crucial transitions between exploration, settlement and exploitation, and apocalyptic retribution—the three major sections of the finished book.[10]

Bradbury's final working chronology is virtually identical to the table of contents surviving in the carbon of the complete typescript he sent Don Congdon on October 10, 1949.[11] Both include twenty-nine titles representing the eighteen stories Bradbury had settled on and the eleven titled bridging passages he wrote to weave the stories into a unified narrative. Final changes came as Doubleday editors reviewed the submitted typescript. Three stories ("The Disease," "They All Had Grandfathers," and "The Fathers") and a bridge ("The Wheel") would be cut in proofs, a process during which the two Bradburys began to form a long lasting and effective author-editor relationship. A December 1949 letter from author Bradbury to editor Bradbury (undated) confirms these cuts, which the two men had made several days earlier by phone. It also reveals the author's concern with Walter Bradbury's reservations about two of the stories that made it though the final cutting process, "The Earth Men" and "Usher II." Neither story was essential to the cycle that Ray Bradbury had woven together during the late summer of 1949. "The Earth Men" was the most expendable of the four stories of first contact; even with bridging and other revisions, it remained the most pulplike in its premise and action. "Usher II" was close to pure fantasy; though given a date in the general chronology, the revenge taken on those who destroy the cultural heritage of Earth blots out any sense of colonial continuity with the rest of the settlement chronicles. But author Bradbury strongly supported the retention of these tales and agreed to revise "The Earth Men" to bring that story's portrayal of the Martians more in line with the masked and exotic creatures presented in the rest of the book.

Both stories are fantastic and violent commentaries on two of Bradbury's favorite themes of the period—the fine line between sanity and psychosis, and the growing menace of cultural censorship in postwar America. Given his determination to include these stories, it is not surprising that Bradbury had considered adding the equally bitter "Payment in Full," which would appear in the February 1950 issue of *Thrilling Wonder Stories*. He had suggested including it during the December 1949 phone conversation with Doubleday's Bradbury, but in his follow-up letter he conceded that the tale was too bitter; in fact, it would never appear in any of his story collections.

THE MARTIAN CHRONICLES   1.

by Ray Bradbury

Chapter One   ROCKET SUMMER

                   The first Mars Rocket lies ready to take off,
                   but the ethical and moral problem is presented
                   "Should man take his evil, his wars, his problems
                   out to the stars, or should he stay behind to
                   solve his problems on Earth first, before
                   contaminating other worlds?" Through a ruse,
                   the protagonist, in the first chapter, succeeds
                   in delaying and destroying the first rocket.

Chapter Two   YLLA

                   On Mars. By inference, we realize that the first
                   trip to Mars is at last coming about, after the
                   initial delay. Ylla, a Martian woman, dreams of
                   the landing of the Rocket. Her husband, at last
                   believing her, goes out and destroys the Earth Men.

Chapter Three   THE EARTH MEN

                   After the failure of the first rocket to return to
                   Earth, when Ylla's husband has killed the men, a
                   second rocket is sent to Mars. In it, is a large,
                   crew, plus a Captain. When they rap at doors,
                   the Martians think them insane. Eventually the
                   Earthmen are thrown into an insane asylum and finally
                   euthanasia is practised upon them. Thus ends the
                   second expedition.

Chapter Four   MARS IS HEAVEN.

                   After the failure of the 2nd Expedition, the Third
                   Expedition very carefully lands upon the opposite
                   side of Mars, where they meet an even cleverer
                   type of Martian. Here, the Captain and his men
                   think they see their home towns, their childhood
                   sweethearts, grandmothers, which the Martians, by
                   a ruse, create mentally. The Captain and his men
                   die. End of the Third Expedition.

Figure 6. The handwritten list represents the earliest known chronological outline of *The Martian Chronicles* as it was conceived during Bradbury's fateful meeting with Doubleday editor Walter Bradbury in June 1949. The first page of a subsequent typewritten digest of contents shows that the early chronicles of contact were clearly identified from the beginning. All four of the principal contact stories carry settled titles except "Mars Is Heaven," an original magazine title that became "The Third Expedition" as *Chronicles* took shape. "Rocket Summer," adapted from an unrelated pulp story, eventually would be replaced by a brief opening bridge chapter bearing the same title.

54,000 WORDS

The Martian Chronicles

	Rocket Summer	— chap. 1
Invasion	Ylla (1)	Chap. -2
Invasion	The Earth Men (2)	Chap. 3
	— DOCTOR STORY —	
Invasion	Mars was Heaven (3)	Chap. 4
Invasion	The Moon Be Still as Bright	Chap. 5
	LOVE STORY HERE ???	
	The Visitor	Chap. 6
toCome	The Death of the Martians (RELIGION STORY)	7
	The Naming of Names	Chap. 8
	(to be altered)	
	The Off Season Picnic	Chap. 9
	These Will Come of the Rains	Chap. -10
	the Millionaire	Chap. -11
	The Long Years —	Chap. 12
	The Empty Towns —	Chap. 13
	?? Mars	— Chap. -14

The mid-book chapters of settlement are clearly provisional in the handwritten outline and would remain so in the digest as well (see table 5). "The Love Story" ("The Love Affair"), "The Visitor," and "The Naming of Names" would eventually be eliminated; "The Death of the Martians (Religion Story)" is probably "The Fire Balloons," which was dropped from the first edition but later restored in other editions. The tentative placement of "The Millionaire [Million-Year] Picnic" with "The Off Season" and "The Naming of Names" indicates the difficulty Bradbury encountered in selecting stories about humans becoming Martians—a concept central to the cultural themes of the completed book. From the Albright Collection, courtesy of Donn Albright and Ray Bradbury.

Table 5. A progression of the stories included in the various working contents developed for *Chronicles* between the June 1949 meeting with Doubleday editor Walter Bradbury and the final contents included in the first American edition. The page containing chapters 14–16 of the contents digest has not been located. The numbers indicate the order of story placement in each version of the contents. The shading highlights all appearances of titles that were included in the published book. Note that the stories of settlement took the longest to develop; in the end Bradbury used the greatest concentration of bridges in the middle of the book to provide a smooth progression through the final selection of settlement stories.

Story and Bridge Titles	Handwritten c. June 1949	Typed digest of contents	First summer chronology	Second summer chronology	Third summer chronology	Submission 8 October 1949	First edition May 1950
Rocket Summer (story)	**1**	**1**	**1**	**1**	**1**	**1**	**1**
Rocket Summer (bridge)							
Ylla	**2**	**2**	**2**	**2**	**2**	**2**	**2**
The Summer Night					**3**	3	**3**
The Earth Men	**3**	**3**	**3**	**3**	**4**	4	**4**
The Taxpayer (bridge)					**5**	5	**5**
The Third Expedition	**4**	**4**	**4**	**4**	**6**	6	**6**
The Disease	4a	5	5	5	7	7	
And the Moon Be Still as Bright	**5**	**6**	**6**	**6**	**8**	**8**	**7**
The Settlers (bridge)				7	**9**	**9**	**8**
They All Had Grandfathers			6a		10	10	
The Green Morning					**11**	**11**	**9**
The Visitor	6						
The Locusts (bridge)					**12**	**12**	**10**
Night Meeting			7a		**13**	**13**	**11**
The Shore (bridge)		7		**13**	**14**	**14**	**12**
The Fire Balloons	7	7	7	9	15	15	

Table 5. (*continued*)

Story and Bridge Titles	Handwritten c. June 1949	Typed digest of contents	First summer chronology	Second summer chronology	Third summer chronology	Submission 8 October 1949	First edition May 1950
Interim (bridge)							
The Musicians (bridge)					16	16	13
Way in the Middle of the Air			13	10	17	17	14
The Wheel (bridge)				11	18	18	15
The Exiles			11	12	19	19	
The Naming of Names (bridge)					20	20	16
Usher II			12	15	21	21	17
The Old Ones (bridge)					22	22	18
The Martian	8	8	9	14	23	23	19
The Naming of Names		9	8	8			
Love Affair	5a	10	10				
The Luggage Store (bridge)				16	24	24	
The Off Season	9	11	14	17	25	25	20
The Watchers (bridge)							21
The Silent Towns	13			19	26	26	22
The Long Years	12	13	16	20	27	27	23
I, Mars	14						24
There Will Come Soft Rains	11	12	15	18	28	28	25
The Million-Year Picnic	10		17	21	29	29	26

On February 17 Bradbury returned proofs to Doubleday, making few corrections in the process: "I found very little in error, after three complete readings. It is a shame that by the time a writer finishes reading his book for the umpteenth time, it reads like nothing more than a battered old telephone directory. The thrill is gone, as the song says."[12] Bradbury now felt that the words were right for every story, but he still was not sure every story was right for the book. In the same letter he noted that "The Off Season" contributed very little to the book and gave Walt Bradbury the option to delete it. But by this time Ray Bradbury had added the final bridge passage ("The Watchers"), which forms a transition between the events of "The Luggage Store" and "The Off-Season" and the events (a few weeks later) of "The Silent Towns." This final addition bolstered "The Off-Season" and perhaps made both author and editor a bit more at ease with that story's fit; it remained in *The Martian Chronicles*, locking in a first-edition chronology of twenty-six chapters—fifteen stories and eleven bridges.

Although fine-tuning the contents had extended from June 1949 to January 1950, Bradbury spent much less time during that period revising the individual stories. Collations of the original texts and the final book version reveal that he made numerous substantive revisions to all the preexisting stories, but few large-scale revisions were necessary. As Bradbury later recalled: "All these stories seemed to fall into a pattern, and they were all about the same people on the same way to the same star. Most of them are not directly related, but there is a general surge."[13] Although many of the original stories shared general characteristics of plot and circumstance, they were as yet largely unrelated variations on the principal themes of first contact, settlement and exploitation, and colonial decline due to trouble back on Earth. Some of the stories would have to be revised to reflect the more detailed Martian culture perfected in such stories as "Ylla"— the bronze-skin, golden-eyed Martians with their ancient achievements, exotic art forms, inscrutable masks, and jaded temperament. The late deletion of "The Disease" led Bradbury to add a six-hundred-word scene near the beginning of "And the Moon Be Still as Bright" to let the fourth expedition discover that all but the most reclusive Martians had succumbed to chicken pox carried by the earlier expeditions. He also added central characters from "The Off Season" and "The Long Years" to the roster of the fourth expedition and revisited its captain in the revised plot of "The Long Years," all in order to weave some of the explorers into the later chronicles of settlement and colonial decline. (These revisions are examined in greater detail in the thematic discussion below.)

The primary creative challenge to the *Chronicles* concept centered on the new bridging chapters that Bradbury developed to form a seamless tapestry. His goal was not only to sustain and extend the narrative but also to relate the experiences of successive waves of settlers, thus more exactly paralleling the American frontier myth. These titled bridges spanned only a page or two and were based on the occasional *pensées* he wrote and set aside, along with his full-blown Martian stories, in the immediate postwar years. He recalled this initial phase of creativity in the introduction to the Avon Books edition: "During the next few years I wrote a series of Martian pensées, Shakespearean 'asides,' wandering thoughts, long-night visions, predawn half-dreams. The French, like St. John Perse, practice this to perfection. It is the half-poem, half-prose paragraph that runs as little as one hundred words or as long as a full page on any subject, summoned by weather, time, architectural façade, fine wine, good victuals, a view of the sea, quick sunsets, or a long sunrise."[14] Later, with the new *Chronicles* project in mind, Bradbury worked a number of these short pieces into bridges. A few were written as the stories locked into place, and two bridges were actually whittled down from existing Martian stories during the summer of 1949.

The first of these represents the only major structural evolution that Bradbury would make in the opening chapters of *Chronicles*. "Rocket Summer" leads off every version of the contents up until publication, where it becomes a single-page opening bridge into the book. But Bradbury's summer 1949 chapter digest reveals that he initially intended to rewrite the earlier lunar-exploration story titled "Rocket Summer" (1947) as a cautionary frame for the entire cycle of stories: "Should man take his evil, his wars, his problems out to the stars, or should he stay behind to solve his problems on earth first, before contaminating other worlds?" (fig. 6). The rest of the summary provides a Martian version of the lunar original, showing how the first rocket is delayed and then destroyed through a ruse mounted by those who want to settle Earth's issues first. But the story is too didactic and the characters too flat, and in the end Bradbury used only the title metaphor and the earlier story's description of rocket exhaust: "It fried the tarmac and a vast deluge of warm air rushed across the country for miles. People sweltered amidst a sudden rocket summer."[15]

At the center of the summer 1949 digest is another story that would be reduced to a bridge in the final book. Chapter 9, "The Naming of Names" (1949), presents a very different concept of Martian settlement (fig. 7). The original published story presents a community of settlers that has named and claimed part of the new frontier but finds itself marooned on Mars by atomic war on Earth. Over time the Red Planet imparts a racial memory of the ancient Martian language and a desire to assume the identities of the old native names and homesteads. Bradbury filters this process through the eyes of the Bittering family; one by one Mars slowly transforms the Bitterings and the other settlers into Martians, and a rescue ship five years later finds only dark and golden-eyed people living far from the colonial settlement. The new crew surveys and names the major landmarks; in this way "The Naming of Names" begins all over again. Bradbury retained this

Chapter Five.   THE DEATH. The Martians die of Earth-brought plague.

Chapter Six: AND THE MOON BE STILL AS BRIGHT

                        The Fourth and successful expedition to Mars.

                        Now, with the Martians dead, save for a few here or
                        there in remote spots, the Earth men come in. But
                        again the moral problem is brought forth. One of
                        the rocket men rebels, tries to kill the other rocket
                        men and the captain, identifies himself with the
                        Martians, runs off into the hills, and has to be
                        hunted, reasoned with, and finally killed.
                        Mars is in the hands of the Invader.

Chapter Seven   THE FATHERS

                        Now, a furious activity has come upon Mars, with
                        Earth men building newaeoidity. And it is inevitable
                        that religion should come to Mars. The Fathers,
                        in a missionary rocket, move to Mars. Their problem:
                        to convert the remaining Martians to God. But the
                        only remaining Martians are some intelligent creatures
                        far to the North, round grey spheroids. The
                        fathers argue among themselves: are the Martians
                        human, have they a soul? or are they animals, not
                        worth bothering with? how to present a man-like
                        Diety to a grey globe? how to represent Christ to
                        them, since Christ, as a man, will be unbelievable
                        to them? the problem is resolved and the Fathers
                        settle into Martian life.

Chapter Eight   THE MARTIAN

                        The last Martian boy on all Mars, comes down to the
                        new community, in the identity of a boy long dead and
                        buried on Earth. The Martian is all things to all
                        people. To one he seems a girl once loved and lost,
                        to another an old man, ten thousand miles away.
                        The Martian boy is coveted for his ability to enchant.
                        And, like the goose that laid the golden eggs, he is
                        destroyed by the Earth men's desires.

Chapter Nine   The Naming of Names.

                        The story of a family in the one bustling community
                        of Mars. Other cities are planned for later, but,
                        at present, only one main town has been completed.
                        And into this town comes Mr. Bittering and his wife
                        and children. Mr. Bittering is afraid of Mars.
                        He begins to notice that Mars is changing all of them,
                        the color of their houses, their vegetables, their
                        eyes, their skins, their hair. He wants to go back to

Figure 7. Pages 2 and 3 of Bradbury's summer 1949 digest of chapters shows an interim
sequence of the middle *Chronicles*. The tentative plot connection between "The Naming of
Names" and "The Off Season" represents an attempt to bring the theme of becoming Martian
to a peak in the middle section of *Chronicles*. Eventually, he would remove "The Naming of
Names" and carry the Martian identity theme through to a climax in the final story, "The
Million-Year Picnic." The final page of the digest, containing the final three stories in this
sixteen-chapter concept of the book, has not been located. The earlier handwritten outline
indicates that "The Million-Year Picnic" had not yet worked its way to the end of the book
(see fig. 6); it likely joined "The Silent Towns" as one of the missing final chapters in the digest.
From the Albright Collection, courtesy of Donn Albright and Ray Bradbury.

Earth, he tries to build a rocket, because all
of the other rockets trying to come to Mars have
been wiped out by a cloud of Meteors, causing a
delay of some two years before more aid can come
through from Earth. In the end, he and his wife
and children go up into the mountains to live,
and their skin turns brown, their eyes yellow.
They become, to all intents and purposes, Martians.
When the Earth Rockets, with aid, finally make it
through to Mars, they find the one city empty,
and colonization must start all over again.

Chapter Ten   LOVE AFFAIR. The ltsayoff an American who finds
                     a Martian woman and tries to build their life
                     together, which ends in failure. She, like the
                     Martian boy, is one of the few remaining Martians
                     who appear now and again upon the scene.

Chapter Eleven: THE OFF SEASON. Now, with the towns growing huger
                     on Mars, a man named Sam sets up a hot-dog stand
                     and desecrates the Martian cities to do it. Mr.
                     Bittering and his family, now become Martians,
                     as we saw in chapter Nine, come down to plead with
                     Sam not to spoil Mars. Sam kills Mr. Bittering,
                     tries to escape from his relatives, and in the end
                     is given papers by the neo-Martians which entitle
                     him to a million acres of land. It is then that
                     the atom war on Earth explodes. Earth seemingly
                     burns in the sky and is dead. Sam's wife, who
                     detests him, laconically states, "Well, Sam, it's
                     looks like an off-season for your hot-dog stand.
                     Have to wait around a million years for your next
                     customers."

Chapter Twelve   THERE WILL COME SOFT RAINS.

                     Brief interlude on Earth. The ruins after the War.

Chapter Thirteen   THE LONG YEARS

                     Now, with all of the colonial peoples of Mars going
                     back to Earth, a few survivors remain on Mars. All
                     others have gone back to help fight the atomic war.
                     An old scientist remains. His wife dies, as do his

basic plot in the digest outline and even worked these same dark, golden-eyed new Martians into the summary for his rewrite of "The Off Season," which had also reached print as a stand-alone story (in 1948). The Bitterings, now living ghosts of the ancient Martians, come back to haunt Sam Parkhill, one of the most single-minded colonial exploiters. But Bradbury eventually dropped "The Naming of Names" completely and eliminated the Bitterings from the rewrite of "The Off Season." Instead, he would retain only the frontier irony of new names for old places in a brief bridge bearing the same title.

This transformation of an existing story into a bridge probably occurred as Bradbury was working the remaining stories into a final sequence. The deletion of "The Naming of Names" reveals a key element in this process. Many of the chosen stories give a sense of humans *becoming* Martians to some degree: "The Earthmen" are mistaken for Martians by the Martians themselves; "The Third Expedition" thinks Mars is heaven, when in reality it is a deadly paradise; and there is a "Night Meeting" out of time between a new settler and an ancient Martian. Spender, the renegade of the fourth expedition in "And the Moon Be Still as Bright," takes on the clothes and identity of one of the last Martians and turns on his shipmates; his rationale and fate (discussed later) set up the cultural thematics of the entire book. In the summer 1949 digest of *Chronicles*, Bradbury tentatively set the culmination of this dynamic late in the middle of the book— he planned to literally turn settlers into Martians through "The Naming of Names" and then bring them back in "The Off Season" to haunt Sam Parkhill with the racial conscience of the displaced culture. By removing "The Naming of Names," Bradbury saved the uncanny effect of "becoming Martian" for the final story of the book. "The Million-Year Picnic," which would soon become the final chapter of *Chronicles*, provides a much more positive variation on this theme through its portrayal of a family that adopts Mars as mankind's last refuge as Earth sinks into the final stages of an atomic war that had already reclaimed the earlier waves of colonial exploitation. With this final structural sequence in place, Bradbury had, in a very real sense, written the greatest bridge of all—the one between author and reader. We *become* Martians by reading the book—we claim it eagerly, for we have earned it in a very personal and literary sense.

Bradbury's constantly evolving concept of *The Martian Chronicles* is reminiscent of his earlier pattern of moving stories in and out of the *Dark Carnival* collection, and indeed this pattern of creative open-endedness and the carnivalization of genres has defined his approach to book-length projects throughout his career. The editorial control that August Derleth had used to reign in this creative pattern during the *Dark Carnival* years was a thing of the past. Bradbury's new relationships with Don Congdon and Doubleday allowed much more space for his unrestricted views of fiction to play out. With Congdon's support, Bradbury tailored a heavily reduced version of "There Will Come Soft Rains" to *Collier's* short-short weekly feature format, and it appeared in the issue of May 6, 1950—the very week that the long version reached bookstores as the penultimate chapter of *Chronicles.*

Bradbury made another trip to New York for the May 4 release date—this time forgoing the exhausting bus ride to take a train. The unexpected surprise of meeting fans who had already read advance copies of *Chronicles* during his Chicago stopover provided a taste of mainstream recognition to come, and he soon turned his attention to the reviews that might confirm this good omen.[16] Rex Lardner's short informational piece appeared in the *New York Times* the same week, but Bradbury was back in Los Angeles when the other major reviews came out. The *Saturday Review of Literature* and the *San Francisco Chronicle* both ran short but upbeat notices. Two editors who knew Bradbury's work well provided much longer reviews for the major Chicago papers—August Derleth's review in the *Tribune* and Anthony Boucher's in the *Sun* provided a context for reading *The Martian Chronicles* as much more than the latest "Doubleday Science Fiction" title.[17] But the book carried that very phrase above a bright red rocket-ship logo on both the spine and front cover of the dust jacket; and the logo also appeared above the liner notes. Clearly, Bradbury needed a breakthrough review by a major-market literary critic, and that opportunity came by way of a chance encounter with Christopher Isherwood in a Los Angeles bookstore early in July 1950. Bradbury recognized him, introduced himself, and placed a store copy of *Chronicles* in his hand. It proved to be a well-placed gift; Bradbury soon wrote to his Doubleday editor with the stunning news that Isherwood would review the book in the new literary journal *Tomorrow:* "And all because I happened to run into Isherwood two weeks ago and give [*sic*] him a copy of the CHRONICLES. Pure coincidence. Isherwood said that people had come to visit him three nights in a row and had sat reading the CHRONICLES instead of talking. I am delighted."[18]

Bradbury asked that Doubleday send copies to other major critics and writers, but Walter Bradbury urged caution—pressure exerted to secure high-profile reviews could backfire on both author and publisher. For now, that answer would suffice. Both author and editor were pleased with sales, which by then had reached five thousand and topped all other titles in the Doubleday Science Fiction group. More significantly, Doubleday had just concluded a deal with Bantam Books for a paperback edition and a thousand-dollar advance, with publication set for mid-1951. *Dark Carnival* had never gone into a paperback edition on either side of the Atlantic, so this break into a new readership with a U.S. mass-market-paperback house was clearly a triumph for Bradbury. And the sale of overseas rights was imminent, for copies of the Doubleday *Chronicles* were beginning to have an effect in Britain.

The Martian stories had actually reached England even before the concept of the book took shape in New York. Through the negotiations of Congdon and his British agent, A. D. Peters, Bradbury was able to retitle and even combine some of the stories for reprint in British periodicals, often very shortly after they appeared in American magazines (see app. A). Beginning in August 1948, *Argosy* of England published eight of the Martian stories, and this preview set up a ready-made reading public for eventual British book publication. Bradbury had, in fact, started working on that possibility well before the May 4 release date in America. In January he asked Doubleday to send Congdon "an extra set of galleys for him to send on to England so that if Hamish Hamilton is interested, they can bring out the Chronicles in England about the same time" as American publication.[19] But this was not to be; Hamilton still carried backlisted stock of *Dark Carnival* and decided against picking up the option on a second Bradbury title.

Hamish Hamilton would remain Bradbury's friend for life, but he was not interested in science fiction titles. Few British publishers were, for that matter, but a breakthrough came most unexpectedly during the fall of 1950. Hugh Wheeler, a minor (and usually pseudonymous) British author of detective fiction, was greatly impressed by the U.S. edition of *The Martian Chronicles* and insisted that his own London publisher, Rupert Hart-Davis, purchase U.K. publishing rights. Hart-Davis was astonished to find that a book with such a title could have such intrinsic literary quality, and in late October he acquired the U.K. rights through A. D. Peters. But neither Congdon nor Peters would be the first to tell Bradbury— he heard the news first from Christopher Isherwood in Los Angeles, for Hart-Davis had immediately asked the English expatriate for an introduction he could use in the new edition. Isherwood had a policy against doing this, but he would later write a significant review for the London *Observer* to help launch the new edition.

English publication also marked the beginning of a series of major postpublication variations in *The Martian Chronicles* that continue to affect readers today. Hart-Davis was still concerned that the title masked the highly unusual imaginative elements and the truly poetic style of the contents, and he did not want the book dismissed as "scientific nonsense" on that basis. On November 10, 1950, he wrote Bradbury and asked him to consider a title change: "A new title without any mention of Mars or planets or rockets would, I believe, help enormously to get the book into the same category as George Orwell's 1984." Bradbury shared Hart-Davis's feelings about the science fiction label and was already trying to get the Doubleday Science Fiction colophon removed from his next book. Hart-Davis initially suggested "Way in the Middle of the Air" as the best candidate for a title story, but eventually both men settled on *The Silver Locusts*—a metaphor that Bradbury used in a bridging chapter ("The Locusts") to describe the earthbound rockets on their launch pads. The new title certainly fit the British publisher's sense of what the book was all about—the metaphor placed science within the context of a poetic imagination more concerned with truth than fact. English reviewers quickly picked up on the fantastic qualities of Bradbury's vision. In his *Punch* review, B. A. Young observed: "scientific fact is for him [Bradbury] only the raw material of fantasy, to be moulded as suits him best, and his real interest is in the aesthetic and moral questions involved when the inhabitants of one planet invade another. By firmly subordinating probability to poetry Mr. Bradbury has created a world of curious beauty, glowing with sympathy and shot through with humour, which the lapidary quality of his writing presents to us in all its strange colours." Isherwood revisited *Chronicles* under its new name for the *Observer*, calling Bradbury "very little of a scientist and very much of a philosopher-poet." He also made it clear that this book, by any title, would more than hold its own in the broader book market. "This philosophic-prophetic fiction is the true legacy of Wells, and is as significant as anything that is being written today."[20]

The Silver Locusts was released in September 1951, sixteen months after American publication but only ten months after Hart-Davis committed to the book. It was typeset from the Doubleday edition, and Bradbury actually allowed Hart-Davis to correct copy for him, thus saving the time of transatlantic proofreading.[21] Sales initially averaged fifty to sixty copies a week, reaching two thousand by mid–February 1952. Hart-Davis considered these figures poor in light of the favorable reviews, but he was convinced that over time a Bradbury public would develop in England. *The Silver Locusts* continued to be a slow but steady seller for many years, and the hardbound edition remained in print for decades. But the book carried more than a new title, for Bradbury made his first postpublication change in contents as well. As early as July 1950, his concerns about "Usher II" resurfaced in his correspondence with Doubleday: "Brad, you were right about USHER II. I should have followed your advice and cut it out of THE MARTIAN CHRONICLES. It is a good story, but time and again people have mentioned it to me as the lump in the cake frosting. I let my love for the story blind me to its position in relation to the whole. I should have taken advantage of your more objective view . . . ah, well, and damn" (ellipsis Bradbury's).[22]

There was nothing he could do about the Doubleday edition, but the British contract opened up new possibilities. When *The Silver Locusts* was released in 1951, it no longer contained "Usher II." To make this work, Bradbury also had to cut the last 150 words from the preceding bridge, "The Naming of Names," which describes those who would react, like the Poe-esque builder of "Usher II," against space-age bureaucrats intent on extending Earth's rules, regulations, red tape, and censorship to Mars. At the same time he restored "The Fathers" as "The Fire Balloons," for he had come to realize that cutting that story from the Doubleday edition at the last minute had been a mistake.[23] The restoration eliminated the awkwardness of three consecutive bridges created by the original excision and restored meaning to the last paragraph of "The Shore" bridge, which alludes to the priests of "The Fire Balloons" as the "men who looked, by their eyes, as if they were on their way to God." In the U.S. edition and all others that do not contain "The Fire Balloons" this passage stands as a nonsensical reading.

In 1953 the publisher Sidgwick and Jackson obtained permission from Hart-Davis to issue a new edition of *Chronicles* in England as the second book in their new venture, the U.K. Science Fiction Book Club (SFBC). This version added a new Martian tale, "The Wilderness," to *The Silver Locusts,* offering their new variant as *The Martian Chronicles,* taking advantage of a title that was showing signs of becoming a perennial seller in America and, just perhaps, an international science fiction and fantasy classic. "The Wilderness" presents a woman's perspective on the eve of departure for Mars, doing so with the tone and language of an American tale of the pioneers. It had appeared in several magazines before Bradbury collected it in the U.S. edition of *The Golden Apples of the Sun,* but its addition to a new British version of *Chronicles* clearly enriched that work as well—"The Wilderness," perhaps more than any other Martian tale, subtly questions the masculine values of science fiction colonization stories.

At least for a time, these British opportunities to fine-tune the collection's contents satisfied Bradbury. He told his good friend Anthony Boucher that the U.K. SFBC contents represents "the definitive edition," adding that this version "should end my additions & corrections to the book for all time." Bradbury was subsequently distracted from thoughts of *Chronicles* by a wonderful but exhausting year (spent largely abroad) working with John Huston on the screenplay for the film adaptation of *Moby Dick* and another two years bringing the better half of the long-awaited *Summer Morning, Summer Night* project to publication in the form of *Dandelion Wine* (1957). During this period, American readership of *Chronicles* was greatly boosted by the successful 1951 paperback edition brought out by Bantam Books. This publisher was only six years old but had quickly become a paperback heavyweight under Ian Ballantine's innovative direction and agreements with the distribution arm of the powerful Curtis Publishing Company. Unlike other major reprint houses, Bantam had moved beyond reliance on mysteries to publish a wide range of titles, and Ballantine was willing to take a chance on Bradbury's mix of science fiction and fantasy. Bantam initially wanted to market *Chronicles* in paper as *The Earth Men,* using Bradbury's tale of the second ill-fated Earth expedition as the title story. Bradbury accepted this possibility without qualm, hoping only that the cover art might not be too lurid.[24] In the end the growing commercial and critical success of *Chronicles* in America finally persuaded Bantam not to change the title, and the first paperback edition was released in June 1951.

The cover art is well executed and, while its weapon-wielding spaceman suggests the pulp origins of some of the stories, sex and aliens are not part of the composition. But Bradbury was astounded to find that a junior editor at Bantam had fabricated much of the final two paragraphs of the prefatory note. After asserting that "Bradbury doesn't care for science," the note closes with an alleged quotation from Bradbury himself: "'I don't like what science is doing to the world,' he says. 'I think science is a good thing to escape from.'" The cautionary message of Bradbury's space-age frontier fantasy was clearly being presented to the public in very different ways by his two American publishers: while Doubleday regarded Bradbury as the most successful author in a new line of science fiction titles, Bantam was portraying him in paperback as antiscientific. Bradbury wanted neither label, but he had more control over Bantam's misleading portrayal; before the month was out, he had forced Bantam to prepare a second printing with the damning paragraphs removed.

When the second paperback printing was exhausted in 1954, Bantam reset the text in a new edition (that setting remained the standard paperback edition until the ninety-fifth printing was reset again in 2001). The prefatory note was completely rewritten, but editors were still fishing for a provocative Bradbury quotation. The result was only slightly less confusing than the original: "He, himself, says: 'Science fiction is a wonderful hammer; I intend to use it, when and if necessary, to bark a few shins or knock a few heads, in order to make people leave people alone.'" In later printings the note was moved to the back of the edition and the "sensational" quotation deleted once and for all. The debate over Bradbury and science was renewed in the late 1950s when Clifton Fadiman's introduction for a new hardback edition found its way into the Bantam paperback, where it remained in all printings until 1970. Incredibly, Fadiman took the milder quotation of the second paperback edition and regressively refashioned it into an approximation of the earlier Bantam fabrication: "He puts his aim all too casually. . . . To this statement he might well add the words 'and leave things alone.' For, unless I misread him, he is telling us, though the lesson is veiled in a shimmering mist of weird fancies, that the place for space travel is in a book, that human beings are still mental and moral children who cannot be trusted with the terrifying toys they have by some tragic accident invented."

The Magazine of Fantasy and Science Fiction's Boucher was disturbed by the observation, and on July 7, 1958, he wrote Bradbury asking for reassurance that Fadiman was off base. A month later Bradbury responded: "No, I assure you, I'm not as anti-scientific as Fadiman makes me out. I'm saddened by the things we humans do with the devices given us. And I'm excited to think these same devices, with changes, might someday give man the channals [sic] whereby his most murderous qualities could find release, could be short-circuited before they ricocheted among men themselves." In this way the extratextual factors of publication—the decisions of editors and the opinions of critics—literally became a part of *The Martian Chronicles* in the sense of the "book as a cultural artifact." Bradbury would have to answer for these extratextual elements of the book for decades, and such complications often obscured public understanding of his never-wavering conviction that science should and must take mankind to the stars. Nevertheless, Bradbury was pleased overall with Fadiman's introduction. He had long regarded Fadiman as a reviewer who, like Isherwood, could propel *Chronicles* into acceptance by other mainstream literary critics.[25] Ironically, the chain of events leading up to that introduction began with one of the most significant scientific events of the space age—the October 1957 launch of *Sputnik* by the Soviets.

Bradbury immediately saw this as a great chance to generate renewed interest in *Chronicles*, but he quickly learned to his dismay that the Doubleday hardback edition had quietly slipped out of print six months earlier.[26] The fact that Doubleday had let this happen to his breakthrough title without telling him was a shock, but he quickly took the opportunity to ask for changes in content. On October 19 he wrote Walter Bradbury and asked first for a complete resetting and redesign of the book in a quality format beyond that of the science fiction series. He also wanted a new introduction that would reflect the new public fascination with the space race—if space was now a mainstream news item, then *The Martian Chronicles* should be marketed as a mainstream novel capable of introducing readers to the moral challenges of the events to come. Finally, Bradbury asked for a change in contents that reflected not only the evolution of the British variations but also the addition of "The Strawberry Window" (1954), an anthologized but otherwise uncollected Martian story.

Even before *Sputnik*, Walter Bradbury had begun planning a hardback reprint. He discouraged his author from tying the book too closely to current events, noting that much of the interest would translate into increased sales for fact books on rocketry rather than fiction titles. He also strongly cautioned against changing contents but reluctantly agreed to reset with new contents and to secure an introduction from one of Ray Bradbury's three choices—Edward R. Murrow, Clifton Fadiman, or Gilbert Highet. In his response, the author offered a rationale for his request for new contents:

> About the revision of CHRONICLES. I have gone over your points again and again. I've thought about this revision for about six years now. In England, the Book Club edition of CHRONICLES has existed for two or three years with THE FIRE BALLOONS and THE WILDERNESS in it. I've always been pleased with that change. Now, when the chance finally comes to add them to CHRONICLES here, I think it will benefit the book. This is one case where I believe revision is okay, and not detrimental. These two stories, plus THE

STRAWBERRY WINDOW, which outlines my beliefs concerning the reason for space-travel, should bring the book up to its final form. . . . I feel we should drop USHER and add the three new stories.[27]

Bradbury's planning went so far as to provide a date prefix and insertion point for "The Strawberry Window." But Anthony Boucher felt that the story was a self-parody that "went overboard" on both idea and style, and he soon convinced Bradbury to withdraw the story from consideration.[28] In the end Bradbury won the new introduction from Clifton Fadiman, a larger paper size with better margins for the text block, and a new title page that eliminated, once and for all, the Doubleday Science Fiction colophon.

But the book was not reset, and no changes were made to the Doubleday text at all. Bradbury was, in effect, a victim of his own success; even with the possibility of a new typesetting, Walt Bradbury soon realized that inclusion of the new Martian stories would mean pulling "The Fire Balloons" from the American edition of *The Illustrated Man* and "The Wilderness" from the American edition of *The Golden Apples of the Sun*. The "Doubleday reprint edition" of *Chronicles* (strictly speaking, a reprint rather than a new edition) was released in June 1958; in August, Bradbury told Anthony Boucher that he would "save revisions for the day when, many years from now, some sort of other special edition is due."[29] But Bradbury's frustrations would continue to build. He had never really been the specialized science fiction author that Doubleday had bargained for in 1949; by the late 1950s he had cast off the science fiction label but was still constricted by Doubleday's limited publicity and design budgets. By 1961, disappointments over *Chronicles* and an impasse over the manuscript of *Something Wicked This Way Comes* would lead Bradbury to larger publishing houses.

Although the Doubleday reprint edition was itself reprinted three more times through 1962, the mainstay of the first American edition text of fifteen stories and eleven bridges continues to be the Bantam paperback, which has never been out of print. The commercial (and intentionally ambiguous) use of the term "edition" obscures the fact that the successive Bantam Pathfinder, Spectra, and Grand Master versions are really reprintings (ninety-four printings through 2000) of the 1954 second Bantam paperback edition. The only significant variation in content is the result of corruption rather than authorial intention—beginning with the sixty-eighth printing (August 1988), the final single-sentence paragraph of the classic "There Will Come Soft Rains" dropped out of the text. This was finally corrected in 2001, when the ninety-fifth printing was completely reset in what amounts to a new (though unadvertised) edition of the ever-available Bantam paperback text.

But opportunities for the "special edition" conceived in the 1958 letter to Boucher soon surfaced and allowed Bradbury to move away from the original

American *Chronicles* contents reflected in the Doubleday and Bantam editions. In the early 1960s Bradbury and Congdon were able to place a successful speculative science essay in *Life* magazine and almost convinced *Life* editor Ralph Graves to publish a chapter of *Something Wicked This Way Comes*. By 1963, this association with Time-Life led to publication of *The Martian Chronicles* in a Time Reading Program Special Edition. For this project, his continually developing vision of a "complete" version of *Chronicles* led him to retain "Usher II" and add both "The Fire Balloons" and "The Wilderness" from the two existing British variations. This "complete" text now contained seventeen stories and eleven bridge chapters and paved the way for other special editions sold outside the mass-market territory staked out by the Bantam paperback.

The "complete" edition next appeared in a new American Science Fiction Book Club edition in 1973.[30] Although the book club was a Doubleday imprint, most of that publisher's Bradbury titles were only available through Bantam paperbacks. Bradbury himself had moved on, first to Simon and Schuster and eventually to Knopf, and he had more leverage with a house that was now less concerned with content overlap between his titles. Other special editions soon followed. A private limited edition was published and marketed successively by the Limited Editions Club (1974), the Heritage Club (1976), and Easton Press (1989). In 1979 Bantam was persuaded to produce a special illustrated trade edition of the "complete" text that ran as a quality paperback alternative to the rack-size mass-market edition.

In 1990 plans for a fortieth-anniversary edition culminated in what has come to be known as the "restored" text of *Chronicles*. For this edition, Bradbury revisited the cuts he and Walter Bradbury made to the American first edition and restored the only excision that he had later come to regret—"The Fire Balloons." The anniversary version reflected what Bradbury had come to see as the ideal American first edition, which—forty years down the road—still included the troublesome "Usher II." Subsequent changes made in creating the 1950 American text (deletion of "The Fire Balloons"), the 1951 *Silver Locusts* text (deletion of "Usher II"), the 1953 English SFBC text (inclusion of "The Wilderness"), and the 1963 "complete" text (inclusion of all stories from any edition) were not part of the 1990 concept.

Bradbury's sixth and final variant text appeared in 1997 in the form of Avon's "updated and revised" edition. His 1994 move from Knopf to Avon provided a chance to bring *Chronicles* out in a new small-format hardbound edition priced to remain in print far longer than any of the special editions. Bradbury took this opportunity to refashion the contents in yet another way—this time he would update it for the realities of the new century, advancing all the chapter date prefixes by thirty years and evaluating the contents to see if any stories had been overtaken by history. The 1997 Avon text includes all the stories moved in and out of earlier variations, but it is not a complete text—Bradbury deleted "Way in the Middle of the Air," a chronicle of the migration of pre-civil-rights-era southern Afro-Americans to Mars.

His decision on both counts is not hard to understand. In moving the date of the first chronicle from 1999 to 2030, he resituated *Chronicles* in a time yet to come and thus synchronized the entire story cycle with our culture's present sense of the pace of interplanetary exploration. He also took the unusual step of refashioning the text itself to include only a twenty-first-century world. The days of de jure segregation—an all-too-present evil to the writer of 1950—is not a reality for those who will go to the stars in the twenty-first century. Ironically, Bradbury had to fight to get this story published in any magazine during the early 1950s; as noted in the thematic discussion that follows, "Way in the Middle of the Air" called into question the facile solutions offered by the mainstream liberals of that day.[31] Nevertheless, the story remains part of the original text through the long-selling Bantam paperback edition and is likely to remain there for a long time to come.

Title variations in two British paperback editions have created further confusion over the years. Corgi's first paperback edition of the *Silver Locusts* (1956) is true to the Hart-Davis first edition, but in 1963 the second paperback edition (published by Corgi's owner Transworld) actually contains the original American first-edition text. The megafirm Grafton published a third paperback edition in 1979 that is true to the *Silver Locusts* text but is, unfortunately, titled *The Martian Chronicles*. These errors probably do not originate with Bradbury; they are more likely the result of an editor's ignorance of the textual history or a publisher's decision to capitalize on the perceived value of one title over another regardless of the text that follows. But in a cultural context, this is a small price to pay for the explosion of textual possibilities that Bradbury has provided and the rich record of extratextual material appended to these various texts (table 6). Over the last fifty years, *The Martian Chronicles* have been introduced by such wide-ranging talents as critics Clifton Fadiman and Martin Gardner, writers Damon Knight and William F. Nolan, and astronomer Sir Fred Hoyle. Bradbury himself has contributed retrospective introductions to the 1990 and 1997 editions. Illustrations by Joe Mugnaini, Karel Thole, and Ian Miller contributed new visions to several U.S. editions; eminent artists and scholars, including Jorge Luis Borges, grace the pages of countless foreign-language editions in ways yet to be assessed.

Traditionally, critics focus on formal characteristics in explaining this kind of textual transformation. *The Martian Chronicles*, along with William Faulkner's *Go Down, Moses* and such bricolage cousins as John Steinbeck's *The Red Pony* and

Table 6. A checklist, in chronological order, of the American and British editions of *The Martian Chronicles*. Successive columns track the six variations in content through five decades. Both title (*MC* or *SL*) and content variations are indicated; the use of the British *Silver Locusts* title with American first-edition *Chronicle* contents (and vice versa) actually creates a seventh and eighth variation. A bibliographical listing of the editions (grouped by variation) appears in entry 50-A of appendix A.

Editions and Texts of *The Martian Chronicles*/ *The Silver Locusts*	American MC text (1950)	English SL text (1951)	English MC text (1953)	complete text (1963)	restored text (1990)	updated text (1997)
Garden City, N.Y.: Doubleday. [May] 1950. American 1st ed. of *The Martian Chronicles*.	MC					
New York: Bantam, May 1951 (mass-market paperback). 2d printing deletes misattributed anti-science statement.	MC					
New York: Bantam Books, 1954. Reset from the 1951 Bantam; 94 printings through 2000.	MC					
New York: Bantam Books, 2001. Reset from the 1954 Bantam; 95 (cumulative) printings through 2001.	MC					
London: Rupert Hart-Davis, [Sept.] 1951. British 1st ed. Title change to *The Silver Locusts*.		SL				
Garden City, N.Y.: Doubleday, [Nov.] 1952. Science Fiction Book Club ed. (6th printing of 1950 edition). Reissued in 1978.	MC					
[London]: Science Fiction Book Club, [1953]. British Science Fiction Book Club ed.			MC			
London: Corgi, [May] 1956 (mass-market paperback).		SL				
Garden City, N.Y.: Doubleday, [May] 1958. American 2d ed. Includes a short preface by Clifton Fadiman.	MC					
London: Transworld, 1963. The *SL* title used with the first British ed. of the original American MC text.	SL					
New York: Time, [Aug.] 1963 (paperback). The 1st "complete text" ed. Introd. Clifton Fadiman.				MC		
Garden City, N.Y.: Doubleday, [June] 1973. Includes a biographical profile and bibliography by William F. Nolan. Illus. Thole.				MC		

Table 6. (*continued*)

Editions and Texts of *The Martian Chronicles*/ *The Silver Locusts*	American MC text (1950)	English SL text (1951)	English MC text (1953)	complete text (1963)	restored text (1990)	updated text (1997)
Avon, Conn.: Limited Editions Club, [Dec.] 1974. New illus. Joe Mungaini. Introd. Martin Gardner.				*MC*		
Avon, Conn.: Heritage Club, 1976. Includes the Gardner introd. and selected Mugnaini illus. from the 1974 Avon ed.				*MC*		
New York: Bantam Books, Sept. 1979. The 1st trade-paperback ed. Illus. Ian Miller.				*MC*		
London: Granada, 1979 (paperback). The British *SL* text used with the *MC* title.		*MC*				
London: Granada, [1980]. The British *SL* text used with the *MC* title.		*MC*				
Norwalk, Conn.: Easton, 1989. The 1974 Avon text signed by the author. With a new introd. by Damon Knight.				*MC*		
New York: Doubleday, [Nov.] 1990. 40th-anniversary ed. New Bradbury introd.: "The Long Road to Mars."					*MC*	
New York: Avon, [Feb.] 1997. New Bradbury introd.: "Green Town, Somewhere on Mars; Mars, Somewhere in Egypt."						*MC*

Anderson's *Winesburg, Ohio,* are considered cycles of stories, something between a story collection and a novel.[32] But in Bradbury's case genre criticism just is not the best way to analyze the evolving nature of the work—the textual record, which contains no identifiable central character, demands a different approach. His kind of textual transformation begins just as Bradbury described it in an interview with Craig Cunningham—certain stories from a large body of related work cluster around a theme in the same way that magnetism attracts particles with common compositional properties. But a much more tangible process follows, a process that Forest L. Ingram describes as selecting, grouping, editing, revising, and bridging the stories to create a completed short-story cycle. Completion in no way implies termination, for Bradbury has never stopped developing *Chronicles.* The complete cycle is always greater than the sum of its parts, but that sum may vary as the text continues to be modified. The invariable result is that *Chronicles* transcends the classification of "science fiction" that is attributed to the constituent stories. Critics sensed this difference from the start, beginning with Christopher Isherwood, whose two early reviews propelled Bradbury from genre notoriety to the mainstream of American letters. For Isherwood and others, the powerful style and imagination created a Martian setting that, in its totality, became a most compelling American parable.

Ray Bradbury's 1990 recollection of his fateful 1949 editorial meeting with Walter Bradbury suggests a root metaphor for the creative process he would apply to *The Martian Chronicles.* In that meeting editor Bradbury asked for a sewn "tapestry" of stories. The phrasing was apt, for author Bradbury quickly began to weave an intricate cloth. In the very process of expanding and linking his fictions, Bradbury implicitly distinguished his woven layers of revision from such formal stages as "story" or "novella" or "novel" in the same way that Roland Barthes explicitly distinguished "text" from the notion of the completed "work." Barthes's poststructural concept of text as "the interweaving of codes" (from the root meaning of "text" as "woven thing") and his eventual conclusion that "each text is . . . its own model" provide useful insights into Bradbury's shaping vision for *The Martian Chronicles.*[33] The concept of an open-ended carnivalized "text" rather than genre classification is the central notion of revision for Bradbury—the weave of *Chronicles* is clearly a unique textual process rather than a formal evolution from story toward novel. Such terms become very elastic and nonrestrictive in Bradbury's revising formula. For both Ray and Walter Bradbury, "novel" was only a publishing category and not an aesthetic notion at all.

In sewing together "some sort of tapestry" with his Martian stories, Bradbury essentially created a text that stands outside genre categories, narrowly defined. Once he transformed his stories into chronicles, rewriting them and bridging them together, they became part of a larger vision of fiction that has never stopped transforming. With this book, Bradbury began a pattern of revision that he would apply to his longer fiction titles for the next half century.

Thematics

Although *The Martian Chronicles* is often justly celebrated as a masterwork of fantasy for its style and appreciated for its "magical" imaginative qualities, it is, in fact, interwoven with philosophical themes, reinvented by Bradbury in his own unique way as a diagnosis of 1950s American culture. It is important in this regard to remember the book's epigraph, which attributes to a future philosopher the statement that "it is good to renew one's wonder" and that "space travel has again made children of us all," for this is an important clue to how the historical field is turned into wondrous art by Bradbury. Before discussing the book's thematics, it is useful to review briefly the cultural role of art according to Nietzsche. According to his book *The Birth of Tragedy*—which is in itself a genetic history of art—Apollo is the ruler over the beautiful illusion of the inner world of fantasy and Dionysus is the god of enchantment, who walks about in the world intoxicated, in ecstasy, himself a work of art. The Apollonian art par excellence is sculpture, and the Dionysian art is music. Together they produce the art worlds of dreams and intoxications. For Nietzsche, culture is essentially the product of the tension between these two artistic impulses. It is a product of man's movement toward the Dionysian apprehension of the abyss from which he has sprung, a process that destroys old Apollonian myths or forms that had previously sustained us. This in turn—if the culture is healthy and respects myth—results in a countermovement that creates a new set of images (which may incorporate parts of the old myths) charged with an awareness of the illusory character of all forms.

According to Nietzsche, in Greek culture it was tragic art alone that was able to maintain a fruitful balance between the two tendencies. But in Bradbury's aesthetic of fantasy (reconstructed in the introduction), it could be said that fantastic art—fully carnivalized by parody, irony, and jokes—roughly takes the place of tragic art for modern culture. Fantasy fulfills the same roles and saving functions; it has the same constant awareness of painful chaos coupled with the will to form beautiful illusions and masks in the interest of life. Therefore, in reading *The Martian Chronicles*, we would expect a critique of worn-out illusions to alternate with the fresh creation of new myths. This alternation of old and new is exactly what structures *Chronicles*: the reader oscillates between Apollonian and Dionysian fantasy, sometimes within the framework of a single story (as in the case of "The Green Morning," where the American folktale of Johnny Appleseed is marvelously rejuvenated).

Bradbury's text carnivalizes Nietzschean philosophical themes through the use of metaphors, myths, and masks. We find that Bradbury's Martian civilization manifests Apollonian tendencies in its constant play of masks. The Martians seem to wear masks on every social occasion. Mr. K of "Ylla" wears an expressionless silver mask when he kills the members of the first expedition; the crew of the second expedition find a whole town full of telepathic, masked citizens who regard their insane members as artists and can only praise the "concentration of wills" that produces what they take to be the "lovely insanity" of the idea of a voyage to Mars from Earth—a planet that they ironically all take to be uninhabited because their scientists have told them so. And the Martian psychologist of this episode, when telling the crew what he takes to be the Martian "truth" about their extraordinarily complete illness, wears a mask painted with three smiles. By the time we get to "The Off Season," at the height of Earth's colonial presence, the Martians themselves have dwindled to little more than masks floating on the wind. On the Dionysian side there is the constant presence of music in all its forms that often violently shatters these masks, especially in the dramatic opera festival in "The Summer Night," where suddenly voices and music from another world emanate from behind the masks of the singers.

The Martians have history books that sing to them when touched, but in "Ylla" these are songs of a beautiful, naive, and illusion-contemplating world that bears comparison with Homer's epic poems, "tales of when the sea was red steam on the shore and ancient men had carried clouds of metal insects and electric spiders into battle." In fact, Bradbury pursues even further a Homeric simile, or extended comparison, when Ylla's sense of apprehension about the approaching rocket of the first expedition from Earth is compared to a thunderstorm. The parallel with Greek civilization is by no means exact, however. The textual evidence also clearly suggests that there were at least three different races of Martians (see below). Nevertheless, there are similarities in that the Martian attitude toward life on the surface seems serene and unclouded—like that conventionally associated with the image of classical Greece—but actually Bradbury's Martians are prone to mental suffering (they are telepathic too) and are deeply in need of artistic and philosophical consolation. At the time of the second expedition, a good deal of their population is insane.

It has rightly been noted by critics that *The Martian Chronicles* evokes an elaborate system of parallels with myths of the American frontier.[34] These parallels serve to guide our understanding of the meaning of the events we witness and aid us in constructing a myth of the rejuvenating wilderness. But merely to focus on this aspect exclusively, as some have done, is to miss the carnivalesque (in Nietzschean terms, "perspectival") treatment of themes in the book. *Chronicles* seeks nothing less than a critique of all life-destroying modes of "emploting" (which is, briefly, the shaping of the bare chronology of events into archetypal patterns of meaning) history, in particular the Christian myth of redemption, the bourgeois doctrine of progress, and any kind of historical thinking that takes us away from the living present of this world by capturing us with longing for an ideal past or a comfortably illusory future. In "There Will Come Soft Rains," Bradbury even demolishes the whole notion of time measured by clocks. And its following story, "The Million-Year Picnic," which ends *Chronicles*, moves us explicitly into a mythical present.

What is more, in addition to being a critique of more traditional and archetypal patterns of meaning belonging to the past, the book is also a defense of history in the poetic or metaphorical mode. *The Martian Chronicles* unveils to what extent the twentieth century's debilitating historical consciousness can be returned to a new capacity to "frolic in images," entertaining the historical field as a poetic phenomena. This ideal of Dionysian-Apollonian history is represented by Bradbury's Martians and their culture. They provide the means for Bradbury as author of this future history to attain once more, but this time self-consciously, a world of mythic apprehensions and a radical innocence. On the thematic level, his use of masks is an example of this radical innocence, for if the Martians mask themselves among themselves, it can only be a form of aesthetic play, hiding nothing when minds are telepathic.

How then is this metaphorical mode of future historiography accomplished; by what rhetorical strategies of the text is the reader persuaded to accept the world portrayed by the text? In theory, we need to distinguish at least three different levels of conceptualization in the historical work: (1) chronicle, (2) story, and (3) mode of emplotment. For the moment, we will ignore the question of ideological implication, and we have already said that the mode of argument is metaphorical. In the writing of any historical work, the first act is to organize its elements into a chronicle by arranging events in the temporal order of their occurrences. Then the chronicle is organized into a story (level two) by the further arrangement or segmentation of events into a "spectacle," a process of happening, by characterizing or encoding them in terms of motifs marking a beginning, middle, and end. This process of exclusion, stress, and subordination is carried out in the interest of constituting a story of a particular kind. Story provides answers to such questions as what happened next, how did it happen, why did things happen this way rather than another, and how did it all come out in the end—in short, questions about the connections between events, which are related to the historian's narrative tactics. The mode of emplotment (level three) answers such concerns as what does it all add up to and what is the point of it all—questions regarding the pattern of the completed whole. According to Northrop Frye, there are at least four different modes of emplotment that answer questions raised at this level: romance, comedy, tragedy, and satire—or in terms of archetypal imagery, summer, spring, autumn, winter. *The Martian Chronicles* is definitely seasonal in its approach to imagery.[35]

The level of chronicle-story is easily summarized and presents no difficulties.[36] In February 1999 the first rocketship from Earth lands on Mars. Its two crew members will immediately be shot dead by a Mr. K with a gun that fires bees. Six months later the crew of a second rocket is subjected to a mercy killing by Mr. Xxx, a psychologist, in the belief that his victims must be incurable Martian lunatics masquerading as Earthmen. In April 2000 the crew of a third rocket is likewise murdered while under a deep hypnosis that persuades them that they are visiting their dead relatives and their childhood homes on Earth. But the crewmen of the fourth expedition, in 2001, are successful not because of their own actions, but by an accident of nature. By that time, almost the entire Martian population has succumbed to an unfamiliar disease carried by earlier expeditions— chicken pox.

After this, the process of colonization goes forward rapidly for the next four years, bringing the total number of settlers up to ninety thousand. Successive waves bring the pioneers, the settlers, old people seeking a place to retire, and finally the entrepreneurs and sophisticates. Then in November 2005, atomic war breaks out on Earth, and nearly all of the colonists return home. (There is a large break in the record here, but "August 2026: There Will Come Soft Rains" shows that wars have continued during this period and destroys any illusion that comfortable life is still available on Earth.) Mars is practically deserted until October 2026, the date of arrival of the Thomas family, a party of war refugees escaping on a private rocket. They, and another family still to come, form the nucleus of a new settlement. It is made clear at the end, however, that interplanetary travel will not be back for centuries, maybe never, so the families literally own an entire world to explore and do with as they please during their own "Million-Year Picnic."

As soon as we try to determine the significance of this "spectacle," however, we run into problems. Any attempt to reach a pattern of the completed whole seems to break down constantly. Each time we are given an indication as to how to emplot a particular story, it is subtly undermined by rhetorical strategies in the episode or segment in question or by other, later perspectives. The book is deeply carnivalized, allowing us to construct no final perspective on events. For example, considered as a large unit, the story of the expeditions can hardly be plotted in the heroic sense of the familiar space operas of E. E. "Doc" Smith, popular with science fiction readers of the 1930s and republished as classics in the 1950s and 1960s. Irony of events seems to predominate in the *Chronicles*, reflected in the fact that the Martians are destroyed not in a space battle, but by what on Earth is a childhood disease. Individual stories present the same difficulties. For example, at the outset one might feel poised to enter a narrative world of romance as the rockets turn winter into summer and the questing hero, Nathaniel York, journeys toward a beautiful Martian woman, Ylla, who desires and dreams of his coming. But York is murdered by her jealous husband as soon as he arrives and is soon forgotten as an episode of wishful thinking.

In other places, we enter into worlds of satire, comedy, and tragic pathos, all subtly carnivalized. In "The Off Season" the object of satiric attack is the commercial instincts of Sam Parkhill, who wants to build a hot dog stand on an ancient Martian highway, but the moral superiority we feel toward this fast-talking embodiment of human greed changes to uneasiness after the ghostly Martians arrive and the entire Earth is destroyed, leaving Sam without any customers in a desert of futility. Likewise in "The Silent Towns," we appear to be moving toward comedy when Walter Gripp hears the beautiful voice of Genevieve Selsor over the telephone and races off to end his loneliness. We anticipate the integration of the hero back into society. But Genevieve turns out to be a grotesquely fat and spoiled child. Gripp prefers the lonely Martian landscape, ten thousand miles of it, between him and such a fate. And "The Long Years" evokes autumnal tragic pathos and isolation with its account of Hathaway's sojourn on Mars, but this pathos is mitigated by the presence of his robot family who never grow old or feel grief, even when he dies. To add to the irony, all three of these stories are in a section of the book chronicling the loss of the frontier rather than the fulfillment of its promise.

Some stories, however, explicitly point toward the ideal of a metaphorical mode of emplotment. Set during the five brief years of colonization, "Night Meeting" provides a lesson in Mars as pure difference. An old man who runs a filling station tells Tomas Gomez, who has stopped his truck to get some gas on his way to a popular festive celebration in honor of one of the new towns, that if he cannot accept Mars for what it is, a play of differences, then he might as well go back to Earth. Time and chronology are especially "crazy" on Mars. More than that: "You know what Mars is? It's like a thing I got for Christmas seventy years ago— don't know if you ever had one—they called them kaleidoscopes, bits of crystal and cloth and beads and pretty junk. You held it up to the sunlight and looked in through [sic] at it, and it took your breath away. All the patterns! Well, that's Mars. Enjoy it. Don't ask it to be nothing else but what it is."[37]

Later on, along the ancient Martian highway, Tomas has an encounter with a time-warped Martian on his way to a carnival. Both Tomas and the Martian Muhe Ca are carnivalized by the experience and the clash of perspectives it brings. They encounter each other through a series of hierarchized thematic opposites: present or past (the master category), real or unreal, and alive or dead, each trying to finalize the other from an "outside" stable perspective. But such stability is made difficult because their bodies are made grotesque to each other. Each can see the stars burning through the translucent limbs of the other. (Bradbury compares the Martian's flesh to the phosphorescent membrane of a gelatinous sea fish; the grotesque body is always open to the world, but here Bradbury extends it to the universe itself.) They become metaphors to each other, each trying to carry meaning over from the strange to the familiar. Tomas has the most trouble accepting this experience and has to label it a dream, quickly speeding off to his party. But the Martian has the deeper wisdom. He does not try to decide in the end who is a ghost and who is real. He recognizes that they have found an "in-between" space where they are neither dead nor alive but "more alive than anything else." He accepts the fact that to him his flesh feels warm and real. That is all he needs. Why delay? The festival fires of carnival await him.

We can interpret this to mean that for Bradbury the thematic field of Mars presented itself as a carnivalesque kaleidoscopic combination of elements—actions, persons, objects, desires—"pretty junk" that allowed him an almost infinite number of new and surprising arrangements, something he must often have felt in arranging his Martian stories into a short-story cycle. Furthermore, these nonlinear combinations of the past with the present are artistic occasions for image making in a symbolic field of meaning never allowed to become frozen in conceptual schemas, whether human or Martian. They result in metaphorical ways of comprehending the world. If Mars *is* a kaleidoscope, there is no single plot by which the definitive truth or lesson to be learned from history is to be communicated. Indeed, this story unsettles the authority of the bare chronicle itself, for we are essentially unable to decide whether to accept the Martian or Tomas as representing the "true" past. Bradbury's appropriation of the carnival chronotope—which emphasizes the lived body—here helps him construct the fantastic notion of metaphorical time.

On the whole though Bradbury's use of carnival concepts in *The Martian Chronicles* creates encounters that are a lot less peaceful than that presented in this enchanting story. Among the "unchronicled" story fragments related to *The Martian Chronicles* are two pages revealing that Bradbury originally intended a carnival to be at the center of the Martian resistance to the invading Earthmen. Although these pages give us only a brief glimpse of this carnival, it is clear that the Martians intend to lure the Earthmen into the festivities and somehow to destroy them. In this passage we see the almost magical Martian carnival being set up:

The Carnival arrived at about seven that night. The sun was just going down among the blue Martian hills, leaving blue lights glimmering along the Highway of the Ancients, when the Martian men, tall and indecisive as vapors, and quite as ghostly blue as the last light in the sky, walked in a line, carrying upon their shoulders a long pole. The pole went back over twenty shoulders and for its length was incredibly light. Wrapped about the fifty foot length was a kind of translucent membrane, something resembling a bat's wing.

The pole was raised outside the American camp, by means of a tiny propeller and vanes at the top. With a soft whirr, the pole rose and stood balanced. Then the [translucent] membranes wrapped around and around the pole gave off a whispering and spread like a giant bat wing, up, up, out, and around in a circle. Now the perfect circle stood against the sky, and the stars glimmered through it and the wind beat upon it making a soft drum sound. From the edges of this remarkable tent top the Martians hung silken festoons, and within the tent chairs that sprang out of discs in the hands of the Martian, the collapsible of all collapsible chairs, were immediately set up. From the teeth of dragons, as it were, comfortable chairs.

As in "Night Meeting," the themes of the ancient highway, the ghostly Martian carnival, and the translucent body are very much in evidence, only here we see the Martians using carnival for the purposes of subjugating the American invaders. When news of the carnival reaches the American camp, the Earthmen decide to attend. In another scene following this one the Martian leader, Wulle, when told that the Americans plan to attend the carnival, remarks that while they (the Martians) have no "atomic weapon" to defend themselves, they nonetheless shall win. We do not know precisely how the Martians planned to win, but from the reference to (metaphorical) dragons' teeth we may infer that it may have involved a transformation of the Greek myth in which King Aeetes raised the dead slain by the hydra to revenge themselves upon Jason who had stolen the golden fleece. In that story the teeth of the slain hydra become seeds that grow skeleton warriors (as seen in a famous stop-motion animation sequence by Ray Harryhausen, one of Bradbury's closest friends, for the 1963 film *Jason and the Argonauts*).

For Nietzsche, the ultimate principle explaining all events in the historical field was the will to power conceived of as a subduing, what he called "becoming master," that inevitably involves a fresh interpretation and an adaptation through which any previous "meaning" or "purpose" is necessarily obscured or even obliterated. Thus understood, historical events do not evolve directly from an origin toward a goal or function as the result of simple cause and effect. The history of a thing in such a view becomes the history of its interpretations, which may have no links with one another. Bradbury does not entirely share this view of the will to power as being the only reality. But actually, there are some aspects of *The Martian Chronicles* that suggest such a principle is operative in this text as well, especially in the sections detailing the invasions. How else, for example, to explain certain events in "The Third Expedition," one of Bradbury's most famous stories.[38]

In this work, nostalgia for the past is appropriated, idealized, and transformed by the Martians for the purposes of defense and reaction. Earth history is subjected to a set of retroactive confiscations, interpretations, and masks. Captain Black and his crew try out a number of logical explanations to rationalize the presence of Earth history on Mars, including time travel and the idea that rocket travel may be older than was previously believed. But each of them eventually succumbs to the emotionally festive music of the welcoming brass band (a Dionysian motif of enchantment) and the reassuring presence of houses, objects, and people from their childhood pasts (an Apollonian motif of illusion). The Martian defense strategy works by dividing up the crewmembers so they can be disposed of individually. Later they are all murdered in their sleep, but not before Captain Black theorizes that what they have experienced is all an illusion in defense of Martian culture.

It is certainly an uncannily chilling thought to consider being murdered by those who are closest to us—Stephen King has said that "The Third Expedition" gave him his first real experience of horror and influenced his own novel *Bag of Bones*—but what makes the Martians continue the illusion after the Earthmen are dead? Why the cemetery, the weeping survivors, the faces of mourning friends "melting like wax," and the brass band playing its mournful dirge? This aspect of the story has bothered some theorists of science fiction who do not understand how, after the nighttime atrocity, a final scene can follow that cannot be explained by the captain's hypothesis about it all being an illusion. Actually, if we consider the endings (both pulp and final) to this story, it is fairly obvious that this is a Martian festival celebrating their victory over the Earthmen with varying degrees of emphasis. In the pulp version the funeral brass band continues to play as the Earthmen's rocket—a fairly obvious symbol of their colonial intentions—is "torn to pieces and strewn about and blown up" while the crowd watches, creating a more directly cruel and Dionysian ending than the final version. In the latter the narrator tells us that after they bury the Earthmen the Martian brass band "marched and slammed" its way back into town from the graveyard playing "Columbia, Gem of the Ocean" (a patriotic song celebrating America that contains the verses "The wine cup, the wine cup bring hither / And fill you it true to the brim") and "everyone took the day off." In this version the Martians retain more of the "at the same time" ambivalence of true carnival. As Bradbury has observed, "The hypnotic effect persisted *after* the death of the Earthmen, for two reasons: the Martians were playing some sort of ironic joke among themselves, at the same time remembering their own peril, at the same time feeling some touch of sadness at the whole encounter. The Martians, therefore, went on creating the illusion of themselves, the city, the cemetery, as a fine sort of dry joke, touched with melancholy."[39]

Bradbury's interpretation seems more in the nature of will to life than will to power, but nonetheless, one should note that what the Martians do—creating new forms of response, new forms of feeling, even sympathizing with their enemies—all goes beyond the mere will to survive and is an aspect of carnivalesque play. This point about the sustainment of illusion being a joke is borne out by an unpublished section of the book, "The Disease" (discussed below).

Every carnivalesque theme in *The Martian Chronicles* seems to have its polyphonic counterpoint somewhere else in the book. Even carnival is carnivalized. This theme of the noble Martian festival celebrating the death of the Earthmen with terrestrial music as a joke is inverted and seen "inside out" (that is, relativized) by a brief bridging story in the approximate center of the book, "The Musicians," in which a group of energetic boys carrying bags of delicious (and strong-smelling) food hike far out into the now dead Martian towns. There they make a game of seeing who can arrive first and be the musician, the first to play music on "the white xylophone bones beneath the outer covering of black flakes" of the bodies of Martians killed by chicken pox (a disease all the human boys have survived). The game is one of transgressing limits, of mingling the remains of dead bodies with those of the living. It also has carnivalized aesthetic qualities because the boys enjoy it best in autumn, when the dry, flaking black flesh of the dead Martians seems most like leaves, making it easier for them to imagine that season on Earth. Thematically, the story underscores the life-death ambivalence of all true carnival celebrations. The grotesque, desiccated bodies are "dismembered" and held in close proximity with the living when the boys fall into the black flakes of mortality (Bradbury's metaphor), their stomachs gurgling and wet, filled with orange pop. Death is placed in close contact with new life, not separated from it. True sons of the carnival spirit, the boys are not appalled by the horrors they see. On the contrary, they revel and dance among them, to their parents' dismay and stern disgust. In fact, the boys are trying to visit all the towns before they are burned away by the firemen, who in cleaning up the towns are "separating the terrible from the normal." The boys play very hard at their transgressive game, eating and sweating among the dead and, in a sense, renewing them through their own bodies in a "musical" way, but the antiseptic firemen eventually take away all the fun. Yet another aspect of humorous carnival debasement occurs in the normalized world. When discovered, the boys are treated to "scalding baths and fatherly beatings."

Much of what Bradbury describes about the now extinct Martian civilization at its height comes through Spender the archaeologist of "—And the Moon Be Still as Bright," another story that provides insight into the value system of *The Martian Chronicles*. Indeed, if the book has a center for its philosophical themes, it should certainly be located here. This story is the longest in the book, originally published as a novelette in *Thrilling Wonder Stories* (June 1948) and lengthened and revised for inclusion in *Chronicles*. According to Spender—whose remarks are pretty much the same in the pulp version—the recently extinct Martians knew how to blend art into their living instead of keeping it separate as on Earth. Spender gains his insights into the alien culture from reading a book of Martian philosophy, which is said to be at least ten thousand years old. Apparently, the Martians went through crises in their development as a civilization, but in creating an artistic culture, they escaped nihilism by knowing when to stop questioning and how to prevent the theoretical side of consciousness from dominating and rigidifying conceptions of the world. This is made clear in Spender's remarks to Captain Wilder:

> "The Martians discovered the secret of life among animals. The animal does not question life. It lives. Its very reason for living *is* life; it enjoys and relishes life. You see—the statuary, the animal symbols, again and again."
>
> "It looks pagan."
>
> "On the contrary, those are God symbols, symbols of life. Man had become too much man and not enough animal on Mars too. And the men of Mars realized that in order to survive they would have to forego asking that one question any longer: *Why live?* Life was its own answer. Life was the propagation of more life and the living of as good a life as possible. The Martians realized that they asked the question 'Why live at all?' at the height of some period of war and despair, when there was no answer. But once the civilization calmed, quieted, and wars ceased, the question became senseless in a new way. Life was now good and needed no arguments."
>
> "It sounds as if the Martians were quite naive."
>
> "Only when it paid to be naive. They quit trying too hard to destroy everything, to humble everything. They blended religion and art and science because, at base, science is no more than an investigation of a miracle we can never explain, and art is an interpretation of that miracle. They never let science crush the aesthetic and the beautiful. It's all simply a matter of degree."[40]

We sense here that Spender is the author's mask. He is even referred to by other members of the crew as "The Lonely One," an epithet the early Bradbury often used for himself. Though Spender's project of turning himself into a Martian fails—in part because he cannot "lie" to himself about his being a real native—he nonetheless embodies Bradbury's first successful attempt to break away from the disillusioned romanticism of *The Masks* (and Spender does refer to his own childhood feelings of identification with Mexican culture). There are a number of Nietzschean notions directly expressed in Spender's speech or suggested by it, especially those having to do with the necessity of the aesthetic and the beautiful. Despite the archaeologist's insistence that the Martians were not pagans but somehow children of God, we understand that they learned how to affirm the life of *this* world. Nietzsche, in his own metahistorical writings, distinguishes three sorts of historical sensibility—the Antiquarian, the Monumental, and the Critical—on the basis of the dominant form of temporal yearning that characterizes each.[41] Spender starts out in the story as an Antiquarian, one who places absolute value on the old simply because it is old. This apparently succors his need for roots in a prior world and stimulates his capacity for reverence, without which he could not live. But after killing several members of his own crew, he realizes that he cannot become a Martian entirely. That part of his project fails, though he remains intent on stopping the invasion.

Captain Wilder tries to assure the alienated Spender that the Earthmen will learn from the Martians. His view represents the Monumental use of the past. It consists of uplifting the manifestly great and heroic as examples of man's power to change his environment and himself. It is oriented toward the future. Of course, men do not learn anything from the Martians, not even how to die philosophically and accept their fates. (See the discussion below of "Payment in Full," a story that Bradbury wanted to include in the original text; Nietzsche's *amor fati* is also evident among the Martians in it.) This is arguably the greatest dramatic irony in the book. In one of the final chronicles, we learn that Captain Wilder has been "kicked upstairs" (that is, promoted) so that he cannot interfere with colonial policy on Mars. When Spender delivers this speech to Wilder in defense of his actions, however, Spender has already arrived at the position Nietzsche characterized as Critical: the judging of both inherited pieties and utopian dreams in terms of present needs and desires. Spender is preparing the way for that creative forgetting, the cultivation of the faculty of "oblivion" without which action in the present is not possible at all—values realized in the last story, "The Million-Year Picnic," where a few humans return and *do* become "Martians."

Before this transformation is possible, the stage of active forgetting must be accomplished. This takes place in "The Long Years," where Hathaway, in order to survive alone on Mars, actively forgets that he has recreated his family as robots, loving them as a real family. But creative forgetting is evident in Spender's references to animals, which, of course, do not possess historical consciousness but only the power to affirm their lives instinctively. What is more, this Dionysian power to affirm life is represented in the Apollonian art of statuary, implying the artistic balance between remembering and forgetting that the Martians had achieved. Nietzsche argues in *The Genealogy of Morals* that mistrust of the riddle of life came when humanity learned to be ashamed of its instincts. With the forming of bad conscience and guilt began the gravest and uncanniest illness from which humanity has not yet recovered, humanity's suffering of itself, which was the result of a forcible sundering from their animal past. All instincts that do not discharge themselves outwardly turn inward, creating what Nietzsche called the internalization of man *(Verinnerlichung)*.[42]

This is no doubt what Spender implies when he says that humans had become too much human on Mars as well (the phrase itself is reminiscent of Nietzsche's phrase "all-too-human"). And how else, incidentally, can one explain the decline of the Martians, who by the time of the second expedition have a good deal of their population locked away in asylums? Sheer will to life is not sufficient in sustaining civilization. At the height of their development, however, the Martians were able to veil the painful knowledge of the absurdity of life with artistic illusions, which allowed them to "forget" the destructive questioning of rationalism. They knew when to stop (that is, before the point of absolute nihilism) and therefore were only apparently naive. As Spender explains, life does not and cannot justify itself; it has no need to do so. Only man feels a need to justify his existence because only man, of all the animals, is conscious of the historical nature of his being and of his modernity at the same time. Nietzsche's way out of this paradox was to argue that only art can justify life to man. Bradbury's argument is parallel: people need a fantastic art with a life-preserving purpose, one in which all ugly and discordant things become transmuted into an aesthetic game that the will, in its utter exuberance, plays with itself.

But to return to Spender's remarks, he says the Martians did not try to provide an answer or solution to the supreme question but rather tried to show how this question might have arisen (that is, during a time of conflict) in the first place. Once this is made clear, it no longer seems important to solve the problem on its own terms. To the Martians, a philosophical problem is a question not to be answered but to be overcome. Thus, the question of the meaning of life becomes "senseless" in a new way—they have the answer before the question ever arises once society regains stability. This only can be what Spender means when he reports that the Martians "blended" science, religion, and art. Surely he does not mean they discovered the meaning of life in some transcendental symbol of God (and what god but Dionysus could be represented by such animal images anyway?). Of course, this whole passage is meant to be taken as a diagnosis of *our* cultural situation—Darwin and Freud are specifically mentioned—in which religion denies art, science denies religion, and philosophy denies science so that modern man is hurled further and further into the depths of an ironic consciousness, deprived of faith in his own reason, imagination, and will and finally is driven to despair of life itself. Spender's argument is thus more than a cultural diagnosis. It contains Bradbury's revaluation of the materialistic and technological values that were prominent in post–World War II America.

Because Spender recites a complete poem by Lord Byron, readers are influenced to emplot this story in a romantic mode. Byron's poem "So We'll Go No More a-Roving" was written in 1817 during the Lenten aftermath of a spell of feverish dissipation in the carnival season at Venice. It expresses romantic sadness at the loss of the heart's loving vitality, though everything in nature remains unchanged. In Bradbury's story, as the crewmen walk through the ruins of the nearest Martian city, Spender recites some stanzas from this poem. He thinks it could have been written as well by the last Martian poet to express his feelings. The temptation is to see Spender's later rebellion as that of a Byronic hero. In fact, the archaeologist is not. True, he certainly is isolated, moody, passionate, and superior to the common run of mankind (represented by Biggs, whom he murders). His self-generated values suggest such a parallel. And he is dissatisfied enough with this, the fate of the world—"the whole crooked grinding greedy setup on Earth"—to be filled with romantic longing for another life, one transformed by the imagination.

Although the Byronic poem he recites expresses in true romantic fashion the feeling of being separated from life—the life of carnival—Spender's rovings ironically bring him "home" to burial in an ancient Martian tomb. Unlike the Byronic hero, his rebellion is not against the limiting presence of God, for he feels no remorse in his "soul" over the murder of his fellow crewmembers. He is not tortured by some vague, archaic guilt no longer understood. Instead he is haunted by the pain of an ironic consciousness—he is very bitter about the fact that his noble Martians were destroyed by a disease that does not even kill children on Earth, saying it is like the Greeks dying of the mumps. His rebellion is mostly against the values of Earth civilization. In effect, Spender attempts to destroy the bourgeois doctrine of progress that stems ultimately from the European Enlightenment of the eighteenth century. There is very little residual optimism in his view of the future for Mars, in which he foresees Earthmen fighting for bases to launch their atomic wars. Ideologically, his actions seem motivated by an extreme anarchism. But although Spender's spirit lives on in later stories, one senses that this is not Bradbury's ultimate position. Besides, Captain Wilder reminds him that the Martians seem to have borne their fate philosophically; there is no evidence that the approaching end of their civilization brought hatred and destruction. The implication is that if Spender is to become a Martian, then he too must learn to accept fate and give up revenge.

This opens the subject of ideological implication, an important element in every historical account of reality. In most recent critiques, Bradbury's books of the 1950s are often accused of a too-easy liberal moralizing or of confused broadmindedness. Actually, these allegations can be shown to be the result of a superficial reading of his work that does not take into account the ironic way in which he treats ideological themes. As far as *The Martian Chronicles* is concerned, Bradbury conveys an apocalyptic vision, using the rhetoric of divine revelation to stage the action in some of his stories.[43] In other words, he insists on transforming the world into something entirely new, not just in reconstituting society on a new basis as the radical or anarchist would. This vision can be seen most clearly in the story "Way in the Middle of the Air," which depicts African Americans leaving the South forever to inhabit Mars. Here Bradbury ridicules liberalism in the character of Samuel Teece, who ironically is not a liberal anyway but instead a racist bigot who just mouths liberal attitudes: "I can't figure out why they left *now*. With things lookin' up. I mean, every day they got more rights. What they *want*, anyway? Here's the poll tax gone, and more and more states passin' anti-lynchin' bills, and all kinds of equal rights. What *more* they want? They make almost as good money as a white man, but there they go."[44]

Liberalism is an ideology in which the basic structure of society is conceived to be sound. Some change is seen as inevitable, but change itself is regarded as being most effective when one works within the system, fine tuning the parts of its mechanism—using the electoral process and the educational system, for example—to advance one's cause. Social equality is therefore projected into the remote future in such a way as to discourage any effort to realize it precipitately in the present. Yet Bradbury's blacks are not hanging around for any such process to happen. They are not impressed by the rescinding of the poll tax or by anything Teece says. They are departing on the rockets, imminently, leaving behind their earthly possessions along the roadside as if "a great bronze trumpet had sounded."

On Mars, presumably, the blacks will no longer be the slaves of anyone, and it is interesting that Bradbury so reverses the usual scale of values in this story that it is the whites who suffer from *ressentiment* and who are forced to compensate themselves with imaginary revenge. Teece, in particular, tries to terrify the blacks into not going by repeatedly telling them horrendous stories about rockets exploding in space. His action is all reaction, the sickness of an impotent will dominated by the past, the opposite pole of the noble mode of valuation according to Nietzsche. Teece lives on one sentiment: rancor.

Bradbury does nothing more with this apocalyptic theme of blacks leaving Earth for Mars in *Chronicles*.[45] In the most recent Avon edition (1997), the entire story is removed. But it is instructive to compare "Way in the Middle of the Air" with "The Other Foot," in *The Illustrated Man*, where blacks have established themselves on Mars but then are visited by a single white survivor of an atomic war; in this story they are the ones who have to give up past hatreds.

"2004–2005: The Naming of Names" (not to be confused with the story "The Naming of Names") is a brief bridge that points toward the will to power as operative in the colonization section of *The Martian Chronicles*. In Nietzsche's philosophy, man's ability to name things, to confiscate things by linguistic means, results in the erection of a second illusory world alongside the first world of pure power relationships. The history of culture thus conceived appeared to him as a process in which the weak vie with the strong for the authority to determine how this second existence will be characterized. If read in this light, the Earthmen in this *pensée* are really the weak ones who, now that the Martians are almost extinct, try to transform the events of the invasion in terms of their own value system. For example, the place where the first Earthmen were killed is called Red Town, the mountain on which Father Peregrine did not redeem the Martians is called Peregrine Mountain (from the story "The Fire Balloons," which Bradbury removed from the first edition), and so on throughout the passage. And Bradbury makes it clear that the old Martian names put up an almost supernatural struggle, for he describes the rockets of the invasion striking at the names like hammers to overcome their resistance.[46]

"Usher II," the story that follows this bridge in most editions, manifests a strong revenge motif, for antiseptic technology is used against itself to create a simulacrum of The House of Usher on Mars, one that eventually kills, in hideous ways prescribed by Edgar Allan Poe, the members of The Society for the Prevention of Fantasy—but especially Garrett, the Investigator of Moral Climates—who have come to Mars to make sure no Earth laws are being violated there. The presence of this story in *The Martian Chronicles* was somewhat "troublesome" for Bradbury. Clearly, he loved it as expressing his authorial position and politics in the 1950s. But the themes do not fit those of *Chronicles* as a colonization narrative, and perhaps the tone is too bitter. The obvious point of the story is that ordinary Earth morality, which represses fantasy, must not be allowed to take over on Mars. Values in the story are not merely negative, however. Although Stendahl may initially seem to be a reactive victim of self-poisoning, having nursed his hatred and anger over the years until he can pay back tit for tat a government that sees fit to ban all escapes from reality, actually his conduct is more in the nature of self-defense. On Earth the tradition of fantasy literature, which he dearly loves, cannot defend itself; the classics are burned without really being read. On Mars, however, it can be made into reality. Stendahl reverses values by having his guests mask themselves, "the very act of putting on a mask revoking their licenses to pick a quarrel with fantasy and horror," Bradbury writes, in sympathy with Stendahl. That character also ironically asks one of his guests before killing him if he does not have the feeling that "all this has happened before," testing his victim's knowledge of the fantasy books he has helped burn. In the war against realism, Bradbury even drops an ironic reference to Sinclair Lewis's *Babbitt* (the very name suggesting to the literate reader *the* model of American middle-class narrow-mindedness and self-satisfaction) when he tells Garrett, "You'll be burning Babbits next!"[47] Since Garrett has just declared his purpose to destroy *any* creature of the imagination, Stendahl's joke relies on our understanding that Babbitt (that is, Garrett) as a literary creation is equally a creature of the imagination.

The original title of "Usher II" was "Carnival of Madness" (see app. A). This title evokes intertextually Poe's "The Cask of Amontillado," which is set, Poe's narrator tells us, "one evening during the supreme madness of the carnival season." Garrett, the "Investigator of Moral Climates," is himself killed by Stendahl in exactly the same way and with much of the same dialogue as Fortunato is in Poe's story. Thus, although the main instrument of Bradbury's revenge against those who would censor and repress fantasy is an artificial robotic incarnation of Poe's House of Usher (which psychoanalytic critics see as a summation of all of Poe's obsessive themes), his story, like Poe's, has a deep connection to the thematic matrices of carnival.

Mikhail Bakhtin has, in fact, given us a very interesting reading of Poe's place in the history of carnivalization, from which we can learn something about Bradbury's place from *The Martian Chronicles*. He argues that in romanticism and symbolism generally, the matrices of carnival are transformed from "the all-encompassing whole of triumphant life" to sharp static contrasts that are not resolved at all but remain in tension, sealed off in the progression of an individual soul and life.[48] At the heart of Poe's story is indeed a complex series of themes derived from the carnival matrix (death, the fool's mask, laughter, the grave), and psychoanalytic critics have argued that the story largely deals with the author's own interior self. They see the victim, Fortunato, as a double of Montresor, who is sealing off his own sexual impulses to return to the womb of his mother (in Marie Bonaparte's famous reading, echoed by Daniel Hoffman).

Bradbury's intertextual reading, however personal, does not get this individualized. His story is about political trends in the field of culture that were affecting his authorship—censorship, for instance—and his use of carnival images as masks returns them to that social context. Bradbury's house murders social groups of people, though the best revenge is taken individually, and thus ironically, on Garrett, who has not read Poe but who could have escaped his fate had he done so.[49] Furthermore, Bradbury gets the kind of revenge that Poe's narrator only wishes for: Montresor wants to be revenged at length and without the possibility of retribution overtaking its redresser; he wants to avenge himself with impunity. But if the psychoanalytic reading of the story is correct in terms of its reading of authorship, then Poe turns out in the end to be his own victim. Not so for Stendahl, who fulfills Poe's wish by destroying the House of Usher in the exact artistic way described in his text (Pikes, the horror film actor, voices Poe's text at the end as Stendahl had at the beginning) and in the process destroys the evidence of murder. The destruction of Usher II is thus not set apart from creative life.

This act of creation and destruction in "Usher II" may not yet have Bakhtin's sense of carnival themes returning to the triumphant context of all-encompassing life—possibly its tone would be too angry, one-sided, and bitter for him, not to mention aristocratic—but it comes close.[50] Incidentally, one of the many intertextual jokes in this story involves not a fantasy writer, but Ernest Hemingway. Stendahl reveals that Garrett's people had forced film producers to abandon making horror films (hence the end of Pikes's career) and exclusively to make and remake Hemingway in "realistic versions." As it turns out, Bakhtin read Hemingway as a writer whose works were on the whole "deeply carnivalized" because of the presence of bullfights and other festivals of a carnival type in his writings: "He had a very keen ear for everything carnivalistic in contemporary life." Now, Bradbury's understanding of Hemingway—a writer whom he truly loves and on whom he has written several fantasies—also goes beyond seeing him simply as a "realistic" writer narrowly conceived. Stendahl says: "My God, how many times have I seen *For Whom the Bell Tolls* done! Thirty different versions. All realistic. Oh, realism! Oh, here, oh, now, oh hell!"[51] (Interestingly, Hemingway himself uses carnival metaphors in chapter 18 of his novel.)

In a sense these ironic and bitter exclamations and curses by Bradbury-Stendahl reveal a society whose official culture is morally fearful and obtuse. Bakhtin's carnival did not exclude realism. On the contrary, his very term for it as an aesthetic mode was "grotesque realism." It is hard to resist plumbing the depths of irony here. Bradbury masks himself as Stendahl—himself a supposed master of psychological realism in such novels as *The Red and the Black*—in order to unmask the stupid rigidity and narrow-minded seriousness of an official culture that cannot even discern the presence of the carnivalesque in the writer it picks to represent the status quo. Bradbury is saying to American culture in the 1950s, "Truly, the bell tolls for thee!" Bakhtin does not discuss such Nietzschean figures as the artist, the nobleman, and the sovereign individual, but nonetheless Stendahl in Bradbury's story double voices many of Montresor's words in Poe's story in a way that subverts the authority of literary culture in the postwar era. For instance, Stendahl requires Garrett to say the exact words of Fortunato, remarking that the entombment of Fortunato-Garrett is indeed a "very good joke"

(Montresor's very words in Poe's story)—that is, the "joke" is one entirely consonant with the spirit of carnival madness. It is important to realize that Poe was not an accepted part of the literary canon of the postwar era, though he was acknowledged as the founder of such popular forms as detective fiction. Bradbury's House of Usher is thus a site of potential resistance to the authority and cultural politics of mainstream 1950s literary culture.

In building the carnivalesque House of Usher II, Stendahl and his factotum Pikes do not construct fantasy so much out of self-hatred and impotent anger as out of strength of the will affirming itself in play.[52] There is a great deal of play with robot simulacrums replacing real humans in the course of the narrative and a deliberate confusion of the imitated with the real at some points. In order to pull off his murders, Stendahl has to convince everyone that he is, in fact, only murdering robots, that is, aesthetic illusions. (Incidentally, Stendahl was one of the few novelists, besides Dostoevsky, admired by Nietzsche for his insights into the *interestedness* of art, in how elements of ego and power mingle in all its aspects, as opposed to the Kantian notion of aesthetic experience as impersonality and disinterestedness.) Stendahl is clearly an *author* in constructing Usher II, his "mechanical sanctuary." The author-artist is the one who gives out of fullness of being. This is the reason why the story's point of view is that of the artist, and it is full of evocative details about the robots—Pikes's desiring machines—that inhabit the house. Readers are invited to revel in its creation, use, and destruction.

Insofar as *The Martian Chronicles* manifests the theme of will to power, then, one can see in these stories the three figures of powerful life Nietzsche mentions in his writings: the artist, the nobleman, and the sovereign individual. What is powerful in the artist is the compulsion to dream and the compulsion voluptuously to destroy illusions. Stendahl in "Usher II" creates a real—and fantastically expensive—House of Usher and then destroys it. He represents the power to intensify exorbitantly one's own presence in the world. As long as one inhabits his artistic world, he controls the present. What is powerful in Bradbury's noble Martians as figures of the will to power is their capacity to induce forgetfulness. They control the past, and it is precisely because the Earthmen cannot forget the past that they are defeated. Further, if Bradbury is correct in his interpretation, his Martians also are noble because a genuine but ambivalent "love of one's enemies"—not conceived along Christian lines—is possible among them (this was to have been made abundantly clear in "Payment in Full"). Spender is the sovereign individual. What is powerful in him is the memory of his own will. He has the capacity to be a man of his word and vows to resist the invasion of Mars by killing off future expeditions. He is the only character who cares deeply about the future of the planet. His is a veritable memory of the future, and it is no accident that Bradbury largely allows him to keep his promise (as Hathaway points out to Captain Wilder twenty years later in "The Long Years," Spender got his way at last). If these three figures of the will were conjoined, they would yield the image of a life fully delivered from the spirit of revenge, from nihilism, and from debilitating historical consciousness itself. In living such a life, one would enter each day as though a new response would have to be invented for each event; one would enter the landscape of childhood as though everything were unexpected, full of promises, dreams, surprises.

Bradbury combines these three figures of the will (the artist, the nobleman, and the sovereign individual) and their traits with just such a landscape in the last story of *The Martian Chronicles* (which was actually the first published in the series, premiering in *Planet Stories*, 1946). But earlier in the book, Bradbury offers a negative picture of the will turned against itself in "The Martian." Here a lonely Martian survivor is able to make old LaFarge and his wife believe that he is their lost son, Tom, by singing to them while they sleep. Later in the story the Martian reveals this practice to LaFarge, so there is no question of deception. The illusion of happiness works as long as it is consciously believed in. The difficulty in sustaining it comes, however, when the Martian becomes trapped in and overloaded by the network of conflicting human desires in the town, which induces a terrifying metamorphosis: "All down the way the pursued and the pursuing, the dream and the dreamers, the quarry and the hounds. All down the way the sudden revealment, the flash of familiar eyes, the cry of an old, old name, the remembrances of other times, the crowd multiplying. Everyone leaping forward as, like an image reflected from ten thousand mirrors, ten thousand eyes, the running dream came and went, a different face to those ahead, those behind, those yet to be met, those unseen."[53]

Illusion building and illusion breaking (Apollonian form and Dionysian metamorphosis) lie at the heart of this tragic story. Borges found in "The Martian" a reversed pathetic version of the Proteus myth.[54] Proteus was master of his changes—an *author* of them—whereas the lonely Martian is subjected to a horrible disfigurement, his face twisted unrecognizably out of shape by the demands of so many others. As always in Bradbury, the mirror represents the world of interiority and regret (see, too, the discussion of *Something Wicked This Way Comes* in chap. 5). Each one of the people in the town wants the elusive running dream to fill some lack, real or imagined, in his or her past life. The will to power is not, however, a hunt to represent the lost desired object, as is the Freudian dream work. Nor is it a will that *longs* for power (this is the reactive stance). Furthermore, the will to power is not passive suffering—it is not a longing for an end that would be the height of its aspiration, the cure for its indigence, and its own termination. The will commands, gives, and proceeds out of plenitude, not out of lack. Because he has aligned himself with lack, the Martian in Bradbury's story has little chance to affirm his becoming-in-illusion. In trying to survive by using the desires of others, he is instead entirely shaped by them.

Before proceeding to the stage of radical innocence, where new myths can be affirmed, and encountering new images, the reader has to be convinced that the old myths of comfort and security have been destroyed. Bradbury's most Dionysian story in this kaleidoscopic cycle is the penultimate "There Will Come Soft Rains." In fact, it has no human characters at all. The reader encounters humanity entirely through its mechanical extensions. Nonetheless, a family remains and functions as an absent center—their images are burned into the side of the house by an atomic blast—around which we see the ironic destruction of their illusions and comforts, for these have been embodied in the technological gadgets and objects that surrounded their lives.

The story follows a completely chronological ordering, that of clock time during a one-day period. The clock voices, in turn, organize the pure chronology into story segments (at four o'clock is the children's hour; accordingly, Bradbury describes events in the nursery). But again it is very difficult to *emplot* this story in any conventional science fiction sense. It is often reprinted in thematic collections as a simple antiwar story showing the tragic effects of atomic conflict. But what is its meaning in the context of *The Martian Chronicles?* The language of the story suggests that the humans are absent gods: "The house was an altar with ten thousand attendants, big, small, servicing, attending, in choirs. But the gods had gone away, and the ritual of the religion continued senselessly, uselessly." It is clear that the situation on Earth is one in which vital myth has been replaced by degenerate meaningless rituals, which must be swept away. The very house itself has become sick, operating "in an old-maidenly preoccupation with self-protection which bordered on a mechanical paranoia."[55]

Since voice clocks figure prominently, punctuating the story into different sections, the story is clearly also about the way in which humans have attempted to master and control time by mechanical inventions like clocks. It is about the deconstruction of our chronological sense of time, which has now become meaningless as the material imagination of fire—and the forces of the natural world—invade the house, upsetting its comforting routines. This defamiliarization of the house and its desiring machines is dramatically accomplished by the recorded recitation of the Sara Teasdale poem "There Will Come Soft Rains," which, ironically, the house recites for the comfort and enjoyment of the woman of the house. To her it was once most familiar, a favorite, in fact. The poem talks about nature not caring if mankind perished utterly. It speaks romantically of nature, Spring, returning to her own archetypal rhythms after mankind's unnoticed disappearance. This voice continues to read poetry in the fiery study, sublimely indifferent as the house collapses.

The various events that occur in the house, including the fire that eventually destroys it, are what make up the field of events, but at the heart of this densely metaphorical story are those alienated machines, which no longer have a human meaning. Because these objects take on a life of their own after the blast, the story has a certain surreal quality to it. Objects seem to possess desires of their own. Hysterical robot mice run through the house trying to keep it clean. In the afternoon, bridge tables sprout from the walls while martinis and egg-salad sandwiches are automatically served. Although some readers first encountered a short version of this story in the pages of *Collier's* magazine, that cut-down text omitted the nursery, the most technologically wonderous room described in the longer *Chronicles* version. The most surreal moments of automatism come appropriately from here, where the glass walls are designed to create illusions through fantasy and color. Even the floor of the nursery is made part of this, part of an attempt to create a total environment of illusion. The projected fantasy in this nursery represents animals on the African veldt (like "The Veldt" in *The Illustrated Man*). Undoubtedly, there is an ironic reference here to the animal images Spender found on Mars. Man on Earth has attempted to completely control his animal nature, reducing it to a child's fantasy. But fire truly liberates these fantasy images as they respond to the real flames destroying the house: "In the nursery the jungle burned. Blue lions roared, purple giraffes bounded off. The panthers ran in circles, changing color, and ten million animals, running before the fire, vanished off towards a distant steaming river."[56]

Fire in this story is an agent for the *deformation* of images, a force of the imagination. It feeds off the Picassos and Matisses in the upper halls, feasts on them like delicacies, and burns the electrical wires until they reveal themselves "as if a surgeon had torn the skin off to let the red veins and capillaries quiver in the scalded air."[57] These apocalyptic and radical transformations—the idea is of a surgeon laying bare the very nerves of our mechanical civilization—prepare us for the new images of man and nature that are to come in the last story.

Bradbury's last story in his chronicles, "The Million-Year Picnic," affirms the innocence of becoming within the context of a new and different family. The title clearly indicates a different sense of festival time as well. The narrator's strategy is self-consciously naive, telling the events from the point of view of a teenage boy whose father, a former state governor, has taken his family to Mars (probably there are echoes in the story's style of Hemingway's rejuvenating fishing trips) on what he calls a fishing trip or a vacation. As William Thomas takes his family down the ancient Martian waterway on a boat, we enter into a mythic and metaphorical apprehension of the world. Everything is new and surprising to the children, from the lonely Martian shrines to the silver ring fish floating and undulating in the canal. They pass by some two hundred cities that are described as dreaming hot summer-day dreams (in terms of Northrop Frye's archetypal imagery, this marks a return to romance) on their quest for one to call their very own. They are unimpeachable monarchs of all they survey. When the children's beautiful mother's eyes are compared to the blue Martian canal water, we know that the landscape is transforming itself also. The father is a pulp science-fiction superman type with a huge sunburnt hawk nose and eyes like agates.

He promises to show the children some Martians, although the mother says they are all dead. Not only does he have this Nietzschean memory of the will but also he has the power to forget the past, for he destroys their rocket—effectively showing us that there is no going back—and makes a bonfire of all his government bonds, stock reports, and a world map. By these actions and by things the father says, we learn that they have come to Mars to establish their own standard of living, which is to live for and in the present. Yet the fantasy of owning an entire world and of taking a million-year picnic to explore it are, it is also made clear, just an Apollonian illusion made by the father for the family's sake. Thus, he is also an artist in seeking to reassure them. The boy, Timothy, senses this: "Just behind the veil of the vacation was not a soft face of laughter, but something hard and bony and perhaps terrifying. Timothy could not lift the veil."

This veil of aesthetic illusion is carefully lifted by the father at the end, when he fulfills his promise by showing the family their reflection in the Martian canal. Surprisingly, they are the Martians who stare back at them for a long, long time. In escaping from Earth, they had been seeking to become Martians all along, to discover their oneiric being. Now they can affirm themselves all the more triumphantly in a fantastic world that allows such affirmations. Yet surely they recognize themselves not as self-identical beings, but as subject to becoming and metamorphosis in this new world. This self-recognition is uncanny and perhaps terrifying, but it produces promising Dionysian shivers in Timothy—a sure sign of the carnivalized fantastic in Bradbury's aesthetics.

This is an altogether appropriate ending for *The Martian Chronicles*. It summarizes the experience of the reader, who has seen old illusions and values destroyed only to be replaced with new and vital ones, oscillating from the Apollonian to the Dionysian poles of fantasy. We are confident that Bradbury's space children will "frolic in images" on this million-year picnic. Throughout the book, the Martian landscape and past are occasions for Bradbury to invent ingenious variations on the will to power: the noble Martians, the artist, the superior man (Spender, Stendahl, and William Thomas), and the interplay of memory and forgetfulness, music and masks—these are all his themes. Bradbury as the historian of Mars is a master of metaphorical identifications. Readers experience a kaleidoscopic transformation of objects and events that occupy the historical field. As many cultural critics after Nietzsche have observed, our overly historical modern consciousness has made us lose all feeling for the strangeness and astonishment of life. For this particularly modern illness Bradbury offers us a homeopathic cure—a return to history in the metaphorical mode. *We* are the Martians.

Several stories and bridges intended for *The Martian Chronicles* never reached print, but the surviving manuscripts reveal how much further Bradbury might have developed his vision of Martian culture (table 7). For instance, there is evidence that he was considering yet another race of Martians. This material includes "The Disease," a four-page story identified in all chronologies but deleted from the first edition prior to publication. The story is told from Yll's (husband of Ylla) point of view and reflects the ravages of chicken pox on the Martian population. Since the disease happens after the third expedition (it is dated "March 2001"), Yll reflects on the "funny story" of that mission: "another ship from the stars and the men from it landing among the Shapers of Dreams. And finding a small town devised of their own memories. And being buried with music and speeches and cheers. A good joke, surely."[58] Apparently, only some Martians—here called Shapers of Dreams—are telepathic or can project dreams. The irony that Yll reflects on in the story is that he killed Ylla's dream; now the dream is killing him.

The only thing that readers often regret about the book is that Bradbury did not give more of a picture of the Martian civilization, his ideal, at its height. There are descriptions of the marvelous flame birds and sand ships and a brief glimpse of a Martian festival (in "Night Meeting"), but these are too impressionistic to completely gratify our desire to enter into a fantastic world in all its materiality. But in another story that Bradbury wrote about Mars—which was probably not intended for inclusion in *The Martian Chronicles*—this need to frolic in images is given full play:

"And here, also, long long ago," said the second Martian, "in the Season of Green Wine, the trees along those far mountain canals would drip a fine green liquor into the canals which flowed to twenty directions in a wonderful tide. They say our ancestors, the ancient Martian men and women, with golden-coin eyes in their brown faces, on spring festival midnights would bathe here. They would swim laughing in the green wine, among flower petals. They would sip the wine as they swam. They would float all through the long clear spring nights, idly, lazily, singing, dreaming wine dreams. Dreams of great wars when clouds of metal insects hovered in the dusky sky. Dreams of great loves, too, until the wine."[59]

Unfortunately, the published extract of this story, called "Christmas on Mars" (according to William F. Nolan sold to *Esquire* for a holiday issue but never published) ends here, but at least one can experience with the Martians an active

Table 7. Bradbury's known Martian stories total thirty-eight (excluding such stories as "The Piper" and "Defense Mech," where Mars provides only an incidental setting). Twenty-two were published prior to *The Martian Chronicles;* twelve of these, along with three new stories (and eleven titled bridge passages), comprise the first-edition text. Two more stories are added in some editions. Another six were subsequently published independently of *Chronicles.* Seven extant story typescripts, four bridges, and four story fragments never reached print.

The Martian Chronicles (15 stories):	Published but unchronicled (16 stories):
"January 1999: Rocket Summer" (bridge)	"The Visitor" (1948)
"February 1999: Ylla"	"The Concrete Mixer" (1949)
"August 1999: The Summer Night"	"I, Mars" (1949)
"August 1999: The Earth Men"	"The One Who Waits" (1949)
"March 2000: The Taxpayer" (bridge)	"The Lonely Ones" (1949)
"April 2000: The Third Expedition"	"The Naming of Names" (1949)
"June 2001:—And the Moon be Still as Bright"	"Holiday" (1949)
"August 2001: The Settlers" (bridge)	"The Mad Wizards of Mars" ("The Exiles," 1949)
"December 2001: The Green Morning"	"Payment in Full" (1950)
"February 2002: The Locusts" (bridge)	"Death Wish" (1950)
"August 2002: Night Meeting"	"The Other Foot" (1951)
"October 2002: The Shore" (bridge)	"The Strawberry Window" (1954)
"February 2003: Interim" (bridge)	"The Lost City of Mars" (1967)
"April 2003: The Musicians" (bridge)	"The Messiah" (1971)
"June 2003: Way in the Middle of the Air"	"The Aqueduct" (1979)
"2004–2005: The Naming of Names" (bridge)	"The Love Affair" (1982)
"April 2005: Usher II"	
"August 2005: The Old Ones" (bridge)	Unpublished stories (7) and bridges (4):
"September 2005: The Martian"	
"November 2005: The Luggage Store" (bridge)	"Christmas on Mars"
"November 2005: The Off Season"	"The Disease" (bridge)
"November 2005: The Watchers" (bridge)	"Fire and the Stars" (bridge)
"December 2005: The Silent Towns"	"Fly away Home"
"April 2026: The Long Years"	"Love Affair" (different from published story)
"August 2026: There Will Come Soft Rains"	"Martian Bulwark"
"October 2026: The Million Year Picnic"	"The Marriage"
	"The Martian Ghosts"
	"They All Had Grandfathers"
Subsequent *Chronicles* (2 stories):	"Thistle-Down and Fire" (bridge)
"The Fire Balloons" (1951)	"The Wheel" (bridge)
"The Wilderness" (1952)	four untitled story fragments

participation, indeed a bathing, in the very substance of their happiness as they enchant themselves with wine, swimming, and discharging Dionysian insights in Apollonian epic myths of Mars, the Red Planet. Such reveries of the healthy will are not again so fully developed until *Dandelion Wine,* Bradbury's lyrical novel of childhood in small-town America in which, he once wrote, "Mars Is Heaven!" would feel right at home as a dream.[60] Clearly, Bradbury thinks of genre in intertextual terms.

In addition to the unpublished stories, bridges, and fragments associated with *The Martian Chronicles*, there are at present some sixteen other published "unchronicled" stories about Mars. They are about it but have never appeared in any edition of *The Martian Chronicles*. (Where they have been collected by Bradbury, we have indicated their presence in app. A.) Some of them occupied definite places in the first chronology ("The Love Affair"); some were pulled from the middle version—summer 1949 revision—of the text ("The Other Foot," *The Illustrated Man)*; some were suggested and then withdrawn at the last moment. This latter is the case with "Payment in Full," a story Bradbury finally considered "a little too unsympathetic and bitter for the tone of the book."[61] Published in *Thrilling Wonder Stories* in February 1950 and collected by William F. Nolan in *Man against Tomorrow* (1965), this story would have been situated in the section after the destruction of Earth. It deals with the crew of a rocket on Mars taking revenge on the Martians, who only want to help and welcome them into their culture. The Martians suggest that the men accept their situation philosophically and allude to a Martian wisdom about defeat—which embodies an aesthetic response to life that is very close in tone and spirit to what Captain Wilder of "—And the Moon Be Still as Bright" discovered among the now nearly extinct Martians: an *amor fati* that enabled them to "accede to racial death" without being devoured by the hatred of Earthmen. The Martian of "Payment in Full" tells them that they must visit the cities and see "the women golden," "the men handsome in bronze masks," and "the flame pictures in the walls, burning and changing." They must "climb the crystal minarets where flowers ten centuries old bloomed forever and forever as delicate as white children, as warm, as tender." And they must hear "the music composed fifty thousand years ago, played on instruments all wire and wind and memory and porcelain throat . . . " (ellipsis Bradbury's).[62] The nearly drunken Earthmen are enraged by such an imputation of wisdom on the part of the Martians. In retaliation they destroy one of the beautiful crystalline cities with their weapons, including the very masks of the Martians. Although this is a very bitter story, it actually gives effective shape and representation to one of the negative figures of the reactive will: revenge. The Earthmen are here figures to be pitied; unlike Stendahl of "Usher II," who is also a figure of revenge, they have no artistic means to affirm life.

It is beyond the scope of this study to discuss in detail every story that Bradbury may have thought of in connection with *The Martian Chronicles*.[63] From an aesthetic point of view—which concerns us here—it is much more interesting to discuss the amount of revision that Bradbury gave to the twelve *Chronicles* chapters originally published as stand-alone stories in magazines. Bradbury's letters to editor Walter Bradbury also indicate how strongly the author felt that *The Martian Chronicles* was a *literary* work. He speaks often about the amount of work he did in revising these stories and states emphatically that he wants their pulp origins to be forgotten by not stating the reprint information on the copyright page. Later, Bradbury fought strongly to have the Doubleday Science Fiction colophon taken off of his next collection, *The Illustrated Man,* because he thought it would sink him with serious literary critics, as he believed it did with *The Martian Chronicles* (the famous Isherwood review occurred because of his own instigation, not Doubleday's). And, indeed, the term does not appear on that book.

What exactly are the literary qualities "added" during revisions of *The Martian Chronicles?* What kinds of things were added? Equally important, what signs of "pulp science-fiction writing" were left out? Actually, Bradbury states in a letter to Walter Bradbury that his typewriter did not know where a good story was finally going to be published and that he put just as much effort into his pulp stories as those published in "slick" magazines such as *Maclean's* or *Charm* (where both "Ylla" and "The Silent Towns" had been published). Many of the stories are, in fact, completely enjoyable—perhaps more so because of the illustrations— in their pulp versions. But it was their shaping into the context of a short-story cycle that modified individual parts into a greater literary whole. The evidence from collations shows unmistakably that Bradbury literally made *thousands* of changes in these stories and at every level of the text, from word to sentence to whole paragraphs. Each of these changes, of course, will make a difference in the reader's aesthetic experience of the text, which reflects thousands of aesthetic choices made by the author. For instance, consider Spender's ten-thousand-year-old Martian philosophy book. Revealingly, in the pulp version this book is made of aluminum, which has "hard" science fiction connotations of modern materials for aircraft and such, but in the revised version it is silver, a change that "aestheticizes" the alien book even more because of the connotation of silver as a precious metal used in fantastic art (one thinks of the use of *mithril* silver in J. R. R. Tolkien's works). Bradbury made thousands of such substantive changes to the text at the word level alone.

Obviously, we cannot discuss all of the revisions and their effect on the whole, which changes in a carnivalized kaleidoscopic manner before our eyes in reading from moment to moment, as Bradbury's metaphor suggests. What we can do is give a brief discussion of some categories of changes Bradbury made, and speculate on why he made them, from our understanding of the general aesthetic intentions of his fantasy. These are perhaps not categories that a textual editor might use, for they only reflect changes in the content and style of the stories that Bradbury made in order to shape a work of literature with a definite aesthetic purpose.

We can distinguish here at least three important categories of (ultimately interrelated) changes keyed to the textual level at which they take effect. First of all, since the organizing principle of *The Martian Chronicles* is a chronology, there are large-scale structural changes that Bradbury made to his pulp stories to accommodate them into the general narrative framework of expeditions, settlers, and Martians. All of the invasion stories were originally first-contact stories. These had to be rewritten so as to reflect their relative position in the expedition section. Furthermore, characters in later stories had to be made aware of the failures of the earlier missions. A large new section added to the fourth expedition (larger, in fact, than most of the bridge passages), for instance, has several functions. It contributes narrative information on the effects of the disease on the Martians and adds two new characters, Sam Parkhill and Hathaway, to the expedition so they will not appear later in "The Off Season" and "The Long Years" unexpectedly.

Another example of this kind of adjustment occurs in "The Third Expedition." Because "Mars Is Heaven!" was originally set in 1960, we have no difficulty in believing that various members of the crew would remember an America set in the early 1920s (some of the songs the Martians use, including Irving Berlin's "Always," date from this period). But when Bradbury moved his whole chronology into the twenty-first century, he had to contrive it so that Captain Black has been kept alive by scientific means past his normal lifespan so he can preserve the nostalgic effect of the songs. It is not that Bradbury wanted to write "hard" science fiction in having Captain Black scientifically rejuvenated—indeed, he barely mentions it in passing—but only because the narrative chronology demands that this character be old enough to remember the songs (eighty years old) and therefore capable of being taken in by the illusion.

These additions and revisions, then, solve problems of narrative continuity and character motivation. They are involved with creating and maintaining the impression of an integrated work of literature. A second category of aesthetic revision can be organized around passages where Bradbury omitted or revised certain "hard" science fiction elements originally present in the pulp stories that might conflict with his goals as a literary fantasist. For example, in "The Million-Year Picnic," he deleted the following passage from the version included in *The Martian Chronicles:* "On both sides of the canal now they saw the great oxygen vines and bushes, planted in irregular diagrams upon the sand; plants with deep reaching roots thrusting miles after the wither [sic] water-gut of the planet; sowed by far-seeing scientists of Earth fifty years before, and only now profuse enough, active enough to give Mars a thin atmospheric shell."[64]

To begin with, "far-seeing" Earth scientists have no role whatsoever in *The Martian Chronicles.* In fact, technology and scientists are severely criticized for their blindness to the realm of the aesthetic; Martian scientists even predict that there is no life on Earth. Moreover, the reference to "fifty years ago" would not jibe with the established chronology (the events on Mars take a little more than a quarter century to unfold, not a half century). Lastly and most important, this information, if allowed to remain in the story, would conflict with the much more fantastic retelling of the Johnny Appleseed folk legend in the earlier story "The Green Morning," where the atmosphere of Mars is changed overnight by trees that grow in an almost magical soil and rain. Undoubtedly, this passage worked well in the context of the extrapolative science fiction pulps, but it has no role in a work that is primarily fantasy.

Two other instances of Bradbury's omission or revision of pulp images—these on the sentence level—come at the end of "Mars Is Heaven!" In the pulp version Captain Black lies in bed at night contemplating the day's events. He eventually realizes with a chill that these seeming humans (including his brother) could really be Martians. He thinks "my brother here on this bed will change form, melt, shift, and become another thing, a terrible thing, a Martian."[65] Part of the horror of this story, which has been justly celebrated by horror writers such as Stephen King, is due to the effect of the indefinite word "thing," which calls up uncanniness in the context of the most familiar, one's family. Bradbury's aesthetic demands that the horrible not be directly represented but approached by indirection and suggestion. The pulp version of this sentence is the same except that the Martian will become not an indefinite thing, allowing for our imagination to work on representing it, but a "one-eyed, green and yellow-toothed Martian." Indeed, the story in the pulp version is decorated with illustrations of various sci-fi monster heads, which are more comically weird and funny than they are horrifying. Again, the passage works fine in the context of pulp science fiction; indeed, it may even be playing with and mocking (that is, carnivalizing) those conventions of representation. But it has no place in Bradbury's literary vision of Mars. Finally, at the end of the pulp version, the Martian crowd tears the rocket apart, blows it up, and strews the pieces all about, a much more directly Dionysian ending than the revised one, where they maintain the illusion for a good while after the Earthmen are dead just for the pleasure of the joke.

The third and final aesthetic category deals with Bradbury's conception of the Martians themselves. Only in two stories considered for inclusion in *The Martian Chronicles* were his Martians originally masked—"Payment in Full" and "The Off Season"—and both are somewhat bitter stories about the clash of aesthetic values with commercial or colonialist impulses. The masked Martians begin to appear in the later stories of 1948 and 1949. Bradbury's decision to mask his Martians throughout, in revisions to such stories as "Ylla" and "The Earth Men," is the most significant literary change he made to the pulp originals. It certainly made a significant difference to some individual works, such as "The Earth Men"—which some critics still complain is too "pulpy"—by creating multiple levels of irony (like the Martian psychologist with three smiles painted on his mask). It seems likely that the uncompleted novel *The Masks* has some influence here, especially in the interview scene with the Martian psychiatrist, which seems to be a reversal of the one Bradbury wrote for his unfinished novel, where the disillusioned romantic hero, not the psychiatrist, wears the mask. Bradbury's fantasy depends heavily on the use of masks, illusions, both in building them up and in destroying them, in order to affirm his life as an artist. One might say with some justice that masks in *The Martian Chronicles* are the aesthetic signs of the mature literary fantasy Bradbury sought, representing his triumph over an earlier and somewhat facile romantic disillusionment.

Beyond these categories of revision, the eleven bridge passages (see table 7) were all deliberately written as a play of stylistic masks: "The bridge passages, written later, were all done under the influence of my favorite poets, from Shakespeare to Gerard Manley Hopkins down to Robert Frost and Dylan Thomas. I knew I had to do something evocative for each, and each was an experiment, much like some of the short French *pensées* I had read years before in various magazines. I imagine Steinbeck's GRAPES OF WRATH influenced me also; the short passages in that novel, that is, the evocative ones."[66] The aesthetic function of the bridges is therefore clear: Bradbury wanted to evoke the literary voices of mainstream authors. "Rocket Summer," which opens *The Martian Chronicles*, in fact develops as a literary reverie, with fire and ice as thematic opposites. Bradbury's rockets create a brief "summer" with their exhaust heat as they leave for Mars from midwinter Ohio. It is an experimental prose poem in which the words "rocket summer" create climates of the imagination reminiscent of Robert Frost.

Masks for the Bradbury of *The Martian Chronicles* assume a polyvalent function and exist at many different levels of the text. The inserted passages masking his Martians enabled him to link up his Mars with carnival themes and to carnivalize the science-fiction genre, the literary masks of other authors enabled him to evoke and criticize the literary mainstream. But masks in *Chronicles* are ultimately reminders of the "Martian" wisdom that illusions—fantasy literature itself—are necessary for the affirmation of life.

3

The Simulacrum of Carnival

Fahrenheit 451

Bradbury's fifth book was his first true novel, evolving from the February 1951 *Galaxy* novella "The Fireman" and, by extension, from a number of cautionary tales of censorship, especially "The Bonfire" (1950) and "Bright Phoenix" (1950; published 1963). Censorship is also thematically central to "Pillar of Fire" (1948), "The Exiles" (1949), and "Usher II" (1950), and this clustering of analogs is a measure of Bradbury's concern with the implications of the politics of that time. Although a lengthy discussion of the contemporary Cold War politics surrounding *Fahrenheit 451* is beyond the scope of this study—we are interested in the larger cultural issues this important work still addresses—any such discussion of the book's politics ought to be grounded in a clear understanding of the novel's origins and development, which this chapter, in part, explores. The book was conceived while Josef Stalin was still in power in Russia and published before Sen. Joseph McCarthy was censured by the U.S. Senate in December 1954. However different their official politics were, both men conducted "show trials" of a sort in which their victims saw themselves as caught up in a kind of evil carnival of public accusation and character defamation and assassination. Probably Stalin's regime could not have survived without them. And in the United States, political paranoia generated by the televised Army-McCarthy hearings, which began in April 1954, was a fact of life for anyone involved in cultural activities at that time.

One often hears, for instance, the phrase "climate of fear" used in connection with this period of American history. Indeed, a letter written at this time to Bradbury by *Fahrenheit* publisher Ian Ballantine mentions McCarthy prominently while addressing Bradbury's worries about sales of the novel and his concern that Ballantine Books might have suffered because of its publication. After observing that McCarthy's speeches to live audiences were, in fact, no longer drawing capacity crowds, Ballantine reflected: "It is an irony of our time that some of the most important things that are happening to us are not talked about because people have been made afraid, and I think that FAHRENHEIT and every other non-conformist book faces the obstacle of this fear. On the other hand, the very importance of the subject of FAHRENHEIT makes the book, of all your books, the one that I find has been read by all the people I generally see. I think that it has made a tremendous impression on those people who are not afraid, and it has added greatly to the respect people feel for you."[1] He went on to assure Bradbury that *Fahrenheit 451* was a book of "frightening importance" (perhaps punning ambivalently on the "climate of fear") and that, far from suffering from having published it, the book had helped his publishing efforts "tremendously." Clearly, people that Ballantine knew were finding a way to talk about McCarthy and the times by reading Bradbury's book.

But Bradbury's use of the system of carnival images in *Fahrenheit 451* should not be narrowly understood as an exterior, mechanical method of defense against censorship, as an enforced adoption of Aesop's language against the obstacles of fear. On the contrary, people who read it at the time were already unafraid, or perhaps made unafraid by reading it. In his remarks to Bradbury, Ballantine hints at the fact that *Fahrenheit 451* was not so much addressing the question of the exterior right to free expression—though some people in society were not speaking out about important issues because of fear of the authorities—as the value of an inner freedom gained through the important "subject matter" of the book. The themes and images of carnival that Bradbury has appropriated suggest a fearless language about the world and about power. One should keep in mind the scene in part 2 of the novel that depicts Montag's angry confrontation with his wife, Mildred, regarding important things that the "idiot bastards" on television never talk to her about—in particular the fear of war at home and the hatred of American consumer society by the rest of the world's poor and starving population, who work while we play. Here Bradbury (almost) directly criticizes the effects of postwar American economic and cultural dominance on the world. Also note the historical irony that Bradbury's frank use of the real language of carnival, which when truly appropriated can address power directly, led to his own censorship. All the abusive language tearing away Mildred's masks, her unconcern and false sense of security, was secretly removed in the Bal-Hi editions of the 1960s and 1970s (see fig. 10). We will revisit this irony as the textual history unfolds.[2]

Regardless, in such an inverted carnival as Bradbury constructs to depict the fears and concerns of postwar America, authorities (or "official culture") impose social masks on a frightened person. One was branded a communist or, in the case of Soviet Russia, a subversive spy for the capitalist West. In *Fahrenheit 451* the mere possession of books is enough to indicate that one is a subversive criminal. Clearly, Bradbury's character Montag is someone who experiences a liberation from such masks. His initial identity as a fireman, an agent of official culture, a "minstrel man" who conducts fiery show trials, is completely discarded (his mask is removed by the young girl Clarisse as discussed in the thematics section). His plot to plant stolen books in the homes of firemen and then turn them in to the authorities also smacks of mocking carnivalesque laughter. But Mildred, his wife, turns in the alarm on him, and when the firemen arrive at his house, Montag can only gaze in disbelief as his neighbors emerge to "watch the carnival" of his own home being destroyed. Montag's victory should largely be understood as a victory over the fool in himself. His actions do very little to change the nature of the state, which self-destructs in an atomic war. Living among the "book people" who constitute a new kind of folk culture, he gains a (joking) understanding that one cannot judge a book by its cover. So in these ways *Fahrenheit*'s appropriation of the great historical stream of carnivalesque imagery and themes is related, by dreamlike thematic reversal (the carnival and its liberating laughter are usually agents of freedom, not oppression), to its contemporary politics.[3]

Bradbury's Texts

Probing the climate of fear is not limited to Bradbury's censorship tales of this period. In fact, "The Fireman" owed its direct inspiration to "The Pedestrian" (1950; published 1951), a story based on an unsettling encounter with authorities during an after-dinner walk in Los Angeles; Bradbury and a friend, the lone pedestrians strolling along a middle stretch of Wilshire Boulevard, were stopped and questioned by police.[4] Within a few days "The Pedestrian" projected this event into a possible future world where addiction to virtual realities such as television has replaced evening walks; in fact, such activity is considered abnormal, and police arrest pedestrians instead of protecting them. As Bradbury began work on a similar dreamlike reversal of standards—one in which firemen start fires instead of stopping them—his character Montag becomes the pedestrian, taking late-night walks down deserted streets. In contrast to the solitary pedestrian of the earlier tale, Montag runs into sixteen-year-old Clarisse McClellan; he has never met her before, but she knows who he is and what he does for a living.

Thus begins Montag's journey of self-discovery in a world where the seductive appeal of constant multimedia entertainment is the real enemy—book burning is only one tool of many used to enslave minds and destroy the human soul. But *Fahrenheit 451* is also a tale that celebrates literature and the powers of literacy. It is built on constant allusions to literature and offers hope for the future through characters who have literally become talking books in the effort to save these works from extinction. In late summer 1950 Bradbury prepared his first draft in the UCLA library, creating a 25,000-word novella in nine days of furious activity surrounded by the very titles that, in many libraries from Waukegan to Los Angeles, had inspired him to become a writer. A close study of the half-dozen surviving forms of the "Fireman"-*Fahrenheit* text shows how Bradbury wove intertextual content into the fabric of the tale to create a work of cultural criticism that is still widely studied today. This evolving metatext, along with the publishing correspondence that documents the rise of this work from story to novel and on to a classic in its own right, also reveals a great deal about Bradbury's development and influence as a mainstream American author.

We now know that this metatext includes a previously unknown novel project dating from 1947, *Where Ignorant Armies Clash by Night.* This project (discussed in detail in the thematic section of this chapter) reveals Bradbury's earliest known creative impulse to write a serious novel about the crisis of values (nihilism) in American culture. If technology and science cannot create values and if God is dead, how is civilization and culture to survive? How are life-affirming values to be created? In Bradbury's aesthetic only artists can create values, but science and technology seem to dominate and indeed threaten to overwhelm culture. His investigation of these ideas resulted in a sixty-six-page manuscript that contains many themes central to what later became *Fahrenheit 451:* an emphasis on the reversal of values (assassins ritually murder people and destroy works of art just as *Fahrenheit*'s firemen do), a focus on a hero who is inwardly disillusioned with this work, and the subsequent pathos of his search for new values (including a reading of Matthew Arnold's poem "Dover Beach" in its entirety). But the ending—at least in one of its versions—is quite bleak because the way out of nihilism is only briefly adumbrated. There may be a group of "book people" living somewhere who are preserving books by memorizing and becoming them, but the hero has no contact with them and dies by state-mandated suicide. Another ending, which is also quite bleak, reached print in revised form a year before *Fahrenheit* ("The Smile," 1952).

The project was intended for a mainstream publisher but never went any further in this "pessimistic" form. More directly, the evolution of *Fahrenheit 451* can be traced back to a complete 140-page typescript titled "Long after Midnight," a clean, fair copy that was almost certainly prepared from a now-lost original composed on the rental typewriters in the basement of the UCLA library. (It was preserved by longtime Bradbury friend and colleague Forrest Ackerman for many years, and although it has now passed into a private collection, a copy survives in William F. Nolan's Bradbury archive at Bowling Green State University.) A subsequent ninety-nine–page typescript titled "The Fire Man" survives in the Pollack Library at California State University, Fullerton (acquired through the efforts of Prof. Willis McNelly during Bradbury's year as writer-in-residence). This last seems to be the direct source of the unlocated final typescript of "The Fireman" submitted to Horace Gold for publication in the February 1951 issue of *Galaxy*.

Fifteen years later, Bradbury would look back at the process of composing this novella and describe it as an "emotional blaze"; the self-imposed nine-day limit would protect him, as much as possible, against rational reflection during the composition process. This was only a variation on the dynamics of his short-story strategy: "I had already learned that self-consciousness is the enemy of all creativity. . . . I must make haste then in order to be emotional, and be emotional in order to be very truthful indeed. Time later, when finished, to go back and 'think' about some unsolved problems, in order to re-emotionalize them and make them 'true.'" The two surviving manuscripts bear the fruits of just this kind of careful revision. As Willis McNelly has noted, "The Fire Man" typescript contains a fairly tight narrative; there are some penciled revisions by Bradbury, but this second draft required little revision prior to magazine publication.[5] In it Bradbury deleted the opening dream sequence of "Long after Midnight," a *1984*-like nightmare in which Montag finds himself caught and reported by a young boy for reading books the fireman has secretly removed from one of his book burnings.

Even without the dream sequence, Bradbury's opening portrayal of Montag as a man in crisis remained in all the early versions of the story. Both drafts, as well as the *Galaxy* version, initially portray Montag as a figure consciously torn between his duty to burn and his impulse to save. Bradbury would take a more subtle approach in revision, recasting Montag as, on the surface, supremely happy with his job, eventually penning the famous opening line, "It was a pleasure to burn." As revised, the unconscious desire to save and read books would begin to surface only after his encounters with Clarisse. But these revisions, and the subsequent transformation of a fast-paced novella into an enduring classic novel, were still two years away.

Bradbury drafted "The Pedestrian," "The Fireman," and a number of other successful stories between submission of *The Martian Chronicles* (October 1949) and submission of his follow-up science-fiction story collection for Doubleday, *The Illustrated Man* (August 1950). By October 1950, Bradbury had sold "The Fireman" to *Galaxy* and was at work on his final revisions.[6] Horace Gold had founded *Galaxy* early in 1950 and was thrilled to have a rare novella-length work of fiction from Bradbury for the fifth issue. His working premise was to form a relationship with authors and readers based on literature rather than money. Gold did not try to tie up a percentage of reprint and book rights, which was a common practice with stories purchased by the pulps, but like Anthony Boucher, who had founded the small-format *Magazine of Fantasy and Science Fiction* a year earlier, he was interested in bringing science fiction into the literary mainstream.

One way of doing this was to buy quality stories and present them in a digest-format periodical with slick-magazine–quality covers illustrated by the best new science-fiction artists. Another way was to strengthen the international market for American science fiction, which was where Gold hoped to make his money. He asked many of his authors to give him first refusal on all stories to ensure steady opportunities to buy quality work, and tried to convince them to sell him international first-serial rights on the stories he purchased. In this way Gold planned to launch international editions of *Galaxy*, but neither Bradbury nor his agent, Don Congdon, were willing to lock into a single magazine that was still struggling to break out of a niche market. Bradbury agreed to international first-serial rights for "The Fireman" but retained the option to offer his new stories without restriction. During November 1950, Bradbury worked on revisions to the first half of the novella, while Gold offered encouragement and a recommendation to end the tale with more pessimism by showing Montag as a flawed guardian of texts. Gold's double irony envisioned Montag unable to recall his texts without massive, Joycean juxtapositions of commercial ads and unrelated literary fragments and the other bookmen unable to detect his helpless corruptions. Bradbury easily avoided this suggestion, for his friend and editor soon realized the implications of the larger issues at work in this novella.[7]

"The Fireman" appeared in *Galaxy* just as Doubleday released *The Illustrated Man*. The strong reception of that collection widened the market for Bradbury stories, and he would not develop "The Fireman" any further for some time. More new stories, as well as revisions to older stories already circulating, occupied him during the rest of the year. Seventeen new stories appeared in periodicals during 1952, and fourteen more followed the next year; nearly all appeared in major-market slicks (see app. A). In fact, Bradbury soon had enough good material for another story collection, and in June 1952 he and Don Congdon persuaded a reluctant Walter Bradbury at Doubleday to offer a contract on the promise that the greatly anticipated (and already contracted) Illinois novel (eventually *Dandelion Wine*) would follow soon after.

Editor Bradbury saw publication of the Illinois novel as the proper path to major writer status, but author Bradbury was already beginning to push beyond the envelope of the Doubleday Science Fiction series on his own terms. He had managed to get the series logo removed from *The Illustrated Man*, though that collection still represented some of his best science fiction of the late 1940s. And the third Doubleday collection, which contained far more fantasy than science fiction, would represent a further step away from science fiction even before its publication in March 1953 as *The Golden Apples of the Sun*. By 1952, Bradbury was also moving into Hollywood ventures; the following year two of his stories were adapted into feature films, and he was under contract to write the screenplay of the Warner Brothers movie *Moby Dick* for John Huston.[8] Yet Bradbury's publishing contracts were making him very little money in proportion to his growing major-market recognition as a book author. Doubleday received half of the paperback royalties as well as a cut of book club, anthology, and second-serial rights, while Bradbury received little in return; the tightly budgeted covers, jackets, and paper of his hardbound titles still reflected the second-level marketing of the science fiction series, and his promotion allowance was minimal. Congdon felt that it was time to force Doubleday to recognize that Bradbury had outgrown a rising author's contract and promotion profile and turned elsewhere to offer book-length material not of interest to Walter Bradbury. In the summer of 1952, Congdon presented a plan to produce a volume of Bradbury's novellas and longer stories—a plan that had earlier failed to interest Doubleday—to Stanley Kauffmann at Ballantine Books.

Both Congdon and Bradbury had watched with interest in 1951 when Bantam founder Ian Ballantine and writer-editor Kauffmann left the paperback giant to start a new kind of firm that would offer authors quality hardback and mass-market paperback editions from the same publishing house—in fact, printed from the same plates. Congdon knew that this kind of efficiency would translate into more royalties for the author. Furthermore, Ballantine was a proven talent— he and his wife, Betty, had introduced Penguin Books to America shortly before World War II, and a decade later Bradbury had seen the Bantam paperback editions of both *The Martian Chronicles* and *The Illustrated Man* reach mass-market popularity largely through the work and planning of Ballantine and Kauffmann.[9]

When Ballantine Books began operations, Congdon wasted no time approaching both men. In August 1952 they agreed to negotiate for the still-untitled collection of novellas and immediately acquired a Bradbury story for a new series of Ballantine hardcover science-fiction anthologies edited by Frederick Pohl.[10] Congdon sent Kauffmann three published novellas to review: "The Fireman," "The Creatures That Time Forgot," and "Pillar of Fire." Kauffmann was impressed with the first two, but Bradbury had begun work on revisions to "The Fireman" and was reluctant to commit it to the collection until he had fully revised and expanded it. Kauffmann agreed to hold that piece for now as long as he could have "The Creatures That Time Forgot." Congdon felt that "The Fireman" could not stand much revision unless Bradbury developed subplots and brought some of the thematic implications into the open. But he shared the excitement of Bradbury's new publishers about the potential of the already excellent novella: "there is such good suspense and such an exciting idea in it that if you can bring about a better sense of texture to the characters and the themes therein, then it should be a humdinger."[11] Bradbury would indeed develop both texture and themes, but he also subdued the play of textuality already established in "The Fireman" in order to better have his readers think of the emerging work as a *book*. It was a very private and personal process, and he would have to leave his agent and editor in suspense until the finished novel finally emerged from the novella.

The evolution of "The Fireman" into *Fahrenheit 451* began gradually; the earliest known evidence survives in two of Bradbury's preliminary outlines for *The Golden Apples of the Sun* (both prepared prior to the summer of 1952, by which time the title and contents for that collection had stabilized). They are undated, but internal evidence indicates priority; the earlier one shows "The Fireman" as the longest selection among other recently published and unpublished stories considered for the Doubleday collection. The list includes titles and word counts for thirteen stories. Bradbury's notes indicate an option for a longer or shorter collection, and in both scenarios "The Fireman" (listed at 35,000 [written over 25,000] words) clearly dominates the ten-story (68,000 word) and thirteen-story (75,000 word) options. It is unclear if Bradbury or Doubleday found the imbalance problematic, but nearly all of the other stories on this list found their way into *Golden Apples*. Another undated (but apparently later) listing of contents reveals another approach to the problem. This one is titled "THE FIRE THAT BURNS a short novel by Ray Bradbury plus ten short stories." Only three or four of these stories would be diverted into *Golden Apples;* the rest seemed destined for a collection explicitly dominated by a revision of his longest published tale.

In November 1952 Kauffmann and Ballantine began to review Bradbury's published stories for ideas about the new collection. In mid-December they submitted a listing of suggested stories, including "The Creatures That Time Forgot." Congdon negotiated a very favorable contract that reflected Ballantine's strong interest in publishing Bradbury, agreeing to a five-thousand-dollar advance on royalties upon publication as well as rights to second-serial and anthology reprints. Any future book-club income would be split equally, but the reduced costs of simultaneous hardback and paperback production allowed Ballantine to offer a generous 8 percent royalty on the paperback sales; since his was primarily a paperback operation (Houghton Mifflin handled hardbound production and sales support), Ballantine took no cut from the paperback royalties. Bradbury personally negotiated a one-thousand-dollar advance on signing and won Ballantine's support for illustrations by Joe Mugnaini.[12]

Bradbury now had a book contract commensurate with his longtime status as a mainstream periodical author and a publisher willing to spend significant sums on promotion to attract more major reviews than ever before. Congdon cleared the last hurdle in early February 1953 by securing Doubleday's promise not to stand in the way. Ballantine's target date for submission was April 15; it only remained for Bradbury to come through with a project to match the opportunity. Up to this point, the contents of the collection had remained quite nebulous, largely because of Bradbury's growing tendency to hold back new and sometimes-revised material until it had fully matured. Congdon had supported and even nurtured this instinct a year earlier as it related to first drafts: "I have a hunch you're right about the validity of rushing a story as you feel it down on paper to get a draft. I think this is particularly true in your case; and as you say, sometimes when you don't get the draft right you are the kind of writer who instinctively knows it, puts the story away and brings it out when you have something new to add to it in the way of conception."[13]

But by autumn, Congdon was becoming concerned about Bradbury's habit of typing revisions of his own work: "Incidentally, why don't you find yourself a good reliable typist to work with on all your things? . . . As a matter of fact, upon checking your story card I see that we have only received 8 new stories from you this year, which astounds me." Much of Bradbury's time was now focused on revising older stories that had either not sold or had not yet been collected in his story collections, and he confessed to Congdon a sense of anxiety that prevented him from releasing any work until he had perfected it.[14] His plan to revise and expand "The Fireman" was a more extensive and fundamentally creative proposition than bridging his Martian stories into a story cycle had been three years earlier, and this challenge was no doubt at the heart of the crisis. Bradbury had three choices: he could move ahead on the "Illinois novel" for Doubleday; revise more stories for the Ballantine collection, focusing on the short novella "The Creatures That Time Forgot"; or continue his much more ambitious expansion of "The Fireman," an even better centerpiece for the new book.

Bradbury soon settled on the latter course. As the winter drew to a close, he sent Ballantine "And the Rock Cried Out" and "The Playground," two well-traveled stories that had recently been through the revision mill and finally, thanks to Congdon's good offices, sold to magazines.[15] He promised to send revised texts from Ballantine's December wish-list of previously published stories as well, but textual evidence from this period suggests that he was actually concentrating on the transformation of "The Fireman." The Pollak Library deposit at California State University, Fullerton, includes nearly two hundred typescript pages from this period of intense activity. Ninety-eight of these leaves represent discarded revisions—runs of pages revising and expanding dialogue by Beatty or Faber, similar expansions of Montag's encounters with Clarisse, and a few pages of outline and literary quotations. The second hundred pages—titled *Fahrenheit 451* and opening with "It was a pleasure to burn"—is a continuous typescript that grew out of the superseded revisions to form a first draft of the novel. This sustained work is itself heavily revised by hand and incomplete, lacking the postapocalyptic ending of the original novella. As Willis McNelly has pointed out, there are a number of transitional titles throughout this material that may have been considered as titles for the entire work or perhaps for the three titled sections that had been part of the text from the beginning.

This two-hundred-page concentration of typescript pages contains evidence of a second "emotional blaze" of creativity, and in fact, Bradbury did return to the basement of the UCLA library to repeat the process of spontaneous composition: "I sat down to another nine-day schedule to add words and scenes and turn the novella into a novel of some 50,000 words. Again, an emotional process. Again, as before, I knew that 'plot' could not be imagined ahead of the event, that you had to trust your main character to live out his time, to run before you. You followed and found his footprints in the snow. Those footprints, after the fact, found in the snow, are 'plot.' But they can only be examined, intelligently, after the emotional sprint, or your actors must quit the stage."[16] But none of this material went forward to either Congdon or Ballantine. The latter continued to work with Joe Mugnaini on line art for the various potential stories, including *Fahrenheit,* which by early April had become the title of the volume and officially replaced "The Creatures That Time Forgot" as the centerpiece of the collection. Ballantine's April 15 deadline was moved back to June 15, but Congdon, Kauffmann, and Ballantine were somewhat anxious.

The months of closely guarded revision (culminating in the nine-day UCLA marathon) began to pay off as the June deadline approached. During this period, Bradbury used his own extensive holograph revisions in the initial *Fahrenheit* typescript as a point of departure for more massive additions and deletions as he worked steadily on a submittable typescript. On June 15 he was still not finished, but he sent Congdon and Ballantine the ribbon copy of the first 126 pages along with a table of contents and a descriptive title page for "8 SHORT STORIES for *FAHRENHEIT 451*" (see fig. 8). Both agent and publisher were greatly impressed by the transformation of the novella, and Ballantine agreed to move the completion date to July 7. Bradbury continued to revise and retype the rest of the UCLA typescript, sending twenty-to-thirty-page installments that both fascinated and frustrated the recipients.[17] The final version was ready in time for a scheduled visit to the coast by Kauffmann in mid-August. Meanwhile, Ballantine had been able to work with his printer to ensure that the late submission would still make the scheduled October release date. But by this time it was impossible to await Bradbury's revisions to the remaining stories, so the "collection" went to press with *Fahrenheit 451* dominating "The Playground" and the concluding "And the Rock Cried Out"—the only stories fully revised and in hand as the book went to press.

Even without a full complement of stories, the development of "The Fireman" into Bradbury's first novel created the publishing event that both Congdon and

RAY BRADBURY'S SHORT STORIES

Creatures Time Forgot *

First Selections:

THE ONE WHO WAITS *	Arkham Sampler, 1949
CHRYSALIS	Amazing Stories, July, 1946
PAYMENT IN FULL *	Thrilling Wonder Stories, Feb 1950
THE WOMEN *	Famous Fantastic Mysteries, Oct 1948
A SOUND OF THUNDER *	Colliers, June 28, 1952
THE OCTOBER GAME	Weird Tales, March, 1948
A LITTLE JOURNEY	Galaxy, August, 1951
A BLADE OF GRASS *	Thrilling Wonder Stories, Dec 1949
DEATH WISH	Planet Stories, Fall 1950
THE WILDERNESS *	Fantasy and Science Fiction, Nov 1952
THE SHAPE OF THINGS *	Thrilling Wonder Stories, Feb 1948
EMBROIDERY *	Marvel Science Fiction, Nov 1951
THE BEAST FROM 20,000 FATHOMS *	Saturday Evening Post, June 23, 1951
FOREVER AND THE EARTH *	Planet Stories, Spring 1950
THE LONELY ONES	Startling Stories, July, 1949
CHANGELING	Super Science, July, 1949
THE SILENCE	Super Science, January, 1949

Alternates:

I, MARS	Super Science, April 1949
SUBTERFUGE	Astounding Stories, April 1943
ASLEEP IN ARMAGEDDON *	Planet Stories, Winter 1948
LAZARUS COME FORTH	Planet Stories, Winter 1944
THE APRIL WITCH *	Saturday Evening Post, April 5, 1952

In Paper covers:

HERE THERE BE TYGERS *	Holt 1951	Pocket Books #908 12/52
KING OF THE GREY SPACES *	Famous Fantastic Mysteries, 12/43	Permabooks P67, 1950
THERE WILL COME SOFT RAINS *		Permabooks P145, Feb 1952
A WHIFF OF SARSAPARILLA		Ballantine March 1953

* those we have in our files.

Figure 8. Ballantine's December 1952 list of suggested titles for the story collection (left) includes Don Congdon's insertion of "The Creatures That Time Forgot" as the possible featured novella. By June, Bradbury's own listing of contents (right) substituted *Fahrenheit 451* as the centerpiece for a collection of eight newer stories. Only two of these, "And the Rock Cried Out" and "The Playground," would be revised in time for publication; four of the remaining six were eventually added to Ballantine's second Bradbury collection, *The October Country* (1955). From the Albright Collection, courtesy of Donn Albright and Ray Bradbury.

june 15th, 1953

contents:

8 SHORT STORIES

for

FAHRENHEIT 451

by

Ray Bradbury

June 15, 1953

Ballantine had hoped for. The textual record of this transformation is preserved today in three locations. In addition to the 200 pages of transitional drafts in California State's Fullerton deposit, the second carbon of the first 126-page submission from the UCLA typescript has been preserved by Donn Albright, Bradbury's principal bibliographer. Albright also holds the complete 221-leaf first carbon of that typescript, including revised and retyped pages of Montag's first encounter with Clarisse, which Bradbury forwarded to Congdon in late July 1953.[18] The final ribbon-copy of the entire 221-leaf UCLA typescript, with the revised replacement pages of the Clarisse encounter as well as many final holograph revisions by Bradbury, is located in William F. Nolan's Bradbury collection at Bowling Green State University in Ohio. This final revised typescript served as printer's copy for the Ballantine first edition. After publication Bradbury had Ballantine return this setting typescript to Nolan, whose *Ray Bradbury Review* (1952) represented the first book-length bibliography of the young author. At that time Nolan was in transition from commercial artist to fulltime writer, but even as his own career blossomed, he would continue to document Bradbury's career for another quarter century. His preservation of the final draft of *Fahrenheit 451* allows a nearly continuous analytical survey of the evolving text.

In order to create his first real novel, Bradbury did a number of things compositionally to expand the text of "The Fireman." He increased the role of cultural criticism by lengthening the speeches of Captain Beatty (named Leahy in "The Fireman"), Faber, and Granger—the three characters who engage Montag in critical discussions. (This is the "ideological" content of the novel to be dealt with primarily in the thematics section.) From its very first stages of development, *Fahrenheit 451* is a fast-paced narrative; any expansion of the character or thematic development in the tradition of the utopian novel runs the risk of becoming too chatty as false prophets and true mentors take turns enlightening the protagonist. Bradbury's challenge throughout the revision was to preserve the narrative pace even as he extended the thematic interactions of characters and enlarged the emotional effect of the action.

Bradbury would limit the play of textuality by cutting back wherever he could let the readers find answers for themselves. A clear example can be traced through revisions of what may be called "the battle of quotations" between Montag and Captain Beatty at the end of part 2 of the novel. Beatty relates a dream in which he and Montag are debating the devil's ability to cite authority for his own gain. Since the dream is Beatty's, the words are presumably all of his own choosing. The Fullerton deposit contains several handwritten and typed sheets of quotations Bradbury intended to use in expanding the passage. His first three penciled quotations are from Nietzsche—more than from any other author—and no doubt were intended to present Beatty's underlying position that books, considered in their textuality, can be "traitors" to the notion of univocal truth. But in subsequent revisions Bradbury chose not to use any of the three, presumably to let readers work out for themselves Beatty's essentially nihilistic perspective.[19] Other actual preexisting passages are cut down and even eliminated to let the reader make connections, and these cuts help preserve the narrative pace even as other passages expanded.

In this process, however, Bradbury dropped some of the more intriguing intellectual arguments of his earlier novella text. In particular, *Fahrenheit* lacks the passage that directly addresses the paradox of books being a product of the technological civilization that is explicitly under attack in the story; the *Galaxy* printing provides the first example of how these more obvious direct attacks on machine civilization were dropped from the novel. Without considering this earlier version, certain critics have pointed out what they take to be Bradbury's lack of awareness on this matter.[20] But besides pointing at the paradox, this and subsequent excised passages notably reflect a psychoanalytic understanding of the nature of textuality. An awareness of contradiction and paradox can be found, for instance, in the following passage, where Montag is among the "hobo intellectuals" who have become books, realizing that these men "were gathered together to watch the machines die, or hope they might die, even while cherishing a last paradoxical love for those very machines which could spin out a material with happiness in the warp and terror in the woof so interblended that a man might go insane trying to tell the design to himself, and his place in it."[21]

This is a very interesting passage for what it tells us about authors and texts. Trying to tell the design to oneself and one's place in it is indeed the central problem of authorship. Bradbury quite correctly says that the author is not outside the design, contemplating it from some point outside the play of textuality. On the contrary, he is part of that design and thereby becomes subject himself to its textual themes, which are organized by a symbolic code that juxtaposes opposites, often reversing themes in a dreamlike manner. Furthermore, Bradbury is here evoking metaphors of textual production and not books as finished products. He has not lapsed, it seems, into the ideology of finished masterpieces. In the novella versions his book people are a lot more fragmented, being mostly chapters and pieces of (sometimes quite different) books. Indeed, Granger refers to himself as a "kaleidoscope" because of the many bits and pieces of books he contains.[22] There is also something threatening to the notion of a stable, rational self being alluded to here. "Material" returns books to their radical or root meaning of text, to their nature as "woven things" (from the past participle of *texere*, "to weave"). Books have texture, as Faber later says in the expanded *Fahrenheit 451*. But textuality threatens "insanity" because of the way it interweaves thematic contradictions—that is, happiness and terror—into a scandalous co-presence and crosses the boundaries of other texts. There is a (nearly unlimited) play of textuality behind all of Bradbury's books, and *Fahrenheit* is no exception. The mass of intertextual citations that make up the novel must be the subject of a future study; nevertheless, it is worth noting that the character of Montag was originally to have been one book, the Book of Job (but then the Bible, the master template of *Fahrenheit,* is not one book but many); instead, he becomes fragments of Ecclesiastes and Revelations.

Other juxtapositions of thematic contradictions are enlarged in revision, and one of the most easily traced (and heavily revised) sites of such a collision centers on Montag's emergence from the water after his flight from the city. In successive paragraphs the sense of well being engendered by his water reverie is immediately contradicted when he steps ashore and is hit with the overwhelming consequence of stepping back into the real world. In revision this contradiction is sharpened to focus the reader's attention on working out an answer to the problem that must be faced if one is to win one's freedom from the world of artificial realities: how to encompass the meaning of the earth.[23] Bradbury wrote three versions of this passage before he was satisfied; the two columns below represent the first and third versions presented for comparison.

He stepped out of the river, and stood on the bank.

The land came running at him. It was a tidal wave. It reared up in a wind through the trees and the trees put out the stars, they were that high, and he was all but knocked down by the darkness and the look of the land and the smell of the million things that filled the wind that iced his body, and set him shivering. He fell back into the water a step and then moved forward under the arch, under the breaking curve of the tidal wave of wind, into the wilderness, his heart thumping, his ears roaring hollow, his mouth shut tight against drowning in this. He whirled about. The dark land spun. The stars poured across his vision like flaming meteors because he spun so fast. He

He stepped from the river.

The land rushed at him, a tidal wave. He was crushed by darkness and the look of the country and the million odors on a wind that iced his body. He fell back under the breaking curve of darkness and sound and smell, his ears roaring. He whirled. The stars poured over his sight like flaming meteors. He wanted to plunge in the river again and let it idle him safely on down somewhere. This dark land rising was like that day in his childhood, swimming, when from nowhere the largest wave in the history of remembering slammed him down in salt mud and green darkness, water burning mouth and nose; retching his stomach, screaming! Too much water!

wanted to plunge on out into the river again and let it idle him safely on down somewhere. He remembered a day as a boy when swimming at the ocean and suddenly out of nowhere the biggest wave in the history of remembering came out of the sea and slammed him into salt and mud and green darkness, and him screaming helplessly at it, with the water choking his mouth and siphoning in his nose and retching his stomach. Things jumped ij [sic] lakes of autumn leaves all about him, there was a pattering down of leaves in the wake of something skittering away, a lizard, a rabbit; a deer, nearby, a whirling about and a rustle, a stir, a whisper. And out of the black marble wall immediately in front of him, a shape. And in the shape, two eyes. The two eyes looking at him. The night looking at him. The forest looking at him.

The Hound! Good Christ, the Hound!

After all the running and all the floating away, the sweating it out and the half-drowning, to come this far and work this hard, and think yourself safe and sigh with relief and come out on the land at last, and what do you find?

The Hound.

Montag gave one last agonized shout as if this were too much, too much for any man.

And the shape exploded away through the trees, the eyes were

Too much land.

Out of the black wall before him, a whisper. A shape. In the shape, two eyes. The night looking at him. The forest, seeing him.

The Hound!

Montag gave one last agonized shout as if this were too much for any man.

The shape exploded away. The eyes vanished. The leaf-piles flew up in a dry shower.

Montag was alone in the wilderness.

gone, and the leaf-piles were cut
aside in a dry shower.
     Montag was left alone in the
wilderness.

Bradbury's intermediate stage of revision inserts a white textual blank space
between too much water and too much land (fig. 9). By textually "spacing" the
shock of Montag's return to land, Bradbury foregrounds the breaks in perception and sensation evident in such an experience: land is first described in terms
of water—of a tidal wave, of a threatened drowning in sensations—instead of
being presented with its own proper imagery because Montag has not yet learned
the meaning of the earth. Bradbury had not been concerned with the structure
of his text when he initially wrote "Long after Midnight" or even "The Fireman."
But as the latter became *Fahrenheit 451*, he paid attention even to the spacing of
his text. Bradbury's revisions here represent a conscious use of the play of textuality that creates an invitation to readers to "fill in" the blanks with their own
imaginations. In many ways these literary reveries were the most significant thematic additions Bradbury made between the published texts of "The Fireman"
and *Fahrenheit*. (We will discuss below a significant reverie of snow that was left
out of the published novel and indicate what was to have been its function in the
text's developing thematic structure.)

     As one might expect, Bradbury was not yet through with variations on his
first novel. For the first time in his career, he held serial and anthology reprinting rights, and in late 1953 Congdon contracted with Hugh Heffner to serialize
Fahrenheit 451 beginning in March 1954 with the second issue of *Playboy*. Heffner's
first issue had not yet reached the newsstands, but he felt that Bradbury would
help him establish the literary dimension that would put the new magazine on
par with *Argosy* and *Esquire*. The three sections of the Ballantine first-edition text
were neatly repackaged into three monthly, illustrated installments.[24]

     Bradbury had to get most of his information on these events secondhand; in
August 1953, just as he finished *Fahrenheit*, John Huston signed him to write the
screenplay for his production of *Moby Dick*. Within a month, Bradbury and his
wife had embarked for Ireland and a grueling nine-month stint with the demanding director. But Bradbury's absence did not diminish Ballantine's impressive
promotional campaign. The publisher sent out a great number of review copies
and secured excellent reviews from Orville Prescott *(New York Times)* and Gilbert
Highet *(Harper's)*. The usually supportive Anthony Boucher and his *Fantasy and
Science Fiction* coeditor Mick McComas wrote the only negative reviews of note,
though Boucher wrote his friend to explain his rationale. Ballantine's 5,000 hardbound printing was released simultaneously with 250,000 paperback copies;

Mugnaini prepared slightly different jacket and cover illustrations, but both featured burning paper-clothed figures of the fireman that would become as famous as the book itself. There was a signed limited edition, and about fifty copies were bound in asbestos boards for collectors.

Ballantine's long-range objective was to sustain a steady seller like *Fahrenheit* through paperback sales, but he would follow the example of Rupert Hart-Davis when it came time to reprint. The British edition did not include the two stories that by now were so heavily overshadowed by the title novel, and Ballantine removed them from all subsequent paperback printings as well. The American hardbound edition was soon out of print—and it remains (along with Ballantine's hardbound first edition of *The October Country*) one of Bradbury's most elusive editions. The 1966 François Truffaut film provided an opportunity for Bradbury to bring *Fahrenheit* back into hardbound availability, and in 1967 Simon and Schuster (Bradbury's primary publisher during the 1960s) brought out a new edition that included the two stories. The fortieth-anniversary edition (1993) represents the only other trade hardbound version in America; Simon and Schuster followed the pattern of other *Fahrenheit* publishers by removing the two stories.

The mass-market paperback soon became a campus classic as well. It has never been out of print but was, unknown to Bradbury or the general public, censored from the mid-1960s through the 1970s. The problem had arisen with Ballantine's 1967 release of the Bal-Hi imprint of *Fahrenheit* along with a number of literary classics for high schools. In 1983 George Guffey collated the first paperback edition (released simultaneously with the hardcover in 1953) against the forty-fourth printing (1977) and found that "by that date fifty-two pages of *Fahrenheit 451* had been completely reset and that, in the process, ninety-eight non-authoritative, substantive changes had been made in the text."[25] Guffey's analysis reveals that the substantive changes involved in this edition (misleadingly listed as a "revised" edition on the copyright page of some printings) included the deletion of expletives, oaths, and references (no matter how subtle) to nudity, drinking, and abortion (see fig. 10). Meanwhile, Ballantine continued to publish the mainline paperback in its original form until 1973, when printings were exhausted; for the next six years, printings of the Bal-Hi censored text were also sold in standard mass-market wrappers. During this period, no uncensored paperback copies were in print. Students brought this fact to the author's attention, and in 1979 Bradbury had Ballantine restore the text to its original form and include an author's afterword discussing this incident in all subsequent printings.

Ballantine eventually released a trade paperback (1996) and now keeps reliable texts of both the mass-market and trade paperback editions in print. The Bradbury-Ballantine association extends beyond this single enduring title, though. In 1955 Ballantine published many of Bradbury's *Dark Carnival* stories (along

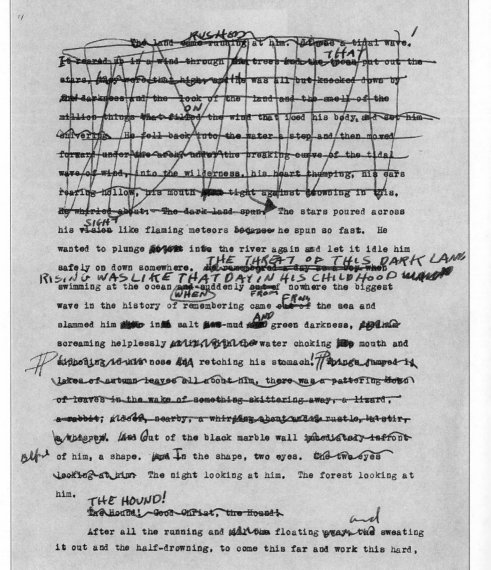

Figure 9. Three stages of revision show how Bradbury's "emotional blaze" of sustained rewriting transitioned into careful revision as he shaped Montag's landfall scene for *Fahrenheit 451*. The first two leaves (from the Fullerton deposit) represent glimpses of the intensive nine-day rewrite and the first revision; the final leaf is from the first ribbon copy of the typescript that Bradbury submitted in stages between June and August 1953. Note Bradbury's instruction to insert space to set off the tranquil water experience from the traumatic return to the reality of the shore. Images courtesy of the Pollak Library, California State University at Fullerton, and Donn Albright; used by permission of Ray Bradbury.

This was all that he wanted now. Some sign that
the immense world would accept him and give him the LONG time ~~that~~

he needed to think all the things that must be thought.

A glass of milk, an apple, a pear.

(SPACE)

He stepped ~~out of~~ FROM the river. ~~and stood on the~~
~~bank.~~

The land rushed at him, a tidal wave. ~~reared up~~
~~by a wind through the trees that put out the stars.~~ He was ~~all~~
~~but knocked down~~ CRUSHED by darkness and the look of the country and
the million odors on the wind that iced his ~~wet~~ body. He fell
back ~~toward the river.~~ ~~Then he moved forward~~ under the breaking
curve ~~of the wave~~ of darkness and sound and smell, ~~into the~~ his
~~wilderness.~~ ~~His~~ ears roar~~ed~~ing, ~~his heart pounded.~~ He whirled ~~to~~
~~stare now here, now there.~~ The stars poured over his sight like
flaming meteors. He wanted to plunge in the river again and
let it idle him safely on down somewhere. This dark land rising
was like that da y in his childhood, swimming, when from nowhere
the largest wave in the history of remembering slammed him down
in salt mud and green darkness, water burning mouth and nose,
retching his stomach, screaming! Too much water!

Too much land.

Out of the black wall before him, a whisper. A shape.
In the shape, two eyes. The night looking at him. The forest,
seeing him.

The Hound!

After all the running and rushing and sweating it out
and half-drowning, to come this far, work this hard, and think

He stepped from the river.

The land rushed at him, a tidal wave. He was
crushed by darkness and the look of the country and the
million odors on a wind that iced his body. He fell back
under the breaking curve of darkness and sound and smell,
his ears roaring. He whirled. The stars poured over his
sight like flaming meteors. He wanted to plunge in the
river again and let it idle him safely on down somewhere.
This dark land rising was like that day in his childhood,
swimming, when from nowhere the largest wave in the
history of remembering slammed him down in salt mud and
green darkness, water burning mouth and nose, retching
his stomach, screaming! Too much water!

Too much land.

Out of the black wall before him, a whisper. A
shape. In the shape, two eyes. The night looking at
him. The forest, seeing him.

The Hound!

After all the running and rushing and sweating
it out and half-drowning, to come this far, work this hard,
and think and think yourself safe and sigh with relief and
come out on the land at last only to find . . .

The Hound!

Montag gave one last agonized shout as if this
were too much for any man.

and the 'family'. That's awful! Think of our investment. Why should I read? What *for*?"

"What for! Why!" said Montag. "I saw the damnedest snake in the world the other night. It was dead but it was alive. It could see but it couldn't see. You want to *see* that snake? It's at Emergency Hospital where they filed a report on all the junk the snake got out of you! Would you like to go and check their file? Maybe you'd look under Guy Montag or maybe under Fear or War. Would you like to go to that house that burnt last night? And rake ashes for the bones of the woman who set fire to her own house! What about Clarisse McClellan, where do we look for her? The morgue! Listen!"

The bombers crossed the sky and crossed the sky over the house, gasping, murmuring, whistling like an immense, invisible fan, circling in emptiness.

"Jesus God," said Montag. "Every hour so many damn things in the sky! How in hell did those bombers get up there every single second of our lives! Why doesn't someone want to talk about it! We've started and won two atomic wars since 1960! Is it because we're having so much fun at home we've forgotten the world? Is it because we're so rich and the rest of the world's so poor and we just don't care if they are? I've heard rumors; the world is starving, but we're well-fed. Is it true, the world works hard and we play? Is that why we're hated so much? I've heard the rumors about hate, too, once in a long while, over the years. Do *you* know why? *I* don't, that's *sure*! Maybe the books can get us half out of the cave. They just *might* stop us from making the same damn insane mistakes! I don't hear those idiot bastards in your parlor talking about it. God, Millie, don't you *see*? An hour a day, two hours, with these books, and maybe . . ."

The telephone rang. Mildred snatched the phone.

"Ann!" She laughed. "Yes, the White Clown's on tonight!"

Montag walked to the kitchen and threw the book

and the family.' That's awful! Think of our investment. Why should I read? What *for*?"

"What for! Why!" said Montag. "I saw the craziest snake in the world the other night. It was dead but it was alive. It could see but it couldn't see. You want to *see* that snake? It's at Emergency Hospital where they filed a report on all the junk the snake got out of you! Would you like to go and check their file? Maybe you'd look under Guy Montag or maybe under Fear or War. Would you like to go to that house that burnt last night? And rake ashes for the bones of the woman who set fire to her own house! What about Clarisse McClellan, where do we look for her? The morgue! Listen!"

The bombers crossed the sky and crossed the sky over the house, gasping, murmuring, whistling like an immense, invisible fan, circling in emptiness.

"Every hour so many things in the sky!" said Montag. "How did those bombers get up there every single second of our lives! Why doesn't some one want to talk about it! We've started and won two atomic wars. Is it because we're having so much fun at home we've forgotten the world? Is it because we're so rich and the rest of the world's so poor and we just don't care if they are? I've heard rumors; the world is starving, but we're well-fed. Is it true, the world works hard and we play? Is that why we're hated so much? I've heard the rumors about hate, too, once in a long while, over the years. Do *you* know why? *I* don't, that's *sure*! Maybe the books can get us half out of the cave. They just *might* stop us from making the same insane mistakes! I don't hear those idiots in your parlor talking about it. Millie, don't you *see*? An hour a day, two hours, with these books, and maybe . . ."

The telephone rang. Mildred snatched the phone.

"Ann!" She laughed. "Yes, the White Clown's on tonight!"

Montag walked to the kitchen and threw the book

Figure 10. A page (above left) from Ballantine's first paperback edition of *Fahrenheit 451* (1953) is compared to the unpublicized resetting of the same page for the printings marketed from 1967 to 1977 as the Bal-Hi "edition." Between 1973 and 1979, the censored text also silently replaced all mass-market printings. Lines of text in the Bal-Hi edition (above right) containing points of variation include lines 1–3, 17, 18, 20, 30, and 31.

with four of the six pieces that were not ready in time for the *Fahrenheit* collection) as *The October Country*. Comic adaptations of many of these weirds were successfully marketed in two further Ballantine paperback collections a decade later (*Tomorrow Midnight* and *The Autumn People*). Although Bradbury would publish most of his major titles with other publishers over his long career, his first Ballantine title remains one of the most universally recognized books of the twentieth century.

Thematics

The main target of *Fahrenheit 451* is not censorship, as is often supposed, but rather mass culture, which Bradbury subjects to a Freudian critique like that given by Theodor W. Adorno and Max Horkeimer in *Dialectic of Enlightenment*.[26] *Fahrenheit* extrapolates into the future certain trends of the American cultural industry (*Kulturindustrie*—the term is Theodor W. Adorno's) observable during the 1950s, particularly the penetration of advertising and marketing techniques into every sphere of society. A central conviction of the book, as it was of "The Firemen," is that enlightenment and our increasingly rationalized civilization have produced not liberation, but further alienation.

The novel shows more clearly than the novella the antilife tendencies latent in what Adorno and Horkeimer call the enlightenment project, tendencies that can only culminate in the reduction of all higher values to a "paste pudding norm," as Captain Beatty, the defender of the status quo, succinctly puts it. Against this tendency toward "normalcy" and universalizing norms, Bradbury pits the protagonist, Montag, who wants to desire differently, not from lack and pseudoneeds created by the culture industry, but from plenitude of the will. The novel explores more fully than the novella the alternative possibilities of desiring things in a different way, suggesting to the reader through reveries of the material imagination an alternative to the values posited by mass culture. In effect, Montag's reveries of the earth help heal the split between man and nature, which rational enlightenment and science have brought about. The book ends by affirming the importance of the earth, which rises, phoenixlike, from the flames of mankind's self-destructive nihilism.

Thus, in its final and published form, *Fahrenheit 451* enacts a three-part diagnosis of the disease of modern man known as nihilism in its complete and incomplete varieties. The first part shows the hero becoming sick, the second deals with his rebellion and search for an antidote, and the third with a revaluation of values in which we learn the true worth of the principles put forth in the second part: the value of literacy, books, and reading in mass culture.

The medical terminology of sickness and health is consonant with Bradbury's own thematics in the novel. Indeed, there is a prominent thematic code in the book that organizes poisons and antidotes, infections and cures, and painkillers and stimulants, particularly with regard to the human bloodstream (as a metaphor for instinctive knowledge) and the stomach (as the capacity to digest or incorporate alien elements), which doubles as an indicator of moral strength, health, and sanity.

Once "infected" with the fever to read the books he normally burns, Montag the fireman is led on a search to find the origin of his unhappiness, and this leads him through certain stages of nihilism (discussed in detail below). However paradoxical it may sound at the outset of this discussion, what Montag discovers is that enlightenment must include a reversal of itself, that is, there should be a limit on enlightenment. He realizes that total science as an ideal leads to nihilism just as surely as Christian otherworldliness does. But any attempt to escape nihilism—understood here in the sense of the negation of the will to live—without reevaluating values simply produces the opposite, making the problem worse. Passing through pessimism, Montag at the end learns wisdom, what Nietzsche called the meaning of the earth, and thereby sets the limits of knowledge at what can be made instinctive, part of a bodily self, reflected symbolically in the bloodstream.

The philosophical position reached at the end, when Montag is living among a group of nomadic book-people, is best described as a determination to admit the necessity of constant revaluation to ourselves without any reservation, to stop telling ourselves tales in the old way. Hence the sense of pathos we feel in some of the speeches made by Granger, the spokesman of the itinerant book-people, a pathos that impels us to seek *new values* not necessarily defined, but nonetheless adumbrated by the novel itself. We learn that the world might be more valuable than once believed; we must see through the human tendency to make ideals fixed and eternal, for that is a denial of life and becoming. While we thought that we accorded the world the highest interpretation and value (the reader's experience in part 2, "The Sieve and the Sand"), we actually may not have given our existence even a moderately fair value.

To trace the itinerary of this revaluation and its stages is our task here. In the opening scene the landscape of this fantastic world is infested with a poisonous mythical monster, the salamander (metaphor for the fire engine) with its hose, described as a "great python spitting its venomous kerosene upon the world." We meet Montag, the agent of this poisoning, whose job it is to burn books that contain the memory of the past, the record of what different men and women have said and done throughout history. He destroys anything that might contradict the state's will to normalize and universalize truth, that is, that everything should be reduced to the thinkable in terms of mass norms. What remains is what Captain Beatty himself, in his own unwittingly ironic way, calls "noncombustible data," the facts of positivism that are supposed to make the people of this society feel brilliant without the need for interpretation.

At the outset, Montag is close to being a pyromaniac. He presides over a comic ritual that provides a carnival for the mass media to televise. Essentially, his nighttime job is entertainment in a society of spectacles, and he thoroughly identifies with it: the poisonous kerosene is perfume to him; a permanent fiery smile grips his face like a mask; and he winks at himself in the fire station mirror, his face burnt black, a minstrel man. When Montag meets his teenage neighbor, Clarisse, however, things begin to change. She has an impish sense of humor unknown to him (her "insanity," as she calls it) and little overt respect for the uniform he wears and its emblems of authority. Her constant wonder and curiosity, her intense *aliveness,* wakens Montag to a real world of sensations outside his ego's identification with its social role. Her function is to activate the dreaming pole of Montag's consciousness, long repressed by this technological society, and to stimulate reveries of the material imagination.

But her observations are also crucial to Montag's unmasking. She tells him, for example, that her education consists of "a lot of funnels and a lot of water poured down the spout and out the bottom, and them telling us it's wine when it's not"; wine is a symbol of health in this novel, as elsewhere in Bradbury. Clarisse diagnoses Montag with a dandelion flower, revealing to him that he really does not love anyone, that unhappiness is his true state of being. She runs off "across the lawn with the mask" that is his social persona, precipitating Montag's first reveries. She also tells him about a fireman who committed suicide by setting a mechanical hound against himself. Semiotically, the hound is one of the most overcoded bearers of the health-sickness distinction. It is an uncanny embodiment of the society's existential problems, which it has tried to banish by means of "healthful" technology, yet the "hounds" have come home, "full of poison wildness, of insanity and nightmare"; it murders its "sick" victims with a numbing dose of procaine. Because of her healthy family environment (which includes, according to her, being spanked when she needed it), Clarisse has been able to resist being shaped by the mass media. It is she who "infects" Montag with the desire to read the books he burns and the need to regain his psychic health.

Montag's wife, Mildred, is the thematic opposite of Clarisse. She embodies just about every form of self-narcotization available in this society and just about every way of avoiding the will to live and its affirmations. Deep down she is empty, suicidal, cruel. She attempts to hide this emptiness by various forms of artificial intoxication. Mildred keeps a miniature radio tamped in her ear at all times. She communicates with Montag by lip reading (training in such a skill having been thoughtfully supplied by the Sea Shell Company). She drives her car down the highways at tremendous rates of speed, hoping to kill an animal or, better yet, a human being. Mildred possesses a blind narcissistic enthusiasm for identifying with "exotic people's lives." Most of all she wants to buy another telescreen for their house, a fourth wall, to "make the dream complete." In appearance she is as thin as a praying mantis from dieting, her hair burnt to a brittle straw by dyeing, and her flesh described as the color of white bacon—not a healthy type to be sure. Mildred is a victim of mass culture and advertising that define desire as a lack and the consumer as someone whose desires can never be fulfilled. When Montag returns home after the book's opening conflagration and his encounter with Clarisse, he finds that his wife has attempted suicide by taking an overdose of sleeping pills. Later she is restored to "health" by an antisuicide team and its machine, which fills her veins with the blood of a stranger. After this experience, Montag's faith in his marriage is profoundly shaken. He wonders whether he really knows this rosy-cheeked woman, or she him. He goes to sleep himself by taking a pill, saying that he does not know anything anymore.

This is the first stage of disorientation associated with nihilism. The second phase begins with Montag's growing alienation from his job, an alienation made complete after an incident in which an old woman chooses to die in the fire that destroys her house and hidden library rather than be taken to the insane asylum. While looting the ruins, Montag is seized with an uncontrollable desire to steal a book for himself after a falling volume accidentally lights in his hand, exposing its beautiful snowy pages painted with words. In this brief moment Montag is able to read one line of the book (which may possibly be a book of fairy tales). It is enough to convince him that there must be something in books that, once experienced, makes living life without them meaningless. He realizes that there is a person, an author behind every book.

As Nietzsche observed, the system of a philosopher may be dead and debunked, but the *person* behind it is incontrovertible; the person simply cannot be killed. The writer's literary force of personality continues to influence others, as Schopenhauer did Nietzsche. Books at this early stage of Montag's nihilism seem to represent a counterideal, offering a kind of transcendence. Metaphorically, books themselves are often compared to upwardly soaring birds, their pages to snowy feathers. They also seem to offer a new relationship to time—the kind of expansive and dreaming time associated with literary reverie. Soon after this incident, an intense physical need to read the books he has stolen overcomes Montag. Now he vomits at the smell of kerosene. A period of convalescence ensues during which the "fever" develops in terms of his search for new values: "So it was the hand that started it all. He felt one hand and then the other work his coat free and let it slump to the floor. He held his pants out into an abyss and let them fall into darkness. His hands had been infected, and soon it would be his arms. He could feel the poison working up his wrists and into his elbows and his shoulders, and then the jump over from shoulder blade to shoulder blade like a spark leaping a gap. His hands were ravenous. And his eyes were beginning to feel hunger, as if they must look at something, anything, everything."[27]

In his culture criticism, Nietzsche distinguishes neatly between one kind of cultural health that is defensive and restrictive and another that is marked by an abundant strength and vitality. Captain Beatty is an example of this former idea (and we will come to him presently), but this passage suggests the idea that Montag's illness will have a positive value and may even strengthen him. True, it exposes old illusions to an abyss, but it also bridges a gap between Montag and himself. Sickness is, then, actually good for him, a desirable challenge stimulating his powers. Montag now wants to see everything outside himself, is ravenously hungry for a world outside the self. Such a sickness, once overcome and incorporated, would leave him in a higher and enhanced state of health. Of course, in a sense this idea of well being collides with the romantic notion of perfect health embodied by Clarisse, for she is somehow untainted, untouched, and untroubled by any "fall" into sickness. She remains the inviolate utopian ideal of the novel, never burnt by the fireflies of any conflagration, and it seems that Bradbury, by having her die early in the novel, never seriously questions that ideal. Montag, however, has to cope with his disease (or "dis-ease," as Bradbury hyphenates it, making us read the word on the ontological level) brought on by her disappearance.

Before Montag can begin to read in earnest, however, Captain Beatty arrives to ask him when he will be well again. He gives Montag what he hopes will be an antidote for his sickness, which consists of a lesson in firemen history. Ironically, that account itself is an incisive indictment of the American culture industry. It describes the many forms of distorted communication taking place in the novel's society, from outright censorship of forbidden books to official state ideology with its leveling of all values to the unconscious and barbaric repetition of the same. Like a machine rotating on the same spot, Beatty's rhetoric gives us the impression of life and vitality, but it actually has none. It is a simulacrum of carnival, little more than a montage of superstructural effects that tells little about the basic economic conditions that led up to the present "utopia."

Beatty idolizes fire, the power of the state to reduce everything to ashy sameness and death. No minority differences are to be tolerated. Fire to him is precisely an antibiotic, an agent of stability and sanitation, for it seemingly destroys the upsurge of threatening new values. Although constantly changing and producing a fascinating world of phenomena, fire is an eternal value to him because it destroys differences. As an advocate of mass culture, he believes that everyone must be the same and desire the same things. Repetition of the same will, in turn, produces the greatest happiness for the greatest number of people. He understands Montag's attraction for books but claims that he himself overcame it. Yet significantly (and despite his apparent air of authority and even "beatitude"), he almost pleads with Montag not to allow "the torrent of melancholy and drear philosophy" to drown his happy world.

What Beatty fears most, we infer, is our present cultural situation with its conflict of interpretations. He only wants people to be crammed full of positivist facts that do not change, even though he ridicules the scientific explanation of fire in terms of friction and molecules as "gobbledygook." Facts are the important things to be desired, worn as emblems on every fireman's arm, like the fact that book paper catches fire and burns at 451 degrees Fahrenheit. His entire history is negative and defensive because he cannot affirm differences that are a result of the will to power playing itself out in events or in art. Beatty really is a nihilist. He argues that modern science has uncovered a bleak and useless existence that has made man feel only bestial and lonely. Beatty knows that man has lost dignity in his own eyes to an incredible extent in trying to equate the universe. And as for books, "Well, Montag, take my word for it, I've had to read a few in my time, to know what I was about, and the books say *nothing!* Nothing you can teach or believe. They're about nonexistent people, figments of imagination, if they're fiction. And if they're nonfiction, it's worse, one professor calling another an idiot, one philosopher screaming down another's gullet. All of them running about, putting out the stars and extinguishing the sun. You come away lost."[28]

Beatty is obsessed with the pessimistic "truth" about life but cannot see the value of literary fictions or their power as borrowed awareness. Why should we be concerned about the fate of a fictional character anyway? Beatty's philosophical position, which Nietzsche would surely have understood in all its implications as a form of nihilism, amounts to an absurd evaluation: because of their pessimism, philosophers put out fires (stars and suns) instead of igniting them as the good optimistic firemen must do. Everyone needs the firemen to provide them with a show that takes away the burden of serious meaning.

Beatty's arguments defend a stage of nihilism Nietzsche calls "the last man."[29] To get an understanding of this stage, one must recall what Nietzsche says about the development of nihilism, which, by the way, he regards as the normal condition of man in culture, for he argues that it is in some fashion always present, *always* at work, before, during, and after the moment of its violent explosion.[30] But insofar as it is the peculiar disease of contemporary man (one requiring a homeopathic remedy), nihilism is also a passing pathological condition. At first, then, it is the disguised expression of a decadent will, of the impotent will to power recoiling from the affirmation of life and changing into negation. At this stage it may appear as the affirmation of grand supersensible values, the Platonic realm of ideas, which also supposedly possesses eternal being. In Nietzsche's view nihilism reactively creates a "true world" that possesses all the attributes life does not have: unity, stability, identity, and such, hence the division into two worlds, appearance and reality, that devalues life in favor of the otherworldly.

According to Nietzsche, as one goes through history, one finds the latent will for negation becoming more and more evident as more and more idols are smashed and replaced with new—and supposedly eternal—ones. The highest values constantly devaluate themselves, until humanity approaches the radical repudiation of all meaning, value, and desirability (see introduction, fig. 2). Eventually, man comes to be so haunted by his own iconoclastic act that he cannot venerate himself, although he was powerful enough to kill God and to put science, or the modern technocratic state, in his place. This is roughly the stage Beatty claims to have passed through. Overtly, he confesses to no disgust with man anymore because he has found the true happiness of life in sameness, in mass culture. Paradoxically, the security of this happiness is derived from a perverse form of reading books that is also a fantastic reversal of enlightenment, in the sense that it idolizes fire and the way fire "consumes" meaning: "He could hear Beatty's voice. 'Sit down, Montag. Watch. Delicately, like the petals of a flower. Light the first page, light the second page. Each becomes a black butterfly. Beautiful, eh? Light the third page from the second and so on, chain smoking, chapter by chapter, all the silly things the words mean, all the false promises, all the second-hand notions and time-worn philosophies.' There sat Beatty, perspiring gently, the floor littered with swarms of black moths that had died in a single storm."[31]

How is this nihilistic happiness in reading to be understood? Certainly, chain smoking is a metaphor for the type of habituated mentality this society is seeking to produce in its consumers. Very little consciousness is required. What is more, here Beatty is doing it for spectacle, showing Montag the progressive consumption of everything having meaning, the growing predominance of empty significations, leading to the indefinite collapse and debacle of all meaning, all the "false promises" and "time-worn" philosophies of the past. The spiritual nihilism of the last man is ironically a product of the promise of the Enlightenment, here symbolized by man's technological control over fire.[32]

One possible interpretation here is that Beatty is parodying the determinate negation of significations that could be subsumed in a dialectical logic of enlightenment (such as that of Hegel). Instead of meaning being enriched by intellectual contradictions, Beatty's nihilistic reading transforms negations into unreadable black butterflies, which furthermore he finds beautiful. It is interesting to note that in the original typescript of the submitted novel, Bradbury had written "fantasies" after "false promises," which if left in would have served to make all the more clear Beatty's hostility to literary fantasy, which can represent a promise as broken (utopian longing can be evoked as unfulfilled). Beatty is one of those who teach contentment through the given norms of society, in this case supported by a cultural industry in which the firemen form a carnivalized sideshow.

The experience of true carnival, however, is not tainted with nihilism. Bradbury's thematics of fantasy in this utopian novel actually depends on the reader recognizing a distinction between two modes of fantasy: the spectacles of the mass media—the simulacrum of carnival—that promise satisfaction but in reality only serve to create anxiety about one's self-image by making an appeal to primitive narcissism, and literary reverie, which represents satisfaction and fulfillment not as a "false" promise, but as a "broken" promise, thereby putting the reader in a negative, or critical, position with regards to the former type of fantasy. The latter type represents true carnival because it creates new values and leads to a healthy (that is, not repressed) self. Clearly, Beatty does not want new values, only their repression. Like a moth fatally attracted to light, Beatty plays out all the dangers inherent in the Western program of enlightenment, which has tended to create a separation of our consciousness from nature through domination. But in the true body of carnival, man is a part of the natural world and the rhythms of life and death.

According to Nietzsche, this acute form of nihilism may abruptly alter its mood or tone, ceasing to be anxious inquietude, becoming instead a complacent quietude. Clearly, Beatty tries to convert Montag from the former to the latter by giving him a lesson in fireman history. He tries to sell his comrade on the idea of being a fireman again, to convert him back to the same. Thus, despite his idolization of fire—which would seem to present a world of changing and novel phenomena—his is really an appeal to sameness. We have in Beatty the experience of a will satisfied with meaninglessness, with nonsense, a will happy that there is no longer any meaning to seek, a will having found a certain comfort in the total absence of meaning and a happiness in the certainty that there is no answer to the question "What for?" He has become Nietzsche's "last man." Frozen at the stage of passive nihilism, rendered uniform, equal, and level, Beatty thinks he has invented happiness. But as Montag realizes in the climactic moment of the novel, *Beatty wants to die.* He deliberately provokes Montag into killing him with a flamethrower. Beatty's happiness is revealed as only apparently beatific. After the lecture, Montag allows that the captain is perhaps right—what is important is happiness. But this thought comes rather from the recognition that Montag himself is not, in fact, happy.

Bradbury constantly represents unhappiness in *Fahrenheit 451* as an emptiness that needs to be filled. Traditionally, beatitude has always been conceived of as a final state. It is always at the end of a certain "itinerary of the soul" that we find it as the fine flower consummating a great labor achieved. Yet happiness for Bradbury must come from affirmation and not negation, not as the end of a process oriented by some desired (and lost) object. Note that in the passage cited above, Beatty's nihilistic happiness-in-reading is also metaphorically a defloration of the text. The pages of the text are first petals that become black butterflies. That Bradbury wants to reject this idea of happiness along with Beatty is made evident in a scene in part 2 where the captain tells Montag of a dream of beatitude. His dream takes the form of a rhetorical battle of citations, with Montag trying to defend the integrity and ideal meaning of literature and Beatty taking the opposite tactic in quoting the books against themselves, displaying, in effect, his interpretive power over the text of this dream. By showing Montag that books can contradict themselves, Beatty apparently wins the battle and seems to stand on the side of reason. The dream ends with Montag climbing on board the salamander with Beatty and the both of them driving back to the firehouse "in beatific silence, all dwindled away to peace." In actuality, they drive off to burn Montag's own house, for Mildred has turned in the alarm on him.

Interestingly, when Bradbury read this novel for Harper Audio, he was careful to pronounce "Beatty" with three syllables so that it sounded like "beatitude." To Nietzsche, of course, an end to the freeplay of interpretation would be precisely an end to life: "There is no solely beatifying interpretation."[33] Although Bradbury may seem to side with Beatty in the sense that he too argues that texts need interpretation, in the end, he wants us to see Beatty's blissfulness as a manifestation of the death instinct, the silent instinct, the end to culture. In thus rejecting Beatty and his beatific readings of literature, we experience a major reversal of values, which prepares the way for a transformation of beatitude from a final to an initial state from which true happiness can then flow. We meet several of these states of being in part 3 of the novel, "Burning Bright."

These moments of plenitude and happiness are presented as "reveries of the material imagination" (the term is Gaston Bachelard's) when the human will spontaneously expresses itself in archetypal images—earth, air, fire, and water. Reverie is the primary means by which the reader, following Montag, explores the natural world and experiences imaginative forces that can create a human relationship to it. The absorption of the subject in fantasy into a material substance is experienced as a dynamic joy that participates in the life of that substance. Literary reverie becomes an act of consciousness by which the imagination overcomes alienation by *becoming* the world.

Before Bachelard's work on the material imagination, critics devoted little interest to Nietzsche's imagery, treating books such as *Thus Spoke Zarathustra* as primarily moral tracts. But Bachelard took Nietzsche's poetic images to be the very substance of his philosophical thought. For example, in his monograph on the German philosopher, Bachelard argues that the first transmutation of values experienced in *Zarathustra* is a transmutation of images. Reverie prepares the reader to experience the moral world of the text. Bachelard has no trouble in showing how and why Nietzsche devotes all his lyrical energy in the book to a change from heavy to light, from the terrestrial climate to the aerial. This creates for the reader a sense of overcoming the spirit of gravity, his primary antagonist. Cold, silence, and height are the components of what Bachelard calls Nietzsche's "oneiric temperament," the favorite region of the imagination in which he finds the image of his will. As he deftly says of the whole dialogic process, "Nietzsche gave the abyss the language of the summits" (*Il a fait parler aux abîmes le langage des sommets*).[34]

Similarly, in *Fahrenheit 451*, reveries of the will and material images are linked to the revaluation of values. They are active at all points in the text—especially in the fire imagery—at various levels of reader awareness. The imagery system of the novel has been a subject of interest among thematic critics, who have demonstrated the extensive use of images drawn from the elements of fire and water, though without linking them to values.[35] Mildred's *ressentiment*, for example, is a poisonous matter that accumulates like green stagnant water to which the eye of technology, as the embodiment of logical techniques, is blind. Fire is initially a force of negation that denies life and history. But in the third part of the novel, Montag experiences a series of reveries that reverse the values associated with these elements. In fact, it is by discovering how to dream well and in becoming master of his reveries that Montag satisfies that intense hunger for material images Clarisse had awakened in him, that is, those leading to a world outside the self. As he floats down a river away from the city, Montag learns to think about time in a reverie that restores his dynamic will to live, giving new values to fire and water. Later, he imagines himself taking on an animal's shape in the forest—thereby recovering his instinctive nature—and discovers a reverie of the forge that restores the power of language, so distorted in the city, to its proper capacity to reveal the meaning of things.

Here it is important to note that reverie is one of the ways in which Bradbury expanded "The Fireman" into a novel that itself brings neglected states of mind to light. Indeed, reverie plays no significant role in the novella, which is mainly concerned with a direct critique of mass culture. To present an alternative to mass culture, in later versions Bradbury greatly expanded the role of Clarisse as an agent of literary reverie. For instance, in the submitted manuscript of August 1953, Bradbury explicitly links the vision of the firelit camp (with the forge as the archetype structuring it) to Clarisse and to the conversations Montag heard while listening outside her house, especially "the rising falling voice of her uncle going on and on, comfortably, warmly, strangely, with wonder and fascination, in the late hours of the night." The entire paragraph makes clear the connection between reverie and the creative use of the powers of language. Although this was deleted in the finished novel, Montag still observes, just before he discovers the campfire, that Clarisse "had walked along here, where he was walking now."

One of the other striking omissions from the published version is a snow reverie that follows the destruction of the city. It is clear from the submitted manuscript that Bradbury originally intended the reveries of the earth that Montag experiences after emerging from the river to threaten to overwhelm him with sensations: "Where did you start? How did you keep your head above the surface of so much to learn? In a silence that was no silence, filled with a thousand wrigglings and shifting, crawlings, with burrowings and flakes of darkness touching at your face, moths, mosquitoes, flies, did you stop at your mouth and nose and eyes and die? Or did you stand, as he was now standing, and let it cover you until you were at the bottom of a stone well of odors and colors and shapes and blowing sounds?"

This passage presents an existential problem, which is also one of knowledge. Montag hungers for a healthful relationship with the earth, yet how can he manage the sensations that it brings? Two paths of struggle with these sensations, both equally fatal to the self, seem open. The first reverie is still based on water, keeping one's head above the surface and one's mouth and nose closed to sensations so that one eventually dies. The other is based on the archetype of the stone well, of water contained in the earth (remember that Montag has just emerged from water) and also leads to a kind of passivity and inundation. It is important to note the thematic paradoxes here: the earth is filled with threatening sensations leading to death and a "silence that was no silence." How does one silence this silence of the earth? How does one make it healthful, poetic, and meaningful?

Partly, this is accomplished by the reverie of the forge, which contains "a silence gathered all about that fire and the silence was in the men's faces, and time was there." This reverie of the forge (which Bachelard discussed as belonging to the thematics of the earth) is in both the novella and novel, but Bradbury no doubt felt the need for a stronger counter-reverie to nature's powers in the submitted manuscript. This took the form of an imagined snowfall, which becomes the very pattern of Montag's thought, truly silencing the earth:

> Montag watched the blood drip from his nose into the earth. He saw the pattern of his thoughts, stunned, shake down. Now it was the faintest blow of snowflakes on the first morning of great falling softness and silence when you squint to see the fine snow in the air and think it'll cover the ground. But it touches ground and vanishes as if eaten by the grass, but that's all right, there's more snow falling and falling, more tiny flecks fluttering

down and you know that if you wait on it patiently there will be the first thin shell of rime and then a sugar-crust and then a thick frosting and then an abundance, enough thoughts and enough thinking in your head so you'll have enough clear drinking water as long as you wish, when ever you want to gather and melt it. The first snow was falling now, in his head.

Since the goal of this reverie is to get the earth and its plurality of meanings into the bloodstream in a healthful way, the passage begins with Montag dripping his own blood into the soil, beginning a kind of dynamic exchange and struggle with nature. This act of sacrifice generates the "pattern of his thoughts" that is equated with snowfall, which is thematically the anti-terrestrial matter Montag needs. Many poets whose imaginations have been attracted to snow have written about how it covers the ground with a whiteness and silence that truly overcomes its meanings, and reveries of snow in literature often manifest the spirit of negation, overturning, and conversion.[36] But Bradbury develops these literary and philosophical meanings in his own unique way. In his reverie the light snow is at first threatened by the grass, which might eat it, but as more falls the values are reversed until the snow becomes a delicious and life-sustaining food. Water is present in potential abundance; it can be eaten whenever Montag wants. Note too the phonetic prominence of the letter f alliterating throughout the passage— faintest, fluttering, falling, flecks—a snowfall of new meaning gathers itself in these words. This is more than just the use of a poetic technique. Matter and thought completely interpenetrate with language: "the first snow was falling now in his head." Bradbury's snowfall reverie equates the pattern of thought present in the image with the language of the text and with fullness of being, with plenitude and clear thought (drinking water).

But Bradbury removed the need for this imaginative counter-reverie when he toned down the threatening nature of the earth for the published version. A complete thematic reading of these passages is beyond the scope of this study. We can, however, give one brief example of language and reverie in the novel that will serve to show how the latter is tied thematically to moral and social codes as well as other texts in a poetic tradition.

American society as depicted in the novel has ceased to be sustained by any organized religion offering a center of meaning outside the self. Nothing replaces this loss of a center, but the mass media has set up grandiose narcissistic images of the self in the form of television media "families" who simulate happiness. Under these cultural circumstances Bradbury contrives to have his protagonist read out loud from the last two stanzas of Matthew Arnold's "Dover Beach," the most commented on poem in the English language. In Montag's society, this constitutes an open act of rebellion. He is asked by one of Mildred's uneasy guests whether or not the presence of the book indicates that he is reading up on "fire-man theory." Montag responds by saying that it is not theory but poetry that the book represents.

The effect of this reading on Mildred and her friends, who are accustomed only to gratifying themselves obliviously with the latest "Clara Dove five-minute romance" on the wall-size television screens, is stunning. One woman sobs un-controllably for her husband lost in the previous war, and another becomes enraged at being exposed to so much "poetry and sickness." Montag himself is overcome by the sudden appearance of authentic communication in the midst of the "empty desert," which is how Bradbury describes Montag's living room when the telescreens are turned off, and the idle chatter stops. It is important to understand here that Arnold's poem has come to signify, for us, the whole problem of modernity: in Nietzschean terms, how does one live meaningfully after the decline of religious beliefs (the death of God) and the demise of the Christian worldview that assigned humanity a clear place in creation? Science is no answer, for it too, as Captain Beatty indicates, only reveals a universe in which nature is indifferent to mankind's purposes.

Is literature then an answer? Is Bradbury appropriating Arnold's poem nos-talgically, yearning after a lost center of culture, longing for some ideal of com-munication whose origins lie in the past? Yes, but only partially. Bradbury is also showing us the real value of "Dover Beach" for our age of mass communications. Arnold subscribed to a liberal ideal of radiant literacy. He conceived of culture as a pursuit of our total perfection based, in part, on our getting to know the best that has been thought and spoken in the past (his famous "touchstones"). Furthermore, for Arnold, culture meant criticism, especially when these touch-stones are applied to the present; without it, man remains a creature limited by self-satisfaction. This ideal of culture and criticism is surely Bradbury's own in the novel, for he makes Arnold's poem resonate in new ways. Unlike the debased romanticism of Clara Dove, Arnold's poem definitely does not have a happy end-ing and therefore no overt appeal to narcissism (though the reverie of the Sea of Faith evokes melancholy to be sure). The speaker of Arnold's poem is trying to enunciate to his beloved how he authentically feels about the state of the world and the possibilities for communication in it, the world that seems to lie before them like a land of dreams but that really has neither joy, nor love, nor peace in it. He has to emerge from darkness to see the landscape that lies about him and to see himself in that landscape.

The poem becomes an instance of the authentic use of language to communi-cate emotions between people. "Fireman theory" will not be capable of explaining away the powerful feelings it evokes. One of the most influential modern theories of literature, Russian formalism, argues that art and its techniques are designed to slow down perception and make us perceive again with a fresh vision what has become worn out and stale, second nature. By building such an interpretive frame around the reading of Arnold's poem, Bradbury, in essence, tells us that as long as humanity remembers one poem from the best of our literature, the effects of habituation, which threaten like fire to devour families, friends, and even fear of war, will find it more difficult to settle in. In particular, the last line of Arnold's poem about ignorant armies clashing by night is "defamiliarized" and rings true in a new way for this society, which has fought and quickly forgotten three atomic wars in the recent past.

The simulacrum of carnival—including three-dimensional "sex magazines"—has almost completely supplanted "authentic" and difficult philosophical meanings evoked by literature such as "Dover Beach." Beatty's earlier comment to Montag that "pleasure lies all about after work" in forms of mass entertainment is probably an ironic echo of the famous line in Arnold's poem about the world lying before the lovers "like a land of dreams." This cultural situation of absolute vulgarity and violence is something Bradbury seems to have been thinking about early in his career and well before the publication of "The Fireman." Among his unpublished novel projects dating from 1947 is *Where Ignorant Armies Clash by Night*, which depicts a situation of near absolute nihilism and vulgarity (in the planned last chapter, published in 1952 as "The Smile," people line up to spit on the Mona Lisa). The story is set in a barren postapocalyptic United States two centuries in the future, in which cultural values have been profoundly inverted. Society is held together by ritualized Roman circuslike ceremonies in which people are murdered by the Assassins, or Great Killers, a guild of honored warrior-killers who also—and this is its thematic link with *Fahrenheit 451*—burn and mutilate books for the adoring crowds. The last copy of the Bible is scheduled to be destroyed during an upcoming carnival in New Orleans. Books have become the center and focus of the democratic crowd's hatred for "elite" culture (such as Shakespeare). The plot in one version has the assassin Muerte—like Montag—begin reading the books he is destroying. This reading in turn provokes a profound crisis of values in which the hero revolts against the democratic masses, discovering "the violence of writing" as he tries to make a copy of the last Shakespeare text before it is destroyed. His story does not end happily. Because of these actions, he becomes one of society's outcasts, not touchable or killable. Finally, a committee of elders comes to him offering death by suicide (poison), considered a highly dishonorable death, and Muerte accepts. Before he dies, he makes a speech in which he identifies with the authors he knows, "I am Byron, I am Shakespeare, I am Poe, I am Plato, . . . " expressing the idea that when he dies, they too will die. Interestingly, Muerte has heard stories of "people who are the books" living somewhere in the world and thinks of organizing them together into one community.

Of course, *Fahrenheit 451* is set at a stage of future nihilism long past that which troubled Arnold, who does lament the loss of a transcendental center (that is, God) that would give meaning to the world, but nevertheless, the poem is not being used nostalgically. Rather, it is being made to serve the function of awakening people to the fact that there is no eternal world of happiness, that one cannot escape the inevitable pain and suffering of life, despite what the illusions of the culture industry may say. Bradbury's reading of Arnold may also suggest here a kind of critique of critique, telling us that the use of tradition is to remind the critique of ideology that humanity can project its emancipation into the future and anticipate an unconstrained and unlimited communication only on the basis of the creative reinterpretation of the cultural heritage. If we had no experience of authentic communication, however restricted and mutilated it was, how could we ever wish it to prevail for all people? He who is unable to reinterpret his past may also be incapable of projecting concretely his interest in emancipation.

Compare *Fahrenheit 451* to *Where Ignorant Armies Clash by Night* with regards to the stages of nihilism. The entire text of Arnold's "Dover Beach" is cited in the unpublished novel because, in that story, his writings have, ironically, become so little known. As in *Fahrenheit*, at the heart of *Ignorant Armies* lies a struggle with the modern crisis of values, with nihilism, which is explained in a speech by the "old man" (unnamed in the manuscript) to the child he is educating. His words show that he is a clear analogue to "wise old man" figures in the utopian-dystopian genre (and to Nietzsche's soothsayer figure in part 2 of *Thus Spoke Zarathustra*): "Everything is futile, all effort is in the end worthless. A man may, of course, still pursue disconnected ends, money, fame, art, science, and may gain pleasure from them. But life is hollow at the center. Hence the dissatisfied, disillusioned, restless, spirit of modern man. Hence Death as a value. If Life has no Value, then give Death a value." It is clear that Muerte (Death) the assassin is an almost allegorical figure, and the perverted carnival over which he presides is an attempt to "make a religion of Meaninglessness." But the perverted carnival can never create new values, not even when it is later supported by the efforts of the full-blown mass media depicted in *Fahrenheit 451*. It remains a performance for spectators, though it is considered an honor to die in such a spectacle.

The wise old man sees no way out of nihilism, which goes in cycles, but thinks that this new religion of Death can at least offer certainty if not hope: "Let man for the first time revoke the natural laws of survival and self-preservation. Self-preservation? For what, for purposes of life? No, no! Man now wades further and further out into the black deep tarpit of Death. Soon he will slide from view. Then the animals will come. The whole thing will start again, from Faith to Faithlessness, from Meaning to Meaninglessness. . . . And this man, this great William Donne [Muerte], is our god, and we his disciples, revolting against meaningless, dying proud and true to our values, cynical as they may seem." This "god," however, is himself infected with a weariness of spirit toward "the wonderfully negative world of killing and being killed" that would have confounded Nietzsche. Muerte sees everyone, including himself, as ignorant and stupid fools "rolling in the filth" of human degradation and desperately wants to smash the system of false entertainments, of "banquets, feasts, and festivals," over which he presides. He remains powerless to do so, however.

Bradbury had plans to introduce another character, William Elliott, who may have been an assassin himself and took to reading books to the crowd. It is he who reads "Dover Beach" to the people before giving it to them, burning it leaf by leaf, "as if hands of fire were turning each page, scanning and burning with the same fire," in a scene whose language looks forward to that of Beatty's nihilistic reading. But in *Ignorant Armies,* the burning pages are caught by the crowd "in eager hands and clenched and popped into mouths like sweetmeats," which suggests a cannibalistic feast. Elliott would subvert the system by pleading with Muerte to spare his life, and indeed he is given a long speech in part of a stage version of the manuscript that Bradbury was working on simultaneously. In this he calls himself "a flame in the wilderness" that can "burn you clean of your oppression and night melancholy" with the good knowledge that "we live and therefore our [*sic,* probably "are"] blessed." But Muerte is unable to affirm his life, to accept the blessing, which is developed in *Fahrenheit 451* as the meaning of the earth, and slays Elliott.

Montag only learns this power of affirmative utopian values through the experience of reading and reverie, which becomes foregrounded in the second part of the novel in such scenes as where Montag's hunger cannot be satisfied by the spectacles of the mass media. Indeed, his society seems to have lost the knowledge of the real feeling of satisfaction or happiness. Another scene, set in a subway, has Montag trying to read from the Bible Jesus' parable of the lilies of the field (in the text of Matthew's gospel) to memorize and understand its import while loudspeakers are blaring out a mindless commercial about dental hygiene. It is only when Montag reaches Faber, an old, retired English teacher, that he receives something like an antidote to his "dis-ease." Faber is a sort of failed Northrop Frye, for he knows that the secular scripture represented by books did nothing to stop the onset of barbarism, but nonetheless he affirms that the media could be used to accommodate Arnold's ideal of radiant literacy. This ideal has not been disproved, even if it has failed to materialize, he seems to say.

Faber tells Montag that he is a "hopeless romantic" for believing that books themselves are what he needs, though Faber does not deny that there are authentic *persons* behind them. He tells Montag that books are hated and feared because they show the pores in the face of life. Furthermore, on close inspection by the intellect, they reveal themselves precisely as texts, which "stitch the patches of the universe together into one garment for us." That is their only magic. And at least they cannot entirely delude readers into believing that they are all of one piece, without gaps, at the origin. The study of literature begins precisely with textual criticism—these "patches" of other texts—and with intertextuality, such as the way in which Bradbury himself appropriates and renews the meaning of Arnold's poem. In books, which can always be shown to be texts, the human will to truth cannot become total. We are allowed the play of interpretation. This is quite unlike the spectacle of the mass media, where the environment is as real as the world: "It *becomes* and is the truth." Nonetheless, and despite these indications of critical reading Faber wants to inculcate in Montag, he first tries to awaken in him a nostalgia for the meaning of the earth. In oneiric terms, Faber introduces him to reveries of the earth and the will by telling him a myth:

> We are living in a time when flowers are trying to live on flowers, instead of growing on good rain and black loam. Even fireworks, for all their prettiness, come from the chemistry of the earth. Yet somehow we think we can grow, feeding on flowers and fireworks, without completing the cycle back to reality. Do you know the legend of Hercules and Antaeus, the giant wrestler, whose strength was incredible so long as he stood firmly on the earth? But when he was held, rootless, in midair, by Hercules, he perished easily. If there isn't something in that legend for us today, in this city, in our time, I am completely insane.[37]

Faber arranges to communicate more of this earthly wisdom by implanting an electronic device in Montag's ear and reading to him from the Bible (exclusively from the Book of Job in "The Fireman," but from Ecclesiastes and Revelations primarily in the finished novel). Listening to the "delicate filigree" of the old man's voice in the following days and nights, Montag's imagination produces its own antidote to the poisons of mass culture through a reverie of the earth. He imagines that fire and water, Montag plus Faber, will combine to form a new substance, a new self, symbolized by wine. Wine is one of Bradbury's major symbols of life, and it is thematically appropriate here because it comes from the soil and "remembers" the climate that produces it. Furthermore, it has long been considered a health-giving liquid that, once in the body, warms and refreshes because it has qualities of both fire and water. It is in itself a living body that balances the heavy and the light, a conjunction of earth and sky, an image of health.

Montag's reverie, which seems to progress in a dialectical fashion, is really an interpretation. He needs this notion to believe in his own value again. Faber destroys Montag's romantic illusions but nonetheless rescues him from total nihilism by providing him with a myth to awaken his dreaming capacity. It fosters in Montag the desire for a kind of instinctive knowledge of the body, though certainly not a longing for another world. These values are, in turn, revalued at the end of part 3.

There are a series of reveries leading up to this revaluation and reversal that come after Montag sets aflame his own house in a conflagration that also kills Beatty, destroys a mechanical hound, and then escapes from the city. The most important of the series for present purposes is the long water reverie. In it, Montag learns to "will backwards," to affirm the passage of time and to liberate himself from the entire weight of the negative. Floating peacefully on his back in a river, looking at the reflected light of the moon, Montag realizes that all knowledge is "solar," that is, active interpretation. As Nietzsche would say, there is no immaculate perception.[38] Montag realizes through reverie that he cannot, like the Moon, simply reflect in contemplation his love of the earth. It must be willed:

> The sun burnt every day. It burnt Time. The world rushed in a circle and turned on its axis and time was busy burning the years and the people anyway, without any help from him. So if *he* burnt things with the firemen and the sun burnt Time, that meant *everything* burnt!
>
> One of them had to stop burning. The sun wouldn't, certainly. So it looked as if it had to be Montag and the people he had worked with until a few short hours ago.[39]

The realization that things go in cycles of nihilism, without the ego consciously willing it, could crush Montag at this point if he were not protected by the water of his reverie. Here again we have the image of nihilism as a fire that inexhaustibly and voraciously appropriates everything strange or new in life with a view to reducing it to sameness. If allowed to progress to the limit, it would reduce all values to falsity (the essence of Beatty's reading of texts). To overcome himself, Montag the fireman vows never to burn again. This is an affirmation, not a negation—one that furthermore affirms everything against which Beatty directed his destructive dialectic. It is the emergence of differences and the will affirming and interpreting itself in time. Montag realizes not only that the world is full of burning of all types and sizes but also that "the guild of the asbestos weaver must open shop very soon," weaving texts that once again will sustain humanity. It is only thus that the becoming of the world can be redeemed, and Montag goes on to dream forward about Clarisse in a vision of the utopian ideal, never burnt by the fireflies of any conflagration. After this reverie, in which he interprets his life backward and forward in time, he emerges from the river a happy man, discovering delight in the miraculous presence of natural objects liberated from the oblivion in which technological thinking casts them.

By bringing Clarisse down to earth onto an idealized image of a farm he remembers from his childhood, Montag has learned the meaning of nature and no longer needs any outside authority to give his life meaning, whether it be the state or books themselves. He goes on to walk through a forest in which he imagines himself an animal, "a thing of brush and liquid eye," until he finds the campfire of the book people, where a collective reverie of the forge is in progress. It is perhaps the strongest image of the human will in the novel. As such, it completely reverses the values previously associated with fire, now becoming humanly warming, and it places time at the service of the men whose voices have the power to talk about everything (that is, language is no longer used for the purposes of domination) as they "look at the world and turn it over with the eyes, as if it were held to the center of the bonfire, a piece of steel these men were shaping."

Among them, Montag is given a new "identity" (if we can call becoming a text anything like becoming self-identical). There is even a joke about not judging a book by its cover, for some of their members have had plastic surgery to disguise themselves. Montag, who has believed that there is a person behind every book, is now self-consciously and playfully becoming a mask. This indicates among other things that he can no longer take his fireman persona—at least insofar as it had been imposed on him by the simulacrum of carnival—so seriously. In fact, Montag is directly told that only the book he has memorized (with the help of Faber) is really important. In the society of the book people, there is a resistance to narcissism.

The social organization of these people is nomadic and antidialectical in structure, described as flexible, very loose, and fragmentary (some people are only chapters of books, as is Montag). The book people are not reconciled to each other in any totalizing vision but rather affirm a radical pluralism. Each man's memorization of a text he loves is the willful and selective affirmation of a self or mask in its positive difference from other masks. They represent a nomadic flow of desire outside the territorial codings of the state into what Bradbury refers to as a "wilderness."

Most Bradbury critics confine their study of the wilderness myth in his writings to *The Martian Chronicles*, but it is clearly operative here as well. Only the myth of the wilderness and its nomads are able to withstand the apocalyptic force of destruction that is finally unleashed in an atomic war, destroying the major cities. It is after this final outbreak of destructive nihilism, however, that Montag learns that man has not valued the earth enough: "Look at the world out there . . . outside me, there beyond my face and the only way to really touch it is to put it where it's finally me, where it's in the blood, where it pumps around a thousand times ten thousand a day."[40]

It would seem that Montag must renew his vow to remain faithful to nature, to give the earth a human meaning. The problem of getting this into the blood was originally taken care of by the snow reverie, which starts with sacrificial blood dripping from Montag's nose into the soil and which follows immediately on the passage cited above. Because of the presence of such strong reveries, even after a nuclear war, man and man's earth appear to him as inexhaustible and still undiscovered. Bradbury's diagnosis of modern culture ends with the emergence of a healthy body that can manifest the meaning of the world.[41] Yet there is hardly an overt myth of the overman (who in Nietzsche's philosophy is the meaning of the earth) in this novel as there was at the end of *The Martian Chronicles*, unless Montag, with his hopeful healing vision of the future, is a presage of one, of a being who is cured of the "sickness of man." The book people themselves are not at all sure that they can "make every future dawn glow with a purer light," and they certainly do not imagine that becoming books affords them any security. Perhaps they correspond to a stage of incomplete nihilism that Nietzsche called "the higher man," those who are the last vestiges of God on earth, in the sense that they desperately uphold an ideal of radiant literacy, the fragility of which they know all to well.[42] After all, even when men possessed books, it did not stop them from destroying themselves, as Faber points out to Montag.

Granger's angry and abusive speech about man being a first cousin to the phoenix, a "silly damn bird" whose origins are "back before Christ," brings the theme of fire back into the text. It is important to understand how this theme of fire is related both to true and inverted carnival. In many respects fire in carnival is an expression of what Bakhtin calls "the ancient ambivalence of the death wish, which also sounds like a wish for renewal and rebirth: die, and live again."[43] Carnival was always utopian for Bakhtin, its fires symbolically destroying the rigidified past and opening onto a new and less terrifying future, more related to the life of the earth and the body. Here, at the end of *Fahrenheit 451*, fire is an agent not only of destruction again but also of renewal, for the phoenix gets himself "born all over again." Clearly, this is different from Beatty's nihilistic use of fire, which destroys all values; his use could never be affirmed and lead to rebirth. And the fact that frank language has been liberated here too (ironically, the expletives, four "damns" and one "goddamn," would be censored in the Bal-Hi version of *Fahrenheit 451*, eliminating much of the emotional effect of this passage and others as well) indicates that Montag is in the presence of a new order of society in which there is no fear of using unofficial language. In addition to the abuse heaped on man—his silly tendency to build funeral pyres and to leap onto them—there is also praise—man remembers "all the damn silly things" he has done in the past and can overcome them if he so desires. Humans are not simply subject to animal drives, like the phoenix, and maybe some day the destructive aspects of carnival will no longer be necessary.

There is a definite suggestion in Granger's speech about the phoenix that cultural nihilism tends to run in cycles (this is also evident in the wise old man's speech to the child in *Where Ignorant Armies Clash by Night*). Is knowing and affirming this "wisdom" of any value? Bradbury seems to suggest that it is without asking us to embrace fully the dread Nietzschean notion of eternal return. That, we take it, is the point of the quotations from chapter 3 of Ecclesiastes. This wisdom book of the Bible is famous, of course, for the assertion that "there is nothing new under the sun" and for the view that there is a time for every purpose under heaven. While some have labeled its author a pessimist weary of life, we think rather that the wisdom of the intertext here is that only when men are aware that nothing is really new can they live with an intensity in which everything can potentially become new. The spectacles of mass culture that Montag has escaped are based on the false illusion of continual newness. Some "disillusionment" is therefore necessary first in order to experience what newness of life truly is. Then we are prepared to understand the value of the tree of life, an image from both the beginning—the garden of Eden—and the end—the Revelation of the New Jerusalem—of the Bible. For Bradbury, the tree of life's real cultural nourishment lies in the ability of mankind's imaginative vision (with twelve kinds of fruit yielded every month—it is an abundant tree) to sustain us in affirming the value and meaning of life in this world.

In this manner *Fahrenheit 451* posits a utopian ideal of ironic enlightenment among the damaged lives of its cultural outsiders ("hobo intellectuals" as they are called in "The Fireman"—they only remember bits and pieces of texts, not whole books), who embrace the ambivalent contradictions of life and textuality and who would not want to abolish them in the name of conformity to social norms, a major preoccupation of the status quo in the 1950s (Beatty tells Montag that society functions best when all are the same). *Fahrenheit* is a book that connects its readers with some of culture's great literary voices, the value of that conversation becoming apparent through the book's critique of mass culture. Indeed, in the novel's last few sentences, Montag is presented as a man who has mastered a great inner emptiness of nihilism and who now feels not emptiness, but a kind of instinctive memory, the "slow stir of words, the slow simmer," that is associated with literary reverie. The promise given by the ending of the novel is that Montag will now speak freely and create values from an initial happiness and plenitude, from a sense of a new beginning, which also revalues the utopian tradition. Quoting from the "defamiliarized" Bible, three times reiterating the word "yes," what could be more appropriate than that Montag, who now embodies the meaning of the Earth, should quote the words of the preacher in Ecclesiastes about the seasons and the words from the Apocalypse of Saint John, one text declaiming all the vanities of this world and the other asserting the need for a new world in the lines about the tree of life, rooted now in *this* world, whose leaves are for the healing of nations? The reader feels assured that these words will be spoken when Montag reaches the earthly city and not the heavenly one.

The most significant thematic development between the text of "The Fireman" and *Fahrenheit 451* was the series of reveries based on the material imagination (earth, air, fire, water) that guide Montag's—and the reader's—growing realization of the meaning of the world in the expanded novel text. In his next book, Bradbury structured an entire novel with reveries that combine these traditional four elements together, his master metaphor *Dandelion Wine*.

4

The Carnival Blaze of Summer

Dandelion Wine

Dandelion Wine, though not ostensibly genre fiction, can often be found in today's bookstores next to Bradbury's other fantasy and science fiction titles. There is a certain logic to this, for all of his Green Town fictions have their roots in the Gothic horror tales that represent his first success as a writer. By the summer of 1945, his outlines for the *Dark Carnival* story collection produced a runaway title story that was already a Green Town novel in progress; he expanded these outlines and sketches into an unproduced screenplay before finally completing the novel in 1962, *Something Wicked This Way Comes. Dandelion Wine* can be traced to the very same creative watershed. While he was developing content variations for *Dark Carnival,* Bradbury was also using some of these same stories to flesh out a novel to be titled *The Small Assassins.* No known chapter drafts survive from this earliest form of the project, but outlines and later chapter drafts document how the initial Ur-novel concept has continued to evolve for nearly six decades. Under the title *Summer Morning, Summer Night,* this project promised to be Bradbury's first chance to develop a true novel from the experiences of his Illinois youth, experiences that had produced such successful short fiction year after year. *Dandelion Wine* was a remarkable first book in this vein, and it has never been out of print since its publication in 1957. But it is nonetheless a novelized story cycle closer (in terms of structure) to *The Martian Chronicles* than to its sister work *Something Wicked.* Although it anchors what Bradbury has always envisioned as his Green Town trilogy—*Dandelion Wine* (1957), *Something Wicked This Way Comes* (1962), and *Farewell Summer* (unpublished)—*Dandelion Wine* is still a prelude to a novel. As we shall see, the rest of the original novel (now titled *Farewell Summer)* survives today as a working manuscript, but it remains a dream deferred.

The original concept behind *Dandelion Wine* was motivated by the same impulses of authorship that produced Bradbury's best horror stories—the need to deal with the fears and guilt of childhood through fiction. His earliest surviving outline for a story collection, *A Child's Garden of Terror* (1944), represented the first gathering of these impulses into a book-length concept; this short-lived outline would provide a nucleus for both *Dark Carnival* and *The Small Assassins*. Looking back after thirty years, Bradbury noted that many of these stories derived from word-association exercises designed to "find out what was hidden in the back of my head. With passion, then, I scared the ideas out into the open and rediscovered my childhood." *The Small Assassins* outline of contents is full of such titles; seven of these—"The Night," "The Poison Sidewalks," "The Baby," "The Man Upstairs," "The Lake," "Reunion," and "The Crowd"—would be shifted to *Dark Carnival*, but they would have been equally effective as chapters in the evolving novel. Bradbury's authorial vision for the initial project survives in three pages of notes prepared in the same way that he prepared individual story notes for Julius Schwartz, who would continue to serve as his agent until 1947. Schwartz usually asked Bradbury to write a simple summary of his subject and the central conflict of the story idea. For the evolving novel, Bradbury began: "I WANT TO WRITE A NOVEL ABOUT . . . a small town and the adults and children who live in that town . . . a novel concerning the vast psychological differences between children and their parents . . . each group, whether children or adults, handled as if they lived in a separate world . . . the children strange, wild, calm, silent and by turns excitable individuals living under their own laws and beliefs . . . the parents unable to comprehend and a bit afraid of the children. I want to get the feel of the small town, the strange wonder of the children, the bewildered suspicion of the adults into the story" (ellipses Bradbury's).[1]

The divisions between the world of the adult and the world of the child are ever present in a child's mind, and Bradbury saw this tension, this constant contest for control, as the thematic center of this project: "THE CONFLICT IN 'the small assassins' IS GOING TO BE . . . between the children and their environment, their parents . . . and between the parents ideas of what the children should be and what the children really ARE . . . the conflict of making children fit into standards and moulds, making ladies and gentlemen out of untrained little creatures. And the children resentfully hating the idea of growing up . . . and the adults themselves wishing again to be children but not able to go back, and are frustrated . . . " (ellipses Bradbury's).[2]

Bradbury's final page of notes, perhaps written later than the initial twenty-four-chapter rough outline of contents, shows how he planned to resolve the plot and the thematic issues in two final chapters (numbered 15 and 16) centering on the two fundamental ways that people are reconciled to the process of aging: falling in love and having children of our own.[3] Many of the story chapters listed in this earliest stage of development were subsequently published as standalone tales, and others still survive in two boxes of draft chapters and transitional bridges. All of the identifiable titles advance the conflict or suggest resolution. The ordering of chapters is problematic at this stage and appears to be more of a list than a progression. But subsequent stages of work show a developing structure in both the incidents of plot and the hierarchy of the town itself.

By late 1946, the novel had begun to coalesce around interactions between children, young adults, and the elderly.[4] The next surviving outline is titled *The Blue Remembered Hills,* and only a few of the twenty-four chapter titles are simple word associations. A number of them are descriptive and imply a developing tension between age groups. Many of the stories may have been drafted or outlined by this time, for each one in the contents outline appears with a word count (ranging from 500 to 3,000) totaling nearly 34,000 words. The outline survives with a draft opening leaf of the first chapter, dated December 11, 1946, but few pages from this phase seem to survive in the two-box nachlass of material for this novel. Other folders have yielded 61 more pages from this period, including two title pages; on one of these Bradbury has typed out two stanzas from the source of his new title, A. E. Houseman's *A Shropshire Lad.* Many of these pages show the evolving war between the young boys and the old men of the town, who seem intent on leading the young toward the same state of decay and impending death that has extinguished their own joy of life.

In 1947, with *Dark Carnival* in print, Bradbury worked with his new agent, Don Congdon, to circulate working manuscripts of two novels—one developed from the vampire family stories of *Dark Carnival* and the other the Green Town novel, now titled *Summer Morning, Summer Night* (table 8). An earlier idea for a third novel, a dark carnival novel set in Green Town, was set aside while Bradbury's muse worked the other chords. The vampire family novel, which (in Bradbury's mind) depended a great deal on illustration and visualization, was also set aside when promising opportunities with publishers and illustrators fell through. As he packaged and repackaged story-collection concepts in the late 1940s, the *Summer Morning, Summer Night* idea continued to evolve as his only active novel in progress.

Bradbury's February 1951 outline includes twenty-six chapters and an estimated length of 65,000 words. Many undated story drafts and mood pieces from this period survive, including an untitled sketch of the age-driven hierarchy of the town that seems to appear in the outline as "The Three Streets." The contrasts presented in this unpublished sketch or bridge reveal the town as a territorial entity:

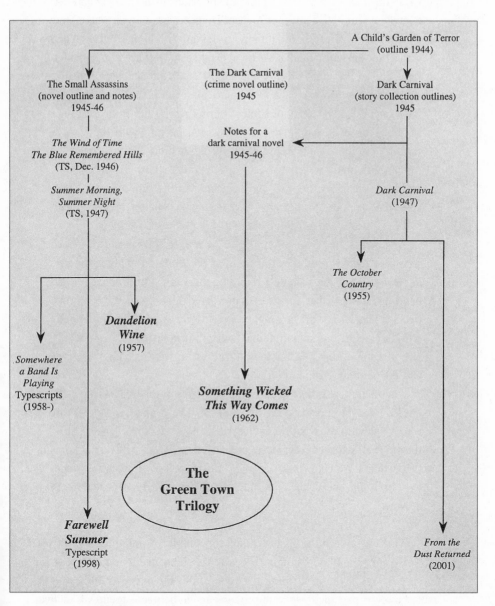

Table 8. The genealogy of the three major literary stems in Bradbury's work that originate in the stories of the mid-1940s. The left and center stems trace the Green Town trilogy, including the unpublished novel *Farewell Summer*. A derivative work that began with material from this yet-unpublished Green Town novel branches from the leftmost stem as a novel manuscript titled *Somewhere a Band Is Playing*. The center and rightmost stems, which are significant in the evolution of *Something Wicked This Way Comes,* appear again in expanded form in the next chapter.

Given time, each town will assemble and populate, in one form or another, a Street of Children, a Street of Ancient Dragons, and a Street where Time Does not Exist. Green Town, Illinois was no different in this. In fact, it had gone at the job with a kind of electrical magnetism. Fertility stimulated fertility, and so the street which seemed most of all, full of shouts, screams, rubber-tire swings, baseballs in mid-air, trees full of summer fruit and boys, boys full of apples, apples full of worms, worms full of the clear juice of life. A street of sleds in winter, snow men melting with the planet's cumbrous nodding of its head toward spring. A street of jacks strewn like robot's teeth on the walks. A street of green ponds, strawberry pools, grape puddles, popsickles dropped and vanishing in the sun. A street where autumn leaves piled for burning, were sewn with children, boned beneath by boys buried deep, unseen by the passing motorist's world.

And across the ravine, what *an abyss of time* [emphasis added] indeed separated their worlds, was the street of the chittering pillbox, the fizzing alka-powder, the soundless rounding thread of electric runabout and hand-thrust wheelchair, the street of powdered dry-nectarine face and rust-freckled fingers. The preying mantis street which smelled like a Mah-Jong set. The [cough] long after midnight street; the candle-flutter, bamboo, rattan, wicker creaking, rustling moth-flicker street which smells of the cave and the mummy even at noon.

And then there is that street of the in-betweens, the timeless ones, the one [*sic*] who never read clocks, who pass calendars without a glance, those who roughly fit into what the industrialists now refer to as "golden time" the age from sixteen or seventeen, perhaps, to 25. Those who do not know that winters are cold, that summers can be tiring. Those who do not look back nor ahead but only in at themselves and immediately about at Now.[5]

The ravine was indeed the great defining topography of young Bradbury's section of Waukegan, Illinois, and in this early sketch he used it as a metaphor for the psychological chasm dividing the young from the old. It is interesting to note, however, that the town here contains an "in between" group whose lives seem to take place already in a perpetual "now," closely akin to the time of the carnival in Western societies and literatures. This group is entirely missing from later versions, and it is fairly easy to see why: it makes for a more dramatic story if carnival time is something that both groups, young and old, will need to struggle over. In another version of this passage, he would develop a more tangible sequence of metaphors to define the communities of young and old:

The street of Old People was a street of dark wreaths and coffin-thin doors, of bleak, rouged colors, of slate roofs like ravens feathers glistering in the summer rains, of trees that sighed their leaves together, of winds that smelled continually of arnica, dust, time, ages, violet water. Up and down it moved women as thin as old fashioned shaped wire soda fountain chairs, and men like withered saplings. You saw them peering from their high bedroom windows, like children who had been put away without supper because of a life misspent. You smelled their milk and bread being warmed for breakfast, you heard the rattle-snake sound of pills shaken in a bottle, as Death prepared to strike. You saw doctors with little black bags knocking on doors or precisely thumbing the bells, and some where in an attic, it seemed, an answering tinkle, a rustle of crepe, a crackle of leather.

How different the street immediately west of this one, a block removed from the ravine and its night influences. Here the trees were smaller, some only seedlings, some large enough for a boy to lash down as a catapult and let fly tin cans into the bright air. Here even the grass seemed a newly purchased carpet, the flower figures fresh in it, the nap smooth and untired. Here were the new small houses, the stucco, the plain fronts, here was the smell of the refrigerator, the sound of Paul Witeman [sic] records through the day, and the rising laughter of children.[6]

Here the streets and the houses are visible and the landscape serves as a tangible frame for the descriptions of sight, sound, and smell as well as metaphors of youth and age. The ravine itself and its "night influences" become in *Dandelion Wine* a more subtle philosophical metaphor for the abyss, representing at night an unnamable and indescribable sense of the wildness and the darkness of destructive impulses. Like all major themes in Bradbury, it is deeply ambivalent. The ravine-abyss is a true carnival chronotope, combining time and space in an organic way. It represents the "intervalic" or in-between space where creativity is free to roam. In its daytime version, the ravine becomes a kind of sanctuary where children play and scheme. Instead of residing on the far side of the gap, the old live on the near side, closer to the children they no longer understand, closer than the children are to the darkness of unknowable things yet to come.

The middle generation of young adults moved into the background as Bradbury continued to develop *Summer Morning, Summer Night*. The struggle for dominance he had initially articulated in *The Small Assassins* outline of the mid-1940s as a struggle between child and adult was becoming a struggle between the young and the old, for the old were a constant reminder of the tyranny of abstract time. The plot, as it evolved during the early 1950s, runs something like this: As summer opens up before them, young Douglas Spaulding and his brother, Tom, declare war on the relentless march of time that will inevitably end summer and return them to school and a sinister progression toward adulthood, old age, and death. A series of accidents puts them at odds with the old men who control the school board and other aspects of town life. A mock epic war breaks out between the two groups, culminating in a midsummer attack by the boys on the town's clock tower, the event that is the thematic center of the evolving novel. The clock tower represents abstract linear time, not the living time of enjoyed experiences most clearly epitomized in the ever returning spectacle of carnival. Time measured out in seconds, minutes, and hours becomes a tormenting reminder of life slipping away. The young silence this clock, but their victory is short lived, for old Colonel Quartermain throws a birthday party for one of the little girls of the neighborhood. His goal is to appear as a friend rather than a foe, for he knows that time is ultimately on his side. The outlines and surviving discards of the novel's development give only hints of how the struggle ends, but two very early ending fragments suggest that the generation gap is finally bridged by tolerance and love. In both cases it is the childbearing generation of young adults who foster this reconciliation, characters introduced in the very earliest outlines but who slowly disappear from the evolving novel.

By the early 1950s, he had a half-dozen Green Town stories in print (and a number of others in progress) that could be used to fill in the adventures of the summer, but as yet there were only a few manuscript chapters involving the central plot and overarching themes of the novel. Drafts of "The Clock Tower" and "The Birthday Party" survive from this period, but connective text and any sense of character development was still largely lacking. Two undated outlines from this general period reinforce the sense that Bradbury considered a wide range of story-chapter combinations and had, in fact, done so since the earliest outlines of 1945–1946 (table 9). In one form or another, nearly all of his published or soon-to-be-published Green Town stories surface in at least one of these early outlines. Other titles lacked specific references to the Green Town topos yet clearly provided plot elements that could be incorporated with revision. But many of these had appeared in *Dark Carnival*, and Bradbury turned more and more to new material in successive outlines. Some of this was eventually discarded as well, and it survives only as fragments or story drafts in the two discard boxes. One of the fragments, "The Crazy Man from Elgin Town," introduced an element of sexuality in the form of a drunken drifter who exposes himself to the boys playing in the ravine; Bradbury opted to delete this glimpse of the grotesque, but he also eliminated more-mainstream glimpses of the carnivalesque as well. "The Circus" is perhaps the best example. In it the theme of carnivalization brings together the literal war and the metaphorical war in a single adventure. Colonel

Quartermain tries to remove all the delightful elements of experiential time by stopping carnival time completely—he works with the various leaders of the chamber of commerce to ban all carnivals, circuses, and even the annual Fourth of July celebrations. The circus is sent packing as soon as it arrives: "There hadn't even been a circus parade. The lions had been silenced outside of town by the Lions inside of town. The elephants had been vanquished by the Elks. The calliope had been throttled and choked with red tape and the entire circus assemblage, band, wagons, and clowns had fled before an Ark of Moose, Eagles and Oddfellows." The animals become doubled metaphor for the two contending views of time. Douglas gains some sense of victory by going out to the abandoned circus grounds and sensing the recent presence of his beloved animals and rides. But this episode was perhaps too nostalgic and digressive for the evolving conflict at the center of the novel, and in fact, this story-chapter has never reached print at all.

Bradbury wanted the novel to develop in a pressure-free environment, in carnival rather than linear time. This was how his individual stories had always come about—first an initial draft created in a spontaneous burst of creative energy, then carefully revised and rewritten over an indefinite period of time. Pressure to finish a story could always be eased by submitting other more-polished tales to Don Congdon while the one in question matured. But a novel manuscript was an entirely different proposition. Bradbury could build the chapters as stories, Twain-like, nursing each one along at its own required pace; but the novel as an overarching entity was a high-profile target, and he found himself constantly under gentle but persistent pressure from Congdon and Doubleday's Walter Bradbury to bring the project to completion. The author needed the book to develop without regard to a clock, evolving in the body's sense of lived time. But the unavoidable outside pressures forced him to live the novel in clock time and led to a creative crisis similar to the one that tortured him throughout the process of transforming "The Fireman" into *Fahrenheit 451* for Ian Ballantine. Bradbury's only recourse was to hold on to his Green Town manuscripts until they were right—however long that might take. And in the case of *Summer Morning, Summer Night,* the battle of wills went on for six years.

Walter Bradbury had read enough of the Green Town stories (both in print and in manuscript) to feel certain that *Summer Morning, Summer Night* would be the breakthrough novel for Ray Bradbury. He had seen the young author develop *The Martian Chronicles* into a unified, sustained work and use the recurring motif of *The Illustrated Man* to link together a much more diffuse sequence of science fiction stories into a very popular collection. Editor Bradbury had seen portions of the Illinois novel before, for Congdon and his client had been shopping the concept since the late 1940s. In 1951 he read the latest version of the manuscript,

Table 9. The four undated outlines prepared prior to the full development of *Summer Morning, Summer Night* appear here in the most likely progression. Many of the early word-association titles of the Ur-novel *The Small Assassins* were moved into the *Dark Carnival* story collection published in 1947. A bibliographical reference keyed to appendix A appears for all titles that can be traced to published Bradbury stories; those unpublished titles with complete or substantial fragment typescripts in the two surviving discard boxes are indicated by the abbreviation MS.

The Small Assassins (c. 1945–46)	The Blue Remembered Hills (c. Dec. 1946)	Summer Morning, Summer Night (c. 1950)	Summer Morning, Summer Night (c. 1950)
The Town	The Opening	First Day of Summer	Summer Night (MS)
The Porches at Night	The General Acts (MS)	Declaration of War	The Night (46–12)
The Children in the Streets	Miss Lieberman's Child Baby	The Green Machine (51–7)	All on a Summer's Night (50–2)
The Game of Anna Anna Anna Anna (MS)	Mr. Terle's Dead Child	The Revolution Grows	Miss Bidwell (50–9)
The Night (46–12)	The Other Old Men	The Night (46–12)	Deep Summer (48–12, as "End of Summer")
The Courthouse Clock (MS)	The Court House Clock (MS)	Deep Summer (48–12, as "End of Summer")	The Witch
The Ravine (MS)	The Message Is Returned, the Other Old Man Is Dead	The Sound of Summer	The Playground (52–7)
The Teacher	The Chess Players (MS)	The Thickening of the Plot	The Magical Kitchen (54–3, as "Dinner at Dawn")
The Poison Sidewalks (46–16, as "Let's Play 'Poison'")	The New Message	Summer Night (MS)	The Blue Remembered Hills
The Baby (46–17, as "The Small Assassin")	The Message Falls into the Hands of the Children	A Story about Love (51–9)	Season of Disbelief (50–22)
The Families	The Crazy Man from Elgin Town Who Understands about Grownups Plan to Undermine Child Patterns (MS)	The Statues (57–7)	The Screaming Woman (51–11)
The Boy Who Wouldn't Grow Up	The Fire—the Candy Factory	Season of Disbelief (50–22)	The Green Machine (51–7)
The Man Upstairs (47–2)	The Anna Anna Anna Words to Forget All Things (MS)	The Court House Clock (MS)	Invisible Boy (45–13)
Carnival		The Magical Kitchen (54–3, as "Dinner at Dawn")	The Great Fire (49–3)
The Lake (44–5)		All on a Summer's Night (50–2)	The Window (50–18)
The Colored Windows			A Story about Love (51–9)

Table 9. (*continued*)

The Small Assassins (c. 1945–46)	The Blue Remembered Hills (c. Dec. 1946)	Summer Morning, Summer Night (c. 1950)	Summer Morning, Summer Night (c. 1950)
I Got Something You Ain't Got! (MS)	The Birth of Miss Lieberman's Child	The River That Went to the Sea (MS)	Long before Dawn (MS, as "A Serious Discussion")
Reunion (44–2)	The Ravine (MS)	The KKK Parade (MS, as Hallowe'en in July)	The Statues (57–7)
The Crowd (43–5)	The Lonely One	Interim: The Circus Grounds (MS)	The Pumpernickel (51–10)
The People Out There	The Runaway Hike	The Gentle Trolley (55–3, as "The Trolley")	The Spring Day
The Sea Shell (44–1)	The Old Men Plan	The Dropping of Summer Apples: The Window (50–18)	Autumn Afternoon (02–2)
The Crazy Man from Elgin Town (MS)	The Lake Forever Young	Lime-Vanilla Ice (54–11, as "The Swan")	
Band Concert	The Night (46–12)		
The Carnival Priest	The Poisoned Food		
	The Fatal Little Girls		
	The Death of the Old Man (possibly 50–18, "The Window")		
	The Ending		

immediately secured a contract for the novel, and made plans to publish it in the fall of 1952. But author Bradbury was not able to pull the various chapters into the kind of seamless whole he had come to envision for his first novel, and his editor reluctantly agreed to postpone the production schedule indefinitely. Meanwhile, Doubleday agreed to publish another story collection, *The Golden Apples of the Sun*, to capitalize on Bradbury's continuing successes in the major-magazine market; but as Congdon noted in June 1952, this was also done to relieve pressure for the Illinois novel.[7] On June 10 Bradbury promised Doubleday in return that he would prepare the collection quickly and get on with the novel:

> I believe I can do this, and give you a book you'll be satisfied with, with-out actually taking too much time away from my Illinois book, for I try to break my routine, working on the Illinois book half a day, and my other stories in the afternoon, or vice-versa. The Illinois book has by no means dragged to a halt, but it *is* going slowly, and there are days, of course, when I am so damned self-conscious of what little reputation I have built for myself that it freezes me entirely. This is both ironic and funny, for it is the very thing I warn the students in short story classes about: don't stop and think or you'll freeze. Get to the typewriter, beat the hell out of it, and no criticism until *after* the first draft. When I manage to follow my own advice and say, "To hell with everything, to hell with the world, to hell with the reader, I'm going to *enjoy* myself!" then things really flow.[8]

But new commitments made it harder for the increasingly popular Bradbury to stick to such a schedule at all. In 1952 he also worked on a contract basis for Universal and other studios and edited the popular anthology *Timeless Stories for Today and Tomorrow* for Bantam.[9] These collaborative projects were more in line with his carnival sense of life but ended up increasing the pressure to complete the novel. The opportunity to turn "The Fireman" into one of Ballantine's first science fiction titles occupied the winter, spring, and summer of 1953. When he left for a nine-month screenwriting trip with the preproduction crew of John Huston's *Moby Dick*, it was apparent to both agent and editor that *Summer Morning, Summer Night* would be delayed further. But the novel would be Bradbury's first priority on his return at the end of May 1954, and shortly after his boat docked in New York, he met with Congdon and Walter Bradbury for a brainstorming session over the last manuscript, which had grown in fitful bursts over the previous three years to at least thirty-three chapters.[10]

This June 2 meeting focused on reorganizing the manuscript, which now had more episodes and characters than readers could easily follow. The next day Walt Bradbury prepared a follow-up memo and sent it off with Ray and Maggie

Bradbury as they returned home to California from their nine-month European odyssey. It reveals that together, author, editor, and agent explored three strategies to streamline the narrative: first, to eliminate some of the peripheral characters by combining their actions within a smaller group of more prominent characters, a strategy that would aid readers in identifying the remaining characters and in following the threads of continuing action through the novel; second, to break down the longer story-chapters and spread them episodically at intervals throughout the novel as parallel plot actions; and third, to develop the personalities of the boys and girls who take part in the summer adventures of Douglas and Tom Spaulding. Walt Bradbury also suggested charting the events, formalizing a cast of characters and their relationships, and even mapping Green Town to aid the process of tightening the narrative flow of events. Within weeks Bradbury had prepared maps and lists of characters and offered to send them to his editor (fig. 11). Walt Bradbury's response underscored the very special enthusiasm he had felt for the project from the beginning: "I can't tell you how much this book means to me: through the months it has become more and more a shining thing that has real being in my mind and heart, and I'm delighted that you're going ahead with it right away. Every weekend when I'm out working in the garden or cutting the lawn or otherwise doing the things one does the beginning of Summer, every little sight, sound and smell reminds me of some line or element in that book."[11]

Through these and other insights, Walt Bradbury joined Don Congdon as a kindred spirit in the Green Town novel, reinforcing the magical, carnivalesque sense of creativity that their author brought to bear on every work of fiction. In this letter Walt Bradbury also suggested that the book open on June 21, the first day of summer. As Ray Bradbury began to refashion the structure of the novel and its constituent story-chapters, he would indeed set the opening events on the longest day of the year. Progress was slow, but by late November 1954, Bradbury had prepared a detailed nine-page single-spaced outline of the revised narrative. Many of the chapters existed as stories, and a number had already been published in that form; the main challenge was to integrate them and develop characters as he had planned back in June. The fully developed outline projected three major sections with a total of twenty-four chapters. It survives within the two boxes of draft discards for the novel but provides a far more unified view of the maturing novel than the unsequenced and incomplete discards can provide.[12]

By this time, the various opening vignettes of earlier drafts had boiled down to a magical predawn moment on the first morning of summer (chap. 1). Bradbury's retrospective self, Douglas Spaulding, awakens and thinks excitedly of the long summer that lies ahead and the new tennis shoes that will carry him through

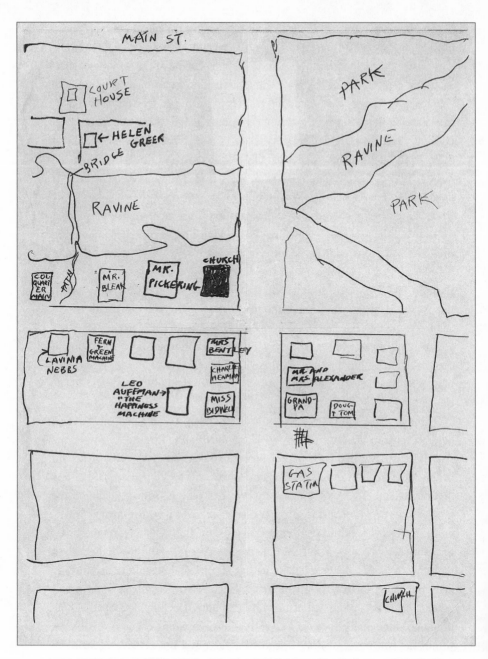

Figure 11. Bradbury's map of the *Summer Morning, Summer Night* locale probably dates from 1954, when he prepared maps, outlines, and character lists for the novel. The setting is a projection of his own childhood neighborhood in Waukegan, Illinois; the homes of the old and young protagonists are identified in relation to the ravine, where key events of the war between the "Grand Army" and the "Grey Army" will be planned or conducted. Some of these characters and their adventures were moved into the developing *Dandelion Wine* project late in 1955. From the Albright Collection, courtesy of Donn Albright and Ray Bradbury.

it. In the new outline Bradbury quickly set up the tensions that he saw as the central motivation for the actions of Douglas, Tom, and the other boys of the town as the novel's plot unfolded: "And in his thoughts, Douglas finds the summer gone already, before it even begins! How, then, to prolong this season, how [to] keep it forever running a golden circle, touching its own tail? With this thought uppermost in his mind, Douglas, with the gesture of a magician summons up and out the rest of the people of the morning town, and the first day of Summer 1928, begins."

At this point Bradbury planned to introduce Douglas's grandfather, sage counselor to people of all ages in Green Town and the only popular figure among the elders of the school board. He is able to maintain a delicate balance between change—mandated by progress and measured in artificial linear time—and tradition, where time is lived and enjoyed rather than measured and controlled. When younger generations of Spauldings try to seed grass that will never need mowing, Grandfather defends the old order of things in a gentle way by declaring the sound of the mowers as a ritual sound of summer (chap. 2). In this way Bradbury was able to incorporate his previously published "The Lawns of Summer" (1952) into the evolving landscape of Green Town.

Later in the morning, Douglas, his younger brother, and the other boys, "released from the prison of the school," rush to the ravine and declare war against the tyranny of time: "In the ravine, the former prisoners cry out their contempt for jails and jailors. They water the creek sands with the one word WAR! that, remembering it later, Douglas realizes was their unconscious declaration of war against the old people" (chap. 3). They rush out of the ravine into the street of old people, shouting and shooting. Douglas accidentally scares Mr. Braling to death with a popgun; old Colonel Quartermain, the most powerful member of the school board, sees it happen.

While the severe and uncompromising Quartermain is absorbed in thoughts about what has just happened, two spinster sisters hit him with their electric car and accidentally break his leg. The old colonel never saw what hit him and blames the accident on Douglas and his bicycle (chap. 4). Douglas, who has seen the second accident, rushes back to the ravine and reflects on these events. The other boys recognize battle lines being formed, but Douglas is not yet ready to see the old men as the awful keepers of time (chap. 5).

The old Spaulding relatives sit out on Grandpa's porch; they talk of recent deaths like old folks do. Douglas flees from this chilling discussion and meets with his new army in the ravine (chaps. 6, 8). Meanwhile, Leo Auffmann, more-or-less the town's idea man and inventor, has been discussing the concept of eternal happiness with the old men in front of the cigar store. He suddenly conceives of the need for a universal happiness machine and goes home to build it (chap. 7).

In this way Bradbury revised an earlier published essay, "The Season of Sitting" (1951), using it to frame the first episode of a long, yet-to-be-published story-chapter, "The Happiness Machine" (1957).

At this point Bradbury worked two of his most successful published Green Town stories into the outline, each a variation on the childhood terrors represented by the ravine near his boyhood home (chap. 9). "The Whole Town's Sleeping" (1950) is the tale of Lavinia Nebbs, who discovers the latest female victim of the Lonely One as she walks with friends through the ravine en route to the theater. The event thrills her more than scares her, and she convinces her friends to continue on to the show. She finally loses her nerve while returning home alone through the ravine, eventually reaching her house safely only to find that the Lonely One is already there, inside, waiting silently. "The Night" (1946) is young Tom's adventure. Douglas has crossed the ravine to play, and Tom is allowed to go get ice cream for himself and his mother. But when Douglas fails to return, both mother and brother brave the terrors of the ravine to call for him. His answering call from the distant playground comes just before they descend into the ravine's dark depths, and the nightmare is averted.

In developing the chronotope of his new outline, Bradbury nested "The Night" inside the darker story and tied them both into the novel's larger plot by having Douglas come across the murder scene just after Lavinia and her friends discover the body: "Douglas, present when the police arrive, is still further shaken by the succession of events during this day and evening, and now decides that he will be the leader in the War against Time, Age, and Death." Instead of going on to play across the ravine, he and some of the boys head for the street of the elderly to serenade Colonel Quartermain with rowdy rhymes. His mother and brother find him returning from this mission, and the happy ending of "The Night" transitions into the final half of Lavinia Nebbs's dark adventure. Meanwhile, Quartermain calls Mr. Bleak for support against the youngsters (chap. 10). Leo Auffmann, working late at night, defines the parameters for his happiness machine (chap. 11).

Earlier in 1954, Bradbury's even darker sequel to Lavinia Nebbs's dark adventure appeared in *Ellery Queen's Mystery Magazine* as "At Midnight, in the Month of June." Frederick Dannay, the editor behind the Ellery Queen persona, had published the original tale in 1950 and finally convinced Bradbury to write the sequel, in which the Lonely One, sitting quietly in an all-night Green Town diner, reflects on his evening of murder.[13] It may have been part of the longest (but unlocated) outline for the novel, the one that Walt Bradbury and Don Congdon had read prior to the June 1954 editing session, but in revising the contents for the new outline, Bradbury avoided the sequel and gave the young librarian a reprieve (chap. 12). She escapes the Lonely One, killing him with scissors in the dark house. Unnerved, she sells her house and joins the other boarders in the home of Grandpa and Grandma Spaulding, next door to Doug and Tom's home. Young Tom develops a crush on Lavinia, leading into Bradbury's published story-chapter "All on a Summer's Night" (1950). In response to living so near to this woman who came so close to death, Douglas gathers his "Grand Army" in the Green Town graveyard and reminds them that death—the manifest tyranny of linear time—is always near. This startling observation allowed Bradbury to introduce "Illumination," a story he was working on but had not yet published: "This, in turn, recalls to Tom the first occasion on which he discovered that he was alive—the day when the opening-out miracle occurred on a special afternoon, when even pain was enjoyable because it was part of living. Now, in the graveyard, Douglas' speech is the closing-up or closing-in miracle of death and darkness, another special afternoon, concerned with inevitable night."

Douglas now puts the army into action against death. The boys have often seen the old men playing chess at tables in the park between their street and the ravine. Earlier in the summer (chap. 10), Douglas had wondered how the players fit into the chronos and topos of Green Town: "The chessboards and the old men, the old men and the chessboards, and the town. The people's lives, moved, like chesspieces, by what agency? . . . By the old men, of course! But if the chessmen were stolen, what then? Something to think about—stealing the chessmen." Now, in the graveyard, Douglas recalls this plan. In fine carnival tradition the war literally becomes a game of chess as the boys set out to rob the fates: "The Chessmen are captured, Douglas sets them out on a chessboard in a cave in the ravine, naming the pawns for the men in his Grand Army, and moving the pawns, the Army, on the board, controlling their every move" (chap. 13). In this way Douglas sends out pawns to spy on the old people; their stories unfold in the middle and final sections of the novel outline.

But Colonel Quartermain has recruited his own "Grey Army [sic]," and in the opening of part two, "The Court House Clock," he begins, with the reluctant help of the more compassionate Mr. Bleak, a counterattack. The elderly have already seen the threat from the children in a fascinating interlude called "Slow Motion, Fast Motion" that inverts the normal metaphors of fast youth and slowing old age: as the children move out to capture the chess pieces, "they are seen by the old people as endlessly afloat in golden tides of slow time, whereas, to the children the old people seem rushing to the grave" (chap. 13). For his first move, Quartermain shuts down the last town trolley and brings the new bus system online; when summer ends, the new buses will "rush the children to school, destiny, destruction, death, more efficiently." This bridge leads into a story that Bradbury would soon publish as "The Trolley" (1955), which describes the trolley conductor's final gift to the children of Green Town—a final ride out to the end of the line for a picnic and back again, no charge.

At midsummer Douglas gets his first report back from Charlie, one of his pawns. "The Trolley" is interwoven with the unpublished tale "Arrival and Departure," the first of Bradbury's stories of the elderly in the novel (chap. 14). Mr. and Mrs. Alexander have been home ill for two years, but now they emerge to see a town that has come to regard them as strangers. After the trolley ride, Douglas's pawn reports how the Alexanders slowly regain their *joie de vivre* as they shop and explore the town, but when they return home, they fade back into inactivity and are again forgotten by the townspeople. They do not venture out again. Later that night Grandfather explains their strange ways to Douglas: "Grandfather, holding a firefly in his cupped hand, shows Douglas what light the power of love can throw upon the miniature world of his half-closed fingers, illuminating this small chamber with warmth and color. Grandpa figures there be isolation and isolation. The Alexanders base theirs on mutual affection and need. Under the circumstances, it's all right. But now—take Miss Bidwell across the street there" (chap. 15). In this way Bradbury bridges into "Miss Bidwell" (1950), revised from an earlier story about a secluded spinster whose guitar-playing beau left her desolate forty years earlier. Over the years she has become a complete recluse, removing the steps from her front and back porches to keep visitors away. Now, as Douglas and Grandpa release the firefly near her home, they are approached by an old man who wants to know if Miss Bidwell still lives there. He wanders off as the two Spauldings wonder if he is the long-lost lover returned (chap. 16).

At this point Bradbury concludes Tom's story, "All on a Summer's Night." The ten year old escorts Lavinia the librarian to a show on the evening of July 4 and then joins Grandpa to launch the last fire balloons of the season (chap. 17). Tom is drummed out of the army for his crush on Lavinia, and Douglas has to come up with a new campaign to keep his remaining pawns in line: "It is at this time that Douglas puts in action his 21-day fast, which he claims will limber up his Army, cut down their maturing rate, keep their bones from growing, and lessen their responsibility to their parents" (chap. 18). As counterpoint, Bradbury brings in two magical tales of food and drink. "Dandelion Wine" (1953), introduces Grandfather's bottling cellar and his day-by-day storehouse of bottled memories from the summer. This brief tale sets up "Dinner at Dawn" (1954), where Grandma's magical kitchen is threatened by the overhelpful aunt who persuades Grandma to forego her wonderful instinctive concoctions for cookbook recipes. The new meals are horrible, prompting Douglas to burn the cookbook and hide Grandma's spectacles. Her cooking magic returns, the great household of relatives and boarders is delighted, and Douglas gives up his fast.

But the unexpected end of the fast is not his only setback. Against his wishes, the girls (led by Isabel, who secretly carries a torch for the boy-general) have formed an auxiliary army. This development bridges into "Season of Disbelief" (1950), another previously published story in which several young girls come to see the elderly widow Mrs. Bentley: "her story begins here, the story of an old woman who cannot *prove* she was ever ten years old. The girls report on Mrs. Bentley to Charlie who reports to Douglas, who agrees that women and girls are a separate race, just as old people are a separate and alien horde from another far dark country" (chap. 19). The middle section of the novel outline closes with the destruction of the courthouse clock, which continues to be the central metaphor for the tyranny of linear time and the hated authority of the old people (chap. 20). The boys demolish the works with a bundle of leftover firecrackers: "Late on a summer's day, the Court House Tower explodes with a grinding, clanging, racheting [*sic*] roar. Everyone in town runs out to look as if the Tower might collapse and fall down dead across their lives. The Clock is indeed stilled, forever. Time has ground to a halt."

But even as the boys celebrate their culminating triumph, the final section of the novel outline, "The Birthday Party," begins with an unexpected tragedy. The next day Douglas's great-grandmother takes herself to bed, says goodbye to three generations of Spauldings, and dies (chap. 21). As "Good-by, Grandma" (1957), this story would not reach print until May 1957, a few months before publication of *Dandelion Wine*. But here, in his November 1954 outline, Bradbury planned in great detail how this story would stand as counterpoint to the clock tower tale as the great turning point of *Summer Morning, Summer Night*:

> Her death proves very well indeed that some greater clock has not stopped ticking in the universe, and that Douglas is powerless to freeze its mechanism. Douglas is stunned, for he had begun almost to believe that the annihilation of the Court House Clock has slowed time almost to a standstill, summer had lingered on, the great river of July had flowed very slowly indeed into the warm lakes of August. But now, in August, Douglas, with his great-grandmother's death, hears Time ticking again, in his veins, in his temples, his throat, his chest. He sees himself beginning to jog along, trot, run, race, rush, flurry, like the old men crashing on toward oblivion. The first smell of autumn floats into his room, the temperature drops warningly. There are signs and portents and warnings of the end of summer, and school and life coming on like a great tidal wave. Douglas lies there listening to the clock ticking in his body.

This remarkable outline sketch for chapter 21 sets in motion the playing out of all the parallel stories of Green Town as well as the main story of war between the young and the old. In the final three chapters, Leo Auffman works feverishly at his invention in the garage until, walking back to his house one evening, he realizes that his own beautiful family, framed in his view through the parlor window, is his true happiness machine. Grandpa places a mandolin in Miss Bidwell's front yard to see if the strange old man who returns every night to her stepless porch is indeed her ancient beau. The mystery man finds it and serenades her to no effect, but the next day she quietly arranges to have her porch steps restored. Mrs. Bentley tries one more time to convince Isabel that she was once as young as she is now; failing, she burns all her mementoes and photographs (chaps. 22, 24). And the colonel decides to defeat Douglas's Grand Army from within. He arranges a birthday party for Isabel, and Douglas realizes, for the first time, that he is in love (chap. 23). The war is over, but questions remain: "[T]he book ends with Quartermain and Bleak asking themselves who has won and who lost, and Douglas and Tom and Charlie saying the same, speaking of all the gains and losses and the equaling-out [*sic*] of their lives. Douglas knows he has won because he has put out his hand to touch the world. But Tom, much younger, feels the sadness of summer gone to never come back the same. They walk on home. And Douglas, that night, puts the town back to sleep again, sadly, happily, on the last day of summer, 1928" (chap. 24).

Walter Bradbury had seen an early version of the outline in late October 1954 while visiting the Bradburys in California, and he was delighted to receive the finished version via Don Congdon a month later. For both agent and editor, the outline eased concern over the distractions that continued to keep author Bradbury away from sustained work on the novel. This was doubly frustrating, since both Congdon and Walt Bradbury felt that the pieces of the novel, the underlying story-chapters, were essentially finished—and had been for months, if not years. Doubleday executives had not forgotten that one of the major delays had been Bradbury's jump to Ballantine to publish *Fahrenheit 451* in 1953, a time when Doubleday technically held the rights to Bradbury's first "novel." Although Walt Bradbury did not block that crucial event in his author's career, he soon pulled hard to get him back on course with the Illinois novel. Nevertheless, the editor understood that some of the distractions were unavoidable; for instance, follow-up complications involving the *Moby Dick* screenplay had to be worked out sooner than later. Ever since his return from Europe in June, Ray Bradbury had shopped his screenplay to Doubleday and other houses to test its publishing potential but had received no firm offers. Late in the year he found to his great distress that John Huston had placed his own name on the shooting script as coauthor. This ended all efforts to publish but led Bradbury into a legal battle for sole credit, a struggle that would continue off and on throughout 1955. In June of that year he won a ruling in his favor from the Writer's Guild of America (West), but Huston quickly made a countercase that, combined with his influence and personality, eventually reversed the earlier ruling.[14] Argued today, the case might turn out differently. Huston certainly made many helpful suggestions and revisions to the screenplay, but there is little doubt that Bradbury was responsible for the vast majority of the text and its structure. And there is no doubt that these frustrating events represented a significant distraction from his work on the Green Town novel.

Other distractions would be far more pleasant but no less tangible. Bradbury's gamble in reworking the *Dark Carnival* collection for Ian Ballantine in 1955 turned into an enduring new title—as *The October Country*, the best of Bradbury's weird fiction remains in print to this day. Walt Bradbury was once again displeased with this digression but felt that his friend should be able to work out his final vision for these stories and thus clear the way for sustained work on the Illinois novel. But the author's growing reputation in many genres and in many countries continued to play havoc with his schedule. In the later half of 1954, he had been deeply involved in the production of "Switch on the Night," his first illustrated children's storybook. He worked especially hard to convey to his illustrator and to his Pantheon editors the kind of presentation he expected, and these labors paid off in the form of a number of excellent reviews.[15] But just as this media project wound down, another surfaced. The very week after finishing the November 1954 outline for *Summer Morning, Summer Night,* Bradbury was approached by MGM's Sam Goldwyn Jr. with a pilot teleplay he had produced from "The Black Ferris" (1948). The year before, Goldwyn had purchased television rights with a seven-year option for film. Bradbury worked through the 1954 holiday season, very informally and without a contract, to extend the teleplay (written by Mel Dinelli) into a rough screen treatment. This was only a preliminary exercise; Bradbury would spend much of 1955 developing a completely new treatment and eventually a full screenplay from old notes and sketches for a dark carnival novel that would eventually become (in both print and screen) *Something Wicked This Way Comes.* This evolution, as well as other Bradbury film projects, would continue throughout the late 1950s.

Summer 1955 brought Bradbury's first major foray into drama. Producer Paul Gregory wanted an appropriate Bradbury work for theater adaptation and quickly bought stage rights to *Fahrenheit 451.* Thrilled with the fact that Charles Laughton would coproduce, Bradbury contracted to write the play himself.[16] By December he had to face another less thrilling fact—Gregory and Laughton let him know, as gently as possible, that he was not yet a successful playwright. Nevertheless, his experience with these two geniuses would pay off later as Bradbury became, in the middle of his career, adept at bringing his shorter fiction to stage and television. In fact, television was already contributing to his time crunch in the mid-1950s. A number of his stories reached the small screen, often using his own teleplays. Six Bradbury tales aired on national networks between July 1955 and November 1956. He was involved to some degree with all of them and wrote two of the teleplays himself—"Shopping for Death," broadcast on CBS's *Alfred Hitchcock Presents* in January 1956, and "The Marked Bullet," which aired on NBC's *Jane Wyman Presents* that November. These were also the last golden years of radio in America, and thirteen new productions of Bradbury stories aired on CBS and NBC Radio during 1955 and 1956. The radioplays were all written by others, but Bradbury and Congdon worked carefully to ensure the quality of these new productions; in fact, Bradbury wrote introductions for two stories ("Hail and Farewell" and "Season of Disbelief") and presented them himself during the 1956 radio season.

Don Congdon continued to handle all the details for the ever increasing volume of Bradbury's literary business and nearly all of his multimedia affairs as well. Bradbury retained Ben Benjamin for his West Coast film and television projects, but Congdon insisted on coordinating these matters in order to ensure that there was no duplication of negotiations.[17] Bradbury's popularity across genres, as well as his own tendency to be too generous with rights in dealing with those he trusted, made this arrangement preferable for all concerned. The correspondence of this period shows that Bradbury now had to pay attention as well to hundreds of foreign-publishing negotiations in dozens of countries around the world. Congdon knew better than others that unavoidable distractions would continue to attend Bradbury's growing reputation at home and abroad. But he was nonetheless disappointed when it became apparent that Bradbury would not make the hoped-for publication date of fall of 1955 for the Green Town novel. In fact, he would miss it by two full years.

The ever-present specter of linear time and its deadline pressures stood in direct conflict with Bradbury's signature habit of revising every story over and over until it was as close to perfection as he could bring it. He could always use other, more mature stories to buy time to develop those in progress. But Bradbury had no such luxury as he struggled to bring together a full-length novel from the *Summer Morning, Summer Night* materials. It was one thing to outline a novel but another to smoothly bridge the stories in a way that would bring his unusual plot to perfection. Art came to imitate life as he struggled to balance his outside commitments with work on his Illinois novel—a novel about a young boy's efforts to destroy the tyranny of time and its ultimate metaphor, death. In the end he was unable to force a solution in the time allotted by his publisher. Bradbury was unable to write at all on the project during the first half of 1955. Instead, he worked as much as his schedule permitted on the less stressful work of background reading. In January he apprised Walt Bradbury of what he was up to: "Right now I am stoking my furnace with much material peripheral to the Illinois book. That is, I am reading books about small towns, books about weather and small town architecture. All of these things, I know, put in, will trip little tabs of memory and give back to me many things I have forgotten."[18] During this period he read, for the first time, Huckleberry Finn.

In this way he hoped to overcome the anxieties of time and deadlines, but the multiple tasks that he and his publishers, agents, and fans had set in motion continued to grow. In July Maggie gave birth to their third daughter—now, on top of everything else, the Bradbury parents were outnumbered by Bradbury children. The next month he presented Walt Bradbury with the news of his new baby and his new stage play in vivid terms of comparative time: "Which brings me, inevitably, to the Illinois book and the simile which occurs to me most often when I stop and look in at my subconscious or whatever in hell it is that ticks in there by night or at noon. . . . it's a clock shop full of clocks all set for different times . . . here's the play, ticking like a time-bomb, set to go off in a few weeks . . . here's an idea for a book in some future year, no more than a whisper of sand in an hour-glass . . . and here's the Illinois book, a grandfather clock, by God, ticking slowly away but moving on toward the hour when it will strike with full and sonorous tone" (ellipses Bradbury's).[19]

He wanted, above all, to see the material from all angles before he finalized it: "Since the Illinois book must speak clearly for all the ideas I have gathered since I was a boy, and try to make sense, I have paced through it now at a dogtrot, now at racing speed, and often standing and just looking at the nearest cow. I'll be back to work on Illinois once the play is finished, in October." He also knew what was at stake; as Walt Bradbury had observed back in February, "Your writing this book is not simply a matter of fulfilling a contract—I'm sure you realize that by now. As they say in Hollywood, this thing 'is bigger than both of us,' and has now achieved the status of something that your talent and your career demands. I have never been more sincere than when I say this can be a really great performance." It would indeed be a great performance, but as the months passed, both men came to realize that the "performance" might better be presented in two "acts."[20]

By the end of the year, both Bradburys had decided to pull out the stories that could be spared from the novel to make a book of Illinois stories that could serve as preamble to the novel.[21] This would remove the pressure of the clock and allow author Bradbury to literally buy time with the work that was already done. Shortly before Christmas he sent his editor a jacket sketch and proposed the title *Green Town, Illinois*. But early in the new year, Macmillan came out with a similar title, and Ray Bradbury immediately proposed *Dandelion Wine* as the new working title for the story collection. Agent and editor felt good about the change, and now it was up to the author to make it all come together. All three realized that this was not just another story collection. In the spring of 1956, as Bradbury began preliminary plans for another of his periodic collections (one that, in 1959, would become *A Medicine for Melancholy*), Walt Bradbury reiterated why *Dandelion Wine* had to come first: "This is vitally important because, as you remember, this was to be not only an interim book before the novel but a curtain-raiser, by its nature, to the novel and thus it is a logical planned publication in your career—rather than 'just another Ray Bradbury collection.'"[22] Here and earlier, Walt Bradbury's carnivalesque use of such terms as "performance" and "curtain-raiser" indicates just how well he understood Ray Bradbury's approach to fiction (unfortunately, no one else at Doubleday really seemed to understand his carnivalesque approach to life at all).

On August 14 Bradbury forwarded a new outline of contents for *Dandelion Wine*. At this point the stories needed reintegrating to create a new and seamless whole, but Bradbury was clearly thinking of this book's relationship to the larger novel that was to follow: "In a way, I see this book as a real preliminary, a basic setting, a revelation of Douglas, that will prepare us for the second book, GREEN TOWN, ILLINOIS, or whatever we decide to title it. All the things that happen to Douglas in the summer of 1928, should come to a full boil in the following summer of 1929." At this point the stories he had extracted did not provide a strong or engaging opening section. He would have to rework the order and come up with a sequence of internal bridges that would make this collection into a unified cycle of stories with an overarching narrative structure. He solved most of these problems by the final week of October 1956, when Walt Bradbury visited during his annual trip to Doubleday's West Coast office. To his great joy he was able to return to New York with the initial *Dandelion Wine* manuscript and another jacket sketch, both items presented by an equally happy author. Rewrites of two early chapters arrived in New York on November 12, and at this point the book was essentially complete.[23]

The transformation from novel to story cycle is striking in its simplicity and creativity (table 10). Bradbury successfully extracted the structure without destroying the source novel through a shift in thematic focus—in *Dandelion Wine*, instead of making war on old people, Douglas and Tom would carry on a more subtle struggle with the concept of time itself. Now the weapons would be a yellow tablet and a Ticonderoga pencil, which Douglas uses to record their discoveries as the summer unfolds. Bradbury wrote or rewrote ten bridges; in each of these the boys write down the revelations of their most recent adventure or in some way prepare themselves for what's just ahead. As days go by, Douglas takes advantage of various "desiring machines" to explore life. Such opportunities to move through time and space come by means of his new tennis shoes, rides on the electric car known as the Green Machine, excursions on the town trolley, and visits to old

Table 10. The two surviving dated outlines for *Summer Morning, Summer Night* show how the survey of various age groups opening the earlier outline was discarded as Bradbury focused more fully on the war between the boys and the old men. Stories brought across from these earlier novel outlines can be seen in Bradbury's reordered and bridged sequence for *Dandelion Wine*. Story-chapters carried over into *Dandelion Wine* from one of the two novel outlines are indicated in bold. Two undated outlines contain other published and unpublished story chapters (see table 9). Unpublished outlines reproduced courtesy of Ray Bradbury.

Summer Morning, Summer Night Outline (20 Feb. 1951)	*Summer Morning, Summer Night* Outline (24 Nov. 1954)	*Dandelion Wine* Page Proofs (Mar. 1957)
First Day of Summer	Part 1: The Chess Players	**Awakening bridge**
The Town	1. First Morning	**"Illumination"**
The Three Streets	**Awakening bridge**	**"Dandelion Wine"**
The Old People	**Summer in the Air**	Running bridge
The Children	2. The Sound of Summer	["**Summer in the Air**"]
The In-Betweens	**The Lawns of Summer**	Revelations bridge 1
The Old Maids	3. The Attack from the Ravine	["**The Season of Sitting**"]
The Night	4. **The Green Machine**	["**The Happiness Machine**" 1]
Summer Night	5. The Quiet Hour	["**The Night**"]
Morning After	6. The Death of So-and-So	["**The Lawns of Summer**"]
The Capture	**The Season of Sitting**	["The Happiness Machine" 2]
The Magical Kitchen	7. **The Happiness Machine** 1	Rugbeating bridge
Season of Disbelief	8. [The Chess Players]	["**Season of Disbelief**"]
The Great Fire	9. **The Whole Town's Sleeping**	Revelations bridge 2
A Story about Love	**The Night**	["The Last, the Very Last"]
The Screaming Woman	10. Midnight	Revelations bridge 3
All on a Summer's Night	11. The Happiness Machine 2	["**The Green Machine**"]
The Green Machine	12. All on a Summer's Night 1	["**The Trolley**"]
Deep Summer	**Illumination**	["**Statues**"]
The Statues	13. Slow Motion, Fast Motion	Revelations bridge 4
The Window		["Exorcism"]
The Blue Remembered Hills	Part 2: The Court House Clock	Revelations bridge 5
The Pumpernickel	14. **The Trolley**	["**The Window**"]
The Playground	Arrival and Departure 1	Revelations bridge 6
Autumn Afternoon	15. Arrival and Departure 2	Dandelion Wine bridge 1
The Loons Fly South (The End)	16. Miss Bidwell 1	["The Swan"; also published as
	17. July Fourth	"Lime-Vanilla Ice"]
	All on a Summer's Night 2	Revelations bridge 7
	18. [The Grand Army Fasts]	["**The Whole Town's Sleeping**"]
	Dandelion Wine	Revelations bridge 8
	The Magical Kitchen	["Good-by, Grandma"; revised
	19. **Season of Disbelief** 1	from **The Beautiful Sleep**]
	20. [The Courthouse Clock]	Revelations bridge 9
		["The Tarot Witch"]
	Part 3: The Birthday Party	Weather bridge
	21. **The Beautiful Sleep**	Junkman bridge
	22. The Happiness Machine 3	["Green Wine for Dreaming"]
	Miss Bidwell 2	Revelations bridge 10
	The Season of Disbelief 2	["Dinner at Dawn"; revised from
	23. The Birthday Party	**The Magical Kitchen**]
	24. The Season of Disbelief 3	Dandelion Wine bridge 2
	The Happiness Machine 4	
	Miss Bidwell 3	
	[Reflections: Who Won?]	

Colonel Freeleigh for recitations of his memories from the last century. Freeleigh's story ("The Last, the Very Last") had not appeared in early outlines of the novel, and in retrieving it for the new collection, Bradbury developed a useful variation on lived, or nonsequential, time. The cumulative effect of these various "machines" sets up the central struggle of the new narrative. Tension builds as, one by one, each breaks down and the boys can no longer depend on them or their owners. As the bridges progress, the boys (and especially Douglas) begin to suffer a crisis of faith in the town, the people, the summer, and life itself. They begin to understand that death comes for all, and they must reconcile this fact in some way to the life that goes on around them. But where is the final insight, the key revelation, that will make sense out of all these complexities?

Bradbury finally decided, quite simply, to put time in a bottle. He could not transfer "The Birthday Party" from the novel, for the unexpected effects of that encounter are central to the further development of both young and old as they sense that love of life is the only thing truly worth fighting for. Instead, he turned to the new title story itself to provide a master metaphor for the new collection. Bradbury moved "Dandelion Wine" to the beginning of the book and wrote two recursive bridges to bring the magic of the bottled summer through the middle and end of the new sequence. Then he inserted a relatively new story, "Green Wine for Dreaming," to resolve the final crisis: Douglas falls ill and is near death until the junkman brings him a reviving draught of life late at night. These two wines, then, become metaphors for the celebration of life. Once again, as in the case of the development of *Fahrenheit 451*, literary reverie became important as the unifying thematic element of one of Bradbury's major fictions. But the scenes of winemaking and drinking are decidedly of more importance in this story because they combine elements of earth, air, fire, and water. (*Fahrenheit 451* mentions wine as a synthesis of the world's sensations only once in the text.) Due to these passages, one could even say that *Dandelion Wine* became that rare thing, a novel of reveries.

Two other new stories joined those that had been brought forward from the last outline of the novel. "Exorcism" and "The Tarot Witch" add carnivalesque elements in the middle of the new collection. "The Tarot Witch" is no doubt the result of Bradbury's parallel work in developing the dark carnival screenplay, for the title character and her master (Mr. Black) suggest characters in what would become Bradbury's first true Green Town novel, *Something Wicked This Way Comes*. Bradbury further reinforced the opening sequence of *Dandelion Wine* by developing a minor chapter section from the middle of the novel—Tom's reverie about life—into "Illumination," a story in its own right. In this version Douglas becomes the central consciousness as he picks blueberries with his father and brother; it is Douglas, rather than Tom, who discovers that he is alive all over.

The introduction of a father to complete the family structure of the Spauldings is just one element of character development that Bradbury brought to a new level as he moved from novel to story cycle. This had been a conscious goal for some time and was perhaps one of the sticking points in the harsher narrative of the original novel. Just before the decision to break up *Summer Morning, Summer Night,* he discussed this aspect with Walter Bradbury: "This year for the first time, I feel I'm beginning to understand characterization. And by the time I'm forty-five or so, with luck and perseverance, I hope to be able to create whole sets of characters with all their incredible different textures intact. Up until now, the mystery of my slowness on the Illinois book has defied me, but now I know that much of it was waiting for the clarification of my ability to characterize."[24]

The new bridges, in combination with the strong selection of story chapters extracted from the novel, allowed Bradbury to breathe life into the two boys and their grandfather—perhaps some of the other story subjects as well. With these challenges successfully met, the prelude volume to the Green Town novel moved closer to publication. Walt Bradbury coordinated the paperwork to incorporate the additional book under the existing contract and set a tentative release date of June 1957.

Accommodating the new book within the existing contract structure was made easier by Walt Bradbury's growing conviction to present *Dandelion Wine* to the public as a novel. The nearly seamless continuity of the manuscript was a key factor, and on December 4 he wrote to describe how this would affect plans for the dust jacket: "We are definitely going to present this book as a novel. There will be some extenuation in the description on the flap copy of what kind of book it is, but I am firmly convinced that one has to apologize to no one in calling it a novel, and therefore we want a jacket that suggests 'big novel' tone."[25] The new design removed such narrowing features from the preliminary jacket as a lawnmower and tennis shoes. The final illustration, by then up-and-coming artist Robert Vickrey, reveals a deep-focused field of dandelions extending to the horizon; the byline on the jacket prominently declares that this book is "A Novel by Ray Bradbury." In this way the original novel remained a protected work in progress, known only to a few writers, editors, and agents, waiting for the muse to return.

Walt Bradbury had first seen a manuscript of the original novel in 1951; now, as 1956 ended, he could be sure that a Green Town novel of sorts would indeed reach print the next year. Meanwhile, Ray Bradbury continued to perfect what was shaping up to be a well-received book. The main problem appeared to be a consequence of unwrapping "The Night" from the dark story of attempted murder, "The Whole Town's Sleeping." The beautiful little family picture of "The Night" had been completely overshadowed inside the murder story, and it now seemed beyond the pale for little Tom and his mother to be looking for Douglas in the ravine on the same night as a murder and an attempted murder by the Lonely One. To avoid this, Bradbury moved it forward in the new chronology to nest within Leo Auffmann's story of "The Happiness Machine." Prior to submission, he had brought "The Happiness Machine" forward in the chronology to complete the opening sequence of *Dandelion Wine.* He had explained his reasoning to Walt Bradbury in earlier correspondence: "I believe there is a way to make the chapter titled THE HAPPINESS MACHINE serve the early sections of the book well. It is this MACHINE that will probably enable me to give structure to all the beginning. The machinery of happiness, after all, is of interest to everyone, to Douglas, Tom, and the other children, as well as to Mr. Auffmann, the inventor."[26]

There was still work to do in the new year, for episodes of "The Happiness Machine" were woven through both "the Night" and "The Lawns of Summer."[27] Bradbury submitted two rewrites of this sequence in January 1957. The first was incorporated into his manuscript setting copy, but the second arrived after galleys were in work. Doubleday compositors and copyeditors tried to make the proper insertions and deletions but depended on Bradbury to check their work when he received galleys on February 11. On the twenty-seventh he sent corrected galleys back to New York with instructions marking the proper sequence of the nested stories. He also wrote new paragraphs to strengthen the final sections of "Dinner at Dawn" and tied up a loose end in "The Green Machine." In detaching the latter from the original novel, he had left the two spinster sisters thinking they had actually run over and killed a "Mr." Quartermain with their silent electric car. The galley revision has Douglas passing a message to the sisters saying "everything's all right." They do not understand what this means and vow to never drive the car again. This seemingly cryptic fix allows readers to know that the old ladies have exaggerated the event, but it effectively advances the overall plot by eliminating the marvelous green machine from the recreations of summer. Readers, however, move on without ever knowing the pivotal role that the tangential Mr. Quartermain once played in the original novel concept.

Bradbury made final galley revisions as well to "The Whole Town's Sleeping," apparently in an effort to make this story more of a piece with the rest of the nostalgic narrative. In January, prior to the galley work, he had expanded the bridge preceding this story. All of this was no doubt in response to his concern that this terror tale might be too dark for the collection. The previous August he had voiced this concern to his editor as he submitted the outline for the new book: "Chapter 29 is of course THE WHOLE TOWN'S SLEEPING, the story about the Lonely One. As before, I am still in doubt as to whether this story is too powerful for such a book as *Dandelion Wine.* It might well destroy the whole light structure of the book."[28] The January revisions convinced Bradbury that he could retain the story within the gentle fabric of the new book; however, the dark sequel "At Midnight, in the Month of June" was still incompatible with Bradbury's need to keep Lavinia alive and was not incorporated in the final mix. The original *Ellery Queen* printings of these stories, which remain outside the nostalgic context of the Green Town book, combine to form one of Bradbury's best extended tales of terror and remind us of the macabre origins of many of the Green Town works.

Page proofs were ready by the end of March. While Bradbury looked them over, bound copies went out to potential reviewers and key readers in the book industry.[29] In April, Clifton Fadiman and the other Bradbury enthusiasts on the Book-of-the-Month Club Editorial Board reluctantly declined to make *Dandelion Wine* a prime selection, but they did designate it as an alternate selection and planned a solid review for a fall issue of *BOMC News.* Rupert Hart-Davis, Bradbury's good friend and British publisher since 1950, also received a proof in April and immediately began negotiations with agents at A. D. Peters, who represented Congdon and the Matson Agency in London. By the end of the month, Congdon and Bradbury had received an offer for a £100 advance to be paid on publication. The offer was in line with the previous British contract for *Fahrenheit 451* and consistent with postwar English publishing practice, especially for an American author with a loyal British readership but who had never broken into the U.K. best-seller lists. For his part, Hart-Davis offered very good royalty rates in return for the ongoing relationship. But Congdon was responsible for arranging the best deal possible and felt that the £100 offer was a minimal advance for any author in the British market. He wanted better for this new book, which was very different from Bradbury's previous science fiction and fantasy titles. This departure in material represented a potential jump to a new level of recognition in both England and America, and Congdon wanted the best effort from publishers. He knew that Bradbury would accept the Hart-Davis offer, but he wanted his client to realize that things could change in the future: "I know, for instance, that Hart-Davis has just become associated with Heinemann, one of the very big publishers, who've taken over his distribution, although this has nothing to do with editorial control, I understand. I do think that if Hart-Davis does not do terribly well with DANDELION WINE, perhaps you should consider moving to a bigger and better publisher, depending of course on what the next book is to be."[30] Hart-Davis would continue to secure Bradbury titles through the 1960s, but Congdon's hunch would prove correct in the long term; Hart-Davis, like so many other small British publishers, would eventually merge into larger conglomerates during the 1970s.

Both agent and author soon turned to another problem closer to home. Minor delays had led Walt Bradbury to shift *Dandelion Wine*'s June release date to early

July; this was not unexpected, and the consensus within Doubleday was that a summer release for this timely summer idyll could only boost sales. But now, with the elusive title finally ready for the public after six years of development and transformation, an unexpected complication delayed release until September. The problem involved first-serial rights to the individual stories, which by contract had to culminate in magazine publication prior to book release.[31] As usual, Bradbury and Congdon had worked diligently to get every self-contained story-chapter serialized in some form prior to book publication. Most had already appeared in print, and in the spring of 1957 the *Saturday Evening Post* had picked up two chapters from *Dandelion Wine* for summer issues, leaving only four chapters to appear without prior serialization: "Statues," "Exorcism" (also known as "Magic!"), "The Tarot Witch," and "Green Wine for Dreaming." With the exception of "Statues," these were relatively late compositions, and there was simply no time to develop variants as stand-alone stories. The *Post* actually moved up the first of their two stories, "Good-By, Grandma," to the May 25 issue, but trouble immediately developed over the second story, "The Happiness Machine." The periodical version was presented in its original form without the two interchapters ("The Night" and "The Lawns of Summer") it would span in *Dandelion Wine*. Illustrations were the major source of the delay, and by the time the graphics were ready, the story had been rescheduled for a September issue. Since these constituted a sunk cost, it would be very expensive for Bradbury to return the purchase price and then buy the story back to compensate the *Post* for their investment. It was better to keep a good working relationship with the magazine, and even Walt Bradbury knew that publication in the *Saturday Evening Post*, whose readership represented the ideal market for *Dandelion Wine*, would offset the consequences of the delay somewhat. Book release was thus rescheduled for September 5.

Bradbury spent much of the summer in England, under contract to Hecht-Hill-Lancaster Productions, writing a screenplay for director Carol Reed based on his early 1950s novella "And the Rock Cried Out" (1953). In August, the Bradburys vacationed in Italy before returning to the States just in time for the release of *Dandelion Wine*. Advance sales for the hardcover had reached nearly seven thousand, and with market release, major book reviews began to come in. These were preceded by the *Library Journal*'s very positive review and a coveted "highly recommended to all libraries" endorsement. The reviewer for the August issue of *Kirkus* was also impressed, noting how well Bradbury accomplished the difficult task of shifting the narrative consciousness from story to story: "Douglas is now a central figure, now a participant, and frequently merely a passer-by in the lives of his elders. This demands rather special handling and understanding."[32] As promised, the August *Book-of-the-Month Club News* included a wonderful review by Basil Davenport. Such kudos continued in the major publications, which began over the weekend following release. The *Saturday Review* of September 7 contained, along with an inset image of Bradbury's jacket photo, a remarkable double-column analysis by Robert Bowen. Bowen established a significant American context for *Dandelion Wine* in a very compelling sequence of observations:

> No other writer since Mark Twain has caught the vitality and innocence of small-town American youth with as fine and mature a perception as Ray Bradbury's.
>
> Beyond this he has chronicled that final tender year of America's youth before the disillusion of The Great Depression and World War II and The Univac Age. He calls back a time now obscured by the inverted sentimentalities of Fitzgerald and Dos Passos. For in the late Twenties much of America did live in an aura of peace and harvest. Families listened together to the Victrola over ice cream; children, parents, grandparents, and great-grandparents did house happily together; and growing boys did love their mothers and respect their elders. As a document alone "Dandelion Wine" is valuable since no other writer of real repute has elected to handle the period according to the terms of its own optimistic truth.[33]

Indeed, Bradbury was now a writer of real repute and had proven his ability to express truth in his prose fiction that was at once special and universal. He provided a lasting and true look at the bedrock American experience that once fed and served the narrower big city and high society worlds chronicled by F. Scott Fitzgerald and John Dos Passos. Other reviewers also sensed that this book was different from what had come before. The *Kirkus* reviewer had noted that Bradbury would no doubt reach beyond his normal reading audience; in the *Herald Tribune Book Review* of September 8, Mary Ross observed that the book would strike a chord with middle-aged and older readers. Her review was generally positive, but she noted that Bradbury's special brand of fantasy seemed to provide his young protagonist with more maturity and sensitivity than one normally finds in a threshold teenager: "The fantasy that has marked the author's earlier writing rules 'Dandelion Wine,' giving adolescence a color and content perhaps evident only in retrospect."[34]

One could question how well young readers might navigate the book, but there was no doubt that readers of all ages would be drawn to this rare glimpse of timeless summer. Perhaps the biggest event of the first weekend after release was a cover review on the first page of the *Chicago Tribune*. In it V. P. Hass proclaimed the novel's core quality throughout the Midwest: "One of the warmest, most refreshing, most appealing evocations of a bygone day that I have ever read or ever hope to read." The review in the September issue of *Harper's* was critical, but

Marc Rivette's very positive review in the November 10 *San Francisco Chronicle* pinpointed the essential quality that any cynic would have to concede in his heart: "He has resisted the temptation—always present in books that look back—to be over poetic, and as a consequence there comes out an honest and genuine portrait, with wonder and delight." As the fall book season drifted toward the holidays, there was no doubt that *Dandelion Wine* was becoming a universal success with mainstream readers and reviewers. The following spring influential Chicago critic Van Allen Bradley presented Bradbury with a 1957 Midland Author's Award for *Dandelion Wine,* which had finished the competition second only to Jessamyn West's new novel, *To See the Dreams.*[35] In a very real sense, Bradbury had come home again to his Illinois roots. Such recognition for this book of Midwest memories was especially timely, for his father had passed away in Los Angeles barely a month after *Dandelion Wine* first reached the public. Bradbury would dedicate his next story collection to this remarkable man and later gave him immortality as the heroic father who bests the dark carnival of his next Green Town saga, *Something Wicked This Way Comes.*

Rupert Hart-Davis released the British edition almost simultaneously with Doubleday's; with few exceptions, he was unable to transmit his enthusiasm to British critics, who generally found *Dandelion Wine* effective in spots but too sentimental overall. The London *Times* reviewer presented a typical summary: "Sentences trail poetic clouds of glory, there are moments of exquisitely exciting description, but even these suggest that Mr. Bradbury is imagining too hard the thoughts he likes to attribute to childhood." The *Times* reviewer found it all "less convincing than the wilder magic of Mr. Bradbury's science fiction." Such attempts to compare *Dandelion Wine* to what was coming to be labeled (especially by his paperback publishers) as his classic science fiction, not to mention occasional efforts to classify *Dandelion Wine* itself as science fiction, would both frustrate and amaze Bradbury for decades. On November 19 Hart-Davis wrote Bradbury with news of steady sales while also conveying his growing realization that "this is not the one with which we are going to break through."[36] He was already looking forward to the next story collection, for Bradbury's collections had done rather well in Britain throughout the 1950s.

Meanwhile, back in the States, Doubleday's November sales totals for *Dandelion Wine* reached nine thousand and headed steadily toward ten thousand by the end of the year. It was a good start toward long-term market prominence, but sales leveled off, as they always did for Bradbury's hardcover editions, just over the ten thousand mark. In part, this was inevitable as readers waited for the following year's mass-market paperback edition, which was already in the works. In December Walt Bradbury negotiated a $5,500 advance from Bantam for a paperback edition scheduled for early 1959. Both Doubleday and Bantam editors knew that the unique content of *Dandelion Wine* eluded most genre labels and would make it a hard book to sell, especially since Bantam had made an industry out of promoting Bradbury as a science fiction author. The advance was not much over previous paperback contracts, but Walt Bradbury assured Don Congdon and Ray Bradbury that agreeing to this contract would ensure Bantam's continued support over the long haul. On his agent's advice Bradbury signed the contract, but Congdon was still concerned about the failure of the hardback sales to break through to another level for this remarkable new book. Since late August he had looked to see if Doubleday would follow through on Walt Bradbury's private enthusiasm with a very public marketing campaign. Doubleday was a large firm, and Congdon had felt for several years that Bradbury's rising prominence had not been matched by a comparable rise in media or point-of-purchase advertising. He was not impressed with what he saw, especially in New York, and in late October he wrote to Walt Bradbury with his concerns.[37]

Walt Bradbury responded with a summary of the advertising campaign, noting that Doubleday had done more in a national context for this book than any of the earlier Bradbury titles. He also reminded Congdon that the campaign included a large 100-by-3 column advertisement in the *New York Times* on September 11 and ran through a list of advertising sources that included the *New York Herald Tribune* as well as major national publishing, library, and trade publications. Congdon did not doubt these particulars but noted that most of the ads amounted to the kind of "list advertising" that helps initial sales for any author but does little to sustain a quality book in the marketplace. Even the daily listing Doubleday ran in the *Herald Tribune* the week of September 16 did little to distinguish Bradbury from other writers appearing on the paper's "Book Page." Congdon knew that the *New York Times* was key to the marketplace life of any new book and recommended that Doubleday place another prominent ad for the Christmas book season. The publisher did little out of the ordinary to promote *Dandelion Wine* over the holidays; instead, Walt Bradbury concentrated on getting *The Martian Chronicles* re-released in a new edition to match the excitement generated by the October launch of *Sputnik*. Despite Walt Bradbury's diligence, it was becoming increasingly hard for Ray Bradbury to keep his titles in print even as his reading public, especially in schools, continued to grow dramatically. With the editor's 1959 departure from Doubleday, Bradbury and Congdon looked seriously for another publishing house.

The Bantam paperback edition of *Dandelion Wine* has never been out of print in America. Eventually, Corgi, Bantam's British subsidiary, was persuaded to venture beyond Bradbury's so-called science fiction titles and in 1965 published British paperback editions of both of the Green Town books, *Dandelion Wine* and *Something Wicked This Way Comes*. In paperback these books have remained in print continuously on both sides of the Atlantic. In May 1958 Best-in-Books published eight chapters (more than one-third of the volume) in their usual condensed-book format. But it was only a matter of time before Doubleday let the first edition lapse, especially after Bradbury's departure for Simon and Schuster in the early 1960s. The author later followed his new editor, Robert Gottlieb, as he moved into an executive position with Knopf in 1968, and he finally won a release of hardback rights from Doubleday for *Dandelion Wine.* Knopf published a new cloth edition in 1975, complete with a Bradbury introduction and a new dust-jacket illustration by his original *Dandelion Wine* jacket artist, Robert Vickrey. But with the steady availability of mass-market paperback editions, it was inevitable that most of Bradbury's titles would go out of print in the increasingly expensive hardbound format. Bradbury's 1994 move to Avon Books was predicated in large part on that publisher's offer to keep attractive small-format hardbacks in print for most of his now-classic titles, and in February 1999 a new Avon edition of *Dandelion Wine* was released in the uniform style of its other Bradbury titles. Morrow's 2000 purchase of Avon has changed the imprint but not the continued availability of these editions.

All of Bradbury's retrospective Green Town projects have been visual as well as lyrical and poetic in their conception, and it became apparent to all associated with *Dandelion Wine* that this first published Green Town book might be easily transferred into other media. Bradbury usually explored film and television possibilities first, but in this case both he and Congdon felt that Broadway options should be explored prior to testing interest in Hollywood. Even before publication, *Dandelion Wine* seemed tailor-made for musical adaptation, and Congdon soon sent copies of the book to New York producers.[38] Eventually, Bradbury authored a stage play and developed two musical productions from this material. In April 1967 the first musical debuted in New York at Lincoln Center, with music by Billy Goldenberg and lyrics by Larry Alexander. Bradbury also developed a second musical in collaboration with well-known pop-music composer Jim Webb in the 1970s, but this project was never produced. The original Lincoln Center production was revised with additional lyrics by Bradbury and performed at (then) California State College, Fullerton (1972), and the University of Tulsa (1989). His stage play has been performed several times; dramatic adaptations by other writers have also been performed, most notably at the Arena Stage in Washington, D.C. (1976).

Dandelion Wine, together with *Something Wicked This Way Comes* and related stories published individually over many years, represent a rich sampling of Bradbury's lifelong habit of returning to the fears and joys of his Illinois childhood for creative inspiration. In his search for a balanced view of life, he would often turn to the grand carnival of memories that enabled him to look at life and death in the right proportion, unclouded by the fear that all too often magnifies death to the point of paralysis in literature and in the surrounding world. When one critic wondered how Bradbury could love the dirty harbor, the dismal coal docks, and the filthy railyards of Waukegan, the author responded by showing just how he could place these aspects of life into a carnival perspective. The railyards provided the game of counting boxcars; the coal turned into a meteor shower as the young Bradbury played around the seasonal coal chute deliveries in his basement: "And again, that supposedly ugly railyard was where carnivals and circuses arrived with elephants who washed the brick pavements with mighty steaming acid waters at five in the dark morning."[39] These childhood memories stand at the center of his creative talent, but Bradbury has often found it difficult to focus them in a sustained work of book-length fiction.

With the completion of the novels *From the Dust Returned* (2001) and *Let's All Kill Constance* (2003), only two novel-length manuscripts remain active and unpublished from earlier years. Not surprisingly, both are novels in the Green Town tradition. Since the late 1950s, Bradbury has worked intermittently on a teleplay that has become a novel in progress titled *Somewhere a Band Is Playing*. It is the tale of a Midwest town very much like Green Town but a little farther off the beaten path. A stranger passing through finds a perfectly normal rural community until he discovers that there are no graveyards. Some of the characters in this novel are borrowed from the early character sketches and story fragments of *Summer Morning, Summer Night*, though with a new twist. The stranger eventually discovers that the people are essentially immortal; they age almost imperceptibly thanks to a special wine made from sunflowers. In the earliest surviving drafts of this manuscript, the elixir is dandelion wine.

The other novel in progress is, of course, the original *Summer Morning, Summer Night*. Bradbury eventually changed the title to *Farewell Summer*, and between 1970 and 1998 rewrote the manuscript to replace the story-chapters removed long ago to create *Dandelion Wine*. The central events—"The Clock Tower" and "The Birthday Party"—remain at the core of the novel, and new episodes join others remaining from the 1954 outline to form a continuous narrative of the war between young and old, which now takes place in the summer of 1929 following the events of *Dandelion Wine*. There are engaging new adventures and a very playful Rabelaisian ending (these and other aspects of the manuscript that reveal the underlying carnivalized structure of the novel are discussed under thematics). But before leaving the textual legacy that surrounds *Dandelion Wine*, it is important to survey the stories that have been left behind. Table 11 charts, as far as can be determined, the three categories of deletions from Bradbury's original Green Town novel. There are the seventeen story–chapters removed from the novel outlines and reworked (with three more-or-less new stories) in 1956–1957 for *Dandelion Wine,* and nine separately published stories that appear in various versions of the novel outlines through 1954. Early weird tales considered in the Ur-novel outline of the mid-1940s could have been effectively incorporated into the evolving work, especially stories such as "The Lake," which is specifically set within the familiar topos of Green Town and Lake Michigan. But only "The Night" continued in the textual history of the novel from this group, and it is the only *Weird Tales*–era piece included.

It is interesting to note that some of the stories carried through into the 1950s outlines disappear from both *Dandelion Wine* and *Farewell Summer.* For instance, young Tom's crush on the librarian recounted in "All on a Summer's Night" has never appeared in a Bradbury collection or novel. "A Story About Love," a variation on this theme involving a high school teacher and the gifted student who loves her, was annotated in one outline as a story about one of Douglas's friends. It too disappeared from both projects, although it is mistakenly credited on the copyright page in every edition of *Dandelion Wine.* "The Pumpernickel" and "At Midnight, in the Month of June" involve the middle generation that Bradbury always found trouble accommodating in the evolving warfare of the novel. "Miss Bidwell" is an enchanting story of long-lost love rekindled without a word spoken between the elderly lovers, but it may be too digressive for the events of the reconstructed novel.

Finally, eleven of the Green Town tales included in various outlines survive in the two discard boxes or elsewhere and remain unpublished to this day. This is the most intriguing category of all, for these stories are complete and may someday be published, as stand-alone Green Town tales, to good effect. Bradbury may, indeed, take them up again, for short fiction has always been his most effective medium. But his stories have also been the building blocks of his novels and novelized story cycles, and it remains to be seen if any of the twenty pieces not incorporated into *Dandelion Wine* might some day be restored to *Farewell Summer.* These are stories of life and death and birth and love, hallmarks of *Dandelion Wine,* which at this point have not been fully breathed into *Farewell Summer. Dandelion Wine* remains an enduring and poetic exploration of the way we all first come to see that life and death are inextricably part of the human condition. Within its pages Douglas Spaulding discovers who he is; in its final form *Farewell Summer* will no doubt tell us who he will become.

Thematics

The phenomenological discovery of self-consciousness, that moment when we discover ourselves as thinking beings enmeshed in a world, can occur in anguish

Table 11. Each of these stories appears in at least one of the early outlines or discard boxes for Bradbury's Green Town novel as it evolved from *The Blue Remembered Hills* (1946) into *Summer Morning, Summer Night* (1947–56). They are arranged in order of first publication as standalone tales; nearly all were first published in major-market slick magazines. Seventeen became untitled chapters of *Dandelion Wine* (1957). None of the remaining twenty stories were carried over into *Farewell Summer,* the post-*Dandelion Wine* form, which remains today a novel in progress. The eleven stories listed at the end of the chronology survive in the discard boxes and elsewhere but remain unpublished today.

Farewell Summer: The Chapters Left Behind

Title	First published (US)	First Collected (US)
The Night"	*Weird Tales* July 1946	*Dandelion Wine* (1957)
"The Great Fire"	*Seventeen* Mar. 1949	*The Golden Apples of the Sun* (1953)
"All on a Summer's Night"	*Today (Phil. Enquirer)* Jan. 22, 1950	Uncollected
"Miss Bidwell"	*Charm* Apr. 1950	Uncollected
"The Window"	*Collier's* Aug. 5, 1950	*Dandelion Wine* (1957)
"The Whole Town's Sleeping"	*McCall's* Sept. 1950	*Dandelion Wine* (1957)
"Season of Disbelief"	*Collier's* Nov. 25, 1950	*Dandelion Wine* (1957)
"The Green Machine"	*Argosy* (U.K.) Mar. 1951	*Dandelion Wine* (1957)
"These Things Happen"	*McCall's* May 1951	*Long after Midnight* (1976)*
"The Pumpernickel"	*Collier's* May 19, 1951	*Long after Midnight* (1976)
"The Screaming Woman"	*Today (Phil. Enquirer)* May 27, 1951	*S Is for Space* (1966)
"The Season of Sitting"	*Charm* Aug. 1951	*Dandelion Wine* (1957)
"The Lawns of Summer"	*Nation's Business* May 1952	*Dandelion Wine* (1957)
"Dandelion Wine"	*Gourmet* June 1953	*Dandelion Wine* (1957)
"The Playground"	*Esquire* Oct. 1953	*Fahrenheit 451* (1953)**
"Dinner at Dawn"	*Everywoman's* Feb. 1954	*Dandelion Wine* (1957)
"At Midnight, in the Month of June"	*Ellery Queen,* June 1954	*The Toynbee Convector* (1988)
"The Swan"	*Cosmopolitan* Sept. 1954	*Dandelion Wine* (1957)
"The Last, the Very Last"	*Reporter* Jun. 2, 1955	*Dandelion Wine* (1957)
"The Trolley"	*Good Housekeeping* July 1955	*Dandelion Wine* (1957)
"Summer in the Air"	*Saturday Evening Post* Feb. 18, 1956	*Dandelion Wine* (1957)
"Illumination"	*Reporter* May 16, 1957	*Dandelion Wine* (1957)
"Good-bye, Grandma"	*Saturday Evening Post* May 25, 1957	*Dandelion Wine* (1957)
"The Happiness Machine"	*Saturday Evening Post* Sept. 14, 1957	*Dandelion Wine* (1957)
"Statues"	*Dandelion Wine* Sept. 1957	*Dandelion Wine* (1957)
"Autumn Afternoon"	*One More for the Road* Apr. 2002	*One More for the Road* (2002)
"Arrival and Departure"	Unpublished	—
"The Beautiful Lady"	Unpublished	—
"The Circus"	Unpublished	—
"The Death of So-and-So"	Unpublished	—
"The Game of Anna Anna Anna"	Unpublished	—
"Hallowe'en in July"	Unpublished	—
"I Got Something You Ain't Got!"	Unpublished	—
"The Love Potion"	Unpublished	—
"Night Meeting"	Unpublished	—
"Summer Nights"	Unpublished	—
"A Serious Conversation"	Unpublished	—

* As "A Story of Love."
** Removed from most editions of *Fahrenheit 451;* in British edition of *The Illustrated Man.*

and suffering or in great joy. In *Dandelion Wine* it is joy and wonder that first find expression. Not surprisingly, given Bradbury's romantic imagination, this moment of awareness occurs in a natural setting. In early June twelve-year-old Douglas Spaulding, his father, and younger brother, Tom, are out walking in the forest around Green Town, Illinois, in search of fox grapes. In breaking the fine lines of a spider's web (metaphor for textuality) with his face earlier that morning, Douglas had the shivery sense, without reason, that something momentous was going to leap upon him on this special day. The feeling of anticipation continues and intensifies in the forest, which Bradbury compares to a great humming loom that weaves sensations together (another metaphor of textuality). Douglas feels himself at odds with his brother and father, who he thinks are driving away with their commonplace talk this encroaching awareness of life as "the terrible prowler, the magnificent runner, the leaper, the shaker of souls."

The father presents nature to the boys as a woven thing (a text of sensations), the sky being woven into the trees and vice versa. But Douglas perceives a wounding of nature, a breaking of the spell of enchantment, when he himself reaches into the thick bush to pick the grapes. Stained with the color of the fruit, his hand seems as if "he had somehow cut the forest and delved his hand in the open wound." This passage enacts a kind of anguished separation from nature, the anguish of individuation. But slowly the feeling of excitement stalks Douglas again over the next few pages until, in a spontaneous wrestling match with his brother, he feels it break down upon him with the force of a tidal wave. So intense is this experience that he is afraid that, when he opens his eyes, the world will have been destroyed. Instead, he finds to his surprise that the world is not only there for his delighted glance but is looking back at him in reciprocity:

And everything, absolutely everything, was there.

The world, like a great iris of an even more gigantic eye, which has also just opened and stretched out to encompass everything, stared back at him.

And he knew what it was that had leaped upon him to stay and would not run away now.

I'm alive, he thought.

His fingers trembled, bright with blood, like the bits of a strange flag now found and before unseen, and him wondering what country and what allegiance he owed to it. Holding Tom, but not knowing him there, he touched his free hand to that blood as if it could be peeled away, held up, turned over. Then he let go of Tom and lay on his back with his hand up in the sky and he was a head from which his eyes peered like sentinels through the portcullis of a strange castle out along a bridge, his arm, to those fingers where the bright pennant of blood quivered in the light.[40]

The same bloody hand associated earlier with an implicit sense of loss and wounding appears again here, now as a part of a body open to the world, transformed, and carnivalized. Similar to the grotesque bodily images of carnival, Douglas's body, through metaphor, has become a castle, and he gazes out through the portcullis at the bridge. Douglas is hardly aware of the presence of his brother now. He is mindful only of the pure becoming of appearances calling him to an adventure in being. "The world slipped bright over the glassy round of his eyeballs like images sparked in a crystal sphere," Bradbury goes on to add, describing the magical astonishment of a such a consciousness. This thematic moment has an affective tonality, typical of Bradbury, expressing his sense of authorship: "I'm *alive,* he thought."[41]

Bradbury describes Douglas Spaulding's consciousness poetically through metaphor as already inhabiting a fantastic world. The strange, enchanted castle is his carnivalized body from which he goes forth in quest of life. The world has drawn near to the body though metaphor. It has become a country whose flag—his fingers filled with blood—Douglas now owes allegiance. In these early sections, then, Bradbury tries to keep his text largely focused on the phenomenology of reading. The reader also feels in the center of a consciousness reflecting the world. Any bloodstained unconscious rifts seem to have been healed, at least temporarily. Nothing outside of this consciousness and its newly discovered joy and freedom—not even the unconscious textual stain of fox grapes—must interfere with the sense of well being. Douglas has achieved a self-contained center of consciousness, and textuality is largely submerged for the moment.

Textuality will return, however, when Douglas begins to write down events in his notepad and interpret them. He decides early in the novel to start making lists of everything that happens during the summer. This is suggested by Tom's "philosophy" of summing up everything he has done in his life, how many peaches eaten, games played, trees climbed, and such. But Douglas feels the need to go further and interpret these bare lists of facts. He wants to know their meaning for his life. All this is quite beyond Tom as Douglas divides his notepad into two parts, front and back, with facts listed in front under the heading "Rituals," and interpretations are written on the back, under the headings "Illuminations, Revelations, and Discoveries." Thus, in a very childlike but nonetheless profound sense, Douglas realizes the double character of life as self-consciousness to be experienced and a text to be interpreted.

When Douglas writes about these things, he enters into the experience of textuality. Bradbury, ever the Dionysian, never allows us to completely forget becoming and change. Feelings of loss and wounding remain to undermine our sense of the stability and the self-contained nature of Douglas's consciousness. We should realize then that Douglas's sense of consciousness and individuation is accompanied not only by a feeling for the newness of the appearances—the crystal sphere previously noted—but also by reminders of the abyss from which it has come. For instance, after this experience of the perfect roundness of being, Douglas closes his eyes to see "spotted leopards pad in the dark." In Nietzschean terms, what are these animals but the forgotten attendants of the god Dionysus, the god of wine and becoming, who brings the end of the spell of individuation?

This ambivalent tension between luminous individuation and the darkness of the body is operative in many of Bradbury's works, but nowhere is it more in evidence than in Douglas Spaulding's consciousness, which is so intensely alive to the nuances of life. At the end of this scene, Douglas wants to shoulder all the pails full of fox grapes, to carry their weight back home, because he wants to feel all he can feel, even pain. He vows, "I mustn't forget, I'm alive, I know I'm alive, I musn't forget it tonight or tomorrow, or the day after that." In order not to forget, Douglas decides he must record his experiences and become a writer. But writing is a paradoxical project because it tends to undermine the idea of consciousness as a self-contained sphere. His writing inevitably brings with it the potential to shatter comfortable illusions of identity.

Textuality also returns in the beating of the boardinghouse rug, where both Tom and Douglas find images of "the whole darn town" in the warp and woof of the carpet.[42] This ritual beating of Green Town is administered twice yearly. In typical carnival fashion the beating is done by the boys symbolically to the boys themselves. They are not spectators but participants, themselves part of the figure in the carpet. Also in typical carnival fashion, the beating not only mocks and degrades ("Take that! Take that!" the beaters, who include Mother, Grandma, and Great-Grandma, rhythmically cry) but also renews the town and orients it toward the future. The boys find signs and traces of past events and objects in the town, such as the various machines that operate in it, as well as signs of the future.

There is probably no clearer statement in all of Bradbury's writings about the "magical" nature of textuality. The carpet is itself connected by thematic threads to other episodes in the novel. Bradbury describes the women and boys performing this ritual beating as looking like "a collection of witches and familiars." Later Tom will be involved in a hilarious episode with a woman, Elmira Brown, who mistakenly thinks she can fashion a witch's potion (the catalog of contents for which is a carnival in itself) with him as an "innocent" who can protect her against the harmful effects of her own magic. And Douglas is also involved later with "magic" writing as a kind of destiny or fate in his adventure with the Tarot Witch (discussed below).

Through this image of textuality, Bradbury encourages us to think of Green Town as an open text carnivalized by various "desiring-machines" (to use a recent characterization of Bradbury's fantasy) that function in it.⁴³ The wire wands beating the carpet is one such machine. Another is Leo Auffmann's Happiness Machine, happily a folly-failure in representing what happiness is (the sound of which is compared to what might emerge from a gargantuan "giant's kitchen on a summer day"). Then there is the Green Machine—an electric car—of Miss Fern and Miss Roberta that Douglas can steal rides on, described as looking "like a little car off the carnival roller coaster"; the Green Town Trolley, a definitive nostalgia machine from the turn of the century about to be taken out of commission; the memory play of Colonel Freeleigh, whose mind is the boys' time machine; the ice house (laughingly called Summer's Ice House); and finally the ravine, described as a "dynamo" that never stops running. And Grandpa even compares the lawnmowers reaping grass to the confetti and serpentine thrown at carnivals.

More overtly a prop from carnival is the Tarot Witch, a fortune-telling machine that is liberated by Douglas and Tom from the money-grubbing hands of Mr. Black, the arcade owner. Her tarot cards contain images from carnival culture— "devils, hanging men, hermits, cardinals and clowns"—and she herself is released from her prison in "the carnival blaze of summer" by Douglas, who fantasizes about her as a beautiful young Italian girl. Although Douglas wants the Tarot Witch to write his fate and fortune as a reward for her release, she gives him a "beautiful blank but promising card" on which his future is open and undetermined.

Perhaps the most carnivalized desiring machine of them all is Grandma Spaulding's kitchen, which produces a banquet that confounds all the known culinary codes. It is described as a gustatory "factory gone wild," thriving on chaos, running with "no prejudice, no tolerance [note the semantic contradiction and ambivalence here] for recipe or formula, save that at the final moment of delivery, mouths watered, blood hammered in response." From the amount of exaggerated and hyperbolic language describing her banquet meals, it is easy to see them as social festivals of victory over the world, as the world made delicious, and not as examples of individual gluttony. While perhaps not entirely Rabelaisian, these meals are their own philosophy of the delight in life itself, explicitly compared to Shakespeare's texts by Grandpa.

Douglas's phenomenological sense of being and plenitude is allowed to continue until it is undermined by changing events. John Huff, "the only living god in the whole of Green Town," leaves him to go to Milwaukee; Colonel Freeleigh, the boys' time machine, dies of old age, as does Douglas's great-grandmother; and the Lonely One murders several women in the town. This serial killer is found to be a plain, ordinary man, "little and red-faced and kind of fat and not much hair." The boys—Tom and Charlie—have to mythologize him in order to make the town exciting again. But for Douglas, death has come a little bit too close (he almost drinks from the glass of lemonade left outside Lavinia Nebbs's house by the killer). In writing about these events in the back of his notepad, Douglas interprets the facts as leading inevitably to the conclusion that he too must die. Writing seems to involve him in the loss of identity, and he cannot complete the concluding line in his tablet about his own death.

In late August Douglas becomes sick, but no one seems to know what exactly is wrong with him. It is Mr. Jonas the junk man who finally cures Douglas's fever with the medicine of liberated imagination, with a reverie of cool stimulating air. Mr. Jonas is the most carnivalized character in the novel. In the blaze of summer, Tom sees him as infernal and ambivalent: "A red-haired man moved along below. Tom, seeing him illumined by the dying but ferocious sun, saw a torch proudly carrying itself [Mr. Jonas has red hair], saw a fiery fox, saw the devil marching in his own country." The language here is typical of the way in which Bradbury uses the children as carnival focalizers of events. What they see is always described in terms of carnival celebration and magical rituals. Mikhail Bakhtin writes that in carnival the devil is no longer the agent of fear that he is in official conceptions of hell; he becomes quite a jovial fellow. Furthermore, the "debasing junk" of the underworld becomes a source of rejuvenation.[44] In carnivalized hell it is the devil himself who gives us the elixir of life.

Regardless, Mr. Jonas considers himself not as an individual, but as "a kind of process, like osmosis, that made various cultures within the city limits available one to another." Douglas is told to drink with his nose while Mr. Jonas reads the carnivalized catalog (which fills an entire page) on a bottle marked "GREEN DUSK FOR DREAMING BRAND PURE NORTHERN AIR." This word reverie provides a healthy and bracing imaginary climate of cold air and white arctic heights that convinces Douglas to affirm his life again. Of course, the bottle does not contain any such substance in reality; it is only Douglas's saving capacity to dream that has been reaffirmed by the carnival language of exaggeration and hyperbole. But it saves him nonetheless. The boy is no longer crushed by the weight of summer. He has overcome the spirit of gravity.

In *Dandelion Wine*, writing leads to the destruction of comfortable illusions, but poetic language—which is particularly governed here by carnivalized modes of reverie—remains as a strong restorative source of pleasure and plenitude in being. Three times the novel sets forth—in June, July, and August 1928—ritual scenes of winemaking that combine and synthesize the scattered archetypal elements of the universe: earth, air, fire, and water. The novel is lifted to a philosophical level by these scenes, becoming, in effect, a novel of reveries. Douglas discovers in them a permanent core of childhood being. They not only lend unity to what would otherwise be a loose collection of episodes rather than a novel but also give shape and meaning to Douglas's maturing self by stimulating his capacity to dream and to interpret his life healthfully through reverie, which itself is a capacity to enjoy life. In a scene during the July brewing of dandelion wine, for instance, Douglas is offered a "thimble-full" of the beverage (the novel is set during Prohibition). After tasting it, he immediately carnivalizes himself by pretending to be a fire-eater.

In reverie, dandelion wine becomes an elixir that can heal the wounds of adult consciousness, the feeling of being separated from the childhood bodily self. As a character, Douglas Spaulding is moving toward maturity and toward accepting the burdens of adult consciousness, which entail acceptance of loss. Douglas, in other words, is becoming *self*-conscious. In the world of Greek myth, the suffering of individuation (the origin and primal cause of all suffering) is like the transformation of the cosmos into air, water, earth, and fire.[45] But intoxicated with wine, the followers of the god Dionysus looked forward to an end of the world torn asunder into elements. Wine, its production and drinking, is also Bradbury's symbol of such a restored oneness with the principle of life. Although the nightmare is given its due in the story of Lavinia Nebbs and the Lonely One, and the ravine that runs through the town represents the abyss, Bradbury for the most part rejects tragic representation.[46] As befits the aesthetics of fantasy as Bradbury understands it, the self in reverie is not brought to the point of tragic annihilation without the comfort of reverie or the promise of rebirth.

In *Dandelion Wine*, language itself takes on the capacity to dream and is capable of granting the reader an intense happiness at being in the world. Bradbury's poetic use of language is nowhere more in evidence than in describing these ritualized scenes of winemaking and drinking. A plenitude of meaning seems to reverberate in "the fine and golden words" of dandelion wine itself, repeated like an echo from scene to scene. In the first scene of winemaking, for instance, Douglas's grandfather lets the fiery golden flowers run amuck on his lawn like the followers of a Dionysian sun. Stare at them, he says, and these seemingly ordinary flowers burn a hole in your retina. The flowers have the dazzle and glitter of a molten sun. Combined with pure rainwater that has been washed by the four winds—"well on its way to wine already"—they are beautified further into images that invite reveries of summer even in the dead of winter. The wine bottles are stored in the cellar of the house, in the earth, instead of in the attic, where Douglas's father tells him "bright illusions" predominate that cannot later be dislodged. Close to the meaning of the earth, Douglas's grandfather sums up the potency of drinking dandelion wine by saying that it does not leave one tied to the past; one has "no regrets and sentimental trash lying about to stumble over forty years from now." To drink dandelion wine is to live the summer over for a minute or two along the way through winter. Healthful also is the spell of language the drink casts. On the book's last page, Douglas, dreaming of dandelion wine, understands now its true value as a life-sustaining fiction:

And if he should forget [the summer past], the dandelion wine stood in the cellar, numbered huge for each and every day. He would go there often, stare straight into the sun until he could stare no more, then close his eyes and consider the burned spots, the fleeting scars left dancing on his warm eyelids; arranging, rearranging each fire and reflection until the pattern was clear. . . .

So thinking, he slept.

And, sleeping, put an end to Summer, 1928.[47]

After the Dionysian dancing of the spots behind the eyelids, Douglas goes off to sleep (that is, loses self-identity), putting an end to the illusions of summer. They can be recovered, however. Such things are possible in the shelter of reverie, in the cellars of being. At the beginning of the novel, Douglas wonders how to make sense of the "interchange" he senses going on between civilization, the town, and "the softly blowing abyss" of the ravine, where a "million deaths and rebirths" happen every hour. Throughout the novel, Bradbury is interested thematically in these borderline and "indefinable" places where a dialogic struggle is ongoing between wild nature and civilization for possession of the landscape. Through the security provided by reverie, Douglas has learned the Dionysian wisdom of the abyss in a manageable way. In fact, he feels so secure that he imagines deliberately staring into the sun to provoke and later master the fleeting "scars" of becoming.

Reversing the familiar optical phenomenon, Nietzsche describes the myths of tragic representation as bright images that healing nature projects to "cure" us after a glance into the dark abyss. Tragic myth is an Apollonian illusion composed of "luminous spots to cure eyes damaged by gruesome night."[48] But in Bradbury's novel reverie creates metaphorical representations that cure us so that we may stare directly into the annihilating sun. Reverie may double the self, it may even bring it to the limits of consciousness (as it does here), but in Bradbury's aesthetics of fantasy, the images of tragic pessimism and representation have themselves been reversed for the affirmation of life.

Farewell Summer, Bradbury's novel in progress that is the planned sequel to *Dandelion Wine*, continues the story of Douglas Spaulding, now entering puberty, as he attempts to delay the forces of life that will bring change to his life and body. The title of the book is a valediction to summer—it opens, in its 1998 version, on October 1—but "farewell summer" is also the name of a flower that grows along the roadside that, when touched, gives an impression of autumn rust: "By every path it looks as if a ruined circus had passed and loosed a trail of ancient iron at every turning of a wheel." These carnivalized flowers permeate the opening landscape (they are only briefly mentioned in the published version of the novel's beginning, "Farewell Summer," contained in *The Stories of Ray Bradbury* [1980]), preparing us for what promises to be Bradbury's most Rabelaisian novel, one in which he explores the ambivalence of what Bakhtin calls the "material bodily lower stratum." Images of the phallus and urination appear prominently in this novel, as well as grotesque images of fetal development, which Douglas sees in a sideshow and which awaken his sexuality.[49] The theme of learning to accept and to affirm the ambivalence of life is very much in evidence.

The plot takes the form of a humorous war between the decrepit old and the boisterous young, the members of the school board of education and the members of Douglas's army of friends. The two groups represent the spheres of official culture and subversive carnival, respectively. As in all carnival wars, seriousness is given a thorough beating, but everyone ends up a winner. Bradbury also makes two playful intertextual references to his other writings (as well as the obvious contextual references to *Dandelion Wine)* in this novel. These references reveal how much Bradbury has become his own influence.

The book opens with a dream (and not a reverie) of Douglas being taken away by a parade of his friends and relatives to a long white steamboat, "a vast ship mourning with the voice of a foghorn," that arrives for him at the lake. Significantly in terms of Bradbury's other stories, the band on shore plays "Columbia, Gem of the Ocean," an intertextual reference to Bradbury's most famous science fiction story, "Mars Is Heaven!" The name of the boat is *Farewell Summer,* and Douglas finds out that he has to make this "brave journey" all by himself. The boy awakes from this nightmare and refuses to embrace the notion of a "farewell" summer, vowing to stop the passage of time. In the ravine he meets up with his brother, Tom, and some other boys who engage in a pissing contest, spelling out their names in the creek sand. Douglas writes "War" in the sand with his urine, and the gang decides to kill the members of the school board, most of whom live along the edge of the ravine, as their first act of war.

The old men are comically exaggerated images of old age and mock each other's growing decrepitude as being "piss-yellow." But they are serious about fixing school policies to limit the freedom of the children in the town, so in that sense they are the rigid and dogmatic enemy to whom all true carnivals are opposed. The first to die is Mr. Braling, an old man who keeps his heart going (he thinks) by listening to a metronome. Douglas fires his cap gun at Braling, upsetting the rhythm of the metronome, and he drops dead. The boy runs off to the ravine, where he is feted as the "arch criminal" of the "great Green Town Confederacy" by the other boys, who now willingly join him in the rebellion. Colonel Quartermain, who had come to Braling's house to discuss school board policy, witnesses what he stubbornly takes to be a murder and vows vengeance on Douglas. The boy later hits him accidentally with his bike ("a damned Hell-fire device," says Quartermain) and puts him in a wheelchair. Throughout the rest of the novel, as chair of the school board (Braling was secretary), the colonel represents the official culture of the town. In fact, he owns both the candy store, from which the boys refuse to eat candy, and the graveyard, which they invade to plan their strategies against the elders.

Leaving out several subplots involving other skirmishes with authority in the town (including an episode of mock fasting that Douglas imposes on his army and an epic description of the candy store that could fit comfortably in the pages of *Gargantua and Pantagruel*), the central episode of the novel is the boys' attack on the courthouse clock, where the school board is meeting to discuss its nefarious plans to "shorten summer vacations, trim Christmas holidays, and cancel the Spring Kite Flying Carnival." Douglas has come to believe that the clock, which "ran this town like a church," is the main agent of official culture that needs to be destroyed. Textually, this is one of the oldest parts of what was planned to be "the Illinois book" *(Summer Morning, Summer Night)* from which both *Farewell Summer* and *Dandelion Wine* derive. (As mentioned previously, because of its slow development, Bradbury compared the Illinois book to a grandfather clock ticking away slowly in his unconscious when he discussed delays with his editor at Doubleday.) Bradbury's symbolic poetic style is at its best in describing the ambivalence of this clock, as when Douglas voices what his grandfather had told him about it:

> The huge round lunar clock was a grist mill, he [the grandfather] said. Shake down all the grains of Time, the big grains of centuries and the small grains of years, and the tiny grains of hours and minutes, and the clock pulverized it, slid it silently out to the four directions of the town in a fine pollen of seconds, carried by cold winds to fall and powder everything! Spores that from that clock lodged in your flesh to pock and wrinkle it, to grow bones to monstrous sizes, to burst feet from shoes like turnips, to inflate bodies like balloons! Oh, how that great machine at the town's center ground and dispensed time in blowing weathers.[50]

In general, the clock is compared to a "lunar" (that is, dead) gristmill that grinds up the organic flow of time into pulverized particles, which it then disseminates throughout the town. So organic is Bradbury's imagination that he cannot help but restore life to the dead stone clock's products—the fine pollen of seconds—through images of pollination. Through this metaphor of metaphor, the gristmill clock now becomes a pollinating flower reminiscent of the farewell summer flowers that open the novel. Although he is afraid of the clock and the "holy place" it inhabits, Douglas manages to stop it, at least temporarily, with a bundle of fire-crackers. Quartermain plans to take revenge on the boys for this escapade by adopting the children's strategy against time. He has a beautiful birthday cake baked for one of the girls in the town, Lisabell (Isabel in the earlier outlines), whose tattered underpants the boys have all seen (and what they revealed of sexual difference as well), and has the party take place in the ravine. Figuring cor-rectly that the fasting boys will be unable to resist such a lure to their appetites, he plans the party as a trap to lure them into celebrating the passage of time. Douglas is smitten with Lisabell when she gives him the first piece of cake and feels himself on a merry-go-round of embarrassed desire. But Quartermain's plan to kill them with kindness backfires when Douglas unexpectedly gives his piece of sweet birthday cake to Quartermain, feeling a strange sort of sympathy for him sitting there in his wheelchair. In a moment that is very reminiscent of *Dan-delion Wine*, Douglas realizes that the old man, whom he has hurt and put in the chair, is really *alive*, and like all living things, he should not be killed. The shared taste of the cake brings love: "Quite suddenly he did not hate anybody. Quite suddenly they were all together here, they all belonged together, because they were all alive." The Nietzschean theme of overcoming revenge and the dead past through the affirmation of life is very prominent here, though in parodic form.

Quartermain, stunned and dismayed, tells his friend on the school board, Mr. Bleak (who dispenses wry ironic humor and wisdom to Quartermain throughout the novel), that he has lost the war. Bleak tells him that the colonel hates Douglas because he was the son he never had. For his part, Douglas is unable to decide who won or lost. One of the "soldiers" in his army, Charlie, reflects on the events of the day by saying that they fought "the first War in history where everybody won." In fact, Quartermain wakes up later that night laughing. What ensues is a hilarious dialog with his phallus, an "old friend" who has not visited him in a long while. He remembers naming his phallus "Junior" when he was fourteen, and they reminisce for awhile. Then Quartermain must say farewell summer to his last erection (which will not say whether it will come again or not). The phallus has carnivalized the colonel's body: "Quartermain's teeth chattered with an outra-geous laugh." It gives Quartermain the idea of setting up certain "medical dis-plays" down by the lake in a tent with a huge question mark over the entryway. In terms of vulgar Freudian symbolism and interpretation, the question mark replaces the phallus, yet as a graphic it still asks the question about whether or not it will return to its erect status once the male member has "entered" the "tent."

Douglas and the boys visit this plywood lean-to museum, a kind of freak show with glass jars filled with fetuses, some human, some animal, in various stages of development. There are no labels on the jars, so Douglas has to guess what this display is all about. Douglas realizes that they are dead babies but does not get sick like Tom does. In fact, he is excited by the schoolgirls who visit the sideshow, and while he watches them in the dark, a "hot liquid pulsed down the inside of his left leg." Douglas comes out to talk to Tom, who is crying, but then goes back in again to explore the world of sexuality. Despite the thinly veiled reference to ejaculation, Bradbury does not here display any gross naturalism. Rather, it is a question of grotesque realism, the style of carnival that reconnects us in healthy ways to the life of the body and the earth. The experience of looking at the fetuses awakens in Douglas the primal ambivalence of life in death. He gives voice to some of them, telling their stories in his imagination. This scene is at least partly autobiographical and reflects an experience Bradbury had at Ocean Park in the summer of 1934 or 1935, which led to the writing of "The Jar" (Dark Carnival).

Later, Douglas and Quartermain meet on the colonel's porch in a scene that is suffused with oceanic metaphors meant to suggest that, as they talk, they are sitting on different ends of a "teeter-tauter [sic]" that gently "masturbates" both of them: "The boards rose to the sky and softly sifted to the ground, with the hard wood between their legs where both could feel it with their crustacean loins, with their shriveled small seabed creatures that now took sustenance from air, now prolapsed back in tidal salts, now roused again with the propulsion of their bodies up, down, down, up, up, down, slowly, slowly."[51] The notion that this is a fantasy scene of mutual pleasure in masturbation is our interpretation, but it seems clearly suggested by the language.

In symbolic terms Douglas has reconnected Quartermain with life, becoming his "son," for the old man has no children through whom he can live. Quartermain suggests that they are like two generals of the Civil War, Grant and Lee. He gives Douglas a glass of lemonade and toasts him to "life." That evening Quartermain and his phallus talk again, his phallus telling him that he is going to leave him but that he is not leaving town. In chapter 30, the last in the novel, the phallus visits Douglas, as we might have expected. Bradbury would not, of course, describe the onset of puberty in purely naturalistic terms alone. The phallus, when asked by Douglas, does not deny that he was present in the jars at the sideshow exhibit, though only "in a way." Here, the phallus should not be interpreted in narrowly Freudian terms. It is the very force of life itself, and it, in fact, tells Douglas not to touch himself. Before that can happen, though, everything has to partake of a carnivalized dialogue that is full of jokes and puns. Douglas names his phallus "Pete":

How's that?
    "Pedro. San Pietro. That's in a book in my grandpa's library. Saints, yes?"
Once.

"Are you a saint?"

No. But not the Devil either. I'm just you. Another way of looking at you.
Ugly. Beautiful. Beautiful. Ugly.[52]

Bradbury's hero in both novels, Douglas Spaulding, has now reached the onset of puberty, a maturational point beyond which Bradbury does not wish to go. It is typical of Bradbury's humor that he connects the name of the phallus inter-textually with a library and the name of a saint. This Dionysian phallus has transformed the lives of countless boys, including that of a saint (once); however, the thematic emphasis is not on the spiritual but on the ambivalence of material bodily life (ugly or beautiful). Bradbury's most Rabelaisian novel ends as Tom comes in to sleep with Douglas, afraid that his brother will "ditch him" because of this newfound maturity. Douglas reassures Tom that he loves him, and the boys fall asleep, thinking about their prospects for fun on Halloween now that summer is finally over.

It seems unlikely that *Farewell Summer* can stand on its own as a complete novel. It exists today as the remains of a much larger work that Bradbury intended to write more than half a century ago, from which *Dandelion Wine*—another "accidental" novel (the term is Bradbury's)—also derives. Despite the evident Rabelaisian nature of its thematic concerns and the fact that it explores the material bodily stratum in ways far beyond where Bradbury has attempted to go before, it does not at this point have the sensuous linguistic textures of *Dandelion Wine* (provided by its rich exploration of poetic language in reveries of the material imagination) or much of a development of its central theme, the war between old and young, which is over far too soon and without much complication. *Dandelion Wine* will likely continue to be the most Dionysian of Bradbury's published fictions about childhood, the distilled essence of all those years of composition. It will stand alone as his best exploration of the dark terrors of the ravine and the ecstatic joys of small-town American life, both themes interwoven with the carnival blaze of summer. But Bradbury picked up another thread of his Green Town fiction, developing his old plan for a dark carnival novel and completing what could very well be considered the center of his canon, *Something Wicked This Way Comes.*

5

Fathering the Carnival

Something Wicked This Way Comes

Bradbury's first Simon and Schuster title remains the most filmic of his major fictions. The evolution of *Something Wicked This Way Comes*—as well as its legacy—is deeply tied to film history; in fact, in 1983 it would become the first feature film of a Bradbury work produced from a Bradbury screenplay. Fathering this work extended over seventeen years; it was his first full-length novel, emerging (unlike the shorter and more focused *Fahrenheit 451)* from materials for a novel dating back to 1945. The project metamorphosed through plans for an experimental graphic novel and blossomed into a full screenplay before reaching print as a book in 1962. The referent for his title—the arrival of a supernatural carnival with nightmare rides—projected his memories of traveling carnival shows of his Midwest youth from nostalgic reality into the dark fantastic. As a novel, it culminates the most productive period of his fiction and sets out in strongly emotional terms his own most heartfelt notions of life, death, and creativity. In this work he reached a peak of character development that he would rarely attain again. By the early 1980s, Stephen King would observe that *Something Wicked*, while certainly not Bradbury's best-known or most acclaimed novel, is arguably his best.[1]

But during the 1940s, Bradbury held back almost every image of this dark carnival from his earliest successes in a new kind of supernatural fiction that, as Darrell Schweitzer has pointed out, "defined the direction in which horror fiction would go, away from haunted English country houses, dark forests, and monsters (Lovecraftian or traditional), toward big cities and their suburbs, and into the mind." Bradbury would soon be an influence on Charles Beaumont and the "California School" of horror and mystery writers that gathered around him, including Richard Matheson, George Clayton Johnson, Chad Oliver, and William

F. Nolan. Clive Barker considers the early stories collected by Bradbury in *Dark Carnival* (1947) as central to the continuing tradition of the fantastic in contemporary literature. King proclaimed *Dark Carnival* "the *Dubliners* of American fantasy," and William F. Nolan believes that every major writer of supernatural fiction has encountered Bradbury's distinctive early work.[2] The history of *Something Wicked* clearly begins here with Bradbury's weird tales, but the historical trail quickly leads to an intertextual mystery: why is the dark carnival absent from *Dark Carnival?*

Bradbury's Texts

Surviving notes from the period 1945–1946 show that Bradbury's ideas for a dark carnival novel are inextricably linked to the evolving concept of his first story collection. The history of *Dark Carnival* is full of clues: an early 1945 outline containing the story title "Carnival" and two possible volume titles, THE DARK CARACEL [*sic*] and DARK CARNIVAL (see fig. 3); the definition of a dark carnival developed in a letter to his editor, August Derleth; and his two word-pictures of a dark-carnival dust jacket, one presented on the outline of contents and one in a letter to Derleth, which adds a child to the jacket composition:

> The cover jacket might possibly illustrate a small carnival that has set up its merry-go-round and side-show tent and banners in a dark green woodland glade at twilight—the entire atmosphere of the picture would be one of remoteness, of a carnival in the wilderness going full steam, but with no one in sight except one small boy in the foreground, tiny, very alone, staring at the moving carousel and the high banners. And on the banners instead of portraits of Fat Ladies, Thin Men and Tattooed Freaks would be pictures of strange, nebulous creatures. And on the carousel, instead of horses sliding up and down the gleaming brass poles, would be other impossible, vaguely, disturbingly delineated creatures of such indistinct cast and line that ones [*sic*] imagination could make them anything in the whole universe.[3]

The impressionistic and misty scenes of this dark carnival are very similar to the dim glances off the midway into terrifying menageries and freak tents that Bradbury would perfect seventeen years later in his novel. In all, the visual images of the imaginary carnival described in his papers of this period are most striking and suggest that he was well on the way to seeing the full potential of carnival to illuminate the secrets of life, death, and creativity. But Bradbury was already developing the germ of a novel from these images, and he held story-length glimpses of the sinister shows out of *Dark Carnival* completely. The early content outlines instead contain weird tales inspired by memories outside of his carnival experiences; seven of these were pulled into *Dark Carnival* from *The Small Assassins*, the Ur-novel from which *Dandelion Wine* and his two unpublished Green Town novel projects descend. His early idea for a full section of stories on carnival simply disappeared as his first collection evolved. The final dust-jacket design was refocused on masks, themselves a symbol of the carnivalesque, but Bradbury deliberately left one direct visual clue in the center of this collage of masks: a carousel horse. It would prove to be a talisman of things to come.[4]

Bradbury continued to move stories in and out of *Dark Carnival* even after he submitted copy to August Derleth in June 1946. But none of these changes brought the carnival back into that collection. Instead, Bradbury was working simultaneously on a novel that seemed to blend his carnival fantasies with the detective fiction he had been publishing successfully during the final years of World War II. An undated outline survives with the title, "DARK CARNIVAL a novel of 70,000 words," prepared on the coarse-wove manila paper he used during the mid-1940s. A two-page opening fragment suggests that the plot idea involved a journey on a carousel into the past to prevent a murder from occurring in the present. The nineteen chapter titles found on the outline have elements in common with the detective stories he had already tired of, and there is no evidence that this form of the novel went any further.

The true origins of *Something Wicked* survive in a much larger nest of materials from this same period, saved in a more contemporary three-prong yellow binder subsequently titled by Bradbury as "Original Materials 'Dark Carnival' which became 'Something Wicked T. W. C.'" The date, also in his hand, reads "Summer 1945 and 1946." The binder contains more than thirty pages of fragments, sketches, and chapter openings for a dark carnival novel that no longer echoes his detective fiction at all.[5] These fragments are also distinctly different from the weird tales he was simultaneously assembling in *Dark Carnival*. They do, however, seem to share the same setting of *The Small Assassins;* eventually, this setting would develop more fully and define *Something Wicked* as a companion Green Town novel to *Dandelion Wine*, but the evolution of contents is distinctly separate for these two books (table 12). The chapter fragments show Bradbury working on early forms of the carnival's supernatural aspects and its effects on the people of his small Midwestern town. There are partial sketches and chapter openings centering on the carnival's arrival and canopy raising, the carnival freaks (including Mr. Electrico), the tunnel of love, the calliope, arcade games, the mirror maze, the Ferris wheel, and the carousel. In nearly every fragment these rides and games, common to so many of the carnivals from Bradbury's youth, have sinister features that can turn deadly without warning. There are three variations on a mirror maze that can trap the viewer in the frozen future of old age and three more variations on husbands who go to the carnival and return home as either old men or young children. Bradbury would develop both of these conceits into major horrors of the final novel.

The story fragments of man-to-boy transformations inspired the first germ of the novel to reach print. In 1948 Bradbury decided to offer an opening episode of the larger concept for publication. "The Black Ferris" presents an evil carnie who rides the Ferris wheel forward and backward to change his age so that he can pose as a child while he preys on the people of the town. This story, which also introduces two local boys—Pete and Hank—who take control of the Ferris and age the carnival master into oblivion, appeared in the May 1948 issue of *Weird Tales*.[6] But the larger carnival fiction would soon languish as Bradbury and Congdon focused on winning a book contract beyond the niche market that *Weird Tales* and Derleth's Arkham House could command. The novel materials, as well as his plan to expand and novelize the vampire stories from his *Dark Carnival* collection, moved to the background as Bradbury's science fiction and wider-market fantasies were transformed into *The Martian Chronicles, The Illustrated Man,* and *The Golden Apples of the Sun. Fahrenheit 451* and his nine-month European excursion to write the *Moby Dick* screenplay took all of 1953 and the first half of 1954.

Even so, the carnival was never far away. In 1952 Bradbury was just beginning his long-term publishing relationship with California artist Joe Mugnaini, whose shadowy drawings and dreamlike paintings would provide illustrations and cover art for some of the writer's most enduring titles. Bradbury would later recall, "Joe Mugnaini and I planned to do THE DARK CARNIVAL, BLACK FERRIS, SOMETHING WICKED THIS WAY COMES complex as an illustrated book with no text, a novel in pictures." A single worksheet for the cover and title survives (fig. 12); Bradbury's light sketch of the carnival train crossing a trestle bridge was made from "The Caravan," a Mugnaini wax and oil painting that, a decade later, would inspire the dust jacket of the British first edition.[7]

Other aspects of this project never moved beyond the planning stage, but it is clear that Bradbury was developing visual images of the novel's plot elements even while the prose remained dormant. Perhaps the most significant of these planned but now lost images was a merry-go-round, for Bradbury's early vision of the carousel as the centerpiece of the carnival had never waned. None of his three 1945–1946 chapter fragments on the carnival's ability to alter age reveals which ride (carousel or Ferris) offers the enchantment. He now saw the carousel, rather than the Ferris wheel of his 1948 trial story, as the device the evil carnival owner would use to cycle back and forth through the aging process. This was no

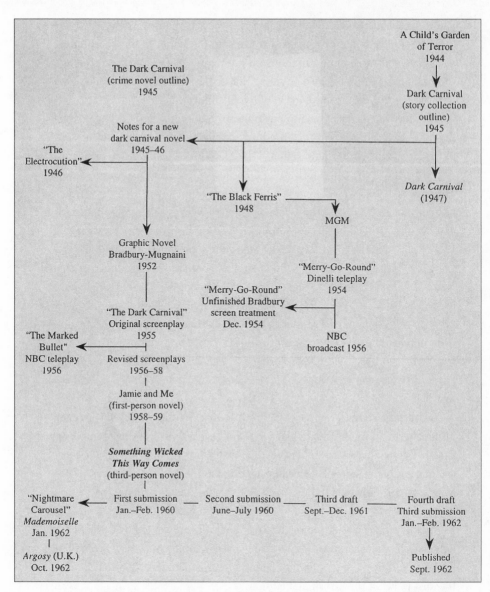

Table 12. The evolution of *Something Wicked This Way Comes* reveals the rich multimedia milestones that underlie the final novel. The textual genealogy is shown in relationship to the early stages of the *Dark Carnival* stem. *Dandelion Wine* and the unpublished novel *Farewell Summer* also originate with the concept for *A Child's Garden of Terror;* this broader genealogy appears in table 8.

doubt a development of his own "novel in pictures" project, but the next stage of inspiration would come, quite unexpectedly, from the pen of a Hollywood scriptwriter.

Film and television adaptations of a half-dozen Bradbury stories were produced between 1951 and 1953, prompting Samuel Goldwyn Jr. to buy the rights to "The Black Ferris" for MGM. He hired Mel Dinelli to write the script, a writer who already knew where Bradbury was going with the plan for the dark carnival novel. In 1949 Dinelli, introducing himself to Bradbury as both a fan and fellow writer, had visited Bradbury at home and received a copy of *Dark Carnival*. During this visit, Bradbury explained to him the curious absence of the carousel from his first story collection, imparting his vision of this ride as the central device of his developing novel. Five years later Dinelli, working with Goldwyn, developed a parallel evolution in the form of a short television script. It aired locally on the *Starlight Summer Theater*, but Goldwyn had difficulty finding a sponsor for national broadcast. During this time, Bradbury returned from overseas work on production of *Moby Dick*, and in early December 1954 Goldwyn showed him the broadcast piece. Bradbury immediately saw the potential for a feature-length film and within two days produced a fifty-page treatment expanding Dinelli's core teleplay along the lines of his own notes for the novel. Dinelli's teleplay was eventually aired on July 10, 1956, as a series pilot for NBC's *Sneak Preview* under the title "Merry-Go-Round."[8] No more came of this project, and Bradbury's expansion of the teleplay remains unlocated. But within a few months, another MGM giant would inspire Bradbury to write a completely original full-length film treatment of the evolving novel.

Once again, the catalyst would be visual.[9] Gene Kelly had recently wrapped production of *Invitation to the Dance,* and in 1955 he arranged a screening for the new film at MGM. The Bradburys had known Kelly for several years and were invited to the screening; they covered the two miles from their Clarkson Road home by bus and greatly enjoyed the movie's three interwoven storylines. The film, and in particular the carnival sequence that opened it, reawakened the long line of Bradbury's circus and carnival experiences, dating back to his childhood viewing of Lon Chaney Sr.'s *Laugh, Clown, Laugh.* The Bradburys had plenty of time to think about the experience that evening—the bus never came, and they decided to walk home. As they walked, Bradbury's wish for a chance to work with Kelly led Maggie to challenge him to find something in his files that could be extended into a screenplay. Within a few days Bradbury was composing his own screen treatment of the now almost fully evolved dark carnival storyline: once Pete and Jim (Hank in "The Black Ferris") have destroyed one of the carnival owners in his own evil device, they become fugitives in their own town as the surviving owner searches them out for revenge. This opening, as well as stored

Figure 12. Bradbury's plan for a novel in pictures was designed to present a textless form of the dark carnival materials through illustrations by Joe Mugnaini. This worksheet for the cover and title dates from 1952. Bradbury's light sketch of the carnival train crossing a Roman arch bridge was based on Mugnaini's "The Caravan." A decade later, Mugnaini further modified the concept to create the British first edition dust jacket of *Something Wicked This Way Comes*. Outline and sketch courtesy of Ray Bradbury; dustjacket illustration courtesy of the Joseph Mugnaini estate.

title suggestions to go with Mugnaini 'CARNIVAL' wax painting.

BETWEEN A DREAM AND A DREAM

FUNERAL FOR CLOWNS

IN THE MIDDLE OF SOMETIME NEVER

WHERE ARE WE GOING AND KKKKKKKK WHERE HAVE WE BEEN!

FLIGHT FROM NOWHERE

HARLEQUINADE!

THE SHADOW TRAIN

by

Ray Bradbury

C

FERROCARILL IN MOTLEY

THE

AND CELEBRATE ETERNITY!

JOURNEY IN DARKNESS

THE MOTLEY TRAIN

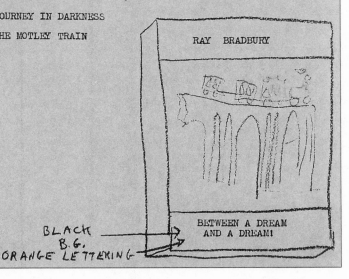

RAY BRADBURY

BETWEEN A DREAM
AND A DREAM!

BLACK
B.G.
ORANGE LETTERING

images from his notes and the "novel in pictures" project, quickly grew into a detailed screen treatment.

Two distinct drafts survive in Bradbury's papers, both titled "The Dark Carnival." The earliest form is a forty-page typewritten draft on legal-size pages that carries the action through to the capture of the boys in the town library by the surviving co-owner, an illustrated man whose tattoos control the tormented carnival freaks who work for him. This typescript is paginated but undated, though discards include dates running from late January through mid-March 1955. A second draft developed from these materials runs to eighty-six pages and is nearly complete. It contains inserts from 1956 and 1957, but it undoubtedly served as the basis for an unlocated typescript submitted to Kelly sometime in the late spring or early summer of 1955. Kelly was fascinated by the project, which was tailor-made for his acting and directing talents, and committed to make it his next film. He soon left for London and Paris to secure backing.

Meanwhile, Bradbury, still intending to work with his actor-friend, explored options for independent backing for the collaboration if MGM failed to support the project at home. There was interest at Columbia, but Kelly was aware that this would jeopardize his own participation; on August 8 he cabled Bradbury with his blessing to proceed with any deals of his own but offered a strong Irish hunch that he could bring in backing from overseas. Bradbury quickly cabled back: "Believe in Irish hunches. . . . No doubt in my mind that Kelly is the man to do it." Unfortunately, Kelly's early 1950s success with such films as *An American in Paris* was fading; *Invitation to the Dance* had not been successful at the box office, and he returned from Europe in September without securing the finances. Bradbury was honored that Kelly had even tried and knew that the project the actor had rekindled could be polished further. Dated inserts in the second draft, as well as discarded pages, show that Bradbury worked on at least one subsequent draft in the middle of 1956; the opening eight pages are dated April 29, 1957.

Bradbury's correspondence reveals that he did indeed circulate revised versions of the Kelly screen treatment through his film and television agent Ben Benjamin of the West Coast–based Famous Artists Agency. Disney declined in December 1955. In May 1957 Hecht-Hill-Lancaster returned it as too fantastic for wide audiences; Bradbury would work in Hollywood and London on retainer with H-H-L through much of 1957 and turn out an excellent screenplay for Carol Read based on "And the Rock Cried Out" (it remains one of the best unproduced Bradbury screenplays). While in London he sent "The Dark Carnival" to Hammer Films, suggesting (through the Peters Agency) that the screenplay would fit in with the studio's recent run of horror films. Hammer executives declined, so in 1958 Bradbury offered "The Dark Carnival" to Twentieth Century Fox, but they were still smarting from an inability to come to terms with him for a film version of

The Illustrated Man and refused the unpublished property.[10] Bradbury would continue to work on unproduced film and television options (primarily involving *The Martian Chronicles*) for two more years, but none of these screenplays were ever produced.

One significant byproduct of "The Dark Carnival" screenplay did make it to television. In 1955 Bradbury created a standalone half-hour teleplay about the bullet trick, a common sideshow illusion where the artist appears to catch a bullet fired by a volunteer from the crowd. Bradbury added the suspense of a deadly love triangle to this game and sold the teleplay to the producers of *Jane Wyman Presents*.[11] It aired as "The Marked Bullet" on November 20, 1956, with Jane Wyman in the role of the illusionist. The love triangle closely followed the plot of "The Electrocution," his 1946 story about an electric-chair illusion in a sideshow. This variation once again demonstrated the intertextual nature of his cross-media authorship—his transfer of storyline from one sideshow act to another is similar to his transfer of the central attraction from Ferris wheel to carousel as "The Dark Carnival" evolved from story to screenplay to novel. Bradbury never published "The Marked Bullet" as a short story; instead, he would write yet another variation on this act into the developing novel. Clearly, the Hollywood interlude had been pivotal—he now had a detailed plot and a great deal of dialog for "The Dark Carnival" project and began to transform these materials into his first full-length novel. The transformation was not continuous—he moved away from the material for six months at a time during 1958 and 1959, eventually finding time to run out a first-person variation of the novel titled *Jamie and Me*. During the first months of 1960, he moved the narrative back into the third person and completed a first draft of the entire novel.[12] This draft would prove to be an ending as well as a beginning—it was the last original work he would ever write for his longtime publisher, Doubleday. In fact, his Doubleday editors would never even see the second draft.

Bradbury experienced growing frustration with Doubleday during the 1950s. His relationship with Walter Bradbury was always trusting and cordial, but periodically Ray Bradbury and his agent, Don Congdon, would point out the failure of Doubleday to increase the relatively small advertising budget and limited review contacts as Bradbury continued to gain popularity among mainstream readers at home and abroad. But by early 1960, other issues needed to be resolved as well. Doubleday was still taking 50 percent of the paperback sales and royalties; any leverage Bradbury had gained in securing full paperback profits from Ballantine for *Fahrenheit 451* (1953) and *The October Country* (1955) was countered in Doubleday's view by Bradbury's vulnerability on two unspoken points: first, that Ballantine, primarily a paperback publisher, could never offer Bradbury large hardback printings or guarantee long-term hardback reprint opportunities; and second, that Bradbury's preference for the short-story form, and his consequent need to periodically publish in the always market-risky short-story-collection format, would put him at a disadvantage with nearly any publisher. Furthermore, Doubleday was growing increasingly weary of Bradbury's move away from science fiction; when he proposed another fantasy collection along the lines of *The Golden Apples of the Sun*, his editors were not willing to offer a better deal. In fact, Bradbury and Congdon had to settle for a two-book deal similar to his earlier contract for *Golden Apples* and *Dandelion Wine*—that is, committing to produce a novel in order to publish another story collection. The contract was signed in the spring of 1958, but Congdon was only able to negotiate a slight increase in the hardback royalty scale and an approval clause for reprints.[13]

But the biggest issue would be the long-term marketing of his titles. Bradbury was still trying to understand how Doubleday let *The Martian Chronicles* hardback edition go out of print in 1957 just as *Sputnik* seemed to launch the *Chronicles* as the great American space-age novel. He secured a new printing with a new introduction by Clifton Fadiman the following year, but Bradbury was frustrated at Doubleday's decision to deny him a new (reset) edition, which would have allowed him to make much-desired changes in content. By 1959, *The Golden Apples of the Sun* was out of print in both hardback and paperback, and the new fantasy collection, released as *A Medicine for Melancholy*, was being advertised on a scale that seemed, from Bradbury's perspective, to assure the same fate in an even shorter period of time. The biggest blow came when Walter Bradbury moved to Henry Holt and Company during the spring of 1959. This move, along with Stanley Kauffmann's move from Ballantine to Knopf, led Bradbury to consider both houses as potential alternatives to Doubleday. But Congdon advised his client to wait and see if these moves by trusted editors of the past would prove to be long-term opportunities for the future.[14] As it turned out, neither Walter Bradbury nor Kauffmann would be able to work with their respective new publishers and could not provide a stable alternative to Doubleday.

By October 1959 Bradbury was determined to force either a renegotiation of the two-book contract (and thus pave the way for better deals in the future) or a release from the agreement. Again Congdon urged caution. From an agent's perspective, the best strategy to get earlier Bradbury titles back in print would be to present Doubleday (or any potential rival press) with a new book that would clearly move him to a higher sales plateau. Congdon sensed that *The Dark Carnival* could be just that book and urged Bradbury to complete the first draft as soon as possible. In November Congdon sounded out Walt Bradbury's successor, Tim Seldes, and discovered that Doubleday held a similar view—delivery of the new novel would indeed open a window for renegotiation. Spurred on by Congdon's advice and embassies, Bradbury began a final period of sustained activity; on April 4, 1960, he sent the first draft of the novel, now titled *Something Wicked This Way Comes,* to Congdon for review. The letter of transmittal for the 377-page, 43-chapter typescript reveals the intensity of the creative process; for the first time in their relationship, Bradbury was sending Congdon a book-length manuscript that was, in large part, unrevised: "Half of the book is first draft, half of it second. . . . The main thing, which I'm sure you're prepared for, is that perhaps never before in the last 13 years, have I sent you a story or book manuscript in quite this almost-but-not quite born state. As you read, I know you will mentally cut some of the more florid metaphors which always encrust my first and second drafts. Sometimes I give myself, on a single page, 4, 5, or 6 similes which, by the fifth draft, dwindle down to one or two really good ones, for proper emphasis."[15]

Congdon wanted a reading from Doubleday as soon as possible and immediately sent a copy to Seldes. In late May Congdon passed along the editor's initial comments to Bradbury, noting that the surface praise and lightly handled suggestions for revision masked the position that Doubleday saw nothing more or less than the usual Bradbury craftsmanship. The implication, from Congdon's viewpoint, was that renegotiation would net no major concessions. But he also felt that the new novel, once revised, would be a book that could command a new level of attention from publishers other than Doubleday. He now urged Bradbury to make his case in writing to Seldes.[16]

On June 2 Bradbury wrote Seldes asking for an editorial board decision on his future with the publishing house. He noted the warm response to his work offered by Walter Bradbury and Seldes over the last eleven years but felt that few others at Doubleday shared their enthusiasm. He cited a need for increased advertising and promotion budgets for the new novel as well as renewed efforts to reprint and promote his earlier titles as fictional forerunners of the space age, which had now become reality. It took Seldes nearly a month to confer with vacationing colleagues, and this was not a good sign. His response went to Congdon with a copy for Bradbury on July 1; it offered to give Bradbury more control of advertising copy and agreed to promote his earlier titles. But Doubleday's initial advertising budget for the new book would only be three thousand dollars, and editorial ideas for republication of the out-of-print titles focused on paperback options and omnibus consolidations of the story collections. Doubleday was a large house with many authors, and it was now clear to Bradbury that his editors were not willing to move him to the next level of marketing visibility. On July 8, after consulting with Congdon, he wrote Seldes to ask for his release from the second half of the current two-book contract: "After eleven years, I think it is time for me to leave Doubleday and to try to find a new publisher who will see me and this fantastic and exciting new Space Age with the same high-spirits in which I approach it. I feel very much like a person who, throwing confetti, serpentines, and my hat to the sky, finds he is the lone celebrant at a party. I need a whole company of people to celebrate and be really excited with me about an Age I believe is the greatest man ever lived in."

Bradbury's use of carnival images was not merely rhetorical. Through its many complex manifestations, carnival expressed his whole approach to writing—and to life. From his point of view, a life worth living requires a crowd of participants, not just spectators. Bradbury needed a high-energy, carnivalized relationship with his chosen genre, his publisher, and his readers. But Walter Bradbury was gone, and Tim Seldes alone did not have the power to increase Doubleday's support. His publisher had become a spectator, and it was time to find a new company of editorial celebrants.

Seldes soon arranged an amicable release. The entire exchange had been carefully developed between author, agent, and editor without acrimony, and the terms of release merely reflected the differing business needs of both parties. He was free to offer his new novel elsewhere, and his advance would be covered by future royalties on his earlier titles and his share of the continuing paperback royalty split on those books. Bradbury would never leave an editor on bad terms and, in fact, would continue to work with Doubleday on derivative anthologies, including two young-adult titles—*R Is for Rocket* (1962) and *S Is for Space* (1966)— and *Twice-22* (1966), an omnibus edition of *The Golden Apples of the Sun* and *A Medicine for Melancholy*. But Bradbury would never again contract new work with Doubleday.

During June and July he worked from a carbon of the initial 377-page submission to produce a new 425-page, 40-chapter typescript of the novel. Meanwhile, Congdon continued to evaluate potential new publishers and soon found high interest where he himself had once worked—Simon and Schuster. He reviewed the new draft in mid-August and then sent it on to Robert Gottlieb at his old firm. Events moved quickly from that point; strong support from the other editors led Gottlieb to offer a contract by mid-September 1960.[17] Simon and Schuster was still a close-knit operation where a commitment to an author brought all departments together to develop an effective marketing strategy. The gifted advertising director Nina Bourne, as well as Bradbury fanatics Peter Schwed and Dick Grossman, were part of Gottlieb's plan to provide what Bradbury needed from a publishing house. On September 9, he outlined his plan for Congdon:

> I understand—and I've made it clear to the others—exactly what it is that Bradbury and you want and expect from a new publisher. You want extra effort. We will give it to you, and it will be an intelligent effort too (I hope). In our favor: Nina is fascinated with the problem of extending

the cult-feeling about Bradbury to a much larger public; and Dick Grossman, who's in charge of marketing (which really means co-ordinating sales
with promotion and publicity) is a violent Bradbury-lover and is already
conniving. Also in our favor: this particular novel, which seems to combine the best features of Bradbury's different themes and manners, is very
promotable. Most in our favor: we want to do it well. Both out of respect
for his writing, and out of a healthy desire to do better with a writer than
anyone else could do.[18]

This attitude had been a Simon and Schuster hallmark since the 1930s, and it
was clearly in tune with Bradbury's own carnival vision of authorship. Gottlieb
was a fairly young sponsoring editor, but he offered the first real chance to put
Bradbury's reputation with the book-buying public on par with his mainstream
reputation as a major-market magazine favorite. And Gottlieb, like Congdon, felt
that this new project was a book that merited a higher level of marketing support than Bradbury had ever before experienced. The contracts were completed
before the end of the month; Bradbury received a five-thousand-dollar advance
on signing, but nearly a year and a half would pass before he was finished revising his new novel.

During the fall of 1960 Bradbury's revisions were interrupted by interference
from a most unlikely source—the head of MGM Studios, Samuel Goldwyn Jr.[19]
By now, Goldwyn knew that the novel was under contract and felt that the
studio still owned rights to the plot elements that had evolved from "The Black
Ferris" story and from the "Merry-Go-Round" teleplay. He renewed his option
for a film version based on these properties and took the position that these rights
would limit Bradbury's ability to market a screenplay based directly on the new
novel. His position was ambivalent. At times Goldwyn seemed willing to engage
Bradbury for a new screenplay; their earlier work on expanding the Dinelli script
had been enjoyable, and the fully developed novel promised an even richer cin-
ematographic experience. But both Congdon and Bradbury knew that this kind
of film was not really in Goldwyn's line and that he had never recovered his
investment from the unsuccessful pilot teleplay. It soon became apparent that,
between the lines, he preferred a buyout—either directly or through a share in
Bradbury's future sale of a new screenplay to another studio.

Goldwyn went so far as to ask that plot elements carried over from the story
and teleplay be removed from the novel as well. Character names such as Cooger,
the carnival owner, could be changed if necessary, but Bradbury knew that the
aging effect of the carnival ride was the central conceit of the novel. In his story
and Dinelli's teleplay, it allows Cooger to assume the appearance of a child in
order to prey on Miss Foley, and it proves to be the means of his own destruction.

As Bradbury's novel developed, the carousel grew into the central symbol of the evil that empowers the carnival masters and enslaves anyone who comes under its influence. On Congdon's advice, Bradbury presented his position to MGM through his own West Coast film and television agent, Ben Benjamin. Bradbury agreed not to use the carousel in any future screenplays as long as Goldwyn maintained his option for an MGM film. But he refused to remove it from the novel. He recounted the whole history of his vision of the carousel as the central image of his dark carnival, his own influence on Dinelli's vision of the work, and his own creative jump from Ferris wheel to merry-go-round as the dark agent of immortality while he worked with Joe Mugnaini on the graphic-novel project. Bradbury noted that these developments predated the Dinelli teleplay and made this clear in his instructions to Benjamin: "These discussions took place in 1952 and were common knowledge among my friends, and in these discussions with Joe we planned on the wonderous merry-go-round which now is in my novel."

Goldwyn maintained his option for the time being and in 1961 contracted Robert Bloch for a feature-length screenplay expansion of the Dinelli teleplay. Bloch delivered the screenplay, but it was never filmed, and Goldwyn eventually allowed his option to lapse. In the meantime Bradbury spent the first half of 1961 working on three very successful teleplays—a dramatization of Stanley Ellin's "The Faith of Aaron Menefee" for NBC's *Alfred Hitchcock Presents* and dramatizations of two new stories of his own, "The Jail" for ABC's *Alcoa Premiere* and "I Sing the Body Electric" for CBS's *The Twilight Zone.* These projects eased the frustration of the unproduced screenplays of earlier years, but Bradbury was turning more and more to adapting his stories to the stage. The previous spring he had transformed his award-winning 1947 radio play "The Meadow" into a stage play for Hollywood's Huntington Hartford Theatre. Veteran stage and screen actors James Whitmore and Strother Martin were part of the project, and they soon convinced Bradbury to bring more of his stories to the stage. Bradbury spent the first half of 1961 dramatizing stories, preparing his first collection of plays for press, and planning *R Is for Rocket,* the first of two young-adult anthologies derived from his older work. This period of activity marked a turning point in the nature of Bradbury's authorship—from now on he would spend less time writing stories as he turned more and more to stage, television, and film adaptations of his work. The decision was not a conscious one; he still wrote a few stories a year and outlined ideas for novels. What he could not know at the time was that a quarter century would pass before he would finish another major novel. But one thing he knew for sure was that he had to publish the one novel he had in hand. By late summer 1961, Congdon and Gottlieb finally persuaded him to return to his revisions for *Something Wicked This Way Comes.*

Bradbury was all too aware that the books based on his Illinois youth seemed the hardest to revise for publication. His first Green Town novel, *Summer Morning, Summer Night*, had wrestled him to a draw; after seven long years under contract, he had only been able to extract the stories of *Dandelion Wine* from that manuscript. Skillful bridging had created a very successful and nearly seamless story cycle, but only a few glimpses of the remaining novel manuscript, now called *Farewell Summer*, would ever reach print. *Something Wicked* represented a similar challenge; he had submitted a long and largely unrevised typescript in early 1960, and his second draft later that year was even longer. Bradbury now faced the most crucial phase of revision and would work from August into December 1961 in an effort to bring the dark carnival to life.

His lifelong conviction that fiction has a life of its own is perhaps most evident in the composition and revision of *Something Wicked*. He had admitted to Congdon that his initial April 1960 submission was in an "almost-but-not quite born state." Bradbury had never submitted work in this state before, but he had also never tried to bring the long-neglected Renaissance tradition of carnival in literature back to life before. He found himself reviving the folk carnival as a literary subject and, in the process, linked himself (and for the first time in a sustained way) to the carnivals he knew so well as a young man. Carnival has always been on the border between art and life, and Bradbury's own close identification with the subject allowed for very little distance between author and narrative. The result is intensity of effect; indeed, effect outshines event in every draft as well as the finished novel. Bradbury's text is itself a carnival. He throws the reader into the hyperbolic play of carnival language—no one is addressed as a mere spectator.

From the beginning of the novel phase of the project, Bradbury allowed for a great deal of textual play and did not impose the conventional narrative control of the novelist on his material. The rational cause-and-effect plot relationship demanded by the narrative code is only a loosely structuring element here. But the explosion of metaphor in *Something Wicked* is as intense as one finds anywhere in Bradbury's fiction, allowing him to create a nonlinear symbolic code where time and logic are reversible. Fathers can be dethroned from positions of authority; fathers can even become sons. Bradbury found the resulting ambivalence both comfortable and vital as he developed this literary equivalent of carnival. He simply did not pass judgment on the evolving work and in a sense let the novel write itself through several difficult stages of revision. In submitting the first draft, his last words to Congdon were "Anyway, the baby is on the way to you. Old Dad? He's just going to sit here in the sun, with his shoes off, for the rest of the day, feeling good."[20]

The material he took up again in the fall of 1961 was quite massive. Bradbury's second submission from the year before totaled 425 pages; it had evolved from a half-first-, half-second-draft original submission of 377 pages and an even earlier 357 pages of discarded variant chapters. The earliest grouping of variants included nearly 100 pages of first-person narrative in young Will's voice, grouped under the running title *Jamie and Me*. In these pages the influence of the *Dandelion Wine* period is evident. Bradbury had read a number of books during 1955–1956, including *Huckleberry Finn*, to enrich his own sense of place and nostalgia as he fashioned *Dandelion Wine* from his larger Green Town manuscript. The initial *Jamie and Me* fragment forms a smooth bridge between the screenplay material and what (in a longer form) would become the final novel, but it also represents an experimental storytelling approach in the tradition of Mark Twain's Huck and Tom narratives. This opening fragment predates all known drafts—a surviving outline of future novels (subsequently dated 1956 or 1957 by Bradbury) schedules *Jamie and Me* for 1959, and holograph revisions show him recasting the narrative in the third person for expansion into the first full draft of the novel. The remaining discards appear to be the first (third-person) draft of roughly the first half of the novel. Two of these discards contain another alternate title, *The Autumn People*. But Bradbury soon settled on the name provided by Shakespeare, his own literary father figure, who dominates over other authors in the library episode at the center of the novel. In fact, the discards also contain an uncanceled series-title page that instantiates the title in an even larger vision of autobiographical fiction:

> *The Illinois Trilogy*
> Dandelion Wine
> Farewell Summer
> Something Wicked This Way Comes

Dandelion Wine had recounted the nostalgic summer events of 1928. *Farewell Summer* was the new title for the *Summer Morning, Summer Night* novel manuscript from which *Dandelion Wine* had been carved; its still largely unpublished episodes recount fictional events from the summer of 1929 in much the same way. *Something Wicked* is clearly the culminating volume in the trilogy; the boys of this novel, two variations on Bradbury's own final Green Town years, are nearly fourteen, a bit older than Bradbury was when in 1932 he encountered the Dill Brothers Combined Traveling Shows and Mr. Electrico dubbed him with the carnival blessing "live forever."[21]

By the fall of 1961 the fiction that had evolved out of fact now ran as follows. Advance posters tell of a strange off-season carnival that will arrive Halloween week, and friends Will and Jim witness the late-night arrival of the carnival train and the supernatural encampment of Cooger and Dark's Pandemonium Shadow

Show. They survey the show and sense that venues such as the mirror maze and the carousel can entrap the unwary in their own subconscious fears and desires. As the story unfolds, their suspicions are confirmed: Cooger reverses the carousel (which is always "out of order" for paying customers) to become a boy and pass himself off as a guest in town; he flees back to the carousel when Will and Jim find him out; and the boys jam it in full throttle as Cooger tries to regain his proper age, leaving him little more than a living skeleton. Mr. Dark, Cooger's partner, afterward seeks to take the boys into the carnival, where they will join all the other freaks enslaved from other towns to serve the two supernatural carnival masters, but the boys are aided by Mr. Ellis, the clownish philosopher-custodian of the town library. Will's father also tries to help the boys, but the other parents and townspeople are unaware of the enslaving powers of the carnival. Dark takes the boys from the library, nearly killing Ellis in the process; but the custodian learns how to combat evil through laughter and enlists Will's father to help save the boys. They rescue Will after beating a deadly version of the bullet trick and escaping from the devouring self-images of the mirror maze. Cooger, who has been artificially preserved in Mr. Electrico's chair, blows apart in the wind before he can be revived on the carousel; Dark tries to lure Jim into a ride on the carousel that will make him the new junior partner in the show. But Dark fails, and he is destroyed along with the enslaving power of his tattoos; the carnival blows away; and the two boys and two men walk home to family and friends who will never guess the truth. Bradbury had worked out much of this plot in writing and revising his first complete screenplay in 1955. The *Jamie and Me* manuscript of 1959 had been a transitional working out of method, and the first two drafts of the novel as a third-person narrative (1960) had been packed to capacity with details of effect and description.

Congdon may not have seen the first-person *Jamie and Me* experiment, but he had carefully read the third-person narratives of the first and second submissions. His August 1960 suggestions for the second submission included a recommendation to differentiate between the boys in order to point up more clearly what is at stake for everyone as the dark carnival settles nearby the small town. The suggestions were practical as well—there are times in the early drafts and discards where it is impossible to tell which boy is speaking.[22] In the evolving third draft, Bradbury did, in fact, carefully delineate the boys, developing Will Halloway more consistently in his words and actions as the practical, well-balanced boy who intuitively gravitates toward traditional patterns of interaction with family and town life. Bradbury also stabilized Jamie as Jim Nightshade, now a fatherless boy living next door with his mother, drawn to the darker mysteries of life and impatient to grow up. In the first two drafts (and in the earlier screen treatments), the boys had shared a common protective source of wisdom—

Mr. Ellis, the erudite elderly custodian at the public library. In the third draft Bradbury made his most significant single revision by subsuming Ellis into the character of Charles Halloway, Will's father. Charles Halloway becomes the thoughtful protector of both boys, but he is nevertheless the natural father of only one. By splitting the circumstances of the two boys in these ways, Bradbury clarified and dramatically advanced a central motivation of the novel: why the carnival has such an irresistible appeal for Jim Nightshade.

But Bradbury was also careful to retain just enough in common between the boys to make their adventures both believable and compelling. Will also enjoys small-town adventures, and he is also curious, in a much more cautious way than Jim, about the strange appearance of the carnival and the dangers it brings to everyone. Even the natural protection provided by Will's father is vulnerable— Charles Halloway, as developed in the third draft, is an older man, and both he and Will sense that they have not really connected as father and son. All these refinements of relationship worked to good effect. The fusing of the two good father figures eliminated the often heavy-handed philosophizing of the clownlike janitor and reduced the overcrowded field of protagonists from four to three. It also made Charles Halloway a believable father. Instead of an archetype of the ideal father, he is debased by all-too-common human frailties—he is an aging man in a humble profession, worries about the present, and fears for the future.

These substantial changes in the third draft brought Will's father into focus as a major character who, along with Cooger and Dark, must fight to win true fathership of the boys. The struggle is one of crowning and decrowning in the traditional sense of literary carnival—by convention, the decrowning of the king represented the central moment in the carnival literature of the Renaissance. The novel itself is deliberately set off into three acts that echo the movement of the crowd at any carnival: "Arrivals," "Pursuits," and "Departures." The first phase of this struggle for control of the boys centers on Cooger and dominates the first third of the novel. The dark-carnival masters have been passing through the same small towns at long intervals, returning when the only evidence of their super-natural longevity is locked away in the dusty library files of old newspapers. When Will and Jim unintentionally endanger this cycle by spinning Cooger around in his own protean device until he's nothing more than a living bag of bones, they have decrowned one of the dark fathers of the carnival. The boys run away in horror, but when they return to the carousel with medics and the police, they find that Dark and the other carnies have stabilized Cooger's failing body in Mr. Electrico's chair. The final scene of "Arrivals" is a carnivalesque parody of a father's blessing; instead of wishing them long and prosperous lives, Cooger showers the boys with sparks from Mr. Electrico's prop sword and curses them to a short, sad life. Figure 13 shows how Bradbury revised the central moment of this scene from the *Jamie and Me* variant, eliminating Will's first-person narrative but retaining the full effect of Cooger's naming "his" boys: "I dub thee—asses and fools. I dub—thee—Mr. Sickly and Mr. Pale. Mr. Scream—ssss—and Mr. Yell." Cooger literally wants to put fear back in the boys with his curse, and screams and yells are, of course, the very manifestation of fear. In all the complete drafts, Bradbury eliminated the final names "Scream" and "Yell"—perhaps to make the reader work a bit harder to "hear" the fear that controls the dark carnival.

The carnivalesque decrowning of Cooger has made him laughable, but he can still invoke fear. The final scene of "Arrivals" is polarized between these two extremes, for there are no neutral terms in a contest with evil. "Pursuits," the second and largest section of the novel, shows Charles Halloway's own decrowning; he uses his self-taught research skills to discover the library archives that document the timeless evil of the carnival, and he tries bravely to bring all his literary knowledge to bear in his fight to save the boys from Dark's revenging hand. But he loses them to Dark in the library, and his own fear paralyzes further action as Dark orders the Dust Witch in for the kill: "The janitor's clock. Stop it." The section ends with Halloway's rediscovery of himself and his realization that laughter can fight fear. Discards from the first draft show how carefully Bradbury worked with this key passage to strengthen its power. His notes for these revisions survive on a remarkable sheet of light blue scratch paper preserved with the discards (fig. 14). His note to check the doubled use of "senseless" in his description of the blind Dust Witch as she gestures to stop the heart of Charles Halloway, who has closed his eyes in fear, is bracketed by two equally important notes about laughter: "Don't give away effect of laughter *too soon*" and "Strengthen laugh discovery growing power & *hope.*"

The comments are framed by faces and eyes directed toward a small man. The figure may represent disconnected doodling, Halloway, or perhaps the author playfully reflecting on the effect of carnival, both in real life and in his novel. The happy caricature is unexpected; these are, after all, notes for a horror novel, and one would expect fear to be central to it. Yet fear is entirely banished by laughter—in the author's life and in his art. Particularly evident is the joyous relativity brought on by carnival laughter, which levels social hierarchies and class distinctions. These drawings certainly stand in sharp contrast to the derisive faces and haunted figure found with Bradbury's unpublished *Masks* manuscript of the late 1940s (see fig. 1). The more upbeat notes and figures found in the first-draft discards of *Something Wicked* suggest Bradbury was working toward a more carefully paced revelation of laughter as the great leveling device in the carnival of life, and his success is best seen through a comparison of the September 1962 published version of this passage with the version as it stood in the discards of

■ take the fire-colored tickets.

Just then, the old *OLD* man somehow managed to raise the prop sword very weakly. From its tip jumped blue-green slithers of sparks. He tapped ~~Will~~ *WILL'S* shoulder with it. ~~─────~~. ~~the~~ *E*lectricity raced through *HIM.* ~~Maaaaa~~*S*parks fell on ~~Jamie.~~ *JIM.* ~~hm~~ *HE* yelled.

The policemen laughed.

The old man's lips hissed again. His *ONE* eye blazed like a dying cats *YELLOW MOON EYE.*

"I dub thee---asses and fools. I dub---- thee--Mr. Sickly and Mr. Pale. Mr. Scream---ssss---and Mr. Yell."

JIM ~~Jim~~ and *WILL* ~~W~~flinched back.

Mr. Electrico finished:

"A short, sad life---for both of you. . ."

Then his mouth shut and his eye closed and he sat ~~────~~ just breathing, just *LETTING* ~~let~~ the sparks *SWARM* ~~around~~ around in his dark blood, ~~like somebae holding a candle in a wind.~~

JIM ~~Jim~~ and *WILL* ~~W~~bolted and ran from the tent.

The internes and the policeman followed, guffawing.

When they reached the police car, *THE BOYS WERE* already in the backseat, waiting for a ride home.

The Illustrated Man was with the~~m~~ *OFFICERS.* He looked into the backseat smiling.

Figure 13. The early "decrowning" of Cooger as Bradbury first composed it for the first-person *Jamie and Me* text of *Something Wicked This Way Comes*. Bradbury's ink revisions removed the exchange from the first person but retained the overt reference to manifestations of fear through the curse of "Mr. Scream and Mr. Yell." Bradbury removed this final curse from the subsequent drafts of the novel. From the Albright Collection, courtesy of Donn Albright and Ray Bradbury.

Figure 14. Bradbury's cryptic note to revise the pivotal library confrontation between Halloway and the Dust Witch is blended into sketched faces looking toward a figure of a man. The happy caricature may echo the central insight of this passage, or it may simply reflect the author's state of mind. From the Albright Collection, courtesy of Donn Albright and Ray Bradbury.

early 1960. (Note that Mr. Ellis has been replaced by Charles Halloway in the third draft; his left hand has been broken by Mr. Dark, and the Dust Witch has almost stopped his tired heart in a dark corner of the library.)[23]

First-Draft Discard
(January 1960)

And then, for no reason at all, for a last look around, perhaps, Mr. Ellis opened his eyes.

He saw the Witch. He saw her fingers tickling the air, tickling at his sight, tickling toward his heart as her lips twitched and her swamp breath inundated him. There was something about her folded flesh, something about her nose, her chin, her dusty ears, her skinny fingers that . . . that . . . that . . .

Mr. Ellis giggled.
Quickly, the thought jumped up in his head, why am I doing this now?
The witch pulled back the merest

First-Edition Text
(September 1962)

And then for no reason, save perhaps for a last look around, because he *did* want to get rid of the pain, and sleep was the way to do that . . . Charles Halloway opened his eyes.

He saw the Witch.

He saw her fingers working at the air, his face, his body, the heart within his body, and the soul within the heart. Her swamp breath flooded him while, with immense curiosity, he watched the poisonous drizzle from her lips, counted the folds in her stitch-wrinkled eyes, the Gila monster neck, the mummy-linen ears, the dry-rivulet river-sand brow. Never in his life had he focused so nearly to a person, as if she were a puzzle, which once touched together might show life's greatest secret. The solution was in her, it would all spring clear this moment, no, the next, no, the next, watch her scorpion fingers! hear her chant as she diddled the air, yes, diddled was it, tickling, tickling, "Slow!" she whispered. "Slow!" And his obedient heart pulled rein. Diddle-tickle went her fingers.

Charles Halloway snorted. Faintly, he giggled.
He caught this. Why? Why am I . . . giggling . . . at such a time!?

inch, as if suddenly feeling the pain from the old man's hand.

The old man saw but did not see this, sensed but did not consider this.

Again, senselessly, he found himself smiling and then letting a little careless laugh out.

"Slow!" cried the Witch, angrily.

He did note her anger.

But still the important thing was, nothing really mattered, life, in the end, was an immense joke of such size you only stood back toward the very end to see it stretch away, and you in its shadow. With death this close he thought of a million silly things he had done in his time, as a boy, boy-man, man, and idiot old goat. He had gathered them up like toys and now, between the stacks, in an instant, the toys of his life loomed, among them the largest silliest toy of all, this woman who called herself witch, tickling, tickling,

The Witch pulled back the merest quarter inch as if some strange but hidden electric light socket, touched with wet whorl, gave shock.

Charles Halloway saw but did not see her flinch, sensed but seemed in no way to consider her withdrawal, for almost immediately, seizing the initiative, she flung herself forward, not touching, but mutely gesticulating at his chest as one might try to spell an antique clock pendulum.

"Slow!" she cried.

Senselessly, he permitted an idiot smile to balloon itself up from somewhere to attach itself with careless ease under his nose.

"Slowest!"

Her new fever, her anxiety which changed itself to anger was even more of a toy to him. A part of his attention, secret until now, leaned forward to scan every pore of her Halloween face. Somehow, irresistibly, the prime thing was: nothing mattered. Life in the end seemed a prank of such size you could only stand off at this end of the corridor to note its meaningless length and its quite unnecessary height, a mountain built to such ridiculous immensities you were dwarfed in its shadow and mocking of its pomp. So with death this near he thought numbly but purely upon a billion vanities, arrivals, departures, idiot excursions of boy, boy-man, man and old-man goat. He had gathered and stacked all manner of that's what she's doing, just tickling the air, what a fool, didn't she know what she was doing, tickling the air, tickle . . .

foibles, devices, playthings of his egotism and now, between all the silly corridors of books, the toys of his life swayed. And none more grotesque than this thing named Witch Gypsy Reader-of-Dust, tickling, that's what! just *tickling* the air! Fool! Didn't she know what she was *doing!*

He opened his mouth.

He opened his mouth and let the blast of hilarity out.

Of itself, like a child born of an unsuspecting parent, one single raw laugh broke free.

The Witch was flung back by his laugh.

The Witch swooned back.

Successive bursts of laughter drive the Dust Witch out of the library, disoriented and barely able to join Dark and the captive boys back at the carnival. It is the beginning of the end for Dark and his powers of enslavement. The revised and greatly expanded text provides a more believable pace for Halloway's saving insight into life, and the additional metaphors support rather than detract from the development of this central passage of the novel.

The various stages of revision also allowed Bradbury to develop sophisticated characterizations to an extent he had rarely attempted previously. Although Halloway and Mr. Dark, developed as two rival father figures, are clearly "prosaic" allegorical types of humanity because of the carnival masks they wear, they are not for that reason flat characters. On the contrary, both are capable of surprising us. Their struggle over the boys and the carnival, over who will "father" the carnival, creates many moments of thematic inversion (explored in detail below). They have a special complexity and multilayeredness that derives from their roles in the carnival chronotope (roughly fool-clown and devil). Among other things, Mr. Dark (the Illustrated Man) surprises Halloway (and the reader) with his ability to handle and mock the Bible, and Halloway himself goes through a surprising revolution in his worldview when he encounters the grotesque in the form of the Dust Witch and understands that life itself is an immense prank being played on him. He comes to accept the darker aspects of life, though only in the right proportion. Evil no longer dominates character out of hand, and this is certainly not what one expects to encounter in a traditional horror novel.

As the final section, "Departures," begins, Halloway is no longer controlled by his book-learned seriousness and his fear of the carnival. Through the insight of his near-death experience, he has been restored as a father who stands a chance of winning back the boys from Dark's control. He now stands in sharp contrast to the carnival owner as a father figure. Despite his seductive appeal, Dark is finally revealed as the "devilish" limiting authority he really is. In cultural terms he is Freud, the threatening contested father of the modern fantastic, who fights with the boys and wrestles for control of their destinies. Charles Halloway has cast off his fear and armed himself with the laughter that destroys seriousness. He is now a father who embraces all of life: the grotesque, the beautiful, and the sublime. In the final contest he is able to decrown Dark and break his control over Will, Jim, and the souls trapped for ages in his carnival.

The freeing of the trapped souls will only come with the destruction of Dark and his enslaving illustrations. Dark's last act of magic proves to be his undoing—while Will and his father attempt to revive Jim, who has nearly lost his soul to the temptation of instant adulthood offered by the carousel, Dark reverses the ride and tries to pass himself off as a lost little boy. Halloway knows him for what he is, though, and senses Dark's plan to murder him. The two would-be fathers play out the final drama in character. Halloway cleverly offers the boy-man the love of a father, a proposition he knows Dark cannot abide. Dark expires in his loving embrace, his body and tattoos blowing away with the rest of the dark carnival on the sudden predawn wind. Halloway revives Jim through the same laughing celebration of life that he experienced in the library and introduces "his" boys to the more balanced carnival of real life that comes with every Green Town dawn.

This fundamental use of carnival's decrowning rituals to restore balance to life is found in the two earlier submissions, but in combining the janitor-father into a single character for the third draft, Bradbury was able to bring the central philosophical illumination of the book into sharper focus. This change also tightened a narrative that sometimes wandered off into a maze of characters and an explosion of metaphors. He completed the third draft by December 1961, and Simon and Schuster tentatively scheduled a summer 1962 release.[24] The final fifty-four-chapter structure was now in place, and the narrative had been tightened to 380 pages. But Bradbury held it back over the holidays and soon began a final sequence of revisions. Between February 12 and 22, 1962, he finalized (in ink) many minor revisions and cuts throughout the typescript. He mailed the fourth and final draft (now 340 pages) directly to Bob Gottlieb in two installments during the final two weeks of February. Gottlieb had to delay the production schedule, but he was pleased to find a tighter narrative that retained the same power of the earlier drafts.

Bradbury soon learned to work effectively with his new editor.[25] At first he expected to make his usual extensive revisions in the galleys, but Gottlieb convinced him to work from his carbon of the final typescript while a Simon and

Schuster copyeditor made a light styling pass through the original to save time. During March, Bradbury made final cuts in the descriptions of the ancient Cooger–Mr. Electrico and the other carnival freaks that protect him from too much scrutiny by the police and the boys in the closing scene of "Arrivals." Gottlieb suggested some trimming in "the father scenes," his shorthand for the detailed library introspections of Will's father at the philosophical center of the novel. Bradbury may have made these changes in the galleys, which he went over closely from April 21 to May 14. Nearly three months had elapsed from his submission of the final draft, and publication was rescheduled for September to provide enough time for reviewers to prime the pump. Bradbury was juggling no less than three other book projects, and this contributed to the minor delays. His first volume of plays, *The Anthem Sprinters* (Dial), and the young-adult collection *R Is for Rocket* (Doubleday) were also scheduled for fall release, and he had already submitted *The Machineries of Joy*, his next story collection, to Gottlieb for review. He was also deeply involved with design issues and was delighted with the dust jacket for *Something Wicked* developed by well-known cover illustrator Gray Foy. Bradbury's good eye for cover art and front-matter design led the production department to make a few changes to color values on the jacket and alter layout of the title page, all to good effect.

Despite these delays, Gottlieb was able to get the text to reviewers well ahead of publication. He sent a number of bound galleys out even before proofs were ready; this way he was able to give Gilbert Highet enough time to read the galleys and write a timely review-article for the September issue of *Book-of-the-Month Club News*. Highet and the other BOMC editors did not select *Something Wicked* as a monthly feature, but his review was very positive and reached a large cross-section of grassroots readers. Congdon's parallel effort for advance publicity began more than a year earlier as he worked closely with Bradbury to place an excerpt with a major-market magazine. Will and Jim's fateful encounter with Cooger and the carousel still had enough of the freestanding structure of the original 1948 "Black Ferris" story to form a publishable excerpt; in early February 1961 Congdon found interest but not a commitment from *Life* editor Ralph Graves, but the agent soon placed the opening excerpt with *Mademoiselle*.[26] This venue had been instrumental in Bradbury's quick rise to mainstream magazine prominence in the mid-1940s, publishing similar Bradbury fantasies each year from 1945 to 1947. During the summer of 1961, Congdon secured a first-serial agreement using an excerpt from the first or second draft, thinking that book publication would be based on this stage of the work. It appeared as "Nightmare Carousel" in the January 1962 issue of *Mademoiselle*, without the significant third- and fourth-draft revisions but recognizable as material that would subsequently appear as chapters 16, 18–19, and 21 of the finished novel.

Bradbury isolated two other excerpts for serial publication but was never able to place them. In late 1960 *Good Housekeeping* rejected one, which was extracted from the complex and introspective library discussions between Charles Halloway and the two boys. In February 1961 Graves of *Life* rejected the other, which consisted of Halloway's library encounter with the Dust Witch bracketed by a new standalone opening and ending designed to work as a Halloween story. *Harper's* declined both in October 1961. Editors at the *Saturday Evening Post* were very interested but, after three separate reviews in the spring and summer of 1962, decided against publication. In September 1962 Bradbury tried *Life* again, where he had enjoyed major national attention for his speculative essay on space, "Cry the Cosmos," earlier in the year. Its editors again declined, noting that there was no time to place a serial excerpt before release of the book. But the real issue was structural—the novel simply had no other self-contained episodes beyond "Nightmare Carousel." And as the publication date approached, it was no easier for advertisers or reviewers to categorize the book itself. Gottlieb and Nina Bourne had faced a similar challenge the year before as they launched *Catch-22* into the literary marketplace. The irreverent satire, dark humor, and experimental structure of Joseph Heller's World War II narrative had demanded an innovative advertising approach. For Heller, Simon and Schuster ran mysterious advertisements containing only the paper soldier from Paul Bacon's dust-jacket design and the title *Catch-22*. A year later Gottlieb and Bourne took the same approach with Bradbury. The *New York Times Book Review* for September 16, 1962, contained a three-column page-length ad featuring Gray Foy's glowing dust devil from the book jacket above the words "Ray Bradbury's long-awaited major novel." The dust devil, spelling out *Something Wicked This Way Comes*, points to a single word at the top of the black background: "Tomorrow." On the eighteenth, the daily *Times* featured the same ad, but the headline now read "Today."[27]

These advertisements exemplified the new level of marketing Gottlieb had promised, and follow-up ads on both coasts picked up on lines from the better reviews.[28] Gottlieb's point was to tell the story of the book, to bring the public in on the publishing event. It was the perfect strategy for Bradbury, who once again had a publisher willing to participate in the carnival of his fiction. Gottlieb understood just what Bradbury was trying to do with this novel, but. it was a tougher proposition for some of the critics. On September 19 the influential Orville Prescott, who had praised *Fahrenheit 451* nearly a decade earlier, came down hard on *Something Wicked* in the *New York Times*. He called Bradbury "the uncrowned king of science-fiction writers" but found his latest fantasy to be overwritten and unengaging. Prescott took the central insight—the leveling, unmasking power of laughter—far too seriously, calling it a "clumsy effort to be significant about the eternal conflict between good and evil." He wanted the traditional enslavement of the horror reader: "if the author does not instantly enslave the reader's imagination he is likely to seem like a little boy wearing a mask and shouting 'Boo!'"[29] These assumptions could not be further from Bradbury's broader philosophical purpose. Good and evil are "transvalued" by the book; it is not evil, but the inner phantasmagoria of fear that evil instills in people and feeds on, that is the focus of Bradbury's thematics.

The weekly *New York Times Book Review* for November 4 featured another harsh blow, this time delivered by an obscure horror and crime writer named Lillian De La Torre. She also wanted to squeeze the plot into a story-length work, maintaining that the barrage of supernatural effects and the unrestrained style were too off trail and too off putting for serious fantasy readers. And like Prescott, she attacked Bradbury's treatment of the genre. Not surprisingly, this instinctive defense of the genre was also at the center of private responses from such close friends and fellow writers as Charles Beaumont and William F. Nolan. Both were uncomfortable with Bradbury's approach to the presence of evil. Beaumont took issue with what he saw as the point of the novel: that evil can be laughed out of the world. Nolan took this line of reasoning even further: "I just flat don't believe that you can deal with true Evil by laughing it out of existence, by fighting a force of darkness with a smile. It is a nice symbolic idea—but the reality of the defeat of Evil did not come across to me with any real force or conviction in the book."[30] Nolan's stance is that of the quintessential horror and mystery writer, and this position is also explicit in both of the *New York Times* reviews. It is the horror genre seen in naturalistic terms—how can laughter defeat the physical manifestation of the supernatural? Laughter confronts fear, laughter wins. A good horror writer cannot suspend disbelief in such a situation.

Most critics and genre writers expected horror pure and simple from *Something Wicked*, not a carnivalization of horror. The genre has always been a literature of fear; one can never put evil away for good. But Bradbury was never a traditional horror writer, and in *Something Wicked* his strategy became downright subversive. His elimination of fear runs counter to the horror writer's need to keep fear central to the tale. Laughter becomes the key to a whole new outlook on life, a philosophy where evil is given its due but is degraded and made laughable through carnivalization. Evil normally separates people from life, but in *Something Wicked* it is relativized, brought down, and reintegrated into life. The evil carnival is no longer taken seriously. In this way laughter is also philosophical and represents a more balanced way of looking at both the light and the dark elements of life. In short, Bradbury gives readers a broader view of life, embraces more of life, than the genre permits. This was hard for most horror writers to accept at the time, but Stephen King's unqualified endorsement suggests that the genre masters of more recent times may be warming to *Something Wicked*—a book that has never been out of print. It makes sense, then, that more favorable reviews initially came from critics and writers who were comfortable judging the novel outside the bounds of the horror tradition.

Gilbert Highet's favorable review for the Book-of-the-Month Club was soon reinforced by Anthony Boucher's remarkable essay headlining the September 16 issue of the *New York Herald Tribune*'s weekly *Books* magazine. Boucher, writing under his house pseudonym of H. H. Holmes, offered a major two-page assessment of the science fiction genre, culminating in a look at Bradbury's almost unique ability to carry science fiction into mainstream literature. His point was that Bradbury, already "consistently recognized as an ambassador and almost as a symbol of S.F. . . . , never really wrote science fiction at all." The essay, which privileges Bradbury's range above that of all other major science fiction writers, ends with a balanced and insightful review of *Something Wicked*. Boucher, a legendary mystery editor and reviewer himself, could not quite see all that operated within Bradbury's carnivalesque exploration of good and evil. But he nevertheless managed to take the longer view that Bradbury implicitly asks of all his readers and found this first full-length novel "superb as pure fantasy narrative." None of the initial reviewers were able to place the book in its true niche. Boucher was certain that it was not an allegory, thus avoiding the trap that snared the *Christian Science Monitor*'s enthusiastic reviewer a few months later. Bradbury offers no philosophical abstractions of good and evil in the tradition of an allegory, for as noted, *Something Wicked* does not follow conventional notions of good and evil. Faith Baldwin, observing in a personal note to Bradbury that the author had simply written truth, perhaps came closest to locating this novel as a complex variation on the moral fables one finds in much of Bradbury's other book-length fictions.[31]

Something Wicked remained a steady seller through a hectic fall season complicated by the unprecedented international anxiety of the Cuban missile crisis. By November, Bradbury had only seen a dozen reviews in major media venues, the fewest for any of his major books to that time. It might have fared better with the earlier summer release that Gottlieb had hoped for—the crowded fall book market and international affairs may have been responsible—but Bradbury never knew for sure. Yet most of the reviews were very good; only the *New Yorker* came across with the same complaints as the two *Times* reviews.[32] Advance orders topped 6,000, prompting Gottlieb to add a second printing of 4,000 to the initial print run of 7,500 before the September 18 release. At the same time, he was able to secure an excellent paperback contract for Bradbury. Despite Bradbury's break with Doubleday, Bantam's Marc Jaffe and Oscar Distel were keen to continue a paperback publishing relationship that had made *The Martian Chronicles*, *The Illustrated Man*, and *Dandelion Wine* perennial sellers. Jaffe initially offered a $5,000 advance on the new novel. Gottlieb negotiated patiently and eventually secured Bradbury's best terms with Bantam so far: a $12,000 guaranteed advance on the first 300,000 copies sold and $4,800 on every additional 100,000 sold. These numbers were based on sales of a sixty-cent book, but Bradbury's demonstrated value as a long-term seller allowed Gottlieb to secure a proportional raise in the payments as paperback prices increased. Congdon was pleased with the Simon and Schuster negotiating effort: "Not only is the advance guarantee decidedly bigger than any of the Doubleday negotiations, but the royalty is approximately 7% for the first 300,000 copies and 8% thereafter—compared with the usual 4% and 6%."[33] This development signified to Bradbury that his new book was continuing to get the level of financial recognition and promotion that he felt his books deserved. Gottlieb's deal with Bantam was particularly gratifying, for Bradbury's paperback editions were now all back in print and were continuing to have a major mass-market presence in homes and schools across America.

October brought Simon and Schuster hardback sales topping eight thousand and a strange letter from Charles Finney, who felt that *Something Wicked* infringed on his own well-known 1930s horror novella, *The Circus of Dr. Lao.* The assertion was really the result of Finney's frustration over his own declining career, for the two works have little in common. Bradbury had been very careful to avoid influences in his fiction, and his own successful 1961 case against CBS and Playhouse 90 for an unauthorized adaptation of *Fahrenheit 451* had helped clarify the application of plagiarism laws to literature.[34] He had known of Finney's strange tale of an Arizona town's confrontation with a macabre circus since the late 1940s. Robert Bloch had recommended it to him in 1947, but Bradbury shied away from it while his own carnivals began to take shape. His eventual reading of Finney's tale resulted from his own growing reputation as an editor. Bradbury's successful edition of Bantam's *Timeless Stories for Today and Tomorrow* (1952) led Bantam's Saul David to plan an anthology of weird tales around another Bradbury introduction. Early in 1953 the new anthology began to take shape around "The Circus of Dr. Lao" as the title story, but Bradbury was busy with *Fahrenheit 451* and the *Moby Dick* screenplay and could not turn attention to the Bantam project until the end of 1954. By this time, the spark of creativity generated by the Goldwyn teleplay and the Gene Kelly screen treatment had grown into a fire, and he delayed work on the anthology until he had the fully developed screenplay for "The Dark Carnival" in the form that he would novelize as *Something Wicked*. With this work behind him, Bradbury finally read Finney's novella and sent Bantam the long-awaited introduction for *The Circus of Dr. Lao and Other Stories* in January 1956.[35]

Finney, of course, knew nothing of Bradbury's independent development of a very different kind of novel; he only knew the sequence of publication. Bradbury related the underlying textual history to Gottlieb, adding that he had found Finney's novella to be very different in approach from his own work and, in fact, an imaginative letdown for him as a reader; this view is also evident in the qualified endorsement he included in his 1956 introduction.[36] Bradbury's own experience with the CBS case, which had been settled in his favor just short of the Supreme Court, offered a clear basis of comparison. There was little similarity in idea and no similarity in incident or plot sequence: "the only resemblance between Finney's novel and mine is he wrote one about a Circus, I wrote one about a carnival. Beyond that gapes the Abyss." His letter to Gottlieb also contains very significant views on originality in authorship, quoting in part from the briefs written in his own successful case:

> The whole thing boils down to: Ideas cannot be copyrighted or protected, but "sequences of texture, sequences of events, based on an Idea, *can.*" For instance, I can write a story tomorrow called TO BUILD A FIRE, using Jack London's title and idea, as long as I challenge my hero differently, and adventure him in such a way that all the textures and details are different and in no way resemble "in sequence" or "any inferred sequence" London's story. Just because London wrote a story about a man freezing to death in the wilds doesn't mean all writers after him must give up trying to write about death by freezing . . . It means they must find fresh ways to use that idea, so as not to infringe on his sequential originality (ellipses Bradbury's).[37]

This note clearly shows how Bradbury situated himself in relation to his dearly loved literary influences. He was confident in his own creative authorship and avoided borrowing. Instead, he tended to bring his masters into his own fiction overtly, using them or their works as actual characters in the play of his fantasies. The living books of *Fahrenheit 451* provide the most celebrated example. In *Something Wicked* the key to understanding Bradbury's carnival comes from Shakespeare's stage, not from any superficial resemblance to Finney's circus. Charles Halloway uses the library and its vast archive of literary traditions to build a defense against the dark carnival. He arranges books in a "great literary clock on a table, like someone learning to tell a new time." Many titles relating to the occult are mentioned, but it is impossible to decode the chronotope—the specific spatio-temporal generic matrix—of the carnival because the clock has no hands, no place in real human time. As Halloway begins to think about the language and freakish faces of the carnival, he realizes that *"Physiognomonie. The Secrets of the Individual's Characters as Found in His Face,"* the book whose pages he is turning, is not the master key to unlocking the "personality" of the carnival either. Men cannot be judged by their faces—a fact enunciated by Duncan in Shakespeare's

Macbeth, the most phantasmagoric and imaginative of all the Bard's plays. So in the middle of the clock of books, Bradbury writes the title of his book, taken from the witches of *Macbeth.* The key to understanding this literary dark carnival is indeed in Shakespeare's lines (so vague, yet so immense), but they must be reimagined, textualized anew. Thus, although Shakespeare can be said to have invented the modern notion of personality, Bradbury must find fresh ways to use textuality in understanding the character of his carnival of evil. Because of its use of masks, the carnival (as analyzed in the thematics section below) is as much a character in the novel as anyone else.[38]

In its originality of events, sequences, and textures, *Something Wicked* is as different from *The Circus of Dr. Lao* as it is from Philip Barry's *Send in the Clowns.* It is not clear if Finney ever realized this fundamental distinction, but there is no evidence that he ever pursued the matter further. Gottlieb was satisfied with Bradbury's position, and the incident was soon forgotten. Hardbound sales continued to do well, and in December *Something Wicked* made the *New York Herald Tribune's* list of the best books of 1962. Gottlieb and Bradbury were already at work on the submitted stories for *The Machineries of Joy* (1964), which had been welcomed by Simon and Schuster. It was clear that his new publisher was willing to consider story collections as the normal vehicle for Bradbury's unique brand of fiction. It was a nice contrast to Doubleday: as Bradbury's story output turned more and more to fantasy in the 1950s, Doubleday had come to view his story collections merely as a price one had to pay for the occasional novelesque story cycle. The move to Simon and Schuster tied Bradbury to a publisher who could appreciate the major-market author he had become rather than the niche-market science fiction author he had once been labeled.

Bradbury and Congdon hoped to see the same process unfold in England, even if it meant, once again, breaking a long association with a publisher. Bradbury had a solid following in the United Kingdom, and British intellectuals on both sides of the Atlantic read him—including Graham Greene, Christopher Isherwood, Aldous Huxley, Kingsley Amis, Gerald Heard, Lord Bertrand Russell, Somerset Maugham, Stephen Spender, and W. H. Auden. But the British market was relatively small, and even with overseas commonwealth distribution, his contracts with Rupert Hart-Davis were not yet in proportion to his reputation. In April 1962 Hart-Davis read a typescript of *Something Wicked* and offered a £150 advance on signing.[39] Congdon's London agents at A. D. Peters were able to get the advance offer up to £250 but cautioned against any hope for further progress. Both Pete Peters and his associate, Margaret Stephens, enjoyed the novel as much as Hart-Davis did, but they also shared his sense that this was not the book to take Bradbury to the higher level in British sales that his long-term reputation warranted. Bradbury and Congdon had heard this from Doubleday two years earlier and asked Peters to shop the novel to three other London publishers (beginning with Gollancz) to see if there was interest. Bradbury also informed Hart-Davis of his plans, for the two men were friends and had no trouble speaking frankly on such issues.

On May 22 Hart-Davis wrote back to affirm his willingness to go higher on the advance but made it clear that this in no way changed his belief that sales would remain problematic. Peters, Stephens, and Hart-Davis all sensed that English readers, expecting what had usually been promoted there as Bradbury's special brand of science fiction, would not know what to do with this long, carnivalesque horror novel. Bradbury wrote again to make his position perfectly clear. For Bradbury, it was not a matter of money upfront or of best-seller status; it was a matter of long-term promotion:

> As for best sellerdom, I don't kid myself that I will ever have that, in the larger degree. But I do believe my books, all of them, could have done better, if more had been done with them. Why do I believe this? Because, everywhere I go in America I find my fans growing up in legions in the schools, not as the result of my hardcover books, but of my softcovers that followed. I find an acceptance, belatedly, on all intellectual levels, for my work, and each time, here in the USA, I have had to go out on my own, and make suggestions, and follow through, in much of the campaigning for my books, on my own.[40]

In his final paragraph he used a military metaphor to show Hart-Davis the kind of participation he wanted from his good friend and long-time British publisher: "I hope you will sympathize with my point and buy the book and go into battle for me. Again, the advance money, while welcome, is not the whole point, but the promotion of the book is." It was, essentially, a variation on his carnival cry to readers and publishers to participate in the creation of the literary work and its cultural success—no one is a spectator. For Bradbury, the advance money was simply a measure of the publisher's commitment to promote, to believe in, the author's book. Hart-Davis responded to the essential issue; in addition to raising the advance offer to £500, he also doubled the promotional budget for *Something Wicked*.[41] Bradbury and Congdon accepted the offer, and his first full-length novel was on its way to release in England.

English release was previewed in October 1962 with British *Argosy*'s reprint of the January 1962 *Mademoiselle* excerpt "Nightmare Carousel." *Argosy* had been a steady market for Bradbury since the late 1940s and welcomed the chance to provide the first view of the novel in England.[42] At the last minute, Bradbury realized that the novel had gone through several significant stages of revision since *Mademoiselle* had purchased the excerpt in the summer of 1961, and in June 1962 he wrote *Argosy* to offer the final version of those chapters forming the excerpt. But the publication had already set the October issue, and "Nightmare Carousel" appeared once again as a preliminary form of the novel's first horrifying adventure.

The British edition of *Something Wicked* was released in March 1963, and once again the critics tried to force-fit the new novel into a traditional genre niche. By that standard, the English critics were just as disappointed as their American counterparts. The *New Statesman* noted, "Ray Bradbury turns from Science Fiction to Gothick fantasy; but it isn't well sustained." The reviewer felt that "the nightmare pursuit and capture of two boys is impressive" but in the final analysis found "too little good horror, and a lot that just suggests the machinations of a black Disney." The *Times Literary Supplement* proclaimed that "[Bradbury] has hit on a finely sinister idea" but considered the horror effect diminished by predictable stylistic effects. "Overwriting has always been Mr. Bradbury's weakness, as though he felt a little ashamed of his chosen genres, horror and science fiction, but hoped that by making them literary enough he would automatically establish their claim to literature."[43] Ironically, none of the critics chose to define or follow the way that Bradbury used the older carnivalesque traditions of literature to level or relativize the effect of fear and thus break out of genre conventions. But his readership in England remained loyal, and Hart-Davis was able to keep *Something Wicked* and most of his earlier titles in print throughout the 1960s.

In the mid-1960s *Something Wicked* received a boost in Britain when Corgi agreed to buy U.K. paperback rights to both of Bradbury's Green Town books. Corgi had published British paperback editions of his science fiction titles and finally agreed to bring out paperbacks of both *Dandelion Wine* and *Something Wicked* in 1965. Meanwhile, the 1963 Bantam paperback edition became a steady seller (and remains in print). As always, Bradbury's hardbound editions eventually slipped out of print, but further moments of market prominence were to come. Once again, he would have to rely on his own promotional skills. Review copies of the novel went out to Harold Prince, who felt that a stage treatment was impossible but that Ingmar Bergman could make an excellent film of it. Bradbury also sent a copy to English director Jack Clayton, who had impressed him with *The Innocents*, a 1961 adaptation of Henry James's master horror novella *The Turn of the Screw*. During the next two decades, he would write three more screenplays of *Something Wicked*, selling the first to Twentieth Century Fox and almost pulling in Clayton to make the film. In the 1970s Bradbury wrote another screenplay that was sold to the Bryna production company of Kirk Douglas. Rights were eventually optioned to his son, Peter Douglas, and under this arrangement Bradbury tried for several years to get Sam Peckinpah, who was deeply interested, to direct the film; again, a deal was never finalized. In 1980 Bradbury's third screenplay was purchased by Disney and lined up to be one of the first films produced under Disney's Touchstone subsidiary. Steven Spielberg was interested in the project but was sidetracked by his whimsical *1941*. Instead of Spielberg, Bradbury was able to lure Jack Clayton out of retirement to make the movie. Substantial post-production reshoots delayed release to 1983, when *Something Wicked* became the third Touchstone film (after *Tron* and *Splash*).[44]

In 1968 Gottlieb had become vice president at Knopf and paved the way for Bradbury to become a Knopf author the following year. The release of the 1983 film persuaded Gottlieb, by then the top executive at Knopf, to bring out a new hardbound edition of *Something Wicked*. But in the late 1980s, Gottlieb moved on to become editor in chief of the *New Yorker*, and it became harder for Bradbury to keep hardbound editions of his books in print with any of his present or past publishers. With the Bantam and Ballantine paperbacks in print, there was little incentive for publishers to bring out hardbound editions except for special projects. Bradbury's 1994 move to Avon led to cloth reprints of the key titles and handsome trade-paper editions of most of the rest. In 1999 Avon released its hardbound edition, but a year earlier *Something Wicked* became the lone mass-market paperback edition in the Avon list of Bradbury titles, joining the Bantam mass-market paperback as an accessible and very popular text of the novel. Despite its long and complicated prepublication history, *Something Wicked* has remained a very stable text in print. All subsequent editions radiate from the Simon and Schuster first edition, which was carefully edited under Bradbury's close supervision. Only the dedication has changed. Leaving his original dedication, which included his two inspirational high school English teachers, in the ever selling Bantam edition, he rededicated both of the new Avon editions to Gene Kelly, who inspired Bradbury with his films and his very personal encouragement so many years ago.

More than any of his major fictions, *Something Wicked* demonstrates in its textual history Bradbury's longstanding ties to the film industry. He began to write for studios in the early 1950s, and over the years this work often focused on one version or another of *Something Wicked*. Publication of the book also marked the beginning of a long period away from sustained story or novel writing. His productivity as a story writer dropped off significantly after 1962 as he turned more and more to writing stage versions of his stories and screenplays of his major fictions. His next book-length work, *The Halloween Tree*, was itself a novella developed out of a deferred animated film project in 1972. In all, nearly a quarter century would intervene between *Something Wicked* and release of another major novel. And many of the publications of his later years would emerge from ideas born in the richly creative midcentury period of his career (1942–62) that culminated in *Something Wicked*. In the best work of this period, he affirmed that laughter is the great unmasking of the seriousness of life. As seen in the thematics discussion below, carnival in *Something Wicked* becomes a master metaphor for Bradbury's life of fiction.

Thematics

Something Wicked This Way Comes raises issues of interpretive reading as no other book by Bradbury does. Critics are divided into those who want to read it as a Christian allegory and those who want to read it as bearing Freudian symbolic or archetypal meanings. The one exception to this rule is Stephen King's deft appreciation of the book in his *Danse Macabre*, which manages to weigh the merits of both readings while suggesting other, more complex ways of understanding it.[45] We do not propose to repeat the details of King's analysis here, but surely this kind of reading of Bradbury's fantasy is an advance over others that try to "decide" on the book's meaning in terms of one interpretive scheme or another as if a fantasy novel were a monologue expressing only one point of view (usually identified with the author of the interpretation). In fact, as we have been at pains to point out earlier in this book, Bradbury's fundamentally carnivalistic view of the fantastic presupposes the ambivalence of themes and the dialogic interaction of metaphors, myths, and masks. This is especially true of *Something Wicked*, which is carnivalized on every level of thematic meaning.

Something Wicked is one of Bradbury's most densely coded books. It uses many "reduced" or indirect forms of laughter, such as parody, irony, jokes, and mocking sarcasm, as well as direct laughter itself. Bradbury's style in this novel piles metaphor upon metaphor, building dense matrices of meaning where codes intersect (the polyphonic musical code alone crosses church music and carnival music with popular tunes) until any literal ground of meaning becomes problematic. These excesses of style—if they can be called that; we think that their function is to evoke the hyperbolic language of carnival—do not mean, however, that the book has become "poetic," losing sight of the prosaic world of everyday life. On the contrary, central to the novel's thematics is the need for building "common cause" with others. In fact, on one level of meaning (the symbolic), it is a concerted attack on the individualistic and romantic (that is, Freudian) use of masks employed by the dark carnival.

Mikhail Bakhtin has demonstrated how profoundly the development of the novel was affected by the adoption of three carnival figures—the rogue, the clown, and the fool—as narrators or central characters. Historically, these "uninvented" figures were needed because of the problem of authorship in the novel genre, which really has no inherent set-and-fixed way to coordinate the authorial position with regards to its narrative's represented world and its public, the readers. Bradbury's authorial position in this novel is complex and needs to be explored in depth, so summarizing it will wait until the end of the chapter. But here let it be noted that, while *Something Wicked* uses the carnival mask of the fool in its main character, the father-fool Charles Halloway, it also invites us to laugh at the fool in all of us.[46] It especially invites us to laugh (with some sympathy) at those "unconnected fools" who are the harvest of the dark carnival. The book takes a stand against lonely, isolated individualism and argues for a collective laughter at everything that is exclusively serious in life (this much is explicitly stated in chap. 39).

King's reading, while acknowledging the role that the "admiring laughter" of the father plays in the book with regard to its sons and recognizing the capacity of Bradbury's "myth-children" to enjoy their terror, does not analyze the all-important role of laughter (in the collective sense belonging to authentic carnival) in this fantasy. Nor does it examine the ways in which the spirit of laughter—increasingly evident in Bradbury's writing from this book onward—might be related to a transvaluation of values. King is content to call the book a "moral horror tale" not so much different from Pinocchio's scary encounter on Pleasure Island, where boys who indulge in their baser desires (smoking cigars and playing snooker, for instance) are turned into donkeys.[47] For King, Bradbury's carnival represents a false freedom to its myth-children, William Halloway and Jim Nightshade; it is a taboo land made magically portable, traveling from place to place and even from time to time with its freight of freaks and its glamorous attractions.

It could be argued that King has read his own moral concerns as a writer of horror—concerns that always involve a threat to normalcy—into *Something Wicked,* but that is not the main concern here. Beyond the obvious appeal of the book's temptation theme and the father-son relationships that are strong in it, laughter—which has such a primal, visceral function for Bradbury as a sign of the capacity to affirm and to enjoy life—is the key to understanding it, for laughter is the primary means by which the fearsome carnival with its evil sideshows is unmasked, defeated, and transformed. Laughter is also the means by which we experience, in the book's third part, a transvaluation of values in which our conventional notions of fatherhood, bad conscience, guilt, and remorse are transformed. What follows is a reading of *Something Wicked* with the intent of showing how laughter, fathership-authorship, and the carnivalization of genre are all interrelated themes in the book.

The first part of *Something Wicked This Way Comes* presents the invasion of a small town in the American Midwest by the denizens of a supernatural traveling carnival, or, more precisely, Cooger and Dark's Pandemonium Shadow Show. Ostensibly, the town with its rules and laws is considered the norm, and the fantasy involves an intrusion of creatures (or ideas) that ordinarily would be confined to some other outside realm of existence.[48] The fortune-telling Dust Witch, for example, embodies our superstitious fear of fate and subjection to chance. As a literary topos, this carnival shares in the notion of a Dionysian eruption or tearing of the social fabric.

In addition to the father-fool as its central interpretive character, Bradbury's carnival still bears many popular-festive carnival images (especially grotesque body images) but is itself double or ambivalent. We hesitate between its two versions. During the day, it acts like a normal carnival that offers the kind of excitement and escape traditionally associated with such entertainments. Yet at night Bradbury's carnival is a machine that runs on bad conscience and regret, evil certainly, but equally pious and serious about itself. It is a paranoid machine run by Mr. Dark, an "illustrated man," who acts as a kind of father to all the freaks. He is clearly a cultural embodiment of the punishing superego of Freudian psychology, which basically defines his role in the internalized Gothic of the novel. The body images of the freaks are imprisoned as magic tattoos on his skin, but he also wears a "brambled suit" of thorns interminably itching, which suggests his relationship to an ascetic ideal.[49] One should remember here that, in its historical origins, carnival was a festive response to the seriousness of the church and official culture of the Middle Ages, which emphasized sin and the punishments of hell and upheld an ascetic ideal for humanity, this world being nothing more than a vale of tears. It was a world of fear and piety that excluded laughter. Mr. Dark's stinging suit is a reminder that he comes from that world, the anti-carnival, not the true carnival.

We soon learn that it is the function of the mirror maze, which operates during the day, to lure people back to the carnival at night by showing them reflections of a part of themselves that they once were or would wish to be so that they are plunged into aching despair. It represents, then, the whole world of interiority and regret—exposed by Friedrich Nietzsche in *On the Geneology of Morals* as the source of all higher values—that can threaten or destroy our capacity to affirm our lives. To the mirror maze is linked the carousel, which seems to run only at night. It can be run at a supernormal speed, forward or backward, and whoever rides it adds or subtracts a year of life per revolution. The carousel offers to repair the damage revealed in the mirror maze by providing maturity or youth—but at a price. The buyer of the ticket becomes a slave to Mr. Dark's shadow show.

Bradbury's fantasies often approach the issue of values by inverting them and then having the reader search for the reasons behind the inversion (*Fahrenheit*

451 has firemen lighting fires instead of putting them out). At the outset we are presented with a reversed-image carnival:

> A carnival should be all growls, roars like timberlands stacked, bundled, rolled and crashed, great explosions of lion dust, men ablaze with working anger, pop bottles jangling, horse buckles shivering, engines and elephants in full stampede through rains of sweat while zebras neighed and trembled like cage trapped in cage.
>
> But this was like old movies, the silent theater haunted with black-and-white ghosts, silvery mouths opening to let moonlight smoke out, gestures made in silence so hushed you could hear the wind fizz the hair on your cheeks.[50]

This carnival—compared to a movie screen that stages desire—sets itself up in the darkest hours of the night. Why does Bradbury reverse the traditional associations belonging to this literary chronotope? We have to remember that he is writing *after* Freud, in a culture that has internalized the Gothic to an extraordinary degree. Tzvetan Todorov has indicated, in a statement that has provoked some controversy, that there is no literature of the fantastic in the twentieth century because psychoanalysis has taken over its themes.[51] This assertion has been largely confirmed, though inadvertently, by recent studies of the American Gothic, such as Mark Edmundson's *Nightmare on Main Street*. Edmundson does not consider the possibility, however, that fantastic literature could take revenge on psychoanalysis for this encroachment by making psychoanalysts figures of fun (or even serial killers themselves; the stories of Clive Barker or films like Brian di Palma's *Dressed to Kill* manifest this widespread tendency) in stories that discredit their authority or show their theories to be fictions. That is the cultural process—carnivalization—that is happening in *Something Wicked*.

Bradbury carnivalizes each genre in which he works. Here it is a question of the horror, or dark fantasy, genre whose themes have been dominated by Freud and based on Oedipal and familial fears. But in *Something Wicked* Bradbury's strategy is less direct than in his short stories and poems. There is no psychoanalyst overtly represented in the literal story. But the carnival itself, because it functions by feeding off the desires of people for lost objects, their guilt and sense of debt, and especially their narcissism, is similar to the psychoanalytic machine as parodied in some recent Nietzschean-inspired anti-Freudian polemics: "the psychoanalyst parks his circus in the dumbfounded unconscious, a real P. T. Barnum in the fields."[52]

Another interpretive issue to be dealt with, then, is the fact that *Something Wicked* speaks to us in the language of images derived from carnival that are indirect and often have a metaphorical and even allegorical significance.[53] But carnival should not be translated into a language of abstract concepts. Instead, one must investigate how carnival laughter, symbols, and its sense of change can be figured by literature and, through understanding them, again regain some sense of participation in it, the authentic use of the carnival being identified, according to Bakhtin, with our sense of carnival having *only just* been transformed into literature. Everything in Bradbury's text, its discourse and themes, strives to achieve this effect.

Here we want to mention that Bradbury conducts his critique of the Freudian view of man (as driven by unconscious desires he can never fulfill and by self-punishment for having those very desires) by the technique of carnivalizing the carnival and by masking his main character as a fool who, because of his "outsidedness," is able to resist its temptations. Fearful things such as Mr. Dark must also be masked in Bradbury's aesthetic. This is not to suggest, however, that *Something Wicked* is purely an allegory. Although his name suggests some such function, Mr. Dark does not represent the abstract allegorical *idea* of the evil father. His image is, in fact, quite ambivalent and derived from carnival images that in origin parodied the ascetic ideal. Mr. Dark is only one of several fathers in the book. It is Cooger whose name comes first in that of the carnival, and he is its (crowned-decrowned) king.

Mr. Dark is, however, the main spokesman for the sinister carnival. His language conveys something of the carnival's attractions, with his talk about life surviving "wildly" in it. He is figured in the novel as an inscribed body that has to be interpreted by Halloway (and Halloway's reading is itself a carnivalized history, a Nietzschean genealogy). In the story the main struggle consists in trying to stop Mr. Dark from "Oedipalizing," or fathering, the entire town. Initially, only the two boys stand in the way of the carnival. Jim Nightshade's father has apparently died. The attraction that Mr. Dark offers him is sexual maturity, the chance to become his own father by riding the nightmare carousel into the future and ruling the carnival with him. Jim is fascinated by the "bramble suit" long before he is seduced by Dark's tattoo images (at least some of them seem to be of phallic origin; Jim hesitates but says he saw a "snake" on Mr. Dark's arm).[54] Will Halloway, Jim's best friend, is able to resist such a temptation because he does have a father—the quiet, scholarly, middle-aged janitor of the local library who has a weak heart.

Will, as his shortened name suggests, has the will to command and obey himself, a prime Nietzschean virtue. He runs because running is its own excuse. Jim runs because "something's up ahead of him," according to Mr. Halloway, who has a deep sympathy with the boys, understanding them from the point of view of the adolescent he once was.[55] But of course, Mr. Halloway is an adult, worried that his age and weak heart do not allow him to be a proper father to Will. The carnival tempts him with restored sexual potency and vitality. Together, Will and his father—who emerges as the real hero of the story—must defeat the carnival and rescue Jim Nightshade from its clutches.

Early in the novel, one of the carnival workers, distributing advertising and putting up posters in the town, shows Halloway what can only be the image of female genitalia on the palm of his hand, which is "covered with fine black silken hair." He leaves a block of ice in an unrented, empty store. This ice block represents "The Most Beautiful Woman in the World." Halloway gazes into it, and Bradbury writes the "truth" about desire staged as lack:

> And yet this vast chunk of wintry glass held nothing but frozen river water.
> No. Not quite empty.
> Halloway felt his heart pound one special time.
> Within the huge winter gem was there not a special vacuum? a voluptuous hollow, a prolonged emptiness which undulated from tip to toe of the ice? and wasn't this vacuum, this emptiness waiting to be filled with summer flesh, was it not shaped somewhat like a . . . woman?
> Yes.
> The ice. And the lovely hollows, the horizontal flow of emptiness within the ice. The lovely nothingness. The exquisite flow of an invisible mermaid daring the ice to capture it.[56]

Charles Halloway wants to leave but instead stands looking for a long time. The desire being staged in this passage, with its emphasis on the captured gaze, suggests that the ice itself is a kind of mirror (and Halloway's name seems to be an echo of the word "hollow"). We are asked to imagine both the representation of a nothingness and something else that flows exquisitely outside that representation, daring desire to capture it. The flow provokes a reverie of warm summer water imprisoned in ice, which eventually suggests the absence of a supernatural mermaid who left behind her voluptuous form.

In the psychoanalytic sense the desire Halloway feels is based precisely on nothing, a feminine void (that is, castration). The fantastic representations of the carnival want to ensnare him in such emptiness. Yet psychoanalytic desiring and the themes of sex and age do not explain everything here. Another, different type of desiring based on the plenitude of the material imagination (of water, which flows outside of forms in this instance) is also present in this passage. The text illustrates very clearly that Bradbury's use of fantastic representation is profoundly ambivalent. There is always life amid death, the lure of beautiful Apollonian forms and the Dionysian flow outside them.

Halloway's views about life at this point are fairly consonant with Christian notions of sin, guilt, and the need for grace. At fifty-four he feels the weight of the world, the spirit of gravity. He is shocked by Jim, who cannot understand the Christian allegorical import of Dante (but Bradbury manages a pun on "Alighieri" and "allegory"), but who is instead fascinated by the literal hell as illustrated by Gustave Doré. At this stage of valuing, Halloway represents classical—and conventional—aesthetic attitudes. His understanding of the carnival is limited initially to the beautiful, as in the figure of the woman, and the sublime. Indeed, the carnival's impending arrival brings with it a sense of the sublime, a "terrified elation" as Bradbury describes it. In response Halloway recites to himself a traditional Christmas carol ("God is not dead, nor doth he Sleep!"), which gives expression to his feelings.

But the mermaid is also a figure, half-human and half-fish, of the "grotesque realism" (the term is Bakhtin's) of carnival. In our interpretation of her image, we can already see that Halloway's experiences with the carnival will not be limited to the classical dualism of the beautiful and the sublime. In the book's second part, Halloway will have to experience and interpret the body of the carnival, which in turn will lead to his rebirth and revaluation of it and its meanings. Halloway will defeat the carnival through an appropriation of its (hidden) laughter, which enables the ambivalent fathering or destruction of Cooger and Dark in the book's third part.

But before that can happen, the reader needs to be dramatically "horrified" by what the carnival can do. Among the supernatural events in the first and early second parts of the book, none is more fully realized and terrifying than the capture of Miss Foley, the boys' seventh-grade schoolteacher. Described as a little woman lost somewhere in her gray fifties, she is nearly drowned in the fathoms of reflections in the mirror maze but is rescued by Jim and Will. Her desire-as-lack is to have once been beautiful. After her experiences with the mirror maze, her house seems haunted by mirrors that threaten her with "billionfold multiplications of self, an army of women marching away to become girls and girls marching away to become infinitely small children."[57] Miss Foley's final metamorphosis into a frightened girl beneath a tree in the cold autumn rain is Bradbury's own image of hell—to be trapped as an adult inside a child's body, unknown even to oneself, with no way to tell the strangeness to anyone. Miss Foley gets more than she desires from the carnival, but in getting it, she severs all ties of love and human time with the community. Even the boys she once taught are unable to do anything about her situation.

The evil agent in this punishment is Mr. Cooger, who is changed into a semblance of her nephew, Robert, by the carousel; changed and crowned by a ruse of Mr. Dark's into Mr. Electrico; and finally decrowned when the freaks cannot get him back to the carousel in time to revive him. The boys spy on this transformation and are aware of his intention to lure Miss Foley back to the carnival to ride on it also. Jim wants to meet the transformed Mr. Cooger out of sheer curiosity, but Will responds to the danger of the situation. What Will sees in Miss Foley's comfortable living room (in the final version, on the right, below) is a quintessential romantic-Freudian mask:[58]

Jamie and Me discards (1959)

Something was standing on the porch looking out at the town. I felt Jamie flinch one way, then another, undecided. I grabbed him tighter. The something on the porch could have been the man, could have been the boy. I smelled the man somehow, and saw the boy a moment later come out in the streetlight. There was his face, round and smooth as a peach. But there were the man's eyes looking out like through the slits of a Sleeping Beauty mask at Hallowe'en. At any moment I expected a crack to appear in the top of the boy's chestnut hair and move down cracking his face in half, splitting his nose, his chin, cleaving like an ax had chopped him down through the neck, the chest, to let a great wet moth heave out beating its wings in the porch dark, a moth big enough to carry us both away from the town forever into hills that never ended. That's how much I felt the other thing inside the thing that said it was a boy that said it was good that never shaved but was all tarantula hair inside.

Something Wicked (1962)

And it was wild and crazy and the floor sank away beneath for there was the pink shiny Halloween mask of a small pretty boy's face, but almost as if holes were cut where the eyes of Mr. Cooger shone out, old, old, eyes as bright as sharp blue stars and the light from those stars taking a million years to get here. And through the little nostrils cut in the shiny wax mask, Mr. Cooger's breath went in steam came out ice. And the Valentine candy tongue moved small behind those trim white candy-kernel teeth.

Mr. Cooger, somewhere behind the eye slits, went *blink-click* with his insect-Kodak pupils. The lenses exploded like suns, then burnt chilly and serene again.

The final passage emphasizes the eyes of the mask, which have no part in the comic masks of carnival that are meant to dispel fear and hide nothing.[59] It expresses, in sweetened images of candy, the individual disconnected human life, not the grotesque body of carnival, which is open to the world (see also fig. 14, which also emphasizes the eyes of individuals). Although it too contains a reference to eyes—in fact, in the earlier version the face beneath the mask is compared to a molting tarantula, a striking image of the fear of dehumanization. In the final version the horror is that the boys can see through the mask. They are not taken in by the ruses of the carnival. The pink, shiny Halloween mask is also linked to another popular-festive holiday, Valentine's Day, which is often celebrated in schools.

Nonetheless, ruses and dissimulation are the laws of life in the romantic carnival, which could not survive if it did not don the mask of the forces against which it struggles. Cooger's mask is scary because, to the boys anyway, it does not entirely hide the horror of chaos beneath it. On the contrary, it lets this stare through in a glance of cold command. And because his eyes are compared to stars and the vast distances traveled by light from sources that may no longer exist (and whose origin is forever unknown), we have the eerie sensation of being looked down upon by a force that is much larger than ourselves. Nephew Robert only seems obedient; actually it is Miss Foley who obeys. Cooger's face appears to have beauty, the sweetness of candy, but underneath lies an abomination of nature, an abyss, which is why Will feels the floor sliding away beneath him.

Soon after this scare, the boys return to the carnival, Jim because he wants to go forward on the carousel, Will because he wants to stop him. Accidentally, while they are fighting, Will pushes the lever forward, and Mr. Cooger is metamorphosed in a shower of electrical sparks into an old, old man. Later, seeking revenge, the carnival comes on a parade through town. For the first time, Will's father is convinced that something wicked has arrived when he has an ominous confrontation with Mr. Dark and the Dust Witch.[60] The parade scene is also the first time we are given an indication that the carnival has a weak spot: its unrelenting seriousness. (It had played church music when it first arrived, another sign of its seriousness.)

During this episode, Mr. Halloway's prankish behavior with a cigar—he is something of a rogue in this scene, pretending not to know who the boys are—causes the Dust Witch to recoil from "the concussion of his fiercely erupted and overly jovial words," which also cause Mr. Dark to go rigid with anger. We are given a strong indication that the carnival cannot abide any attack on its seriousness and "piety," especially the enjoyment of life in an expenditure without reserve. When Mr. Halloway puffs a cigar, everything goes up in smoke of enjoyment; nothing, save his enjoyment, remains. But the carnival, we may infer, wants to make human pain and negativity a resource, to make it work for them. Mr. Dark talks openly later in the book about "investing in our securities" and offers ostensibly free tickets to the boys.[61] Here, the reader begins to suspect, however, that there is something deceptive about the economy of the carnival that needs to be unmasked.

The unmasking occurs in the books interpretive chapters. Following the parade through town, Mr. Halloway repairs to the library with an invitation to Mr. Dark to come and find him there. The setting is already symbolic of reading and interpretation. By the end of the book's second part, we are astonished not by supernatural events, but by the eight full chapters set in the town's library that are devoted to interpretation of the carnival (chaps. 37–44). These argue against our seeing the carnival as an allegory of abstract ideas, urging us rather to interpret it as a body with a certain history.

When the boys arrive and give a precise summary of the fantastic events in the plot thus far (that now become "facts" to interpret), we enter into what Mr. Halloway calls a "history of the carnival." Actually, it is no conventional history at all but approximates a Nietzschean genealogy that examines the emergence and descent of things one normally thinks of as being without history—negative emotions such as fear and unhappiness, conscience and regret, and instincts. According to Michel Foucault, Nietzschean genealogy is "history in the form of a concerted carnival."[62] Halloway's history of the carnival does not, in fact, trace in the carnival a gradual curve of evolution from an origin or describe a linear development in the conventional historical sense. Rather, it is sensitive to the carnival's periodic invasions of the "real" world, its struggles, plunderings, disguises, ploys, and above all its recurrence, in the process isolating different scenes where it engaged in different roles. It is best understood as a carnivalized history:

> The stuff of nightmare is their plain bread. They butter it with pain. They set their clocks by death-watch beetles, and thrive the centuries. They were the men with the leather-ribbon whips who sweated up the Pyramids seasoning it with other people's salt and other people's cracked hearts. They coursed Europe on the White Horses of the Plague. They whispered to Caesar that he was mortal, then sold daggers at half-price in the grand March sale. Some must have been lazing clowns, foot props for emperors, princes, and epileptic popes. Then out on the road, Gypsies in time, their populations grew as the world grew, spread, and there was more delicious variety of pain to thrive on. The train put wheels under them and here they run down the long road out of the Gothic and baroque; look at their wagons and coaches, the carving like medieval shrines, all of it stuff once drawn by horses, mules, or, maybe, men.[63]

This entire highly engaging genealogical analysis by Halloway—of which we have only reproduced a small sample here—proceeds through a series of what

Nietzsche calls emergences *(Entstehung)*, moments of arising. An emergence is an entry of forces onto the scene of history through a play of dominations. It designates a place of confrontation that later becomes stabilized in social forms such as rituals, in meticulous procedures that impose rights and obligations. Thus these "autumn people" (as Halloway earlier calls them) become "foot props for emperors, princes, and epileptic popes." But no single unified origin is posited as giving rise to the carnival, nor is there a fall into sin or a promise of redemption. On the contrary, throughout this history, Halloway stresses the strategies of the weak against the strong, not good against evil. (Could the carnival of evil have had the same values in such different historical periods as the Gothic and the baroque?) A form of the dark carnival arises whenever and wherever people begin to feed on what Nietzsche calls man's progressive internalization of instinct, giving rise to bad conscience and even higher morality, especially ascetic ideals.[64] Interestingly, the carvings on the wagons are described as "medieval shrines," making the dark carnival allude to the pious seriousness of the Middle Ages.

The genealogy begins with the simple prehistoric *Schadenfreude,* the malicious delight of one man in another's misfortune, and thereafter (passing from father to son—an Oedipal structure is suggested) grows until it takes on the qualities of a machine threatening to dominate the earth. As Halloway patiently explains to Jim in the passage immediately preceding this, the carnival is not evil but bad, for from it comes "nothing for something," nothingness in return for the investment of desire. (A similar deconstructive analysis of the binary oppositions, for example, "good" and "bad," that structure our moral values can be found in Nietzsche's *On the Geneology of Morals,* which we suggest as an intertext here.)

The second part of Halloway's genealogy takes the form of a descent *(Herkunft)* that is involved with the body and everything that touches it: diet, climate, soil. Something of this is already evident in the passage quoted above, which is strongly phrased in such metaphors ("The stuff of nightmare is their plain bread. They butter it with pain"). But the body metaphor becomes dominant in the next chapter (forty), in which the bodily image of the carnival is analyzed, and where the soul itself becomes a kind of body that oxidizes need, want, and desire. Halloway here gives an instinctive Nietzschean analysis of the "black candle-power" of the carnival, whose fuel is "the raw stuffs of terror, the excruciating agony of guilt, the scream from real or imagined wounds."

In Foucault's analysis descent "attaches itself to the body," inscribing itself in the nervous system, in the temperament.[65] Descent establishes marks of its power and engraves memories on things, creating stigmata that can be read by the genealogist. Through his analysis of its descent, Halloway is able to interpret the carnival as a machine that inscribes desires, failings, and errors on the bodies of its victims, the people who join it, abandoning wives, husbands, and friends.

In Halloway's interpretation—which he stresses is incomplete and subject to a lot of guesswork—the carnival becomes a body and the freaks are read as ironic inscriptions on an inscribed surface of events. The mirror maze transforms these individualized people who want a "change of body, change of personal environment" into freakish living images of their "original sins." The primary sins are narcissism and not bothering to form common causes with others. For instance, the lightening-rod salesman, whom the boys meet at the beginning of the novel, is figured as someone who never stays around with others to face the storms. The carnival turns him not into a boy, but into a dwarf, "a mean ball of grotesque tripes, all self-involved."

A few comments on the nature of the carnival body as it develops in the novel is necessary at this point, for that body represents collectivities and crowds whose nature may be misunderstood. At the end of the novel's first section, we see how Mr. Dark's body bears the living tattoos, the illustrations of all the stories of the freaks he dominates. Although they are described as a collective identity, as a "picture crowd flooded raw upon his chest," the freaks are not allowed to speak in their own voice, to tell their own stories.[66] They have to serve the evil of Mr. Dark's narrative monopoly:

> Mr. Dark came carrying his panoply of friends, his jewel-case assortment of calligraphical reptiles which lay sunning themselves at midnight on his flesh. With him strode the stitch-inked *Tyrannosaurus rex* which lent to his haunches a machined and ancient wellspring mineral-oil glide. As the thunder lizard strode, all glass-bead pomp, so strode Mr. Dark, armored with vile lightening scribbles of carnivores and sheep blasted by that thunder and arun before storms of juggernaut flesh. It was the pterodactyl kite and scythe which raised his arms almost to fly the marbled vaults. And with the inked and stenciled flashburnt shapes of pistoned or bladed doom, came his usual crowd of hangers-on, spectators gripped to each limb, seated on shoulder blades, peering from his jungled chest, hung upside down in microscopic millions in his armpit vaults screaming bat-screams for encounters, ready for the hunt and if need be the kill.[67]

The passage goes on for another lengthy sentence. On the whole it evokes a sense of Mr. Dark's tyrannical and predatory power over the carnival. It is composed of dinosaur metaphors and metaphors of metaphors. The narrative of events is halted by the outbreak of a profusion of bodily metaphors—consider the series pterodactyl-kite-scythe, which signifies by resemblance the deadly mechanisms that lift Mr. Dark's stitch-inked arms. Everything happens on the surface of a fantasized body that Dark has somehow made appealing to the boys, who he knows are interested in dinosaurs. (Earlier, stripped bare to the navel, he is seen stinging himself with a tattoo needle, adding a picture to his left palm, undoubtedly the image of Jim's face.)[68]

The crowds depicted on this social body, though they seem full of life, are not really free. In true carnivals no one is just a spectator. No one is outside the play of carnival, everyone is a participant in its life and subject to it. The freaks should be able to speak with their own true voices to each other, yet they appear as themselves only as masked by their sins. Because his body contains so many "spectators," Mr. Dark is thus the *author* of the carnival, one who seeks to master and control all of its narrative meanings. Bradbury wants very much to defeat this notion of authorship in all its seriousness with the notion of the author as someone who creates himself and sees himself created as self and other, as both man and mask. (Julia Kristeva describes the notion of carnivalesque authorship in exactly these terms.)[69] In intellectual terms the Illustrated Man, as Dark prefers to call himself, is a congeries of inscribed images, a text threatening to dissociate itself, held together by the appropriative force of his will.

Mr. Dark tries to tempt Halloway with restored youth and vitality if he will tell him where the boys are hiding in the library. Halloway refuses, but his heart is too weak to put up a fight. His attempt to do battle with Dark among books, he now realizes, has not really amounted to much in terms of action, and Dark taunts him with this knowledge. When Halloway asks him if he has read the Bible, Dark takes the copy from him with ease: "Do you expect me to fall away into so many Dead Sea scrolls of flesh before you? Myths, unfortunately, are just that. Life, and by life I could mean so many fascinating things, goes on, makes shift for itself, survives wildly, and I not the least wild among many. Your King James and his literary version of some rather stuffy poetic materials is worth about *this* much of my time and sweat."[70] Dark then throws the Bible into the wastebasket.

Because Mr. Dark can read the Bible and discard it as if it were rubbish—a still shocking act of carnivalization, decrowning what was for many centuries the center of our literary culture—we understand that words, not even the Word of God in the soaring poetic cadences of the King James Version, are going to be sufficient to defeat the carnival. There is no question either of any genealogical word of "truth" that would make Dark's body fall away into textuality, into "Dead Sea scrolls of flesh." As Halloway realizes that he is being mocked and debased in his efforts to understand the carnival as both book and text, he lies helpless on the floor of the library, thrown down by Mr. Dark's power. Dark then goes off in search of the boys, "my two precious human books," so he can turn their pages. Having caught them and sealed their lips with a magic dragonfly spell, he leaves Halloway in the unsavory company of the Dust Witch, who has been instructed to stop his heart.

At this point something rather unexpected, though not entirely unprepared for, happens. Looking up at the wizened Dust Witch's mask, at her "Halloween face" with an intense scrutiny as she tries to kill him "as if she were a puzzle, which once touched together might show life's greatest secret" (in the last revised draft, Bradbury had originally typed "hidden values" but wrote "life's greatest secret" over it, which indicates that he was thinking of a transvaluation of values in this scene), Halloway is still trying to interpret what that secret may be when— and the phonetic resemblance between "Halloway" and "Halloween" may also be a dialogic jest on his own mask here—he begins to spontaneously and uncontrollably giggle.

The central passage from chapter 44 cited above in compared texts is highly significant in terms of its carnivalized thematics and requires extensive comment. First of all, it is the literal turning point of the novel, the pivot around which the story changes because, as the penultimate sentence indicates, laughter and freedom are breaking free and turning the tide against a "grotesque" horror. When raw laughter is born from Halloway, its "unsuspecting parent" (in the last revised draft, Bradbury had written "unsuspecting father," which makes the birth directly related to fathering the carnival), we sense a reappropriation of the true function of folk carnival, which had become perverted by Mr. Dark. Of great significance is the fact that the laughter is described as "raw." It is not undergoing sublimation of any sort, neither religious, mystical, nor philosophical. It has not been filtered through the corrupted institutions of the dark carnival that prey on isolated individuals. This laughter remains outside of official falsification and lies, exploding and ripping away masks and pretensions. The passage goes on to register Halloway's acute awareness of a "joke" rushing through his body, "letting hilarity spring forth of its own volition along his throat . . . , whipping shrapnel in all directions." As Lionel Trilling has observed (in a quote reproduced in the front matter), no great novel exits that does not have a joke at its very heart.

Bradbury's use of laughter and the joke is still more complex. According to Bakhtin, the themes of carnival laughter were expressed in a number of characteristic comic images. Always in them can be discerned "the defeat of fear presented in a droll and monstrous form, the symbols of power and violence turned inside out, the comic images of death and bodies gaily rent asunder. All that was terrifying becomes grotesque." Furthermore, Bakhtin goes on to add, in carnival even death becomes pregnant. In the true carnival symptoms of pregnancy or of procreative power are not hidden but abound, and a joyous recreation of an Earth without fear is expected. At the end of the novel, Halloway and the boys experience the world "as it must have been in the first year of Creation, and Joy not yet thrown from the Garden."[71] This "final" victory over fear is not its abstract elimination, however.

Bradbury has adapted these carnivalesque images to our modernist sensibilities about meaning. The Dust Witch, the embodiment of human desires to understand such serious notions as fate, desire, and fortune, seems funny to Halloway because she is blind to her own interpretive activities. By tickling and interpreting Halloway, she is trying to give him a heart attack, but instead she only makes him laugh. All the reading and interpretive activities he has engaged in, all those books, seem like "playthings of his egotism and swaying toys of his life" now. As the Illustrated Man points out to Halloway, biblical images of him as the Devil are myths, and myths, unfortunately, are just that. As interpretations, they cannot help Halloway defeat the carnival. Life, however, "goes on, makes shift for itself, survives wildly." In other words, a myth or a metaphor simply *is* a mask of the play of interpretive forces. Mr. Dark can see, touch, and even read from the Bible, a fact that surprises Halloway. Life as the will to power interprets, using any number of masks. This is the "great secret of life" that Halloway learns and appropriates from the carnival.

Second, Halloway begins to see himself, it is clear, not as a stable person who is either good or evil, but as a succession of arrivals and departures (the names of *Something Wicked*'s first and last sections). Having gained this radical perspective, this "joyful relativity" from the carnival itself, Halloway realizes that the only thing possible to do at this extreme moment is to push this ridiculous masquerade to its limits, to risk a revaluation of all values. In looking so closely at the witch's mask and at her efforts to stop his heart by negating his love of life, Halloway at least realizes that he too, although "good," must give up any claims to substantial identity, to a metaphysical essence that defines reality once and for all.

It is important to realize that Halloway *has* gone beyond conventional notions of good and evil in this passage. He no longer believes in these or in the specter of Christian guilt. Therefore, the carnival, which represents the whole world of interiority and regret, can have no claim on him any longer. It is not normalcy that is restored at the end (as in King's reading of the novel, in which the Dionysian only disrupts and threatens normalcy that is then restored, missing entirely the ambivalence of carnival). Halloway ends up believing in a kind of pure exteriority of meaning, in the playful surfaces of things instead of the profound "depths" of meaning, an appreciation that is brought to him though his intense scrutiny of the Dust Witch's mask. Through saying "yes" to life's essential meaninglessness and suffering and to death itself, he overcomes the carnival and himself. Halloway realizes he has been granted this power "all because he accepted everything at last, accepted the carnival, the hills beyond, the people in the hills, Jim, Will, and above all himself and *all of life*, and, accepting, threw back his head for a second time tonight and showed his acceptance with sound" (emphasis added).[72] Laughter, not meaning, will defeat the carnival.

Laughter brings the serious things of life—which usually occupy a position above us—close at hand so that they can be mocked. Laughter has brought Halloway to understand the partial nature of all one-sided ideological positions. His actions after this transformative experience disrupt the restrictive economy of the master-slave dialectic on which the carnival runs. Making use of the unsuspected Dionysian power of laughter, Halloway bursts apart the carnival at its seams, shattering the mirror maze with its anguish of petty narcissism, which is the very motor of the carnival's machine, which gives nothing (it seems the very spirit of Hegelian negation) for something. Eventually, he slays the Dust Witch with a bullet on which he has marked his smile. No aspect of displaced carnivalesque humor is too "childish" or baroque for Bradbury to appropriate and use in his war against the internalized Gothic and its regime of guilt and self-punishment.

The laughter that is born from the Dust Witch's "tickling" is not just a physiological response. It opens up a new philosophical understanding of the world, revealing the joyful relativity of all structure and order, of all authority and hierarchical positions. In Nietzschean terms it would mark the birth of the overman and a more joyous and higher psychic life. To laugh at "evil" requires discipline and strength, an entire method that understands evil's byways and techniques and actively appropriates them: "Not by wrath does one kill, but by laughter. Come, let us kill the spirit of gravity!"[73] In Nietzsche's later philosophy, laughter is an antidote for afflictions produced by the spirit of gravity that makes life a burden. So in Bradbury's text also, when the Dust Witch comes with her "weights and pressures of despair" to read his pain and regret and to make him part of the carnival, Halloway laughs, prompted by her ticklings. Actually, he does more than simply laugh: he laughs hysterically, guffaws, and hollers with mirth. His laughter is the deeply primal bodily laughter of the carnival reborn and released in all of its ambivalent life.

After these Dionysian insights, Halloway is no longer an interpreter of literary myths in the library, but someone who experiences a rebirth through the ambivalent death of the carnival (he had, in fact, told the boys earlier that "Death doesn't exist; it never did, it never will" but explained to them that the carnival feeds off of the fear of death). As a Dionysian father, however, he has to teach young Will the value of laughter for life. Will must learn to affirm life; he must abandon will-negating moods brought on by the carnival. Only then can he and Will bring Jim back to life with mirth, harmonica playing, and mimic dancing— all true aspects of carnival culture. Halloway even kills Mr. Dark, who has transformed himself into a boy, Jed, with a loving fatherly embrace. Halloway literally kills with kindness. Before he dies, Jed groaningly accuses Halloway of being "evil" in a nice carnivalesque reversal of perspectives.

Mr. Dark's illustrations disperse and melt away, leaving the freaks with no body in which to recognize themselves any longer, with no "common cause" to unite them. This dispersal of the romantic-Freudian machine that was Cooger and Dark's Pandemonium Shadow Show is in itself a rather dismal affair, for it seems we will never know who the freaks really were as they are liberated into intensities and differences, for they disappear in all directions like shadows, Miss Foley and the others captured from Green Town leaving with them. The true horror of Miss Foley's transformation is that she is no longer connected to a social body in human lived time.

We know that the carnival of interiority is finished, though it may return again under different masks. The haters and despisers of life will always be around, Halloway seems to imply: "The fight's just begun." Indeed, Bradbury will struggle again with such "autumn people" and "pessimist" thinkers in *Death Is a Lonely Business*. But laughter will be available also as a principle that affirms life, as a balm that makes light of our wounds. "We *can't* take them seriously," Halloway tells his son, "them" being the "night people" of the carnival in whatever form they may take.

Although expressed in carnival images, Bradbury's authorial position (a notion that encompasses the author-hero relationship in the world of the novel and also the relationship of the author to his readers) in this novel is complex and philosophical. Fathering the carnival with a fool character and his laughter does not mean that Bradbury's position of authorship dispenses with seriousness altogether. Bradbury still wants to be taken seriously as an author, but it is a question of an "open" seriousness, one that eschews the dogmatic and the hierarchical notion of author represented by Mr. Dark. Some readers of this novel cannot understand how evil can be defeated so easily by laughter alone. But it is not evil as a metaphysical essence that Bradbury is out to destroy. What he wants to destroy is the fear on which evil feeds. With this book, Bradbury serves his readers "official" fair warning that henceforth those who read him without laughter, without finding the joke at the very heart of his works, might as well not be reading him at all.

Through the ambivalence of carnival—it has always represented both death and life for him since he met the real Mr. Electrico (who curses the boys in this novel instead of giving them a blessing, see fig. 13)—Bradbury addresses his own authorship of the fantastic. The father-fool's ritual debasement by the carnival and the Dust Witch gives birth to a new and world-embracing "raw" laughter outside of the need for social masks that hide the person inside. It now seems entirely appropriate for Halloway as Nietzschean father to kill this "son" Jed, who represents the poisoned ruses and formal disguises of psychoanalysis insofar as they have penetrated the horror and dark fantasy genre. By making his fantasy responsive to the situation of the fantastic after Freud, by carnivalizing the whole tragic nature of interiority (repression, guilt, anguish) that Freud's work represents in our literary culture for him, Bradbury has written a new chapter in the history of laughter. *Something Wicked This Way Comes* remains his favorite book and is (in our judgment) his best use of metaphor, myth, and mask to create a literary carnival. Because of its intense focus on carnivalization on all levels of the text, and especially because of its use of laughter, the novel exists on the boundary between art and life as if carnival itself had *only just* come to claim its rights in literature.

Something Wicked is the culmination of Bradbury's aesthetics of carnival in the fantasy genre. But he went on to use the mask of the fool to transform the detective genre as well.

6

Corpse Carnivals

A Memory of Murder, Death Is a Lonely Business,
A Graveyard for Lunatics, and *Let's All Kill Constance!*

Bradbury's early development as a professional writer took a brief but significant detour during the mid-1940s as he successfully placed seventeen stories in the major detective magazines of that day. He would continue to build a larger reputation with his unique brand of weird fiction during this same period, eventually placing twenty-five stories in *Weird Tales* from 1942 through 1948. But Bradbury's beloved science fiction stories did not meet with the same level of success during the war years, and for a time he turned where his natural ability to write compelling five-thousand-word tales of the darker aspects of life led him. Bradbury never saw this foray into the world of crime fiction as an end in itself and would always see such stories as a useful but unfinished stage of his development as an author. His immediate postwar success in the science fiction pulps, as well as his simultaneous movement into the mainstream magazine market with enduring tales of fantasy and small-town reminiscence, led him away from the detective-mystery culture after 1948.

Subtle reminders of these origins would surface from time to time in his contributions to *Ellery Queen Mystery Magazine* as well as other, larger major-market periodicals. Even in his original pulp tales, his instinctive carnivalization of characters and plots was decidedly off-trail from the conventional detective story. Nearly four decades later, these stories returned to the public eye in a way that Bradbury had never anticipated; this, along with his rekindled interest in the great detective writers of the 1940s and a growing sense of nostalgia for that zany and youthful period of his own life, led Bradbury to begin a new and very different phase of detective fiction. He would eventually write three complete but interlocked detective mystery novels in his own inimitable style.

In the process he would turn the genre on its ear by centering the novels on a version of his younger self, projected as a fully carnivalized writer-detective. What he had done with the horror novel in *Something Wicked This Way Comes* he would now do with the crime novel in *Death Is a Lonely Business* (1985). In this novel he formed a typically Bradburian nostalgia for his own beloved past—this time to his early twenties and his life as a writer of detective tales, closeted in a small office-apartment on Figuroa Street deep in the rich narrative life of the Los Angeles Bario—combined with a search for creative potentialities that lay in the future. This complex temporality involving both author and hero subsequently supplied enough material for *A Graveyard for Lunatics* (1991) as well as the recently published conclusion to this trilogy, *Let's All Kill Constance!* (2003). In these three books he would weave together the tenement characters with Venice Pier carnival exotics, movie moguls, reclusive film stars, and elusive murderers inspired by his own vividly remembered experiences, beginning with his adolescent arrival in 1930s Los Angeles and running through his early years of film work in 1950s Hollywood. Just why he would want to engage the genre of detective fiction in three novels when he was thought of primarily as a fantasy and science fiction short-story writer is investigated below. Bradbury has always been a writer who combines nostalgia for the past with a love of surprising and unpredetermined futures, but the detective genre represented the greatest aesthetic challenge to this notion of creative freedom—and perhaps the greatest surprises of his career.

Bradbury's Texts

Bradbury's sojourn into detective pulp fiction began with the help of his first agent, Julius Schwartz. Bradbury had met Schwartz at the inaugural 1939 Science Fiction WorldCon in New York, where he also made contact with a number of science fiction and weird-pulp editors. In 1941 Schwartz began to work with the young writer as an agent for the pulps. He witnessed a dramatic development within the first year as Bradbury began to produce his own kind of quality horror stories for *Weird Tales* and other niche-market magazines. In the late summer of 1942, Mike Tilden, a good friend of Schwartz, became editor of *Detective Tales;* in early September, Schwartz suggested to Bradbury that they begin to submit stories to *Detective Tales* and other genre pulps owned by Popular Publications.[1] It was a good fit in a general sense, for Henry Steeger, who had founded Popular Publications with Harold Goldsmith in 1932, was influenced by offshoots of the carnivalesque in dramatic literature, including Gothic melodramas and the darker twentieth-century French tradition of Grand Guignol. He started *Dime Detective* as a cut-rate competitor for the fifteen-cent *Black Mask* and the next year turned his *Dime Mystery* magazine into what became known as the first of the "shudder" pulps by bringing Grand Guignol's brand of visualized terror to what had been, in its first issues, merely a companion magazine for *Dime Detective*.[2] Bradbury never went as far in his fiction as the sometimes sadistic Grand Guignol tradition, but the occasional "grue" in his stories and the high emotional effect of his prose clearly evolved from the same carnivalesque literary roots. His very first published crime story, "Killer, Come Back to Me!" (1944), had been submitted as "Autopsy," for this retrospective look at a dead bank robber's last weeks is literally "read" from his exposed organs during autopsy. This gruesome reading of the past, laid out as if it were a simple tea-leaf reading of the future, was prime material for Popular Publications. It appeared in Mike Tilden's relatively tame *Detective Tales*, but Bradbury would eventually place five stories in the more sensational *Dime Mystery* shudder pulp.

Author and agent focused on the more conventional magazines in the Popular stable, which included *Detective Tales, Dime Mystery*, and *Flynn's Detective*. Tilden edited the first two titles, and Alden Norton, who was also editorial director for Popular, edited *Flynn's*. By the early 1940s, Popular had bought *Black Mask* but maintained its tradition as a niche for writers of the newer, distinctively American "hard-boiled" detective tradition. This was the first great American crime pulp, founded in 1920 by H. L. Mencken and George Jean Nathan to support their other more genteel publications. In its pages they had published the pioneering detective mysteries of Dashiell Hammett and the early stories of Raymond Chandler. At first Schwartz did not offer Bradbury to *Black Mask* or its digest-format competitor, *Ellery Queen;* instead, he decided to work up to these venerable venues by way of the other magazines.[3] Both Tilden and Norton were captivated by Bradbury's style and emotional power but found his unconventional plotting problematic. By the very circumstances of crime publishing in the pulps, Bradbury would have to conform, to some degree, with certain traditional notions of plotting and logical development. Detective fiction is essentially logical, and the ratiocinative principles of Edgar Allen Poe virtually require an author to work out a story from the end back to the beginning. Bradbury's instinctive need to let his characters tell their own stories ran counter to this tradition, and he would never compromise this process. In the end he rewrote his tales just enough to be acceptable for the pulps and became a distinct talent in his brief engagement with the field.

Bradbury did not go into the field unprepared. His reading and filmgoing passions had prepared him in a general way already, and during the previous year, Henry Kuttner and Leigh Brackett had led him into a deeper study of the works of James Cain, Dashiell Hammett, and Raymond Chandler. Kuttner had even lent him copies of the genre masterworks and had reawakened Bradbury's earlier interest in the late Thorne Smith.[4] Smith's light mysteries and comic whodunits were very much in the tradition of carnival literature; in fact, his Topper series and other popular sellers had earned him the title of "the American Rabelais" well before his premature death in 1934. During 1942, Kuttner was writing what Schwartz called his "Thorne Smith novel" for review at Random House. He would begin to collaborate with his wife, science fiction writer C. L. Moore, on the first of four detective novels where the crime solver was a psychoanalyst. Four decades later, in *Death Is a Lonely Business*, Bradbury would fashion a protagonist very much in the tradition of the American Rabelais and would reverse the Kuttner-Moore formula to transform a psychoanalyst from healer to murderer.

Bradbury found Tilden more accepting of his initial approach to detective and murder mysteries than Norton and published more in the magazines that Tilden edited than in any of the others. Seven Bradbury crime stories reached print in 1944 and five more in 1945. His wartime output was all the more impressive in light of the paper shortage that led many pulps across all genres to shorten each issue or even publish fewer issues per year. Tilden continued to ask for the five-thousand-word stories that Bradbury found so easy to generate, but his growing success in the science fiction pulps left less and less time for the mysteries. The money was relatively good—1¼ to 1½ cents per word on acceptance; in contrast, *Weird Tales* held all their writers to a penny a word and paid only on publication. But Bradbury would only publish five more crime pieces between 1946 and 1948 and would never again appear in the pages of the detective pulps. After the summer of 1945, he was placing more and more stories in the major-market slicks and by the early 1950s was done with the pulps altogether. Nevertheless, his run was impressive; he had placed five stories in *Detective Tales*, three in *New Detective*, and soon won over Alden Norton with a sale for *Flynn's Detective Fiction*. He would have placed more in that venue if Norton had not had to shut down production near the end of 1944. Despite good sales, the paper shortage led Norton to suspend *Flynn's* for the duration of the war to support circulation of the even more successful romance series published by Popular. Bradbury also placed five stories in *Dime Mystery*, the syndicate's first magazine packaged in the Grand Guignol tradition. By the early war years, a more conservative reaction to the sometimes sadistic and gruesome tortures of the magazine's first decade had led the publishers to tone it down considerably, and as a result Bradbury's stories fit in.[5] But it is significant that his work found its way so easily into the most theatrical of the crime pulps, for these were clearly descended from the spectacle elements of carnival.

Of the early tales, "Yesterday I Lived!" (1944), the story of a studio cop's efforts to solve the on-set murder of a cherished actress, contains the best combination of plotting and imaginative power. As Bradbury's science fiction and fantasy matured, so did the stories he placed in the detective pulps. "The Small Assassin"

(1946) would prove to be an enduring part of the Bradbury canon; its fantastic plot of a baby intent on murdering the parents who forced it from the safety of the womb into the pain and trauma of the real world is only marginally a detective tale, and Bradbury had no trouble bringing it into *Dark Carnival* and five subsequent collections. In 1948 he made his last and most masterful appearance in the detective magazines. *Detective Book*, run by a different publishing syndicate, accepted "Touch and Go," later known to Bradbury's fantasy and science fiction readership as "The Fruit at the Bottom of the Bowl." This story would be collected with other selections from his established fantasy and science fiction canon in *The Golden Apples of the Sun* (1953). It is important to note that from the late 1940s on, Bradbury would continue, on occasion, to turn his now fully developed narrative talents to subjects of crime and punishment. A few of these stories would appear in *Ellery Queen* (which by the early 1950s had absorbed the venerable *Black Mask*) but most often in major-market magazines. Bradbury would eventually embrace most of these later stories into his periodic and always popular story collections. His most chilling Green Town tales, "The Whole Town's Sleeping" (1950) and "At Midnight, in the Month of June" (1954), certainly evolved from his journeyman stint with the crime magazines; in fact, the latter story won *Ellery Queen*'s 1954 prize for best sequel in a special issue that published both stories. But other much more fantastic elements shape most of Bradbury's later crime stories, and in these tales the fantastic often operates within the tradition of the carnivalesque in literature.

Intimations of this evolving playfulness can be seen in the pulp period; in fact, it is no small irony that his editors added their own textual layer of meaning by replacing most of Bradbury's titles with new titles of their own (see app. A). But the underlying conceits remain, especially in such stories as "The Coffin," one of the word-association stories first published in *Dark Carnival* but almost immediately reprinted in *Dime Mystery* under the more enigmatic title "Wake for the Living." No matter what the title, it remains a play on the coffin as metaphor for the leveling effect of death. The coffin is capable of conducting the service and burying the occupant; it is the greatest invention of one monomaniacal brother and the emotionless killer of his avaricious, fratricidal sibling. The unwitnessed, automatic burial alive is darkly humorous and macabre, simultaneously entertaining and shocking. But Bradbury was unable to take the next step within the confines of the established genre. "The Very Gentle Murders" (1994) illustrates just how far beyond the rules of the field Bradbury tried to go; although the story was not published until 1994, correspondence reveals that it was offered to his crime magazine editors in the mid-1940s but rejected. It is the tale of the last days of Mr. and Mrs. Enderby, a painfully aging couple sick of life but far sicker of each other's company, who spend all their waking hours devising secret plans for domestic murder. Conventional structural elements such as motive simply do not apply here. When each realizes what the other is up to, Mr. Enderby sees that they will have to dispense with such conventions: "'Motives are Bilge,' he said. 'We are two querulous old pots with nothing to do but kick off, and make a circus of *that*. But how much better the dying game if we write a few rules, act it neatly, with no one the wiser.'" Bradbury's characters write the need for purpose entirely out of the story and center the mystery on a darkly humorous murder endgame. Eventually, the authorities, who see the crime scene as a simple murder-suicide pact, impose motives that have nothing to do with reality. Early in his career, Bradbury could not win publication for this carnivalesque parody of the motive convention. Another generation of editors would eventually place this story in the May 1994 issue of *Ellery Queen*.

For decades, Bradbury would pull back from this playfully creative assault on the crime-writing establishment. He had no ego invested in this form and took his search for the fundamental insights of life to a wider range of readers and the nearly logic-free world of fantasy. His occasional return to the realm of crime and punishment was so far distant from genre characteristics that none of the later tales have ever been categorized as serious crime fiction at all. One of his early detective pulps, "The Trunk Lady," led within a few years to four fantasies exploring variations on the same theme: the mannequin radio play (1947) and story, "And So Died Riabouchinska" (1953), and his "marionette" trilogy, a mixed science fiction and fantasy group that includes "Marionettes, Inc." (1949), "Changeling" (1949), and "Punishment without Crime" (1950). "The Wonderful Death of Dudley Stone" (1954) offers a metaphorical murder of authorship. "The Town Where No One Got Off" (1958) explodes the distinction between random and premeditated homicide through a deadpan parody of paranoiac fantasies. "My Perfect Murder" (1971), like the story of Dudley Stone, explores what can happen when a premeditated murder proves unnecessary. In "A Touch of Petulance" (1980), a wife-murderer moves back in time to warn his youthful self of what the future holds for the young man and his bride. The fundamental elements of murder mystery lurk within many Bradbury fantasies of the last half-century, but none of these stories marked a return to the genre he had explored as a developing writer in the mid-1940s. In these fantasies the narrative center rests with either the murderer or the victim. In other words, none of these stories has a detective.

All this changed, rather quickly, in the early 1980s when a crucial sequence of circumstances led Bradbury to explore the carnivalesque possibilities of the detective genre in earnest. In the end this significant shift in his career would fully establish Bradbury's credentials as a novelist. His intense but successful struggle to produce *Something Wicked This Way Comes*, his first full-length novel, was followed by rewarding experiments beyond novels and stories that would occupy him for the next two decades. The 1960s saw the flowering of Bradbury as a mature stage writer able to successfully adapt his own stories to drama. In the 1970s he drew great satisfaction from writing verse and marketing it, with the able advice and assistance of Nancy Nicholas at Knopf, in three popular and entertaining collections of his poems. In between he turned an unproduced animated feature into the short juvenile novel *The Halloween Tree*, which, like his other so-called juvenile and young-adult books, was really intended for the child in all people. He became a highly prized public speaker for a wide range of audiences and settled into a regular routine of speaking engagements that continued for decades. Yet story writing continued as well, although at a much slower rate than before. And throughout these years he would continue to work on film and television projects as he had since the early 1950s. In the early 1980s Disney's movie version of *Something Wicked* became the first Bradbury work filmed from a Bradbury script, and he was laying the groundwork for his own television series. But these promising media developments were interrupted by some unpleasant ghosts from the past.

There were fifteen ghosts, to be exact. As work on the Disney film wound down in 1982, Bradbury was approached by Joel Silverstein, who had interested Dell Books in a collection of Bradbury's early detective-mystery stories. Bradbury found that rights to his Popular Publications stories were now owned by Robert Weinberg, who had agreed to work with Silverstein on the project. Bradbury knew only too well how this state of affairs had come about. Julius Schwartz had been an excellent agent during Bradbury's years as a pulp writer, but he made one decision that would come to haunt his client—he allowed Popular Publications to buy all rights to the sixteen Bradbury detective stories they published between 1944 and 1948. This was not an uncommon practice and in itself might not have developed into a problem at all. Over the years, Bradbury had asked for and (often with only a token payment) received his rights returned by various pulp syndicates as his stories were adapted to other media, anthologized, or revised for his own story collections. When "Killer Come Back to Me!" his first detective story to appear in a Popular Publications magazine, was adapted by other writers for national radio broadcast on NBC's *Mollé Mystery Theater* in 1946, Popular released their rights in the story so Bradbury could pursue film negotiations as well. But by 1953, when Bradbury needed releases on some of the other stories for comic adaptations by William F. Gaines's EC editors and artists, Alden Norton retained the rights and asked for 25 percent of the income in return for granting Bradbury permission to use them. From Norton's perspective, it was only good business sense; Bradbury was now a major writer, and the EC comics reached millions of readers with every issue. But Bradbury felt betrayed by editors he had always trusted and favored at Popular and limited the comic adaptations to tales he could buy back from Standard Publications *(Weird Tales)* and other syndicates with no such strings attached.

Norton was not interested in doing anything on his own with these stories, and over the years, Bradbury himself made no effort to collect or reprint tales that he felt, with the exception of "The Small Assassin," were inferior to his mature work. But now someone was willing (and able) to collect these pieces under Bradbury's name regardless of the author's desires. Bradbury decided to take an active part in the collection and, in the end, won back everything he had lost. First, he held out the two stories he did control: "Killer, Come Back to Me!" which he had purchased from Popular in the late 1940s, and "Touch and Go," which he had originally placed with a different syndicate and subsequently revised into an integral part of *The Golden Apples of the Sun.* Next, in an effort to provide the best possible entry into the collection, he supplied his own introduction and led off the collection with the strongest story, "The Small Assassin." And when the new collection, aptly titled *A Memory of Murder,* was released in 1983, Bradbury secured new copyright control over these fifteen stories as well. He limited the entire edition to a single paperback print run; it could not be reprinted, reissued in hardback, or marketed overseas. It remains a difficult book to find today and no doubt will remain so for a long, long time. Nevertheless, Bradbury revisited all of these stories in writing an introduction that placed them in the larger context of his life of fiction, and he revisited as well the detectives he had invented to solve the imagined crimes of a bygone day.

Two Bradbury detectives reached print via Popular, but one vanished after just a single appearance. "Hell's Half-Hour" had originally been titled "Mr. Priory Meets Mr. Caldwell" before its publication in the March 1945 issue of *New Detective;* in this tale Bradbury had started to develop police lieutenant Chris Priory into a crime solver that Julius Schwartz thought might merit development into a series.[6] But Priory has no personality at all, and his words and actions are narrated by an assistant equally devoid of character. Filtered through this oblique narrative strategy, Priory seems little more than a voice through which Bradbury experiments with ratiocenative plotting. By revealing only selective knowledge of the character's actions, Bradbury withholds Priory's key insight until the final paragraph: that the half hour it took to murder a blind man in a confined room can only mean that the murderer is also blind. With this insight, the lieutenant is able to narrow the possible suspects and quickly finger the murderer. But the final confrontation, like the rest of the story, reads much better as a radio script. Detective Priory would undoubtedly have been more effective in a radio play, but nothing further came of this protagonist in either genre.

The only true detective developed in print by Bradbury during the pulp years is the partly carnivalized "Douser" Mulligan, a diminutive detective-joker found in two published stories—"Half-Pint Homicide" 1944) and "Four-Way Funeral" (1944)—and one unpublished manuscript. At this time, Raymond Chandler loomed large in Bradbury's consciousness, for his good friend and mentor Leigh Brackett was at work on the screenplay of *The Big Sleep*. The Douser represents a parodic treatment of the typical Chandler detective, but in the final analysis Bradbury is largely ineffective in sustaining even a carnivalized form of detective fiction. David Mogen, who published the first detailed discussion of Bradbury's detective fiction in 1986, notes that the ex-cop Douser is too whimsical to carry a story, let alone a series: "[T]iny in stature, unarmed, he destroys his sinister opponents with his genius for provocation, for simply bugging them until they self-destruct. A hero whom Bradbury's ingenuity cannot entirely save from silliness, Douser consciously parodies the prototype hero from which he departs."[7] Bradbury's approach is certainly intriguing, but even in this most carnivalesque of fiction genres, the Douser proved to be a dead end. The ideal Bradbury crime solver would have to evolve into something more like Thorne Smith's eccentric, bumbling, and often fantastic characters who are able, nevertheless, to function credibly in the dark, lonely corners of the real world. By the early 1980s, Bradbury had come to admire a new crime writer who represented an effective blend of the zany, semiserious Thorne Smith characters and the hard-boiled heroes of Chandler and Hammett. The writer was James Crumley, and his 1978 novel *The Last Good Kiss* became an instant Bradbury favorite.

Meanwhile, Bradbury's good friend William F. Nolan reawakened his interest in Sam Spade and the other defining sleuths created by the original hard-boiled detective, Dashiell Hammett. As Bradbury was navigating his way through the unwanted publication of *A Memory of Murder*, Nolan was writing a biography of Hammett, and Bradbury often read drafts of his friend's insightful commentary. This reintroduction to old detectives created by himself and others, his discovery of Crumley's more contemporary carnivalesque counterpoint to the hard-boiled masters, and his own growing sense of nostalgia for the days when he was writing in the same vein, all combined to focus Bradbury once again on the detective genre in a creative context. Nostalgia struck first, even before the unexpected detour into *A Memory of Murder*. In his late fifties Bradbury was drawn to some of the surviving unpublished manuscripts of his twenties, and by 1977 he was working with an unpublished detective story titled "Where Everything Ends." This complete twenty-three-page work had been submitted to Alden Norton in early 1944. Norton felt it was well written but too vaguely plotted, rejecting it in late March with a note to Schwartz that was becoming increasingly familiar: "As I've told you many times, if this Bradbury guy can combine undeniable talent for good writing with a few plots that can really hang together he will be outstandingly good."[8]

The plot was already engaging as a general idea, even without detailed development. Detective Steve Michaels and his partner Charlie Brandon are investigating extortion in the small oil fields found along one of the canals in California's Venice Beach area. As the story opens, Brandon has already been found dead near the end of the canal, close to a rather bizarre landmark—circus wagons and animal cages that had been dumped there years before. As the murders mount up, Michaels is baffled by the lack of physical evidence until he realizes that the murderer moves about in the waterway itself; he is a deadly and silent swimmer who waits for his victims beneath the various drains along the canal wall. He has been extorting the smalltime oilmen, but the game has turned deadly. Michaels enters the murderer's domain and is attacked underwater. He is able to drown his assailant and shoves his body into one of the submerged circus cages at the spot where his partner had been murdered.

This early story provided a good setting for a novel, and a waterborne murderer could be used effectively to sustain a longer narrative. But the story's original protagonist was too obsessed with avenging his partner and too much of a hard-boiled tribute to the old masters to fit well in an original Bradbury plot. The work stalled, for Bradbury had not yet fully reconnected with the early years of his fiction. Then came his discovery of Crumley and the unexpected work on *A Memory of Murder*. As Nolan worked away on his Hammett book, Bradbury turned back to the germ of a novel, with a new focus on characterization. A carnival world lurked within every crime story, and even the hard-boiled heroes could appreciate the unexpected jokes of life. Bradbury would go a step further in developing a protagonist for his first sustained detective narrative, and he would take his cue from his own earlier novel, *Something Wicked This Way Comes*. In that work he had developed a typically carnivalesque protagonist in Charles Halloway, but he had fashioned him into a resourceful and perceptive student of human nature who could save the two boys from Mr. Dark. For this new novel, Bradbury turned to his own past and fashioned that remembered young writer into an engaging first-person narrator—goodhearted, incredibly naive, but a keen observer of events. This would be Bradbury's most direct entry into one of his own works, for the narrator-hero is never even named. There is no need, for author and hero are nearly one, though they do not coincide in terms of narrative knowledge (even though Bradbury will try to resist his surplus of meanings with regard to his hero—as author he already knows everything the hero must discover as a surprise). The narrator is not methodical, and he distrusts the rigid logic of classical detection, but he has great empathy and intuits the truth behind the unfolding mystery. Like Charles Halloway, he is "the fool who knows." As the plot developed, Bradbury provided himself with a more-traditional police detective to share the crime-solving duties. He is methodical but also understands and appreciates what Bradbury's character brings to the case. The detective can also be a bit zany himself; not surprisingly, his name is Crumley.

But how would the plot unfold? Again, Bradbury would reach into memory, and certainly there were no better memories of those exciting days than the time he spent in his daytime office-apartment on Figuroa Street. The people of that tenement world had found their way into some of his detective pulp stories as well as such better-known tales as "En La Noche" ("Torrid Sacrifice" [1952]), "Sun and Shadow" (1953), "The Wonderful Ice Cream Suit" ("The Magic Ice Cream Suit" [1958]), and "Massinello Pietro" (1964). He missed those people, and he missed the big red streetcars that took him all over Los Angeles and out to Venice Beach, where his family had moved in 1941. Nolan had urged him to bring this world into his longer fiction, and now Bradbury realized that the circumstances were right. He opened the new book with a glimpse of Venice, and it is useful to see how the opening of the 1943 story evolved forty years later into the opening of a novel.[9]

"Where Everything Ends" (1943–44)	*Death Is a Lonely Business* (1985)
In the old days a circus had dumped its ancient red wagons and yellow-painted cages into the canal. It looked as if a long parade had rolled and rumbled off the rim to pile up and rust brown under the grey motionless waters. There were about ten cages, wheels turned up, the paint of old years flaking like leaves from a calendar.	Venice, California, in the old days had much to recommend it to people who liked to be sad. It had fog almost every night and along the shore the moaning of the oil well machinery and the slap of dark water in the canals and the hiss of sand against the windows of your house when the wind came up and sang among the open places and along the empty walks.
Steve Michaels stood on the edge of it, looking down and seeing it through a red mist.	Those were the days when the Venice pier was falling apart and dying in the sea and you could find there the bones of a vast dinosaur, the rollercoaster, being covered by the shifting tides.
Thirty years ago this was called Venice by the Sea, California. Like Italy. Gondolas had skimmed brightly, with green lanterns in the night, up and down, people singing, everything clean and new. That was all gone. Now it was a dump for empty cages.	At the end of one long canal you could find old circus wagons that had been rolled and dumped, and in the cages, at midnight, if you looked, things lived—fish and crayfish moving with the tide; and it was all the circuses of time somehow gone to doom and rusting away.

Originally, he had looked back in time to the town's early-twentieth-century hey-day. For the novel, he concentrated on the mood and atmosphere of his remem-bered Venice of the late 1940s, when the famous amusement park on the pier is about to be taken down forever. In contrast to the original story, there is not even a memory of Venice in its heyday: "How the lion cages got in the canal no one knew. For that matter, no one seemed to remember how the canals had gotten there in the middle of an old town somehow fallen to seed. . . . But there they were, the canals and, at the end of one, a dark green and oil scummed water-way, the ancient circus wagons and cages, flaking their white enamel and gold paint and rusting their thick bars."[10]

As the novel opens, Bradbury's young hero is riding one of the red street-cars through this tired canal town. Here for the first time he senses, but does not turn to see, a water-soaked stranger who will become all too familiar as the plot unfolds. Later, on foot, he crosses a canal bridge and discovers, floating in one of the circus cages, the killer's first victim. The hero's search for the murderer takes the character through Bradbury's own world of the 1940s and to such fic-tional friends as the immense Fanny Florianna, first found in his pulp detective story "The Long Night" (1944), Massinello Pietro, and other story elements from the author's long career. The novel quickly became autobiographical, with Brad-bury at center and glimpses of his canon spread throughout the text. Canon, of course, implies a fixed set of meanings and texts. But because as author Brad-bury does not entirely coincide with his younger self, we see these stories against the fictionalized background of his early struggles with novel form. *Death Is a Lonely Business* constantly exploits this tension to carnivalize the detective genre and presents its author's younger self as a fool who knows.

In this way Bradbury's first detective novel centered on his early struggle with the novel form, a struggle we now know to have involved at least three develop-ing novels in the mid- and late-1940s. This struggle was largely masked by his remarkable successes with short fiction, for during the same period he quickly rose to major-market prominence. In revisiting it here he rejoined a lifelong chal-lenge with conventional form, for detective fiction from Poe to the present has always been plotted out in reverse, in advance of the writing process. As always, Bradbury turned loose his remembered characters and let them write the story in outright contradiction of the rules of the game. But the creative effort involved in writing a "first novel" holds the narrative together, for the young author-narrator is able to use the materials of death to breathe life into his fiction. He will face his creative demon in the form of A. L. Shrank, the carnival-pier psycho-analyst who represents the Freudian threat of creative death. It turns out that he is also the waterborne murderer. But Bradbury as young author is not done in by Freudian anxiety over his creative forefathers in the genre. He is able to fight off Shrank's final attempt at murder, leaving the lifeless murderer in the circus cages at the bottom of the canal. In the process he also sells stories and takes a giant step toward becoming the great American novelist.

Writing about death in the face of death gave Bradbury a sense of living on. It was a key moment in his career, for as he entered his fifth decade as a professional author, he needed an effective way to wrestle with these issues. In the late 1970s his preliminary title had been *Death Rides Fast.* When he settled on *Death Is a Lonely Business,* he was, in fact, practicing the advice he had given to a younger writer in 1963. Mentioning the real violence he had personally witnessed in Los Angeles, Bradbury asked the question "What is murder?" and explored how it is reimagined and brought back to the reader through its disturbing contact with the author's "soul."

> I knew a man and wife once at a tenement downtown in LA, she shot him, he died crying in her arms, weeping for a priest, and she wept her tears down on him. This was murder, of a big dumb blundering slob human by his unkempt slutty dumb slob wife, but suddenly there they were, he had done bad things to her but loved her, and she had done this thing to him but loved him and now he was dying, and her crying on him and kissing him and sorry for that awful moment she had fired the pistol, but it was too late and now he was dead, and her picture in the papers. Or one night a young man waited out front of the tenement in his car, I saw him there, and three hours later he was found, stark naked, in his big empty rich house a mile away, his head bashed in by someone never found. This was death and murder to me, too, and I remember the far image of the young man who was to die, who didn't know it, a few hours later, how lonely my memory is of him, as if he were on a ship going out in a harbor on a trip and me not knowing and him not knowing, and him in the papers the next day. Death. Violence. Sex. Murder. I have seen it several times as it brushed by over my hair-ends and fingertips in my life. Death Is a Lonely Business is the overall response one has to it.[11]

Bradbury's remarks form a kind of meditation on murder, narrative knowledge, and the "scene of suffering" (the term is Geoffrey Hartman's). Murder and violence are mainly considered in their effect on the author's own psyche as a reflection of loneliness in the author's soul. "Death is a lonely business"—whispered in his ear by Shrank, who is the unseen streetcar passenger in the opening scene of the novel—becomes the working title of the novel that Bradbury as narrator is struggling to write, a title that he later transfers to the novel being written by Elmo Crumley, the "real" detective-writer of the book. He has his narrator-self adopt a new title, *Downwind from Death,* one that mocks the overpowering smell of corpses that attaches itself to Shrank. These creative encounters with the scene of suffering and death in the "outer" novel are clearly an advance over his pulp fiction and always have unexpected carnivalesque—as well as doubling or mir-roring—consequences. They are corpse carnivals.

By September 1984 Bradbury had sent the novel on to his agent, Don Cong-don, for transmittal to his editors at Knopf. Congdon felt the novel was in good shape and was relieved that it would not need the comprehensive revisions that had kept *Something Wicked This Way Comes* in limbo between author, agent, and editor for nearly two years after its 1960 submission. He did encounter some confusion identifying certain characters and following sequences of events in the first fifty pages and urged revision at these points as he passed the manuscript over to Knopf for editorial review. By this time Bradbury was well established with Knopf, where he had moved in 1968. This move had reunited him with Robert Gottlieb, who had left Simon and Schuster the previous year to become editor-in-chief at Knopf. During the 1970s Gottlieb had asked Nancy Nicholas, a well-respected editor, to work with Bradbury on three successive poetry volumes. She continued to work with him on his fiction titles as well until leaving for a position with Simon and Schuster in 1985, when Gottlieb once again took over to see the novel through its final stages of production. By early October both Nicholas and Gottlieb had read the manuscript, and they agreed that revision was most needed in the final third of the text.[12] Nicholas was aware that Bradbury, working in the classic habits of a master short-story writer, had been writing the episodes in short bursts of self-contained prose. But there were over one hun-dred chapters, and from midpoint on the transitions seemed choppy. She also asked for revisions to make the full introduction of the villain Shrank, which hap-pens in midbook, more significant for the reader.

William Nolan also reviewed the early manuscript and made a significant observation about character presentation. He found that many chapters ended with the author-narrator deeply affected by the developing tragedies of this mys-tery novel, often to the point of tears. Although Nolan had long understood Bradbury's carnival approach to fiction and had written a 1980 survey of this ele-ment for the private printing of Bradbury's *The Last Circus and The Electriocution,* he also felt that the narrator could be toughened up just a bit. Bradbury agreed, and in revision he gave his narrator-self a slightly greater degree of emotional dis-tance without altering the essential autobiographical characteristic of deep com-passion.[13] Bradbury worked on revisions through the fall but received his most focused advice over the holidays from Sid Stebel, a California writer and well-known creative-writing consultant who had been a part of his writing group for many years. Stebel felt that the key to revising was structural; he recommended that Bradbury compress the first fifty pages to clear up the confusions Congdon had noted, but most importantly he suggested getting the action going sooner. This strategy in revision would engage the reader early on, which would be crucial to the book's success. He also advised Bradbury to work in mid-manuscript on bringing out a clearer pattern of suspects. This would counter any confusion created by the explosion of new characters in the middle of the novel (a problem that Nicholas had also seen). Finally, Stebel noted that while Bradbury needed to foreground the suspects, he also needed to suppress hints about the big surprise—the return of Constance Rattigan, a famous but reclusive film star who has been given up for dead in the first half of the narrative. In this way Stebel was able to help Bradbury move only as far as he needed in the direction of classic mystery storytelling and did so without diminishing the hallmark characteristics that made the novel a significant new chapter in Bradbury's life of fiction.

And it was indeed a new chapter, for once again Bradbury had turned a genre on its ear by carnivalizing it. He had delightfully subverted horror genre conventions years earlier in *Something Wicked,* and now in *Death Is a Lonely Business,* he was able to significantly extend the established traditions of full-length detective fiction in a similar way. He let the characters, rather than the rules of logical crime-solving, tell him how the novel would play out. And he also presented the reader with a fully carnivalized protagonist, an "idiot savant" hero who solves the murders instinctively, while Crumley, the likeable but conventional ratiocinative detective, brings up the rear. Bradbury developed enough classic mystery storytelling to structure his narrative for readers and critics, but in the end he told his own story (the early fears and triumphs of his career) without disturbing the illusion of fiction or preempting any creative surprises—always of paramount importance to Bradbury—that might develop in the course of writing the novel.

Nicholas received Bradbury's last significant revisions in February 1985 and supervised final copyediting before galleys. Together, they worked out the design of the chapter breaks, which by this time numbered 117. The problem was eventually solved with the help of designer Irish Weinstein. Instead of numbered chapters with full page-breaks, there would be interior page-breaks between what really amounted to episodic sections rather than formal chapters. These would be highlighted with an oversize rubric for the first letter of the first word, but otherwise the narrative flow would not be interrupted at all. The book was released in October 1985 and received generally positive reviews. It was Bradbury's first novel in more than two decades and established both a range and prominence in this genre that had taken more than forty years to develop.

By this time he was deep into work on the first season of *Ray Bradbury Theater,* a venture into sustained television production that had been in the works for several years and a cherished dream since the 1950s. It was a very different proposition from the *Twilight Zone,* which had drawn on a stable of core writers that included such Bradbury-influenced talents as Richard Mathesen, Charles Beaumont, and George Clayton Johnson. Only one Bradbury teleplay had become an original *Twilight Zone* episode, but now he was able to bring a number of his classic stories to television through his own adaptations. The first season of *Ray Bradbury Theater* featured six stories aired on HBO during the 1985–1986 season (the series debut coincided with two Bradbury-authored teleplays on CBS's new *Twilight Zone* series as well).[14] He continued to write teleplays for *Ray Bradbury Theater,* which after a year in transition had moved to the USA Network for four additional seasons. Bradbury wrote a total of sixty-five teleplays from his stories for the series, which left less time for new fiction. His story output remained low during the 1980s, although he was able to publish a new collection, *The Toynbee Convector,* in 1988.

Despite this shift in focus to television, Bradbury was able to sustain his new life in fiction as a novel writer through a continuation of the first novel's narrative of the 1940s into memories of the 1950s, for he had found an open-ended way to deal with the issues of authorship in his fiction by tapping these memories. While working on the early seasons of *Ray Bradbury Theater* he developed a new fictional core mystery for a second autobiographical mystery novel, which would have its roots in two sources. For the central theme he drew on an encounter at sea during a cruise to Europe around 1980, which he recently recalled:

> I went down to my stateroom, and on the way there, I passed a man who walked by with some people, and he had this horribly destroyed face. It looked like he had shoved his face into a furnace and been burnt, that his face was wax, so it all melted. His face was so horrible that a few seconds after I passed him, I burst into tears. I didn't know who he was, but I couldn't imagine how a man could live with that face, you know, terrible, terrible, terrible. So that night, at dinner, down below in the dining room, I saw the man seated at a table about forty feet away, with his wife and his daughter, and they were laughing and enjoying themselves and drinking champagne. And it struck me like a blow, you know, now here's a man that should have killed himself years ago, out of despair, and here he is with his wife and his daughter who made him forget that he was ugly. So, the gifts of love right in front of you, a metaphor you put on the screen if you had a way of doing it.
>
> So that shocked me so much that love could do this for that man, that when I got to Paris, I had my portable battery-operated typewriter with me, which was completely silent, it didn't make a sound. So every night at

midnight Maggie would go to bed and go to sleep. The room was completely dark, not one light, and I sat in my room with my battery-operated typewriter and I began to write *A Graveyard for Lunatics,* starting with this man that I saw on board ship, who shocked me with his face, and the love of his wife and daughter, transfiguring him. So that's how it all began. I was in Paris for two weeks, and I wrote a hundred pages about this man, and *The Phantom of the Opera,* that's what it's all about, and the Hunchback, and all the weird people I've met in my life, to see if they'd write a book for me. And by God, gradually, when I got home with these pages, I began to think about Ray Harryhausen, and the various studios I worked at, and everything began to fall in place.[15]

Bradbury's occasional contract studio work and that of his boyhood friend Ray Harryhausen had sometimes overlapped during the 1950s, and he decided to use his own screenwriting encounters as well as some of Harryhausen's pioneering adventures in science fiction and fantasy film animation as creative starting points for the new detective novel. But he still needed an opening jolt to bring his author-narrator into the adventure, just as he had done with the discovery of the murder victim in the submerged circus cages to open *Death Is a Lonely Business.* Here again, one of his old pulp detective stories gathered up for *A Memory of Murder* provided a clue. "Yesterday I Lived" had been one of the better pulp tales. The studio cop's route to solving the popular actress's murder opens and closes with references to her gravestone, for the studio is right next door to a cemetery that holds more than one late lamented star of the past. In midstory Sgt. Cleve Morris pauses to reflect on the irony: "Funny Hollywood. It builds a studio next door to a graveyard. Right over that wall there. Sometimes it seemed everyone in movietown tried to scale that wall. Some poured themselves over in a whiskey tide, some smoked themselves over; all of them looked forward to an office in Hollywood Cemetery—with no phones."[16] MGM was, in fact, next door to the cemetery, and Bradbury would enlarge this metaphor in both directions to set up the opening of *A Graveyard for Lunatics:*

And then I got the idea, since I used to go over the wall (I'd go over the graveyard when I was a kid. I couldn't get into the studio any other way— I'd go over the wall, and climb down the other side) and walk around like I belonged to the studio. That's the great secret—don't look as if you're a fugitive, look like you belong there. So I never got kicked out—occasionally, but most of the time I walked around like I belonged there. So I started with that then, and once I got the idea of this strange man being up on the wall, and him falling, then the book began to gather steam, and I let the characters carry it ahead. It took about two years, finally, before the book was finished.[17]

The novel opens in 1954 as the author-narrator is hired to write science fiction screenplays for one of the major Hollywood studios. An anonymous note sends him out to the adjacent graveyard with the promise that a "great revelation awaits you. Material for a best-selling novel or superb screenplay. Don't miss it!" There he finds a body, balanced on a ladder above the graveyard wall, facing into the studio. It has the face of J. C. Arbuthnot, the studio's founder, and this terrifies the narrator—everyone knows that Arbuthnot had been killed in a horrible car crash two decades earlier. During breaks in his studio writing (his assigned film is titled *Death Rides Fast)*, the Bradbury-narrator works with his friend and special-effects genius Roy Holdstrom to solve the crime, but the first thing they discover is that the body is only a cleverly constructed mannequin. As promised in the note, the mystery opens up a new novel, but of course, it is a story written from the inside out as the older Bradbury again combines autobiography and fiction to sustain a novel. In creating his fictional Maximus Films, Bradbury packed in everything he knew about the last years of the Hollywood studio system. With the help of Elmo Crumley (who has just published the traditional detective novel he was writing within the pages of *Death Is a Lonely Business)*, the narrator discovers that Arbuthnot survived the accident as a horribly disfigured phantom and has been living a shadow life in secret prohibition-era passages that run between the graveyard and the studio. Four studio employees have protected the secret for years, but the graveyard mannequin suggests that one of them is blackmailing the boss, who still eludes both detectives—the narrator has only seen him once across a room, his true identity still only guessed at, early in the novel. One by one the insiders disappear, but conventional detective work hits a dead end. Finally, the author-narrator is called to the studio (now closed for a two-month renovation) to meet with the elusive man-monster.

At this point, the new detective novel became problematic for Bradbury. He had allowed his characters to write a fascinating and highly imaginative narrative, but there seemed no convincing way to resolve it. To simply attribute the disappearances to the monster mogul's obsession with secrecy would not provide the payoff that this engaging work had so far promised. Sid Stebel reviewed this stage of the manuscript and suggested that Bradbury develop the full consequences of the relationship between the author-narrator and the monster. This was indeed the heart of the problem; in *A Graveyard for Lunatics,* the villain is very different from the predatory A. L. Shrank. The disfigured J. C. Arbuthnot has led a tormented existence, secretly running the studio wisely with the help of a few insiders. He has only killed to stop betrayal and prevent his horrible existence from becoming public. What higher threat does he pose to the narrator? To get by this creative roadblock, Bradbury turned to the larger issue of authorship, which had been essential to the earlier detective novel, in order to finish the new one. Arbuthnot reveals to the hero-character that he is now dying of cancer and that he had hired the promising young writer on the hunch that he would have the creative ability to succeed him as studio head. But news of his illness had prompted one of the insiders to threaten betrayal of everything, including the love triangle that had led to his disfigurement so many years ago. Only one trusted confidant remains, his mouthpiece Manny Leiber, who has functioned as the apparent studio head all these years. In his dying moments Arbuthnot offers the narrator everything, including Leiber's job:

"Last chance? Last offer?" His voice was fading.
"And give up my wife and my writing and my life?"
"Ah," whispered the voice. And a final "Yes. . . ."

With this turn, Bradbury created an existential moment where his author-narrator again faces creative death in the same magnitude that he faced in *Death Is a Lonely Business.* In the earlier novel, the psychoanalyst Shrank threatened oblivion through anxiety of influence. In *Graveyard for Lunatics,* the studio mogul Arbuthnot makes a seductive promise to a young man who has grown up worshipping film classics and yearning for a chance to bring his own stories to the silver screen. But the consequences are just as deadly as before, for the narrator will pay a heavy price if he accepts. The studio will become his life, to the exclusion of his unwritten novels and his unborn children. It will bring him only transitory fame; without a family or a life of fiction, he will die when it dies. To embrace Hollywood would mean the death of the author.

Stebel offered another suggestion that helped Bradbury add symmetry to the novel. Why not provide a cautionary "story within a story" to illustrate in concrete terms the consequences of taking over the reins of the studio? Earlier Roy Holdstrom had proven that he could reproduce Arbuthnot's horror—his one look at the terrible face inspired him to recreate it in his special-effects workshop at the studio. In the fully developed conclusion of *A Graveyard for Lunatics,* the narrator finds out that his pal, who has also disappeared along the way, actually changed places with the monster mogul for a time. The shock of seeing Holdstrom in his mask drives Arbuthnot temporarily out of his senses. Using his mask and his ability to mimic voices, Holdstrom masquerades as the voice behind the office wall who whispers studio decisions to Manny Leiber. The power corrupts, and Holdstrom comes close to consummating murder himself. Sobered by his own transformation, and realizing that Arbuthnot is indeed dying, he releases him so that he can make his final offer of power to the narrator. The novel opens with the mannequin corpse, a double for Arbuthnot as he once was. It concludes with Roy's monstrous mask, a double for any who try to assume Arbuthnot's tragic legacy. With these revisions and the powerful conclusion in place, the adventures of the two young filmmakers effectively bridge the action of the novel in tandem from beginning to end.

The manuscript arrived at Knopf early in 1989; Nancy Nicholas had departed for Simon and Schuster four years earlier, and in 1987 Bob Gottlieb left the top job at Knopf to take over the *New Yorker* magazine a few blocks away. Before leaving, he had asked Managing Editor Kathy Hourigan to take over as Ray's sponsoring editor.[18] They would form an excellent working relationship during the development and editing of *The Toynbee Convector* collection, which was published in 1988. The following year she began to work with him on the new novel manuscript, which had come in with a number of minor continuity problems. This was not unexpected, for the short bursts of episode-length composition had occurred over a long period of time with interruptions for successive seasons of writing for *Ray Bradbury Theater*. Hourigan sent a number of suggestions in late March, and Bradbury made revisions to smooth out the narrative flow and any minor inconsistencies caused by the revised conclusion. The novel was released in July 1990 with multiple dedications to Sid Stebel, who helped him solve the mystery, and to the Hollywood masters who inspired it. Once again the major eastern newspapers did not publish significant reviews, but a number of West Coast reviews were generally favorable. *Time* magazine and the usual readers and publishers of periodicals also weighed in with positive comments. Many of the critics were uncertain of a genre niche for the novel, but most found that the engaging portraits of individual studio production artists and the satirical images of the dictatorial studio bosses established a very effective and entertaining look back at the last days of the Hollywood studio system.

British publication of the two detective novels was unremarkable, for Bradbury's long relationship with Rupert Hart-Davis was now only on a personal basis. In the 1970s his publishing house was swallowed up by the larger conglomerates, beginning with McGibbon and later Granada. Both of Bradbury's detective novels were published in Britain by Grafton and eventually marketed in paperback for both the domestic and overseas commonwealth markets by the same house. In America, Knopf found Bantam most willing to continue its longstanding agreement to publish Bradbury's paperback editions. *Death Is a Lonely Business* appeared in a mass-market edition in 1987, but after publication of the sequel Bantam editors decided to bring out both novels in matching large format trade-paperback editions in 1992. A year later, Bradbury had moved from Knopf to Avon, accepting their guarantee to keep all of his titles in print. This became necessary for the detective novels as the century closed, and Avon published a new trade-paperback edition of *Death Is a Lonely Business* in 1999. Transitions within the HarperCollins publishing conglomerate affected the companion edition of *A Graveyard for Lunatics*. The trade-paper edition appeared in 2001, though under the HarperCollins-Perennial imprint. Bradbury's interest in the visual presentation of his books has never diminished, and the new Perennial wrapper features a design based on Bradbury's own sense of the carnival that is Hollywood.[19]

Since 1990 Bradbury has continued to perfect early story ideas and bring them to print, often with new stories, in three new collections. He has also finished *From the Dust Returned,* the vampire family novel first conceived in the late 1940s. These recursive explorations of his past authorship turned once again to the detective form and led to the completion of a third novel, *Let's All Kill Constance!* (2003). Each of the earlier novels in this trilogy brought closure to a particular adventure while maintaining a distinct sense of openendedness that mirrors Bradbury's own perception of his career as a writer. In developing *Constance,* he worked off and on for nearly a decade to unravel the mysterious past and uncertain future of his author-hero's favorite actress-companion, Constance Rattigan. It is once again a book within a book, but this time it is a metaphor for creativity itself—Constance arrives with her "Book of the Dead," which contains the record of all the people who have intersected with her life. Bradbury considers the early stages of this manuscript to be the most primitive launching of any of the detective novels:

> I just got Constance herself, showing up at night with the Book of the Dead. I didn't know where it was going to take me, but all these strange people were in her book, and we [the hero and Crumley] suspected that a lot of them were dead. . . . So I had to start a search then, to find all the people that are marked in her Book of the Dead, and see if they were really dead and then if necessary stop their being killed. . . . So the characters wrote the book. I went to one character after another to see what they had to say. I hadn't the faintest idea where in hell I was going. . . . I wasn't sure if she was killing the other people, one by one, and of course it turns out by the time you finish the book, Constance is killing herself.[20]

As they die one by one, Crumley is convinced by circumstantial evidence that Constance herself is the murderer. And once again the hero, the "fool who knows," continues to solve the murders ahead of the traditional detective. As Crumley is forced to give up a reasoned approach, Bradbury as hero remembers his life-changing meeting with Mr. Electrico at age twelve and turns it into a parable of hope to inspire the policeman (and himself) to continue the investigation. Thus, out of his very latest detective novel comes one of his greatest surprises: Mr. Electrico, who is the direct agent of carnivalization in Bradbury's life of fiction, arrives on the scene to help him finish his novel.

Bradbury's struggle as an author is effectively mirrored in his mask as the "fool who knows." He stands outside the novel he is writing, but he also participates in it. This is a hallmark of his unique brand of detective fiction as it has evolved late in his remarkable career. He is an author looking back on his previous work, and these novels are an oblique reflection of his creative process. From a textual perspective, we can see how the chapter-episodes were expanded from early stories, from ideas for stories, and from life experiences. They show an evolving authorial intention that makes room for creative surprises, instead of an intention given all at once. They also show how Bradbury has become his own literary influence (considered more fully in the conclusion). From an aesthetic perspective, the most fascinating aspect of the narration is the double identity of the narrator as both character and author. Bradbury tries to keep the character from knowing what is next in autobiographical terms while his created character runs off with the fictional dimension of each novel. Later, during revision, Bradbury works on the necessary structural continuities, but in essence there is no grand design in place at the beginning of the creative process. There is little sense of closure in these novels either, for Bradbury has consistently developed each out of the one before it. Each one is a celebration of a life of fiction, but both author and hero take the process seriously, for creativity is as precious as life itself. By stopping creative death in much of his book-length fiction, Bradbury has carnivalized the creative process across an ever-widening range of genres. The carnival tradition in literature has allowed him to break out of the rigid cause-and-effect conventions of detective fiction and establish a unique narrative form of his own.

Thematics

Bradbury's detective fiction falls into two distinct periods of his career, one from about 1944 to 1949, when he wrote some fifteen stories for pulp detective magazines such as *Detective Tales* and *Dime Mystery,* and the other from 1984 to 1989, when he authorized a collection of these early stories while writing two new novels that revisited and reworked his vision of the genre. Detective fiction remains present as a by-no-means-minor part of his early output and plays a major role—two novels within five years of each other from an author who has always considered himself a short-story writer—in his recent achievements. But why did Bradbury's talent take so long to develop and express itself in this genre? Or, to ask a related question, what is the thematic difference between the early detective fiction and that of his recent novels? Bradbury was never particularly proud of his early detective stories, calling them "walking wounded," and only participated in reprinting some of them for the Dell paperback *A Memory of Murder* (1984) because Knopf was going to publish his first mystery-suspense novel, *Death Is a Lonely Business,* the following year.

In his introduction to *A Memory of Murder,* Bradbury claims that his talent for intuitive writing was hampered by detective tales: "they required hard thinking, prevented my flow, [and] damaged my ability to use my intuition to the full." Apparently for Bradbury, the writing of detective fiction requires that he trust too much in reason. Indeed, the very success of detective fiction seems to depend on a mechanically plotted or logically motivated world, which Bradbury would have felt very uneasy with since this type of narrative plane would seem to rule out the notion of unforeseen creative possibilities. If everything is determined, then nothing is free. At the heart of Bradbury's relationship to this genre, then, is the difficulty of grappling with its mechanical and manipulative aspects (especially evident in his novel about how a film studio operates—*A Graveyard for Lunatics*). Yet there were undoubtedly attractions of the genre beyond the small amount of money Bradbury was paid for writing these early stories. To a young writer who reflected on society as a kind of carnival of masks, the notion of identity posed by detective fiction could not help but be of great interest. As Geoffrey Hartman points out: "[In the world of detective fiction,] Identities are roles changed from time to time yet as physically clear as warts or fingerprints. Your only hope is not being trapped by your *role* into an *identity.* Once you are marked, or the bite is on you, fun is over. It is, consequently, a clownish world: grotesque, manic, evasive, hilariously sad. Chandleresque is not far from Chaplinesque."[21]

Given his attraction to circuses and carnivals, it is probably no accident that some of Bradbury's early detective stories manifest a preoccupation with themes of identity in a carnivalesque world similar to what Hartman describes. In "Corpse Carnival," for instance, a surviving Siamese twin searches among circus freaks for the murderer of his once-conjoined twin brother. Throughout the story, the perverse personality of this murdered twin still haunts the survivor like a distorting mirror, and the reader suspects what is finally revealed not to be true— that he himself is the murderer. The original title of this story was "One Minus One" (1945; published under the pseudonym "D. R. Banat"), which plays a joke on the grotesque body revealed by carnival—the hero is indeed one person minus the other, his double. The difference of his identity is zero (death), which is the solution to the mystery. These cognitive jokes played on the unity of the subjecthero in the context of detective fiction help carnivalize the genre and are developed in the later novels to embrace the paradox of Bradbury the hero not knowing what Bradbury the author must already know, the solution to the mystery. Incidentally, the title to this story—"Corpse Carnival"—was given to it by an editor (as was the case with many of Bradbury's detective stories), which indicates that publishers in the field were pointing up some of the carnivalesque properties of Bradbury's stories.

"The Candy Skull" takes place during the masked festivities honoring the Day of the Dead in Mexico as the protagonist confronts the murderer of his American friend, whose corpse has been interred with the mummies. In other stories we often see characters hilariously struggling to avoid being trapped into identities that are constructed by someone trying to frame them (as in the Douser stories, where the criminals are victims framed by the detective's lies). This trend of manic humor becomes full blown in the autobiographical novels. In *Death Is a Lonely Business*, personified Death is trying to trap ("finalize" is the Bakhtinian term) the young Bradbury, who ends up putting Death to death in a drowned circus cage. *A Graveyard for Lunatics* especially describes a carnivalesque world dominated by images of a Hollywood film studio next to a graveyard, images that seem all at once grotesque, evasive, and hilariously sad.

In order to provide an overview of the thematic concerns of Bradbury's early detective fiction, one must discuss some of these pulp stories, indicating where Bradbury wrestled with the problems of realistic motivation in a genre whose compositional aesthetic requires the opposite of what he values: the true creative freedom of the unforeseen. Then Geoffrey Hartman's ideas about the nature of detective fiction return. Hartman delineates the main artistic problems of the genre, especially the problem of narrative approaches to what he takes to lie at the center of detective fiction: the scene of suffering. Bradbury's detective fiction is structured by such Freudian themes. This discussion will give us a broad base of understanding from which to investigate the thematic network of Bradbury's three detective novels, where the carnivalization of these same themes takes place.

One of the most insistent effects of rationalism in these early pulp stories has to do with the motivation Bradbury gives to his characters. Like many writers in the genre, he seized upon then-current Freudian notions of personality and society to make the actions of his characters believable and real. For example, in his first published crime novelette, "Killer Come Back to Me!" (1944; still uncollected), the main character, Broghman, does not understand how his own unconscious need for a mother has allowed a dominating woman to make him over into the image of her dead gangster-lover until she explains it to him. He himself tries clumsily to explain the mob's acceptance of him as the original leader: "He was near enough to the original, so they made him into a kind of duplicate of the old boss. Something strictly from a psychological text. Something for mind doctors to kick around. Mob instinct, leader instinct, desire to put upon a pedestal. . . .

No matter how a psychiatrist explained it—the wishful thinking, the acceptance of a new shape from the old mould, he was *in!*"[22]

This is a clear example of others "finalizing"' a character's identity and fate, which he largely accepts. But even where the main character puts up more of an intellectual struggle with the need of others to fix his identity, the reasons for behavior can indeed sound like casebook Freudian examples. Published two years later, "A Careful Man Dies" (1946) presents a hemophiliac character who likes to flirt with death because, he says, it sets up an exciting tension in him between ego instincts and the death instinct, between "self preservation and the will to die tugging back and forth." Robert Douglas, the main character, also explains at some length to his friend Jerry that his (Jerry's) problems with women have to do with his "Oedipus complex," in which he never resolved his idealization of women. And Bradbury's only detective creation, Douser Mulligan, states in "Half-Pint Homicide" (his first story appearance) that in his dealings with criminals—whom he drives to the point of apoplexy by being a nuisance—to them he is an embodiment of the reality principle: "I was death, irritation, and stuff he'd never really known." In the clownish inverted world of Bradbury's detective fiction, criminals are governed by the pleasure principle; the detective represents the demands of the reality principle.

Many of these stories, if not all of them, reveal a scene of suffering or pathos that resembles the Freudian primal scene in its effects (see discussion below) and that is often quite richly and vividly presented, as the pulp tradition demanded. But Bradbury adds touches of carnivalization to his scenes. In "It Burns Me Up!" a dead man imagines a young girl looking in on the scene of his murder, "framed"' momentarily by a window: "I am now immortal! Caught in that child's mind I shall be dead forevermore, and on dark nights I will stride drunkenly through the shivering corridors of her body. And she will waken shrieking, ripping the bedclothes apart. Someday her husband will feel her red fingernails in his fleshy arm, and that will be me, in the middle dark, reaching out a constricting claw to clutch again at life."[23]

This is clearly an instance of the finalization of a character's identity by the other who, in this instance, witnesses the scene of suffering. But the dead man also gives an identity and self-image to the girl. The primal scene of the narrator's dead, mutilated body is crucial for them both and acts as a kind of traumatic event, reflecting the psychic temporality and causality of deferred action, the Freudian *Nachträglichkeit.* Psychoanalysis is often rebuked for its alleged reduction of all human actions and desires to the level of the infantile past; this would seem to deny the possibilities of human freedom. But Jacques Lacan is responsible for drawing attention to the importance of the term *nachträglich* in Freud's texts, where it indicates that psychic causation in interpretation can appear to work backward, the effect of an event occurring only after considerable delay.[24] This "working backward" is also a part of Bradbury's carnivalization of the notion of identity here. Far from using the reductive Freudianism of childhood cause leading to adult effect, Bradbury seems to be structuring the temporality of this scene as a kind of a deferred action. The little girl who witnesses the death in the present clearly does not understand "what is wrong with the man." It is only later, presumably at the onset of sexual awareness, that the scene takes on a devastating new meaning. Indeed, it creates a frenzied effectiveness (the girl's ripping apart the bedclothes seems a violent Dionysian act, the repetition of unconscious desires clawing their way into consciousness) through which the dead narrator lives on.

Actually, the scene bears an overdetermined meaning in its conflation of several effects of primal fantasies, according to Freud. The origin of the self (he will be born again through her) in seduction, which governs the origin and emergence of sexuality (he will come "striding drunkenly through the corridors of her body"), and displacement, or reversal of castration anxiety. The red phallic fingernails of the girl ("that will be me") penetrate into the fleshy arm of the husband, who has been made passive.

But repetition of the primal scene does not structure the narrative. It is just being used here to define character reaction and motivation. The narrator resorts to the imagination of such a scene in order to overcome his feeling of passiveness in being dead and in having his image captured by prying reporters. But repetition does structure another of these early stories, "Yesterday I Lived!" In this piece a glamour-struck desk sergeant at a movie studio solves the murder of his favorite actress during the making of a film by watching her death scene over and over. The mechanical nature of the film image allows the agonized detective to watch her actual death repeatedly (and also the outtakes, which show her "real" feelings toward members of the cast) until he can "splice out the innocents" and uncover the true murderer—ironically, her cinematographer.

The murderer's name is actually scratched on the film by one of his other victims, but it is a long time before the detective actually "sees" the name because he takes the traces to be imperfections in the film stock. Moreover, the sergeant does not initially suspect the cinematographer because he is not "visible" in the death scene: "Diana looked at the camera when she died. She looked at you. We never thought of that. In the theater you always feel as if she were looking at the audience, not the man behind the camera." Thus, the detective has to break with the illusion of the cinematic gaze—and with it his attraction to the beautiful film star—in order to make the invisible visible, no matter how violent or terrifying the truth of the scene of suffering may be. This story forces us to think about the mechanical apparatus of film, to look behind the film surface or screen and beyond the enjoyment of the illusions produced by it.

The necessity of breaking with the glamorous image of the film star in order to solve the mystery destroys the hero's capacity to feel anything but a murderous rage himself. The story ends with the detective smashing the face of the cinematographer with his fists again and again. Because the film laboratory is described as "a huge dark mortuary building with dead-end passages and labyrinths," this story prefigures the use of the Hollywood studio-graveyard metaphors of *A Graveyard for Lunatics.*

One story in which the mechanical actually does seem to triumph over the living in a parodic kind of way is "Wake for the Living" (retitled "The Coffin" for other collections). In this story an inventor named Charles Braling builds, through a "carnival of labor," an economy casket designed to murder his good-for-nothing younger brother, Richard, who continually mocks him during the construction process. Charles pretends throughout to be building the "economy" casket only for himself (he expects to die soon) but speaks of the money it might save morticians and poor families if it were mass produced. After Charles dies, Richard has him buried in a cheap wooden coffin and explores the casket for himself, expecting to find money. As soon as he lies down inside it, however, a series of mechanical devices take effect—he is drugged by a needle, his blood is drained— all accompanied by music and flowers, the aesthetic things he so loved in his life—while the casket, in a "mechanical transcribed funeral," delivers an oration, rolls out the door, and buries itself in the backyard.

This story depends on the development of elaborate joke structures about the expense of funerals. It was successfully adapted by EC Comics artist Jack Davis for *The Haunt of Fear* (no. 16, December 1952). Davis's comic style, which later helped make *Mad* magazine famous, is well suited to the tone of the story. There are some nice "Freudian" touches to it. Governed by the pleasure principle, at first Richard appears to be enjoying the aesthetics of the funeral, pretending to himself to be dead, until he hears the funeral orator Charles pronounce his name. He tries to reassure himself that his name is just a "slip of the tongue" for Charles himself. But at the end the coffin keeps repeating Richard's name over and over again, mechanically, after he is dead because the recording is stuck: "Nobody minded. Nobody was listening." "The Coffin" stages the scene of suffering as a mechanical tour de force. It is a good joke played on a character who is entirely narcissistic and venal, who has always had things done for him throughout his life.

"The Trunk Lady" stages its scene of murder in the context of family desires and secrets. It also plays a game of identities with a mannequin. A young boy, Johnny Menlo, finds the corpse of a beautiful woman in a trunk in his family's attic. Near the corpse is the fragment of a letter asking some unknown interlocutor to allow her to become "Johnny's teacher," for that would justify her presence in the house. The adults who are throwing a party try to convince Johnny that the body he saw was just a mannequin—for which the boy's cousin William designs dresses—but the boy continues to believe stubbornly in his own perceptions of the primal scene, which are tinged with eroticism. Although Johnny feels himself too old for bedtime stories, that night he listens with interest when his Uncle Flinny tells him a romantic story about a beautiful young girl who falls in love with a knight and marries him. Their happiness is destroyed by a "Dark One," who kidnaps the beautiful woman and runs away with her. Although Johnny suspects other members of the family, eventually the boy's "snooping" leads him to discover that his uncle had, indeed, committed the murder on his own daughter (the Dark One of the mirroring story) whom he had long blamed for the death of his wife during childbirth. It was the uncle who substituted the mannequin. This motive for murder—the ambivalent carnival theme of life and death—is also explored in one of Bradbury's most memorable stories, "The Small Assassin" (discussed later), which is enough of a weird tale that its detective elements seem merely an incitement for the uncanny effect it produces.

Bradbury's early pulp detective stories are sometimes entertaining in their humor, but one cannot take them seriously. For the most part, they are parodic imitations of pulp-fiction detective style (Hammett and Chandler mostly) and show little originality in plotting, though "Hell's Half Hour" is a ratiocinative tale in the manner of Poe. At their worst they seem obvious and manipulative. For the most part, they do not develop original characters and motivations either, though one character—Fannie Florianna of "The Long Night"—does reappear as one of the "Lonelies" in *Death is a Lonely Business*.[25] Yet Bradbury still regards "The Small Assassin" as one of the best stories. Indeed, it can still raise a chill due to its uncanny reversal of roles and identities and to its modern use of the fantastic after Freud: a baby that hates its mother because of the birth trauma; a mother who wants to murder her child because she believes it is trying to kill her, though no one suspects him of being capable of murder until it is too late. We actually hesitate in this story between a rationalistic explanation of the mother's hatred (the psychiatrist says it is all due to "ambivalence") and a socially uncanny one, offered reluctantly by the father, that the child has, in fact, somehow been born completely aware, embodying "something different" that has yet to be thought.[26]

The latter explanation turns out to be right. The psychiatrist must abandon his theory of ambivalence and himself try to kill the baby with a scalpel. But "realistic" Freudian theories about the child resenting being cast out from the bliss and security of the womb—"this disenchantment, this rude breaking of the spell," as the father says—still serve to motivate his behavior. With the exception then of "The Small Assassin," which has become something of a horror classic (although published in *Dime Mystery* in November 1946, it can function as weird or horror and is included in *Dark Carnival* and *The October Country*), these stories did little to advance Bradbury's career or to establish his distinctive voice.

Nonetheless, they do provide an interesting thematic counterpoint to his later detective fiction, in which Freud is denied any final authority. The examples above should be sufficient to indicate the enormous influence (or perhaps "use" is a better term) of Freud on Bradbury's early career. Because the demands of pulp detective fiction require a kind of realistic look at the sufferings of our world, Bradbury as detective writer was often forced to put on other narrative voices as masks. Take, for instance, the opening paragraph of his first crime novelette, "Killer Come Back to Me!": "If you've never watched an autopsy, then this is what they do. They cut the body down the middle. Not all the way, but far enough for you to see everything from collar-bones to kidneys. When the peels of flesh are tethered back with bright surgical clamps, the various organs thus exposed are examined closely before being sliced out with an expert move of the scalpel. They are then set aside for chemical analysis. The brain is removed from its case by the simple expedient of lifting the skull off in a circle from the ears up."[27]

This passage goes on for several more paragraphs. We find out later that the narrator-pathologist performing this autopsy is the dead criminal's brother. The matter-of-fact, cold, forensic, looking-directly-at-death perception this paragraph stages—without evident metaphor—is thus all the more shocking and quite unlike anything in Bradbury's mature poetic style. Compare this to the metaphorical "autopsy" of the vampire by the eleven-year-old boy in "The Man Upstairs" (published only three years later, in 1947, but in a slick magazine, *Harper's*), and one can immediately see the difference in direct and indirect presentation of the scene of suffering. The "autopsy" of the chicken that opens this story is, in fact, a metaphorical staging of what Douglas will later do to the vampire, which is never directly described for the reader, though the boy proudly displays the strange guts of the vampire to his grandmother.

Returning to Geoffrey Hartman's discussion of the narrative world of detective fiction and staying close to the fate of reading in detective fiction, both in its pulp versions and in the *nouveau roman* of Robbe-Grillet, Hartman's analysis touches upon artistic qualities of the genre that are relevant also to our understanding of Bradbury's later authorship and use of it. He argues that "the relentless center or focus of detective fiction" is some scene of bodily agony, mutilation, murder, or wounding, which he calls "the scene of suffering." Hartman begins his discussion of detective fiction with Aristotle and *Oedipus Rex*, arguing that recognition and reversal in detective stories—the Aristotelian *peripeteia*—serve mainly to reveal the violence of the scene, though the real violence is perpetrated on the psyche (or the "soul," as Bradbury himself argues in a 1963 letter). *Peripeteia* functions primarily as "an unmasking:" "The reversal in detective stories is more like an unmasking; and the recognition that takes place when the mask falls is not prepared for by dramatic irony. It is a belated, almost last minute affair, subordinating the reader's intelligence to such hero-detectives as Ross Macdonald's Archer, who is no Apollo, but who does roam the California scene with cleansing or catalysing effect."[28]

Hartman goes on to suggest that it is the absence of direct and vivid representation of the scene of suffering that separates literary or artistic detective fiction from its pulp uses. Anticipating our arguments below, we should mention here that Bradbury's more recent authorship of detective fiction mainly works on this "artistic" aspect of detective fiction, on the poetic and metaphorical absence of the scene of suffering (so vividly presented in his pulp detective fiction) that nonetheless structures the narrative. In *A Graveyard for Lunatics*, Bradbury adds the further complication of using aesthetic masks in order that the scene of suffering can be contemplated without fear.

To reconstruct the evidence for this narrative event is the desire of the detective tale, according to Hartman, and he has no trouble linking this desire to Freud's notion of the primal scene as a structuring element in the detective novel. In psychoanalysis, as in much detective fiction, a lifetime may depend on a moment, on one traumatic recognition. The scene itself seems always "too fast" for our perception, and the detective's reconstruction always has something phantasmagoric about it, which may manifest itself in the language of puns, riddles, and mime. Many of Bradbury's titles for his detective fiction are, in fact, puns or riddles that allude to the sufferings of the primal scene. ("It Burns Me Up!" for instance, is an allusion not only to a dead man's anger but also to his cremation, which ends the story; the double meaning of *Death Is a Lonely Business* also depends on wordplay.) Lastly, in detective fiction we want to see the "ocular proof" of the scene of suffering, which moreover, is always tied to a definite location.

Hartman feels that American detective fiction such as that of Raymond Chandler and Ross Macdonald reflects a "naive reality-hunger," a tendency to vivify perception throughout with images that "flash around us like guns" and displays a decisive visual reanimation of the scene of suffering in which "the horror of the visible is clearly preferred to what is unknown or invisible." The European *nouveau roman* (manifest in a film such as *Last Year at Marienbad*), however, refuses us any such definitive visual scene and deploys many ruses to defer ultimate meaning. In fact, the whole middle section of most mystery novels is made up of such deferrals (or "clues") of meaning anyway, but the problem posed by the story is usually resolved at the end of formula-based pulp detective fiction. Hartman concludes that the detective novel can never become art because of this relentless reduction of everything—except perhaps the motives of the detective—to overt and vulnerable gestures. It is this "voracious formalism" that dooms it to seem unreal, however "real" the world it describes. For Hartman, detective fiction cannot get over "its love-hate relationship for the mechanical and the manipulative" and is destined to produce only "machined narratives" no matter how hard it tries to distance itself from them. And as for its literary ability to embody the unfinalized consciousness of another life from the inside, "Instead of a Jamesian reticence that, at best, chastens the detective urge—our urge to know or penetrate intimately another person's world—the crime novel incites it artificially by a continuous, self-cancelling series of overstatements, drawing us into one false hypothesis or flashy scene after another."[29]

One may question Hartman's insistence that Ross Macdonald and other American writers of detective fiction have been unable to transform the genre into art (when all is finished, he says, nothing is re-readable) and truly satisfy our "reality-hunger," but what of Bradbury's two autobiographical detective novels? To the reader unfamiliar with carnivalization, these novels certainly seem overburdened with flashy scenes and exaggerated language. But Bradbury's autobiographical detective fictions are a part of his ongoing carnivalization of genres, achieving artistic form by focusing on the aesthetic play of masking and unmasking the scene of suffering rather than revealing it directly. In this manner Bradbury as author and character is himself not trapped into an identity he has not himself freely chosen. Through this play, he hopes to avoid any determinism of the plot.

Bradbury's first novel in twenty-three years, *Death Is a Lonely Business*, is a detective story that is also an oblique projection of his own creative processes. It is still largely a clownish world. The clownish atmosphere is evident in Bradbury's description of the first murder scene: "We looked like a mob of miserable clowns abandoned on the bridge, looking down at our drowned circus."[30] The hero, an autobiographical stand-in for Bradbury as a young man, is a penniless and love-starved writer living in the carnivalized atmosphere of fog-bound, dilapidated Venice, California, in the late 1940s, writing his early detective and weird stories for *Dime Mystery Magazine* and *Weird Tales*. It seems that death is stalking and killing the "Lonelies"—eccentrics living their lives on the edge of despair or in the past—and the plot of the book centers on finding out who death's agent really is before it can kill the hero. Death also stalks "Bradbury" indirectly in the figure of A. L. Shrank, whom the young author must defeat with the help of a "real" detective, Elmo Crumley (also a writer of detective fiction).

But in the middle part of the novel, which is taken up by a string of murders, Bradbury gives us glimpses into the lives of the Lonelies with a kind of reticence that reveals not their literal death, but their death in life. The scene of suffering is always approached in a metaphorical and imaginative way. "Bradbury" discovers through the details of each murder scene that the Lonelies are waiting for death to come to them, some half-welcoming him. From the writings scratched on the walls of William Smith's room, he deduces a "terrible sentence of lone-liness and despair." Smith will be the first victim; a later victim, Fanny Florianna, is so obese that she could suffocate in her sleep: "Fat, as Murderer, was always with her." "Bradbury" visits the carnivalized scene of suffering bodies not as a literal detective, but as someone in search of creative metaphor. For he himself is a blocked writer, "going through that long desert known as Dry Spell, Arizona." Shrank, who first approaches "Bradbury" from behind while he is riding home on a red trolley car in the rain, cannot be seen directly but is, in fact, an aspect of creativity as in all carnivalized literature. He whispers in Bradbury's ear the title of his unfinished novel, "death is a lonely business."

A. L. Shrank turns out to be a pretentious, reclusive little fellow (whose facial appearance "Bradbury" compares to the daguerreotype photos of Poe) whose name and library, stocked with "pessimists" such as Spengler, Schopenhauer, Freud, and "dread Nietzsche," suggest his significance. For Shrank is a "shrink," that is, a psychoanalyst, or "meadow doctor to lost creatures," as he calls himself. On the level of authorship, Bradbury's struggle with Shrank is that of tempta-tion, of allowing himself to be influenced by mainstream psychoanalytic culture. One of Shrank's patients is a narcissistic actor named John Wilkes Hopwood, who tells "Bradbury" that he should go into analysis with Shrank. Hopwood, bi-sexual but preferring men, also invites the young writer up to the Carousel Apart-ments (as the name suggests, it is located near a carousel and the inhabitants are carnivalized denizens of Hollywood), suggesting that he might meet Aldous Huxley there. The protagonist's response to this invitation is revealing: "I was filled with an inexpressible and insufferable need that I had to force myself to repress. Huxley was a madness in my life, a terrible hunger. I longed to be that bright, that witty, that toweringly supreme. To think, I might meet him."

Bradbury reveals some central anxieties of his early authorship in this passage. For him, Huxley represents the whole trend of intellectualism in our literary cul-ture, an ideal to which Bradbury aspires but that he needs to repress, for, trust-ing as he does in romantic notions of intuition, imagination, and spontaneous will, he can never become such a self-consciously intellectual author.

"Bradbury" clearly indicates that he is strongly attracted to the cultured worlds of Hopwood, Huxley, and Shrank, but how can he deal with such ambivalence since their world would destroy his deepest creative impulses? The answer is that the writer has to carnivalize that world thoroughly before he can appropriate it to himself in a healthful manner. "Bradbury" jokingly refers to Shrank as "Sig-mund Freud's Munchkin son," and this phrase offers yet another "clue" to the workings of Bradbury's authorship. Due to the effects of literary condensation, some mechanisms of humorous meaning in this joke need to be unpacked. First of all, the epithet makes Shrank the *American* son (and not the father) of Sigmund

Freud by way of the cheerful anti-intellectualism of L. Frank Baum. Through this mock patronymic, Bradbury is "shrinking" psychoanalysis down to size. In terms of the cultural reception of Freud in America, it may well be, as Lacan asserts, that Freudian psychology at this time had, in fact, already become a shrunken-down version of Freud, who had originally concentrated his writings on the effects of the unconscious on the ego—which is not master in its own house—and not on the ego's adjustment to society. Jokes are, of course, one of the primary means by which the unconscious makes itself felt in conscious social life (Freud studied them in his *Jokes and their Relation to the Unconscious*). It might be objected here that Bradbury's use of jokes in this novel confirms the Freudian notion of humor as a defense mechanism veiling violence, but this would be to miss the liberating effects of language in *Death Is a Lonely Business* that link it to carnival and the need to dispel anxiety and fear. The intertextual process functions more like a joke, one in which Bradbury carnivalizes Freud through evoking Baum's Oz (which Baum always said was designed to leave out the terrors of the European fairytale).

Interesting too is the intertextual connection Bradbury's Mars has with Baum's Oz in the American fantasy tradition. Martin Gardner points out in an introduction to a 1974 edition of *The Martian Chronicles* that Mars—or Tyrr as it is known to the Martians—before the invasion is Bradbury's Oz. So Bradbury is giving us a broad hint here about how he will overcome his creative anxieties. But his fears about the influence of psychoanalytic culture shrinking his literary self are not so easily dismissed. At this point in his career, Bradbury was still composing his Martian tales (he does refer to writing the story that later became "Ylla") that would make him famous. "Bradbury" *is* fascinated by Shrank, yet afraid to talk to him, because he seems to know everything about him and because of the dire knowledge of literary melancholy (read anxiety of influence) he possesses. Listening at Shrank's door, he wonders: "In there, between precipice shelves of dusty books, did I hear Sigmund Freud whispering a penis is only a penis but a good cigar is a smoke? Hamlet dying and taking everyone along? Virginia Woolf, like drowned Ophelia, stretched out to dry on that couch, telling her sad tale? Tarot cards being shuffled? Heads being felt like cantaloupes? Pens scratching?"[31]

Bradbury imagines here a scene of instruction in psychoanalytic culture that expresses his ambivalent desires. In this scene Freud, significantly, *precedes* the list of literary writers and is represented by one of the jokes reported of him (in which he made fun of "Freudian symbolism" narrowly interpreted). Not wanting to be shaped into a melancholy "modernist" writer such as Virginia Woolf, whose life ended in suicide, Bradbury knows that, however tempted, he must struggle against this scene of instruction, defending himself with laughter and his own brand of carnivalized humor. Bradbury uses jokes to dispel his fear of Freud, the Freud who tried to think rationally about the irrational in human nature. Not coincidentally, this is the Freud Bradbury himself used to provide character motivation in his early pulp detective stories. And for "Bradbury" the writer-hero of this novel, Freud represents the need to overcome his journeyman efforts and transform himself into an artist.

"Bradbury" laughs when he discerns the theme of Shrank's library: it is full of one-sidedly serious and pessimistic books and is unrelieved by anything remotely humorous. He banters with Shrank about the unrelieved monotony of his collection and asks for some variety: "How about the *Savanarola Joke Book* or *The Funny Sayings of Jack the Ripper.*"

The connection of Shrank himself with detective fiction is made clear when Bradbury reveals that Shrank is also Poe. Soon after this first glimpse of the library, while visiting Mr. Shapeshade's cinema, "Bradbury" finds himself *behind* the movie screen with the "ghosts" of film actors during the last silent-movie show on the Venice pier. Shrank, glimpsed in this phantasmagoric scene, is described as "the Poe eye in the projectionist's window." So Bradbury must also reject Poe, whose ratiocinative techniques of composition in the detective tale have doomed it to being too mechanical (though he certainly used Poe the horror writer as a figure of rage in such carnivalized Martian stories as "Usher II" and "The Exiles").

Thus, *Death is Lonely Business* is as much about Bradbury's influences and struggles with precursors (both in literature and in film) as it is about murder. Its real subject is creative death. Scenes of instruction can also be a form of death to a writer if the precursor is allowed to be too strong, as Harold Bloom has shown. "Bradbury" tells Elmo Crumley that he does not want Shrank's help because he would "sink me down with Schopenhauer and Nietzsche," never to rise again. Nietzsche, a "pessimist" like Freud, must not be allowed to enjoy any final authority in the novel. They must both be mocked and decrowned.

But how does this decrowning happen? "Dread" Nietzsche is mentioned several times in the book as a pessimist to be avoided, but being a denier of influence himself, he is less of a threat than Freud.[32] Perhaps the best way to examine his decrowning is through one of the novel's intertextual literary dreams. Besides jokes, dreams were Freud's prime territory and evidence for unconscious conflicts.

I had two dreams that night.

In the first, A. L Shrank's Sigmund Freud Schopenhauer tarot card shop was knocked to flinders by the great hungry steamshovel, so off in the tide floated the Marquis de Sade and Thomas De Quincey, and Mark Twain's sick daughters and Sartre on a truly bad day, drowning in the dark waters over the shine of the shooting gallery rifles.

The second dream was a newsreel I had seen of the Russian royal family, lined up by their graves, and shot so that they jerked and jumped like a silent film projection, knocked, blown away, end over end, like popped corks, into the pit. It made you gasp with horrid laughter. Inhuman. Hilarious. Bam!

There went Sam, Jimmy, Pietro, canary lady, Fannie, Cal, old lion-cage man, Constance, Shrank, Crumley, Peg, and *me!*

Bam!

I slammed awake, sweating ice.[33]

These dreams of philosophy, literature, and cinema are both double and doubling. They represent a working through of the narrator's creative anxieties and state of mind, described earlier as "furious with fate, and confounded by funerals." First, there is the destruction of A. L. Shrank's psychoanalytic shop, which is located on the Venice pier, where many of the carnival amusements are located, including the Venice Cinema and the shooting gallery, both of which the narrator had visited earlier in the day and are destined to be destroyed. In this context of destruction, Freud and psychoanalysis; the philosopher of the will, Schopenhauer (the philosophical father of Nietzsche); and tarot cards are all thrown together as various ways human beings have supposed that character and fate can be deciphered from cryptic signs.

As for the creative works released by this semioclasm, the Marquis de Sade and Thomas De Quincey need perhaps no commentary here; they are famous literary figures of eccentric deviancy whose lives ended badly. But the unexpected reference to Mark Twain's daughters seems incongruous and requires some comment. The death of Twain's favorite daughter, Suzy, following hard upon his bankruptcy, left the author in a black mood that lasted from 1896 until 1904. Filled with despair and self-reproach during this period, Twain filled rooms with manuscripts, most of which were fragments. His comic genius was ill-adapted to the expression of despair, and not much of significance emerged from this period (except for *The Mysterious Stranger,* which was left unfinished). This explains his incongruous presence among the other authors mentioned. Jean-Paul Sartre was, of course, the spokesman of postwar existentialism, famous for such chilling assertions as "hell is other people" and "man is a useless passion" and for arguing that man must avoid sliding into inauthentic modes of existence that hide these basic facts. Sartre on a bad day on the Venice amusement pier would then be a "truly" incongruous sight.

It was Sartre, however, who gave us perhaps the most compelling phenomenological understanding of the existential situation contained in dreams. For him, the dreamer exists in a narrative world without freedom and devoid of choices, trapped because he does not know he is dreaming. One cannot articulate the essential and authentic act of self-reflection.[34] Now, all these authors from Shrank's library are drowning in the dark tidal waters of what "Bradbury" takes to be one-sided despair, in which the light of the shooting-gallery rifles is reflected (the gallery is perhaps already submerged or flooded). They cannot articulate any broader perspective on life than that contained in their worldviews, finalized by their own works. They lack the ongoing freedom and openness to the future that "Bradbury" associates with creative consciousness. It is their funeral.

The "shine" of the rifles provides a thematic link to the next dream, fusing amusement with murder, in which the Russian royal family is being executed in a newsreel. They too seem imprisoned in the film itself, but their "jerking" deaths are represented as provoking laughter (the "popped corks" suggests the opening of a bottle in celebration of revolution). The carnival themes are sharply ambivalent: the inhuman and the hilarious, murder and amusement, literary life outside of the normal, and laughter emerging from the horror of death. Yet the dreams are meant to be taken together in order to give us a wider range of meaning taken from the totality of life. They double as corpse carnivals that strive together to embrace the totality of life, which does contain terrible things indeed.

It is also possible to interpret the dream in Nietzschean terms, as the struggle of the creative will with the dead past. In Nietzsche's philosophy the creative will always appears as a liberator and agent of open freedom and future possibility, yet consciousness here is imprisoned in a dream. In this situation the creative will cannot change the past, which becomes a necessity. Therefore, it resorts to the spirit of revenge. The assassination of the Romanovs is an example of such madness, the madness of the revengeful will attempting to change the past that mocks the present with laughter. It was Nietzsche's view that mankind needed to be delivered from the spirit of revenge, which he saw masked and at play in all systems of punishment and justice.[35] The writer-hero's double dream may be figuring a way out of such an anguished dilemma of the creative will.

At any rate, there follows a list of all those murdered—and those who the hero thinks are about to be—in the course of the novel (the hero does not yet know, nor do we, that Shrank is the real killer) that ends with the hero's girlfriend and himself. The author, of course, is not asleep as his hero is. Although "murdered" as hero, Bradbury the author is not finalized in the dream as the other characters are. Instead, the dream logic makes it possible for him to combine laughter with death and murder, and for the crisis-ridden character or author to live on. Author and hero do not entirely coincide in this novel; if they did, it would certainly mean creative death. The hero had been expressing his rage in the shooting gallery earlier, firing at targets until he was "impotent," so it is likely that the shooting of the Romanovs is Bradbury's own ritual dream act of decrowning. His authorial mask throughout this book is that of the *fool who knows,* a mask enabling him to preserve a certain position of relative "outsidedness" to the novel's events while participating in them.[36] Unlike the victims of the dream, he can formulate a self-reflective consciousness. Indeed, Bradbury wants us to realize here that, in enjoying the execution of the Romanovs as entertainment (in what must have been a staged "documentary" film), we are all complicit in murder. Indeed, Bradbury derives his own creativity from death, though he is not finalized by it.

This ambivalent dream logic of death and creativity is extended to the entire thematic network of novel, which makes brief summary difficult since every theme is given a carnival treatment while author and hero are kept from coinciding (one can approach this level of understanding Bradbury's authorship only on *re*-reading, as we are doing here). But certainly clues themselves become carnivalized (for example, the ticket "confetti" found on the first corpse and the Janus newspaper found in Fannie Florianna's apartment). Both the hero and Elmo Crumley are themselves carnivalized figures-authors described as "loud fools and laughing detectives doing maniac things to typewriters."[37]

The question arises, though, if not Poe-Freud or Huxley, just who will be a good literary father for Bradbury? In discussing the issue of the motivation for murder, Detective Crumley tosses a copy of Shakespeare on the kitchen table and gives the young "Bradbury" a lecture on "meaningless malignity," that is a crib from Samuel Taylor Coleridge (who used the term "motiveless malignity" to describe the character of Iago in Shakespeare's *Othello*). An experienced "real" investigator, Crumley tells the young writer that in his experience, psychiatry seldom helps in explaining criminal or deviant behavior because the causes are "buried so deep it would take nitro to blast them out." This statement is clearly a criticism of Bradbury's pulp detective fictions, where Freudian motivations are right on the surface. It is also an attack on the notion of causality and determinism. Here we have one of the many oblique reflections on Bradbury's struggle with the authorship of major form in the detective genre. Somehow, Bradbury needs to discover characters who live on in their unfinalizedness. This is hard to accomplish in a short story. He needs the fictional and perpsectival space of the novel—a major form that does not have any predetermined role or identity for its hero—to sustain him in such a creative venture, which is one of the reasons why Bradbury depicts himself in this novel as working on an unfinished novel.

Crumley then forces the young "Bradbury," who naively seems to think that clues are his muse, to see that in the final analysis, there may be "no motives, no root systems, no clues" with which to understand a murderer. Bradbury is clearly upstaging the influence of Freud to replace it with an earlier, more powerful literary" precursor, Shakespeare, an interpretation that he has made more explicitly in subsequent correspondence: "Have read little Freud or Jung. All my psychoanalytic education comes from Shakespeare's subconscious haunts that inspired and educated Freud and Jung. The creative artist always, I repeat, always precedes the analytical one. Shakespeare the father intuitionist, taught sons Freud and Jung. I always return to the original Artist. Old Will continues to teach me, late in life, along with G. B. Shaw."[38]

This may, in fact, be a disavowal made in good faith, but we have clearly seen the use of Freud in Bradbury's early detective fiction. The author also felt the need to enact the same upstaging of Freud in a poem entitled "Shakespeare the Father, Freud the Son." It opens with the line "Old Will invented Freud" and goes on to assert that "gay Vienna's demi-dwarf on Old Bard's shoulder rides." But *Death Is a Lonely Business* was written after Bradbury's great laughing carnivalization of psychoanalysis in *Something Wicked This Way Comes,* where Shakespeare is the center of a great literary clock constructed by Halloway in the library (the title of that book, of course, comes from lines spoken by the grotesque witches in *Macbeth*).[39] There are also aspects of *Something Wicked*'s understanding of death in this detective novel as well. Death is not something one can know directly, but only through its masks of fear.

The writer-hero's final confrontation with Shrank is described in language that reveals a carnivalized world of detective fiction in all its depths of irony. Just as Hartman indicates, it is a clownish world, grotesque, manic, evasive, and hilariously sad. But carnivalization deepens and broadens the themes presented and enables the hero to evade being finalized in a clownish identity. Throughout the confrontation, "Bradbury" is very afraid that he is going to give way to "the terrible laugh of dread," when what is called for is ratiocination, for some of the clues are so hilarious (a set of false teeth, for instance): "I was poised on the near rim of hysteria, panic, terror, delight at my own perception, my own revulsion, my own sadness. I might dance, strike, or shriek at any moment." But in order to overcome Shrank, "Bradbury" first diminishes and decrowns him by referring to his malodorous smell (he is nicknamed "The Armpit") and by affirming the life of the author, for he believes fervently that he is not going to end up as a Lonely but is instead going to write "damned fine books and be loved." He freely curses and abuses Shrank, who dispensed death indirectly by fear and intimidation. Weakened by this outburst of direct and uninhibited fearless language, Shrank retreats, only to try and drown "Bradbury" later in the submerged circus cages in the canals of Venice. In a final act of carnivalization, Shrank himself dies in the lion cage because he cannot kill "Bradbury" directly. He himself is "caged" in the submerged circus of the unconscious.

Death Is a Lonely Business can be understood, then, as an autobiographical detective fantasy exploring the theme of the death of the author, who must struggle with finalization in all of its forms. In the end we realize the hidden pun or twist in the title: Death is not only a business concerning Lonelies but also the business *of* a Lonely, A. L. Shrank himself. "Bradbury" freely acknowledges that death is what has often given creative inspiration to his work. He has, in fact, been writing stories about the Lonelies and their deaths throughout the novel, and Shrank has been following him, enabling those deaths, a fact with which Shrank taunts him ("You were my good dog of death"). But "Bradbury" has foiled the attempt of death to "finalize" his identity from the outside. On the contrary, he plans to "live forever" through his books. True to the ambivalence of carnival, death has been both a threat and a creative inspiration. Shrank himself is shrunken and emptied of hope because he "shrank" from life and hated it. He dies the death of the last Lonely, "caged" by Bradbury in the drowned circus.

Bradbury's sequel, *A Graveyard for Lunatics,* explores the link between this carnivalized version of detective fiction and film, particularly the "madness" of the Hollywood studio production system, which made films into a mechanically based "factory" of dreams. He treats the studio system—in which the creative screenwriter was often just an anonymous cog in a gigantic machine—as a madhouse. In this novel everyone from the producer to the director to the actors manifests some form of psychic abnormality. Not the least in this cast of crazies is a manic-depressive drunken actor, who identifies with his screen role as Jesus Christ and manifests the stigmata of crucifixion, whom Bradbury tries to "save." From paranoia to schizophrenia, from obsessive neurosis to the perversions, the book runs the gamut of psychic afflictions. Also woven into the plot is one catatonic character—the wife of the studio head—locked away in an asylum, who chooses madness rather than face the horror of her lover's death and the mutilation of her husband, and the studio physician, Doc Phillips, whose function it is to "cure incurable egos." Bradbury refers to his adolescent self in the novel as "the Crazy," one who was himself utterly mad about film. Now as a young writer with a successful book to his credit, he works inside the film factory, "a victim of my own romance and infatuated madness over films that controlled life when it ran out of control beyond the Spanish wrought-iron front gates [that is, outside the studio]."

Thus the thematic links between madness and creativity are clearly established, but once again the author must struggle with creative death, for screenwriters are not remembered by the studio system. The novel opens on Halloween 1954, a few years after the end of *Death Is a Lonely Business.* "Bradbury" and his friend Roy Holdstrom (a character based on special-effects wizard Ray Harryhausen) have been hired by Maximus Films to "write, build, and birth the most incredibly hideous animal in Hollywood history." This apotheosis of the monster film— which also represents the apotheosis of their personal egos—has the working title of *The Beast.* Such a creature first has to be imagined, however. "Bradbury" can only approach such a fearful vision through the writer's art, through metaphor. Holdstrom, however, can work from real-life models. His art is made to be *seen.*

Although "Bradbury" is mad about movies, film itself has difficulty in relating metaphor. One of the primary effects of cinema illusion is that the audience often takes what it sees on the screen to be literally and really there and not a symbol for something else. Early in the book "Bradbury" argues with the studio head, Manny Leiber, that "the scare comes from night shadows, things unseen." Leiber rejects this aesthetic of suggestion for the crude notion that "people want to see what scares them." This is one place where Bradbury's novel reflects 1980s debates about the nature of horror film, with splatterpunks taking the vulgar position that everything must be shown. Some of his pulp horror fictions for *Weird Tales* (for instance, "The Maiden" [1947]), were written in this Grand Guignol mode and were gruesome enough to inspire EC horror comics during the 1950s, but body horror and gore was never the real center of his aesthetic. "Bradbury" is forced, at least initially, to write his screenplay around an absent center, leaving room for the monster. What will fill this void is a scene of suffering, one that demands masking and unmasking.

Holdstrom and "Bradbury" first encounter the primary victim of the scene of suffering at a Hollywood restaurant, where they see a man with a disfigured face. Enraptured by the hideous disfigurement, Holdstrom models his beast on it but is soon hastily fired from the studio, disappearing mysteriously after his work is destroyed. It is finally revealed that the whole chain of events is a practical joke played by Stanislaw Groc, a cosmetologist employed by the studio, himself a resemblance, or mask, of Conrad Veidt in *The Man Who Laughs*. Described by Bradbury as a man hardly larger than one of the midget actors who played munchkins in *The Wizard of Oz*, Groc is a pessimist and a clear parallel with A. L. Shrank. He wants to reveal to the world—although his motive may involve blackmail—that J. C. Arbuthnot, once head of Maximus Films but thought to have died in a car accident, still lives, though nearly insane and horribly mutilated. What is more, though dying of cancer, Arbuthnot still directs the studio, giving orders to Leiber through a tunnel or mirror connecting the studio with the graveyard. Groc contrives to have "Bradbury" and Holdstrom hired by the studio to do a monster picture and arranges for them to see the disfigured Arbuthnot in the restaurant. Arbuthnot then becomes the living model for Holdstrom's beast, but the studio (Leiber) is embarrassed and threatened to the point of destroying Holdstrom's work and firing him after only three minutes of test film have been made. Finding out just why the studio is acting so strangely toward Holdstrom's art—which after all is designed to show the monster in all of its horrid detail—involves us and "Bradbury" in mystery, seeming madness, and the aesthetics of fantastic representation.

Once again Bradbury uses the conventions of the detective genre in order to fictionalize his creative anxieties during this early period of his career and to explore aesthetic problems. The plot of the novel is very convoluted and nearly baroque in its intertwining of themes, with "Bradbury" and Elmo Crumley running down one misleading clue after another. Another complication is added by the fact that Holdstrom, who we think is dead, goes mad in this section of the book and impersonates the beast, imprisoning the original Arbuthnot and taking over direction of the studio. Here Bradbury takes the manipulative devices of detective fiction to the limit as we race back and forth in a hyperventilated fashion from the studio, where "Bradbury" is working on an ending for a religious spectacle about the life of Christ, to the graveyard: "Half of me saw this [chasing Arbuthnot, who is really Holdstrom] as manhunt, the other as Keystone farce."

As Geoffrey Hartman observes, Chandleresque is not far from Chaplinesque in detective fiction. But Bradbury's world of Keystone detective comedy is even more anarchic and carnivalized. Everyone, it seems, is wearing a mask or a mask beneath a mask. At the studio party that preceded the car accident in which Arbuthnot was mutilated (the scene of suffering), "All the masked people ran off in their masks." People from this party, including the director Fritz Wong (based on director Fritz Lang, who once wanted to film *The Martian Chronicles*), stage manage the scene of suffering so that the studio will survive the scandal. "Bradbury" tells Groc, who sewed up Arbuthnot's face after the accident, that "There's a mask behind your mask and another under that," suggesting that the scene of unmasking required by detective fiction is problematic in this novel. "Bradbury" alone seems totally naive and is referred to variously by the more experienced characters in the novel's narrative world as the "true sainted fool" (Groc) or "the real honest-to-God idiot savant" (Arbuthnot). Both terms, of course, refer to literary versions of the fool of carnival, who can stand outside of society's conventions and expose them. It is the authorial mask that Bradbury chooses to wear in both detective novels.[40]

Near the denouement we are told that *The Beast* was an "impossible film" all along. Holdstrom's three minutes showed that it was at least possible to put such a creature on film, *but only as a mask.* In viewing the fragmentary footage, "Bradbury" is at first overcome with terror—uncannily, the beast seems to be looking directly at him (normally film does not return our gaze)—but then realizes that it is Holdstrom himself *pretending* to be the beast, wearing makeup. But even before it was filmed, the model clay head was already described as "the finest work he [Holdstrom] has ever done, a proper thing to glide from a far-traveling light-year ship, a hunter of midnight paths across the stars, a dreamer alone behind his terrible, awful, most dreadfully appalling mask." The filmic beast, while horrific in effect, is revealed as a product of the interplay of a mask beneath a mask. But the real beast (Arbuthnot) is himself the joke at the center of the novel: "He proved that life was a joke! Imagine! To *prove* such a thing."

In many ways then, this book explores the problematic relationship of film to Bradbury's authorship, which depends on the notion of representations that must also be recognized as masks hiding more terrifying truths of the soul one dare not confront directly. It is significant that Bradbury never allows his writer-hero to catch up in his screenplay to Roy Holdstrom's "mad wish" to pursue and trap the most terrible face in the world, a wish that causes him eventually to slide deliriously into murdering Doc Phillips. Instead, Bradbury constantly approaches the horror of the visible with metaphorical language, which is often related to film. In his television scenario on the modern horror film, "Death Warmed Over," Bradbury was prepared to accept certain horror films, such as *The Phantom of the Opera*, where masking and unmasking is quite prominent thematically, as dreams that were more powerful and more beautiful than death.[41] In the following scene, the mirror in Manny Leiber's office becomes a metaphorical space—a film screen—that captures "Bradbury's" gaze, calling up childhood memories (of Alice, from Lewis Carroll's *Through the Looking Glass*) and a sequence of images from *Phantom:*

> And suddenly it was—
> Nineteen twenty-six. The opera singer in her dressing room and a voice behind the mirror urging, teaching, prompting, desiring her to step through the glass, a terrible Alice . . . dissolved in images, melting to descend to the underworld, led by the man in the dark cloak *and white mask* to a gondola that drifted on dark canal waters to a buried palace and a bed shape like a coffin. (emphasis added)[42]

Through the mechanism of identification, Bradbury is Alice, falling into the dark abyss of *The Phantom of the Opera*, a film he saw when he was six years old. The invisible world of thought and language, however, still seems preferable to the madness of literal representation, which the mirror is and the studio purveys. Arbuthnot, the beast, actually wants to make "Bradbury" his son by giving him the studio before he dies. But recognizing that this scenario is a Freudian one of the internalized Gothic—for Arbuthnot was "the super-ego," invisible behind the mirror for so many years, and Manny Leiber "the ego"—he refuses Arbuthnot, whom "Bradbury" tells us speaks with "the voice of my father."

With this rejection of the madness and power of film, "Bradbury" reaffirms his sole desire: to be a writer and finish his novel. In essence the priestlike "Bradbury" hears Arbuthnot's confession: "'I forgive you!' I shouted at the man's terrible mask." Every terrifying thing in his world must become an aesthetic mask, even the real Arbuthnot, who represents the temptation of selling out to film. But only the carnivalized word has the power to free us. The novel appropriately ends with "Bradbury" forgiving madness and the need for masks—both in himself and in others, including Roy Holdstrom—and with the affirmation of life and hope.

Bradbury's latest murder mystery, *Let's All Kill Constance!* developed from one character, Constance Rattigan, who is in both previous books. A former movie star, Constance presents "Bradbury" with two "Books of the Dead," a phone book from 1900 and her personal address book, as clues to a mystery and then disappears herself. Certain names in the latter text are marked with a red-inked circle and a crucifix. As it turns out, this Book of the Dead (mentioned briefly in *Death Is a Lonely Business*) becomes a text of clues, containing both victims and suspects, for this novel. The story then becomes a search to find out whether or not certain people on the list are really dead or to stop their being killed if they are not. For most of the book we are not sure whether it is Constance herself who is killing people or someone else. But it turns out that she is killing herself—that is, her identification with her numerous film roles (masks) that have submerged her real self—which emerges when "Bradbury" talks her out of the literal tomb she has built for herself.

The novel was obviously fun for Bradbury to write and full of surprises. From the opening lines it plays with the reader ("Shouldn't Constance have her own book?" he asks), and Bradbury says that he allowed the characters to write the book as he visited with them one by one.[43] In many respects it is even more playful, manic, and carnivalized than the previous two books. We can only give something of the flavor of its discourse here, but like all of Bradbury's major works of fiction, it depends on the interplay of metaphor, myths, and masks. Once again, Bradbury the narrator is wearing the mask of the fool who knows and is referred to in the narrative variously as "the Crazy" or "the Martian." "Bradbury" first visits the detective Elmo Crumley (whose novel *Death Is a Lonely Business* has finally been published). Elmo is at first reluctant to join the investigation: "Look, Willie [for Shakespeare], I'm an old man and can't take those graveyard carousels and crocodile men snorkeling the canals at midnight." But he is intrigued and finally agrees that something is amiss. They become convinced that Rattigan is running away "from Death, from one of the names in the book."

The first name they investigate in Constance's personal Book of the Dead is Clarence Rattigan (described as a "mummy" who once was her husband named Overholt—Constance made him change *his* last name for the marriage). He lives on a mountain, Mount Lowe, surrounded in his house by huge piles of newspapers and movie memorabilia, many of which are cited in the text. Clarence says that Constance red circled his name because she wants "Bradbury" to write her autobiography. From this point on, newspaper titles come in to play in the discourse of the novel as additional intertextual clues. Clarence also explains the origin of the name "California" and the name of the next character on the list in the Book of the Dead.

Apparently, the Hispanics who conquered California carried certain books with them. One described the myth of an Amazon queen ruling in a land of milk and honey, Queen Califa. When the conquerors first saw the native peoples and country, they were moved to name the new land after her. Now Califa (Alma Crown) is a character in the novel, a psychic who "prognosticated our [that is, Constance and Clarence's] predestined marriage." And her name is marked with a "more than enormous crucifix by an almost circus banner name" in the Book of the Dead. She lives in an area of Los Angeles, which is ethnically carnivalized, a "real free-for-all stewpot of Mexicans, Gypsies, stovepipe-out-the-window Irish, white trash and black." It turns out that this fortuneteller is the proprietor of Queen Califa's Psychic Research Lodge, dead center of Bunker Hill. Although many detective novels contain psychics as typical characters, Queen Califa's gargantuan proportions are clearly meant to evoke the presence of carnival:

> I saw an immense woman in an immense crimson velvet queen's robe receding on roller wheels in a metal throne across the hardwood floor to the far side of the room. She stopped by a table on which rested not one, but four crystal balls, coruscant with light from a green and amber Tiffany lamp. Queen Califa, astrologer, palmist, phrenologist, past and futurist, sank inside three hundred mountainous pounds of too-too-solid flesh, her stare flashing X-rays.[44]

As the fool who knows, "Bradbury" revives Califa's own waning power to prognosticate when she tries to read his palm. Both she and Clarence die early in the novel under suspicious circumstances. And since Califa demonizes Constance's character during this interview, the pair of detectives begin to suspect Constance as the murderer.

They next visit Constance's brother, Fr. Seamus Rattigan, described as a "skeleton-thin Florentine Renaissance priest" whose lips are "ravenous for salvation." He is a priest at Saint Vibiana's Cathedral who has just heard Constance's confession. The effect of this confessional discourse on her brother is profound: "Here was Savanarola begging God to forgive his wild perorations, and God silent, with Constance's ghost burning from his eyes, and peering from his skull." The priest is presented as a "sinner-saint" of the Renaissance (Savanarola, it is pointed out in the text, made Botticelli burn his paintings in 1492). The Renaissance was the period in which the carnivalization of literature reached its peak, where such an ambivalent figure as a "sinner/saint" would have appeared in literature with religious themes. (From this point on there are significant last-minute deletions by Bradbury, which appear bracketed as necessary.)

Father Seamus calls "Bradbury" an "idiot savant," one in whom others feel the need to confide (implicitly making him into a priest). "Bradbury" replies: "My face. I look in mirrors but never catch myself. The expression always changes before I can trap it. It's got to be a blend of the Boy Jesus and Genghis Khan [or maybe innocent nerd and hyperventilator]. It drives my friends crazy." This is a good summary of the authorial mask Bradbury wears throughout his detective novels and makes the notion of noncoincidence of author and mask, on which Bradbury's aesthetic depends, evident.

The investigators then move on to a more fully carnivalized location that they revisit several times in the novel: Grauman's Chinese Theater. (It is also known to the narrator as "Uncle Sid's fake Chinese Palace," founded by Sid Grauman, the "cinema monkey man." Bradbury here playfully mocks the institution he was so fascinated with as a young man.) Outside they meet Constance in masculine disguise, her feet in the impressions of her own in the sidewalk along Hollywood Boulevard. Constance leaves them clues to follow by standing in other footprints. Then the two men accost Clyde Rustler, the projectionist, who we later learn is Constance's father. Henry, the blind African American from the previous two novels, is also back. When first encountered, he is standing in the prints of Bill Robinson's (the black tap dancer) shoes at Grauman's. Together they explore the basement of the theater, looking for more clues among its dressing-room mirrors. All of what they find has to do with early films.

Next they visit J. Wallington Bradford, a homosexual friend of Constance, who describes her sexual escapades: "Constance invented Freud, tossed in Jung and Darwin, [wrote *their* books first]." His description of her is a parody of androgyny (as he himself is a parody of the Hollywood "Queen"). To him, Constance is a "tomboy with suspicious breasts." It is he, however, who provides the key to understanding her real desires. He tells them that Constance is imprisoned in her film roles and is saying, through the clues she has been leaving behind ["untie, unbind, give me back who I was"]. This symbolic unbinding is the work of the rest of the novel.

Next on the list is Alberto Quickly, a ninety-year-old actor who first taught Constance. He was known in vaudeville as Mr. Metaphor and runs a small theater in his apartment. He reveals that Constance had many roles and identities: "Katy was Alice in Wonderland, Molly was Molly in *Mad Molly O'Day*. Polly was *Polly of the Circus,* same year. Katy, Molly, Polly, Constance. A whirlwind [storm]. Blew into town nameless, blew out famous. I taught her to shout, 'I'm Polly [of the Circus].' Producers cried, 'You are, you *are!*' [and whipped out contracts]." The carnivalized atmosphere of her (almost mythical) film career is made obvious in these remarks linking it metaphorically to the circus world.

After a visit with Fritz Wong, one of Constance's directors, they go back to Grauman's basement, where they find a multiplication of masks but no further information: ["all those Alberto Quickly personas, faces. There are dozens of masks and faces here. Basement mirror names. A glass catacomb"]. Desperate for clues, with Constance's character and legend looking more and more tarnished, "Bradbury" has to persuade Crumley not to give up on Constance. Somehow he knows that she is not the person demonized in the stories about her. In an extraordinary passage, "Bradbury" revisits the Mr. Electrico story, the decisive event of the real Bradbury's life of authorship, and tells it to Crumley as a parable of hope. He relates that Mr. Electrico was "a carnival magician" who carried on with his performances despite knowing that people came to his show hoping to see him electrocute himself. And this defrocked Presbyterian minister gave his spectators his blessing despite their desires to see him fry: "All I know is somehow [by paying attention], burning me with his great eyes, he gave me my future. Leaving the carnival I stood by the carousel, heard the calliope playing 'Beautiful Ohio' and I wept. I knew something incredible had happened, something wonderful and nameless. Within three weeks, twelve years old, I started to write."[45]

Crumley is not entirely persuaded by the Mr. Electrico story (or by the notion of reincarnation, which is central to it) and does not want to be a participant in carnival. He responds at first with cynicism, saying that Mr. Electrico saw in "Bradbury" a "romantic sap, a dumpster for magic." But "Bradbury" still wants to use the hope inspired by Mr. Electrico's story to solve the mystery, referring in a joking manner to lines of poetry he wrote about Freud and God: "And Freud spoils kids and spares the rod, to justify Man's ways towards God." He does not want Constance to be "finalized," her character and life cut off from the future, by Freudian interpretations of her past.

Eventually, operating on his intuitions about Constance as much as deductive logic, "Bradbury" explains the mystery to a waiting audience of Wong, Crumley, and blind Henry. Constance had not really committed any of the murders (and they were not really murders, just accidents). She was just trying to erase signs of her former identities, her masks. Gathered outside her several tombs at Forest Lawn Cemetery, the group learns that Constance has buried herself over and over again under different names: "When she was done with one act, one face, one mask, she hired a tomb and stashed herself away." Thus the title of the book is revealed as a joke. It is not "Shall we all kill Constance?" but Constance is killing her various selves over a period of years. Fritz Wong loves the explanation and wants to do a film of it, with "Bradbury" writing the screenplay. Then they find a final unlocked tomb with Constance's name (Rattigan) on it. All the stolen scraps of her past are there. Descending into the crypt alone, "Bradbury" finds Constance in a kind of trance. In effect, "Bradbury" becomes the priest who cleanses this "den of iniquity" and brings Constance back to life. Constance asks him about her many masks: "Are they gone?" As the novel ends, Constance goes swimming with the seals, the implication being that she will be brought in by the sea, all fresh and new, with a chance to live a new life.

In his detective novels Bradbury expanded his aesthetic of metaphors, myths, and masks to include an oblique commentary on his own creative struggles with the form. The history of the novel is indebted to carnival figures such as the clown, the rogue, and the fool, which first enabled writers to find a position of authorship from which they could criticize the society they saw around them. Bradbury's detective novels construct this struggle of authorship in a modern context as both a nostalgic longing for the past and a hope for an undetermined future, difficult tasks to accomplish in a narrative world that has depended so much on deterministic plotting and mechanistic causality. In all three books Bradbury succeeds in turning the detective novel into an exploration of the freedom of art by carnivalizing the genre, by turning its conventions inside out. Far from being the hard-boiled detective, Bradbury is deeply affected by the scene of suffering, which for him has to be approached indirectly by metaphor so that its full terrors do not panic and freeze the heart. And far from being the ratiocinative character the genre demands, Bradbury the hero and author solves his mysteries by exploring the hilariously sad world of the narrative while wearing the mask of the *fool who knows*. In the novel form at least—and this assertion must be understood as not applying to his early detective fiction collected in *A Memory of Murder*—Bradbury does not create narrative worlds in which his creative freedom is in any sense finalized or trapped in a clownish identity. On the contrary, he lives on through his masks and metaphors, through his life of fiction.

Bradbury's life of fiction is often accompanied by "carnival sideshows" of fantasy and science fiction story collections, which provide interesting points of comparison to his main attractions.

7

Carnival Sideshows

The Fantasy and Science Fiction Story Collections

The concept of "final authorial intention" seldom surfaces in a discussion of Bradbury's fiction. His half-dozen variations on *The Martian Chronicles* (most still in print, even after fifty years) offer little indication that he will ever reveal a preferred form for one of his best-known book-length fictions. Each version represents a settled intention for *Chronicles* at a particular period of Bradbury's career. No one form supersedes another in any linear or authoritative sense, for in his mind each one represents a valued milestone of creative achievement. For many years, *The October Country* has seemed to represent his preferred form of presentation for the corpus of weird tales that established his early reputation as a unique and engaging stylist. Yet in recent years he has released a new (though limited) edition of *Dark Carnival*, where all but four of the nineteen *October Country* tales were first collected. He is equally satisfied with editions of *Fahrenheit 451* as a standalone novel or in its original format as the title work in a collection of stories. The same pattern is apparent in the eighteen fantasy and science fiction story collections he has published at regular intervals over the last fifty years. A number of his early and best-known fantasy and science fiction story collections have been repackaged for new generations of readers, while individual stories from these earlier titles have also found their way into specialized collections (*R Is for Rocket, S Is for Space*, and *Dinosaur Tales*) and two retrospective compilations (*The Vintage Bradbury* and the *Stories of Ray Bradbury*). He has just released *Bradbury Stories*, a third compilation that draws from six decades of story publication—a record which (in all genres) amounts to an impressive total of four hundred distinct tales.

It is not easy to establish a reliable count of published stories, for Bradbury has rewritten and retitled dozens of previously released tales for his collections and novels. Scores of others are at least lightly revised as they are collected. And the collections themselves are just as unstable as they initially evolve; the content of each one is constantly modified from the time that Bradbury first plans a collection until exhausted but enthusiastic editors finally release it to the public. With the exception of *The Illustrated Man,* the structural elements of these collections cannot be considered integral units of creativity in the same sense as the major fictions that constitute the central focus of this book. But each one does reveal a great deal about Bradbury's career-long habit of periodically collecting his stories to give them lives beyond the ephemeral magazine publication by which most of them first reached print. From a textual perspective, the most fascinating aspect of these collections is the way that book publication can unintentionally mask the creative sequence of his story canon. Successive generations of readers have at least a vague idea of the chronology and the period of publication for the story collections, but they tend not to scrutinize the copyright page or (in recent decades) Bradbury's introductory references to the genesis of the individual stories gathered in his collections.

Bradbury has reached far back in his publishing career in preparing many of his collections. The origins of previously unpublished stories first printed in these volumes is explored below as we survey the fantasy and science fiction collections that remain the foundation of his literary canon. There is no doubt that the stories Bradbury conceived during the 1940s and 1950s represent a watershed of creativity. In later decades, as work in other media has left less time for story writing, he has wisely revisited the unpublished ideas of that period to enrich his collections with previously unpublished gems that now, late in life, he has made the time to polish. Authorial intent is a very elusive concept in any study of Bradbury's fiction; the structure he ends up with in a published story collection is rarely what he started out with, for such volumes, like his individual stories, seem to compose themselves. Nevertheless, it is possible to see how Bradbury has tended to rely on the fruits of his first two decades as a creative writer as he periodically adds chapters to his life of fiction.

Bradbury's Texts

Bradbury worked feverishly during his June 1949 trip to New York to produce book outlines that would fit Doubleday editor Walter Bradbury's desire for a novel or a novelized story cycle that could be marketed as a unified book-length fiction. Before he left the city, Doubleday offered to publish two of his concepts. Bradbury returned home with a signed contract for two books: *The Martian Chronicles,* due on September 1, 1949, was to be developed from his Martian stories into a novelized story cycle, and *The Creatures That Time Forgot*, which was described in the contract as a story to be revised into a fifty-thousand-word novel, by February 1, 1950.[1] This second book proposal had originally been marketed as a short novella and published in the fall 1946 issue of *Planet Stories*. It is a fascinating tale of colonists who have been trapped for generations on a planet that has accelerated human metabolic rates to fantastic levels; people are born, grow to adulthood, age, and die within eight days. The blazing hot days and the arctic nights leave only a few minutes at dawn and dusk when the people can leave the caves they inhabit to gather the plant life that grows incredibly fast during those short interludes. Against all odds, a young man and woman manage to collect enough knowledge of the past to escape from the planet and its metabolic nightmare. The power of this novella is found in Bradbury's haunting and highly emotional descriptions of the constant presence of death, which has all but extinguished the qualities of love and hope that make us human. Both Don Congdon and Bradbury initially felt that an expansion of this long story could sustain a novel, but Bradbury was not yet ready to extend a single story in this way. He had become adept at creating story-length masterpieces in a single sitting, but he took weeks and sometimes months to revise and had not made the creative leap to novel-length authorship. During the middle and late 1940s, he had outlined several novel proposals from sequences of his Green Town stories and his weird tales, but thus far he had only succeeded in transforming the Martian stories into a unified book.

Fortunately, Walt Bradbury sensed that *The Martian Chronicles* would be a very significant book for Doubleday's new science fiction series and was increasingly impressed with the consistent quality of the young author's prolific output of short stories. With *Chronicles* in hand, Doubleday permitted Bradbury to renegotiate the second book into a story collection and extended his deadline into the summer of 1950. An index for the collection, dated May 20, 1950, contains many of the titles eventually selected for publication (fig. 15). Bradbury wrote to Doubleday in July promising to meet the August 15 deadline; he also made his case for marketing the new book beyond the science fiction genre. Specifically, he wanted separate sections for fantasy stories and science fiction stories and asked that the Doubleday Science Fiction colophon be omitted from the dust jacket and cover. He also submitted his first suggestion for a title story, "The Illustrated Man," a weird-horror fantasy about a carnival grotesque that Bradbury had just published in the July issue of *Esquire*. Editor Bradbury agreed to publish the book without the science fiction colophon as a "book of short stories by Ray Bradbury." But he resisted a departure from the science-fiction-oriented contents and felt that "The Illustrated Man" ran too far afield from that focus. Given little room to wiggle on contents, Ray Bradbury agreed with his editor's assessment:

"It would make a wow of a title, but the story is—well—different. I think we can safely eliminate it. I'll try to think of a new title in the next two weeks."[2]

By the end of July, Bradbury offered a new title that he felt would counter the thread of pessimism running through the selection of stories.[3] We cannot be sure of this title, but it may have been "Frost and Fire," which he had considered in an earlier stage of outlining when the tentative table of contents still contained "The Creatures That Time Forgot." This was a good metaphor for that novella and would eventually become the title of this tale more than a decade later in *R Is for Rocket.* Three weeks later Bradbury submitted the manuscript, which contained a major shift in contents from what Doubleday was expecting. Bradbury had removed "The Playground," "The Vacation," and "The Pedestrian," which he and Congdon had not yet been able to sell to the magazines. He also eliminated "Payment in Full," which had already appeared in a science fiction pulp but was perhaps the most brutally pessimistic story in his preliminary outlines for the collection. He added an unsold science fiction story, "No Particular Night or Morning," and "The Highway," a snapshot look at Americans in Mexico just after a nuclear war has forever changed the way the less-developed world will look at American culture (its much longer sequel, "And the Rock Cried Out," is one of his finest stories and his best unproduced screenplay). Bradbury was still not quite sure of the contents; he wanted to include "Pillar of Fire," another of his short novellas, and offered to drop "The Exiles" to accommodate inclusion of the longer tale.[4] But the collection was already longer than *The Martian Chronicles,* and the twelve-thousand-word novella was not included in the new book. Each previously published story in the final submission was slightly revised from its magazine version; as a group they represented the best of his distinct variety of short science fiction, including four "unchronicled" Martian tales. A few had appeared in major-market magazines, but the basic concept of the book left Bradbury at ease with the idea of presenting the best remaining stories of his pulp science-fiction years. In contrast to his frantic attempts to reshape *Dark Carnival* after it was already in galleys at Arkham House, he stopped transforming the contents of his new Doubleday collection at the point of manuscript submission.

But there was one more surprise for Doubleday, and it would help transform the book into a science fiction classic. The manuscript Bradbury submitted on August 19 included an entirely new and innovative approach to naming the collection. He was able to restore his "wow of a title" by sketching out an entirely different illustrated-man framing device: while on a walking tour of Wisconsin, Bradbury's narrator offers the hospitality of his food and campfire to a strange drifter, an illustrated man who has been banned from every carnival around because his tattoos predict the future. As they settle into sleep around the campfire, the drowsing narrator is enthralled by a tattoo that begins to move and tell

"FROST AND FIRE" — (TENTATIVE TITLE?)

contents of a book of SCIENCE FICTION STORIES by RAY BRADBURY

~~22~~		
29 L	THE CONCRETE MIXER	7,000 words
15 L	KALEIDOSCOPE	3,000 words.
23 L	THE VELDT	5,000 words.
20	THE FOX AND THE FOREST ("TO THE FUTURE")	5,000 words.
	~~LONG BEFORE DAWN (new story, unpublished)~~	~~words.~~
18 L	THE ROCKET MAN	4,000 words.
20	THE VISITOR	4,000 words.
22 L	DEATH BY RAIN	4,000 words.
	~~FOREVER AND THE EARTH~~	
17 L	MARIONETTES, INC.	3,000 words.
21 / 15	~~THE MAN~~ ZERO HOUR	3,000 words.
12 L	THE CITY (published as "PURPOSE")	3,000 words.
15 L	~~THRESHOLD TO THE STARS~~ (THE ROCKET)	3,000 words.
26 L	THE FATHERS	7,000 words.
20 L	THE OTHER FOOT	5,000 words.
7	~~THE VACATION~~	~~2,000 words~~
5	THE HIGHWAY	2,000 WORDS
20 / 12 IX	THE EXILES	5,000 WORDS
	~~PAYMENT IN FULL~~	~~3,000 words.~~
5 L	THE LAST NIGHT OF THE WORLD	2,000 words.
7 L	~~THE PEDESTRIAN~~	~~2,000 words.~~

~~347~~
315 pages

TOTAL: 78,000 WORDS. ~~131,000 words~~

O.K. MAY 20, 1950

Ray Bradbury

Figure 15. Bradbury almost certainly took this tentative index for what would become *The Illustrated Man* to New York during his trip to help launch *The Martian Chronicles* and consult with his Doubleday editor, Walter Bradbury. The author's signature and an apparent date of review are at the lower right. "Frost and Fire" would eventually become the reprint title of Bradbury's 1946 novella, "The Creatures That Time Forgot," in *R Is for Rocket* (1962). This novella (as "The People That Time Forgot") and another, "Pillar of Fire," have been crossed out of the index to reduce the collection from 131,000 words to 78,000 words. This was the approximate size of the final volume. *Frost and Fire* had been the tentative title in earlier undated outlines as well and may have resurfaced as the interim title Bradbury used during the summer of 1950 while he developed two very different versions of "The Illustrated Man" as possible title-story concepts. From the Albright Collection, courtesy of Donn Albright and Ray Bradbury.

a story. In this way Bradbury introduces the group of eighteen stories that compose the new collection. He added short bridges into the second and third stories as the narrator awakens to focus on new tattoos that tell new stories. There are no more bridges afterward, for by now the reader has entered the fantastic dream world of the narrator, and the collection moves from illustration to illustration without the aid of any textual bridges. After the eighteen stories have run their course, the narrator awakens again, near dawn, and focuses on the one tattoo that has yet to resolve itself into an illustration. It now offers a terrifying scene—the narrator being strangled by the illustrated man. This epilogue closes with the narrator running away from the still-sleeping illustrated man toward the next town in a desperate attempt to alter his own future. Bradbury's narrator has continued to run off into history; the new carnivalized title, and its overarching "Illustrated Man" prologue and epilogue, have since sold millions of copies at home and abroad. For the next forty-six years, the original but unrelated story "The Illustrated Man" never found its way into a Bradbury collection, although he did include it in his first midcareer compilation, *The Vintage Bradbury* (1965). Then, in preparation for a new hardbound 1997 edition in Avon's uniform format of Bradbury titles, he added "The Illustrated Man" as a surprise nineteenth story (a surprise even for the copyeditor, whose liner notes describe the "eighteen startling visions" of this collection).

Bradbury read proofs in November 1950. He made few changes, and *The Illustrated Man* was published in late February 1951, just as the last few stories scheduled for magazine publication reached the newsstands. The science fiction colophon was removed from the dust jacket but was stamped, much less conspicuously, on the cover spine beneath the jacket. Bradbury was persuaded to compromise on the byline as well; the dust jacket reads "stories by the author of *The Martian Chronicles*," which ran counter to his purpose in removing the colophon but did build effectively on the association with Bradbury's earlier success. He felt that this book could be marketed within the book trade as a science fiction collection, but he wanted the textual evidence of this genre association minimized to give the book the best chance possible with mainstream reviewers and critics. Walt Bradbury understood that his author now cast a shadow far beyond the science fiction genre and helped with the physical design of this book as much as possible.[5]

Doubleday also secured deals for subsequent editions that consolidated Bradbury's new relationships with subsidiary publishers. Bantam contracted for the American paperback, and Rupert Hart-Davis bought the U.K. rights. Since Bradbury had managed to replace "Usher II" with "The Fire Balloons" in the British edition of *Chronicles* (published by Hart-Davis as *The Silver Locusts* in 1951), the latter story would have to be pulled from the 1952 U.K. edition of *The Illustrated*

Man. In the end Bradbury and Hart-Davis decided to make it a full swap and replaced "The Fire Balloons" with "Usher II" in this and all subsequent British editions of the collection. But there were other problems. "The Exiles" and "The Rocket Man" had been published in *Maclean's* of Canada, which apparently held exclusive rights in England as well. These two stories, as well as "The Concrete Mixer," were deleted, and "The Playground" was added to make up at least part of the lost content. Other news from Britain was more favorable. On June 1, 1952, *The Illustrated Man* was honored in London with an International Fantasy Award. Bradbury won the third-place fiction award and, in doing so, stood with distinguished company. John Collier's *Fancies and Goodnights* placed first, while John Wyndham took second place with *The Day of the Triffids.* In America all three were Doubleday authors.[6]

But as time went by, Bradbury once again began to feel the drag of story collections that showcased the pulp stories he was beginning to leave far behind. He had felt the same about *Dark Carnival* even before that collection was published, and despite good reviews, he was beginning to feel the same way about *The Illustrated Man.* A year after publication he wrote to Walt Bradbury hoping to make changes when the book went into the next printing:

> I would like to stand the *complete* expense of cutting out two stories THE VISITOR and NO PARTICULAR NIGHT OR MORNING. I want to replace them with better stories. Even if I have to write new ones, believe me. I'll stand all costs of setting up new stories in type, and repaging costs. To be really happy, I'd also like to cut out THE CONCRETE MIXER and THE EXILES, but this would probably be pushing you too far. It would make me feel better anyway, if I could cut two of the stories and replace them with better ones so that, in its last printings, anyway, the book would be nearer to what I intended. I am most serious in this request and I do not expect Doubleday to stand any of the cost whatsoever. It was my mistake in judgment, originally, that allowed me to let several not so good stories slip into the book.[7]

Bradbury would make similar requests for changes in *The Martian Chronicles* a few years later and for very much the same reasons. It was an impulse that would gnaw at him throughout the 1950s as he periodically looked back, from the vantage point of a writer who had reached more-mainstream markets, at the pulp roots of the two books that had established his critical reputation. Walt Bradbury firmly resisted this impulse from the beginning. He explained his rationale in a way that his author clearly understood. Setting aside issues of cost and the library cataloging chaos that would inevitably ensue from such changes, Walt Bradbury argued that two different texts would be a disservice to his readers—both early and later readers would feel cheated. Bradbury's instinctive habit of continually revising his stories had spread to his view of the story collections as well, and through the 1950s he looked to such interludes as reimpressions, or new editions, to revisit his first two major titles in much the same way he would revise his individual stories between submissions to various magazines or between magazine and book appearances. Although he used the past tense in describing the proposed changes in *The Illustrated Man* as "what I intended," his notion of intentionality was always in flux, referring to a "now" that was constantly slipping into future plateaus of creativity and recognition. On February 18, 1952, Walt Bradbury offered this firm counterpoint: "A published collection of short stories is an entity, complete, and, in the literary tradition, irrevocable. Many authors, like you, have regretted an original selection, but you don't change them, any more than a novelist would rewrite an already published novel because he wasn't satisfied with the original story."[8] He was generalizing, of course, and implicitly discounting such famous revising hands as Ralph Waldo Emerson, Henry James, and Walt Whitman. But Bradbury was always concerned for his readers and accepted the reader-based points of the Doubleday argument. And as his career continued to evolve and broaden into successes in other media, Bradbury came to see *The Illustrated Man* as an important milestone in a particularly exciting time of his career. The Bantam paperback continues to reflect this early intention, although the variant British editions are still in print throughout the commonwealth. And there is, of course, the 1997 Avon hardbound edition in America, which places the standalone story "The Illustrated Man" within the framework of the prologue-epilogue.

One story in this collection, "The Fire Balloons," which is in some editions of *The Martian Chronicles* (most recently, the 1997 Avon edition) requires some comment as an important "sideshow" because of the way in which it critiques old myths and illusions through the carnivalization of ideas. The story's central metaphor and title is taken from the paper balloons sent up on the Fourth of July celebrations of Bradbury's youth. In this way it is linked thematically to festival and also helps convey a sense of wonder about the other race of Martians revealed in the story. Nonhuman in appearance, they are round luminous spheres of blue light. Father Peregrine, the story's central character, is being sent to Mars to bring religion to the aliens but wonders if the aliens will understand human concepts of sin and salvation because of their different senses and bodies. He has himself written a "little book" that suggests "the possibility of unrecognizable sin." The idea strikes some of his fellow missionaries as nonserious and circus-like in its assertion of the possibility that new bodies may involve new sins (an adventuresome idea in which Father Peregrine obviously delights) as a mere juggling of mirrors. But he responds to his critics by comparing the church to a static "posed circus tableaux" that has trouble with new ideas. Although he is well aware of his "serious" task in saving the Martians, Father Peregrine asserts that God himself is not serious: "The Lord is not serious. In fact, it is a little hard to know what else He is except loving. And love has to do with humor, doesn't it?"⁹ Father Peregrine suggests that God laughs at us, loving us all the more because we appeal to his sense of humor.

Father Peregrine's experiences with the Martians are comic in the broad sense. After the Martians save him from an accidental fall (certainly there is a pun on fall and the Fall), he speculates that they may not have experienced Original Sin and may live in a state of God's grace. He then attempts suicide, risking his own soul in sin several times more in order to prove them human, "to find the man behind the mask, the human behind the inhuman." After an attempt to build a temple for the Martians in which Christ appears in their own image, the Martians finally explain to Father Peregrine telepathically that "each of us is a temple unto himself," and therefore they have no need of a church. The Martians themselves only have legends about how the racial transformation into the incorporeal came about, but it is clear that because they no longer have bodies, they no longer sin. Father Peregrine undergoes the final stages of carnivalization when he wonders, "What church could compare with the fireworks of the pure soul?" He now has to imagine a Christian church thriving without the body of Christ, at least in its human form.

In 1952 William F. Nolan, not yet a professional writer himself, published in book form the first comprehensive assessment of Bradbury's career. His *Ray Bradbury Review* included the first full bibliography of Bradbury's career and essays on the importance of carnival concepts in his writing, but it is even more interesting to see Nolan's snapshot of what Bradbury was working on just after publication of *The Illustrated Man.* Two novels were in development, including a Mexican piece centering on a psychological study of fear: "The narrative concerns the gradual disintegration of a woman's mind, as loneliness and terror replace the sane security of her past life." The material for this concept came directly from Bradbury's autumn 1945 trip to Mexico with Grant Beach and drew on the occasional tensions that developed between the two road-weary travelers, as well as the constant sense of violence that Bradbury found simmering just below the surface of life in the dusty towns of mid-century Mexico. He had actually penned a table of contents and more than two-dozen pages of material for this novel during and immediately after the trip under the initial title of *The Fear of Death Is Death.* By early 1950 Bradbury had decided on a different approach, based on some of his longest and best short fiction to date. His excellent novella, "The Next in Line," was to serve as the basis for the novel's conclusion, while his yet-unpublished prequel story "Interval in Sunlight" would provide both the new title and the interior progression of events that the author envisioned for the middle of the book (see app. B). But he only penned thirty-three pages of bridging narrative over the next three years and apparently never developed more than a few pages for the opening third of the novel. "Interval in Sunlight," finally published in the March 1954 issue of *Esquire,* was the only tangible result of this project.

It is unclear if any work was done toward the second novel mentioned in Nolan's *Ray Bradbury Review,* but by the summer of 1951 Bradbury had signed a contract with Doubleday for a third work-in-progress—an autobiographical cycle of stories based on his Illinois childhood, bridged and unified like *The Martian Chronicles* into novel form.[10] Of these three projects, only a prequel to the Illinois novel, *Dandelion Wine,* would ever reach print, and even that book would take six more years. By 1952 it was apparent that Bradbury's hallmark habit of writing in story-length creative bursts would not easily sustain a novel-length concept. He continued to produce a remarkable range and number of quality stories, knowing that eventually groups of these building blocks would lock together to form novels. With *Something Wicked This Way Comes* (1962), he would indeed find a way to write a full-length novel from a single story concept, but for the rest of the very productive 1950s, Bradbury would produce story collections.

Even before *The Illustrated Man* reached print, Don Congdon had suggested that Bradbury either collect several of his science fiction novellas into book form or turn one into a novel. They both sensed that the novella could be Bradbury's most likely bridge into the longer form. In late 1950 Congdon encouraged his client to continue his transformation of "The Next in Line" and some of his unpublished Mexican stories involving psychologically vulnerable American protagonists into a short novel of fifty to sixty thousand words. After making some progress, Bradbury decided to secure a contract for the Illinois book instead and tried to pull that group of stories into a novel during the next year. But by the summer of 1952, it was apparent that the Illinois project needed more time, and Walt Bradbury agreed to take the pressure off by accepting Bradbury's proposal for another story collection. Doubleday held him to a tight timetable on developing the collection, and Bradbury quickly prepared a series of outlines. Two of these included his long novella "The Fireman," but he soon decided to gather only stories of his standard five-to-six-thousand-word length instead. He not only considered a number of stories published since 1950 but also considered some new ones. On June 10, 1952, he sent Doubleday a sixteen-story index with a cover letter suggesting that a new story, "The Golden Apples of the Sun," should supply the title for the new collection (fig. 16). Walt Bradbury liked the title but preferred one that they had kicked around before, from the unpublished story "Perhaps We Are Going Away." Ray Bradbury soon convinced his editor that his first choice was more distinctive, for that line from Yeats's "The Song of the Wandering Aengus" provides not only a very lyrical but also a very memorable title. "Perhaps We Are Going Away," a less substantial story that did not reach print until 1962, was never used as a title story for any Bradbury collection.[11]

"The Golden Apples of the Sun" was one of his best new stories, a stimulating fantasy with science fiction trappings, and it represented Bradbury's growing desire to bring his fantasy tales into the Doubleday canon of titles. A week after providing the story index, he sent some magazine tearsheets for recently published stories for Walt Bradbury's review and suggested as well that the new collection include a section devoted to his realistic fiction. He recommended four such titles: "I See You Never," "Power House," "Invisible Boy," and "The Big Black and White Game." Walt Bradbury penciled these new titles into the June 10 index, and all four were added to the final table of contents. These were older stories published between 1945 and 1948, but they represented his first wave of success in the major-market magazines; in fact, "Powerhouse" was an O. Henry Award Story from 1948. Bradbury was determined to extend the range of the collection, but at the same time he was unsure how fans of his more recent fantasy stories would respond. He suggested grouping the realistic titles together and adding the following word of warning to the opening of the book: "These stories are not fantasies in any sense of the word. They are 'realistic' stories. Rather than be shocked by too sudden a contact with more mundane affairs, afficionados of more imaginative stories may feel free to skip this entire section, and start reading . . . where all is once again dreams and visions and portents of things to come."[12] This idea was a variation on his impulse to keep his collections moving toward what he was doing in the "now," but he knew that these particular pieces symbolized how he had gotten to where he now stood. Furthermore, they were quality stories that still appealed to readers, and they had no links to the pulps.

Bradbury finally decided to be more subtle about the older stories and blended the science fiction, fantasy, and realistic tales without an authorial preamble that might be seen as patronizing. The more-or-less-random mix was effective, but *The Golden Apples of the Sun* lacked any narrative concept like that of *The Illustrated Man*. Instead, Bradbury decided to link the stories visually, for by now he had developed an excellent eye for art in general and book design in particular. As he began work in earnest on the new collection, Bradbury purchased his first oil painting. It was by Joe Mugnaini, a California artist whose unique paintings and line art instantly attracted Bradbury. The two became great friends, and during the summer of 1952, they experimented with a novel-in-pictures based on Bradbury's old outlines for a dark carnival novel. In a June 1952 letter to Doubleday, Bradbury announced that he had an excellent idea for the dust jacket and wanted to commission Mugnaini to execute it. The Doubleday staff quickly

THE BEAST FROM 20,000 FATHOMS (Sat.Eve.Post)

THE SOUND OF THUNDER (Collier's, June 28, 1952)

THE APRIL WITCH (Sat.Eve.Post, April, 1952)

THE PLAYGROUND

THE PEDESTRIAN (The Reporter, 1951)

THE WILDERNESS (Phila.Inquirer)

THE FLYING MACHINE

THE MEADOW (Best One Act Plays of 1947-48, adapted to short story)

THE WATCHFUL POKER-CHIP
OF M.MATISSE

AND THE ROCK CRIED OUT

A SCENT OF SARSAPARILLA

EMBROIDERY (Marvel Science)

THE GARBAGE COLLECTORS

THE MURDERER

TOUCH AND GO

THE GOLDEN KITE, THE SILVER WIND

Brad: The above list is the result of my culling and re-culling,
        and listing and re-listing all of my stories during the
        past six months. I've actually been thinking about a new
        book of such stories for quite a time now. I realize that,
        actually, more than half of this list will be meaningless
        to you. I enclose this Index merely to show you that I
        have given this particular project thought, and that it
        will not be a rushed and second-hand piece of work. R.

Figure 16. This story index for *The Golden Apples of the Sun* was sent to Doubleday on June 10, 1952. A week later Bradbury suggested that the collection also include four realistic stories from his 1940s break into major-market magazines. The handwritten titles in the right margin record Doubleday editor Walter Bradbury's decision to include these older stories; his annotation reads: "Power House—O. Henry 48," "I See You Never—New Yorker," "Invisible Boy," and "The Big Black & White Game." Ray Bradbury's explanatory note to Walt Bradbury concerning the initial index titles appears at the bottom. From the Lilly Library, courtesy of the Lilly Library, Indiana University, Bloomington, Indiana, and Ray Bradbury.

learned that Mugnaini was a marvelous fresh talent and a real joy to work with. Bradbury had wanted illustrations for individual stories, but the cost associated with producing and inserting the plates was prohibitive. Doubleday suggested smaller chapter headings done as line art, but even smoother paper might not provide enough definition for the reduced images. Mugnaini supplied samples of line, brush, and simulated woodcut approaches. Doubleday could not go with the lighter-weight paper required for line drawings—it would reduce the volume bulk considerably and risk customer irritation at the prospect of paying three dollars for a slim book. There was no lowering the price with artwork involved, but Mugnaini was able to provide excellent definition on the rougher, bulkier paper with a brush approach.[13]

By now it was October, and with the March 1953 publication date looming, the book still lacked illustrations and a title story. Bradbury had forwarded a total of twenty-four stories during August. In addition to the sixteen from the June index and the four realistic pieces of the 1940s, he submitted "The Great Wide World Over There," "En La Noche" ("Torrid Sacrifice"), "Sun and Shadow," and "Hail and Farewell." While he continued to work on the title story in Los Angeles, author and editor worked cross-country to finalize the contents. Bradbury felt too close to the stories to be sure about any of them—by his own count, he had revised each one, even those previously published, from six to ten times. He sensed that "Embroidery" and "The Murderer" were the weakest, but Walt Bradbury liked all except the unpublished "And the Rock Cried Out" ("The Millionth Murder") and the old pulp detective story "Touch and Go." The author had no time to rework "And the Rock Cried Out" and reluctantly dropped it from the volume, but he retained "Touch and Go" as "The Fruit at the Bottom of the Bowl." The original title had been Bradbury's pun on the central conceit of the story, a murderer's obsession with removing all evidence of his touch from the murdered man's home. When he remembers that he has been a frequent visitor over the years, he obsessively polishes every object in the house, including the contents of a fruit bowl. (Mugnaini ended all lingering doubts in Walt Bradbury's mind with a fascinating rendering of the table setting of fruit.)

By the end of the summer, Bradbury also decided to drop the off-trail weird story "The Watchful Poker Chip" and the otherwise obligated "A Scent of Sarsaparilla," which was scheduled for a new Ballantine anthology of science fiction writers. After more than ten rewrites, Bradbury finally submitted the title story in early November, and the twenty-two-story field seemed ready to go at last. Mugnaini's rendering of Bradbury's jacket design was already at press; it suggested a reader's eye formed out of Mugnaini's representation of the full Yeats couplet: "The Silver Apples of the Moon, / The Golden Apples of the Sun." During November and December, the artist completed magnificent illustrated headpieces for every story and accommodated a late substitution when it was determined that "The Playground" would not appear in *Esquire* prior to the March release date. "The Great Fire" was hastily substituted, along with a Mugnaini headpiece. The book was published in late March 1953 to accommodate a late sale of "Hail and Farwell" to the *Philadelphia Enquirer* for the March 29 issue of *Today*.

Bradbury had carefully mixed the story types prior to galleys and finally had a collection that in his mind seemed to represent his best work. Only one story, "Embroidery," had appeared in the pulps. With the exception of the very fine realistic stories he had pulled forward from the 1940s, all of the previously published titles in the collection had appeared in magazines within the previous twenty months. There were also six new and previously unpublished stories: "The Flying Machine," "The Garbage Collector," "The Meadow," "The Murderer," and the title story itself. *The Golden Apples of the Sun* received fine reviews, and the Mugnaini illustrations captured the fantastic underlying so many of these stories. The Bantam paperback edition retained them as well, and these images have become an integral part of the story collection for several generations of readers. Rupert Hart-Davis published the U.K. edition, eliminating two stories that he felt would not appeal to British readers, "The Big Black and White Game," an American baseball story, and "The Great Fire," a story slanted toward the *Seventeen* reader's market. Corgi's 1956 paperback edition followed suit, but all subsequent British editions are unabridged.

Bradbury had wanted his new collection to carry the best review comments that his first two Doubleday titles had earned, including the important critical observations of Christopher Isherwood and Angus Wilson. Walt Bradbury felt that this strategy would awaken reviewer suspicions that the kind words of courteous British critics may be masking tougher assessments back home. He agreed to his friend's request, but out of respect for the American booktrade's wariness of overseas critics, he took these comments off the back of the jacket cover and the top of the front flap and moved them to the bottom of the back flap to minimize the appearance of hype. Part of the editor's concern stemmed from the fact that he had finally convinced his superiors at Doubleday to reach out for more-mainstream critics to review Bradbury's new book. He also got the house science fiction colophon removed from the spine of this collection, completing (at least symbolically) Bradbury's move away from that Doubleday book series. But in spite of these efforts by their friend and editor, both Congdon and Bradbury were beginning to feel that Doubleday could do more to market an author who was bringing in good hardbound sales on every book and excellent royalties on his paperback contracts, which were shared equally between author and publisher. Congdon also felt that his client's willingness to pay for the Mugnaini illustration plates, while a relatively small expense, should be reimbursed from future profits. For his part, Walt Bradbury made it clear that he was just following trade practice in making the author responsible for the content of the book, which included both the words and the beautifully integrated illustrations (all of which were copyrighted in Bradbury's name). But his patient and reasonable explanations could not keep the author and his agent from beginning to feel that they should give Doubleday some competition to bid against.[14]

Another publisher was already very interested in securing a Bradbury story collection. Ian Ballantine's new publishing house promised both hardbound and paperbound editions backed by established distribution and bookselling networks. During the fall of 1952 Ballantine and his editor, Stanley Kauffmann, expressed interest in a collection that could include one or two of Bradbury's novellas. Two years earlier Congdon had found no interest in the novellas at Doubleday, and with that publisher's reluctant approval, Bradbury began to assemble a collection for Ballantine in December 1952 that could include one of three previously published novellas: "The Fireman," "Pillar of Fire," or "The Creatures That Time Forgot." The latter title was Kauffmann's favorite, but Bradbury spent much of 1953 transforming "The Fireman" into *Fahrenheit 451*. (Chapter 3 describes the intensive process of rewriting that produced this novel, first published as the title work in a lopsided story collection that also included two late deletions from *The Golden Apples of the Sun:* "And the Rock Cried Out" and "The Playground.") Bradbury would also continue to work outside of his Doubleday commitments to bring the best of his *Dark Carnival* weird tales (and a few newer ones) to a wider market as *The October Country* (1955). He was very careful to present these stories as a backward glance at an earlier phase of his career so that reviewers and readers would not mistake the new title for a step backward in creativity. These Ballantine titles allowed Bradbury to publish volumes regularly while he was wrestling with the Illinois novel he was obligated to complete for Doubleday.

In the middle and late 1950s, Bradbury would develop two Illinois projects in an effort to extend his undisputed credentials as a master of the short story into the production of a true novel. In the United States, only Poe had attained the reputation Bradbury enjoyed without developing into a successful novelist, and Bradbury knew that his autobiographical Green Town material offered the best chance to make the transition to long fiction. Walt Bradbury agreed, for he felt that only a novel carved from the retrospective Illinois material would allow his author to break completely out of the science fiction label that his first three Doubleday books had helped establish.[15] *The Golden Apples of the Sun* had reached a wider range of major-market reviewers than either of the earlier titles, and both author and agent had to concede that this was progress. But it was clear that Doubleday executives still saw Bradbury as a niche author within their large and highly compartmentalized stable of authors. Advertising continued to use Bradbury's successful titles to promote the Doubleday science-fiction series and the associated Science Fiction Book Club. And from the perspective of the company's higher echelon, Bradbury's success was relative. He sold better than most of the other authors they had recruited for the science fiction series, but without a wider-market book, he would never be a best-selling writer worthy of promotion, from the company's perspective, to the first or second tier of Doubleday authors.

In 1957 Bradbury gave Doubleday that title. *Dandelion Wine* was only the curtain raiser for the promised novel, but with its publication Bradbury broke into a new range of book-length fiction. Still, Walt Bradbury's enthusiastic support could not convince the publisher to risk a major production and marketing outlay on Ray Bradbury's fourth Doubleday book. The results were predictable; Bradbury sold very well, eventually reaching the ten-thousand-sales level that the earlier books would generally achieve. But he would never be a hardbound bestseller, largely because Doubleday did not expect him to be one. Sales records for the first two decades of Bradbury's Doubleday titles suggest that the house was quite satisfied to make their expenses back on each successive Bradbury book launching and then allow the Bantam paperback to reach six and seven figures in sales, for Doubleday would always receive 50 percent of that royalty base. In a sense Bradbury was a victim of his own success. He reached millions of readers through library copies of his hardbound titles and the mass-market sales of his paperbacks. As long as he was associated with a major publishing house for his hardbound editions, he would be vulnerable to this kind of limited marketing. Walter Bradbury was an excellent editor and friend, well respected throughout the New York publishing scene, but he was not high enough in the hierarchy to significantly change the way that Bradbury's first editions would be marketed.

Bradbury and Congdon decided that the best plan would be to continue to work on the two Green Town novels, but Bradbury's transformation of his dark carnival screenplay into *Something Wicked This Way Comes* would continue into the 1960s, and still another decade would pass before he would begin to pull the *Summer Morning, Summer Night* novel materials into a post–*Dandelion Wine* structure. Bradbury's work on television and film projects also increased during the late 1950s, and although this began to slow his production of stories, he was still publishing enough and writing enough to plan another collection before the end of the decade. Ian Ballantine was still a strong paperback rival to the Doubleday-Bantam connection, but he had been forced to pull back from his hardbound publishing program and did not represent a viable alternative for Bradbury in that regard. In May 1958 Bradbury signed a two-book contract for a new story collection and the novel that was developing from the dark carnival screenplay. It was similar to the two-book contract for *The Golden Apples of the Sun* and *Dandelion*

Wine, but Don Congdon was able to secure a better royalty rate on the hardbound edition as well as right of approval on book club and paperback reprint sales.[16]

Bradbury wasted no time in finalizing the story collection, which would buy him the time he needed to complete the new Green Town novel. A month before the contract offer, he sent Congdon his usual conflated package of unpublished typescripts and published tearsheets for the stories he wanted to consider for the new collection. His plans can be traced back much further, though. Bradbury periodically wrote out indexes for future story collections or lists of future novels, and two indexes survive from the post–*Golden Apples* period. An eleven-story index titled *In the Eye of the Beholder* is dated May 7, 1953, and an undated ten-story list titled *Butterfly in Amber* contains working titles for manuscripts of the same period. These listings represent very preliminary thoughts, for only one of these stories, "Fahrenheit 92" ("Shopping for Death," 1954), was even published during the 1950s and only two others, "Tyrannosaurus Rex" ("The Prehistoric Producer," 1962) and "Magic Show" ("Quicker Than the Eye," 1995), can be traced to published stories at all.

The full contents of his April 1958 submission are not fully known, but he apparently sent in at least twenty-five stories. A half-dozen were considered for the title piece.[17] Walt Bradbury was still holding out for his pet title, "Perhaps We Are Going Away," but no such story was submitted. Ray Bradbury initially wanted "Icarus Montgolfier Wright," one of his favorite recent stories about the history of flight, but it seemed to mask the fact that this was a collection. He then suggested "I Sing the Body Electric!" but this was a teleplay that he was having trouble transforming into a story (another decade would pass before he succeeded). In June Walt Bradbury suggested "The Town Where No One Got Off" as the title story and "The Wonderful Ice Cream Suit" as the alternate. Ray Bradbury had reservations about the former, and both men agreed that the latter might lead readers to think that the volume only contained the highly popular *Saturday Evening Post* story that was here collected. Such confusion could be clarified by the addition of "and Other Stories," but this was clearly too mechanical and awkward. Bradbury then proposed a new story that he had not yet submitted, "A Medicine for Melancholy." Walt Bradbury's early reservations (based on a reductionistic reading of the words "Medicine" and "Melancholy") were quickly swept aside by strongly favorable responses by other Doubleday staff. But Walt Bradbury, along with Don Congdon, wanted the author to drop "Almost the End of the World" and four older stories that represented the best of his uncollected pulp publications—"Referent," "Asleep in Armageddon," "The One Who Waits," and "Here There Be Tygers." The newer tale was not very substantial, and the older ones could prove a problem with readers expecting the very latest fiction. He realized that this time the older pulp stories might prove to be more of a liability than the major-market realistic fiction he had pulled forward into *The Golden Apples of the Sun* five years earlier. He deleted all five, and production went forward, like his last Doubleday collection, with twenty-two titles.

In mid-July Bradbury sent in the title story, "A Medicine for Melancholy," which proved to be a delightful fantasy and a skillful homage to the sexual masquerades of Casanova's *Memoirs*. But the title itself came from the occult medicines found in the works of Albertus Magnus.[18] It certainly set the tone for a collection that reflected Bradbury's full flowering as a master of fantasy. "The Strawberry Window" and "The End of the Beginning" provided richly imaginative commentary on space travel that reflected his own excitement over the world's accelerating plunge into the space age. "The First Night of Lent" and "The Great Collision of Monday Last" transformed autobiographical episodes from his 1953–1954 Irish screenwriting sojourn with John Huston into modern folklore. But "The Smile," a story of a postapocalyptic America in which the Mona Lisa is ritually destroyed in a culturally debased festival, had its roots in one of Bradbury's unfinished novels.[19] Joe Mugnaini's jacket painting, based on Bradbury's own concept of magical vessels bursting with fantastic contents, signaled that *A Medicine for Melancholy* would pick up where *The Golden Apples of the Sun* had left off. Meanwhile in London, Rupert Hart-Davis was delighted to have another Bradbury collection, but he went further than he ever had before to make a Bradbury volume more appealing to British audiences.[20] Hart-Davis felt that the two Irish stories were grounded too much in reality for the overall mood of fantasy in the book and thought that "All Summer in a Day" was more in line with the tone of earlier collections. He asked Bradbury to delete these stories as well as the American title piece. He wanted him to replace these with the still-unwritten "I Sing the Body Electric!" which he felt would make a great title story no matter what the content, and add another work that had never appeared in England, "And the Rock Cried Out." In 1954 Hart-Davis had deleted the latter along with "The Playground" from *Fahrenheit 451* to issue that title as a standalone novel in England; now that Bradbury had turned it into a British screenplay for Carol Reed, Hart-Davis wanted to have the original story for the new collection in case the film ever materialized (which it did not).

Bradbury supplied "And the Rock Cried Out" but had already set aside "I Sing the Body Electric!" for a later time. Instead, he sent Hart-Davis the five stories that had been discarded from the American version of the book over the summer, "Almost the End of the World" and the four older pulps. Hart-Davis accepted all but "The One Who Waits," which seemed, like "All Summer in a Day," to belong to the period of the earlier collections. Bradbury completely reworked the story sequence to accommodate this radical shift in content, revised and retitled "The Shore Line at Sunset" as "The Sunset Harp," and restored "Asleep in Armageddon" to its original 1940s title, "Perchance to Dream." In the end "The Day It Rained Forever," which had just become Bradbury's third *Best American Short Stories* winner, became the title story in England.[21] *The Day It Rained Forever* was released in late February 1959, just two weeks after the American release of *A Medicine for Melancholy,* but it is essentially a distinct collection. Bradbury's sense of this distinction is implied in the separate dedications. *Medicine for Melancholy* is dedicated to three new discoveries—the love of his father and the "new world" of insight found through his new friendships with Bernard Berenson and Nicky Mariano. *The Day It Rained Forever* is dedicated to Rupert Hart-Davis, who never wavered in his attempts to bring Bradbury to major-author status in England. The differences between the two collections offer striking evidence of his fluid sense of development in his collected short fiction. Bradbury's quick reaction to the challenges facing British publication led to a completely different book that was just as well conceived as its erstwhile American twin.

Doubleday executives were not thrilled with the kind of fantasy stories that had crept into *The Golden Apples of the Sun* and had now fairly exploded through *Medicine for Melancholy.* House executives apparently discounted the possibility that slower sales for these volumes could be the result of minimal increases in production or marketing allocations for these books.[22] Both *The Martian Chronicles* and *The Illustrated Man* had moved into new hardbound editions, and *Dandelion Wine* progressed slowly but surely toward five figures in sales. By contrast, *Golden Apples* was not reprinted when its initial impressions (totaling just over 8,000 copies) sold out in September 1958. *Medicine for Melancholy* was never reprinted at all and went out of print in September 1960 with just under 5,500 copies sold.[23] Doubleday's failure to market Bradbury as a major author, coupled with Walt Bradbury's departure for Holt in April 1959, led him and Congdon to demand a full reassessment of support from the house upon submission of *Something Wicked This Way Comes.* Doubleday's reluctance to change the status quo led Bradbury to move, on Don Congdon's advice, to Simon and Schuster during the summer of 1960. But Bradbury was not quite finished with Doubleday; a year after his longtime publisher released him from his contract obligations for the new novel, Doubleday and Bradbury agreed to continue with a pair of special story collections originally intended for young readers. Over the next six years, the resulting volumes—*R Is for Rocket* and *S Is for Space*—would evolve into two of Bradbury's most enduring and popular collections for readers of all ages.

He had suggested a collection of "Bradbury's Space Stories" to an enthusiastic Tim Seldes at Doubleday in November 1959, but the ensuing break with that publisher over *Something Wicked* ended any discussion for the time being.[24] As he made his transition from Doubleday to Simon and Schuster, his idea for a specialized story collection took another turn. For years, Bradbury had been urged by librarians and teachers to write a collection of stories for young adults and teenage readers. His first impulse was to issue *Dandelion Wine* in a teenage edition as a warm up for a new story collection for the same market. He explored the first possibility late in 1960, but hardbound sales of *Dandelion Wine* had slowed considerably, and he foresaw no interest. Within two years, Doubleday let the title go out of print. His only viable option was long term; he could secure a release from Doubleday for *Dandelion Wine*, complete the *Farewell Summer* sequel, and eventually get his new publisher to market both titles in a special juvenile or young-adult format. But Bradbury has yet to complete the sequel, and the idea for juvenile editions of this and other enduring titles never went further than a December 1960 discussion with Don Congdon. Instead, he immediately merged his ideas for a teenage readers series and a specialized collection of space stories.

Bradbury had no trouble coming up with a manuscript—the stories for such a collection were already published and even to some extent collected piecemeal in his earlier story volumes, but they had not been brought together in a dedicated collection. By February, Congdon had already sent Bradbury's new package of stories on to Bob Gottlieb at Simon and Schuster. Gottlieb was interested but not persuaded; he felt that most teen readers could read Bradbury without a specialized collection, and he was reluctant to include stories brought forward from earlier books.[25] For his part, Bradbury saw no problem bringing appropriate stories forward from his earlier titles, especially as he watched the hardbound editions of both *The Golden Apples of the Sun* and *A Medicine for Melancholy* go out of print. During the spring and summer of 1961, Congdon presented the concept to various publishers, including Little, Brown, and eventually found rekindled interest back at Doubleday. Contracts were signed in October for a two-book series, and for once Doubleday's widespread book empire seemed ready to pull harder for a Bradbury title. The two volumes would be midwifed by Doubleday's Books for Young Readers Division, whose distinctive double-dolphin logo was already a symbol of success in that specialized market. Division editors would work closely with the Institutional Department to coordinate sales to libraries and schools. Readers up to age sixteen represented the main focus for these books, and the first Bradbury collection was scheduled for release in October 1962—just in time for Children's Book Week.[26]

The collection led off with Bradbury's first quality science-fiction story, "King of the Gray Spaces," and he soon turned it into the title story as "R Is for Rocket." The first of his sustained science-fiction novellas, "The Creatures That Time Forgot," finally found a home toward the end of the collection as "Frost and Fire."[27] In between these two he pulled forward twelve of his signature science-fiction tales from *The Illustrated Man* (four), *The Golden Apples of the Sun* (three), *A Medicine for Melancholy* (four), and that collection's fraternal twin, *The Day It Rained*

Forever (one). Most are space stories or a blend of science fiction and fantasy. Then he closed the volume with *Dark Carnival*'s "Uncle Einar," the grounded vampire who finds a whimsical way to return to the air as a child's kite, and two *Dandelion Wine* chapter-stories featuring young Douglas Spaulding. The first of these, "The Time Machine" (originally "The Last, the Very Last"), offers time travel through the memories of old Colonel Freeleigh. It was paired with "The Sound of Summer Running" (originally "Summer in the Air") to close the collection with more-reachable boyhood adventures and a glimpse of the boy who grew up to write these tales. In June, Bradbury read galleys and made one final adjustment by placing "The End of the Beginning" right after "R Is for Rocket" to provide a second space-age story before the more earthbound dinosaur fantasy "The Fog Horn." He also removed the last traces of profanity from several of the stories to ensure that the book would not be restricted to the young-adult section of American libraries; he did this freely for *R Is for Rocket,* not knowing that in a few years Ballantine editors would secretly censor *Fahrenheit 451* in an ill-advised attempt to make their new Bal-Hi edition less offensive to school districts.[28]

The space age seemed to stimulate Bradbury's creativity in a wide range of projects. Earlier in the year he worked with Joe Mugnaini and others to produce an animated film version of "Icarus Montgolfier Wright," and by year's end this prelude to the space age had garnered Bradbury an Academy Award nomination. In early September his *Life* magazine essay "Cry the Cosmos" became an instant success and led readers to regard the author of *The Martian Chronicles* as an unofficial lay spokesman for the American space program. *Newsweek* published a space issue in early October that included prominent quotations from Bradbury. *R Is for Rocket* was released the same month, and Doubleday's publicity department worked hard to get review copies in the hands of juvenile reviewers as well as to many of the mainstream critics who were likely to notice and comment on any new Bradbury title. But as always in his dealings with Doubleday, Bradbury had difficulty with executives in charge of the advertising and production budgets.

Doubleday did include *R Is for Rocket* in a major advertisement that coincided with the book's release date, placing it in such major papers as the *Chicago Tribune, San Francisco Chronicle, New York Times,* and the *New York Herald Tribune.* But these were little more than list ads covering all of its large offering of new titles and represented nothing out of the ordinary. Bradbury wrote frequently to executives at the company and finally secured a major ad of his own in the November 25 *New York Times Book Review.* It promoted *R Is for Rocket* as well as all the earlier Bradbury titles, an unusual move typically reserved for authors with a string of best sellers. But Bradbury was, of course, a mainstay in the mass-paperback market, and this was one of the few occasions that he had been able to convince the publishers to plow some of their half-share in his paperback royalties back into advertising for his hardbound editions. Doubleday was not spending much of their own money on these ads, and Bradbury had only gotten this much out of his publisher by writing constantly to a wide range of company executives. In this way he discovered that a major error had been made in the production budget for the new collection.[29] The Books for Young Readers production coordinator had limited the first printing to 4,500 copies, which was standard for most books in this category but failed to take into account Bradbury's established sales record or the name recognition he brought into the field. In November *R Is for Rocket* won a special award from the Los Angeles Public Library, but bookstores in this major market found that the title was out of stock due to the short initial print run. By December, a second and a third printing filled the shelves again, and although sales remained strong, Bradbury had not yet convinced Doubleday management that his collections for young readers would reach the potential he saw for them.

Nearly four years would pass before Bradbury was able to pull together the second volume, which soon took on the companion title *S Is for Space.* By the end of 1962, he was fully engaged in transforming many of his best stories into stage plays and was devoting more time to the actual production of performances all around the country. These projects took up a great deal of time and resources, and Bradbury also continued to write screenplays and explore ventures in other media as well. His stories continued to appear, but he would only publish fourteen new ones over the next five years. Nevertheless, in early 1966 he sent Doubleday twenty-two stories for *S Is for Space.* This mix was out of balance with the earlier seventeen-story format of *R Is for Rocket* and included perhaps too many general fantasy selections. Doubleday set galleys for the full group of submissions, but Bradbury cut six from the concluding galley sheets, where he had placed a number of the wider-topic tales. He retained the first thirteen stories in order, and these remained in the final release. But he cut six of the last nine, including "The Black Ferris," "Referent," "A Weather of Statues" ("Statues"), "The Drummer Boy of Shiloh," "The Sea Shell," and "The Veldt." "The Black Ferris" and "The Veldt" were too disturbing for young readers, and both "Referent" and "The Sea Shell" were early pulp explorations of psychoanalysis, reverie, and illness that also did not transfer well to this market. The other two were fine stories of childhood, but they tipped the balance of contents too far toward general fantasy tales. He also dropped "The Pedestrian" but soon restored it, deciding that this cautionary tale about a world obsessed with media entertainment would not be lost on his youngest readers. The final sixteen-story format of *S Is for Space* made it a better companion for the earlier volume, although his editor's front-flap text reflected the rapid changes in content prior to publication with an incorrect claim that "Mr. Bradbury has selected twenty-two of his best-known stories for this collection" (the *New York Times* reviewer quoted on the back flap is closer to the mark, claiming only seventeen stories).

S Is for Space includes ten stories brought forward from *The Illustrated Man* (two), *The Golden Apples of the Sun* (four), *A Medicine for Melancholy* (three), and his new Simon and Schuster collection, *The Machineries of Joy* (one). Bradbury also pulled a chapter each from *The Martian Chronicles* ("The Million-Year Picnic") and *Dandelion Wine* ("The Trolley") into the new collection. Once again he added four previously uncollected stories, and he decided to open the volume with two of these. "Chrysalis" is one of his earliest and most revised science-fiction stories. Scientists cannot agree if their patient, trapped in a metamorphic insectlike transformation, will emerge a degenerate menace or a new stage of superman. He emerges with no physiological differences from a normal man, and the medical staff is both relieved and disappointed. But only the reader sees the surprise conclusion, which derives from a third and most alien possibility, totally overlooked by the scientists. Quite possibly Bradbury is carnivalizing in this story the Nietzschean idea of the superman, which had been absorbed and used by the science fiction community during the 1930s. After an initial rejection from John Campbell's *Astounding Science Fiction,* Bradbury worked on this story from 1942 to 1946 before finally placing it in the July 1946 issue of *Amazing Stories.* He received continuous feedback during the war years from Henry Kuttner as he refined "Chrysalis," and this extended sequence of mentored revision helped Bradbury fully develop his own distinct kind of science fiction.

"Pillar of Fire" followed "Chrysalis" in the opening pages of *S Is for Space.* It is the second of his three science fiction novellas, appearing in the summer 1948 issue of *Planet Stories* two years after publication of "The Creatures That Time Forgot" and three years before "The Fireman" began its evolution into *Fahrenheit 451.* "Pillar of Fire" was the last of these novellas to be worked into a Bradbury volume, and its inclusion in *S Is for Space* risked an extended plunge into terror for young readers. It is the most carnivalized text of the three novellas. (The clues it offers into Bradbury's strategy of carnivalization in his longer fiction are fully discussed in the thematics section of this chapter.) Both "Chrysalis" and "Pillar of Fire" are thematically rich, but in very fundamental terms they deal with transformations and identity in ways that Bradbury extended through the entire collection. All sixteen tales explore special ways that people are different or are about to be made different by the passage of time. Some of these metamorphoses are terrifying, as the dead walk among the living ("Pillar of Fire"), or darkly humorous, as alien mushrooms take over the living ("Come into My Cellar). There is literal time travel ("Time in Thy Flight") and metaphorical time travel ("The Trolley" and "The Smile"). Humans become Martians ("The Million-Year Picnic" and "Dark They Were, and Golden-Eyed"), pedestrians become criminals

("The Pedestrian"), a child is really a midget ("Hail and Farewell"), and an idealistic inventor becomes an enemy of the state ("The Flying Machine"). Some children control the fate of adults ("Zero Hour" and "The Screaming Woman"), and others gain the power to shape their own destinies ("Invisible Boy" and "Icarus Montgolfier Wright"). It is a rich collection, subtly crafted from stories old and new, and clearly assembled with the care for readers that Bradbury has brought to bear in many of his collections and novels.

Both *R Is for Rocket* and *S Is for Space* were published with striking dust jackets by Joe Mugnaini that once again captured a sense of the fantastic world that Bradbury had crafted between the covers. And in a very few years, this two-volume series would prove Doubleday's executives dead wrong about sales. Despite the competition from Bantam's six-figure sales history for the subsequent paperback editions, the original Doubleday hardbound editions became remarkable sellers within this specialized market. By the end of 1972, *R Is for Rocket* had sold nearly 37,000 copies in both trade and library bindings, and *S Is for Space* had sold nearly 28,000, making these two titles second only to *The Martian Chronicles* in terms of total hardbound sales.[30] This ranking order has probably not changed in more-recent decades; except for a fortieth-anniversary edition of *Chronicles*, Doubleday has not reissued any other Bradbury titles since a book club edition of *The Illustrated Man* appeared in 1969.

Bradbury had less to do with other specialized collections of his work. In the mid-1960s Ballantine Books put together two collections of the EC comic adaptations of Bradbury stories that had been carefully developed directly from Bradbury's story texts more than a decade earlier by William M. Gaines and his editor Al Feldstein. The best sixteen of these graphic adaptations were collected in two Ballantine mass-market paperbacks, *The Autumn People* (1965) and *Tomorrow Midnight* (1966), with brief introductions by Bradbury. Although Feldstein was careful to use Bradbury's words for his adaptations, these graphic collections contain no Bradbury stories at all. The only subsequent young-reader's collection of actual Bradbury stories is *Dinosaur Tales* (1983), a concept developed by Byron Preiss and sold to Bantam for trade and eventual mass-market-paperback editions. Preiss secured seven of the best graphic illustrators to collaborate on this collection, and Bradbury provided four dinosaur stories. Three had been previously published and collected: "The Fog Horn" and "A Sound of Thunder" from *The Golden Apples of the Sun* and "Tyrannosaurus Rex" from *The Machineries of Joy*. Bradbury added a newer dinosaur tale to open the volume, a previously unpublished Green Town story titled "Besides a Dinosaur, Whatta Ya Wanna Be When You Grow Up?" Bradbury was sold on the concept by the illustrators Preiss had gathered, including Bill Stout, Steranko, Moebius, David Weisner, Overton Loyd, Kenneth Smith, and Gahan Wilson. They provided illustrations for the four stories and two dinosaur poems supplied by the author. Although the content revolves around a Bradburian view of dinosaurs, he provided no conceptual structures for the volume itself. It was marketed as "A Byron Preiss Book," and that accurately reflects the origins of the concept and the collection as it has continued in Bantam paperback and Barnes and Noble hardbound editions.

Bradbury's initial move into young reader collections in 1962 coincided with the development of his next major story collection. In February of that year he submitted the final manuscript of *Something Wicked This Way Comes* to Simon and Schuster, and within a few weeks he sent Bob Gottlieb another submission composed of published or circulating stories titled *The Machineries of Joy*. It was a wide-ranging collection of both new and old material, and after receiving a favorable reaction from Gottlieb in May, Bradbury worked on and off through the summer of 1962 revising some of the selections. In early June he described the process for his editor: "There isn't much to be done to most of the stories, but I will go over each one for minor cuts and deletions, especially on some of the older science-fiction tales, parts of which are now a trifle naïve in the light of our fast-advancing Space people." He also addressed Gottlieb's concern that the two Irish stories in the submission might strike an odd note. Bradbury decided to keep both in order to maintain a rich mixture of heterogeneous forms: "Let us be rocket men, let us be sea creatures, let us be Irish, and let us be dogmatic priests bewildered by the whole damn affair. Let the book be a revolving door, and you never guessing if you'll come out in patio or lobby, raw air or false illumination. Let us throw the compass overboard, Bob, and steer for the rocks."[31] These remarks indicate Bradbury's willingness to risk confounding his more timid readers and point toward a notion of authorship and metaphorical shipwreck that affirms the spirit of carnival in which the author may wear many different masks.

The Machineries of Joy included two stories from the 1940s, "El Dia De Muerte," set in Mexico City during the annual Day of Death observances, and "The One Who Waits," an uncollected weird tale originally published in August Derleth's *Arkham Sampler*. Two overlooked but fascinating stories from the early 1950s were also collected: "A Flight of Ravens," based on a Bradbury encounter with the New York publishing elite, and the last of his marionette or mannequin crime stories, "And So Died Riabouchinska," which was based on his unpublished radio script of 1947. "Almost the End of the World," one of Bradbury's frequent fables on television culture during the 1950s, appeared in the American edition only; since Rupert Hart-Davis had already slipped this tale into *The Day It Rained Forever*, it was deleted from his British edition of *The Machineries of Joy*. Bradbury selected the remaining fifteen stories in the collection from the twenty-one works he had published between 1960 and 1963. Four appeared in the *Saturday Evening Post*, but eight of the others—more than half of the stories selected from the 1960s—

had appeared in *Playboy*. He had appeared in both magazines periodically since the early 1950s, but *Playboy* found his more recent style particularly in step with the times. This included the title story, which opens the collection with a priest's search for a meaningful accommodation between religious faith and the wonders of the unfolding space age. It was one of the first of many variations on this theme that would appear more and more frequently in Bradbury's short fiction.[32] Beginning with *The Machineries of Joy*, his newer stories would focus less on plot and more on dialogue intended to explore links between the rapidly receding past and the terrifyingly uncertain future. His technique would often involve humor and nearly always unfold through the voices of fantastic or whimsical characters rather than fully drawn realistic characterizations. This became a hallmark narrative pattern for his newer stories, and even the older unpublished manuscripts he has taken up in more recent decades have been colored with this mood.

The Machineries of Joy would be the first major collection since *The Illustrated Man* to appear without a Joe Mugnaini dust jacket; in fact, there was no original cover art at all, just a montage of machines and diagrams forming a very loose association with the title story's allusion to the elusive metaphorical machineries that manufacture contentment and happiness within the human heart. Bradbury's own design was discarded, and the lack of a distinct artistic concept was unfortunate.[33] (Mugnaini's art would forever be associated with Bradbury's greatest short fiction, and the two would remain lifelong friends.) *The Machineries of Joy* was also Bradbury's only new book for Simon and Schuster. He would place his next collection with Knopf and thereby rejoin his good friend and editor Bob Gottlieb, who had moved to Knopf along with advertising mainstay Nina Bourne in 1967. Bradbury signed on at Knopf in October 1968, and by February 1969, he had signed a contract and stabilized the contents. Gottlieb heartily endorsed Bradbury's choice of "I Sing the Body Electric!" ("The Beautiful One Is Here") as the lead story, and it soon became the title story as well. The book was released as a seventeen-story collection in October 1969. Following a by now-familiar pattern, Bradbury included four stories from much earlier times. There were three previously uncollected pulps: "Tomorrow's Child" ("The Shape of Things"), an off-trail but engaging science fiction tale of interdimensional childbirth; "The Women," a siren-song weird tale; and "Night Call, Collect" ("I, Mars"). "The Tombling Day" had appeared in the literary journal *Shenandoah* (November 1952), but it was perhaps even older than the pulp selections, having been drafted no later than 1947.[34] All of these stood up well over time and proved to be excellent companions for the more recent tales.

The other thirteen stories were published in the 1964–1969 period, but several had older roots. "I Sing the Body Electric!" was developed from a teleplay that Bradbury had written in the late 1950s; an uninspired but memorable production of this "electric grandmother" fable aired during the 1962 season of *The Twilight Zone*, but Bradbury had drafted a story version around 1958. "The Lost City of Mars" is an unchronicled Martian tale that reprises several characters from the fourth expedition of *The Martian Chronicles;* it had been, for a time, woven into Bradbury's 1962 *Chronicles* screenplay. William F. Nolan subsequently read the script and noticed that in this part of the screenplay, Bradbury had lapsed into fully narrative prose; with Nolan's encouragement, Bradbury subsequently returned to the original short story and revised it for publication.[35] These thirteen represent nearly all of his published story production in the middle and late 1960s; only three stories published from 1964 until the release of *I Sing the Body Electric!* in the fall of 1969 were held out. He had published no stories at all in 1968, and this was the first year since 1940 without a professional story magazine publication. Bradbury's creativity was unabated; he had simply shifted his attention to drama, film, consultancies, and speaking engagements and away from the regular production of original stories. The preparation of *I Sing the Body Electric!* stimulated him to publish eight stories in 1969 (including the two first published in that collection), but he would not reach that total again in a single year for two decades.

Two of the stories with older roots develop significant variations in Bradbury's carnival of science fiction themes, suggesting how machines might be made to serve the purposes of life. They require some brief discussion here. In "The Lost City of Mars," Bradbury's focus seems to be on a new character, the drunken poet Harpwell, who interfaces with a machine in an ancient Martian city. Each of the characters experiences the machine in different ways related to their desires, but Harpwell, described as a person "insulted with Christian guilt, and gone mad from the need of destruction," is cured from despair, self-punishment, and his death wish when the machine makes him live through the fantasy of his own death repeatedly in a variety of fantastic scenarios. The virtual experiences this machine provides set him free. He is "off the Christian hook" of internalized guilt and at last able to affirm his life. This story is practically an allegory of the need to overcome both the internalization of guilt brought about by Christian culture and the Freudian death wish. It carnivalizes both Nietzschean and Freudian ideas in the context of virtual reality well before that notion became a popular theme in science fiction.

The other story contains one of Bradbury's more delightful attempts to carnivalize the robot story. Bradbury feels humankind must build what he calls "empathy machines" or "compensating machines" to survive in our technological culture, and the artist has a central role to play in their design. These issues come to a focus in "I Sing the Body Electric!" a story revolving around the experiences of three children growing up with a robot grandmother. After losing their mother, the children, together with their father, have a "humanoid-genre mini-circuited, rechargeable AC-DC Mark V Electrical Grandmother" made for them by Guido Fantoccini (whose name means "shadow puppet" in Italian). Fantoccini is obviously an artist Bradbury admires, one concerned to destroy certain myths about machines, or as the Grandmother later phrases it, "to invent machines to give the lie to the ancient lying truth" about them, a nice Nietzschean turn of phrase. At any rate, the children, except for the girl, Agatha, are enormously happy with this robot that somehow manages to give the impression of imperfection while anticipating their desires. Agatha holds back her affection because she does not want to suffer another human loss and thinks the machine can die. But when the grandmother saves her from a speeding car by pushing her out of danger and allowing herself to be hit instead, then quickly reviving, Agatha learns to love her also. Cars are the technological villains of the story, described by the grandmother as "the greatest destroyer of souls in history" because they appeal to our primitive and paranoid instincts for self-destruction.

One critic who has written on the story, Wayne Johnson, says that it "reveals, in spite of itself, the essential narcissism behind the robot-as-human fantasy."[36] Johnson thinks that the robot grandmother is reinforcing the children's narcissism because she shows each one the face that pleases them most, to each a different face. But early in the story this ruse is discovered by the eldest boy, who is also the narrator, when he takes some photographs of the grandmother. The boy's reaction to this discovery contradicts this premise, for instead of outrage at being thus deceived, he has nothing but praise for the clever and wise artist Fantoccini. He does not tell his brother and sister. The illusion does not seem to have done him any harm, for he knows that "Hers was a mask that was all a mask," and the artist who made her is therefore superficial out of profundity. Far from reinforcing their narcissism, the robot grandmother enables the children to live it as a form of play. Once again, a Freudian notion is given a carnivalized treatment through a science fiction theme. A child who is haunted by her past is given the opportunity to affirm an openness toward life through the healthful and artistic use of technology.

If one counts the two Irish stories of this collection, which were written in the early 1960s, more than half of the stories included in *I Sing the Body Electric!* were recovered and reworked from earlier years. Bradbury's five subsequent story collections reflect his continuing rediscovery of manuscripts and even published stories from his first two decades as a professional writer (see table 13). These were works of quality (even those that ended up in the pulps could have found their way into more-mainstream publications) but were set aside, often unfinished, as Bradbury turned to screenwriting, to fashioning stories and plays from his Irish experiences, and to the major book-length fiction projects through which he transformed his mastery of short fiction into wide-ranging success as a novelist. His rediscovery of these materials began in earnest in 1974, when William F. Nolan took a break from his own writing career to prepare a major companion and reference book covering Bradbury's career to that point. By the time that *The Ray Bradbury Companion* appeared in 1975, Nolan had revisited every facet of Bradbury's early career and found thirteen stories published prior to the mid-1960s that merited revision and presentation for both old and new Bradbury readers.

Nolan's efforts and advice led Bradbury to refashion these tales and nine newer stories into *Long after Midnight*. Bradbury found a rhythm in this work and successfully revised twelve of the older pieces for the new collection. There was great range in his selections. "One Timeless Spring" (1946), a nostalgic look at childhood distrust of square meals and packaged treats, was an early prelude to one of the *Summer Morning, Summer Night* chapters that has yet to reach print in any form. "Getting through Sunday Somehow" ("Tread Lightly to the Music") was an uncollected Irish story from the early 1960s. Only "I, Rocket" failed to pass muster; it was pulled from galleys and replaced with "The Better Part of Wisdom," which was just out in a late-summer issue of *Harper's*. But the collection still retained a dozen older publications, compared to only ten from more recent times. Bradbury found that he could return to a gruesome tale like "The October Game" or a pessimistic Martian fable like "The Blue Bottle" ("Death Wish") and seat them comfortably within a wide-ranging mix of old and new works. He would dedicate the volume to Nolan, who had helped him form a carnival parade of stories from an unexpected combination of moods and tones. Nolan also singled out the perfect title story. Bradbury's original title story was "Getting through Sunday Somehow," but Nolan convinced him to use the more mood-evoking "Long after Midnight."[37] This title had cycled through several manuscripts before sticking to a 1962 short story; it had also been the original working title for the evolving *Fahrenheit 451* manuscripts and would represent this new collection of forgotten favorites very well.

As ever, Bradbury appreciated the work his editors and agent brought to each new collection, and he had by now developed an excellent working relationship with Nancy Nicholas at Knopf. Bob Gottlieb's responsibilities as chief executive led him to ask Nicholas, an experienced editor, to work on Bradbury's volumes of verse in the early 1970s. She continued as his sponsoring editor with *Long after Midnight*, and Bradbury depended a great deal on her sense of presentation as the stories were brought together into the final sequence. She was also an excellent editor of fiction and had great command of Bradbury's work from the early days of *Dark Carnival* on through his widening mastery of the story cycle and novel. She knew that his natural style was short fiction. Years later she would reflect on this aspect of his genius: "He naturally wrote three-four-five thousand words. And he'd been doing it since he was a kid. And he just cranked those out—he had an idea, and he wrote it. One of the things that's so charming about Ray's mind is, I get the sense that his ideas come out like eggs, just completely formed, as opposed to writers who struggle line by line, fussing. He gets a good idea and knows how to put it down." With Bradbury, of course, the fussing came in revision, but many of the stories brought out of the distant past for *Long after Midnight* had already gone through a tempering process prior to original maga-zine appearances. In nearly every case he found it much easier to revise for this book. The result was seamless and sold well. But neither of his first two Knopf story collections received the kind of major reviews that his earlier titles received. Knopf was now marketing Bradbury in three genres, and he had been critical of house efforts to sustain sales campaigns for *I Sing the Body Electric!* or the 1972 release of *The Halloween Tree;* but during this period, Knopf generally responded well to his wishes, and the lack of reviews was perhaps more the result of Brad-bury's diminishing presence in major-market magazines during the 1970s.[38] Between 1970 and 1980, only seven new Bradbury stories appeared in American slicks. His career was developing in many directions, and with great success, but he was not able to maintain the pace of new fiction that had been a hallmark of his creativity in earlier decades.

After Nolan's research for *The Ray Bradbury Companion* had unearthed some unpublished early Bradbury stories that showed great potential, in 1977 and 1978 he and Donn Albright, then a professional artist and professor at Brooklyn's Pratt Institute, began a systematic search of the surviving manuscripts with Bradbury's help. In 1947 Bradbury had burned all but a handful of manuscripts from earlier times, but a larger number of quality stories and story fragments remained from the late 1940s and early 1950s. Despite his own heavy writing commitments, Nolan continued to review and make recommendations based on the original-manuscript searches of the late 1970s, but Albright would take the lead in seek-ing out and reconstructing older manuscripts during the next two decades. The first fruits of this work were collected in *The Toynbee Convector,* Bradbury's final volume of stories published by Knopf. By this time, Nancy Nicholas and Bob Gottlieb had worked with Bradbury in defining the best of his first four decades of published fiction for *The Stories of Ray Bradbury* (1980). But Nicholas departed for Simon and Schuster in 1985, and by early 1987, Gottlieb was headed to the top job at *The New Yorker*. In early 1987, as Bradbury prepared to send in the first submissions for the new collection, Gottlieb asked Knopf's managing editor, Kathy Hourigan, to take over as Bradbury's editor.[39] The transition was smooth; Hourigan rarely had the chance to work with individual authors anymore, but she would have several months to review stories before Bradbury reached a crit-ical mass of material.

Between February and June 1987, Bradbury submitted twenty-three stories that included eight older tales.[40] Two were early magazine publications, but a half-dozen were unpublished stories that Bradbury had selected from the group Albright and Nolan had urged him to complete: "The Last Circus," "A Touch of Petulance," "Colonel Stonesteel's Genuine Home-Made Truly Egyptian Mummy," "The Love Affair," "One Night in Your Life," and "West of October." These six dated from the 1948–1950 period; during the 1980s Bradbury completed them all and brought them into an effective mix of new and old. By year's end he and Hourigan set the sequence, and *The Toynbee Convector* was published in May 1988. Despite its wide range of stories, the title story was the only science fiction tale, and even that story's premise of time travel is not what it seems to be. The time travel in the story turns out to be a hoax, a lie of a beautiful future concocted to enable our present society to survive the crisis of modernity with its "incipient nihilism." There is perhaps no clearer fictional statement of Bradbury's philosophy of the lie as necessary for life. But the move away from science fiction in this collection was no accident. Both Gottlieb and Hourigan had urged him to include other kinds of stories since his reputation had by then transcended Bantam's ubiquitous honorific, "Greatest Living Science Fiction Author."[41] He would continue to speak and write widely in real-world forums about human aspirations in space, but the evolving complexities of the technology and the growing sophistication of science fiction readers ran counter to Bradbury's intuitive focus on the human equation in science fiction and the need for fictions and masks. He would pursue other avenues of creativity to the near exclusion of science fiction in his subsequent collections.

The next two years were devoted to two major autobiographical fictions— his second detective novel, *A Graveyard for Lunatics*, and the fusing of his older Irish stories into the larger fabric of *Green Shadows, White Whale*. He would also wind down a very successful six-year run of teleplays for *The Ray Bradbury Theater*. And he would make perhaps his final change in publishers as he departed Knopf for Avon in 1994. He had been disappointed when Knopf let *The Halloween Tree* go out of print in the early 1990s and had been unable to persuade them to reissue his older titles in new hardbound editions. Both Knopf and Bradbury knew that he needed the kind of teamwork that could only be provided by a publisher that could combine the reprint advantages of a paperback publisher with hardbound reissues of his older titles in a uniform edition. Bradbury had found a pioneering form of this relationship in his Ballantine editions of *Fahrenheit 451* and *The October Country*, but Ballantine was unable to sustain this kind of versatility and returned to a predominantly paperback operation. But in the early 1990s, Lou Aronica of Avon made Bradbury an offer he could not refuse. Avon would guarantee that his back titles would remain in print and established both a small-format hardbound series and a large-format trade-paperback series that covered all the Doubleday and Knopf volumes in Bradbury's canon that were no longer in print beyond the Bantam mass-market paperbacks. And Avon would publish full-size hardbound editions of all new Bradbury titles.

Knopf understood the magnitude of this offer and gave Bradbury full support in his transition.[42] The change would result in three more story collections during the sixth decade of his professional career. Throughout the 1990s, he would pursue a wide range of short fiction, not only writing new stories but also turning to a number of the manuscripts that Albright had reconstructed from Bradbury's oldest surviving files. *Quicker Than the Eye* (1996) contains twenty-one selections, and thirteen of these are stories first written in the 1940s and 1950s. "The Electrocution" is a circus story that actually reached print in earlier times, but the other twelve are recovered manuscripts completed and published between 1994 and 1996. A year later Bradbury brought out *Driving Blind*, another well-received collection that includes eleven older stories along with ten others developed from manuscripts and published in 1997 (see table 13).

One of the older stories is "That Old Dog Lying in the Dust," which has its origins in a trip through Mexican border towns nearly a year before his major mask-collecting trip deep into Mexico with Grant Beach. During the winter of 1944–1945, he offered to write an article for *Argosy* on a Mexican circus he had encountered, "one of the most intrigueing [*sic*], hilarious, outre circuses I've ever seen . . . which is a microscopic satire on our huge American tent shows."[43] Decades later the essay appeared in *Westways* (October 1974) as "Mexicali Mirage" before Bradbury finally turned it into fiction. The story is remarkable for the way in which Bradbury and a traveling friend become enthusiastic participants in a run-down parodic one-ring circus despite the obvious gaffes of the performers and the pathetic appearance of a yawning lion. In its welcoming celebration of the muscled woman, Lucy-Lucretia, who is the show's central performer, the story literally carnivalizes carnival. It stands in contrast to "The Last Circus," a story with equally old roots that Bradbury had collected a decade earlier in *The Toynbee Convector*. If "The Last Circus" offers a more nostalgic look at the disappearance of circuses from our culture, "An Old Dog Lying in the Dust" playfully extends this nostalgia into parody.

Bradbury's most recent collection, *One More for the Road* (2002), includes ten older stories and fifteen others published or completed after 1997; one of the older ten, "With Smiles as Wide as Summer," is a short-short in the *Dandelion Wine* tradition written during the mid-1950s and buried in the obscure travel magazine *Clipper* until Nolan discovered it in a Bradbury file drawer in the 1970s. Not surprisingly, five more of the older selections were completed by Bradbury from Albright's manuscript discoveries of forgotten tales. There are important threads connecting many of these recovered stories to larger components of

Bradbury's life of fiction. Bradbury's selection of "Mr. Pale" for *Driving Blind* and "The Enemy in the Wheat" for *One More for the Road* has just such a resonance, for Albright has been able to connect both stories to the original table of contents for *The October Country*. All but four of the new stories intended for that collection were deleted during the spring of 1955; many were soon published and collected, but these two would not be completed for another forty years.

Table 13 offers a recapitulation of the new and old fiction in the six story collections that Bradbury has published since the late 1960s. These volumes pick up nearly all of his stories published after 1963; the dozen or so uncollected stories are mostly nostalgic shorts for noncommercial publications or vignettes that are unlikely to appear in any future Bradbury collections.[44] Of the 129 collected stories of the last three decades, 59 are developed from unfinished manuscripts or published stories of the mid-1940s through the early 1960s. This was the period of Bradbury's rapid development as a master storyteller and included as well his first triumphs as a novelist. Later editors also sensed that those early decades represented Bradbury's most concentrated period of pure creativity. Nancy Nicholas, whose thirteen years as Bradbury's editor exceeded in length even the tenure of Doubleday's Walt Bradbury, has perhaps found the perfect analogy for his kind of genius: "It's like being a musical prodigy or a physicist, I think. . . . The fertile stuff comes when you're still young enough to . . . suspend good sense and let your mind go that way. His mind just took you places that you couldn't imagine."[45] Like a prodigy, Bradbury has never lost the gift of creative genius; but like most geniuses, a particular watershed period underlies and echoes through all that follows.

Without doubt, Bradbury's late-career publication of new stories is deeply grounded in the creative materials generated during the 1940s and 1950s, a time when he had just come into his full power as a uniquely imaginative talent. If the later story collections derive much of their richness from that period, the first fruits of those decades—the five major Doubleday collections—continue to have a commanding presence in the literary marketplace. Bradbury's sense of authorship is perhaps most apparent in the way he has worked to keep these early masterworks in print through several new configurations that have extended their life through a half century of market prominence. His first success took advantage of publicity generated by director François Truffaut's 1966 release of *Fahrenheit 451*. This prompted Simon and Schuster to overcome the general market wariness of reprint editions to bring out a new hardbound edition of the novel shortly after the film's release. (Ballantine, no longer in a position to reprint the original hardbound edition, signed over the rights.) But these events also encouraged another former publisher to bring two Bradbury story collections back into hardbound availability. Doubleday repackaged *The Golden Apples of the Sun* and *A Medicine*

Table 13. Bradbury's rediscovery of his best, unpublished manuscripts of the first two decades of his career is evident from the textual history of his last six story collections. Each story's identifying number, which reveals the year of publication and its ordinal position of publication within that year, is keyed to appendix A. Every collection includes at least one previously published story from Bradbury's earliest period of major-market success, and *Long after Midnight* reflects the care with which Bradbury worked with William F. Nolan to revise many of the best of these that remained uncollected during the mid-1970s. But all the other later collections include a number of previously unpublished stories presented alongside of his newer compositions. The stories revised from older manuscripts include the approximate date of the original draft in parenthesis (those revised from pre-1964 manuscripts or publications are indicated in boldface). Knopf's *The Stories of Ray Bradbury* (1980), a major retrospective compilation of his short fiction to that point, was different in scope and purpose from his periodic story collections and is not included in this table.

Bradbury's Later Story Collections (1969–2002)

Stories revised from pre-1964 manuscripts or publications are indicated in boldface

The Knopf Collections			The Avon/Morrow Collections		
I Sing the Body Electric! (1969)	Long After Midnight (1976)	The Toynbee Convector (1988)	Quicker Than the Eye (1996)	Driving Blind (1997)	One More for the Road (2002)
48–2	**46–5**	**45–4**	**46–13**	**48–12**	**47–15**
48–17	**46–6**	**54–7**	94–1	**93–2 (1948)**	**61–3 (1955)**
49–7	**48–3**	**80–1 (1950)**	**94–2 (1947)**	**95–3 (1950)**	66–3
52–11 (1946)	**50–5**	**80–2 (1950)**	94–5	**97–2 (1960)**	81–1
64–2	**50–7**	**81–2 (1949)**	94–6	97–3	93–1
64–3	**50–21**	**82–1 (1948)**	**95–1 (1950)**	97–4	**94–3 (1949)**
65–1 (1962)	**51–9**	84–1	95–2	**97–5 (1948)**	00–1
66–1	**51–10**	84–2	**95–4 (1959)**	**97–6 (1945)**	00–2
66–4	**52–6**	84–3	95–5	97–7	01–2
67–1 (1949)	**54–5**	84–4	**95–6 (1951)**	97–8	02–1
69–1	**62–5**	84–5	**95–7 (1951)**	**97–9 (1950)**	**02–2 (1947)**
69–2 (1958)	**62–8**	85–1	96–1	**97–10 (1950)**	02–3
69–3	71–1	85–2	**96–2 (1950)**	97–11	**02–4 (1950)**
69–4 (1963)	71–2	87–1	**96–3 (1951)**	97–12	02–5

Table 13. (*continued*)

Bradbury's Later Story Collections (1969–2002)

Stories revised from pre-1964 manuscripts or publications are indicated in boldface

| | The Knopf Collections | | | The Avon/Morrow Collections | |
I Sing the Body Electric! (1969)	Long After Midnight (1976)	The Toynbee Convector (1988)	Quicker Than the Eye (1996)	Driving Blind (1997)	One More for the Road (2002)
69–5 (1962)	72–1	88–1	**96–4 (1948)**	97–13	02–6
69–6	73–1	88–2	**96–5 (1948)**	**97–14 (1950)**	02–7
69–8	73–2	88–3	96–6	97–15	02–8
	75–3	89–4	**96–7 (1950)**	97–16 (1974)	02–9
	76–1	88–5	**96–8 (1950)**	**97–17 (1947)**	02–10
	76–2	**88–6 (1950)**	**96–9 (1949)**	97–18	02–11
	76–3	88–7	96–10	97–19	**02–12 (1950)**
	76–4	**88–8 (1949)**			02–13
		88–9			02–14
					02–15
					02–16 (1949)

for Melancholy in a single volume and retitled these forty-four collected stories *Twice Twenty-Two*. The small trade edition soon went out of print, but the book club edition remained in stock through periodic reprintings into the early 1970s.

The mass market Bantam paperback editions have always represented the fundamental market resource for Bradbury's Doubleday titles. Innovative packaging, such as the boxed sets *Six Masterpieces of Tomorrow* (1969) and *The Best of Ray Bradbury* (1976), helped keep most of the collections available in paperback. But by the 1980s, only *The Illustrated Man* remained in print, and Bantam convinced Bradbury to permit combined editions of the other collections in a two-volume concept titled *Classic Stories 1 and 2* (1990). The idea was to combine *The Golden Apples of the Sun* with *R Is for Rocket* as volume 1 and *A Medicine for Melancholy* with *S Is for Space* as volume 2. Since the two young-reader volumes were derived in part from the earlier story collections, Bantam would be able to cut the redundant pieces. The editors worked out a complicated scheme to make sure that the fourteen stories duplicated between the four volumes could be eliminated as the four were collapsed into two. Unfortunately, there was a major problem with the first volume. As appendix A documents in greater detail, the editors somehow dropped "The Golden Apples of the Sun" completely; only the little sun peeking out of the cover of volume 1 remained. This error was not corrected until the third printing, when the entire second half of the book was reset and repaginated. In the process Bradbury's original introduction to *R Is for Rocket*, which had been useful as an internal divider between what was left of the two collections in the first two printings, was eliminated, perhaps to compensate in some small way for the increased size of the third and subsequent printings.

This concept was confusing enough for bibliographers and longtime Bradbury readers, but Avon's late-1990s trade-paperback alternative was even trickier. Its contents are identical to *Classic Stories 1 and 2*, but the Bantam series title is dropped completely. Instead, Avon marketed these volumes as *The Golden Apples of the Sun and Other Stories* (1997) and *A Medicine for Melancholy and Other Stories* (1998). These titles further obscure the relationship between the four original collections and essentially dismember the young-reader books entirely. A third volume extends this series where no Bradbury conflation has gone before. *I Sing the Body Electric! and Other Stories* (1998) includes the title collection complete but slips in the first half of *Long after Midnight* (eleven selections) as *and Other Stories*. The genealogical chart of these variations in table 14 suggests that the overall confusion is perhaps a small price to pay for quality large-format paperbacks that, in concert with the Avon hardbound editions and the rack-size Ballantine and Bantam paperbacks, provide accessible editions for nearly all of Bradbury's significant fiction. Of his major press fiction releases, only *The Machineries of Joy* remains unavailable today.

But nine of the selections from *The Machineries of Joy* are available within the largest of Bradbury's collections, *The Stories of Ray Bradbury* (1980). In fact, this compilation and its forerunner, *The Vintage Bradbury* (1965), are still in print today. It is important to remember that his sense of authorship also includes these two carefully planned backward glances at his career as a storyteller. This is the third and final category of Bradbury's short-fiction publications, one that embraces the periodic collections as well as the young-reader series. Of all of Bradbury's fiction volumes, only these two are immutable—he has shown no inclination to tamper with the contents of either. They are his only true time capsules in fiction, and one can draw useful conclusions from a brief look at the way they were assembled.

Bantam's Saul David first approached Bradbury and Don Congdon with the idea for a selected compilation in the fall of 1959.[46] Science fiction collections in general were slumping at that time, and although *The Martian Chronicles* and *The Illustrated Man* continued to be perennial sellers for Bantam, later collections were not projecting well. David suggested to Congdon that a Bradbury compilation of his best work would boost the general market and stimulate sales of his own earlier books. Bradbury had edited two very successful multiple-author anthologies for Bantam, but he had not yet settled on an approach to take with his own work. Five years later he would be able to draw from a half-dozen collections and decided to bring the sense of pleasure and wonder he felt for his publications to this unfamiliar task. He opted to avoid any sense of locking in a rigid process of selection. Fifteen years later he would work with Knopf's Bob Gottlieb and Nancy Nicholas to survey the full range of his best stories, but for *The Vintage Bradbury*, he was selective in a way that more accurately reveals his own personal favorites through the mid-1960s. There are few surprises here; most of his favorites have been discussed by Bradbury in various introductions, articles, and interviews. Three of his four most-often-anthologized stories—"The Fog Horn," "There Will Come Soft Rains," and "The Small Assassin"—appear here; "A Sound of Thunder" is the only top anthologized title omitted from this volume, but it appears in seven other Bradbury collections.

The Vintage Bradbury includes pieces from every one of his earlier story collections and three of his four book-length fictions—including three chapters from *The Martian Chronicles* ("Ylla," "Night Meeting," and "There Will Come Soft Rains") and four from *Dandelion Wine* ("Illumination," "Dandelion Wine," "Statues," and "Green Wine for Dreaming"). These selections serve as a reminder that, even as revised and bridged for these novelized story cycles, the component chapters remain essentially self-contained stories. Even *Fahrenheit 451* was initially marketed as a story collection, and one of its two original companion stories ("And the Rock Cried Out") is included here. But the remaining eighteen stories

Table 14. Bradbury has managed to keep nearly all of his fantasy and science fiction collections in print by working with Bantam and Avon to repackage some of them in larger configurations. The genealogy of the various commercial editions is outlined above for the older fantasy and science fiction collections. His two retrospective compilations, *The Vintage Bradbury* (1965) and *The Stories of Ray Bradbury* (1980), are not shown here; they have never been out of print. Selections from *The Machineries of Joy* are available in these two volumes. Publishing data courtesy of Ray Bradbury and Donn Albright.

Bradbury's F&SF Story Collections

Timeline	1950	1955	1960	1965	1970	1975	1980	1985	1990	1995	2000
The Illustrated Man (1951)											
Doubleday (hb)											
Bantam (pb)											
Avon (hb)											
The Golden Apples of the Sun (1953)											
Doubleday (hb)											
Bantam (pb)				*Twice 22*					*Classic Stories 1*		
Avon (trade pb)							*The Golden Apples of the Sun and Other Stories*				
A Medicine for Melancholy (1959)											
Doubleday (hb)											
Bantam (pb))				*Twice 22*					*Classic Stories 2*		
Avon (trade pb)							*A Medicine for Melancholy and Other Stories*				
R Is for Rocket (1962)											
Doubleday (hb)											
Bantam (pb)									*Classic Stories 1*		
Avon (trade pb)							*The Golden Apples of the Sun and Other Stories*				
The Machineries of Joy (1964)											
Simon and Schuster (hb)											
Bantam (pb)											
Timeline	1950	1955	1960	1965	1970	1975	1980	1985	1990	1995	2000

Table 14. (continued)

Timeline	1950	1955	1960	1965	1970	1975	1980	1985	1990	1995	2000

S Is for Space (1966)
Doubleday (hb)
Bantam (pb) — *Classic Stories 2*
Avon (trade pb) — *A Medicine for Melancholy and Other Stories*

I Sing the Body Electric! (1969)
Knopf (hb)
Bantam (pb)
Avon (trade pb) — *I Sing the Body Electric! and Other Stories*

Long after Midnight (1976)
Knopf (hb)
Bantam (pb)
Avon (trade pb, first eleven stories only) — *I Sing the Body Electric! and Other Stories*

The Toynbee Convector (1988)
Knopf (hb)
Bantam (pb)

Timeline	1950	1955	1960	1965	1970	1975	1980	1985	1990	1995	2000

in *Vintage Bradbury* showcase the five story collections of the 1950s, which have come to represent his best sustained work: *The Illustrated Man* (three), *The Golden Apples of the Sun* (five), *The October Country* (three), *A Medicine for Melancholy* (four), and the widely divergent British version of the latter, *The Day It Rained Forever* (one). *The October Country* carried forward fifteen stories from *Dark Carnival*, Bradbury's first story collection; but only two of these older works ("Skeleton" and "The Small Assassin") were favored enough to make it into *Vintage Bradbury*. Only one, "The Anthem Sprinters," appears from *The Machineries of Joy*, perhaps indicating the relative weakness of that collection but possibly reflecting a decision not to interfere with the most recent collection's marketability. The original story "The Illustrated Man," rather than the more famous framing prologue-epilogue of *Illustrated Man*, is the only previously uncollected story among the twenty-six selections. The *Dandelion Wine* story-chapters are grouped in the middle of the compilation, but there are no other chronological or bibliographical patterns in the sequence of the others.

The introduction by Gilbert Highet offers one of the most glowing appreciations of Bradbury's work ever written, but it is also concise, to the point, and compelling. Highet identifies the hallmarks of Bradbury's creative individuality—his style: "A curious mixture of poetry and colloquialism"; his subjects: "Whatever they are, they are not realistic. But they are human"; and his relationship to the genre: fantasy and speculative themes in transition, "dreams turning out true, truth dissolving into dreams," and the adult world "transformed into exciting and sometimes appalling fantasy in the minds of children." Highet offers one of the best brief arguments against labeling Bradbury a science fiction writer: "He knows little about science; he cares even less. He is a visionary. Technology he scarcely admires and scarcely uses. If it occupies his mind at all, it is not as a convenience or a source of extra muscle-power, but as a possible extension of the abilities of the human spirit."[47] Most significantly, Highet attempts to situate Bradbury's work within a Western fantasy tradition that includes Aristophanes, Lucian, Villiers de l'Isle-Adam, Poe, Wells, Kipling, Barrie, and Kafka. In Highet's estimation, Bradbury's fantasies enlarge rather than degrade human life and span the full subject range—cosmic horrors, tortuous puzzles, future utopias, and boyhood memories—of his predecessors.

This introduction frames *The Vintage Bradbury* and thus sets it off from any of Bradbury's periodic story collections before or since. Highet's remarks, while stressing the unique individuality of Bradbury's authorship, also situate him in the "great time" of the Western fantasy tradition. No longer was he simply to be understood as a writer concerned merely with contemporary problems, but one whose writings had deep historical roots in fantasy literature of previous literary epochs. Highet even suggests that Bradbury's stories really take place in "the world of the spirit." This deep rooting in the past of the human spirit, in Highet's view, also gave Bradbury his literary future and the possibility of meanings in his works that were not yet fully realized: "He has been misunderstood. He has been underestimated. He will gain a wider and more thoughtful public than he had at first; and his work will last." Highet points at the carnival ambivalence of meanings in Bradbury still to be discovered when he says that the author is *both* "a pessimist and an optimist." He implies that future readers will need to understand these aspects of Bradbury's authorship if they are to grasp his uniqueness as a writer. Bradbury's literary reputation has continued to grow, of course, even if the misunderstanding of his works still occasionally occurs.

Fifteen years later Bradbury would have much more distance between himself and his earlier work. As the 1970s drew to a close, he was completing a decade in which he had published only seven major-market stories and only fourteen in all. He still had his favorites, but now he could see more clearly those that were truly significant in his development as a writer. His great popularity among publishers and educators had led to an impressive number of commercial anthology and textbook appearances, and he was thus able to see which stories had come to be regarded as "essential Bradbury" in a cultural context. In the end he combined all these perspectives and decided to be as inclusive as possible. Bradbury characteristically extended the decision-making process to the editors he had come to trust at Knopf, Bob Gottlieb and Nancy Nicholas. They found a surprising degree of agreement in the selections, but then they were all building a volume with an eye toward establishing a canon that would have the widest possible appeal. Readers would always forgive the inclusion of a lesser tale, but they would never forgive the exclusion of a time-tested favorite.

In the end *The Stories of Ray Bradbury* became a "light" version of every story collection he had ever fashioned from his first four decades as a professional writer. Through this defining look back, it is possible to see a remarkable consistency in quality as his career opens in *Dark Carnival* and the collections that follow. Even more than twenty years after it release, there is no sense of premature closure to the compilation. A reader familiar with Bradbury's individual books can discern from this single volume that the first quarter century of his career has produced the most enduring work. In 1980 the one hundred selections in *The Stories of Ray Bradbury* represented one-third of his total output of short fiction to that time (excluding rewrites, retitlings, and the integration of certain stories into story cycles and novels). Bradbury has since published another hundred stories, prompting him to bring out a third compilation, *Bradbury Stories* (2003). Yet today, marketed only in the expensive first hardbound edition, *The Stories of Ray Bradbury* continues to sell. And it has never been out of print. As a consequence, *Bradbury Stories* was designed as a companion rather than a replacement—it surveys nearly six full decades of Bradbury's fiction, but there is no duplication between the two volumes.

The Stories of Ray Bradbury received one prominent review by Thomas M. Disch, himself a science fiction writer of the "New Wave" and author of a history of science fiction, in *The New York Times Book Review*.[48] The review is full of the deliberate misunderstandings that still plague Bradbury's reception as a science fiction author. Sarcastic to the point of insult about Bradbury's status as a writer of serious science fiction (Disch has elsewhere compared Bradbury to childlike comedian Pee-wee Herman) and entitled "Tops in Brand Name Recognition," Disch's review focuses entirely on the stories brought forward to the new collection from pulp origins in *Weird Tales,* such as "The Night" and especially "The Black Ferris," which he subjects to an abusive reading. He parts company with Bradbury's view of himself as an enthusiastic carnival entertainer and presents him as one who masks inferior writing and false naiveté: "There's the choice—love Ray Bradbury, out there beyond embarrassment, or be enrolled among those loveless, zestless critics who never go to the circus." Disch's review is an exact historical reversal of Highet's concerns. He makes no attempt to consider the finer pieces collected in the volume and simply ends by saying that Bradbury is not in the same league as fantasy writers such as Hans Christian Andersen or A. A. Milne. Disch's review should probably be read as an attempt to decrown Bradbury as the king of science fiction writers, a title that he never really acceded to anyway. It is a hasty piece of carnival abuse—"Only readers who would profess Rod McKuen to be America's greatest poet, or Kahlil Gibran its noblest philosopher, could unblushingly commend Mr. Bradbury's stories as literature"—directed at Bradbury's image in the publishing field and not a considered attempt to assess the larger significance of his writings or how they might carnivalize genres.

Critics aside, an examination of the textual record contained beneath the surface of every one of his collections is quite revealing. The continuing popularity of *The Stories of Ray Bradbury,* as well as the significant proportion of previously uncollected and even unpublished early stories in the collections of the last three decades, implies that the first twenty years of his life of fiction produced an incredibly rich wellspring of creativity that continues to resonate in his work of the new century. Such textual evidence underlies an even more remarkable phenomena of book culture—Bradbury has been able to keep an incredible range of his fiction in print for successive generations of readers (table 15). The continuing availability of the best of his weird fiction through *The October Country* is only slightly less remarkable than his ability to keep Avon and Morrow, Bantam, and millions of readers committed to his five major Doubleday collections after all these years. In their various forms, all of his periodic fantasy and

Table 15. The table identifies the number of stories or story-chapters shared between Bradbury's story collections and his novelized story cycles; the latter category includes *The Martian Chronicles* (MC), *Dandelion Wine* (DW), *Green Shadows, White Whale* (GS), and *From the Dust Returned* (FDR). The total number of stories in each source volume is indicated under the title abbreviation at the top of the respective column. Many of these stories were revised or rewritten from magazine appearances (see appendix A for a story-by-story listing of publication). Those shared between two or more Bradbury books were all reconfigured, and many were revised or rewritten yet again for the later collections and novels. A story may appear in a number of later volumes; for instance, the table shows that the twenty-seven stories first collected in *Dark Carnival* (DC) appear sixty-two times in later Bradbury works. The novel *Fahrenheit 451* (*F451*) appears here because it was originally published as a story collection with two short stories; these two appear a total of three times in later collections.

Intertextuality of Bradbury's Stories and Book Chapters

	DC 27	MC 15	IM 19	GA 22	F451 2	OC 19	DW 19	MM 22	DRF 23	RR 17	MJ 21	SS 16	IS 17	LAM 22	SRB 100	TC 23
OC	OC 15															
DW	DW 1															
DRF	DRF 1			DRF 18	DRF 1											
RR	RR 1		RR 4	RR 3			RR 2	RR 4	RR 1							
SA	SA 13					SA [13]										
MJ									MJ 1							
VB	VB 2	VB 3	VB 3	VB 5	VB 1	VB 2	VB 4	VB 4	VB 1		VB 1					
T22				T22 22				T22 22								
SS	SS 1	SS 1	SS 2	SS 4			SS 1	SS 3			SS 1					
SRB	SRB 16	SRB 6	SRB 10	SRB 14	SRB 1	SRB 1	SRB 4	SRB 12		SRB 1	SRB 9	SRB 1	SRB 9	SRB 11		
DT				DT 2							DT 1					
MeM	MeM 2															
TC	TC 1															
CSJ	CSJ 1		CSJ 4	CSJ 18			CSJ 2	CSJ 3	CSJ 1	CSJ 2						
CS2		CS2 1	CS2 2	CS2 3			CS2 1	CS2 19			CS2 1	CS2 4				
GS								GS 2			GS 2		GS 3	GS 1	GS 1	GS 2
IS&OS													IS&OS 17	IS&OS 11		
FDR	FDR 2			FDR 1												FDR 2
BS	BS 7	BS 6	BS 6	BS 6	BS 1	BS 5	BS 5	BS 5	BS 5	BS 4	BS 7	BS 8	BS 7	BS 9		BS 12
	62	17	31	96	4	21	19	74	9	7	22	13	36	32	1	16

science fiction collections (and the ever available Vintage and Knopf compilations of his best stories) have kept more than three hundred Bradbury stories in print. Coupled with the new Avon compilation and the continuing availability of all his major book-length fiction, these short-story collections fill out a remarkably extensive legacy of productivity that is both culturally significant in its popular appeal and deeply literary in its underlying form.

Thematics

A textual survey of the major story collections reveals three extended short stories, often called novellas by his original pulp editors, that move toward novelization of his ideas. They represent a significant point of evolution between short and long fiction; Bradbury developed them to a certain length beyond the short-story template that his fictions usually settled into, but only the last one—"The Fireman"—reached its full potential in a novel. The others reached novelistic potential in other genres. "The Creatures That Time Forgot," eventually "Frost and Fire," appeared as a short film, *The Quest,* and was later published as a graphic novel adapted by DC Comics (with Bradbury's approval but without his active participation). "Pillar of Fire," written between the other two, was evolved by Bradbury into the title piece of one of his first collections of stage plays.

"Pillar of Fire" clearly manifests textual and thematic carnivalization. Since a detailed thematic study of Bradbury's story collections is beyond the scope of this study, let us instead examine how carnivalization, intertextuality, and authorship all interact in the context of this extended story, which is also one of the longest he has written (comprising forty pages in *S Is for Space* and originally published in *Planet Stories* [1948]). It is a work rich in pulp imagination, with the transgressive bodily images associated with carnival prominently displayed. It has on that account perhaps few "literary" qualities, but it is remarkable for its politics of the revolutionary outsider. To situate this politics of fantasy, one may compare Nietzsche's ideas to those of Mikhail Bakhtin and carnival, both of whom contrast a stifling official culture with a vital unofficial one. Nietzsche's recuperation of the Dionysian parallels Bakhtin's recuperation of the forbidden, the repressed, the grotesque, and the noncanonical. Both celebrate the body not as a self-contained system delineated by the ego, but as the site of dispersion and multiplicity. In addition, the idea of a "corpse carnival," the notion that life and death are one ambivalent theme in Bradbury, comes into play here. All of these aspects of carnivalization become thematic concerns in this story.

In "Pillar of Fire" the Apollonian sun of rationality and the Dionysian dark side of the mind encounter one another, as they often do in Bradbury's fantasy, only this time the encounter takes the form of a bitter social struggle that ends in the death of the imagination. The theme of madness as a strategy of resistance is unusual in a pulp context (which aims primarily at entertainment), but Bradbury deemed this story important enough to rework it into a successful play because of its theme, and indeed, the play is something of a warning about the death of the imagination in contemporary technological society. It remains the closest Bradbury has ever come in his published fiction to the creation of an abject hero and a bitter carnival.

According to Bradbury, it was a rehearsal for *Fahrenheit 451*. But the protagonists are reverse images of each other: Montag, who is trying to stop burning, is reversed in William Lantry, the last dead man "reborn" into an antiseptically clean, utopian society that has destroyed his grave and all other graveyards on Earth. Lantry is obsessed to the point of extreme paranoia with burning down this society. The fact that both stories involve the suppression of works of fantastic fiction is a strong parallel, but still, Bradbury's protagonist in "Pillar of Fire" realizes only belatedly that he is the last person remembering all the old books of fantasy and imagination and that with his death, they die also. Besides, Lantry is essentially motivated, until almost the end of the story, by the spirit of revenge, something Nietzsche hoped to deliver man from.[49]

In order to bring out the all-important political aspects of fantasy in this story, we draw on the work of Gilles Deleuze and Felix Guattari, French anti-Freudians, to discuss the political implications of madness or delirium.[50] Although their critical vocabulary is often strange and even a bit bizarre, they acknowledge they were preceded in their ideas by literary authors, many of whom they mention in their study. Deleuze and Guattari see no serious objection to using terms inherited from psychiatry in order to characterize social investments of the unconscious, provided these terms are stripped of the familial connotations that would make them into simple projections. What is important to them is that delirium be recognized as having a primarily social content.

At first glance Deleuze and Guattari may seem to present a rather simplistic model of the activities of desire in the social field. But in investigating the relationship between the two poles of delirium, paranoia and schizophrenia, Deleuze and Guattari are quick to point out that doubtless there are astonishing oscillations of the unconscious from one extreme to the other. A revolutionary group can turn fascist, and fascism can, in turn, give rise to revolutionary or nomadic desires. Fortunately, they give many literary examples to support their argument, drawing frequently on fantasy and horror writers and on utopian novels (Bradbury's story "The Veldt," from *The Illustrated Man*, is briefly discussed as an example of group fantasy).

They make the interesting assertion that it is the destiny of American literature to be initially a crossing of limits and frontiers, causing deterritorialized flows of desire to circulate only to recode this flow along the shores of moralizing, Puritan, and "familialist" territories. The classic case of this kind of authorship seems to be Jack Kerouac, who initially took such a nomadic voyage out (especially in *On the Road)*, but who ended by affirming—against radicals and friends of the 1950s such as Alan Ginsberg—the dream of a Great America and the racial superiority of his French Breton ancestors. Bradbury's story of authorship here moves in the opposite direction, constructing a paranoid narrative that eventually moves toward the schizo-revolutionary pole of carnivalization.

"Pillar of Fire" evokes familiar themes and figures from pulp horror and science fiction, especially the zombie, which it subjects to a thoroughly carnivalized interpretation: zombies are usually depicted as inarticulate automatons, the subhuman slaves of others, and not as having revolutionary potential. It seems designed to make readers hesitate between a supernatural and a scientific explanation of the uncanny events that happen when William Lantry rises from the grave in the year 2349 A.D. Is Lantry really one of the walking dead, or is he an extraordinary case of suspended animation? The reader suspects from the outset that he is a zombie and has these suspicions confirmed at the end. Appropriately, the story is set in Salem—prime Puritan territory with a history of persecution of witches—where the last graveyard had been preserved as a tourist attraction by the government as a reminder of a barbaric custom. But now this graveyard too (as well as alien tombs on Mars; the story intertextually evokes Bradbury's Martian stories) is scheduled by authorities for destruction. The state seeks thereby to make absolute its control over the world of darkness, death, and decay and over all writers whose imaginations are attracted to it. We learn from Lantry's visit to a library that the Great Burning of 2265 destroyed all of the "unclean" writings of the past, including the works of Poe, Lovecraft, and Ambrose Bierce, among others. Lantry realizes with a shock that if he is destroyed, all memory of such literature will be destroyed as well, for he is the last person, or rather the last *dead* person, to remember them.

The society Lantry is reborn into could be described in Nietzschean terms as an extreme Apollonian culture, as is evident from the symbolism it employs. It worships the sun of rationality, emblazoned everywhere on public buildings. The dead of this society are burned in a centralized rite, in incinerators that are warm, cozy temples where soothing music plays and the fear of death is abolished through ceremonies that deify fire (here the story intertextually evokes "The Fireman" and *Fahrenheit 451*). As Lantry watches the operation of the Salem Incinerator, slowly the golden coffins of the dead roll in, covered with sun symbols, and after a brief ceremony they are cast into a flue. On the altar are written the words "We that are born of the sun return to the sun," a reversal of the words normally spoken at Christian burials, where the meaning of the earth is at least partially evoked.

It is these gigantic incinerators as myths of an Apollonian culture that Lantry wants to explode and carnivalize (he repeatedly compares his efforts to destroy them as reinaugurating the Fourth of July). Because deviant behavior is not expected, he manages to infiltrate the Salem Incinerator and destroy it easily, killing hundreds of people in the surrounding towns. He hopes thereby to effect a revolution, to "manufacture friends" by creating more walking dead. But in this rational world, the dead remain dead. Because they never imagined while living that the dead might walk, they cannot be resurrected by Lantry's magical procedures. He draws symbols of long-dead sorcerers on the floor of the makeshift morgue next to the bodies and chants his own magic formulas, all to no avail. Eventually, he is picked up by the authorities and is interrogated by a man named McClure, who is this century's version of a psychoanalyst and something of a detective as well. McClure tries to analyze his mortified behavior, his paleness and lack of breath, as a self-induced psychosis but is himself slowly unnerved when he finds that Lantry is the real thing, one of the walking dead.

He is a logical impossibility to a mind such as McClure's. After a brief struggle in which Lantry tries to murder McClure, he is subdued and condemned to a second death by the state, a death that is also the death of every fantastic writer in history, for only Lantry remembers them. If this were a Christian fantasy in the mode of J. R. R. Tolkien or C. S. Lewis, the evident compassion of McClure for his victim would have resulted in his conversion to the imagination at the end, thereby saving the hero. But no, Bradbury really wants us to feel the shock of seeing the imagination die forever, and on this level of response, the story is quite effective. The second death, the death of the imagination, becomes more terrible than physical death.

Bradbury's "Pillar of Fire" clearly does invest the social field in a manner described in the *Anti-Oedipus*. Thematically, it is constituted by a delirious oscillation between the two poles of the unconscious that Deleuze and Guattari describe. But Bradbury's fantasy goes in a direction opposite to that which they ascribe to American literature, that is, from paranoia to schizophrenia (these terms are not meant in the clinical sense but only designate different investments of the social field). If the task of their "schizoanalysis" is to learn—sometimes with help from literary texts—what desiring machines are, how they work in investing the social field, then Bradbury's story has much to tell. The passage quoted below is an investment of the first type, the paranoiac pole, which emerges from what Deleuze and Guattari call "the body without organs" (the term actually comes from the writings of Antonin Artaud). The body without organs is the social field initially inhabited only by molecular desiring-machines on its surface.

In Bradbury's story it is represented by dead bodies that the state is attempting to eliminate:

> Hatred was a blood in him, it went up down around and through, up down around and through. It was a heart in him, not beating, true, but warm. He was—what? Resentment. Envy. They said he could not lie any longer in his coffin in the cemetery. He had *wanted to.* He had never had any particular desire to get up and walk around. It had been enough, all these centuries, to lie in the deep box and feel, but *not feel* the ticking of the million insect watches in the earth around, the moves of worms like so many deep thoughts in the soil.
>
> But then they had come and said, "Out you go and into the furnace!" And that is the worst thing you can say to any man. You cannot tell him what to do. . . . They had given birth to him with all their practices and ignorances.[51]

Lantry arises from the catatonic body without organs because a fascisizing and sovereign state apparatus has selected him and subjected him to its will. His delirium—which intensifies in a passage we have omitted—begins as a direct investment of the social field. He was perfectly content to remain a body without organs himself, swarming with worms and bacilli, "not feeling the ticking of the million insect watches (the desiring machines) in the earth around" him. But the fascisizing machine tears up the body of the earth, divides it up into new territories and structures. And so Lantry becomes a reactive paranoid, and this is exactly how Bradbury directs that the character should be played in the stage version of the story.[52]

As Deleuze and Guattari point out, the body without organs is the model of death; it is not death that serves as the model of catatonia. In their opinion, horror authors have understood this very well.[53] There is no real death in the unconscious, only carnivalized flows of desire between desiring machines. Lantry's behavior, according to them, would be the political behavior of the paranoid, consisting in the organizing of masses and packs. The paranoid manipulates crowds; he opposes them to one another, maneuvers them. This is clearly what Lantry intends to do, hanging around the makeshift morgue where the dead bodies have been laid out in rows on the ground, hoping to resurrect and mobilize them into an army of the dead against the state, which has banished the word "dead" from the language.

In the end Lantry realizes that his war machine had no hope of ever materializing. But when McClure tells him that he will die of loneliness anyway because he is a freak, one of a kind, we pass to the schizophrenic pole. But Lantry, in a moment of extreme carnivalization, realizes that he himself is a crowd of people, both fictional and real. The passage accompanying this schizophrenic voyage is too lengthy to quote in full, but after saying that he is Poe and Bierce and a host of other fantastic creatures besides, Lantry goes on to add: "I am a mask, a skull mask behind an oak tree on the last day of October. I am a poison apple bobbing in a water tub for child noses to bump at, for child teeth to snap . . . I am a black candle lighted before an inverted cross. I am a coffin lid, a sheet with eyes, a foot-step on a black stairwell. I am Dunsany and Machen and I am the Legend of Sleepy Hollow. I am the Monkey's Paw and I am the Phantom Rickshaw. I am the Cat and the Canary, the Gorilla, the Bat. I am the ghost of Hamlet's father on the castle wall."[54]

The full list contains many names in the literary history of the fantastic, and the name of the father—that is, Hamlet's father on the castle wall—which ends the delirium, is just another name among many (but Bradbury always seems to want to discover his authorship in relation to Shakespeare his father). In addition, this corpse carnival of masks affirms a host of depersonalized part-objects and intensities that connect the flows of desire to organs and desiring machines such as the apple and the child's teeth that bite it. Through his masks, Lantry (and by implication Bradbury himself) finds a way to affirm a multiplicity of identities in the true Dionysian manner. However negative his situation may be, his desires flow outside the structures of the state's Apollonian model of death, with no apparent desire to return and be represented in it. He had wanted to escape to Mars, where tombs still existed. As a carnival-schizo-revolutionary, Lantry believes that escape may still be possible, even at this extreme point. But his body is given to the incinerators while he imagines being walled up in the catacomb of Poe's "The Cask of Amontillado." (Poe's story of revenge is set during carnival time, as Bakhtin points out in one of his few discussions of thematic carnivalization in the short-story form; "Usher II" in *The Martian Chronicles* also uses this story, but in a thematically reversed way.) His existence ends with a wild scream and "much laughter." Withdrawal, saying I am not of your kind (of the superior Apollonian race), but one who belongs eternally to the inferior race (the freaks), sweeps away social masks on leaving or, at least, can cause a piece of the system to get lost in the shuffle. Here carnivalization and intertextuality are agents of fear, but that is entirely appropriate since fear is creative, "the thing against which man built all his lanterned cities and his many children." What matters is to break through the rigidity of social walls, to make society *afraid* again.

There is an emotional intensity to this story that goes quite beyond the play of "signifires" and linguistic representations. "Pillar of Fire" provides a good example of the ways in which Bradbury's fantasy directly invests the social field with desire while playing off of different genres (in this case, horror, science fiction, and detective fiction) in order to create a sense of dislocation in the reader. This experience of delirium has two major poles of investment. Instead of a linguistic structure, Deleuze and Guattari find the unconscious to be a kind of Nietzschean flux, manifesting astonishing oscillations from one pole of delirium to the other. In their view, it is not Oedipal structures, the name of the father, which is invested by the unconscious, but every name in history.[55]

This story is so emblematic of the situation of authorship in the fantastic after Freud that an argument could be made that it self-consciously carnivalizes the very idea (argued by Tzvetan Todorov) that fantastic literature arises from the absence of a referent in the real world: "Labels without referents you cry! . . . Frankly, I don't believe in you either," says Lantry with scorn when he thinks of the violence already done to creatures of the imagination such as vampires, zombies, and ghosts by the normalized citizens of this society.[56] In Bradbury's story, however, Lantry really *is* dead but thinks of the people who inhabit this utopia without imagination as completely dead, deader than he ever was, because they do not know that their culture is founded on the carnival ambivalence of light and dark, life and death.

"Pillar of Fire," a story that was almost included in *The Illustrated Man* but was dropped because of length, reflects Bradbury's growing concerns in the late 1940s and early 1950s with the politics of authorship in the fantastic. Facing an increasingly rationalized culture that tended to put fantasy and science fiction at its margins, Bradbury invented a story in which the death of the imagination is given real force and a certain cultural priority over literal death. Bradbury carnivalizes the science fiction genre by inverting and inserting themes from horror: a mortified zombie becomes a hero and bearer of revolutionary potential when he realizes that he is the last "living" person to remember the great works of the fantastic and their authors. This literature represents the story's intertextual field, which in the last pages becomes the multiple masks of the hero, Lantry. But does he, in effect, achieve a kind of victory by making the citizens of this utopia afraid of the dark again? Does he dismantle their Apollonian myths? Are the regenerative effects of a true literary carnival in evidence?

This is, indeed, partly the case, because of the way in which the story evokes the presence of carnival through its use of intertextuality. It is forced to evoke such literary meanings as it has (intertextually and allusively) because of its pulp origins. When we restore the literary intertext, however, we realize that the second death, the death of the imagination, is staged within the context of Poe's "The Cask of Amontillado." Bradbury is taking what was obviously a personal story by Poe (psychoanalytic critics usually read it as the entombing of his own fearful unconscious desires) and making it directly invest the social field. Undoubtedly, the story expresses real emotions and concerns on Bradbury's part, but it tries to turn his fears against those who would do the entombing: the repressive state and its surrogates (the detective and psychoanalyst McClure), and to unmask them.

At this length, and in this pulp context, it is hard to develop the ambivalent and nuanced play of themes associated with literary carnival in a novel. Still, the story does achieve a certain regenerative effect in its language. Although Lantry says (to himself, but dialogically to others he wants to frighten and to have taste the morbid wine of the fantastic), "One more drink, dear friends, of Amontillado, before the burning." In fact, in this "catacomb" where he is to be metaphorically entombed, he realizes that "there is no bottle of Amontillado," and there is not in Poe's story, either; it is just a lure used by Montresor to ensnare his drunken victim. So the story works through a thematic series: burial, disentombment, burial (entombment), except that the final return to the earth will not be allowed, the cycle of life growing out of death being destroyed by fire. This is a story in which the meaning of the earth (figured in other stories as dandelion wine) will be cut short, entirely forgotten, due to the efforts of social reformers.

In terms of authorship, Bradbury now sees this story as a rehearsal for *Fahrenheit 451*. Indeed, in both stories he uses his heroes to rage against attempts by social reformers to suppress the imagination. The difference is Bradbury's hero Montag *searches* for the meaning of the earth—a much longer philosophical quest—whereas Lantry *is* the meaning of the earth, come back to haunt the graveless society. He already embodies the meaning. So the two figures are closely related. Montag is the one who wants to discover and save; Lantry is what needs to be saved. The intermediate form of the extended short story, or novella, works fine for Lantry, but Bradbury needed the longer space of the novel to fully explore the effects of mass culture on the carnival tradition (which survives as a simulacrum in *Fahrenheit*), and to have his hero discover the meaning of the earth for himself. In this way two of Bradbury's three early novellas were points of exploration in the carnivalization of genres that he would develop fully in *Something Wicked This Way Comes* and the detective novels of his later years.[57]

8

Conclusions

A Carnival Sense of Life

Throughout this study, we have endeavored to avoid a naive "biographism" in which literary ideas and themes would become mere facts of the author's life. We have focused instead on the story of Bradbury's authorship as it has unfolded in the publishing history and the textual and thematic development of his writings. But, as we have observed, Bradbury's biographical life is deeply connected with the life of folk and popular culture in such forms as carnivals, circuses, and magic shows. By his own account, these were the catalysts that, around the age of thirteen, made him undertake the pursuit of writing. Films were also influential even earlier. *The Phantom of the Opera* and *The Hunchback of Notre Dame*, which he saw at a very young age, were probably Bradbury's earliest exposure to the carnivalized fantastic. These films in the Gothic or romantic tradition confront the viewer with the grotesque body and the dramatic play of masking and unmasking that is at the heart of carnival and of Bradbury's major fiction. Newsreels and exhibitions of Howard Carter's King Tut discoveries also introduced him to the world of mummies and ancient exotic magic, which was to have a profound effect on his imagination. Halloween, which was festively celebrated in Bradbury's family, was clearly an influence on his aesthetic as well.

It seems to have been a very deep-rooted authorial intention of Bradbury from the beginning of his career to write a novel that involved carnival themes and ideas. *The Masks*, his abandoned novel project of the late 1940s, is infused with such concepts. But the remaining fragments of that book show a preoccupation with romantic irony and psychoanalysis, which Bradbury could not sustain for the length of a novel. In the end, the novel was just too "pessimistic" for him. At around the same time (1947), Bradbury was also writing *Where Ignorant Armies Clash by Night*, another novel project imbued with carnival concepts, though in the form of debased social rituals that are intended to ward off the problem of nihilism. It is clear that this project was in many respects a rehearsal for what later became *Fahrenheit 451*. Both of these novels attempted to deal in major form with significant themes in culture and society. They were designed for mainstream publication. Both, however, end with the death of the hero, for Bradbury had not yet found a healthful way to overcome these problems. But he never abandoned his faith in carnival as having great significance for his authorship. The process first appears distinctly in his published works, with the shaping of his first story collection, *Dark Carnival*, a molding that went well past the galley stages of that book, to the exasperation of August Derleth, its publisher. Clearly for Bradbury, the creative process was not over even when it *was* over. *Dark Carnival* also has extensive intertextual and thematic relationships with a book Bradbury did not finish until more than a half century had elapsed, *From the Dust Returned*, which is his most recent exploration of the carnivalesque.

Apart from the direct influences mentioned above, carnival also entered Bradbury's life through literature. Carnivalization was an important feature of much of the literature Bradbury was exposed to at a young age (the Oz books and later Edgar Allen Poe). An important historical and cultural process, carnivalization profoundly shaped the growth and development of the novel, which borrowed the masks of the clown, the fool, and the rogue to establish its position of authorship. We have analyzed how Bradbury expanded on carnivalization as both a textual process and a theme in his writings, contributing to his deepening conception of authorship with each succeeding book. While every novelistic text is necessarily its own model and must be discussed as such, metaphor, myth, and especially masks were global textual processes at work in all of Bradbury's major fiction. His authorial position in each work draws on the masks of carnival as he attempted to solve the aesthetic problem of the whole creation, even affecting such "paratexts" as the covers and the actual physical appearance of his books. Bradbury shares the dust-jacket liner notes with the artist who designed the cover of *Dark Carnival*, George Barrows, and *The Halloween Tree* has masks by Joe Mugnaini as each of its chapter headings.

Carnivalization allowed Bradbury to play imaginatively with the speech genres of carnival life. Various forms of "reduced" laughter such as jokes, parodies, and hyperbolic humor appear early in his fan writings for *Futuria Fantasia* and were well suited to his personality, though not always acceptable to his sought-after publishers (especially the more formulaic pulp magazines) or his friends. Bradbury's correspondence shows some of this language too (as we have been at pains to point out). In their happier moments, Bradbury's letters and manuscripts are often decorated on the margins with carnivalesque figures looking in on the text. One difficulty in understanding his writings has been the role that these carnival elements—especially laughter and masks—play in his aesthetics of fantasy. Bradbury's mature works for the most part do not speak in conceptual categories but in the language of images and metaphors that often need to be "unpacked" for their philosophical content. This stylistic feature of his writings is, in fact, fairly typical of all carnivalized literature. It has earned Bradbury high praise in some literary critical circles, but it has also been a source of difficulty to those who prefer programmatic rationalism in such genres as science fiction.[1]

In other more-tendentious writings such as "Death Warmed Over," where Bradbury's philosophical themes are more directly conceptualized, his metaphors point toward a view of the world in which art is fundamentally discordant with the truth. He has consistently pursued a notion of authorship that holds that the primary function of art is to mask the intolerable truths of life, which need to be revealed in a manageable fashion so that life can be affirmed. This means that the artist must be akin to the entertainer, someone who can construct fantastic fictions (myths) in which we can all believe for awhile. This central notion of his authorship has been stated in many interviews and essays at different times in his career but perhaps nowhere more clearly than this: "We must be entertainers— carnival people, circus people, playwrights, poets, tellers of tales in the streets of Baghdad, we're all of the same family that exists throughout history to explain ourselves to one another."[2] It is a nonexclusive notion of authorship that embraces both Shakespeare, among the great entertainers, and carnival people such as Mr. Electrico as among the most inspiring "authors," all in the same family.

As a matter of fact, Bradbury's ideas about the science fiction author resisting through carnival the "ghettoization" of science fiction by the mainstream have a certain warrant in science-fiction criticism itself. As early as 1953, Anthony Boucher remarked that the distinction between "popular" and "serious" fiction was strictly an invention of the twentieth century, mentioning Shakespeare and Dickens in particular as examples of earlier authors whose texts transcend those very distinctions. According to Boucher, this invidious distinction "would have startled the wits out of any playwright of the greatest period of our language, the Elizabethan Age." Boucher argued that one of the things—and perhaps the main thing, ideologically—supporting this distinction was "a new school of criticism" that dominated the critical journals and English departments of his day and that insisted on a sharp distinction between commercial appeal and literary quality. Boucher is undoubtedly referring to the formalist approach of the New Criticism, which tried to cut off texts from their "extrinsic" social history and to read them as self-contained verbal icons.[3]

For our part, we have tried to read Bradbury's texts as seeking to undermine this distinction through the social process of carnivalization. For those aware of the history of carnivalization, Bradbury's open family has some justification. For many of the authors Mikhail Bakhtin discusses in his history of literary carnivals, Shakespeare was the paragon of an "open" seriousness toward life and literary ideas. He could embrace both the grotesque and the sublime and give us perhaps the greatest expression of nihilism in literature—the "tomorrow" speech in *Macbeth*—without becoming a nihilist himself. For such Renaissance authors as François Rabelais, laughter was just as admissible in great literature, answering to universal problems, as seriousness. Once again, this is a typical feature of carnivalized literature. It should be noted too that carnivalization in the modern period, while taking a critical stance toward fixity of meaning and seeking to "relativize" literature both high and low, is never nihilistic. On the contrary, it remains a powerful means to affirm the life of the author.[4]

The laughter of carnival, which becomes paramount in Bradbury's writings with the publication of *Something Wicked This Way Comes* (with its title from Shakespeare's *Macbeth)* in 1962, is really a philosophical notion for him. In all of its forms, laughter helps bring terrifying things down to a human level, represents a victory over fear, is a universal principle that heals and regenerates, and removes the burden and dead weight of the past, restoring to all an open future. In its political forms it is related to freedom of spirit and freedom of speech *(Fahrenheit 451)*. The important role of parody and satire functioning as social criticism in Bradbury's writings has been pointed out frequently in this study and does not bear repeating here. Critics who feel that he is *merely* an entertainer— Harold Bloom, for instance—because of the presence of so many literary forms of humor in his writings are simply missing the important dimension of his work that takes up a cultural struggle with such "serious" thinkers as Nietzsche and Freud, who have been so influential in defining the nature of the author in modern culture in a predominantly negative fashion (roughly as alienated outsider and neurotic, guilt-ridden agonist).[5]

Bradbury did, indeed, begin his literary career by authoring pulp fiction in the Gothic tradition, which is haunted by a past of severe and punishing figures of the imagination and offers a view of life that says, fundamentally, people are doomed to guilt, self-punishment, mourning, and dismal death. Poe is the exemplary American writer in this mode, to whom Bradbury has often compared himself. Some of Bradbury's early stories collected in *Dark Carnival* certainly were conceived with this internalized Gothic in mind ("Cistern" and "The Lake" are the stories mentioned herein, but Gothic sadomasochism is also prominently displayed in such stories as "The Maiden"). And the analogies with Poe's authorship seem fair enough.

But if Bradbury had published nothing after *Dark Carnival* and had remained a minor writer of Gothic fictions, one still could not comfortably argue that he was a writer "haunted" by the specter of his past. On the contrary, we have been at pains to show how his writings, especially when they were shaped into collections and novelistic projects, manifest a continuing carnivalization of the worldviews they contain. *Dark Carnival* embraces both the dark and the lighter sides of the Gothic tradition, containing such stories as "The Homecoming" and "Uncle Einar," which are festive celebrations of otherness, as well as "Interim," which explores the ambivalent image of pregnant death. The chapter on *Dark Carnival* and *The October Country* indicates just how much Bradbury struggled to write a literary carnival in which the demands of the Gothic past are recognized yet profoundly transformed.[6] We know from recent interviews that, as he matured and became less anxious than he had been with *Dark Carnival* to establish himself as a mainstream author of literary carnivals, Bradbury wanted to unmask the pretensions of our official literary culture, which supports the notion of author as a stable category of seriousness outside the play of textuality (the point of such a story as "The Wonderful Death of Dudley Stone" [1954], collected in *October Country*).[7]

For us, Bradbury's authorship involves far more than mere entertainment. His fiction is really a borderline phenomenon like carnival, operating between the serious and the nonserious in culture and often disrupting that very opposition. Indeed, we have found it to be a manifold and fascinating field of investigation where one finds a popular-nostalgic yearning for the past combined with an unabashed creative desire to live on in an unpredetermined future not circumscribed by that past (a variation on the carnival "chronotope," which mocks at the notion of the death of the author). In the science fiction writings for which he became famous, Bradbury seemed willing to entertain almost any idea or theme that the genre suggested and to combine those with intertexts from mainstream literature. He has given us his own unique take on space travel, invasions, aliens, time travel, robots, and the planet Mars. In his Martian stories and fragments, the ambivalent life of carnival appears to renew conventions about the Red Planet that had become stale (Bradbury fills the Martian canals with wine, not water). Individually, stories such as "Usher II" (published as "Carnival of Madness" in the pulp *Thrilling Wonder Stories)* and "The Exiles" were his response to a culture that increasingly embraced realism and marginalized or rationalized the fantastic. Perhaps they are a little too steeped in the notion of revenge to be entirely free of Gothic influence, but on the whole *The Martian Chronicles* moves toward a post-Gothic affirmation of life, creating a cycle of stories in which no one ideological position, high or low, is allowed the final word. The delights of reading a story such as "Night Meeting," with its perceptual clash of carnival time, both human (prosaic) and Martian (high romantic) serve to indicate how Bradbury maintained an "open" intellectual seriousness toward the genre, testing and discarding ideas once they became rigidified. This story in particular rings in some new changes on the science fiction theme of parallel worlds. Throughout his lifetime, the text of *Chronicles* has remained fluid. For Bradbury, the creative process involved in creating this masterpiece is still ongoing.

Bradbury's only book that seems to have had a fairly direct and untroubled genealogy is *Fahrenheit 451*, which he wrote in a blaze of creativity. Although it clearly addressed issues of free speech for its original audience, *Fahrenheit* is much more than a book about censorship. It has its thematic roots in *Where Ignorant Armies Clash by Night*, which addresses the problem of nihilism in culture. In the earliest versions of the narrative, the protagonist, Montag, recognizes that he is a fool who does not know anything about the world around him. In the novel he realizes that he has rediscovered the meaning of the earth, an antidote to the nihilism created by the simulacrum of carnival. One of the ways Montag (re)discovers this meaning is through literary reverie, which evolved in complex forms during the revisions and expansion of the novella. These reveries have a direct emotional effect and meaning to a reader concerned with the problem of modernity. For many, Montag has become a figure of the modern, spiritually sensitive individual struggling with the contemporary crisis in values (that is, nihilism) in the wake of the collapse of the Christian worldview that assigned humanity a clear place in the universe.

The creative process behind the authorship of *Dandelion Wine* was also quite fluid and complex, involving multiple intentions over the years, but it was finally "completed" by the addition of reveries of winemaking and wine drinking, making it a novel of reveries. Originally centered on a carnivalized war between the old and the young in a small town in Illinois, nothing much of that storyline survives in the published novel (though that material, much revised to include Bradbury's Rabelaisian take on puberty, is contained in the unpublished *Farewell Summer*). Bradbury's narrative worlds are often models of the struggle for creative human freedom in time, and *Dandelion Wine* in all its versions shows a preoccupation with this theme. In fact, the main incident of that work was originally an attack by children on the clock dominating the town. Bradbury has privately offered the view that his classic science-fiction story, "Mars Is Heaven!" which depends so much for its effect on the strength of nostalgia for an idyllic childhood, would be right at home as a dream in the context of *Dandelion Wine*, so it is obvious that the creative process of this book is not finished either.[8]

Bradbury's most frequent position of authorship in his later writings, particularly his detective fiction, is that of *the fool who knows*. Detective fiction requires a ratiocinative subject, usually the detective, at the center of its perceptions of a fated world, but Bradbury places the fool—himself—at the center of these novels. This position, derived from carnival masks, gives him a certain "outsidedness" to the events depicted in the narrative world (he can never be killed by them), yet he remains a participant in those dire events and in the life of carnival. To fully understand Bradbury's use of the detective genre—which itself has extensive historical roots in cultural time—one must clearly see first the textual play of carnivalization, starting with Bradbury's pulp detective fiction in short-story form and then perceive his authorship of complex semi-autobiographical detective novels. The opposition between serious and nonserious is something that these writings attempt to dismantle with various "reduced" forms of carnival laughter: hyperbolic exaggeration, parodies, sarcasm, and clownish intertextual jokes.

Bradbury's intertextuality is multifarious and drawn from two areas of culture usually kept separate: "serious" literature and popular culture. Although he writes in popular genres, his work also manifests a more than passing interest in mainstream literature insofar as it too participates in the carnival tradition of the Renaissance and romantic periods.[9] In his earliest statements about the nature of science fiction, Bradbury mentions Rabelais as one of the founders of a literature of open ideas, to which, in his view, science fiction is heir. *The Masks* was thus an aesthetic failure for Bradbury: he soon discovered that the romantic use of carnival masks led to guilt and despair and a profound separation from life. But this failure in turn led to a discovery of the post-Gothic affirmative uses of masks in *The Martian Chronicles*. The theme of masking and unmasking—the most complex aspect of carnival—has remained central to his aesthetic of fantasy ever since.

The center of the Bradbury canon lies in the fully carnivalized *Something Wicked This Way Comes*, where carnival laughter becomes a philosophical view of life, involving the reader in a "joyful relativity" and an "open" seriousness toward ideas. Laughter, which is so forceful in this book, is not simply a bodily reaction. It is rightfully a philosophical experience, as it was during the Renaissance when the carnivalization of literature was at its peak.[10] At the heart of *Something Wicked* is the modern problem of values, of good and evil, which needs to be overcome. In this novel Bradbury stands out as a moralist concerned to show us how much our moral valuations are rooted in fear, regret, and guilt. Here carnivalization attacks the dark carnival of the ascetic ideal as a prelude to a new way of valuing based on common causes and laughter at the darker aspects of life.

Bradbury also struggles darkly both with Freud and internalized Gothic fantasy in *Something Wicked*. Mr. Dark is, among other things, clearly a representation of the punishing superego of Freudian psychology. After this book, Bradbury's intertextual literary fathers are generally given a mirthful interpretation if they appear too rigid, one-sided, and punishing (or "pessimistic"' might be a better word; Poe, Bradbury's father in the Gothic, is gently mocked in *Death Is a Lonely Business*). Freud, and especially Nietzsche—whose genealogical carnivals of history Bradbury made use of in understanding his own involvement with the Gothic tradition and its immersion in regret, guilt, and revenge—have no final authority in his texts after *Something Wicked*. The central act of carnival is the decrowning or crowning of the carnival king. In *Something Wicked* Bradbury even decrowns his own father in carnival, Mr. Electrico, who taught him that in the midway there can be no spectators, all must participate, even the dead. To understand it one has constantly to be a participant in its life. But even carnival, if it becomes trapped and haunted by the past—especially in the case of the internalized Gothic carnival presided over by Freud—needs to be carnivalized.

The laughter that Bradbury uncovers in *Something Wicked*, while it renews and regenerates the genre, is also directed at himself. Although Charles Halloway was its first example, Bradbury has adopted the narrative mask of the fool in his later detective fiction trying to undermine the genre's preoccupation with ratiocination. In these semi-autobiographical novels, Bradbury has again reinvented himself in complex ways—many of them involving techniques of carnival self-mockery—while remaining faithful to the field and its insistence on a scene of suffering. But however much Bradbury may write about the grotesques and "Lonelies" he knew early in his career, all the while wearing the mask of the fool, he does so in order *not* to become one of them. Bradbury embraces life in all its ambivalence and wants his readers to embrace him on an equal footing. Thus, even at their most ratiocinative, the plots of his detective novels allow him a textual "loophole," which is open to the future, through which he escapes death and finalization. This out is tied to his faith in the carnival sense of life, its fictions and need for masks, allowing him to live on in his characters and readers.[11]

It is something of a temporal paradox that his detective fictions are structured by a search for an open future while constantly evoking a strong sense of nostalgia for the past, for the completed and finalized (that is, the dead). They take the literary form of corpse carnivals and are full of jokes, puns, and laughter at death. In them Bradbury as author and character never completely coincides with his past self (that is, he is never finalized or dead). He always manages to discover what Bakhtin calls an "unrealized surplus of humanness" available to him from the use of these masks of his previous authorial selves, some unrealized and surprising potential that needs to be actualized in the course of the mystery (mysteries that have taken on religious overtones of the "holy fool" in the last two novels).[12] These books mirror Bradbury's early creative struggles with major form—novels such as *Summer Morning, Summer Night* and *The Masks* (left unfinished but uncovered and presented in this study).

It would seem that Bradbury wanted to create a novel in which the carnival sense of time would predominate, and detective fiction, with its emphasis on deterministic plotting, clearly represented a real challenge to his talents. It is no easy task to combine a sense of creative openness and potentiality with nostalgia for a completed past, but in the process Bradbury fully carnivalized the detective genre, which is already based, in its more literary forms, on the main character's struggle not to be trapped by his role into a clownish identity (a struggle that usually ends in failure, as Geoffrey Hartman has implied). He did this by making himself a character—who is never named as other than a fool—in a quasi-autobiographical detective novel. Thus, author and hero are set in a constant open-ended "loophole" dialogue with each other, for even though logically Bradbury the author must know the end of the story, Bradbury the character does not.[13] These three novels represent, then, something of an artistic milestone for Bradbury, who always thought of himself as a short-story writer. It will take time, however, for critics and lovers of detective fiction to understand what he has done with the genre and decide whether or not they find it legitimate.

It remains to discuss Bradbury's authorship in other novelistic writings that, while not fully carnivalized, nonetheless form a part of the life of fiction, for they too make dramatic use of processes central to his aesthetic: the dialogical interplay of metaphors, myths, and masks. Those works are *The Halloween Tree* (1972), *Green Shadows, White Whale* (1992), and *From the Dust Returned* (2001).

In its general outlines, the textual evolution of *The Halloween Tree* echoed that of *Something Wicked This Way Comes.* The catalyst was, once again, a film—this time, however, it was an animated teleplay, the 1968 first airing of the Charley Brown Halloween special, *The Great Pumpkin.* Bradbury was a great admirer of the work of Charles Schultz but felt that the Peanuts special was a letdown: "They promised the kids the Great Pumpkin would arrive, but it never did. You can't do that. It's like shooting Santa Claus in the chimney, or the Easter Bunny doesn't show."[14] Bradbury understood the point of the program but was moved to create an alternative that celebrated rather than consoled. He quickly found a kindred spirit in his good friend Chuck Jones, the creative genius behind decades of Warner Brothers cartoon characters who was at that time with MGM. Bradbury turned to a visual inspiration of his own making, a 1960 painting of a "Halloween Tree" full of carved and illuminated pumpkins. The tree became the central metaphor for the new project—a history of Halloween that would trace the branching evolution of this ancient celebration down through time. But a budget crisis led MGM to eliminate the animation unit, and Bradbury was left with a screenplay and no producer. As he had done with *Something Wicked,* he soon transformed the teleplay into a short novel.

The Halloween Tree was published by Knopf in 1972, but neither Bradbury nor Don Congdon were satisfied with the advertising and marketing strategies. Bob Gottlieb coordinated a first-class production, once again uniting Bradbury with his longtime illustrator, Joe Mugnaini. But Bradbury could not convince anyone at Knopf that *The Halloween Tree* should be marketed as a Bradbury title rather than as a juvenile publication.[15] Despite a narrowly focused advertising campaign that did little to exploit the wider-market appeal of the author's name, the book became a perennial seller far beyond the targeted audience of juvenile library readers. In 1993 Bradbury worked closely with Hanna-Barbera to produce an Emmy Award–winning animated film that has joined the shorter Peanuts classic as an annual fall television event.

To study *The Halloween Tree* as an example of carnivalization across media would be an interesting topic, but one beyond the scope of this study. The novel presents Bradbury's philosophical and cultural ideas about fantastic art in a more monologic fashion than is usual in his fully carnivalized works, but still it reveals a good deal about his authorship.[16] Because it takes place on Halloween, Bradbury's favorite holiday, the delight and pleasure he finds in this carnivalesque celebration is communicated vividly to the reader through the book's rhetorical strategies, which mimic those of "trick or treat." The play of masking and unmasking in particular, which is at the heart of all Bradbury fantasy, is festively employed to make the world itself seem a fable. As the philosopher of Halloween, Death himself removes the ancient mask he has worn under the reign of univocal truth to put on the plurality of masks demanded by Dionysian enchantment, actively working with the protagonists of the book to remove the fear of him and to affirm life.

The plot has a doubly interwoven structure, taking the form of a quest for the origins of Halloween—a philosophical-historical fable—and the search for a boy named Pipkin, who disappears mysteriously at the beginning of Halloween night. Pipkin's worshipful gang of friends, led by Tom Skelton, who is our center of orientation in the novel, are led on this quest by personified Death, masked under the wonderfully sonorous name of Carapace Clavicle Moundshroud. After tearing apart the old and many-layered circus posters that decorate the side of a barn, in a scene carefully constructed to suggest or mime the ritual *sparagmos* associated with the god Dionysus, the boys and Moundshroud construct a "kite of destructions" out the fragmented pictures of animals. Hanging onto this kite as a stabilizing tail, they fly backward in time and space to ancient Egypt, where they witness the rituals devoted to the death and rebirth of the god Osiris, then spy on similar celebrations going on in Greece and Rome, with the help of a giant telescope mounted on top of a pyramid. From there they fly onward to the Celtic festivals of Samhain (according to folklorists, the actual origin of Halloween). During the Middle Ages, they reconstruct the symbolic Christian art imprisoning the terror of chaos on the frozen facades of Notre Dame Cathedral, and lastly they visit contemporary Mexico, where the sugary festivities for the Day of the Dead are in progress.

At each of these historical stages, the boys also encounter Pipkin, who is elusively masked in various forms—for example, as a dead Egyptian prince recently mummified and as a gargoyle of Notre Dame—and at each stage the significance of the masks and costumes is explained by Moundshroud. But in Mexico Death makes a bargain with them. He will let Pipkin (who is actually sick in the hospital with appendicitis) live if they will each agree to forfeit a year from the end of their lives. The boys unselfishly agree to this risk, and Moundshroud returns them home, where a restored Pipkin is waiting for them. The ostensible moral to be drawn seems to be that common cause, the sharing of love and risks together, gives significance to life even in the face of death. Thus the book is something of a thematic pendant to *Something Wicked This Way Comes*.

Moundshroud is at the outset given an unambiguous bestowal of authority by Bradbury to convey his carnivalized (and quasi-Nietzschean) themes. Throughout the novel, Moundshroud comments in official tones on the dramatic scenes the narrative stages. Yet on closer inspection, it turns out to be a strange kind of authority, becoming problematic when Death himself takes up certain philosophical assertions about the nature of religion and morality. Death in this text often speaks as a demystifier, as a critical (if not entirely rational) philosopher, yet he never seems to question openly his own authority to make such assertions. Yet in true carnivalesque fashion, Death foresees the time when he will no longer be feared. At the end of the novel, Moundshroud delivers a new myth, foreseeing that "when you reach the stars, boy, yes, and live there forever, all your fears will go, and Death himself will die."[17]

His discourse on the origin of Halloween presents human history as a long struggle and labor in the face of death, fear of death being the underlying sameness, the "truth" that generates a variety of surface figures of the spirit: religious forms, systems of moral values, even artistic styles such as the medieval grotesque that generated the gargoyles decorating Notre Dame. It is, then, a largely Nietzschean view of man's cultural history. But is this goal of banishing the fear of death really the goal of humanity's development? No, it is rather the end to one narrative of history, in which the primordial terror of risking one's life gives meaning to human life, and the beginning of another, the colonization of space. Bradbury's central theme of living forever is paradoxically fully enunciated only by Death himself (masked as Moundshroud).

Since all children's books have both child and adult perspectives in dialogue with one another (some meanings of which can be shared by both audiences), it is possible to read this text as supporting a more fully carnivalized reading in which we become aware of an even more playful unmasking in which Death decrowns and deconstructs his own authority. The text hints at this deeper understanding when Moundshroud delights the boys (and the reader) with his deliciously frightening tricks *and* treats, which go beyond anything we have experienced before on any ordinary Halloween. To travel with Death on his "kite of destructions" is indeed an intoxicating Dionysian experience of dispersal in space and time. Like the boys, we are bored with the town where "all the people who met them at doors looked like candy factory duplicates of their own mothers and fathers. It was like never leaving home."[18] The text here hints at a more radical notion of Halloween as other than a brief festival in which normalcy (adults ruling over children) is only temporarily overturned. It points toward the longing for deeper, further transformations. We are led to feel that Halloween should be a continuing carnivalesque festival, and we search for more thematic reversals.

One such reversal is that Moundshroud approaches the absolute risk of death for the boys only in play. It is actually *he* who needs life and laughter at the simulacrum of death he has become.[19] This much is evident in some of the scenes set in Mexico, where the boys are able to eat death as bits of a candy skull and where they meet their own doubles in a sacrificial ceremony (chap. 19). The economy of these ritual scenes goes beyond that of dialectics and of death giving a meaning to life. It is rather an example of high-spirited play before the work of death. Furthermore, the miniaturization of art objects and the display of corpses create a dramatic situation in which the boys can watch themselves die, feigning to die (but to make it seem that there are still some risks involved, Bradbury has Tom Skelton wonder whether the skulls are poisoned). In these spectacles and representations, it is always a question of an *other*, but in such cases the death of the other is always the image of one's own demise. The boys find enjoyment in eating the candy fragments of Pipkin's skull bearing the letters of his name (another Dionysian *sparagmos*). In these rituals and representations, the primordial terror and negativity of death is not allowed to become so serious. And this, Bradbury says, is the life-preserving function of carnivalized fantastic art.

Another thing that belies Death's ultimate authority is that throughout the text a constant game of masking and unmasking is being played, often accompanying the representational scenes. Initially, the reader has to match up each character with his costume, and this is not easily done because the boys do not want their "identities" given away to Moundshroud so easily and quickly. And in the spirit of Halloween, Death plays along with this game, although he knows who they are all along. Indeed, Tom Skelton in one scene claims to be *all* the boys, and Death allows this assertion to go unquestioned (chap. 5), for he is the greatest master of masking, himself appearing in various guises in the story, from Moundshroud to a mummy to the Vendor of Skulls. If, therefore, he does have any authority in this story on the philosophical level, it is the sovereignty of laughter that makes the seriousness of meaning appear inscribed in play.[20]

One scene that admirably demonstrates Death's sovereignty (but not authority) occurs when the boys first cross the ravine, a literary topos that always represents the abyss in Bradbury (as in *Dandelion Wine*) to call on the House of

Haunts (chap. 5). They demand a conventional trick or treat, but Moundshroud defeats their expectations by denying them a treat and promising them a trick, slamming the door in their faces. The boys then go around the corner of the house, finding the luminously beautiful Halloween Tree, its black branches laden with candle-lit pumpkins. Tom Skelton immediately understands it to be a celebration, but of what he does not know. Suddenly, while they are staring in fascination at the tree, Death springs at them from a pile of leaves. The boys start to run away, terrified, but he reaches up a bony hand and peels off his white skull face. Moundshroud roars with laughter at this "trick," which on the philosophical level is a violation of the principle of identity, so dear to philosophers from Plato to Edmund Husserl. Death is masked as himself, and the unmasking only leads to a mask more reassuring and convincing to the boys (the character of Moundshroud). It would seem that there is no naked essence of truth lying behind the mask. Behind the mask of appearances is nothing, or rather another mask. For to be a mask, the mask must obscure its very nature, and thus it continually generates a sequence of masks, without there being any person, any self, or any self-identical ego behind the appearances. The same sort of play with masking and appearances exists with the character of Pipkin, whose life story cannot be one of identity (chap. 10).

Throughout the novel, *The Halloween Tree* makes extensive use of the two most basic modes of narrative mediation available to the storyteller, telling and showing, which cooperate in making claims on our belief and in persuading us to believe in a world of fantasy. Moundshroud treats and tricks us with them to the point of satiety. Interestingly, the distinction between the two modes is made by Death himself as storyteller. After tricking the boys in front of the Halloween Tree, he promises to treat them to the story of Halloween, its origins, and what it celebrates by telling them about it. But he quickly changes his mind and, opting for a combination of the two modes, declares: "'Then wouldn't it be fun for you to find out?' asked Mr. Moundshroud. 'I'll tell you! No, I'll *show* you!'"[21]

Here in his character of Moundshroud, Bradbury explicitly acknowledges the interplay of rhetorical modes staged by the novel. The two modes, in fact, work together, supporting each other's claims to authority. Chapter 13, for example, is a kind of phantasmagoria that tells and shows the defeat of the druidic priests by the Roman legions, who are then in turn overcome by the onset of Christianity. Although phantasmagorical description predominates in this chapter, Moundshroud's interpretation of these images, his scrutiny of the violence of religious history, is quasi-Nietzschean in the way it emphasizes the continual birth, death, and rebirth of myths.

Moundshroud clearly wants the boys to believe that there are such things as events. His telling is subordinated to a dramatic presentation of the Dionysian flows that are periodically trapped in the Apollonian images of religious idols, a process that momentarily fixes the cultural imagination in forms and saves it from endless wandering. But there are no permanent or eternal gods; they succumb in turn to new gods (created by humanity, it is clearly implied). It is also implied that these myths help humanity at various historical stages to interpret their struggles with others, quite in the manner, one supposes, that the pagan rituals of the druids were assimilated to the body of Christian doctrine.

This telling and showing of rhetorical strategy is employed throughout the book, especially as we witness the prehistoric "origin" of Halloween in chapter 10, where Death's commentary is most lengthy. In the Egyptian tomb beyond the walls painted with hieroglyphics, Moundshroud causes a fantasy of apeman, fire, and saber-toothed tiger magically to appear. Then he carefully stage manages this fantasy so that the boys see the apeman seize a flaming branch lit by lightning and with it drive off a menacing tiger, afterward tossing the fiery branch into a pile of autumn leaves with a laugh.

Moundshroud, in his historico-philosophical commentary, observes: "The days of the Long Cold are done. Because of this brave, new-thinking man, summer lives in the winter cave." Death, it seems, is no Darwinian. On the contrary, he presents the struggle against the primordial terror of death as primarily a manifestation of the will to power, which for Bradbury is the will to life. Already, as the apeman snorts and laughs in triumph, much more is being staged than just the instinct for self-preservation. His actions are also an expansion of power in which he risked his life. Nietzsche always insisted that the Darwinian struggle for existence was too simple a notion, perhaps only a temporary exception of the will to life. In nature he found not that conditions of stress are dominant, but that overflow and squandering were operative, even to the point of absurdity. Likewise in Moundshroud's commentary, *courage* and new thinking are the ways by which humanity discovers its intellect, in spite of the fear that is the implied background of these events.

Nor is this simply a restaging of the technological discovery and control of fire. If it were, it would probably belong in the Museum of Natural History and not in a fantasy of the origins of Halloween. Rather, fire gives humanity time to think, to philosophize, and to discover the world in reverie: "Only by night fires was the caveman, beast-man, able at last to turn his thoughts on a spit and baste them with wonder," says Moundshroud about the next stage of development. In effect, he is saying that Halloween began "with such long thoughts at night, boys. And always at the center of it, fire."

Moundshroud's commentary seems to follow the Bachelard ontology of reverie, for the depicted primitives are going to eat their world—or rather consume the extra pleasure (the gastronomic value) that fire gives to food, which goes quite beyond utilitarian values.[22] For Bradbury, fire gives material form to the earliest festivities, and it is in joy and not in sorrow that humanity discovers its intellect. Furthermore, the conquest of the superfluous (basting thoughts with wonder) in Bradbury's text gives a greater spiritual excitement than the conquest of the necessary—the fight with the saber-toothed tiger. True, the extremities of cold are driven back by fire also, but humanity is seen nonetheless as a creation of desire, not a creation of need or lack. In Moundshroud's anthropological speculations, where the caves of primitives are invaded by "ghosts" of the dead and terrible memories (the influence of Gothic romanticism on Bradbury can be read here too), it suffices to toss more twigs on the fire to banish nightmares. Thus are presented the first attempts to master the world of fears through fantastic representation.

Before returning the boys home to the ordinary world, Moundshroud shows them the function and structure of the House of Haunts, Bradbury's structure of fantastic fiction. But precisely because it is a structure, however lively its description may be—and Gothic techniques of exaggeration are nowhere more in evidence than in the rhetoric evoking this vast cemetery of a house—we are led to have doubts about its ability to contain Dionysian experience. Moundshroud commands all the boys to slide down a gigantic banister to the respective historical levels where they think their individual disguises and masks belong, telling them that the celebrations they have witnessed are in essence all the *same*. But can the reader's experience of difference and dispersal in time and space, and such a lengthy play of masking and unmasking as indicated (in part), be contained within such creaking Gothic machinery? Moundshroud leads us to believe that it is all one, that all the celebrations are the same. This should rather be taken—on the adult level of reading we are pursuing here—to mean that the truth about life is always horrible and will negating. We can grant that the House of Haunts is a workable metaphor, but it is a static metaphor that can never contain the reader's temporal experience of the fantastic, as Moundshroud describes it when they are all settled in the niches of the house: "Night and day. Summer and winter, boys. Seedtime and harvest. Life and death. That's what Halloween is, all rolled up in one. Noon and midnight. Being born, boys. Rolling over, playing dead like dogs, lads. And getting up again, barking, racing through thousands of years of death each day and each night Halloween, boys, every night, every single night dark and fearful until at last you made it and hid in cities."[23]

To add our own commentary on this passage, both forces in Bradburian fantasy, the Apollonian and the Dionysian, pursue life, though in each case in a radically different way. A sense of ambivalent unity is emphasized by the language of the above quotation, which embraces opposites: life-death, night-day, summer-winter, change-identity. The Dionysian element strains after universality, which will blot out boundaries and embrace all extremes. The Apollonian element strives for unity of life too but rather emphasizes certain masks drawn from the whole of cultural history, which it subordinates to a structure entailing individuality. The Dionysian strives after a unity of the whole, and the Apollonian aspires toward a clarity attainable from a particular perspective, a mask, hence the various levels of the house—the masks of cultural history—from which the boys are capable of understanding their roles in the fantasy. But however one understands the book, on the level of the child or of the adult, it is certain that Moundshroud is telling the boys that death is only a part of the larger life of carnival uncovered in this story of Halloween's origins.

Bradbury uses incantatory poetry several times in the text to convey the radical pleasure in the dispersal of identity that true Halloween requires. We can close our discussion with an example of it, the very verse in which Death speaks of tearing himself apart, to the boys' unbounded delight:

> O autumn winds that bake and burn
> And all the world to darkness turn,
> Now storm and seize and make of me. . . .
> A swarm of leaves from Autumn's Tree![24]

On the adult level, the powers of recurrence in the Dionysian world must not be understood as the return of *something* that is one, an ego that is ever the same (even though Moundshroud tells the boys that it is Pipkin—the same—who is masked at different historical times). What recurs is the life of fictions. The carnival recurs, but in *The Halloween Tree* there is recurrence not of the same essence masked by different appearances, but the play of ever divergent appearances. Once again Bradbury carnivalizes the genre in which he works. Adults are carnivalized by their experience of reading *The Halloween Tree* far more than its child readers, who need more reassurance. Traditional philosophical fantasy from J. R. R. Tolkien through C. S. Lewis to Ursula LeGuin has always provided the reader that reassurance with a glimpse into the essence of things, but *The Halloween Tree* is a break with that metaphysical tradition. It is Bradbury's celebration of nonidentity.

Two decades later Bradbury took on a very different interpretive challenge in developing *Green Shadows, White Whale* out of his experiences in Ireland. He had been part of John Huston's intense world of creativity during 1953–1954 as screenwriter for the preproduction crew of the movie *Moby Dick,* but he had kept the highs and lows of this experience to himself for nearly four decades. He was in his final years with Knopf when his own editor, Kathy Hourigan, was working with Katherine Hepburn on a brief memoir of John Huston and the making of

The African Queen. Bradbury was more fascinated by what Hepburn left unsaid in this slim volume and tried once again to find a way to present Huston in all his complexity through a truthful but compassionate lens:

> I waited thirty-five years. . . . I never said a word. I was offered a chance to write articles for *Harper's Bazaar* and other magazines, and I refused because I don't believe in gossip. . . . But on the other hand, I'd written all these stories indirectly connected to Huston, and most of them rather happy, and fascinating—like the fox hunt, that gives you a lot of ideas about John without hurting him. . . . So I said, what the hell, it's time for me to quit holding off and do a book that's shaded in both directions, and when you're done you won't hate John. I think you'll sympathize with him a little bit, and you'll know when he was an SOB.[25]

His title offered a more subtle echo of Peter Viertel's devastatingly accurate *White Hunter, Black Heart*, which chronicled Huston's earlier odyssey with the cast and crew of *The African Queen*. Bradbury's own Irish stories, inspired as they were by the *Moby Dick* experience, helped him take a more compassionate tone than Viertel. But the result was more than a novelized story cycle; unlike *The Martian Chronicles* or *Dandelion Wine*, the stories are connected by sustained narrative chapters rather than short chapter-bridges. In all, he would rework eleven of his Irish stories and an essay-story, "The Hunt-Wedding" (1992), for the new novel. Most of the stories had been written from the mid-1950s through the mid-1960s, the decade after his Irish interlude. Publication was scattered on down through all the major story collections, and Bradbury subsequently adapted many of these richly lyrical tales to stage. But for *Green Shadows, White Whale*, he would scatter the stories through a narrative of his own life, the story of a young writer entering a defining moment of his career.

Like all of Bradbury's extended fiction, *Green Shadows, White Whale* uses metaphors, myths, and masks to interpret its subject matter. A major portion of the book details Bradbury's visit to Ireland, fictionalizing his encounter with two "Beasts," the director, John Huston, and Herman Melville's White Whale. Imagining an incredible future for himself as a screenwriter for a genius director, the young writer soon learns that Huston is a very difficult man to work for and even portrays the director as someone bent on destroying him. Bradbury records several attempts by Huston to humiliate him and his creative efforts in front of others, playing a masculine game that Bradbury says he never really understood (though he suggests homoerotic reasons). But to be fair to the ambivalence of that relationship, Bradbury presents Huston in a more favorable light in chapter 13, where the director helps him deal with the beggars that surround his hotel and particularly to overcome his feelings of guilt when one of them, to whom he has resisted giving money, commits suicide.

Bradbury presents Huston as a womanizer and eventually wins out over him by writing a story about him being destroyed by a banshee, which he delivers to him instead of the required screenplay pages. The writing of this story effects a kind of literary revenge, and Bradbury's restaging of an Irish myth represents an overcoming of his "feminine" position in relation to the director. In Irish myth and folklore, the banshee is believed to presage a death in the family by wailing outside the house; it seems clear that Bradbury identifies with the banshee of the story. This "poetic justice" works very well in the context of the novel. But as an assertion of the writer's will over that of the director, it never occurred in real life. Bradbury's real relationship with Huston remained deeply ambivalent and was exacerbated by his struggle with the Screen Writers' Guild over the screenplay credits for *Moby Dick*. Nor did his earlier visit to Ireland, supposedly in 1939, actually occur; Bradbury invented this trip primarily to motivate the romantic aesthetics of some of the Irish material. (In chapter 23, for instance, Bradbury is overcome with a feeling of "incredible mystery" when he recognizes that a beggar's child, first seen in 1939, is still young.) It also is a bit too reactive and motivated by the spirit of revenge to be a fully carnivalized use of myth.

Toward the end of the novel, Bradbury revisits his creative struggles with Melville's novel. His victory over the whale—how to capture the literary force of Melville's novel on film—comes when, struggling through his last days in Ireland, he finds a central metaphor holding the entire screenplay together: "What nailed it fast [the screenplay] was hammering the Spanish gold ounce to the mast. If I hadn't fastened on that for starters, the other metaphors . . . might not have surfaced to swim in the bleached shadow of the Whale."[26] According to Bradbury, this central metaphor acts as a "solar presence" in the screenplay, a center of meaning that controls all of the various tropes he was able eventually to glean from Melville's pages, enabling him to identify (that is, mask) himself with Melville's style. Bradbury thinks of metaphor as a revelation of the workings of Melville's mind, as the way in which Melville establishes intimacy with his reader. An objective reading of the screenplay, however, reveals Bradbury's version ending not in metaphor, but in the literal death of the White Whale, which was never intended by Melville. Indeed, as critics have observed, Bradbury's version seems closer on some points—the whale's destruction, in its death, of the ship—to Steven Spielberg's *Jaws* than to Melville's book.

For most of the novel, Bradbury is largely a spectator and a cultural outsider trying to understand the nature of the Irish, a position that is incompatible with true carnival. But chapter 26 stages a humorous encounter with George Bernard Shaw (figured as the devil in a Punch and Judy puppet show) in a Dublin pub that gives at least a partial answer to the philosophical question of Irishness: "The Irish. From a little they glean so much: squeeze the last ounce of joy from a flower with no petals, a night with no stars, a day with no sun. One seed and you lift a beanstalk forest to shake down giants of converse. The Irish? You step off a cliff and . . . fall *up!*"[27]

Although he is sensitive to Irish turns of phrase, Bradbury's Irish ultimately turns out to be a reflection of his own concerns (voiced through the mask of Shaw) about affirming the life of the imagination even in the presence of overwhelming negativity.[28] This, of course, belies the suicide of the beggar on the bridge, with which Bradbury never does come to terms. Despite its skillful deployment of metaphors, myths, and masks, *Green Shadows, White Whale* remains his least carnivalized novel.

While the stories at the heart of that book allow us to see how this novel was thirty-five years in the making, Bradbury's next novel, *From the Dust Returned* (2001), has a textual history that stretches back for more than fifty years. His vampire family stories date to the same mid-1940s creative watershed that generated the origins of *Dark Carnival* and the Green Town trilogy. Three of the vampire stories appeared in *Dark Carnival*: "The Homecoming" (1946), "The Traveler" (1946), and "Uncle Einar" (1947). "Trip to Cranamockett" was pulled from the galleys and finally found its way into the *Toynbee Convector* as "West of October" (1988). As early as June 1948, Bradbury and Congdon had offered a proposal for a novel based on these stories to Knopf, but Bradbury was unable to pull together enough unified material to secure a contract. This early concept was titled *He Who Hath Wings* and later surfaced among Bradbury's many undated concept outlines of the 1950s as *The Gentle Teeth, the Wondrous Wings*. But with the passing years, only two other vampire tales, "The April Witch" (1952) and "On the Orient, North" (1988), reached print as standalone stories. Then in the mid-1990s, Bradbury began to develop the novel in earnest. A new story, "From the Dust Returned" (1994), placed the gentle vampire family in opposition to the daylight world for the first time and hinted at how he might resolve the fate of his fantastics in this larger context. The story was eventually split by a brief "interchapter" and used to conclude the principal action of the novel as chapter 21, "Return to the Dust," and chapter 23, "The Gift." But in terms of structure, the final novel is more than the sum of its story-based parts. The interchapters are often slim, but they unfold a larger story of human destiny and authorial creativity than the preexisting stories alone can span.

In terms of degree of carnivalization, *From the Dust Returned* lies between the two previous novelistic projects. On the one hand, it has the ambiance and poetic ritual of *The Halloween Tree*; it also has a child as its "main" character. On the other hand, that character, Timothy, although adopted by the supernatural Elliott family and intimately familiar with its haunts, does not undergo carnivalization to any great degree and remains, by choice, a mortal outsider to the family, whose historian he becomes. True, he is deeply ambivalent—a proper carnivalesque attitude to be sure—about wanting to be like the family. But he is from the outset marked by his "otherness" ("outsidedness" in Bakhtin's terminology), which needs to be maintained in order for the story of the family, and their narrative image, to emerge. Early in the novel he is gently mocked and toyed with by certain family members on their arrival: "And in the roundabout centrifuge, Timothy with mindless joy was hurled by the whirl and spin to be flung against a wall and held fast by the concussion, where, *motionless, forlorn, he could only watch* the carousel of shapes and sizes of mist and fog and smoke faces and legs with hooves that, jounced, struck sparks as someone peeled him off the wall in jolts!" (emphasis added).[29] Tossed against the wall by the "mindless joy" of the carousel, Timothy remains external to the family's carnivalized meanings. He is not a rider on the carousal, not a participant. In addition, because *From the Dust Returned* is made up of short stories written at many different times in Bradbury's career (Timothy is a character in some of them) and has been assembled without much editorial attention to continuities, being loosely organized by the homecoming, gathering, and dispersal and destruction of the Elliott family, the thematic structure of the book can at times seem contradictory.

Bradbury's most enchanting and poetic character, the telepathic Cecy, has these kinds of problems. She seems to have a greater range of powers in some stories than in others, no doubt because of the different plot requirements of those stories when written individually. For instance, early in the novel she has a mind-reading range of ten thousand miles, but later she can only travel a few miles, which necessitates a train journey in chapter 10. This latter story—under the title "Trip to Cranamockett"—was pulled by Bradbury from *Dark Carnival* during the galley stages of that book because he evidently considered it too "pulpy." When he revised it for publication in *From the Dust Returned* so many years later (it was also a story in *The Toynbee Convector* called "West of October," which is its current chapter title), he could hardly change the original narrative and structure without radically altering the thematics of the story. And although some editorial effort clearly was made to disambiguate, by means of italics, who is talking when Cecy inhabits other characters and makes them speak, this has the effect of reducing the play of meaning and the double voicing that readers experience in the original versions of these stories.

Nonetheless, these are not major problems.[30] The book is richly satisfying and coherent on many levels of meaning. Metaphor is used throughout to evoke a many-layered sense of otherness in the house and in each of its inhabitants. In fact, "to inhabit" is probably a key theme in the book, as one's consciousness can live inside of many others, human or nonhuman. Cecy helps Timothy overcome his sense of alienation by causing his mind to inhabit that of Uncle Einar and others in the family. She can even live in the one-celled animals in a well or help several others live inside of one, with comic effect. For instance, the young men who inhabit Grandpere's mind feel a sexual desire that he no longer wishes to acknowledge, but his "mummy" eyes cannot help but look: "The young woman curved, leaning as the train pushed or pulled her; as pretty as something you won at a carnival by knocking over milk bottles." And Cecy herself, although "innocent," has experienced vicariously many forms of sexual desire. Her carnal experiences are sometimes evoked through textual metaphors: "I have *sewn* my way though bedroom windows on a thousand summer nights" (emphasis added).

As is to be expected in such a situation, the family has many myths and legends about itself. Some of these Timothy records and remembers, which are told to him by Nef, "A Thousand Times Great Grandmere," an ancient Egyptian mummy residing in the high attic of the house, which is itself storied. Indeed, the house's arrival and construction is "the stuff of further legends, myths, or drunken nonsense." Because of the size and variety of its inhabitants, it is "a puzzle inside an enigma inside a mystery." Thematically, it is the Gothic House of Haunts of *The Halloween Tree* renovated and revisited. Of course, there are the obvious intertextual thematic affinities to Charles Addams's own (in)famously perverse cartoon family. Bradbury's house is, in fact, depicted on the dust jacket through the magic of Charles Addams's illustration. (Bradbury discusses the origins of this project, in which he actively sought Addams's involvement, in a revealing afterword to his novel.)

Yet Bradbury's family is gentler and somehow more sympathetic in its construction of otherness than Addams's Gomez, Morticia, and Uncle Fester, though it is none-the-less comic for all that. Cecy's treatment of the drunken uncle, John the Terrible, who betrays some of the family members to the "normals," is typical. For punishment, she fills his head with the sounds of church bells, and he drops dead (this was originally a *Dark Carnival* story, as are most of the stories involving her). When it is discovered that foundling Timothy is not like the others—his face can be reflected in a mirror—he is nonetheless taken in by the dark lady of the house, given the name of a saint, and eased in his anguish by Cecy, who enters his mind to let him know they are one. Even Arach the Spider becomes his playmate, forming on the small child's hand "a nightmare papal ring" that makes him, in play, the crowned king of this carnival.

Despite the depths of mysteries alluded to, the family of the house is compelled to define itself later in the book, forming an "Autumn council" in chapter 14, "The October People," for just such a purpose. This is the most overtly philosophical chapter of the book. It seems that some of their kind have been made extinct by human wars raging in the world, but it is made clear that these con-flicts are not just physical. The threats to the family are ideological, involving them in a struggle to maintain self-definition in a world that is increasingly nihilistic. They realize that, since over the centuries the family had not attempted to define itself, others have begun to do it for them to their detriment. Not sur-prisingly, the family attempts self-definition with a debate structured by certain key words—"metaphor," "myth," and "mask"—the very organizing principles of Bradbury's aesthetic. The role of these in defining and protecting the family is explicitly discussed. After it decides that isolated metaphors, however striking and poetic, are too nebulous, the council, led by the father of all darkness, comes to understand that their fate is intimately bound up with that of the normal world and its growing disbelief. Then follows a kind of genealogy like that given to the carnival in *Something Wicked This Way Comes*. We learn that masks have been a crucial part of the family's defense against the world.

> The world is at war. They do not name us the Enemy, no, for that would give us flesh and substance. You must see the face or the mask in order to strike through one to deface the other [the intertextual allusion here is to Melville's *Moby Dick*]. They war against us by pretending, no, assuring each other we have no flesh and substance. It is a figment war. And if we believe as these disbelievers believe, we will flake our bones to litter the winds. . . . As long as they believed in their sermoned lives, and disbelieved in us, we had more than a mythical flesh. We had something to fight for to survive.[31]

In this passage, from which we have provided only a small extract, we can begin to see some of the remarkable semantic depths Bradbury's themes have acquired over the half century it took him to realize this project. The text has roots in Bradbury's writings of the late 1940s where fictional beings struggle to survive in a culture of disbelief ("The Exiles," "Pillar of Fire," and "Usher II," in particu-lar). But instead of reactive anger against those unable to tolerate fictions—the stance of these early stories—we now find an active philosophical and creative response to a far more desperate cultural situation: how can they fight without appearing to fight? How can they make people believe in them only up to a point? (This situation is actually explored in an earlier chapter, where a ghost is kept alive by reading from fiction.) This entire discussion, of course, also figures Brad-bury's own creative struggles with the creatures of his imagination. Against the forces of disbelief in this "figment war," the council eventually decides on a sug-gestion made by Timothy, involving a kind of dissemination of its members, to be conducted by Cecy, in which they will inhabit, temporarily, the "empty bodies and empty lives" of certain normal people (presumably, in a nice irony, those who do not believe in them), themselves escaping to otherness.

Before the dissemination of the family (which is not in any sense a "finalization" of its meanings) and destruction of the house, we are treated to one of Bradbury's most treasured stories in which Uncle Einar makes himself into a kite to play with his children. This story of an old and well-known character in Bradbury's fiction is followed by that of a new and intensely carnivalized one: Mademoiselle Angelina Marguerite, who was "perhaps strange, to some grotesque, to many a nightmare, but most certainly a puzzle of inverted life." This character—dug out of the grave by Timothy and his father—is born again from the soil as a young woman who gradually gets younger and younger. After being exhumed, she is laid out under a tree to the sound of much laughter. Timothy, as outsider, does not understand the meaning of this ritual:

> "How can they *laugh?*" cried Timothy.
> "Dear child," said his mother. It is a triumph over death. Everything turned upside down. She is not buried, but *unburied,* a grand reason for joy. Fetch wine!"[32]

The theme of pregnant death—prominent is such early stories as "Interim"—is here given a fully carnivalized and joyous treatment. Initially, Timothy does not understand the ambivalent laughter of carnival or this family for whom death is not a serious matter. But as Angelina Marguerite explains herself to him, in a speech that is perfused with Shakespearean meaning, he begins to understand the celebration, the laughter, and the wine. His real gift to the family—his "sublime destiny," as his mother puts it—will be the "outsidedness" he provides for them; his "surplus of meaning" will be their survival. In a beautifully poetic passage that begins with the words "We are the granaries of dark remembrance," Nef tells Timothy of all the deaths, the semantic depths of the family, which he must preserve. "Only death," she says, with typical carnival ambivalence, "can set the world free to be born again, that is your sweet burden."

As always, Bradbury's poignant poetic images tell us much about his literary meanings and how he reinvents himself and his authorship in each succeeding book. But those meanings themselves need to be "unpacked" into the language of literary criticism to be properly understood. Once again, Mikhail Bakhtin's reflections on the nature of language are helpful to us. He points out that we all make meanings out of the language of others; we are always recontextualizing meanings taken out of the past and creating new ones that point openly toward the future. This is the very life of social discourse, of which literature is a part. It is especially evident in literary works separated from us by great historical time, literary works that, Bakhtin argues, may not even reach their full potential until centuries later (this is the problem of "great time," which structures literary history). The literary historian and critic must always be aware of the historical otherness out of which current identities are made: "Others' assimilated words, eternally living, and creatively renewed in new contexts; and others' inert, dead words, 'word-mummies.'"[33]

It is important to remember that Nef herself is a mummy whose discourse with Timothy exists in these two registers (life and death); she speaks to Timothy in the present while her body is covered with ancient hieroglyphs representing the family, which he has to learn to read. Later, when Timothy escapes the holocaust of the burning house with Nef in a bundle under his arm, he is accosted by a passerby in a truck who wants to know what he is carrying. His answer is both a disguise—for he does not reveal to the stranger what he is carrying— and a truth about Bradbury's own love for popular culture: "'Collect 'em,' said Timothy. 'Old newspapers. Comic strips. Old magazines. Headlines, heck, some before the Rough Riders. Some before Bull Run. Trash and junk.' The bundle under his arm rustled in the night wind. 'Great junk, swell trash.'"

The ambivalences are striking: *great* junk, *swell* trash. It seems that Timothy in his lying has learned something of the life of carnival. Bradbury's great gift has been to reinvent himself through his popular-festive imagination, through such child characters as Timothy, who undoubtedly is another expression of Bradbury's own inner child still very much fascinated by the life of carnival. We have insisted throughout this study, following Bakhtin, that carnival is a form of life; it is a borderline phenomenon occurring on the boundaries of art and life.[34] Bradbury's texts frequently construct their meanings—sometimes uneasily and with great anxiety, as was the case with *Dark Carnival*—on the boundaries of publishing categories, between "pulp" and "slick," and literary meanings, between "serious" and "nonserious," literature and trash aesthetics. *From the Dust Returned*, therefore, has a rich semantic depth in Bradbury's own career, finishing (but not finalizing) a book project that began over fifty years earlier.

Thus, *From the Dust Returned* is richly dialogic with popular culture and the literary mainstream as well: Shakespeare, Dickens, Poe, Melville, all are intertextually cited. But one should be mindful of the fact that the book is subtitled *A Family Remembrance*. The Bradbury of this late novel is not haunted by characters he created early in his career. On the contrary, he, in effect, becomes his own influence by welcoming them home. Despite the dispersal and dissemination of his carnival family over the years, he has brought them together, with new members, one joyous last time. Bradbury's family will live on (Timothy wisely leaves Nef in the care of a famous Egyptologist who can hear her voice), and we— who must be fans of popular culture as well as literary scholars if we want to understand the life of carnival in his writings—are left with the assurance that nothing in Bradbury's texts, both published and unpublished, is absolutely dead.

We have referred very little in this study to the externals of Bradbury's career and his many awards and distinctions. But surely his recent National Book Award for lifetime achievement, which graces the cover of *From the Dust Returns*, indicates that his writings have now entered into the "great time" of our literary culture and will survive.[35] This study, of necessity, says little of his work in film, theater, and television or considers how carnivalization might develop across media (evident in a story such as "The Wonderful Ice Cream Suit" [1958], which has been a short story, a play, and a film).[36] As Ray Bradbury's works are studied further and in different contexts, we believe that other scholars too will eventually come to participate in the life of carnival. Then every meaning will have its homecoming festival.[37]

A Conversation with Ray Bradbury

Excerpts from an interview conducted at
Palm Springs, October 21, 2002

Q. Carnival is the crucial experience defining the origins of your authorship, as you have defined it on many occasions previously. But we have noticed that in your writings it is at once a source of life and death. Isn't that a rather ambivalent gift?

A. Well, I suppose that's because of Mr. Electrico. I still don't know, all these years later, why he said what he said to me. He looked into my face, that day down by the shore, after we'd been talking for five minutes and he says, "You know, we've met before." I said, "No sir, I've never met you." He said, "No, you were my best friend in the battle of the Ardennes forest, outside of Paris, in October, 1918. You were wounded, and you died in my arms. But now here you are, back in the world, with a new name, a new face. The light shining out of your eyes is the soul of my dead friend. Welcome back to the world."

Now, why did he say that? He didn't know me. It's the electricity, the ambience of people. Every once in awhile, at a book signing, or a lecture, someone comes up that has a certain fire in their face. A young man or a young woman, it doesn't matter, but you look at them and get the same impulse to say "Live forever! Whatever it is you've got." I couldn't see myself, I never saw myself. Even today, I see photographs and I don't know who in the hell that is. But it must have been something, because he said that, and when I left the carnival, that afternoon, I stood by the carousel and I watched the horses going around and around to "Beautiful Ohio," and I wept. I knew something had happened, and it *had* happened—within weeks I became a writer full time. And it was that impulse of his, and looking at the carnival turning around and around, that caused me to move on into my life.

And that was the day of my uncle Lester's funeral. So I was running away from death, and running toward life. My uncle Lester was shot in a holdup and he was in the hospital for three days, and he died, I think, on a Wednesday. There was a funeral Labor Day morning, Saturday, and coming back from the graveyard, I told my father, "Stop the car, I've got to get out!" Because I could see the carnival down by the lake, the flags and the tents. And my father stopped the car. He was furious. He said, "You've got to come home! There's going to be a wake for your uncle." I said, "No, I can't do that." Twelve years old—I went against my family, and my dad drove off. He was furious with me, and I ran down the hill. I didn't know what I was doing. I was running away from death, though. I was running towards life, wasn't I?

As I look back on it now, I was running toward Mr. Electrico to ask him how to live forever. I knew I couldn't ask him, but I had to *try* to ask him. And I get down there and he's sitting on a bench, almost like he's waiting for me. I approached him very shyly, and I had a magic trick in my pocket, thank God, a ball-and-vase trick, and I held that out to him. I said "Can you show me how to do this?" He took it and showed me how to make the trick work and gave it back to me. And then he looked in my face, and said, "Would you like to see all these strange people over here?" I said, "Oh, yes, sir!" He said, "Come on." So he went over to the tent and he hit it with his cane. He said, "Clean up your language! Clean up your language!" He took me in and introduced me to The Skeleton Man, The Fat Lady, The Illustrated Man, and the acrobats. And then he took me down to the beach and we talked. It's a miracle.

Q. Masks and metaphors are not just literary, but also a part of the life—your life—of carnival?

A. When I put *The Martian Chronicles* on at the El Ray Theater, I had my Martians on stage, and during rehearsals one night I went over to the County Museum of Art on Wilshire there [in Los Angeles] and they had a traveling exhibit of Tutankhamen. I walked in and I looked at him, the mask lying there in the sarcophagus, a beautiful golden mask, and I said, "That's one of my Martians!" And I walked back to the theatre and looked on the stage, and my Martians were there with their golden masks, and I said, "My God, that's Tutankhamen. So the metaphors are interchangeable. I didn't know I was doing that. That's the great thing—to do all this without knowing it.

Q. Laughter, particularly the laughter evoked by carnival, takes center stage in your writings with the publication of *Something Wicked This Way Comes* in 1962. Is laughter still important to your authorship and outlook on life, even now?

A. I have an epigraph from Melville's *Moby Dick* in *Something Wicked This Way Comes*. The character Stubb says "I know not all that may be coming, but be it what it will. I'll go to it laughing." Laughter is the best answer to everything. And I learned that lesson from Melville, and I learned it from Aldous Huxley and Gerald Heard. I went to lectures of Heard's at the Vedanta Temple and he spoke of laughter—the Great Laugh—and during my last three years, after my stroke, I learned that truth. There comes a point when your frailties assail you. When you can't walk well enough, your arm doesn't work, you can't speak very well, and then you suddenly say, "This is very funny." You've either got to laugh at it, or you are destroyed by it. So you throw back your head and say, "Wow!" I'll be goddamned!" That allows you to go on. But you have to learn that personally in life. . . . the time comes, finally, maybe when you're lying in bed late at night, you add up all these things and you say," You know, that's ridiculous! That's really ridiculous!" That you would let all these stupid things—they're very serious when they happen one by one—but when you add them up, it's ridiculous. Sure you have days when you are not happy, but the Great Laugh is the cleanser.

Key to Abbreviations

These abbreviations are used primarily to save space in the appendix Year-by-Year listings of Bradbury's published fiction and in the tables used throughout the volume to present textual histories of Bradbury's work. Abbreviations used primarily in notes for unpublished materials are limited to designations for the major repositories of Bradbury's letters: Lilly (Indiana University), Ransom (University of Texas, Austin), Madison (State Historical Society, Wisconsin), and Butler (Columbia University). Letters cited or quoted are located in Bradbury's personal papers are so indicated; Albright Collection refers to those Bradbury manuscripts in the personal collection of Donn Albright (Westfield, New Jersey). The following abbreviations for Bradbury's published volumes have evolved from those used in "The Stories of Ray Bradbury: An Annotated Checklist" (1992).

AS	*The Anthem Sprinters and Other Antics*
BB	*Bloch and Bradbury*
BS	*Bradbury Stories*
CS1	*Classic Stories 1*
CS2	*Classic Stories 2*
DB	*Driving Blind*
DC	*Dark Carnival*
DLB	*Death Is a Lonely Business*
DRF	*The Day It Rained Forever*
DT	*Dinosaur Tales*
DW	*Dandelion Wine*
F451	*Fahrenheit 451*
FDR	*From the Dust Returned*
GA	*The Golden Apples of the Sun*
GL	*A Graveyard for Lunatics*
GS	*Green Shadows, White Whale*
HT	*The Halloween Tree*
IM	*The Illustrated Man*
IS	*I Sing the Body Electric!*

LAKC	*Let's All Kill Constance!*
LAM	*Long After Midnight*
LCE	*"The Last Circus" and "The Electrocution"*
MC	*The Martian Chronicles*
MEM	*A Memory of Murder*
MJ	*The Machineries of Joy*
MM	*A Medicine for Melancholy*
NRB	*The Novels of Ray Bradbury* [omnibus]
OC	*The October Country*
OM	*One More for the Road*
PF	*Pillar of Fire and Other Plays*
QE	*Quicker Than the Eye*
RB	*Ray Bradbury*. (London: Harrap, 1975)
RB2	*Ray Bradbury* [omnibus]
RBOS	*Ray Bradbury on Stage: A Chrestomathy of His Plays.*
RR	*R Is for Rocket*
SA	*The Small Assassin*
SL	*The Silver Locusts*
SRB	*The Stories of Ray Bradbury*
SS	*S Is for Space*
SW	*Something Wicked This Way Comes*
T22	*Twice 22*
TC	*The Toynbee Convector*
TS	*To Sing Strange Songs*
VB	*The Vintage Bradbury*
WICS	*The Wonderful Ice Cream Suit and Other Plays.*

A given story's first book appearance is indicated by the abbreviation FBA. Many of Bradbury's first editions are not readily available to readers today. Page references throughout this volume are keyed to the most accessible editions (the Bantam, Dell, or Avon mass-market paperbacks) unless otherwise indicated.

Bradbury's Fiction, Year-by-Year

Books

All of Bradbury's fiction published in book form is listed and described in chronological order. Retitled and "remixed" collections, which generally have involved Bradbury's collaboration, are also included as well as his children's storybooks and a number of special-format fiction "books" published with little or no participation by the author. For example, he took no active role in assembling omnibus editions combining multiple volumes within a single binding or in marketing paperbound boxed-sets. Other volumes, such as *Bloch and Bradbury* and the two U.K. textbooks *Ray Bradbury* and *To Sing Strange Songs*, were the concepts of independent editors and required little more than permission from Bradbury. These volumes, along with a number of educational and private editions of single stories in booklet form, were outside projects handled primarily by Bradbury's agent, Don Congdon.

Bradbury took a more active role in preparing stage adaptations of his stories for book publication, although educational editions of individual plays were generally arranged by Congdon. EC Comics' sequential art adaptations of his stories closely followed the story texts, and Bradbury wrote the introductions when these strips were collected in book form. These stage and comic-strip adaptations are closely tied to the original texts and are included in the story-by-story listings of each year. Since they play an important role in any study of Bradbury's fiction, books containing these adaptations are also listed.

Bradbury's book publications appear ahead of the individual story publications within each year group, with reference numbers keyed to year of publication and sequence within the year. In this system *The Golden Apples of the Sun*, Bradbury's first book of 1953, is designated 53-A. *Fahrenheit 451*, published later that year, is designated 53-B. This system does not serve a descriptive bibliographical function; it simply provides a quick chronological reference to year and sequence of fiction publication within a year. Dates of publication given here for first editions represent the copyright office deposit date or, for British firsts, the English Catalog of Books; if this is not known, the publisher's release date or the copyright page date is used and so indicated.

Adaptations of Bradbury's fiction volumes for radio, television, and film are noted in the comments section that follows each title's contents; books adapted by Bradbury are so indicated.

Adaptations of individual stories are indicated in the story-by-story listings. A number of Bradbury's fiction volumes have been recorded by him and other readers and marketed in both LP phonograph and audiotape formats; these presumably do not vary from the published texts and are not listed here.

Stories

Bradbury's individual stories appear by title, arranged by date of first publication. Seasonal (quarterly) publications precede monthly publications of the same season; monthly periodicals precede those published by date within the month. If first publication occurs within a book, the title is listed by the book's copyright office deposit date or as close to that date as can be determined; multiple stories first appearing in the same Bradbury collection or novel are listed in alphabetical order for ease of reference. Each title's entry is comprehensive—it includes citations for subsequent publication in periodicals and in Bradbury's own story collections, novels, and other genre forms. References to periodicals include full title and issue date. Cross-references to Bradbury's story collections and novels appear in italic print, using the abbreviations listed above. The following terms are used to define the publishing history of the fiction:

REPRINTED—The title is subsequently published in a newspaper, journal, or other periodical or reprinted under separate cover as a single-story book.

COLLECTED—The title appears in a Bradbury novel, novelized story cycle, or story collection. Individual story entries identify titles that were revised or rewritten for collections and novels. With the exception of *Bloch and Bradbury*, collections were planned and prepared by Bradbury and contain only his stories.

BRIDGED—The title was rewritten by Bradbury and bridged into other titles for inclusion in a novelized story collection *(The Martian Chronicles; Dandelion Wine; Green Shadows, White Whale)*.

ANTHOLOGIZED—The title appears in an anthology containing stories by other authors. Bradbury edited only two such books *(Timeless Tales* and *The Circus of Dr. Lao)*, but his fiction has been published more than 650 times in commercial anthologies. Every known appearance is listed for each story; this anthology history includes book titles and publication dates. Many anthologies have also been published in the United Kingdom, but these editions are identified here only if the U.K. edition varies in title or content, is historically significant, or if it lacks a U.S. counterpart. Bradbury's work has also appeared over 750 times in educational (textbook) anthologies, including English-language textbooks overseas. A total count of textbook appearances is given for each story as well as the volume title and date of the first textbook appearance.

Adapted—The title has been adapted (by Bradbury or other writers) and has been broadcast on radio or television, released as a film, published as a stage play, or printed as a graphic (comic) book. Dates of first broadcast or publication are also included when known. Adaptations of Bradbury's novels and story collections are listed in the book entries. By definition, the adaptations listing excludes original screenplays, stage plays, and teleplays that have never evolved into story form (very few titles fall into this category). Unpublished manuscript adaptations are not included, nor are performed but unpublished stage adaptations. Phonograph and audiotape recordings of stories are not considered adaptations and are not listed.

If a story has a printing history beyond first publication, reprints will be logged first, then appearances in Bradbury's collections or novels. Appearances in trade and textbook anthologies come next, followed by references to radio, television, stage, film, and comic-strip adaptations of the material by Bradbury and others (adaptations by Bradbury are so noted). Every appearance includes a date. Taken together, the publishing history allows the reader to see just how Bradbury worked—sometimes simultaneously—between reprinted, collected, and dramatized forms of a story. A new title may signal deeper revision, or it may merely reflect publishing or copyright requirements. Entries indicate Bradbury' known revisions, rewrites, or even conflations. Further scholarship will undoubtedly turn up more.

For the stories, a number identifying the year and sequence of publication within that year precedes each title; for example, 50–16 identifies "The Illustrated Man" as the sixteenth story published in 1950. This numbering scheme follows (with corrections and updates) the system developed in "The Stories of Ray Bradbury: An Annotated Finding List," *Bulletin of Bibliography* 49, no. 1 (Mar. 1992): 27–51. A cumulative number (indicating where each story falls in Bradbury's total story count) follows each title. For example, "The Illustrated Man" is followed by the number 155, which identifies this work as Bradbury's 155th published story. Bear in mind that his 400 published stories have been reprinted thousands of times; in that process many have been revised, retitled, and sometimes completely rewritten in ways that make the original four hundred publications merely the point of departure for the serious student of Bradbury's short fiction.

Title changes appear in the publication history. Unless a separate title is specifically listed, all the printings of a given story have the original title. Many stories are far better known under subsequent titles created when Bradbury revised them for his story collections. For ease of reference, both the original title and (in parenthesis) the better-known title will open entries for such stories. Entries also indicate Bradbury's use or disuse of the date prefix attached to stories that become chapters of *The Martian Chronicles*.

1938

Stories

38–1 "Hollerbochen's Dilemma" (1)
  Imagination! Jan. 1938. Reprinted *Burroughsian* 1 (Jan. 1957). Anthologized *Horrors Unseen* (FBA, 1974).
38–2 "The Death of Mr. McCarthy" (anon.) (2)
  Blue and White Daily [Los Angeles High School], Apr. 21, 1938. Attributed to Bradbury in 1995 (Albright).
38–3 "Hollerbochen Comes Back" (3)
  [*Mikros*] Nov. 1938.

1939

Stories

39–1 "How to Run a Successful Ghost Agency" (as Brian Eldred) (4)
  D'Journal Mar. 1939.

39–2 "Mummy Dust" (as Cecil Clayborne Cunningham) (5)
D'Journal May 1939. Attributed to Bradbury in 1995 (Albright).

39–3 "Don't Get Technatal" (as Ron Reynolds) (6)
Futuria Fantasia summer 1939.

39–4 "Gold" (7)
Science Fiction Fan Aug. 1939.

39–5 "The Pendulum" (anon.) (8)
Futuria Fantasia fall 1939. Anthologized *Horrors Unknown* (FBA, 1971). Developed into "Pendulum" (41–6) with Henry Hasse.

1940

Stories

40–1 "The Fight of the Good Ship Clarissa" (anon.) (9)
Futuria Fantasia winter 1940.[1]

40–2 "The Maiden of Jirbu" (with Bob Tucker) (10)
Polaris Mar. 1940.

40–3 "Tale of the Tortletwitch" (as Guy Amory) (11)
Spaceways Apr. 1940. Reprinted *Remembrance of Things Past* Aug. 1962.

40–4 "Luana the Living" (12)
Polaris June 1940. Anthologized *Horrors in Hiding* (FBA, 1973).

40–5 "The Piper" (as Ron Reynolds) (13)
Futuria Fantasia 4 [Sept. 1940]. Anthologized *Futures to Infinity* (FBA, 1970). Developed into "The Piper" (43–1), with Ray Bradbury byline. Bradbury's first Martian tale, it remains "unchronicled."

40–6 "The Last Man" (14)
The Damn Thing Nov. 1940.

40–7 "The Tale of the Terrible Typer" (15)
Fantasite Nov. 1940.

40–8 "It's Not the Heat, It's the Hu—" (16)
Script Nov. 2, 1940. Bradbury's first appearance in a commercial general-market periodical.

40–9 "Genie Trouble" (17)
The Damn Thing Dec. 1940.

1941

Stories

41–1 "How Am I Today, Doctor?" (18)
The Damn Thing Feb. 1941.

41–2 "The Trouble with Humans Is People" (19)
The Damn Thing Mar. 1941.

41–3 "Tale of the Mangledomvritch" (20)
Snide [June] 1941.

41–4 "Wilber and His Germ" (21)
Script May 24, 1941. A fictional prose-poem that served as the basis for "Fever Dream" (48–11).

41–5 "To Make a Long Story Much Much Shorter" (22)

Script July 5, 1941. Anthologized *The Best of Rob Wagner's Script* (1985).

41–6 "Pendulum" (with Henry Hasse) (23)

Super Science Stories Nov. 1941. Reprinted *Super Science Stories* (Canada) Aug. 1942, *Famous Fantastic Mysteries* June 1953. Anthologized *Horrors Unknown* (FBA, 1971). Developed from "The Pendulum" (39–5). Bradbury's first story sale, earning $27.50.[2] This is his first appearance in the "pulps."

1942

Stories

42–1 "Eat, Drink, and Be Wary" (24)

Astounding Science Fiction July 1942.

42–2 "The Candle" (25)

Weird Tales Nov. 1942. Reprinted *Weird Tales* (Canada) Mar. 1943. Anthologized *The First Book of Unknown Tales of Horror* (FBA, U.K., 1976). Henry Kuttner wrote the last two hundred words.[3]

1943

Stories

43–1 "The Piper" (26)

Thrilling Wonder Stories Feb. 1943. Reprinted *Fantastic Story* spring 1955. Anthologized *The Future Makers* (FBA, 1968), *Science Fiction Special 5* (U.K., 1971). Developed from "The Piper" (40–5), which had appeared under the pseudonym Ron Reynolds.

43–2 "The Wind" (27)

Weird Tales Mar. 1943. Reprinted *Weird Tales* (Canada) July 1943, *Mysterious Traveler* Nov. 1951, *The Diversifier* July 1977; reprinted *Argosy* (U.K.) Nov. 1951, as "Valley of the Winds." Revised and collected *DC* (FBA, 1947), *OC* (1955), *RB* (1975), *BS* (2003). Anthologized *Alfred Hitchcock Presents: Stories My Mother Never Told Me* (1963), *Great Science-Fiction* (1965), *Far Out* (U.K., 1974), *Nature's Revenge* (1978), *The Penguin Book of Ghost Stories* (U.K., 1984). Adapted for radio and broadcast on *Radio City Playhouse* (NBC), Oct. 30, 1949. Adapted (TV) by Bradbury for *Ray Bradbury Theater* (USA), July 28, 1989.

43–3 "Gabriel's Horn" (with Henry Hasse) (28)

Captain Future spring 1943.

43–4 "Subterfuge" (29)

Astonishing Stories Apr. 1943. Reprinted *Super Science Stories* (Canada) Dec. 1943. Anthologized *Assignment in Tomorrow* (FBA, 1954), *Eight Strange Tales* (1972).

43–5 "The Crowd" (30)

Weird Tales May 1943. Reprinted *Weird Tales* (Canada) Sept. 1943, *Mysterious Traveler Mystery Reader 5* 1952, *Cavalier* Jan. 1959; *DC* revised version reprinted *Shock* May 1960; *DC* revised version revised again and reprinted *Argosy* (U.K.) May 1949. Revised and collected *DC* (FBA, 1947), *OC* (1955), *SA* (1962), *SRB* (1980). Deleted *OC*—Ace U.K. edition only (1961). Anthologized *Terror in the Modern Vein* (1955), *Dark Imaginings* (1978), *Uncanny Tales of Unearthly and Unexpected Horror* (1983), *The Dark Descent* (1987), *Mists from Beyond* (1993), *Weird Tales, Seven Decades of Terror* (1997), *Great Ghost Stories* (U.K., 1997). Anthologized in three textbooks, beginning with *Impact* (1971). Adapted (with heavy modification) for radio and broadcast on *Suspense* (CBS), Sept. 21, 1950; adapted

(TV, without credit) for broadcast on *Journey to the Unknown*, Nov. 14, 1968, as "Somewhere in a Crowd"; adapted (TV) by Bradbury for *Ray Bradbury Theater* (HBO), July 2, 1985.

43–6 "The Scythe" (31)

Weird Tales July 1943. Reprinted *Weird Tales* (Canada) Nov. 1943, *Cavalier* Oct. 1959. Revised and collected *DC* (FBA, 1947), *OC* (1955), *RB* (1975), *SRB* (1980). Deleted *DC* U.K. edition (1948). Anthologized *Legends for the Dark* (U.K., 1968), *Summoned from the Tomb* (U.K., 1973), *Stories of Terror* (U.K., 1982), *Isaac Asimov Presents Tales of the Occult* (1989), *Mystery Stories* (U.S., U.K., 1996). Anthologized in two textbooks, beginning with *The Discovery of Fiction* (1967). First 500–600 words written by Leigh Brackett.

43–7 "Doodad" (32)

Astounding Science Fiction Sept. 1943. Reprinted *Astounding Science Fiction* (U.K.) Dec. 1943. Anthologized *Strange Signposts* (FBA, 1966), *Alien Earth and Other Stories* (1967), *Wizards of Odd* (U.K., 1996; U.S., 1997). Manuscript title: "Everything Instead of Something."

43–8 "And Watch the Fountains" (33)

Astounding Science Fiction Sept. 1943.

43–9 "Promotion to Satellite" (34)

Thrilling Wonder Stories fall 1943. Reprinted *Fantastic Story* summer 1954.

43–10 "The Ducker" (35)

Weird Tales Nov. 1943. Reprinted *Weird Tales* (Canada) Mar. 1944. Anthologized *Weird Legacies* (FBA, U.K., 1977). A forerunner for "Bang! You're Dead!" (44–12).

43–11 "King of the Gray Spaces" ("R Is for Rocket") (36)

Famous Fantastic Mysteries Dec. 1943. Reprinted *Super Science Stories* (Canada) Aug. 1944, as "King of the Grey Spaces." Revised and collected *RR* (1962), *CS1* (1990), as "R Is for Rocket." Anthologized *The Science Fiction Galaxy* (FBA, 1950), *Every Boy's Book of Science Fiction* (1951); anthologized *Space 9* (U.K., 1985), as "R Is for Rocket." Adapted to comic-strip form by Al Feldstein (John Severin and Will Elder, illustrators) for EC Publications in *Weird Fantasy* 19 (May–June 1953), as "King of the Grey Spaces"; EC version collected in *Tomorrow Midnight* (Ballantine, 1966).

1944

Stories

44–1 "The Sea Shell" (37)

Weird Tales Jan. 1944. Reprinted *Weird Tales* (Canada) May 1944, *Short Stories* Feb. 1958. Collected *DC* (2001 Gauntlet edition only). Anthologized *The Fantastic Pulps* (FBA, 1975).

44–2 "Reunion" (38)

Weird Tales Mar. 1944. Reprinted *Weird Tales* (Canada) July 1944, *Weird Tales* fall 1984. Collected *DC* (1947). Deleted *DC* U.K. edition (1948).

44–3 "The Monster Maker" (39)

Planet Stories spring 1944. Reprinted (in two parts) *Spacemen* Oct. 1962, Jan. 1963 (as Leonard Spaulding). Manuscript title: "Pirates in Profile."

44–4 "I, Rocket" (40)

Amazing Stories May 1944. Reprinted *Amazing Stories* Apr. 1961. Anthologized *The Human Zero* (FBA, 1967), *Amazing Science Fiction Anthology: The War Years, 1936–1945* (1987). Adapted to comic-strip form by Al Feldstein (Al Williamson, illustrator) for EC

Publications in *Weird Fantasy* 20 (July–Aug. 1953); EC version collected in *Tomorrow Midnight* (Ballantine, 1966). Revised for *LAM* (1976) but deleted by Bradbury in galleys.

44–5　"The Lake" (41)

Weird Tales May 1944. Reprinted *Weird Tales* (Canada) Sept. 1944, *Shenandoah Review* spring 1951, *Short Stories* Dec. 1957, *Man from U.N.C.L.E.* Feb. 1967, *Scholastic Voice* Apr. 1, 1983. Collected *DC* (1947), *OC* (1955), *SA* (1962), *SRB* (1980). Deleted *OC*—Ace U.K. edition only (1961). Anthologized *Who Knocks* (FBA, 1946; U.K., 1964), *The Ghoul Keepers* (1961), *Masters of Shades and Shadows* (1978), *The Arbor House Celebrity Book of Horror Stories* (1982), *Young Ghosts* (1985; U.K., as *Asimov's Ghosts*, 1986), *Asimov's Ghosts and Monsters* (U.K., 1988), *Visions of Fantasy* (1989). Anthologized in one textbook, *Road-Runner 2* (Sweden, 1986). Adapted for radio and broadcast on *Radio City Playhouse* (NBC), Oct. 16, 1949. Adapted (TV) by Bradbury for *Ray Bradbury Theater* (USA), July 21, 1989. Adapted to comic-strip form by Al Feldstein (Joe Orlando, illustrator) for EC Publications in *The Vault of Horror* 31 (June–July 1953); EC version collected in *The Autumn People* (Ballantine, 1965).

44–6　"Morgue Ship" (42)

Planet Stories summer 1944.

44–7　"There Was an Old Woman" (43)

First published *Weird Tales* July 1944. Reprinted *Weird Tales* (Canada) Nov. 1944, *Argosy* (U.K.) Aug. 1949. Revised and collected *DC* (FBA, 1947), *OC* (1955), *SRB* (1980). Adapted for radio and broadcast with other stories and a Bradbury interview as "October Country," an ABC Halloween special, Oct. 31, 1984. Adapted (TV) by Bradbury for *Ray Bradbury Theater* (USA), May 21, 1988. Adapted to comic-strip form by Al Feldstein (Graham Ingels, illustrator) for EC Publications in *Tales from the Crypt* 34 (Feb.–Mar. 1953); EC version collected in *The Autumn People* (Ballantine, 1965).

44–8　"Killer, Come Back to Me!" (44)

Detective Tales July 1944. Reprinted *Detective Tales* (Canada) Jan. 1945, *Detective Tales* Apr. 1952, as "Murder Is My Business." Adapted for radio and broadcast on *Mollé Mystery Theatre* (NBC) May 17, 1946. Manuscript title: "Autopsy."

44–9　"The Long Night" (45)

New Detective July 1944, *New Detective* (Canada) Dec. 1944. Collected *MEM* (FBA, 1984).

44–10　"Yesterday I Lived!" (46)

Flynn's Detective Fiction Aug. 1944. Collected *MEM* (FBA, 1984). Anthologized *Great Detectives* (1984). Manuscript title: "No Phones, Private Coffin."

44–11　"The Trunk Lady" (47)

Detective Tales Sept. 1944. Reprinted *New Detective* Aug. 1952, *Detective Tales Magazine* (U.K.) Aug. 1960, *Mike Shayne Mystery Magazine* July 1965. Collected *MEM* (1984). Anthologized *Horror Times Ten* (FBA, 1967).

44–12　"Bang! You're Dead!" (48)

Weird Tales Sept. 1944. Reprinted *Weird Tales* (Canada) Jan. 1945. Collected *DC* (2001 Gauntlet edition only). Anthologized *Weird Tales* (FBA, 1976).

44–13　"And Then—the Silence" (49)

Super Science Stories (Canada) Oct. 1944. Reprinted *Super Science Stories* Jan. 1949, *Super Science Stories 1* (U.K.) Oct. 1949, as "The Silence."

44–14　"Half-Pint Homicide" (50)

Detective Tales Nov. 1944. Collected *MEM* (FBA, 1984). Manuscript title: "Enter the Douser."

44–15 "The Jar" (51)

Weird Tales Nov. 1944. Reprinted Weird Tales (Canada) July 1945 (as by Edward Banks), Short Stories Oct. 1958, Cavalier Feb. 1959, Short Stories (U.K.) Mar. 1959, Suspense (U.K.) Apr. 1959. Collected DC (FBA, 1947), OC (1955), SRB (1980). Anthologized The Sleeping and the Dead (1947; U.K., 1963), Fear and Trembling (1948), Suddenly (1965), Dr. Caligari's Black Book (U.K., 1968), Getting Even (1978). Adapted (TV) for Alfred Hitchcock Hour (CBS), Feb. 14, 1964; adapted (TV) for Alfred Hitchcock Presents (USA), Apr. 6, 1986; adapted (TV) by Bradbury for Ray Bradbury Theater (USA), Jan. 17, 1992.

44–16 "It Burns Me Up!" (52)

Dime Mystery Nov. 1944. Reprinted Strange Detective Mysteries (Canada) Dec. 1944. Collected MEM (1984). Anthologized Hauntings and Horrors (FBA, 1969). Adapted to comic-strip form for Ray Bradbury Comics 2 (Apr. 1993) Manuscript title: "The Forgotten Man."

44–17 "Undersea Guardians" (53)

Amazing Stories Dec. 1944. Reprinted Fantastic Jan. 1968. Anthologized The Second Book of Unknown Tales of Horror (FBA, U.K., 1978), Mysterious Sea Stories (1985), Combat! Great Tales of World War II (1992).

44–18 "Four-Way Funeral" (54)

Detective Tales Dec. 1944. Collected MEM (FBA, 1984). Manuscript title: "The Very Bewildered Corpses."

44–19 "Lazarus Come Forth" (55)

Planet Stories winter 1944.

1945

Stories

45–1 "The Poems" (56)

Weird Tales Jan. 1945. Reprinted Weird Tales (Canada) Mar. 1945. Collected DC (FBA, 2001 Gauntlet edition only), BS (2003). Anthologized Masterpieces of Terror and the Unknown (1993).

45–2 "'I'm Not So Dumb!'" (57)

Detective Tales Feb. 1945. Collected MEM (FBA, 1984).

45–3 "Hell's Half-Hour" (58)

New Detective Mar. 1945. Collected MEM (FBA, 1984). Manuscript title: "Mr. Priory Meets Mr. Caldwell."

45–4 "The Tombstone" (59)

Weird Tales Mar. 1945. Reprinted Weird Tales (Canada) May 1945, Strange Tales 1 (U.K.) Feb. 1946; reprinted Argosy (U.K.) Jan. 1952, as "Exit Mr. White." Collected DC (FBA, 1947), SA (1962), TC (1988). Adapted (TV) by Bradbury for Ray Bradbury Theater (USA), Oct. 29, 1992.

45–5 "Skeleton" (60)

Script Apr. 28, 1945. Unrelated to Weird Tales story of same title (45–11).

45–6 "The Watchers" (61)

Weird Tales May 1945. Reprinted Weird Tales (Canada) July 1945 (as Edward Banks), Showpiece Jan.–Mar. 1973, Weird Tales summer 1973. Collected BB (1969), BS (2003). Anthologized Rue Morgue No. 1 (FBA, 1946), I Can't Sleep at Night (1966). This story should not be confused with "November 2005: The Watchers," an unrelated MC bridge passage.

45–7 "Dead Men Rise Up Never" (62)

Dime Mystery July 1945. Reprinted Strange Detective Mysteries (Canada) Aug. 1945. Collected MEM (FBA, 1984). Manuscript title: "The Sea Cure."

45–8 "Corpse-Carnival" (as D. R. Banat) (63)

Dime Mystery July 1945. Reprinted *Strange Detective Mysteries* (Canada) Aug. 1945. Collected *MEM* (FBA, 1984). Anthologized *Night Screams* (1996). Manuscript title: "One Minus One."

45–9 "The Dead Man" (64)

Weird Tales July 1945. Reprinted *Weird Tales* (Canada) Sept. 1945, *Short Stories* June 1958, *Broadside* Sept.–Nov. 1972. Revised and collected *DC* (FBA, 1947), *SA* (1962), *BB* (1969), *BS* (2003). Anthologized *I Can't Sleep at Night* (1966), *Masters of Darkness* (1986), *The Complete Masters of Darkness* (1990). Adapted (TV) by Bradbury for *Ray Bradbury Theater* (USA), Sept. 26, 1992.

45–10 "The Big Black and White Game" (65)

American Mercury Aug. 1945. Collected *GA* (1953), *T22* (1966), *SRB* (1980), *CS1* (1990). Deleted *GA* U.K. edition (1953). Anthologized *Best American Short Stories of 1946* (FBA, 1946), *On the Diamond* (1987), *Great Baseball Stories* (1990).

45–11 "Skeleton" (66)

Weird Tales Sept. 1945. Reprinted *Weird Tales* (Canada) Nov. 1945, *Rex Stout's Mystery Magazine* 6 Oct. 1946, *Shock* Sept. 1960. Revised and collected *DC* (FBA, 1947), *OC* (1955), *VB* (1965), *SRB* (1980). Anthologized *Best Horror Stories* (U.K., 1957), *Spine Chillers* (U.K., 1961), *Famous Monster Tales* (1967), *Strange Beasts and Unnatural Monsters* (1968), *Christopher Lee: From the Archives of Evil Number 2* (1976), *The Best Horror Stories* (U.K., 1977; deleted from U.S. edition, 1990), *Venomous Tales of Villainy and Vengeance* (1984). Adapted (TV) by Bradbury for *Ray Bradbury Theater* (USA), Feb. 6, 1988. Adapted to comic-strip form for *Ray Bradbury's Tales of Terror Special* 1 (May 1994). Unrelated to *Script* story of same title (45–5).

45–12 "The Long Way Home" (67)

Dime Mystery Nov. 1945. Reprinted *Strange Detective Mysteries* (Canada) Dec. 1945. Collected *MEM* (FBA, 1984). Manuscript title: "The Long Way Around."

45–13 "Invisible Boy" (68)

Mademoiselle Nov. 1945. Reprinted *Story Digest* Nov. 1946 (condensed); reprinted *Argosy* (U.K.) Apr. 1952, as "The Invisible Boy." Revised and collected *GA* (FBA, 1953), *VB* (1965), *T22* (1966), *SS* (1966), *SRB* (1980), *CS2* (1990). Anthologized *Invisible Man* (1960), *40 Best Stories from* Mademoiselle (1960, as "The Invisible Boy"), *Famous Tales of the Fantastic* (1965); *Some Things Fierce and Fatal* (1971); *Authors' Choice 2* (1973); *A Chilling Collection* (1980); *Isaac Asimov's Magical Worlds of Fantasy 4: Spells* (1985; U.K., 1988); *Country Ways* (1988); *The Trick of the Tale* (U.K., 1991); *The Wizard's Den* (2001). Adapted (TV) and broadcast on *CBS Library: Robbers, Rooftops and Witches*, Apr. 21, 1982.

1946

Stories

46–1 "Final Victim" (with Henry Hasse) (69)

Amazing Stories Feb. 1946. Reprinted *Amazing Stories* Aug. 1965.

46–2 "The Traveller" (70)

Weird Tales Mar. 1946. Reprinted *Weird Tales* (Canada) May 1946. Revised and collected *DC* (FBA, 1947) as "The Traveler" ("The Traveller," U.K. edition); *SRB* (1980), as "The Traveler." Collected *OC*—Ace U.K. edition only (1961). Rewritten as a chapter in *FDR* (2001). Anthologized *Beyond Midnight* (1976), *Witches and Warlocks* (1989).

46–3 "Defense Mech" (71)

Planet Stories spring 1946.

46–4 "Rocket Skin" (72)
Thrilling Wonder Stories spring 1946.

46–5 "The Miracles of Jamie" (73)
Charm Apr. 1946. Collected *LAM* (FBA, 1976), *BS* (2003).

46–6 "One Timeless Spring" (74)
Collier's Apr. 13, 1946. Reprinted *Literary Cavalcade* Apr. 1977. Collected *LAM* (FBA, 1976). Anthologized in one textbook, *Harper and Row English* (1983).

46–7 "The Smiling People" (75)
Weird Tales May 1946. Reprinted *Weird Tales* (Canada) July 1946, *Mike Shayne Mystery Magazine* Jan. 1971, *Weird Tales* fall 1973. Revised and collected *DC* (1947), *SA* (1962), *BS* (2003). Anthologized *The Night Side* (FBA, 1947; U.K., 1966), *Giant Mystery Reader* (1951), *The 10th Fontana Book of Great Horror Stories* (U.K., 1977).

46–8 "Her Eyes, Her Lips, Her Limbs" (as William Elliott) (76)
Californian June 1946.

46–9 "Lorelei of the Red Mist" (with Leigh Brackett) (77)
Planet Stories summer 1946. Reprinted *Tops in Science Fiction* fall 1953. Anthologized *Three Times Infinity* (FBA, abridged, 1958), *The Human Equation* (FBA, complete, 1971), *The Best of Planet Stories 1* (1975), *Isaac Asimov Presents the Great Science Fiction Stories 8: 1946* (1982), *Isaac Asimov Presents the Golden Years of Science Fiction Fourth Series* (1984), *Echoes of Valor II* (1989). Manuscript title: "Red Sea of Venus."

46–10 "The Million-Year Picnic" (78)
Planet Stories summer 1946. Reprinted *Argosy* (U.K.) Feb. 1950, as "The Long Weekend"; reprinted *Tops in Science Fiction* spring 1953, *Tops in Science Fiction 1* (U.K.) 1954. Collected *MC* (1950), *SL* (1951), as "October 2026: The Million-Year Picnic"; *SS* (1966), *SRB* (1980), *CS2* (1990), as "The Million-Year Picnic." Anthologized *Strange Ports of Call* (FBA, 1948), *Invasion from Mars* (1949), *Worlds of Wonder* (1951), *Beyond Tomorrow* (1965), *Science Fiction of the 40s* (1978), *The Road to Science Fiction 3* (1979), *Alien Worlds* (U.K., 1981), *Isaac Asimov Presents the Great Science Fiction Stories 8: 1946* (1982), *Isaac Asimov Presents the Golden Years of Science Fiction*, 4th ser. (1984), *SFWA Grandmasters* vol. 2 (2000). Anthologized in six textbooks, beginning with *American Literature* (1967); some include the *MC* date prefix in the title. Adapted for radio and broadcast with four other *MC* stories as "MC" on *Dimension X* (NBC), Aug. 18, 1950. Adapted (TV) and broadcast as part of the *MC* miniseries (NBC), Jan. 27–29, 1980. Adapted to comic-strip form by Al Feldstein (John Severin and Will Elder, illustrators) for EC Publications in *Weird Fantasy* 21 (Sept.–Oct. 1953), issue includes a letter by Bradbury. Manuscript title: "Family Outing."

46–11 "Chrysalis" (79)
Amazing Stories July 1946. Reprinted *Amazing Stories* Oct. 1965. Collected *SS* (FBA, 1966), *CS2* (1990). Anthologized *Amazing Science Fiction Anthology: The Wild Years 1946–1955* (1987).

46–12 "The Night" (80)
Weird Tales July 1946. Reprinted *Weird Tales* (Canada) Sept. 1946, *Man from U.N.C.L.E.* Jan. 1968, *Starwind* spring 1976. Collected *DC* (FBA, 1947), *SA* (1962), *SRB* (1980); rewritten and bridged into *DW* (1957), untitled. Anthologized *Suspense Stories* (1949). Anthologized in two textbooks, beginning with *Enjoying English 9* (1975); textbook title variations include "Ice Cream on a Summer's Evening." The *Starwind* reprint includes a prefatory description by Bradbury of the story's origin.

46–13 "The Electrocution" (as William Elliott) (81)
Californian Aug. 1946. Collected *LCE* (FBA, [Aug.] 1980, with Ray Bradbury byline), *QE* (1996).

46–14 "The Creatures That Time Forgot" ("Frost and Fire") (82)

Planet Stories fall 1946. Revised and collected *RR* (FBA, 1962), *SRB* (1980), *CS1* (1990), as "Frost and Fire." Anthologized *13 Short Horror Novels* (1987), as "Frost and Fire." Adapted (almost beyond recognition) to comic-strip form by Klaus Janson and published as a separate issue by DC Comics (1985), as "Frost and Fire." Adapted to film by Saul Bass and produced as the short feature *Quest* (1980s). Manuscript title: "Eight Day Wonder."

46–15 "Homecoming" (83)

Mademoiselle Oct. 1946 (as revised from original *DC* submission). Reprinted *Avon Fantasy Reader 3*, 1947; original version reprinted *Argosy* (U.K.) Sept. 1949, *Famous Fantastic Mysteries* Dec. 1952, as "The Homecoming." Original version collected *DC* (1947), as "The Homecoming"; revised version revised again and collected *OC* (1955), *SRB* (1980), as "Homecoming." Rewritten as a chapter in *FDR* (2001). Anthologized *Prize Stories of 1947: The O. Henry Awards* (FBA, 1947), *Best Black Magic Stories* (U.K., 1960), *Alfred Hitchcock's Monster Museum* (1965), *The Evil People* (1968), *Dying of Fright* (1976), *The Fantasy Hall of Fame* (1983), *Young Monsters* (1985; U.K., as *Asimov's Monsters*, 1986), *Vampire* (U.K., 1985), *Asimov's Ghosts and Monsters* (U.K., 1988), *Famous Fantastic Mysteries* (1991), *The Oxford Book of Fantasy Stories* (U.K., 1994), *Virtuous Vampires* (1996), *Vampires, Wine and Roses* (as "The Homecoming," 1997). Anthologized in one textbook, *The Supernatural in Fiction* (1973). Adapted to comic-strip form for *The Ray Bradbury Chronicles* vol. 3 (Nov. 1992). The *OC* paperback (mass market only) includes Bradbury's final revisions, introduced in galleys pulled between the hardback and paperback editions, and corrects a major transposition error introduced in the hardback edition; unfortunately, this error carries through to the recent Ballantine trade paperback and Avon hardbound editions.

46–16 "Let's Play 'Poison'" (84)

Weird Tales Nov. 1946. Reprinted *Weird Tales* (Canada) Jan. 1947, *All-Mystery* Oct.–Dec. 1950, *Mike Shayne Mystery Magazine* Nov. 1962, *Read* Dec. 4, 1970. Collected *DC* (FBA, 1947), *SA* (1962), *RB* (1975), *BS* (2003). Anthologized *Little Monsters* (1969), *Weird Tales: 32 Unearthed Terrors* (1988). Adapted (TV) by Bradbury for *Ray Bradbury Theater* (USA), Feb. 14, 1992. Adapted to comic-strip form by Al Feldstein (Jack Davis, illustrator) for EC Publications in *The Vault of Horror* 29 (Feb.–Mar. 1953); EC version collected in *The Autumn People* (Ballantine, 1965).

46–17 "The Small Assassin" (85)

Dime Mystery Nov. 1946. Reprinted *Suspense* Apr. 1951. Collected and successively revised *DC* (FBA, 1947), *OC* (1955), *SA* (1962), *VB* (1965), *SRB* (1980), *MEM* (1984). Deleted *OC*—Ace U.K. edition only (1961). Anthologized *Children of Wonder* (1953), *In the Dead of Night* (1961), *Tales of Terror and Suspense* (1963), *A Chamber of Horrors* (1965), *Shock* (1965), *Best Tales of Terror 2* (U.K., 1965), *Nightfrights* (1972), *Young Demons* (1972), *Classic Crime Stories* (1975), *Horror Stories* (U.K., 1978), *Deadly Doings* (1989), *The Horror Hall of Fame* (1991; U.K., 1992), *The Fantasy Hall of Fame* (1998), *Arkham's Masters of Horror* (2000). Adapted (TV) by Bradbury for *Ray Bradbury Theater* (USA), Apr. 9, 1988. Adapted to comic-strip form by Al Feldstein (George Evans, illustrator) for EC Publications in *Shock Suspenstories* 7 (Feb.–Mar. 1953); EC version collected in *The Autumn People* (Ballantine, 1965).

46–18 "A Careful Man Dies" (86)

New Detective Nov. 1946. Reprinted *Gamma* Sept. 1965 (ed. by William F. Nolan). Collected *MEM* (FBA, 1984). Anthologized *Urban Horrors* (1990).

1947

Books

47-A   *Dark Carnival*

Story collection. Sauk City, Wis.: Arkham House, [May 4], 1947; London: Hamish Hamilton [Nov. 1948]; limited edition (700 signed, 300 unsigned), Springfield, Pa.: Gauntlet, 2001. Contents (U.S. edition only): "The Homecoming"; "Skeleton"; "The Jar"; "The Lake"; "The Maiden"; "The Tombstone"; "The Smiling People"; "The Emissary"; "The Traveler"; "The Small Assassin"; "The Crowd"; "Reunion"; "The Handler"; "The Coffin"; "Interim"; "Jack-in-the-Box"; "The Scythe"; "Let's Play 'Poison'"; "Uncle Einar"; "The Wind"; "The Night"; "There Was an Old Woman"; "The Dead Man"; "The Man Upstairs"; "The Night Sets"; "Cistern"; "The Next in Line." U.K. first edition deletes "The Maiden"; "Reunion"; "The Coffin"; "Interim"; "Jack-in-the-Box"; "The Scythe"; and "The Night Sets"—the remaining stories appear in the order of the first U.S. edition. See also *OC* (55-B) and *SA* (62-A) for later evolutions of stories from this collection. The Gauntlet limited edition adds four previously uncollected stories first published in *Weird Tales:* "The Sea Shell"; "Bang! You're Dead!"; "The Poems"; and "The Watchers." These are placed between afterwords by Clive Barker ("The Last Unknown") and Bradbury (untitled); includes a new introduction by Bradbury, "Dark Carnival Revisited."

Stories

47-1   "The Handler" (87)

Weird Tales Jan. 1947. Reprinted *Weird Tales* (Canada) Mar. 1947, *Copy* spring 1950, *Satellite Science Fiction* Mar. 1959. Collected *DC* (FBA, 1947), *SA* (1962), *BB* (1969), *BS* (2003). Anthologized *Brrrr!* (1959), *The Unexpected* (1961), *Tales of Terror* (U.K., 1967). Adapted (TV) by Bradbury for *Ray Bradbury Theater* (USA), Oct. 26, 1992. Adapted to comic-strip form by Al Feldstein (Graham Ingels, illustrator) for EC Publications in *Tales From the Crypt* 36 (June–July 1953); EC version collected in *The Autumn People* (Ballantine, 1965).

47-2   "The Man Upstairs" (88)

Harper's Mar. 1947 (as revised from original *DC* submission). Reprinted *Avon Fantasy Reader 4*, 1947, *Argosy* (U.K.) Dec. 1951, *New Liberty* (Canada) Aug. 1952. Original version collected *DC* (FBA, 1947), *SA* (1962); revised version collected *OC* (1955), *SRB* (1980). Deleted *OC*—Ace U.K. edition only (1961). Anthologized *Harper's Magazine Reader* (1953), *The Vampire* (U.K., 1963), *Black Magic* (1967), *The 5th Fontana Book of Great Horror Stories* (1970), *The Beaver Book of Horror Stories* (U.K., 1981). Anthologized in one textbook, *Literature of the Supernatural* (1974). Adapted (TV) by Bradbury for *Ray Bradbury Theater* (USA), Mar. 5, 1988.

47-3   "Rocket Summer" (89)

Planet Stories spring 1947. This story should not be confused with the *MC* bridge, "January 1999: Rocket Summer."

47-4   "Tomorrow and Tomorrow" (90)

Fantastic Adventures May 1947. Reprinted *Fantastic* Nov. 1965. Anthologized *Time Untamed* (FBA, 1967). Opening passages by Leigh Brackett.[4]

47-5   "The Cistern" (91)

Mademoiselle May 1947 (as revised from original *DC* submission). Original version collected *DC* (FBA, 1947), as "Cistern." Revised version collected *OC* (1955), *SA* (1962), *BS* (2003), as "The Cistern." Deleted *OC*—Ace U.K. edition only (1961).

47–6 "The Coffin" (92)

DC (FBA, [May 10], 1947). Reprinted *Dime Mystery* Sept. 1947, as "Wake for the Living"; reprinted *Scholastic Voice* Oct. 29, 1982, as "The Coffin." Collected *SRB* (1980), *MEM* (1984), as "Wake for the Living." Deleted *DC* U.K. edition (1948). Anthologized *Modern Masterpieces of Science Fiction* (1965), *The Pulps* (1970), as "Wake for the Living"; anthologized *The Television Late Night Horror Omnibus* (U.K., 1993; U.S., as *Great Tales of Horror*, 1993), as "The Coffin." Adapted (TV) by Bradbury for *Ray Bradbury Theater* (USA), May 7, 1988. Adapted to comic-strip form by Al Feldstein (Jack Davis, illustrator) for EC Publications in *The Haunt of Fear* 16 (Nov.–Dec. 1952), as "The Coffin!"; EC version collected in *The Autumn People* (Ballantine, 1965); reprinted *Haunt of Fear*, n.s., 4 (Mar. 1992).

47–7 "The Emissary" (93)

DC (FBA, [May 10], 1947). Revised and reprinted *New Story* July 1951; rewritten *OC* version reprinted *Shock* July 1960, *Weird Worlds* 6 1980, *Scholastic Voice* Oct. 16, 1987, *Scholastic Scope* Oct. 18, 1991. Rewritten and collected *OC* (1955), *SRB* (1980). Anthologized *Best Tales of Terror [One]* (U.K., 1962), *The Fourth Pan Book of Horror Stories* (U.K., 1963; U.S., 1970), *The Hounds of Hell* (1974), *The Hell of Mirrors* (U.K., 1974), *Ghostly and Ghastly* (U.K., 1977), *A Dog's Life* (1978), *Thrillers, Chillers, and Killers* (1979), *Ghosts That Haunt You* (U.K., 1980), *Roger Caras' Treasury of Great Dog Stories* (1987), *Ghost Stories* (U.K., 1988), *Dark Voices* (U.K., 1990), *The Greatest Dog Stories* (2001). Anthologized in one textbook, *Ripples* (Singapore, 1992). Adapted for radio and broadcast, with other stories, and a Bradbury interview as "October Country," an ABC Halloween special, Oct. 31, 1984; adapted (TV) by Bradbury for *Ray Bradbury Theater* (USA), Feb. 13, 1988. Adapted (without credit) to comic-strip form by Al Feldstein (Jack Kamen, illustrator) for EC Publications in *Vault of Horror* 22 (Dec. 1951–Jan. 1952), as "What the Dog Dragged In."

47–8 "Interim" (94)

DC (FBA, [May 10], 1947). Reprinted *Weird Tales* July 1947 and (Canada) Sept. 1947. Deleted *DC* U.K. edition (1948). Anthologized *Fiends and Creatures* (1975), *A Fantasy Reader* (1981), *Weird Tales* (1988). Not related to *Epoch* story of same title (47–15).

47–9 "Jack-in-the-Box" (95)

DC (FBA, [May 10], 1947). Reprinted *Avon Fantasy Reader 17* 1951. Deleted *DC* U.K. edition (1948). Revised and collected *OC* (1955), *SA* (1962), *SRB* (1980). Deleted *OC*—Ace U.K. edition only (1961).

47–10 "The Maiden" (96)

DC (FBA, [May 10], 1947). Deleted *DC* U.K. edition (1948). Anthologized *Lovers and Other Monsters* (Guild America, 1992).

47–11 "The Next in Line" (97)

DC (FBA, [May 10], 1947). Reprinted (abridged) *Playboy* Dec. 1955. Collected *OC* (1955), *SA* (1962), *MG* (1978), *SRB* (1980). Deleted *OC*—Ace U.K. edition only (1961). Anthologized *The Fontana Book of Great Horror Stories* (1966).

47–12 "The Night Sets" (98)

DC (FBA, [May 10], 1947). Deleted *DC* U.K. edition (1948).

47–13 "Uncle Einar" (99)

DC (FBA, [May 10], 1947). Reprinted *Argosy* (U.K.) Oct. 1949, *Read* Sept. 1, 1963, *Weird Worlds* 8 1981. Revised and collected *OC* (1955), *RR* (1962), *TS* (1979), *SRB* (1980), *CS1* (1990). Rewritten as a chapter in *FDR* (2001). Anthologized *Haunting Tales* (1973), *Masterpieces of Fantasy and Enchantment* (1988). Anthologized in one textbook, *Daybook 7*

(1999). Adapted to comic-strip form for *Ray Bradbury's Tales of Terror* Special 1 (May 1994).

47–14 "El Dia De Muerte" (100)
Touchstone fall 1947. Reprinted *Gamma 2* 1963, as "Sombra Y Sol." Collected *MJ* (FBA, 1964).

47–15 "Interim" ("Time Intervening") (101)
Epoch fall 1947. Reprinted *Ray Bradbury Review* Jan. 1952, as "Time Intervening"; reprinted *Eureka Literary Magazine* spring 1994. Collected *OM* (2002), *BS* (2003), as "Time Intervening." Anthologized *Timescape* (FBA, U.K., 1997; U.S., as *Time Travelers*, 1998), as "Time Intervening." Not related to *Weird Tales* story of the same title (47–8).

47–16 "Zero Hour" (102)
Planet Stories fall 1947. Reprinted *Avon Fantasy Reader 8* 1948, *Read* Sept. 9, 1983. Collected *IM* (1951), *SS* (1966), *RB* (1975), *CS2* (1990), *BS* (2003). Anthologized *Invasion from Mars* (FBA, 1949), *My Best Science Fiction Story* (1949), *Best SF Two* (U.K., 1956), *The Best Science Fiction Stories* (U.K., 1977), *Isaac Asimov Presents the Great S F Stories 9 (1947)* (1983), *Isaac Asimov Presents the Golden Years of Science Fiction Fifth Series* (1985), *The World Treasury of Science Fiction* (1989), *Bruce Coville's Book of Aliens* (1994; U.K., as *Bruce Coville's Book of Aliens and Ghosts*, 1996), *Supernatural Stories* (U.K., 1995; U.S., 1996). Anthologized in six textbooks, beginning with *Aspects of Science Fiction* (U.K., 1959). Adapted for radio and broadcast on *Dimension X* (NBC), June 17, 1950; *X Minus 1* (NBC) Dec. 5, 1956; adapted again and broadcast on *Escape* (CBS), Oct. 4, 1953; adapted and broadcast on *Suspense* (CBS), Apr. 5, 1955, May 18, 1958; adapted and broadcast on *Experiment in Drama* (NBC), Aug. 27, 1973; adapted and broadcast on *Lights Out* (NBC), July 23, 1951; adapted by Bradbury for *Ray Bradbury Theater* (USA), Jan. 10, 1992. Adapted to comic-strip form by Al Feldstein (Jack Kamen, illustrator) for EC Publications in *Weird Fantasy 18* (Mar.–Apr. 1953). Manuscript title: "The Children's Hour."

47–17 "I See You Never" (103)
New Yorker Nov. 8, 1947. Reprinted *Literary Cavalcade* (Feb. 1998). Collected *GA* (1953), *T22* (1966), *CS1* (1990), *BS* (2003). Anthologized *Best American Short Stories of 1948* (FBA, 1948), *75 Short Masterpieces* (1961), *The World's Best Short Short Stories* (1967), *Sudden Fiction* (1986). Anthologized in twenty textbooks, beginning with *Modern English Readings*, 7th ed. (1956). Two other textbooks are notable: the story received significant critical endorsement and classroom exposure through the classic textbook, Cleanth Brooks and Robert Penn Warren, *Understanding Fiction* (2d ed., 1959), and Cleanth Brooks, *The Scope of Fiction* (1960).

47–18 "The Irritated People" (104)
Thrilling Wonder Stories Dec. 1947. Reprinted *Wonder Story Annual* 1953, *Science Fiction Yearbook 1* 1967.

1948

Stories

48–1 "The Candy Skull" (105)
Dime Mystery Jan. 1948. Reprinted *Detective Tales Magazine* (U.K.) Nov. 1960. Collected *MEM* (1984). Anthologized *Masters of Horror* (FBA, 1968), *Hallowe'en Hauntings* (U.K., 1984), *The Second Black Lizard Anthology of Crime Fiction* (1988), *Homicidal Acts* (1989).

48–2 "The Shape of Things" ("Tomorrow's Child") (106)

Thrilling Wonder Stories Feb. 1948. Reprinted *Argosy* (U.K.) Apr. 1970, as "Tomorrow's Child." Collected *IS* (1969), *SRB* (1980), as "Tomorrow's Child." Anthologized *Travelers of Space* (FBA, 1951), *The Shape of Things* (1965), *The Unspeakable People* (1969), *Tales Out of Time* (1979); anthologized *Space 2* (U.K., 1974), as "Tomorrow's Child." Adapted (TV) by Bradbury for *Ray Bradbury Theater* (USA), Aug. 14, 1982, as "Tomorrow's Child."

48–3 "The October Game" (107)

Weird Tales Mar. 1948. Reprinted *Weird Tales* (Canada) Mar. 1948, *Alfred Hitchcock's Mystery Magazine* June 1957, *Alfred Hitchcock's Mystery Sampler* spring 1958, *Mike Shayne Mystery Magazine* Nov. 1963. Collected *LAM* (1976), *SRB* (1980). Anthologized *Alfred Hitchcock Presents: Stories They Wouldn't Let Me Do on T.V.* (FBA, 1957), *13 Ways to Dispose of a Body* (1966), *Christopher Lee's New Chamber of Horrors* (U.K., 1974), *Gooseflesh!* (1974), *Deadly Nightshade* (1977), *The World Fantasy Awards 2* (1980), *65 Great Tales of Horror* (U.K., 1981), *13 Horrors of Halloween* (1983), *Nursery Crimes* (1993). Anthologized in one textbook, *Man to Himself* (1970). Adapted to comic-strip form by Al Feldstein (Jack Kamen, illustrator) for EC Publications in *Shock Suspenstories* 9 (June–July 1953).

48–4 "Powerhouse" (108)

Charm Mar. 1948. Collected *GA* (1953), *T22* (1966), *SRB* (1980), *CS1* (1990). Anthologized *Prize Stories of 1948: The O. Henry Awards* (FBA, 1948).

48–5 "Jonah of the Jove Run" (109)

Planet Stories spring 1948. Manuscript title: "The Calculator."

48–6 "The Black Ferris" (110)

Weird Tales May 1948. Reprinted *Weird Tales* (Canada) May 1948, *Outré* Oct. 1997. Revised and bridged into *SW* (1962), chap. 18; original collected *SRB* (1980). Anthologized *The Dark Side* (FBA—original, 1965), *The Devil's Generation* (1973), *A Treasury of Modern Fantasy* (1981), *American Fantasy Tradition* (2002), *Beware!* (2002). Anthologized in two textbooks, beginning with *Scope Reading 3* (1967); textbook title variations include "The Ferris Wheel." Adapted (TV) as a series pilot and broadcast on *Sneak Preview* (NBC), July 10, 1956, as "Merry-Go-Round"; adapted (TV) by Bradbury for *Ray Bradbury Theater* (USA), Aug. 10, 1990. Adapted to comic-strip form by Al Feldstein (Jack Davis, illustrator) for EC Publications in *The Haunt of Fear* 18 (Mar.–Apr. 1953; issue also contains a letter by Bradbury). Adapted again (without credit) to comic-strip form by Len Wein (Berni Wrightson, illustrator) for DC Publications in *The House of Mystery* 221 (Jan. 1974), as "He Who Laughs Last." William F. Nolan's headnote to the *Outré* reprinting surveys the way this story grew into an unproduced screenplay (as "Dark Carnival") and eventually into the novel and film *SW*.

48–7 " . . . And the Moon be Still as Bright" (111)

Thrilling Wonder Stories June 1948. Revised and collected *MC* (1950), *SL* (1951), *BS* (2003), as "June 2001:—And the Moon Be Still as Bright." Anthologized *Best Science Fiction Stories: 1949* (FBA, 1949), *Science Fiction Omnibus* (1952), *The Best Science Fiction Stories* (U.K., 1977). Anthologized in one textbook, *Other Worlds* (U.K., 1990). Adapted for radio and broadcast with four other *MC* stories as "MC" on *Dimension X* (NBC), Aug. 18, 1950; again as a standalone radio play on *Dimension X*, Sept. 29, 1950, and *X Minus 1* (NBC), May 8, 1955. Adapted (TV) by Bradbury for *Ray Bradbury Theater* (USA), Oct. 19, 1990.

48–8 "Pillar of Fire" (112)

Planet Stories summer 1948. Collected *SS* (1966), *CS2* (1990). Anthologized *The Other Side of the Moon* (FBA, 1949; U.K., 1956), *A Treasury of Great Science Fiction* vol. 1 (1959),

The Midnight People (U.K., 1968; as *Vampires at Midnight,* 1970), *Tomorrow Sucks* (1994). Adapted to stage by Bradbury and collected *PF* (1975), *RBOS* (1991). Adapted for radio and broadcast on *2000X* (2001).

[48–9   Bradbury ghosted the opening section of "The Undead Die," by E. Everett Evans (*Weird Tales,* July 1948). This tale is provided an entry, but is not given a number in Bradbury's total story count.]

48–10   "The Earth Men" (113)

Thrilling Wonder Stories Aug. 1948. Reprinted *Esquire* Nov. 1950, combined with "The Spring Night" as "The Great Hallucination"; reprinted *Argosy* (U.K.) Feb. 1951, combined with "The Spring Night" as "Danger Wears Three Faces"; reprinted *A Treasury of Great S.F. Stories 1* 1964. Revised and collected *MC* (1950), *SL* (1951), as "August 1999: The Earth Men"; collected as revised *SRB* (1980), but without title prefix. Anthologized *The Other Side of the Moon* (FBA, 1949; U.K., 1956), *Toward Infinity* (1968). Anthologized in two textbooks, beginning with *Currents* (1971). Adapted for radio and broadcast on *Escape* (CBS), July 25, 1951. Adapted to stage and separately printed *Literary Cavalcade* Apr. 1977, as *MC.* Adapted (TV) by Bradbury for *Ray Bradbury Theater* (USA), Jan. 3, 1992.

48–11   "Fever Dream" (114)

Weird Tales Sept. 1948. Reprinted *Weird Tales* (Canada) Sept. 1948, *Short Stories* Feb. 1959, *Swingle* Sept. 1975, *Weird Worlds 5* 1980; reprinted *Lab World* July 1979, as "Creation: The Moment of Touch"; reprinted as an illustrated book (New York: St. Martin's, 1987). Rewritten and collected *MM* (FBA, 1959), *DRF* (1959), *VB* (1965), *BB* (1969), *RB* (1975), *TS* (1979), *SRB* (1980), *CS2* (1990). Anthologized *Beyond the Curtain of Dark* (1966), *Tales of the Uncanny* (U.K., 1968), *Supernatural* (Australia, 1974), *The Ghost's Companion* (1975), *Tales from beyond the Grave* (1982), *Horrifying and Hideous Hauntings* (1986), *Shape Changers* (1999). Anthologized in ten textbooks, beginning with *Designs for Reading: Short Stories* (1969). The underlying idea for this story can be traced back to the prose poem "Wilbur and His Germ" (41–4). The 1987 illustrated book version (a "Glow in the Dark Book," with illustrations by Darrel Anderson) lists the *Weird Tales* copyright but follows the text Bradbury revised for *MM* (1959).

48–12   "End of Summer" (115)

Script Sept. 1948. Collected *DB* (FBA, 1997).

48–13   "The Long Years" (116)

Maclean's (Canada) Sept. 15, 1948 (inadvertently as by "Roy" Bradbury). Reprinted *Argosy* (U.K.) Mar. 1949; reprinted *Planet Stories* spring 1949, *Planet Stories* (Canada) spring 1949, *American Science Fiction 19* (Australia) [1953], as "Dwellers in Silence." Revised and collected *MC* (FBA, 1950), *SL* (1951), *BS* (2003), as "April 2026: The Long Years." Anthologized *Best Science Fiction Stories: 1950* (1950; deleted U.K. edition, 1951), *Science Fiction Omnibus* (1952), as "Dwellers in Silence." Anthologized twice in textbooks, beginning with *Fiction for Composition* (1968); textbook title variations include "Dwellers in Silence." Adapted for radio as "Dwellers in Silence" and broadcast on *Dimension X* (NBC), July 19, 1951; and on *X Minus 1* (NBC), Nov. 10, 1955. Adapted (TV) by Bradbury under original title for *Ray Bradbury Theater* (USA), Nov. 16, 1990. Adapted to comic-strip form by Al Feldstein (Joe Orlando, illustrator) for EC Publications in *Weird Science 17* (Jan.–Feb. 1953; issue includes a letter from Bradbury). EC version collected in *Tomorrow Midnight* (Ballantine, 1966).

48–14   "Mars Is Heaven!" ("April 2000: The Third Expedition") (117)

Planet Stories fall 1948. Reprinted *Esquire* Dec. 1950; reprinted *Argosy* (U.K.) Apr. 1950, as "Circumstantial Evidence"; *Coronet* June 1950, as "They Landed on Mars" (condensed);

Authentic Science Fiction 29 (U.K.) Jan. 1952, as "Welcome Brothers"; *Suspense* (U.K.) Nov. 1958, as "While Earthmen Sleep." Revised and collected *MC* (1950), *SL* (1951), as "April 2000: The Third Expedition"; collected as revised *SRB* (1980), as "Mars Is Heaven!" Anthologized *Best Science Fiction Stories 1949* (FBA, 1949), *Shot in the Dark* (1950), *Science Fiction Omnibus* (1952), *Best Horror Stories* (U.K., 1957), *Worlds to Come* (1967), *Science Fiction Hall of Fame v1* (1970), *Isaac Asimov Presents the Great S F Stories 10 (1948)* (1983), *Isaac Asimov Presents the Golden Years of Science Fiction, Fifth Series* (1985); anthologized *Space Odyssey* (1983), as "The Third Expedition"; anthologized *Read into the Millenium* (1999), as "April 2000: The Third Expedition." Anthologized in seven textbooks, beginning with *Perception* (1969); textbook title variations include "April 2000: The Third Expedition." Adapted for radio and broadcast on *Escape* (CBS), June 2, 1950; *Dimension X* (NBC), Aug. 18, 1950; and *X Minus 1* (NBC), May 8, 1955; adapted for *ABC Radio Workshop* (Mar. 16, 1953), as "Think." Adapted (TV, without credit) for broadcast on *Wide World Mystery* (ABC), Oct. 21, 1975, as "Distant Early Warning"; adapted (TV) by Bradbury for *Ray Bradbury Theater* under the original title (USA), July 20, 1990. Adapted to comic-strip form by Al Feldstein (Wally Wood, illustrator) for EC Publications in *Weird Science* 18 (Mar.–Apr. 1953); EC version collected in *Tomorrow Midnight* (Ballantine, 1966) and subsequently anthologized in the textbook *What's Happening* (1969). Bradbury adapted parts of "Mars Is Heaven!" and "Ylla" (50–1) to comic-strip form (illustrated by Doug Wildey and John Cassone from a Joe Mugnaini concept) for *West* (*Los Angeles Times*, Mar. 12, 1972), as "MC" (issue includes a Bradbury article, "Where Are the Golden-Eyed Martians?"). Influenced the basic premise of Stephen King's *Bag of Bones* (Bradbury's title appears as an epigraph).

48–15 "Referent" (as Brett Sterling) (118)
Thrilling Wonder Stories Oct. 1948. Revised and collected *DRF* (1959). Revised and anthologized *Imagination Unlimited* (FBA, 1952; U.K., 1953) with Ray Bradbury byline.

48–16 "The Square Pegs" (119)
Thrilling Wonder Stories Oct. 1948.

48–17 "The Women" (120)
Famous Fantastic Mysteries Oct. 1948. Reprinted *Argosy* May 1974. Collected *IS* (1969), *SRB* (1980). Anthologized *The Fiend in You* (FBA, 1962), *Sea Cursed* (1992), *Splash!* (1996).

48–18 "The Visitor" (121)
Startling Stories Nov. 1948. Reprinted *Science Fiction Yearbook 5* 1971. Collected *IM* (FBA, 1951), BS (2003). Adapted to comic-strip form for *Ray Bradbury's The Illustrated Man Special* 1 (1993). An "unchronicled" Martian tale.

48–19 "The Off Season" (122)
Thrilling Wonder Stories Dec. 1948. Revised and collected *MC* (FBA, 1950), *SL* (1951), as "November 2005: The Off Season"; collected *SRB* (1980), as "The Off Season." Anthologized in *The SF Collection* (U.K., 1994). Anthologized in one textbook, *Apples and Oranges* (1995). Adapted for radio and broadcast with four other *MC* stories as "MC" on *Dimension X* (NBC), Aug. 18, 1950. Adapted to comic-strip form for *Ray Bradbury's Martian Chronicles Spaceman Special* (June 1994).

48–20 "Asleep in Armageddon" (123)
Planet Stories winter 1948. Reprinted *Avon Fantasy Reader 11* 1949, *Argosy* (U.K.) Feb. 1952, *Authentic Science Fiction 33* (U.K.) May 15, 1953, *Beyond the Stars 211* (Australia) [1955]. Collected *DRF* (1959), as "Perchance to Dream." Anthologized *Possible Worlds of Science Fiction* (FBA, 1951; U.K., 1952), *Asleep in Armageddon* (U.K., 1962), *Between Time and Terror* (1995).

48–21 "Touch and Go" ("The Fruit at the Bottom of the Bowl") (124)

Detective Book winter 1948. Reprinted *Ellery Queen Mystery Magazine* Jan. 1953, *Argosy* (U.K.) Mar. 1954, *Cavalier* Feb. 1960, as "The Fruit at the Bottom of the Bowl"; reprinted *Men* Mar. 1962, as "The Last Fingerprint." Collected *GA* (FBA, 1953), *VB* (1965), *T22* (1966), *CS1* (1990), *BS* (2003), as "The Fruit at the Bottom of the Bowl." Anthologized *Ellery Queen's 1962 Anthology* (1962), *Ellery Queen's 12* (1964), *Best Murder Stories* (U.K., 1965), *Mystery and Suspense Stories* (U.K., 1977), *Murder Most Foul* (1984), as "The Fruit at the Bottom of the Bowl." Anthologized in one textbook, *Horror* (1978), as "The Fruit at the Bottom of the Bowl." Adapted (TV) by Bradbury for *Ray Bradbury Theater* (USA), Jan. 23, 1988. Adapted to comic-strip form by Al Feldstein (Johnny Craig, illustrator) for EC Publications in Crime *Suspenstories* 17 (June–July 1953); EC version collected in *The Autumn People* (Ballantine, 1965).

1949

Stories

49–1 "The Spring Night" (125)

Arkham Sampler 2, no. 1 (winter 1949). Reprinted *Esquire* Nov. 1950, combined with "The Earth Men" as "The Great Hallucination"; reprinted *Argosy* (U.K.) Feb. 1951, combined with "The Earthmen" as "Danger Wears Three Faces." Revised and collected *MC* (FBA, 1950), *SL* (1951), as "August 2005: The Summer Night."

49–2 "The Man" (126)

Thrilling Wonder Stories Feb. 1949. Reprinted *Newsday* Apr. 12, 1952, *Boy's Life* Dec. 1961. Collected *IM* (1951), *SS* (1966), *CS2* (1990), *BS* (2003). Anthologized *Best Science Fiction Stories, 1950* (FBA, 1950; deleted U.K. edition, 1951), *Science Fiction Omnibus* (1952), *The Boy's Life Book of Outer Space Stories* (1964). Adapted (TV) for broadcast on *Out There* (CBS), Dec. 23, 1951. Adapted to comic-strip form (Howard S. Taylor, illustrator) for *Kaleidoscope* 1 (1967).

49–3 "The Great Fire" (127)

Seventeen Mar. 1949. Collected *GA* (1953), *T22* (1966), *SRB* (1980), *CS1* (1990). Deleted *GA* U.K. edition (1953). Anthologized *The Best Humor of 1949–1950* (FBA, 1950), *Nineteen From Seventeen* (1952).

49–4 "The Silent Towns" (128)

Charm Mar. 1949. Revised and collected *MC* (FBA, 1950), *SL* (1951), as "December 2005: The Silent Towns"; collected as revised *SRB* (1980), as "The Silent Towns." Adapted (TV) by Bradbury for Ray Bradbury Theater (USA), Oct. 10, 1992. Adapted to comic-strip form by Al Feldstein (Reed Crandall, illustrator) for EC Publications in *Weird Fantasy* 22 (Nov.–Dec. 1953).

49–5 "Marionettes, Inc." (129)

Startling Stories Mar. 1949. Reprinted *Thrills Incorporated* 8 (Australia) 1950, as "Synthetic Alibi" (as by D. K. Garton); reprinted *Argosy* (U.K.) June 1951, as "No Strings Attached"; reprinted *Science Fiction Yearbook* 4 1970, *Read* Jan. 3, 1975, *The Japan Times* 36–39 (Sept. 4, 11, 18, 25, 1992). Collected *IM* (FBA, 1951), *RB* (1975), *SRB* (1980). Anthologized *Tall Short Stories* (1959; U.K., as *Tall Stories*), *Hilton Bedside Book Volume 6* (1964), as "No Strings Attached." Anthologized in four textbooks, beginning with *Me, Myself, and I* (1975); textbook title variations include "Wondercopy." Adapted for radio and broadcast on *Dimension X* (NBC), Aug. 30, 1951, and on *X Minus 1* (NBC), Dec. 21, 1955. Adapted (TV) for broadcast on *Alfred Hitchcock Presents* (CBS), Nov. 9, 1958, as "Design for Loving"; adapted (TV) by Bradbury for *Ray Bradbury Theater* (HBO), May 21, 1985. Adapted to comic-strip form for *The Ray Bradbury Chronicles* vol. 1 (July 1992). The first of three "Marionette" or human "stand-in" concept stories that Bradbury published during this period; the others are "Changeling" (49–10) and "Punishment without Crime" (50–5).

49–6   "The Concrete Mixer" (130)

Thrilling Wonder Stories Apr. 1949. Reprinted *Playboy* Jan. 1955. Revised and collected *IM* (FBA, 1951). Deleted *IM* U.K. edition (1952). Adapted (TV) by Bradbury for *Ray Bradbury Theater* (USA), Jan. 31, 1992.

49–7   "I, Mars" ("Night Call, Collect") (131)

Super Science Stories Apr. 1949. Rewritten and collected *IS* (1969), *SRB* (1980), as "Night Call, Collect." Anthologized *A Wilderness of Stars* (FBA, 1969), *Tales of Terror from Outer Space* (U.K., 1975), *The Weekend Book of Science Fiction* (U.K., 1981). An "unchronicled" Martian tale.

49–8   "The One Who Waits" (132)

Arkham Sampler summer 1949. Reprinted *Magazine of Fantasy and Science Fiction* Feb. 1951, *Argosy* (U.K.) Feb. 1951, *Science Fiction Monthly 8* (U.K.) 1974. Collected *MJ* (1964), *SRB* (1980). Anthologized *Far Boundaries* (FBA, 1951; U.K., 1965), *Three Stances of Modern Fiction* (textbook, 1972), *Space 7* (U.K., 1981). Anthologized in three textbooks, beginning with *Headway* (1970). Adapted to comic-strip form by Al Feldstein (Al Williamson, illustrator) for EC Publications in *Weird Science* 19 (May–June 1953, issue also contains a letter by Bradbury); EC version collected in *Tomorrow Midnight* (Ballantine, 1966). An "unchronicled" Martian tale.

49–9   "The Lonely Ones" (133)

Startling Stories July 1949. Collected *BS* (2003). An "unchronicled" Martian tale; a simpler variation on the themes developed in "Impossible" ("The Martian," 49–15).

49–10   "Changeling" (134)

Super Science Stories July 1949. Reprinted *King* (U.K.) July 1966, as "The Changeling." Anthologized *The Pseudo-People* (FBA, 1965; U.K. anthology titled *Almost Human*, 1966), *The Monster Makers* (1974), *Terrors, Torments, and Traumas* (1978). Anthologized in one textbook, *Enjoying Stories* (1986). Adapted to comic-strip form by Al Feldstein (Jack Kamen, illustrator) for EC Publications in *Weird Science* 20 (July–Aug. 1953), as "Surprise Package." The second of Bradbury's three "marionette" tales of this period, the others being "Marionettes, Inc." (49–5) and "Punishment without Crime" (50–5).

49–11   "The Naming of Names" ("Dark They Were, and Golden-Eyed") (135)

Thrilling Wonder Stories Aug. 1949. Reprinted *Argosy* (U.K.) Mar. 1959, as "Dark and Golden Eyed"; reprinted *Great Science Fiction Stories 3* 1966; reprinted as a single-story book (New York: Writers' Voices, 1991), as "Dark They Were, and Golden-Eyed." Rewritten and collected *MM* (1959), *DRF* (1959), *SS* (1966), *T22* (1966), *SRB* (1980), *CS2* (1990), as "Dark They Were, and Golden-Eyed." Anthologized *Best from Startling Stories* (FBA, 1953; U.K., 1954), *Science and Sorcery* (1953), *The Other Dimension* (1972), *Gates to Tomorrow* (1973), *Alien Visitors* (1996), *Masterpieces* (2001). Anthologized in twenty-six textbooks, beginning with *New Trails* (1958); textbook title variations include "Dark They Were, and Golden Eyed." Adapted to comic-strip form for *The Ray Bradbury Chronicles* vol. 1 (July 1992), as "Dark They Were, and Golden-Eyed."

49–12   "Holiday" (136)

Arkham Sampler autumn 1949. Anthologized *Far Boundaries* (FBA, 1951; U.K., 1965). An "unchronicled" Martian tale.

49-13 "The Mad Wizards of Mars" ("The Exiles") (137)

Maclean's (Canada) Sept. 15, 1949. Revised from FBA version and reprinted *Magazine of Fantasy and Science Fiction* winter–spring 1950, as "The Exiles." Revised again and collected *IM* (1951), *RR* (1962), *CS1* (1990), *BS* (2003), as "The Exiles." Deleted *IM* U.K. edition (1952). Anthologized *Beyond Time and Space* (FBA, 1950), as "The Exiles." Revised from reprint and anthologized *The Witchcraft Reader* (1969), as "The Mad Wizards of Mars." Anthologized in two textbooks, beginning with *Decades of Science Fiction* (1998); textbook title variations include "The Exiles" and "From *The Illustrated Man*." An "unchronicled" Martian tale.

49-14 "Kaleidoscope" (138)

Thrilling Wonder Stories Oct. 1949. Revised and collected *IM* (FBA, 1951), *VB* (1965), *SRB* (1980). Anthologized *Omnibus of Science Fiction* (1952; U.K., as *Strange Travels in Science Fiction*, 1954), *Great Stories of Space Travel* (1963), *Best SF Six* (U.K., 1966), *History of the Science Fiction Magazine V. 3 1946–1955* (1976), *The Best Science Fiction Stories* (U.K., 1977), *The Arbor House Treasury of Modern Science Fiction* (1980), *Isaac Asimov Presents the Great S F Stories 11 (1949)* (1984), *Isaac Asimov Presents the Golden Years of Science Fiction, Sixth Series* (1988), *Tales from Space* (1998). Anthologized in two textbooks, beginning with *Space Suits and Gumshoes* (Toronto, 1972). Adapted for radio and broadcast on *Dimension X* (NBC), Sept. 15, 1951, and on *Suspense* (CBS), July 12, 1955. Adapted to stage by Bradbury and collected *PF* (1975), *RBOS* (1991); reprinted separately (Woodstock, Ill.: Dramatic, 1986). Adapted (without credit) to comic-strip form by Al Feldstein (Wally Wood, illustrator) for EC Publications in *Weird Fantasy* 13 (May–June 1952), combined with "The Rocket Man" (51–8) as "Home to Stay." Adapted to comic-strip form for *Ray Bradbury's Martian Chronicles Spaceman Special* (June 1994).

49-15 "Impossible" ("The Martian") (139)

Super Science Stories Nov. 1949. Collected *MC* (FBA, 1950), *SL* (1951), as "September 2005: The Martian." Adapted for radio and broadcast with other *MC* stories as "MC" on *Dimension X* (NBC), Aug. 18, 1950. Adapted (TV) as part of the *MC* miniseries (NBC), Jan. 27–29, 1980; adapted (TV) by Bradbury for *Ray Bradbury Theater* (USA), Feb. 21, 1992.

49-16 "A Blade of Grass" (140)

Thrilling Wonder Stories Dec. 1949. Reprinted *Thrilling Wonder Stories* (U.K.) May 1950. Collected *BS* (2003).

1950

Books

50-A *The Martian Chronicles / The Silver Locusts*
Novelized story cycle.

A1 The American first edition of *MC* ([May 4], 1950): fifteen stories, eleven bridge passages. Editions: Garden City, N.Y.: Doubleday, [May] 1950; New York: Bantam, May 1951 (paperback); Garden City, N.Y.: Doubleday, [Nov.] 1952 (Science Fiction Book Club, reissued 1978); New York: Bantam, 1954 (reset paperback); Garden City, N.Y.: Doubleday, [May] 1958; New York: Bantam, 2001 (reset paperback); as *SL*—London: Transworld, 1963. Collected in the omnibus *RB2* (87-E). Contents: "January 1999: Rocket Summer" (bridge); "February 1999: Ylla"; "August 1999: The Summer Night"; "August 1999: The Earth Men"; "March 2000: The Taxpayer" (bridge); "April 2000: The Third Expedition"; "June 2001: And the Moon Be Still as Bright"; "August 2001: The Settlers" (bridge); "December 2001: The Green Morning"; "February 2002: The Locusts" (bridge); "August 2002: Night Meeting"; "October 2002: The Shore" (bridge); "February 2003: Interim" (bridge); "April 2003: The Musicians" (bridge); "June 2003: Way in the Middle of the Air"; "2004–2005: The Naming of Names" (bridge); "April 2005: Usher II"; "August 2005: The Old Ones" (bridge); "September 2005: The Martian"; "November 2005: The Luggage Store" (bridge); "November 2005: The Off Season"; "November 2005: The Watchers" (bridge); "December 2005: The Silent Towns"; "April 2026: The Long Years"; "August 2026: There Will Come Soft Rains"; "October 2026: The Million-Year Picnic."

A2 The U.K. first edition of *SL* (1951): fifteen stories, eleven bridge passages. Editions: London: Rupert Hart-Davis, [Sept.] 1951; London: Corgi, [May] 1956 (paperback). As *MC*—London and New York: Granada, 1979 (paperback); London and New York: Granada, 1980. Contents: Deletes "April 2005: Usher II" and adds "November 2002: The Fire Balloons."

A3 The U.K. Science Fiction Book Club edition of *MC* (1953): sixteen stories, eleven bridge passages. Editions: [London]: Science Fiction Book Club, 1953. Contents : Adds "May 2003: The Wilderness" to *SL* text.

A4 The "complete" text of *MC* (1963): seventeen stories, eleven bridge passages. Editions: New York: Time, [Aug.] 1963 (paperback); Garden City, N.Y.: Doubleday, [June] 1973; Avon, Conn.: Limited Editions Club, [Dec.] 1974; Avon, Conn.: Heritage Club, 1976; New York: Bantam, Sept. 1979 (first large-format trade paperback); Norwalk, Conn.: Easton, 1989. Contents: The original first-edition U.S. *MC* text plus "November 2002: The Fire Balloons" and "May 2003: The Wilderness."

A5 The "restored" original text of *MC* (1990): sixteen stories, eleven bridge passages. Editions: New York: Doubleday, [Nov.] 1990, fortieth-anniversary edition. Contents: Restores "November 2002: The Fire Balloons" to the original U.S. text but does not include "May 2003: The Wilderness."

A6 The "updated and revised" text of *MC* (1997): sixteen stories, eleven bridge passages. Editions: New York: Avon, [Feb.] 1997. Contents: Shifts the dates in the chapter-title prefixes a quarter century into the future and deletes the outdated "Way in the Middle of the Air" from the "complete" U.S. text.

General notes, 50-A1–6: One bridge passage, "2004–2005: The Naming of Names," was collected as a stand-alone story in *BS* (2003); another bridge, "March 2000: The Taxpayer," reprinted in *Scholastic Scope* (Mar. 6, 2000). Three other bridge passages anthologized in textbooks, with their *MC* title prefixes: "The Locusts" (*From Experience*, 1972); "The Luggage Store" (*Focus on Composition*, 1978); and "The Settlers" (*Starting Points in Language*, 1973). Two bridges have appeared in textbooks under variant titles: "Rocket Summer" (*The Language Lens*, 1974), combined with "Ylla" as "From a City on Earth"; and "The Settlers" (*In Common*, 1975), as "There's Work for You in the Sky." Two bridge passages, ("Rocket Summer" and "The Locusts") were adapted to comic-strip form for *The Ray Bradbury Chronicles* vol. 2 (July 1992). Anthologized *MC* stories are listed under the individual story/chapter titles; excerpts titled *MC* have been anthologized in six textbooks, beginning with a grouping of untitled bridge passages in *Fictional Chronicle 4* (1973). Five stories ("Ylla," "And the Moon Be Still as Bright," "There Will Come Soft Rains," "The Off Season," and "The Million-Year Picnic") adapted to radio and broadcast on *Dimension X* (NBC) as "The Martian Chronicles." *MC* adapted to stage by Candace Sorensen and published in one textbook, *Theatre for Youth* (1986). Many chapters of the "complete" text (50-A3) adapted (TV) as a miniseries (NBC), airing Jan. 27–29, 1980, and subsequently marketed in a number of video formats. Audio recordings of the full novel (versions unspecified) and excerpts have been marketed on LP and audio tape a number of times.

Stories

50–1 "I'll Not Ask for Wine" ("Ylla") (141)

Maclean's (Canada) Jan. 1, 1950. Reprinted *Argosy* (U.K.) July 1950, as "I'll Not Look for Wine"; revised and reprinted *Avon Fantasy Reader 14*, 1950, as "Ylla." Collected as revised *MC* (FBA, 1950), *SL* (1951), *BS* (2003), as "February 1999: Ylla"; *VB* (1965), as "Ylla." Anthologized *The Outer Reaches* (1951; U.K., 1963), *200 Years of Great American Short Stories* (1975), *Treasury of Great Short Stories* (U.K., 1984), *Space Movies II* (1996), *Vintage Science Fiction* (U.K., 1999), as "Ylla." Anthologized in two textbooks, beginning with *Ginn Elements of English 8* (1970); textbook title variations include "Ylla," with and without the *MC* date prefix. Adapted for radio and broadcast with four other *MC* stories as "MC" on *Dimension X* (NBC), Aug. 18, 1950. Bradbury adapted parts of "Ylla" and "Mars Is Heaven!" (48–14) to comic-strip form (illustrated by Doug Wildey and John Cassone from a Joe Mugnaini concept) for *West* (*Los Angeles Times*, Mar. 12, 1972), as "MC" (issue includes a Bradbury article, "Where Are the Golden-Eyed Martians?").

50–2 "All on a Summer's Night" (142)

(Philadelphia Enquirer) Today Jan. 22, 1950. Collected *BS* (2003).

50–3 "Payment in Full" (143)

Thrilling Wonder Stories Feb. 1950. Anthologized *Man against Tomorrow* (FBA, 1965). An "unchronicled" Martian tale. Announced in *Startling Stories* (July 1949) as a coming attraction but printed instead in *Thrilling Wonder Stories*.

50–4 "Outcast of the Stars" ("The Rocket") (144)

Super Science Stories Mar. 1950. Reprinted *Literary Cavalcade* Apr. 1959, *Practical English* Sept. 14, 1960, *Scholastic Voice* Dec. 13, 1979, as "The Rocket." Collected *IM* (FBA, 1951), *RR* (1962), *CS1* (1990), *BS* (2003), as "The Rocket." Anthologized in nine textbooks, beginning with *New Horizons Book 3* (1962); textbook title variations include "The Rocket" and "R Is for Rocket." Adapted for radio and broadcast as "The Rocket" on *NBC Presents: Short Story*, Jan. 4, 1952. Adapted (TV) for broadcast on *CBS Television Workshop*, Mar. 16, 1952, as "The Rocket." Adapted to comic-strip form by Al Feldstein (Joe Orlando, illustrator) for EC Publications in *Weird Science* 22 (Nov.–Dec. 1953); EC version collected in *Tomorrow Midnight* (Ballantine, 1966).

50–5 "Punishment without Crime" (145)

Other Worlds Mar. 1950. Reprinted *Honey* (U.K.) Nov. 1977. Collected *LAM* (1976), *SRB* (1980). Anthologized *Science Fiction Terror Tales* (FBA, 1955). Adapted (TV) by Bradbury for *Ray Bradbury Theater* (USA), Apr. 16, 1988. Adapted to comic-strip form by Al Feldstein (Jack Kamen, illustrator) for EC Publications in *Weird Science* 21 (Sept.–Oct. 1953); EC version collected in *Tomorrow Midnight* (Ballantine, 1966). Adapted again to comic-strip form for *The Ray Bradbury Chronicles* vol. 2 (July 1992). Manuscript title: "Behold, Thou Art Fair."

50–6 "The Highway" (as Leonard Spaulding) (146)

Copy spring 1950. Reprinted *Newsday* Mar. 15, 1952, *The New York Post* Dec. 4, 1955, with Ray Bradbury byline. Collected *IM* (FBA, 1951). Anthologized *Stories for Here and Now* (1951). Anthologized in three textbooks, beginning with *Ten Tales in English* (London, 1966).

50–7   "Forever and the Earth" (147)

Planet Stories spring 1950. Reprinted Planet Stories 2 (U.K.) [July] 1950. Collected LAM (1976), BS (2003). Anthologized Big Book of Science Fiction (FBA, 1950), Sinister, Strange, and Supernatural (1981). Anthologized in two textbooks, beginning with On Writing by Writers (1966). Adapted for radio and broadcast on NPR, July 2, 1976. Dramatized as a radio play and printed separately (Athens, Ohio: Croissant, 1984).

50–8   "Carnival of Madness" ("Usher II") (148)

Thrilling Wonder Stories Apr. 1950. Reprinted Argosy (U.K.) Nov. 1950, as "The Second House of Usher"; reprinted Esquire Nov. 1951, as "The Immortality of Horror." Revised and collected MC (FBA, 1950), BS (2003), as "April 2005: Usher II." Deleted SL (1951) and MC U.K. editions (1953). Collected IM U.K. edition only (1952), as "Usher II." Anthologized in three textbooks, beginning with United States in Literature (1979); text-book title variations include "April 2005: Usher II." Adapted (TV) by Bradbury for Ray Bradbury Theater (USA), Aug. 17, 1990, as "Usher II." Adapted to comic-strip form for Ray Bradbury Comics 4 (Aug. 1993), as "Usher II."

50–9   "Miss Bidwell" ("A Far Away Guitar") (149)

Charm Apr. 1950. Reprinted Argosy (U.K.) Mar. 1952, as "A Far Away Guitar." Collected BS (2003), as "A Far Away Guitar."

50–10   "December 2001: The Green Morning" (150)

MC (FBA, [May 4], 1950), SL (1951). Reprinted Read Dec. 1, 1960, as "December 2001: The Green Mountains." Anthologized The Green America Book (1980). Anthologized in seven textbooks, beginning with The Study of Literature (1964).

50–11   "August 2002: Night Meeting" (151)

MC (FBA, [May 4], 1950), SL (1951). Reprinted Identity 1974; reprinted Weird Worlds 1 1978, as "Night Meeting." Collected VB (1965), as "Night Meeting." Anthologized Science Fiction Adventures in Dimension (1953). Anthologized in eleven textbooks, beginning with Grooving the Symbol (1970). Adapted to comic-strip form for The Ray Bradbury Chronicles vol. 2 (July 1992), as "Night Meeting."

50–12   "June 2003: Way in the Middle of the Air" (152)

MC (FBA, [May 4], 1950), SL (1951). Reprinted Other Worlds July 1950, as "Way in the Middle of the Air"; reprinted Duke Aug. 1957, as "The Day the Negroes Left Earth." Collected BS (2003). Anthologized Human and Other Beings (1963), as "Way in the Middle of the Air." Deleted from the Avon edition of MC (1997).

50–13   "There Will Come Soft Rains" (153)

Collier's May 6, 1950 (as Collier's issue-ending "short-short" feature, the first of four Bradbury stories to be so honored). Reprinted Argosy (U.K.) Aug. 1950, The New York Post Mar. 13, 1955, Scholastic Scope Apr. 5, 1971. Reprinted as single-story book (89-B). Long version collected MC (FBA, 1950), SL (1951), as "August 2026: There Will Come Soft Rains"; collected VB (1965), SRB (1980), without title prefix. Anthologized Adventures in Tomorrow (1951; U.K., 1953), Beyond the End of Time (1952), Of Men and Machines (1963), The Vintage Anthology of Science Fantasy (1966), Utopian Literature (1968), 21 Great Stories (1969), In Dreams Awake (1975), Science Fiction and Fantasy (1977), Space 6 (U.K., 1980), After the End (1981), Science Fiction A to Z (1982), Isaac Asimov Presents the Great S F Stories 12 (1950) (1984), Top Science Fiction (U.K., 1984), Beyond Armageddon (1985), Isaac Asimov Presents the Golden Years of Science Fiction, 6th ser. (1988), The Oxford Book of American Short Stories (1992; U.K., 1994), The American Short Story (1994), The Puffin Book of Science Fiction (U.K., 1993), SFWA Grandmasters vol. 2 (2000). Anthologized in seventy-four textbooks, beginning with The Informal Reader (1955); textbook title variations include the *MC* date prefix. Adapted for radio and broadcast on *Dimension X* (NBC), June 17, 1950, *X Minus 1* (NBC), Dec. 5, 1956, *Experiment in Drama* (NBC), Aug. 27, 1973; adapted for radio and broadcast with four other *MC* stories as "MC" on *Dimension X* (NBC), Aug. 18, 1950. Adapted to comic-strip form by Al Feldstein (Wally Wood, illustrator) for EC Publications in *Weird Fantasy* 17 (Jan.–Feb. 1953); EC version collected in *Tomorrow Midnight* (Ballantine, 1966). Adapted again to comic-strip form for *The Ray Bradbury Chronicles* vol. 3 (Nov. 1992).

50–14 "To the Future" ("The Fox and the Forest") (154)

Collier's May 13, 1950. Reprinted *Argosy* (U.K.) Sept. 1950, as "Escape"; reprinted *Mysterious Traveler* Jan. 1952; reprinted *Everybody's Digest* July 1951 (condensed), *The New York Post* Mar. 30, 1952, as "The Fox and the Forest." Rewritten and collected *IM* (FBA, 1951), *VB* (1965), *SRB* (1980), as "The Fox and the Forest." Anthologized *Alfred Hitchcock Presents: Stories Not for the Nervous* (1965); anthologized *Best Science Fiction Stories: 1951* (1951; U.K., as *BSFS Second Series*, 1952), as "The Fox in [*sic*] the Forest"; anthologized *Tell Me a Story* (1957), *Breath of Danger* (U.K., 1966), as "The Fox and the Forest." Anthologized in three textbooks, beginning with *Freedoms* (1969); textbook title variations include "The Fox and the Forest." Adapted for radio and broadcast on *Dimension X* (NBC), May 27, 1950; *X Minus 1* (NBC), Dec. 14, 1955. In his classic short story "The Neighbors," Jack Finney has his main characters speak of reading this story as events in their lives take a similar eerie turn toward the future.

50–15 "Death-by-Rain" ("The Long Rain") (155)

Planet Stories summer 1950. Reprinted *Planet Stories 3* (U.K.) [Jan.] 1951; reprinted *Cavalcade* Mar. 1959, *Scholastic Scope* Oct. 11, 1972, as "The Long Rain." Collected *IM* (FBA, 1951), *RR* (1962), *SRB* (1980), *CS1* (1990), as "The Long Rain." Anthologized in three textbooks, beginning with *Science Fictions* (1971), all as "The Long Rain." Adapted for the Warner Brothers film *The Illustrated Man* (1969); adapted (TV) by Bradbury for *Ray Bradbury Theater* (USA), Sept. 19, 1992, as "The Long Rain."

50–16 "The Illustrated Man" (156)

Esquire July 1950. Reprinted *Argosy* (U.K.) Oct. 1950, *Esquire* Oct. 1973, *Scholastic Voice* Sept. 23, 1976. Collected *VB* (1965), *IM* (1997, Avon edition only), *BS* (2003). Anthologized *In the Grip of Terror* (FBA, 1951), *The Esquire Treasury* (1953; U.K., 1954), *Stories for the Dead of Night* (1957), *Great Stories about Show Business* (1957), *The Eighth Pan Book of Horror Stories* (U.K., 1967), *Esquire: The Best of Forty Years* (1973), *Horrors, Horrors, Horrors* (1978), *Lust, Violence, Sin, Magic* (1993), *Reel Futures* (1994), *Dorothy Parker's Elbow* (2002, abridged). Anthologized in three textbooks, beginning with *Kaleidoscope* (1970). A radically different concept of this story became "Prologue/Epilogue: The Illustrated Man," *IM* (1951).

50–17 "Purpose" ("The City") (157)

Startling Stories July 1950. Reprinted *A Treasury of Great S.F. Stories 2* (1965). Collected *IM* (FBA, 1951), *SRB* (1980), as "The City." Anthologized *Science Fiction: A Historical Anthology* (1983); anthologized *SFWA Grandmasters* vol. 2 (2000), as "The City." Anthologized in two textbooks, beginning with *Responding: Four* (1973), all as "The City." Adapted to comic-strip form for *Ray Bradbury Comics* 4 (Aug. 1993), as "The City."

50–18 "The Window" (158)

Collier's Aug. 5, 1950. Reprinted *Argosy* (U.K.) May 1952, *The New York Post* Dec. 11, 1955; reprinted *Scholastic Scope* Oct. 11, 1972, as "The Long Distance Telephone Call." Collected *DW* (FBA, 1957), untitled; *SRB* (1980), as "Calling Mexico." The second of Bradbury's stories to appear in *Collier's* "Short Short" story feature, following "There

Will Come Soft Rains" (50–13) and preceding "The Pumpernickel" (51–10) and "The Marriage Mender" (54–1).

50–19 "The Whole Town's Sleeping" (159)

McCall's Sept. 1950. Reprinted *Woman's Journal* (U.K.) Dec. 1950, *Argosy* (U.K.) July 1951, *Ellery Queen's Mystery Magazine* (U.S. and U.K.) June 1954. Revised and Collected *DW* (FBA, 1957), untitled; *BS* (2003). Anthologized *Alfred Hitchcock Presents: Stories for Late at Night* (1961), *The Masque of the Red Death* (U.K., 1964), *Argosy Bedside Book* (1965), *Best Horror Stories 3* (U.K., 1972), *Great Short Tales of Mystery and Terror* (1982), *Tales of Fear and Frightening Phenomena* (1982); anthologized *Read All About It* (1994), as "The Ravine." Anthologized in seven textbooks, beginning with *Literature for Enjoyment* (Canada, 1967). Adapted (prior to publication) for radio and broadcast on *Suspense* (CBS), July 15, 1948, as "Summer Night"; adapted (TV) and broadcast on *Suspense* (CBS), Feb. 19, 1952, as "Summer Night"; adapted for radio under the original title and broadcast on *ABC Radio Workshop,* Mar. 16, 1953; adapted again for radio under the original title and broadcast on *Suspense* (CBS), June 14, 1955, Aug. 31, 1958. Adapted to stage and printed *Scholastic Scope* Sept. 7, 1984, as *The Lonely One.* Adapted (TV) by Bradbury for *Ray Bradbury Theater* as "The Lonely One" (USA), July 10, 1992. The sequel to this story, "At Midnight, in the Month of June" (54–7), was not included in *DW.*

50–20 "The World the Children Made" ("The Veldt") (160)

Saturday Evening Post Sept. 23, 1950. Reprinted as single-story book, *The Veldt* (82-B, 87-D). Collected *IM* (1951), *VB* (1965), *RB* (1975), *SRB* (1980), as "The Veldt"; collected *IM* U.K. first edition only (1952), as "The Veld." Anthologized *Saturday Evening Post Stories* (FBA, 1950), *Reading for Pleasure* (1957); anthologized *Beyond the Barriers of Space and Time* (1954; U.K., 1955), *The Britannica Library of Great American Writing vol. 2* (1960), *More Horror Stories* (U.K., 1962), *Master's Choice* (1966), *World Zero Minus* (U.K., 1971), *Past, Present, and Future Perfect* (1973), *Space 3* (U.K., 1976), *The Best Horror Stories* (U.K., 1977; U.S., 1990), *Breaking Away* (1987), *The Puffin Book of Ghosts and Ghouls* (U.K., 1992; U.S., as *Ghosts, Ghouls and Other Nightmares,* 1995), *Simulations* (1993), *American Gothic Tales* (1996), *The Young Oxford Book of Nasty Endings* (U.K., 1997), *Science Fiction Classics* (1999), and *Technohorror* (1999), as "The Veldt" ("The Veld" in some of the U.K. anthologies). Anthologized in twenty-six textbooks, beginning with *Second Orbit* (London, 1965); textbook title variations include "The Veldt." Adapted for radio and broadcast as "The Veldt" on *Dimension X* (NBC), Aug 9, 1951; *X Minus 1* (NBC), Aug. 4, 1955. Adapted to stage by Bradbury and collected *WICS* (1972), *RBOS* (1991); reprinted *Literary Cavalcade* Dec. 1972; reprinted separately (Woodstock, Ill.: Dramatic Publications, 1988), all as *The Veldt.* Adapted (TV) by Bradbury for *Ray Bradbury Theater* (USA), Nov. 10, 1989, as "The Veldt." Adapted to comic-strip form for *The Ray Bradbury Chronicles* vol. 3 (Nov. 1992).

50–21 "Death Wish" ("The Blue Bottle") (161)

Planet Stories fall 1950. Reprinted *Planet Stories 5* (U.K.) [June] 1953, *Orion's Child* May–June 1984, as "The Blue Bottle." Rewritten and collected *LAM* (1976), *SRB* (1980), as "The Blue Bottle." Anthologized *A Sea of Space* (FBA, 1970), as "The Blue Bottle," ed. by William F. Nolan. Anthologized in one textbook, *Another Page* (1981), as "The Blue Bottle." The rewritten and retitled form was prepared for William F. Nolan's *A Sea of Space* anthology (1970) and was the source for the *LAM* and *SRB* versions.

50–22 "Season of Disbelief" (162)

Collier's Nov. 25, 1950. Collected *DW* (FBA, 1957), untitled; *BS* (2003). Adapted by others for *CBS Radio Workshop,* Feb. 17, 1956, with an introduction written and read by Bradbury.

50–23 "The Bonfire" (163)

> *Torquasian Times* winter 1950–51. Revised, corrected, and reprinted *Gauntlet 2* (FBA, 1991). *Torquasian Times* was an amateur publication; the *Gauntlet* version represents the first professional printing of this story.

50–24 "The Year 2150 A.D." (164)

> *Shangri-LA* 1950. Reprinted *Vertex* June 1973, as "In the Year 2150 A.D." Anthologized *Worlds in Small* (Canada, 1992).

1951

Books

51-A *The Illustrated Man*

> Story collection. Garden City, N.Y.: Doubleday, [Feb. 23], 1951; New York: Bantam, 1952 (paperback); London: Rupert Hart-Davis, [June 20], 1952; New York: Bantam, 1954 (reset paperback); London: Corgi, 1955 (paperback); Garden City, N.Y.: Doubleday, [1969]; London: Panther, 1977 (paperback); [London]: Heinemann, 1991; Cutchogue, N.Y.: Buccaneer, 1994 (library edition); London: HarperCollins Flamingo, 1995 (large-format trade paperback); Springfield, Pa.: Gauntlet, 1996 (limited edition); New York: Avon, 1997, with a new introduction; Thorndike, Maine: G. K. Hall, 1999 (large-print edition; reissued, Bath, U.K.: Chivers, 1999). Collected in the omnibus *RB2* (87-E). Contents: "Prologue: The Illustrated Man"; "The Veldt"; "Kaleidoscope"; "The Other Foot"; "The Highway"; "The Man"; "The Long Rain"; "The Rocket Man"; "The Fire Balloons"; "The Last Night of the World"; "The Exiles"; "No Particular Night or Morning"; "The Fox and the Forest"; "The Visitor"; "The Concrete Mixer"; "Marionettes, Inc."; "The City; Zero Hour"; "The Rocket"; "Epilogue [The Illustrated Man]." With the exception of the Corgi paperback (1955), all U.K. editions delete "The Rocket Man," "The Fire Balloons," "The Exiles," and "The Concrete Mixer." These editions add "Usher II" and "The Playground." The 1997 Avon edition adds "The Illustrated Man" (50–16) as a twentieth story. The "Prologue/Epilogue" and three stories ("The Veldt," "The Long Rain," and "The Last Night of the World") were adapted (by others) for the Warner Brothers/Seven Arts film, *The Illustrated Man* (1969).

51-B *The Silver Locusts / The Martian Chronicles*
      See 50-A.

Stories

51–1 "The Fireman" (165)

> *Galaxy* Feb. 1951. Anthologized *Science Fiction Origins* (FBA, 1980). Revised and expanded into *F451* (53-B).

51–2 "The Last Night of the World" (166)

> *Esquire* Feb. 1951. Reprinted *The New York Post* June 22, 1952, *World Digest* (U.K.) Jan. 1953, *Literary Cavalcade* Jan. 1984. Collected *IM* (FBA, 1951), *RB* (1975), *SRB* (1980). Anthologized *The Edge of the Chair* (1967), *Wolf's Complete Book of Terror* (1979). Anthologized in seven textbooks, beginning with *Voices of Man* (1970).

51–3 "Prologue: The Illustrated Man"; "Epilogue" (167)

> *IM* (FBA, [Feb. 23], 1951). A "frame" story based on the character developed for "The Illustrated Man" (50–16) and used to structure *IM*. Adapted to comic-strip form for *Ray Bradbury's The Illustrated Man Special* 1 (1993).

51–4   "The Fire Balloons" (168)

    IM (FBA, [Feb. 23], 1951). Reprinted *Imagination* Apr. 1951, as "In This Sign"; reprinted *And It Is Divine* Dec. 1975 (abridged). Collected *MC* (1950, some later U.S. and all U.K. editions), *SL* (1951), *SRB* (1980). Deleted *IM* U.K. edition (1952). Anthologized *Best SF [One]* (U.K., 1955), *Contact* (1963), *Special Wonder: The Anthony Boucher Memorial Anthology* (1970), *The New Awareness* (1975), *Angels and Awakenings* (1980), *Isaac Asimov Presents the Great S F Stories 13 (1951)* (1985); anthologized *Looking Forward* (1953; U.K., 1955), *Chronicles of a Comer* (1974), as "In This Sign." A follow-on story, "The Messiah," describes a subsequent encounter between Father Peregrine and a more substantial Martian survivor, but this story was never added to *MC*. (Beware the network TV adaptation of *MC*, which includes "The Messiah" as part of the *MC* sequence.)

51–5   "No Particular Night or Morning" (169)

    IM (FBA, [Feb. 23], 1951). Collected *SRB* (1980). Anthologized in one textbook, *Thought Fugues* (1996).

51–6   "The Other Foot" (170)

    New Story Mar. 1951. Reprinted *Duke* June 1957, as "The Last White Man." Reprinted twice as a single-story book (82-A, 87-C). Collected *IM* (FBA, 1951), *RB* (1975). Anthologized *Best American Short Stories, 1952* (1952), *Fifty Best American Short Stories, 1915–1965* (1965). Anthologized in eight textbooks, beginning with *Life in Literature* (Canada, 1966). Adapted to stage and published in the textbook *Elephants Are Dainty Birds* (1978). An "unchronicled" Martian tale.

51–7   "The Green Machine" (171)

    Argosy (U.K.) Mar. 1951. Collected *DW* (FBA, 1957), untitled.

51–8   "The Rocket Man" (172)

    Maclean's (Canada) Mar. 1, 1951. Reprinted *Argosy* Feb. 1952, *Scholastic Voice* May 1, 1981. Collected *IM* (FBA, 1951), *RR* (1962), *SRB* (1980), *CS1* (1990). Deleted *IM* U.K. edition (1952). Anthologized in five textbooks, beginning with *Family* (1972). Adapted (without credit) to comic-strip form by Al Feldstein (Wally Wood, illustrator) for EC Publications in *Weird Fantasy* 13 (May–June 1952), combined with "Kaleidoscope" (49–14) as "Home to Stay."

51–9   "These Things Happen" (173)

    McCall's May 1951. Reprinted *Argosy* (U.K.) Sept. 1951, as "A Story about Love"; *Magpie* (U.K.) Mar. 1953, as "The Years Cannot Be Hurried"; *Eastern Review* Jan. 1977, as "A Story of Love"; *Honey* (U.K.) Nov. 1977, as "A Love Story"; *Reader's Digest* (U.S.) Feb. 1983 and (Canada) Mar. 1986, as "I'll Never Forget You" (condensed). Collected *LAM* (FBA, 1976), *SRB* (1980), as "A Story of Love." Anthologized in one textbook, *Reading and Writing from Literature* (1997), as "A Story about Love."

51–10   "The Pumpernickel" (174)

    Collier's May 19, 1951. Reprinted *Argosy* (U.K.) Oct. 1951. Collected *LAM* (FBA, 1976), *BS* (2003). A *Collier's* "Short Short" story—the third of four tales that Bradbury placed in this feature during the early 1950s (see also 50–13, 50–18, 54–1).

51–11   "The Screaming Woman" (175)

    (Philadelphia Enquirer) Today May 27, 1951, with revised upbeat ending. Reprinted *Suspense* winter 1952, *The Saint Detective Magazine* (U.S.) Sept. 1955 and (U.K.) Aug. 1957, *Suspense* (U.K.) Jan. 1959, *Argosy* (U.K.) Oct. 1964, *Scholastic Scope* Oct. 11, 1972, *Reader's Digest* (U.S. and Canada) May 1984 (condensed). Collected *SS* (1966), *SRB* (1980), *CS2* (1990). Anthologized *The Graveyard Reader* (FBA, 1958), *The Ghost Finders* (U.K., 1978), *Tune in for Fear* (U.K., 1985), *Night Shadows* (2001); original dark ending restored in

Best of Whispers (1994). Anthologized in three textbooks, beginning with *Real and Fantastic* (1970). Adapted (TV) for broadcast as the *Universal-ABC Movie of the Week*, Jan. 29, 1972; adapted (TV) by Bradbury for *Ray Bradbury Theater* (HBO), Feb. 22, 1986. Adapted to stage by Bradbury and printed in *Scholastic Voice* Mar. 21, 1986. Adapted to comic-strip form by Al Feldstein (Jack Kamen, illustrator) for EC Publications in *Crime Suspenstories* 15 (Feb.–Mar. 1953); EC version collected in *The Autumn People* (Ballantine, 1965). Bradbury's original story outline was adapted by others for radio and broadcast on *Suspense* (CBS), Nov. 25, 1948.

51–12   "The Beast from 20,000 Fathoms" ("The Fog Horn") (176)
Saturday Evening Post June 23, 1951. Reprinted *Argosy* (U.K.) Aug. 1951, *Literary Cavalcade* Dec. 1974, *Cricket* Oct.–Nov. 1993, as "The Fog Horn"; reprinted *Saturday Evening Post* Sept. 1981, with original title; reprinted *Reader's Digest* (U.S. and Canada) Nov. 1983 (condensed), as "Up from the Deep." Reprinted as a single-story book (87-B), as "The Fog Horn." Collected *GA* (1953), *RR* (1962), *VB* (1965), *T22* (1966), *RB* (1975), *SRB* (1980), *DT* (illustrated, 1983), *CS1* (1990), as "The Fog Horn." Anthologized *Saturday Evening Post Stories, 1951* (FBA, 1951), *The Saturday Evening Post Reader of Sea Stories* (1962), *The Ghouls* (1971), *Movie Monsters* (U.K., 1988); anthologized *Tell Me a Story* (1957), *Mystery and Adventure Stories for Boys* (U.K., 1962), *The Best of Both Worlds* (1968), *The Hilton Bedside Book Volume 7* (1968), *The Sea-Green Horse* (1970), *Author's Choice [1]* (1970), *Monsters, Monsters, Monsters* (1974), *The Big Book of Boys' Adventure Stories* (U.K., 1977), *Creepy Creatures* (U.K., 1978), *The Best Animal Stories of Science Fiction and Fantasy* (1979), *Top Fantasy* (U.K., 1985), *The Big Book of Adventure Stories* (U.K., 1986), *Cinemonsters* (1987), *The Monster Book of Monsters* (1988), *Lighthouse Horrors* (1993), *Fossils* (excerpts, 1994), *Dinosaurs* (1996), as "The Fog Horn." Anthologized in forty textbooks, beginning with *Modern Tales of Adventure and Suspense* (1961); textbook title variations include "The Fog Horn" and "Up from the Deep." Adapted by Bradbury for stage and collected *PF* (1975), *RBOS* (1991), as *The Fog Horn*. Major plot elements borrowed (without credit) in comic-strip form by Al Feldstein (John Rosenberger, illustrator) for EC Publications in *Tales of Horror* 7 (Oct. 1953), as "The Beast from the Deep." Adapted to comic-strip form for *Ray Bradbury Comics* 3 (June 1993), as "The Fog Horn." His original title was "The Fog Horn," but *Post* editors persuaded him to use the more exciting "Beast from 20,000 Fathoms" instead. Bradbury later restored the original title for the eight story collections in which this work appears.[5]

51–13   "A Little Journey" (177)
Galaxy Aug. 1951. Collected *BS* (2003). Anthologized *Galaxy Reader of Science Fiction* (FBA, 1952), *Rod Serling's Other Worlds* (1978).

51–14   "The Season of Sitting" (178)
Charm Aug. 1951. Collected *DW* (1957), untitled. A nonfiction article rewritten as the unnumbered fourth story-chapter of *DW*.

51–15   "The Pedestrian" (179)
Reporter Aug. 7, 1951. Reprinted *Magazine of Fantasy and Science Fiction* Feb. 1952, *New Liberty* (Canada) Jan. 1954, *Magazine of Science Fiction* (U.K.) May 1954, *Magazine of Fantasy and Science Fiction 1* (Australia) [Nov.] 1954, *American Science Fiction 39* (Australia) [1955], *Scholastic Scope* Oct. 11, 1972, *Looking Ahead* 1980 and [Sept.] 1981, *Literary Cavalcade* Mar. 1980, *Walking* May 1987, *Scholastic Scope* Oct. 8, 1993. Reprinted as a single-story book (64-B). Collected *GA* (1953), *T22* (1966), *SS* (1966), *CS2* (1990), *BS* (2003). Anthologized *Best Science Fiction Stories: 1952* (FBA, 1952), *Timeless Stories for Today and Tomorrow* (1952), *Off-Beat* (U.K., 1961), *Decade: The 1950s* (1976), *The Great Late Future*

(1976), *Strange Planets* (U.K., 1977), *Tomorrow's TV* (1982), *The World Treasury of Children's Literature Book Three* (1985), *Isaac Asimov Presents the Great SF Stories 14 (1952)* (1986), *A Century of Science Fiction* (1996), *Writing Los Angeles* (2002). Anthologized in thirty-eight textbooks, beginning with *Adventures in American Literature* (1958). Adapted for stage by Bradbury and published as a book (66-E). Adapted (TV) by Bradbury for *Ray Bradbury Theater* (USA), Aug. 4, 1989.

51–16 "Embroidery" (180)

Marvel Science Fiction Nov. 1951. Collected *GA* (FBA, 1953), *T22* (1966), *SRB* (1980), *CS1* (1990). Anthologized in one textbook, *The Whole Story* (U.K., 1988).

51–17 "Here There Be Tygers" (181)

First published as revised for *New Tales of Space and Time* (New York: Holt, 1951). Original version printed *Amazing Stories* Apr.–May 1953; revised version reprinted *Suspense* (U.K.) June 1959, *Argosy* (U.K.) Mar. 1965, *Mother Earth News* Jan.–Feb. 1978. Revised version collected *DRF* (1959), *RR* (1962), *CS1* (1990). Anthologized *New Tales of Space and Time* (FBA and first printed, 1951; U.K., 1952). Anthologized in one textbook, *Tomorrow, and Tomorrow, and Tomorrow . . .* (1974). Adapted (TV) by Bradbury for *Ray Bradbury Theater* (USA), Nov. 30, 1990. Scripted by Bradbury but never produced for *The Twilight Zone*.

1952

Stories

52–1 "A Flight of Ravens" (182)

California Quarterly winter 1952. Collected *MJ* (FBA, 1964). The surviving manuscript is titled "A Short Wait between Lives."

52–2 "The April Witch" (183)

Saturday Evening Post Apr. 5, 1952. Reprinted *Argosy* (U.K.) Mar. 1953, *Saturday Evening Post* June 1985, *After Hours* 6 spring 1990. Reprinted as a single-story book (87-A). Collected *GA* (FBA, 1953), *T22* (1966), *TS* (1979), *SRB* (1980), *CS1* (1990). Rewritten as a chapter in *FDR* (2001), as "The Wandering Witch." Anthologized *Fantasy Tales* (1977–78), *Young Witches and Warlocks* (1987), *The Ultimate Witch* (1993). Anthologized in one textbook, A *Midsummer Night's Dream and Related Readings* (1997). Adapted to comic-strip form for *Ray Bradbury Comics* 5 (Oct. 1993).

52–3 "The Wilderness" (184)

(Philadelphia Enquirer) Today Apr. 6, 1952. Rewritten and reprinted *Magazine of Fantasy and Science Fiction* Nov. 1952; reprinted *Everybody's Digest* Sept. 1953, as "Honeymoon on Mars." Collected *GA* (FBA, 1953), *MC* (1950, later editions), *T22* (1966), *SRB* (1980), *CS1* (1990). Anthologized *Stories for Tomorrow* (1954; U.K., 1955), *Universe Ahead* (1975). Anthologized in two textbooks, beginning with *Exploring Life through Literature* (1964).

52–4 "The Lawns of Summer" (185)

Nation's Business May 1952. Reprinted *Argosy* (U.K.) Aug. 1954. Collected *DW* (FBA, 1957), untitled.

52–5 "Love Contest" (as Leonard Douglas) (186)

Saturday Evening Post May 23, 1952.

52–6 "A Piece of Wood" (187)

Esquire June 1952. Reprinted *Scholastic Scope* Jan. 7, 1983. Collected *LAM* (FBA, 1976), *SRB* (1980). Anthologized in four textbooks, beginning with *American Short Stories*

(Germany, 1985). Adapted to comic-strip form for *The Ray Bradbury Chronicles* vol. 2 (July 1992).

52–7 "The Playground" (188)

IM, London: Hart-Davis (FBA, [June 20], 1952). Rewritten and reprinted *Esquire* Oct. 1953, *Soho International* (U.K.) 1973. Collected *F451* (1953, certain editions), *SRB* (1980). Not included in *IM* U.S. editions (1951). Anthologized *Portals of Tomorrow* (1954; U.K., 1956), *Twisted* (1962), *Black Water* (1983), *Ready or Not* (1987). Anthologized in five textbooks, beginning with *Literature: An Introduction* (1960). Adapted (TV) by Bradbury for *Ray Bradbury Theater* (HBO), June 4, 1985.

52–8 "A Sound of Thunder" (189)

Collier's June 28, 1952, with the final paragraphs altered by the editors. Reprinted *Argosy* (U.K.) Oct. 1952, Aug. 1956; restored and reprinted *All-Story Braille Magazine* Apr.–May 1953, *Senior Scholastic* Nov. 18, 1953, *Planet Stories* Jan. 1954, *Planet Stories 11* (U.K.) [July] 1954, *Playboy* June 1956, Jan. 1989, *Everybody's* (U.K.) Aug. 25, 1956, *Wonder Stories* 1957, 1963, *Best from Playboy 2* (1968), *Social Education* Dec. 1971, *Literary Cavalcade* Apr. 1974, *The Japan Times* May 28, June 4, 11, 18, 25, July 2, 1993. Revised (with original ending restored) and collected *GA* (FBA, 1953), *RR* (1962), *T22* (1966), *RB* (1975), *TS* (1979), *SRB* (1980), *DT* (illustrated, 1983), *CS1* (1990). Anthologized *Science Fiction for People Who Hate Science Fiction* (1966), *Science Fiction through the Ages 2* (U.K., 1966), *The Stars and Under* (U.K., 1968), *Eco-Fiction* (1971), *Masterpieces of Science Fiction* (1978), *Tales Out of Time* (1979), *Space 5* (U.K., 1979), *Wide-Angle Lens* (1980), *Behold the Mighty Dinosaur* (1981), *Stories of the Future* (U.K., 1981), *Caught in the Organ Draft* (1983), *Isaac Asimov Presents the Great S F Stories 14 (1952)* (1986), *Science Fiction Stories* (Germany, 1993), *Tales in Time* (1997), *The Young Oxford Book of Time Warp Stories* (U.K., 1001), *The Best Time Travel Stories of All Time* (2003). Anthologized in forty-two textbooks, beginning with *Aspects of Science Fiction* (U.K., 1959). Adapted (TV) by Bradbury for *Ray Bradbury Theater* (USA), Aug. 11, 1989. Adapted to comic-strip form by Al Feldstein (Al Williamson, illustrator) for EC Publications in *Weird Science-Fantasy 25* (Sept. 1954; issue includes a letter by Bradbury). Adapted again to comic-strip form for *Ray Bradbury Comics 1* (Feb. 1993).

52–9 "The Smile" (190)

Fantastic summer 1952. Reprinted *The Sunday Chronicle* (U.K.) Sept. 12, 1954, *Amazing Stories* Dec. 1967, *Social Education* Feb. 1973, *Bananas Yearbook* 1977. Reprinted as a single-story book (91-C). Collected *MM* (1959), *DRF* (1959), *SS* (1966), *RB* (1975), *CS2* (1990), *BS* (2003). Anthologized *Worlds of Tomorrow* (FBA, 1953; U.K., 1954), *Transformations* (1973), *Perry Rhodan 75* (1975), *Ackermanthology* (1997). Anthologized in four textbooks, beginning with *Spectrum 2* (1969). An earlier form of this story was originally the final chapter of the unpublished novel, *Where Ignorant Armies Clash by Night* (1947).

52–10 "The Secret" (191)

IT summer 1952. Original composition: c. 1940. Intended for a pre-war fanzine, and finally published a dozen years later in Bob Chambers's fanzine *It*.

52–11 "Cora and the Great Wide World" (192)

Maclean's (Canada) Aug. 15, 1952. Collected *GA* (FBA, 1953), *T22* (1966), *SRB* (1980), *CS1* (1990), as "The Great Wide World Over There." Adapted (TV) for broadcast on *Windows* (CBS), July 22, 1955 as "The World Out There"; adapted (TV) and broadcast in syndication on *Studio 57*, May 20, 1956, and possibly earlier; adapted (TV) by Bradbury for *Ray Bradbury Theater* (USA), Oct. 28, 1992, as "Great Wide World Over There."

52–12　"The Tombling Day" (193)

Shenandoah autumn 1952. Reprinted *Satellite Science Fiction* June 1958. Collected *IS* (1969), *SRB* (1980). Anthologized *Supernatural Reader* (FBA, 1953; U.K., 1957), *Mysterious, Menacing, and Macabre* (1981). Original composition: 1946.

52–13　"Torrid Sacrifice" ("En La Noche") (194)

Cavalier Nov. 1952. Reprinted *Argosy* (U.K.) Nov. 1953, as "The Price of Silence." Collected *GA* (FBA, 1953), *T22* (1966), *CS1* (1990), as "En La Noche." Anthologized *A Treasury of Ribaldry* (1956), as "En La Noche."

52–14　"The Gift" (195)

Esquire Dec. 1952. Reprinted *Literary Cavalcade* Dec. 19, 1953, *Fantastic* July 1959, *Scholastic Scope* Dec. 9, 1964, *Strange Fantasy* fall 1969, *Pizzazz* Dec. 1977, *The (North San Luis Obispo) Country News Christmas Storybook* Nov. 20, 1991, *Your View* fall–winter 1994. Collected *MM* (FBA, 1959), *DRF* (1959), *RR* (1962), *T22* (1966), *RB* (1975), *CS2* (1990). Anthologized *14 Favorite Christmas Stories* (1964), *70 Finest Stories for Young Readers* (1974), *Young Star Travelers* (1986), *Keeping Christmas* (1990), *Christmas Stars* (1992). Anthologized in twelve textbooks, beginning with *Life and Adventure* (1962). Adapted to comic-strip form ("Fritz," illustrator) for *Xanadu* (summer 1970); adapted again (James Denney, illustrator) for *Myrrh* (Jan. 1981).

1953

Books

53-A　*The Golden Apples of the Sun*

Story collection. See also 66-A, 90-A, 97-B. Garden City, N.Y.: Doubleday, [Mar. 19], 1953; New York: Bantam, 1954 (paperback); London: Rupert Hart-Davis, 1953; London: Corgi, 1956 (paperback); New York: Bantam, 1961 (reset paperback); [London]: Corgi, [1964] (paperback); Westport, Conn.: Greenwood, 1971; New York: Bantam, 1979 (reset paperback); [London]: Heinemann 1990; [Shelton, Conn.: First Edition Library, 1993], facsimile of the Doubleday first edition; London: Earthlight, 2000 (paperback). Collected in the omnibus *RB2* (87-E). Contents: "The Fog Horn"; "The Pedestrian"; "The April Witch"; "The Wilderness"; "The Fruit at the Bottom of the Bowl"; "Invisible Boy"; "The Flying Machine"; "The Murderer"; "The Golden Kite, the Silver Wind"; "I See You Never"; "Embroidery"; "The Big Black and White Game"; "A Sound of Thunder"; "The Great Wide World Over There"; "Powerhouse"; "En La Noche"; "Sun and Shadow"; "The Meadow"; "The Garbage Collector"; "The Great Fire"; "Hail and Farewell"; "The Golden Apples of the Sun." The U.K. first (1953) and first-paperback (1956) editions delete "The Big Black and White Game" and "The Great Fire"; subsequent U.K. editions are unabridged. *T22* (66-A) combines *GA* and *MM* (59-B); Bantam's *CS1* (90-A) and Avon's *The Golden Apples of the Sun and Other Stories* (97-B) each combine the stories of *GA* and *RR* (62-C).

53-B　*Fahrenheit 451*

Novel (certain editions include stories).

Bound as a story collection: New York: Ballantine, [Oct.] 1953; New York: Ballantine, [Oct.] 1953 (mass-market paperback); New York: Simon and Schuster, 1967; New York: Del Rey/Ballantine, 1981 (large-format trade paperback); New York: Limited Editions Club, 1982, with a new foreword (reprinted, Norwalk, Conn.: Easton, 2000); London: Collins Educational, 1985; Evanston, Ill.: McDougal Littell, 1998 (a critical edition of *F451* without the other two Bradbury stories but bound with censorship stories by other writers and retitled *Fahrenheit 451 and Related Readings*). Contents: *Fahrenheit 451;* "The Playground"; "And the Rock Cried Out."

Bound as a novel: New York: Ballantine, 1953 (paperback, second and all subsequent printings and editions); London: Rupert Hart-Davis, [Mar.] 1954; [London]: Science Fiction Book Club, [1955]; London: Corgi, 1957 (paperback); Toronto: MacMillan of Canada, [1968]; Vancouver: Fitzenry and Whiteside, [1972]; Bath, U.K.: Chivers, [1988]; New York: Simon and Schuster, fortieth-anniversary edition, 1993; London: HarperCollins, Flamingo, 1993 (large-format trade and mass-market paperbacks); Cutchogue, N.Y.: Buccaneer, 1994; London: HarperCollins Voyager, 1996 (school-series paperback); New York: Ballantine, 1996 (large-format trade paperback), with Limited Editions Club foreword included as an afterword; Thorndike, Maine: G. K. Hall, 1997 (large-print edition). Collected in the omnibus volumes *NRB* (84-C), *RB2* (87-E). Contents: *Fahrenheit 451* only. Reprinted as a serial in *Playboy* (Mar., Apr., May 1954). Excerpts reprinted in *The Bookseller* (U.K.), Feb. 20, 1954, as "The Last Book Burning—and After." Excerpts have been anthologized in sixteen textbooks, beginning with *The Creative Arts: Four Representative Types* (1968); textbook title variations include "The Happiness Boys" and "The Mechanical Hound." Adapted (TV, without credit) for broadcast on *Playhouse 90* (CBS), Oct. 3, 1957, as "A Sound of Different Drummers"; adapted to stage by Bradbury and published as *Fahrenheit 451* (see 86-E); adapted under François Truffaut's direction for the Universal film *Fahrenheit 451* (1966). Originally developed from "The Fireman" (51–1).

Stories

53–1 "The Golden Kite, the Silver Wind" (196)

Epoch winter 1953. Reprinted *Read* Feb. 2, 1990, *Scholastic Scope* Sept. 8, 1997. Collected *GA* (FBA, 1953), *T22* (1966), *SRB* (1980), *CS1* (1990). Anthologized *The Book of Fantasy* (1988). Anthologized in five textbooks, beginning with *Stories* (1957).

53–2 "A Scent of Sarsaparilla" (197)

Star Science Fiction Stories, New York: Ballantine, [Feb.] 1953. Revised and reprinted *Argosy* (U.K.) Oct. 1953, as "Scent of Summer." Collected *MM* (1959), *DRF* (1959), *T22* (1966), *SRB* (1980), *CS2* (1990). Anthologized *Star Science Fiction Stories [No. 1]* (FBA, 1953; U.K., 1954), *Stories for Tomorrow* (1954), *Mad Scientists* (1980). Adapted as an opera and performed at 1953 WesterCon in San Francisco.

53–3 "Sun and Shadow" (198)

Reporter Mar. 17, 1953. Reprinted *Argosy* (U.K.) Feb. 1955. Reprinted as a single-story book (57-A). Collected *GA* (FBA, 1953), *VB* (1965), *T22* (1966), *CS1* (1990). Anthologized *Prize Articles 1954* (1954), *Tell Me a Story* (1957). Anthologized in nine textbooks, beginning with *A Search for Awareness* (1966). Adapted (TV) by Bradbury for *Ray Bradbury Theater* (USA), Oct. 3, 1992.[6]

53–4 "The Flying Machine" (199)

GA (FBA, [Mar. 19], 1953). Reprinted *Playboy* Aug. 1954, *Children's Digest* Mar. 1973. Collected *SS* (1966), *T22* (1966), *CS1* (1990), *BS* (2003). Anthologized in thirty-two textbooks, beginning with *Invitation to Short Stories* (Canada, 1958). Adapted for stage by Bradbury and printed separately (86-B). Adapted to comic-strip form by Al Feldstein (Bernie Krigstein, illustrator) for EC Publications in *Weird Science-Fantasy* 23 (Mar. 1954).

53–5 "The Garbage Collector" (200)

GA (FBA, [Mar. 19], 1953). Reprinted *Nation* Oct. 10, 1953, as "Garbage Collector." Collected *T22* (1966), *CS1* (1990), *BS* (2003). Anthologized in three textbooks, beginning with *Current Thinking and Writing*, 3d ser. (1956).

53–6   "The Golden Apples of the Sun" (201)

   GA (FBA, [Mar. 19], 1953). Reprinted *The Observer* (U.K.) Sept. 27, 1953, *Planet Sto-ries* Nov. 1953,. *Planet Stories 9* (U.K.) [Mar.] 1954, *Argosy* (U.K.) July 1955, *Science Fic-tion Monthly 13* (Australia) Sept. 1956, *Sky* 1964. Collected *RR* (1962), *T22* (1966), *SRB* (1980). Accidentally omitted *CS1* (1990) until 3d printing (1995). Anthologized *Adventure Stories* (1988). Anthologized in six textbooks, beginning with *Our Heritage* (Canada, 1963). Adapted to comic-strip form for *The Ray Bradbury Chronicles* vol. 1 (July 1992).

53–7   "The Meadow" (202)

   GA (FBA, [Mar. 19], 1953). Reprinted *Argosy* (U.K.) Sept. 1953, as "Meadow of the World"; reprinted *Esquire* Dec. 1953. Collected *T22* (1966), *CS1* (1990), *BS* (2003). Anthologized *Hollywood Unreel* (1982). Anthologized in two textbooks, beginning with *Story: Adventures in Living* (1968). Developed from Bradbury's *The Meadow*, a one-act play broadcast on *World Security Workshop* (ABC), Jan. 2, 1947; published in *The Best One-Act Plays of 1947–48* (New York: Dodd, Mead, 1948). Play anthologized in one text-book, *Plays to Remember* (1967).

53–8   "The Murderer" (203)

   GA (FBA, [Mar. 19], 1953). Reprinted *Argosy* (U.K.) June 1953, *Adam* 2, no. 11 (1958), *MD* Nov. 1975 (excerpts). Collected *GA* (1953), *T22* (1966), *SRB* (1980), *CS1* (1990). Anthologized *Science Fiction Stories* (U.K., 1975). Anthologized in five textbooks, begin-ning with *The Storytellers Two* (1971). Adapted (TV) for broadcast on PBS (WGBH), Oct. 12, 1976; adapted (TV) by Bradbury for *Ray Bradbury Theater* (USA), July 27, 1990.

53–9   "Hail and Farewell" (204)

   (Philadelphia Enquirer) Today Mar. 29, 1953. Reprinted *Argosy* (U.K.) Sept. 1954. Col-lected *GA* (FBA, 1953), *VB* (1965), *T22* (1966), *SS* (1966), *T22* (1966), *SRB* (1980), *CS2* (1990). Anthologized *Young Mutants* (1984; U.K., as *Asimov's Mutants*, 1986), *The Immor-tals* (1984), *Just Fantastic* (Canada, 1993). Anthologized in six textbooks, beginning with *Portfolio* (1973). Adapted by others (along with "Season of Disbelief") for *CBS Radio Workshop*, Feb. 17, 1956, with an introduction written and read by Bradbury; adapted to stage by Bradbury; printed in *Scholastic Scope* Sept. 7, 1984. Adapted (TV) by Brad-bury for *Ray Bradbury Theater* (USA), Sept. 29, 1989.

53–10   "Bullet with a Name" (205)

   Argosy Apr. 1953.

53–11   "Dandelion Wine" (206)

   Gourmet June 1953. Reprinted *Gourmet* Sept. 2001. Collected *DW* (FBA, 1957), untitled; *VB* (1965). Anthologized *Endless Feasts* (2002).

53–12   "And So Died Riabouchinska" (207)

   The Saint Detective Magazine June–July 1953. Reprinted *Argosy* (U.K.) July 1954, as "The Golden Box"; reprinted *The Saint Detective Magazine* (U.K.) Mar. 1957. Collected *MJ* (FBA, 1964), *SRB* (1980). Anthologized *Hitchcock in Prime Time* (1985), *Masterpieces of Mystery and Suspense* (1988). Adapted for radio from Bradbury's 1947 radio-script out-line by other writers and broadcast on *Suspense* (CBS), Nov. 13, 1947, as "Riabouchin-ska"; story version adapted (TV) for broadcast on *Alfred Hitchcock Presents* (CBS), Feb. 12, 1956; adapted (TV) by Bradbury for *Ray Bradbury Theater* (USA), May 28, 1988, as "Riabouchinska."

53–13   "Time in Thy Flight" (208)

   Fantastic Universe June–July 1953. Reprinted *Gamma 1* 1963, *Literary Cavalcade* Nov. 1980, *The Reading Connection* 1, no. 4 (1980) and 7 (1984), *Land's End Catalog* 1989. Collected *SS* (FBA, 1966), *CS2* (1990), *BS* (2003). Anthologized in twelve textbooks, beginning with *The Young America Level 14* (1972). Adapted to comic-strip form (Ron Wilbur, illustrator) for *Rocket's Blast Comic Collector* (Oct. 1976).

53–14 "The Millionth Murder" ("And the Rock Cried Out") (209)
Manhunt Sept. 1953. Reprinted *Manhunt* (U.K.) May 1954; reprinted *Merrick News Annual* Sept. 1965, as "And the Rock Cried Out." Rewritten and collected *F451* (FBA, 1953, certain editions), *DRF* (1959), *VB* (1965), *BS* (2003), as "And the Rock Cried Out." Anthologized in four textbooks, beginning with *Studies in the Short Story* (1968), all as "And the Rock Cried Out." Adapted by Bradbury for director Carol Reed as a screenplay, "And the Rock Cried Out," but unproduced.

1954

Stories

54–1 "The Marriage Mender" (210)
Collier's Jan. 22, 1954. Reprinted *Housewife* (U.K.) Apr. 1954, *Escapade* Aug. 1958; reprinted *Eros* summer 1962, as "A Bed for Marie." Collected *MM* (1959), *DRF* (1959), *T22* (1966), *CS2* (1990). Anthologized *Wild Sweet Wine* (FBA, 1957), *Anthology of Best Short-Short Stories*, vol. 7 (1959). Bradbury's initial working title was "Calliope." A surviving typescript (UCLA) is titled "The Pipe Organ" and is annotated "original version 1952." As "The Marriage Mender," it became his fourth and final "Short Short" feature in *Collier's*, following "There Will Come Soft Rains" (50–13) "The Window" (50–18), and "The Pumpernickel" (51–10). This story scheduled for *OC* (1955) but deleted prior to publication.

54–2 "The Dwarf" (211)
Fantastic Jan.–Feb. 1954. Reprinted *Cavalier* Jan. 1960, *Amazing Stories* Nov. 1968. Collected *OC* (FBA, 1955), *VB* (1965), *BS* (2003). Anthologized *Horror Anthology* (U.K., 1965), *The Freak Show* (1970), *The Penguin Book of Horror Stories* (U.K., 1984). Anthologized in two textbooks, beginning with *The Quickening Pulse Book 5* (1982). Adapted (TV) by Bradbury for *Ray Bradbury Theater* (USA), July 7, 1989. A presentation copy of the manuscript survives in Leigh Brackett Papers, Eastern New Mexico University, Portales.

54–3 "Dinner at Dawn" (212)
Everywoman's Feb. 1954. Collected *DW* (FBA, 1957), untitled.

54–4 "All Summer in a Day" (213)
Magazine of Fantasy and Science Fiction Mar. 1954. Reprinted *The New York Post* Dec. 5, 1954, *Magazine of Fantasy and Science Fiction 1* (U.K.) Dec. 1959, *Weird Worlds 3* 1979, *Scholastic Scope* Apr. 6, 1990 (condensed), *Verbicide 5* (Spring 2002). Collected *MM* (1959), *T22* (1966), *TS* (1979), *SRB* (1980), *CS2* (1990). Anthologized *The Best from Fantasy and Science Fiction*, 4th ser. (FBA, 1955), *Tomorrow's Children* (1966; U.K., 1974), *Voyages* (1971), *Space Opera* (1974), *Peter Davison's Book of Alien Planets* (U.K., 1983), *Children of the Future* (1984), *SFWA Grandmasters* vol. 2 (2000). Anthologized in seventy-three textbooks, beginning with *Short Stories I* (1961). Adapted (TV) for broadcast on PBS, Aug. 15, 1982. Adapted to stage and published in one textbook *Lobstick* (1988).

54–5 "Interval in Sunlight" (214)
Esquire Mar. 1954. Revised and collected *LAM* (FBA, 1976), *SRB* (1980).

54–6 "The Watchful Poker Chip" (215)
Beyond Mar. 1954. Reprinted *Help!* Jan. 1961, as "The Watchful Poker Chip of H. Matisse." Collected *OC* (FBA, 1955), *VB* (1965), *BS* (2003), as "The Watchful Poker Chip of H. Matisse." Anthologized *Beyond* (1963). Anthologized in one textbook, *Literature IV* (1969), as "The Watchful Poker Chip of H. Matisse."

54–7　"At Midnight, in the Month of June" (216)

　　　Ellery Queen's Mystery Magazine June 1954. Reprinted *Ellery Queen's Mystery Magazine* (U.K.) June 1954. Collected *TC* (1988), *BS* (2003). Anthologized *Night Chills* (FBA, 1975). This story picks up from the final paragraph of "The Whole Town's Sleeping" (50–19) but was not included when the earlier story was refashioned into a chapter of *DW*.

54–8　"Shopping for Death" ("Touched with Fire") (217)

　　　First published *Maclean's* (Canada) June 1, 1954. Reprinted *Argosy* (U.K.) Nov. 1954, as "Shopping for Murder"; reprinted *The Saint Detective Magazine* Feb. 1955, and (U.K.) Dec. 1956; reprinted *Help!* Apr. 1961, as "Touched with Fire." Revised and collected *OC* (1955), *SRB* (1980), as "Touched with Fire." Anthologized *Best Detective Stories of the Year—1955* (FBA, 1955). Adapted (TV) by Bradbury and broadcast on *Alfred Hitchcock Presents* (CBS), Jan. 29, 1956; adapted (TV) by Bradbury for *Ray Bradbury Theater* (USA), Aug. 3, 1990, as "Touched with Fire." Adapted to comic-strip form for *Ray Bradbury Comics* 2 (Apr. 1993), as "Touched by [*sic*] Fire."

54–9　"They Knew What They Wanted" (218)

　　　Saturday Evening Post June 26, 1954. Manuscript title: "Family Portrait."

54–10　"The Wonderful Death of Dudley Stone" (219)

　　　Charm July 1954. Reprinted *Argosy* (U.K.) Apr. 1956, as "Chance of a Lifetime"; reprinted *Mystery Digest* Nov. 1957, *Ellery Queen's Mystery Magazine* Dec. 1983; reprinted as single-story book *WD* (85-B). Collected *OC* (FBA, 1955), *BS* (2003). Anthologized *The Haunted Hour* (1995). Adapted for radio and broadcast with other stories and a Bradbury interview as *October Country* (ABC Halloween special), Oct. 31, 1984. Adapted (TV) by Bradbury for *Ray Bradbury Theater* (USA), Aug. 18, 1989. A surviving typescript (UCLA) is dated "June 52–June 53" and titled "The Incredible Death of Dudley Stone."

54–11　"The Swan" (220)

　　　Cosmopolitan Sept. 1954. Reprinted *Argosy* (U.K.) June 1955, as "Lime-Vanilla Ice." Collected *DW* (FBA, 1957), untitled; *BS* (2003).

54–12　"The Strawberry Window" (221)

　　　Star Science Fiction Stories 3 (New York: Ballantine, 1954). Reprinted *Argosy* (U.K.) Aug. 1955. Collected *MM* (1959), *DRF* (1959), *RR* (1962), *T22* (1966), *SRB* (1980), *CS1* (1990). Anthologized *Star Science Fiction Stories No.3* (FBA and first printed, 1954). An "unchronicled" Martian tale.

1955

Books

55-A　*Switch on the Night*

　　　Children's picture book. With illustrations by Madeleine Gekiere: New York: Pantheon, [Mar.] 1955; London: Rupert Hart-Davis, [Nov.] 1955; New York: Pantheon, 1963 (library edition). New edition, with illustrations by Leo and Diane Dillon: New York: Knopf, 1993 (trade and library bindings); New York: Knopf, 2000. Anthologized *The Golden Treasury of Children's Literature* (with house illustrations, 1966); *The Oxford Book of Story Poems* (unillustrated, 1990); *What a Wonderful World* (U.K., 1998). Original version anthologized in five textbooks, beginning with *Taking Off* (1970).

55-B　*The October Country*

　　　Story collection. See also *SA* (62-A). New York: Ballantine, [Oct.] 1955; New York: Ballantine, 1956 (mass-market paperback); London: Ruper Hart-Davis, [July] 1956; London: Ace, 1961 (abridged paperback); New York: Knopf, 1970; New York: Ballantine, 1996, with a new Bradbury foreword (large-format trade paperback); Springfield, Pa.: Gauntlet, 1997; London: Earthlight, 1998 (paperback); New York: Avon, 1999, with a new Bradbury introduction. Contents: "The Dwarf"; "The Next in Line"; "The Watchful Poker Chip of H. Matisse"; "Skeleton"; "The Jar"; "The Lake"; "The Emissary"; "Touched with Fire"; "The Small Assassin"; "The Crowd"; "Jack-in-the-Box"; "The Scythe"; "Uncle Einar"; "The Wind"; "The Man Upstairs"; "There Was an Old Woman"; "The Cistern"; "Homecoming"; "The Wonderful Death of Dudley Stone." The U.K. Ace paperback (1961) deletes "The Next in Line," "The Lake," "The Small Assassin," "The Crowd," "Jack-in-the-Box," "The Man Upstairs," and "The Cistern" and adds "The Traveller." Fifteen of the nineteen *OC* stories were revised or rewritten from *DC* (47-A).

Stories

55–1   "Marvels and Miracles—Pass It On!" (222)
      New York Times Magazine Mar. 20, 1955. Reprinted *World Digest* (U.K.) Nov. 1955, as "My Interview with Jules Verne"; reprinted *Galileo 1* Sept. 1976.

55–2   "The Last, the Very Last" (223)
      Reporter June 2, 1955. Reprinted *Boy's Life* May 1987, as "The Time Machine." Collected *DW* (1957), untitled; collected *RR* (1962), *CS1* (1990), as "The Time Machine." Anthologized *The Reporter Reader* (FBA, 1956). Anthologized in three textbooks, beginning with *Here and Now* (1968), all as "The Death of Colonel Freeleigh." Adapted to stage by Bradbury and printed as *A Device Out of Time* (86-F).

55–3   "The Trolley" (224)
      Good Housekeeping July 1955. Reprinted *Argosy* (U.K.) Mar. 1956, as "The Enchanted Trolley." Collected *DW* (1957), untitled; collected *SS* (1966), *RB* (1975), *CS2* (1990), *BS* (2003). Anthologized in one textbook, *Winterfall* (1981).[7]

55–4   "The Dragon" (225)
      Esquire Aug. 1955. Reprinted *Magazine of Fantasy and Science Fiction* Mar. 1956, *Adam Bedside Reader 3* 1960, *Literary Cavalcade* Jan. 1964, *Knight* May 1966. Reprinted as a single-story book, *The Dragon* (88-A). Collected *MM* (FBA, 1959), *DRF* (1959), *RR* (1962), *T22* (1966), *CS1* (1990), *BS* (2003). Anthologized *Dragons* (1997). Anthologized in ten textbooks, beginning with *Adventures in Appreciation*, vol. 1 (1963). Adapted to comic-strip form for *The Ray Bradbury Chronicles* vol. 1 (July 1992).

55–5   "The Mice" (226)
      Escapade Oct. 1955. Revised and collected *MM* (FBA, 1959), *DRF* (1959), *VB* (1965), *T22* (1966), *CS2* (1990), as "The Little Mice."

1956

Stories

56–1   "Summer in the Air" ("The Sound of Summer Running") (227)
      Saturday Evening Post Feb. 18, 1956. Reprinted *Argosy* (U.K.) Sept. 1956; reprinted *Crossroads* July–Aug. 1980, as "Wings of Summer"; reprinted *Reader's Digest* (U.S. and Canada) June 1981, as "Magic Sneakers" (condensed); reprinted *Saturday Evening Post* Oct. 1983. Collected *DW* (1957), untitled; collected *RR* (1962), *CS1* (1990), and *BS* (2003), as "The Sound of Summer Running." Anthologized *Saturday Evening Post Stories, 1956* (FBA, 1956–57); anthologized *Anthology of Best Short-Short Stories, V5* (1957), as "Sneakers"; anthologized *Teen-Age Treasury of Imagination and Discovery* (1962), as "Royal Crown Cream-Sponge Para Litefoot Tennis Shoes"; anthologized *Help Wanted* (1997),

as "From Dandelion Wine." Anthologized in sixteen textbooks, beginning with *Reading Roundup* (1958); textbook title variations include "New Sneakers" and "The Sound of Summer Running." Adapted to stage and published in two textbooks, beginning with *Students Anthology* (1986), as *Wings of Summer*.[8]

56–2   "The First Night of Lent" (228)

    Playboy Mar. 1956. Reprinted *Argosy* (U.K.) Apr. 1957. Collected *MM* (1959), *T22* (1966), *CS2* (1990), *BS* (2003). Anthologized *The Third Playboy Annual* (FBA, 1957), *Playboy's Short-Shorts* (1970).

56–3   "Icarus Montgolfier Wright" (229)

    Magazine of Fantasy and Science Fiction May 1956. Reprinted *Space World* June 1961, *The Antiquer* Nov. 1965. Collected *MM* (1959), *DRF* (1959), *T22* (1966), *SS* (1966), *TS* (1979), *CS2* (1990), *BS* (2003). Anthologized *The Best from Fantasy and Science Fiction*, 6th ser. (FBA, 1957). Adapted by Bradbury (with George Clayton Johnson) and produced as an animated film (Academy Award nomination, 1962).

56–4   "Next Stop, the Stars" ("The End of the Beginning") (230)

    Maclean's (Canada) Oct. 27, 1956. Reprinted *Colorado Review 1* winter 1956–57, as "The End of the Beginning"; reprinted *Amazing Stories* July 1959, *Science Fiction Greats 16* winter 1969. Collected *MM* (FBA, 1959), *DRF* (1959), *RR* (1962), *T22* (1966), *SRB* (1980), *CS1* (1990), as "The End of the Beginning." Anthologized *Science Fiction Showcase* (1959; U.K., 1966), *Skylife* (2000), as "The End of the Beginning." Anthologized in one textbook, *World History: Continuity and Change* (1997).

56–5   "The Time of Going Away" (231)

    Reporter Nov. 29, 1956. Reprinted *Grail* Sept. 1957. Collected *MM* (FBA, 1959), *DRF* (1959), *T22* (1966), *CS2* (1990).

1957

Books

57-A   *Sun and Shadow*

    Single story (53–3) in book format, privately printed. Berkeley, Calif.: [Quenian], 1957.

57-B   *Dandelion Wine*

    Novel (stories collected and bridged into novel form). Garden City, N.Y.: Doubleday, [Sept. 5], 1957; London: Rupert Hart-Davis, [Oct.] 1957; New York: Bantam, 1959 (paperback); London: Corgi, 1965 (paperback); New York: Knopf, 1975; New York: Bantam, 1977 (reset paperback); London: Grafton, 1977 (paperback); New York: Easton, 1988; New York: Avon, 1999; Thorndike, Maine: G. K. Hall, 1999 (large-print edition); London: Earthlight, 2000, (large-format trade paperback). Collected in the omnibus volumes *NRB* (84-C), *RB2* (87-E). Contents: ["Illumination"]; ["Dandelion Wine"]; ["Summer in the Air"]; ["The Season of Sitting"]; ["The Lawns of Summer"]; ["The Happiness Machine," used as opening and closing frame for "The Night"]; ["Season of Disbelief"]; ["The Last, the Very Last"]; ["The Green Machine"]; ["The Trolley"]; ["Statues"]; ["Exorcism"]; ["The Window"]; ["The Swan"]; ["The Whole Town's Sleeping"]; ["Good-by, Grandma"]; ["The Tarot Witch"]; ["Green Wine for Dreaming"]; ["Dinner at Dawn"]. A condensed version of *DW* was anthologized in *Best-in-Books* (1958). Excerpts anthologized in four textbooks, beginning with *Make Yourself Clear*, 2d ed. (1976); all others are titled "Summer Rituals." Adapted to stage and anthologized in two textbooks, beginning with *Readers Theatre Handbook* (1967). Adapted to stage by Bradbury and published (excerpts) in *Readers Theatre 3* (1973).

Stories

57–1 "In a Season of Calm Weather" ("Picasso Summer") (232)
Playboy Jan. 1957. Reprinted *Argosy* (U.K.) Sept. 1958, as "Sea Change"; reprinted *Literary Cavalcade* Jan. 1977 [1978]; reprinted *Horizon* Apr. 1980, as "Picasso Summer." Collected *MM* (FBA, 1959), *DRF* (1959), *T22* (1966), *CS2* (1990); collected *SRB* (1980), as "Picasso Summer." Anthologized *The Permanent Playboy* (1959), *Best Fantasy Stories* (U.K., 1962), *The Twentieth Anniversary Playboy Reader* (1974), *Playboy Stories: The Best Forty Years of Short Fiction* (1994; paperback titled *Playboy Book of Short Stories*). Anthologized in four textbooks, beginning with *Probing Common Ground* (1974); textbook title variations include "Picasso Summer." Adapted by Bradbury (as Douglas Spaulding) and Edwin Boyd (as Ed Weinberger) and produced for film as *Picasso Summer* (1972). Adapted to comic-strip form for *Ray Bradbury Comics* 5 (Oct. 1993), as "Picasso Summer."

57–2 "Illumination" (233)
Reporter May 16, 1957. Collected *DW* (1957), untitled; *VB* (1965), *TS* (1979). Anthologized in one textbook, *The Insistent Present* (1970), as "The Subtlest of Incidents."

57–3 "Good-by, Grandma" (234)
Saturday Evening Post May 25, 1957. Reprinted *Families* Dec. 1981, as "The Leave-Taking" (condensed); reprinted *The Country Gentleman* spring 1982, *Reader's Digest*, July 1983 (condensed), *Saturday Evening Post* July–Aug. 1988 and June 2003, *Voices* 1989. Collected *DW* (FBA, 1957), untitled; *SRB* (1980), as "The Leave-Taking." Anthologized *Saturday Evening Post Stories, 1957* (1957–58), *Anthology of Best Short-Short Stories*, vol. 5 (1958). Anthologized in twenty-two textbooks, beginning with *How to Improve Your Reading* (1963); textbook title variations include "Great-Grandma," "Hail and Farewell to Grandma," and "Grandma."

57–4 "The Day It Rained Forever" (235)
Harper's July 1957. Collected *MM* (1959), *DRF* (1959), *T22* (1966), *SRB* (1980), *CS2* (1990). Anthologized *Best American Short Stories, 1958* (FBA, 1958). Anthologized in two textbooks, beginning with *Literature for Listening* (1968). Adapted (TV) by Bradbury for *Ray Bradbury Theater* (USA), Aug. 29, 1990.

57–5 ["Exorcism"] (236)
DW (FBA, [Sept. 5], 1957, untitled. Collected *SRB* (1980). Anthologized *The Witch's Brew* (2002). Adapted (TV) by Bradbury for *Ray Bradbury Theater* (USA), Aug. 22, 1990. Prepublication title, "Magic!"[9]

57–6 ["Green Wine for Dreaming"] (237)
DW (FBA, [Sept. 5], 1957), untitled. Collected *VB* (1965).

57–7 ["Statues"] (238)
DW (FBA, [Sept. 5], 1957), untitled. Reprinted *Off-Beat* 4 1959. Collected *VB* (1965). Anthologized *Who Do You Think You Are?* (1993), as "Good Grief." Anthologized in four textbooks, beginning with *Enjoying English* 10 (1964); textbook title variations include "Statues Are Best."

57–8 ["The Tarot Witch"] (239)
DW (FBA, [Sept. 5], 1957), untitled. Titled by author.

57–9 "The Happiness Machine" (240)
Saturday Evening Post Sept. 14, 1957. Collected *DW* (FBA, 1957), untitled; *SRB* (1980). Anthologized in two textbooks, beginning with *Psychology and Personal Growth* (1998). Adapted (TV) by Bradbury for *Ray Bradbury Theater* (USA), July 17, 1992.

57–10 "Almost the End of the World" (241)
Reporter Dec. 26, 1957. Collected *DRF* (FBA, 1959), *MJ* (1964), *BS* (2003). Deleted *MJ* U.K. edition (1964).

Stories

58–1 "The Headpiece" (242)

Lilliput (U.K.), May 1958. Collected *MM* (FBA, 1959), *DRF* (1959), *T22* (1966), *CS2* (1990). Anthologized *The Midnight Penthouse* (U.K., 1968).

58–2 "The Town Where No One Got Off" (243)

Ellery Queen's Mystery Magazine Oct. 1958. Reprinted *Argosy* (U.K.) July 1959, as "Back of Beyond." Collected *MM* (1959), *DRF* (1959), *T22* (1966), *SRB* (1980), *CS2* (1990). Anthologized *Ellery Queen's 14th Mystery Annual* (FBA, 1958; U.k. edition omits Bradbury), *The Town Where No One Got Off* (U.K., 1990; U.S., as *Journey into Fear*, 1991), *Stranger* (2002). Anthologized in seven textbooks, beginning with *The Cities* (1968). Adapted (TV) by Bradbury for *Ray Bradbury Theater* (HBO), Feb. 22, 1986.

58–3 "The Magic White Suit" ("The Wonderful Ice Cream Suit") (244)

Saturday Evening Post Oct. 4, 1958. Reprinted *Argosy* (U.K.) May 1959, as "Ice Cream Suit." Collected *MM* (1959), *DRF* (1959), *VB* (1965), *T22* (1966), *SRB* (1980), *CS2* (1990), as "The Wonderful Ice Cream Suit." Anthologized *Saturday Evening Post Stories, 1958* (FBA, 1959), *The Chicano* (1971). Anthologized in seven textbooks, beginning with *Modern Fiction* vol. 3 (1967), all as "The Wonderful Ice Cream Suit." Adapted to stage by Bradbury for *Rendezvous* (1958); rewritten and collected *WICS* (1972), *RBOS* (1991); and rewrite published separately (86-C), all as *The Wonderful Ice Cream Suit*. Adapted to film by Bradbury and produced (for video) by Disney as *The Wonderful Ice Cream Suit* (1998).

58–4 "The Great Collision of Monday Last" (245)

Contact 1 1958. Revised and reprinted *Argosy* (U.K.) Nov. 1958, as "The Collision of Monday." Original version collected *MM* (FBA, 1959), *T22* (1966), *CS2* (1990), *BS* (2003). Rewritten and bridged into *GS* as the untitled chap. 4. Adapted to stage by Bradbury and collected *AS* (1963), *RBOS* (1991). Adapted to stage again by Bradbury in combination with "The Cold Wind and the Warm" (64–2) and published in book form as *Falling Upward* (89-A). Bradbury initially sold the story to the *Saturday Evening Post* but was not willing to expand the text as desired by *Post* editors.

Books

59-A *A Medicine for Melancholy*

Story collection. See also 59-B, 66-A, 90-B, and 98-A. Garden City, N.Y.: Doubleday, [Feb. 5], 1959; New York: Bantam, 1960 (mass-market paperback). Contents: "In a Season of Calm Weather"; "The Dragon"; "A Medicine for Melancholy"; "The End of the Beginning"; "The Wonderful Ice Cream Suit"; "Fever Dream"; "The Marriage Mender"; "The Town Where No One Got Off"; "A Scent of Sarsaparilla"; "Icarus Montgolfier Wright"; "The Headpiece"; "Dark They Were, and Golden-Eyed"; "The Smile"; "The First Night of Lent"; "The Time of Going Away"; "All Summer in a Day"; "The Gift"; "The Great Collision of Monday Last"; "The Little Mice"; "The Shore Line at Sunset"; "The Strawberry Window"; "The Day It Rained Forever." *DRF* (59-B) is the heavily altered U.K. form of this collection. *T22* (66-A) combines *GA* (53-A) and *MM;* Bantam's *CS2* (90-B) and Avon's *A Medicine for Melancholy and Other Stories* (98-A) combine *MM* and *SS* (66-C).

59-B *The Day It Rained Forever*

Story collection. See also *MM* (59-A). London: Rupert Hart-Davis, [Feb. 20], 1959; London: Science Fiction Book Club, 1960; London: Penguin, 1963 (large-format trade paperback). Contents: "The Day It Rained Forever"; "In a Season of Calm Weather";

"The Dragon"; "The End of the Beginning"; "The Wonderful Ice-Cream Suit"; "Fever Dream"; "Referent"; "The Marriage Mender"; "The Town Where No One Got Off"; "Icarus Montgolfier Wright"; "Almost the End of the World"; "Dark They Were, and Golden-Eyed"; "The Smile"; "Here There Be Tygers"; "The Headpiece"; "Perchance to Dream"; "The Time of Going Away"; "The Gift"; "The Little Mice"; "The Sunset Harp"; "A Scent of Sarsaparilla"; "And the Rock Cried Out"; "The Strawberry Window." *DRF* is the heavily altered U.K. form of *MM*, deleting four stories: "A Medicine for Melancholy"; "The First Night of Lent"; "All Summer in a Day"; "The Great Collision of Monday Last." Five stories are added: "Referent"; "Almost the End of the World"; "Here There Be Tygers"; "Perchance to Dream"; "And the Rock Cried Out." "The Shore Line at Sunset" is retitled "The Sunset Harp."

Stories

59–1 "A Medicine for Melancholy" (246)

    MM (FBA, [Feb. 5], 1959). Reprinted *Tales of Topper 1* 1961. Collected *VB* (1965), *T22* (1966), *SRB* (1980), *CS2* (1990).

59–2 "The Shoreline at Sunset" (247)

    Magazine of Fantasy and Science Fiction Mar. 1959. Reprinted *Argosy* (U.K.) June 1959, as "The Sunset Harp"; reprinted *Venture Science Fiction* (Australia) Nov. 1964. Collected *MM* (FBA, 1959), *T22* (1966), *CS2* (1990), as "The Shore Line at Sunset"; *DRF* (1959), as "The Sunset Harp"; *SRB* (1980), as "The Shoreline at Sunset." Anthologized *The Year's Best S-F: 5th Annual Edition* (1960; U.K., as *The Best of Sci-Fi 5*, 1966), *Great American Short Stories* (1977), *Large Type Reader: Selections from Reader's Digest Condensed Books* vol. 2 (1991).

59–3 "A Wild Night in Galway" (248)

    Harper's Aug. 1959. Reprinted *Argosy* (U.K.) Feb. 1960, as "Wild in Galway." Collected *BS* (2003). Anthologized *The Wild Night Company* (FBA, 1970), with introduction. A typescript of the story (UCLA) bears the title "A Wild Night in Ireland." It is a preliminary draft, and Bradbury's annotation states that the story is "based on a fragment of conversation with Ben Maddow, returned from Ireland, at lunch, Dec. 15, 1958."

1960

Stories

60–1 "Forever Voyage" ("And the Sailor, Home from the Sea") (249)

    Saturday Evening Post Jan. 9, 1960. Reprinted *Argosy* (U.K.) June 1960, *Saturday Evening Post*, July–Aug. 1983. Collected *MJ* (FBA, 1964), *BS* (2003), as "And the Sailor, Home from the Sea."

60–2 "Death and the Maiden" (250)

    Magazine of Fantasy and Science Fiction Mar. 1960. Reprinted *Suspense* (U.K.) July 1960. Collected *MJ* (FBA, 1964), *BS* (2003). Adapted (TV, without credit) for broadcast on *The Twilight Zone* (CBS), Jan. 5, 1962, as "Nothing in the Dark."

60–3 "The Drummer Boy of Shiloh" (251)

    Saturday Evening Post Apr. 30, 1960. Reprinted *Argosy* (U.K.) Sept. 1960, *Reader's Digest* Apr. 1961, *Counterpoint in Literature* 1967, 1974, *Read* Mar. 28, 1986. Collected *MJ* (1964), *BS* (2003). Anthologized *Saturday Evening Post Stories, 1961* (FBA, 1961), *Reader's Digest New Treasury for Young Readers* (1963), *Transformations II* (1974). Anthologized in seventeen textbooks, beginning with *Prose and Poetry Journeys* (1964).

60–4 "The Best of All Possible Worlds" (252)

Playboy Aug. 1960. Reprinted Argosy (U.K.) Nov. 1960. Collected MJ (FBA, 1964), SRB (1980). Anthologized The Bedside Playboy (1963), Playboy's Stories for Swinging Readers (1969).

60–5 "Very LATE in the Evening" (253)

Playboy Dec. 1960. Collected MJ (FBA, 1964), SRB (1980), as "Some Live like Lazarus." Anthologized The Best from Playboy 1 (1964). Adapted by Bradbury for Ray Bradbury Theater (USA), Oct. 24, 1992, as "Some Live like Lazarus."

1961

Stories

61–1 "The Beggar on the Dublin Bridge" (254)

Saturday Evening Post Jan. 14, 1961. Reprinted Argosy (U.K.) May 1961, Saturday Evening Post Jan.–Feb. 1985. Collected MJ (1964), BS (2003), as "The Beggar on O'Connell Bridge." Bridged to other Irish stories and rewritten for inclusion in GS (as untitled chap. 13). Anthologized Saturday Evening Post Stories, 1962 (FBA, 1962), Short Story: A Thematic Anthology (1965). Anthologized in two textbooks, beginning with Literature 6 (1970).

61–2 "The Illustrated Woman" (255)

Playboy Mar. 1961. Reprinted Argosy (U.K.) July 1961. Collected MJ (1964), SRB (1980). Anthologized Tales of Love and Horror (FBA, 1961). Anthologized in one textbook, Discovery and Recollection (1970).

61–3 "With Smiles as Wide as Summer" (256)

Clipper Nov.–Dec. 1961. Collected OM (2002). Original composition: c. 1955.

1962

Books

62-A *The Small Assassin*

Story collection. See also OC (55-B). London: New English Library Ace edition, 1962 (paperback); London, Grafton, 1976 (paperback). Contents: "The Small Assassin"; "The Next in Line"; "The Lake"; "The Crowd"; "Jack-in-the-Box"; "The Man Upstairs"; "The Cistern"; "The Tombstone"; "The Smiling People"; "The Handler"; "Let's Play 'Poison'"; "The Night"; "The Dead Man." Contains the seven OC stories deleted from the abridged U.K. Ace paperback (55-B) and the six remaining stories from the U.K. edition of DC (47-A).

62-B *Something Wicked This Way Comes*

Novel. New York: Simon and Schuster, 1962; London: Rupert Hart-Davis, 1963; New York: Bantam, 1963 (paperback); London: Corgi, 1965 (paperback); New York: Knopf, 1983; New York: Easton, 1988; New York: Avon, 1998 (paperback); London: Earthlight, 1998 (large-format trade paperback); New York: Avon, 1999; [Springfield, Pa.]: Gauntlet, 1999 (limited edition); Thorndike, Maine: Center Point, 2000 (large-print edition). Collected in the omnibus NRB (84-C). Contents: The novel includes revised and expanded forms of "The Black Ferris" (48–6) and "Nightmare Carousel" (62–2) embedded in an unpublished screenplay adapted from "The Black Ferris" and subsequently expanded into a novel. The library confrontation scene was anthologized Magic and Madness in the Library (1999). Adapted by Bradbury for the Disney-Touchstone film, Something Wicked This Way Comes (1983).

62-C   *R Is for Rocket*

Story collection (young adult). See also 90-A, 97-B. Garden City, N.Y.: Doubleday, [1962]; New York: Bantam, [1965] (paperback); London: Rupert Hart-Davis, 1968; London: Pan, [1972] (paperback). Contents: "R Is for Rocket"; "The End of the Beginning"; "The Fog Horn"; "The Rocket"; "The Rocket Man"; "The Golden Apples of the Sun"; "A Sound of Thunder"; "The Long Rain"; "The Exiles"; "Here There Be Tygers"; "The Strawberry Window"; "The Dragon"; "The Gift"; "Frost and Fire"; "Uncle Einar"; "The Time Machine"; "The Sound of Summer Running."

Stories

62–1   "A Miracle of Rare Device" (257)

Playboy Jan. 1962. Reprinted *Argosy* (U.K.) Jan. 1963. Collected *MJ* (1964). Anthologized *The Worlds of Science Fiction* (FBA, 1963), *The Year's Best S-F: 8th Annual Edition* (1963), *The Fully Automated Love Life of Henry Keanridge* (1971). Anthologized in three textbooks, beginning with *Contact Two* (U.K., 1969). Adapted (TV) by Bradbury for *Ray Bradbury Theater* (USA), July 14, 1989. The title originates with Coleridge's description of the "pleasure-dome with caves of ice" in "Kubla Khan" (verse 35).

62–2   "Nightmare Carousel" (258)

Mademoiselle Jan. 1962. Reprinted *Argosy* (U.K.) Oct. 1962; reprinted *Gauntlet* 18 (1999), as "Night Carousel." Revised and collected *SW* (FBA, 1962), untitled. A re-working of "The Black Ferris" (48–6) to form the climactic chapters of "Arrivals" (Part 1 of *SW*).

62–3   "Perhaps We Are Going Away" (259)

Topper Jan. 1962. Collected *MJ* (FBA, 1964). Anthologized in one textbook, *The Conscious Reader* (1974).

62–4   "The Prehistoric Producer" ("Tyrannosaurus Rex") (260)

Saturday Evening Post June 23, 1962. Reprinted *Argosy* (U.K.) Apr. 1963. Collected *MJ* (FBA, 1964), *SRB* (1980), *DT* (illustrated, 1983), as "Tyrannosaurus Rex." Anthologized *The Hollywood Nightmare* (1971). Adapted (TV) by Bradbury for *Ray Bradbury Theater* (USA), May 14, 1988, as "Tyrannosaurus Rex." Adapted to comic-strip form for *Ray Bradbury Comics* 1 (Feb. 1993), as "Tyrannosaurus Rex."

62–5   "Tread Lightly to the Music" ("Getting Through Sunday Somehow") (261)

Cavalier Oct. 1962. Collected *LAM* (FBA, 1976), *BS* (2003), as "Getting through Sunday Somehow."

62–6   "Come into My Cellar" ("Boys! Raise Giant Mushrooms in *Your* Cellar!") (262)

Galaxy Oct. 1962. Reprinted *Galaxy* 94 (U.K.) Oct. 1962, *Argosy* (U.K.) Mar. 1963. Collected *SS* (1966), *CS2* (1990); collected *MJ* (1964), *TS* (1979), *SRB* (1980), as "Boys! Raise Giant Mushrooms in *Your* Cellar!" Anthologized *17 X Infinity* (FBA, 1963), *The Seventh Galaxy Reader* (1964), *Nightmare Garden* (1976), Bruce Coville's Book of Spinetinglers II (1997); anthologized *Dangerous Vegetables* (1998), as "Boys! Raise Giant Mushrooms in *Your* Cellar!" Story adapted from Bradbury's original teleplay for *Alfred Hitchcock Presents* (CBS), Nov. 29, 1959, titled "Special Delivery"; adapted again by Bradbury for *Ray Bradbury Theater* (USA), Nov. 17, 1989, as "Boys! Raise Giant Mushrooms in *Your* Cellar!" Adapted to comic-strip form for *The Ray Bradbury Chronicles* vol. 2 (July 1992).

62–7   "The Machineries of Joy" (263)

Playboy Dec. 1962. Reprinted *Argosy* (U.K.) July 1963. Collected *MJ* (FBA, 1964), *BS* (2003). Anthologized *Transit of Earth* (1971).

62–8   "The Long-after-Midnight Girl" (264)

Eros winter 1962. Collected *LAM* (FBA, 1976), *SRB* (revised, 1980), as "Long after Midnight." The *SRB* text deletes the last single-sentence paragraph of the story.

1963

Books

63-A   *The Anthem Sprinters and Other Antics*
Collected plays (from stories). New York: Dial, [Oct.] 1963; New York: Dial, [Oct.] 1963(paperback). Contents: *The Great Collision of Monday Last; The First Night of Lent; A Clear View of an Irish Mist; The Anthem Sprinters;* "The Queen's Own Evaders" (afterword). All except *A Clear View of an Irish Mist* were adapted from published stories (see 56–2, 58–4, 63–3, 91-B).

Stories

63–1   "To the Chicago Abyss" (265)
Magazine of Fantasy and Science Fiction May 1963. Reprinted *Magazine of Fantasy and Science Fiction* (U.K.) Sept. 1963, *Argosy* (U.K.) Mar. 1966, as "Abyss." Collected *MJ* (FBA, 1964). Anthologized *The Best from Fantasy and Science Fiction* (1974), *Beyond Armageddon* (1985). Anthologized in four textbooks, beginning with *Science Fiction: The Future* (1971). Adapted by Bradbury for stage and collected *WICS* (1972), *RBOS* (1991); play anthologized in one textbook, *Nova* (1977); reprinted as a single-play book (88-D). Adapted (TV) by Bradbury for *Ray Bradbury Theater* (USA), Sept. 22, 1989.

63–2   "Bright Phoenix" (266)
Magazine of Fantasy and Science Fiction May 1963. Reprinted *Magazine of Fantasy and Science Fiction* (U.K.) Sept. 1963, *Argosy* (U.K.) Nov. 1963, *Gauntlet* 2 (1991). Collected *BS* (2003). Anthologized *Tales of Dungeons and Dragons* (FBA, U.K., 1986), with a Bradbury introduction. The manuscript dates back to 1948 and may be considered an early variation of material developed in *F451* (53-B). The *Gauntlet* reprinting includes an introduction by William F. Nolan.

63–3   "The Queen's Own Evaders" ("The Anthem Sprinters") (267)
Playboy June 1963. Reprinted *The Deanna Durbin Society Newsletter* (U.K.) spring 1992, as "The Anthem Sprinters." Rewritten and collected *MJ* (FBA, 1964), *VB* (1965), *SRB* (1980), as "The Anthem Sprinters." Bridged as rewritten into *GS* (untitled chap. 29). Anthologized in one textbook, *Fictional Memoir 4* (1974), as "The Anthem Sprinters." Adapted (stage) by Bradbury and collected *AS* (1963), *RBOS* (1991), as *The Anthem Sprinters;* adapted (TV) by Bradbury for *Ray Bradbury Theater* (USA), Aug. 21, 1992, as "The Anthem Sprinters." Not to be confused with "The Queen's Own Evaders," the afterword to *AS*.

63–4   "The Life Work of Juan Diaz" (268)
Playboy Sept. 1963. Reprinted *Argosy* (U.K.) Mar. 1964. Collected *MJ* (FBA, 1964), *BS* (2003). Anthologized *Playboy Book of Horror and the Supernatural* (1967). Anthologized in one textbook, *Short Stories* (1969). Adapted (TV) by Bradbury and broadcast on *Alfred Hitchcock Hour* (NBC), Oct. 26, 1964.

63–5   "The Vacation" (269)
Playboy Dec. 1963. Reprinted *Argosy* (U.K.) May 1964, as "Holiday." Collected *MJ* (FBA, 1964), *SRB* (1980). Anthologized *The Twelfth Anniversary Playboy Reader* (1965), *The Playboy Book of Science Fiction and Fantasy* (1966), *The Storm before the Calm* (1972), *Isaac Asimov's Magical Worlds of Fantasy 7: Magical Wishes* (1986), *A Magic-Lover's Treasure*

of the Fantastic (1998). Anthologized in three textbooks, beginning with *Basic College Issues* (1969).

1964

Books

64-A *The Machineries of Joy*
Story collection. New York: Simon and Schuster, [Feb.] 1964; New York: Bantam, 1965 (paperback); London: Ruper Hart-Davis, 1964; London: Corgi, 1966 (paperback); London: Earthlight 2000. Contents: "The Machineries of Joy"; "The One Who Waits"; "Tyrannosaurus Rex"; "The Vacation"; "The Drummer Boy of Shiloh"; "Boys! Raise Giant Mushrooms in *Your* Cellar"; "Almost the End of the World"; "Perhaps We Are Going Away"; "And the Sailor, Home from the Sea"; "El Dia De Muerte"; "The Illustrated Woman"; "Some Live like Lazarus"; "A Miracle of Rare Device"; "And So Died Riabouchinska"; "The Beggar on O'Connell Bridge"; "Death and the Maiden"; "A Flight of Ravens"; "The Best of All Possible Worlds"; "The Lifework of Juan Diaz"; "To the Chicago Abyss"; "The Anthem Sprinters." U.K. editions delete "Almost the End of the World."

64-B *The Pedestrian*
Single story (51–15) in book format, privately printed. Glendale, Calif.: [Roy A. Squires, Sept. 1964].

Stories

64–1 "Massinello Pietro" (270)
Connoisseur's World Apr. 1964. This story was originally projected for the August 1958 issue of *Escapade* under the tentative title "What Have I Done?" Ultimately, *Escapade* published a reprint of "The Marriage Mender" (54–1) instead.

64–2 "The Cold Wind and the Warm" (271)
Harper's July 1964. Collected *IS* (FBA, 1969), *BS* (2003). Anthologized *Meanwhile in Another Part of the Forest* (U.S., U.K., 1994). Adapted to stage by Bradbury in combination with "The Great Collision of Monday Last" (58–4) and published in book form as *Falling Upward* (89-A).

64–3 "Heavy-Set" (272)
Playboy Oct. 1964. Reprinted *Weekend Telegraph* (U.K.) Dec. 3, 1965. Collected *IS* (1969), *BS* (2003). Anthologized *The Playboy Book of Horror and the Supernatural* (FBA, 1967), *The Elephant Man and Other Freaks* (U.K., 1980), *Shudder Again* (1993), *October Dreams* (2000).

1965

Books

65-A *The Vintage Bradbury*
Story collection (retrospective compilation). New York: Vintage, [Aug.] 1965; New York: Vintage, [Sept] 1965 (paperback); New York: Vintage, 1990 (large-format trade paperback). Contents: "The Watchful Poker Chip of H. Matisse"; "The Veldt"; "Hail and Farewell"; "A Medicine for Melancholy"; "The Fruit at the Bottom of the Bowl"; "Ylla"; "The Little Mice"; "The Small Assassin"; "The Anthem Sprinters"; "And the Rock Cried Out"; "Invisible Boy"; "Night Meeting"; "The Fox and the Forest"; "Skeleton"; "Illumination"; "Dandelion Wine"; "Statues"; "Green Wine for Dreaming"; "Kaleidoscope";

"Sun and Shadow"; "The Illustrated Man"; "The Fog Horn"; "The Dwarf"; "Fever Dream"; "The Wonderful Ice Cream Suit"; "There Will Come Soft Rains"; introduction by Gilbert Highet. A retrospective collection, pulling stories and chapters from *DC, MC, IM, GA, OC, DW, MM,* and *MJ.*

65-B   *The Autumn People*
Collection of EC comic-strip adaptations of stories. New York: Ballantine [Oct.] 1965 (paperback). Foreword by Bradbury; close textual adaptations by Al Feldstein. Contents: Adaptations of "There Was an Old Woman"; "The Screaming Woman"; "Touch and Go"; "The Small Assassin"; "The Handler"; "The Lake"; "The Coffin"; "Let's Play 'Poison.'"

Stories
65-1   "The Kilimanjaro Machine" (273)
Life Jan. 22, 1965. Reprinted *Argosy* (U.K.) June 1965. Rewritten and collected *IS* (FBA, 1969), *BS* (2003), as "The Kilimanjaro Device." Anthologized *Fateful Choices* (2001), as "The Kilimanjaro Device." Anthologized in one textbook, *Philosophy,* 6th ed. (1994), as "The Kilimanjaro Device."

1966

Books
66-A   *Twice 22*
Story collection omnibus. Garden City, N.Y.: Doubleday, [Jan.] 1966; reissued as the Science Fiction Book Club edition, 1966. Contents: contains *GA* (53-A) and *MM* (59-A), complete, bound together in the original order.

66-B   *Tomorrow Midnight*
Collection of EC comic-strip adaptations of stories. New York: Ballantine [June] 1966 (paperback). Introduction by Bradbury; close textual adaptations by Al Feldstein. Contents: Adaptations of "Punishment without Crime"; "I, Rocket"; "King of the Grey Spaces"; "The One Who Waits"; "The Long Years"; "There Will Come Soft Rains"; "Mars Is Heaven!"; "Outcast of the Stars."

66-C   *S Is for Space*
Story collection (young adult). See also 90-B, 98-A. Garden City, N.Y.: Doubleday, [Aug.] 1966 (trade and library edition); London: Rupert Hart-Davis, 1968; New York: Bantam, 1970 (paperback); London: Pan, 1972 (paperback). Contents: "Chrysalis"; "Pillar of Fire"; "Zero Hour"; "The Man"; "Time in Thy Flight"; "The Pedestrian"; "Hail and Farewell"; "Invisible Boy"; "Come into My Cellar"; "The Million-Year Picnic"; "The Screaming Woman"; "The Smile"; "Dark They Were, and Golden-Eyed"; "The Trolley"; "The Flying Machine"; "Icarus Montgolfier Wright"; and an introduction.

66-D   *The Day It Rained Forever—A Comedy in One Act*
Play adapted by Bradbury from his story (57–4). New York: Samuel French, [Dec.] 1966. Contains Bradbury's production note.

66-E   *The Pedestrian—A Fantasy in One Act*
Play adapted by Bradbury from his story (51–15). New York: Samuel French, [Dec.] 1966. Contains Bradbury's production note.

Stories
66-1   "The Best of Times" ("Any Friend of Nicholas Nickleby's Is a Friend of Mine.") (274)
McCall's Jan. 1966. Rewritten and collected *IS* (FBA, 1969), *BS* (2003), as "Any Friend of Nicholas Nickleby's Is a Friend of Mine." Anthologized *The Peregrine Reader* (1997),

as "Any Friend of Nicholas Nickleby's Is a Friend of Mine." Adapted (TV) and broadcast on *American Playhouse: Sense of Humor* (PBS), Feb. 9, 1982, as "Any Friend of Nicholas Nickleby [*sic*] Is a Friend of Mine."

66–2   "The Blue Flag of John Folk" (275)
Two Bells June 1966.

66–3   "The Year the Glop-Monster Won the Golden Lion at Cannes" ("The Dragon Danced at Midnight") (276)
Cavalier July 1966. Collected *OM* (FBA, 2002), as "The Dragon Danced at Midnight." Anthologized *Knights of Madness* (U.K., 1998; U.S., 1000).

66–4   "The Man in the Rorschach Shirt" (277)
Playboy Oct. 1966. Reprinted *Vision* 1980. Collected *IS* (FBA, 1969), *BS* (2003). Anthologized *Transit of Earth* (1971), *The Pocket Playboy 4* (1974). Anthologized in two textbooks, beginning with *Introductory Psychology through Science Fiction* (1974).

1967

Stories

67–1   "The Lost City of Mars" (278)
Playboy Jan. 1967. Excerpt reprinted *Psychology Today* Apr. 1969, as "Swing Low Sweet Chariot"; reprinted *The Daily Sketch* (U.K.) Oct. 14–15 1969. Collected *IS* (1969). Anthologized *3 to the Highest Power* (FBA, 1968), *Mars, We Love You* (1971; U.K., as *The Book of Mars*, 1976), *Last Train to Limbo* (1971), *The Playboy Book of Science Fiction* (1998).

1969

Books

69-A   *Bloch and Bradbury*
Dual-author story collection. Ed. Kurt Singer. New York and Canada: Tower, 1969 (paperback); London: Sphere, 1970 (paperback), retitled *Fever Dream and Other Fantasies;* [Chicago: Peacock], 1972 (paperback). Contents: "The Watchers"; "Fever Dream"; "The Dead Man"; "The Handler"; and six stories by Robert Bloch. The 1972 edition is expanded but contains no new material by Bradbury.

69-B   *I Sing the Body Electric!*
Story collection. New York: Knopf, [Oct. 24], 1969; London: Rupert Hart-Davis, 1970; New York: Knopf, 1970 (Science Fiction Book Club reissue); New York: Bantam, 1971 (paperback); London: Corgi, 1971 (paperback); London: Earthlight, 1998 (paperback); Avon, 1998 (large-format trade paperback), expanded and retitled *I Sing the Body Electric! and Other Stories*. Contents: "The Kilimanjaro Device"; "The Terrible Conflagration up at the Place"; "Tomorrow's Child"; "The Women"; "The Inspired Chicken Motel"; "Downwind from Gettysburg"; "Yes, We'll Gather at the River"; "The Cold Wind and the Warm"; "Night Call, Collect"; "The Haunting of the New"; "I Sing the Body Electric!"; "The Tombling Day"; "Any Friend of Nicholas Nickleby's Is a Friend of Mine"; "Heavy-Set"; "The Man in the Rorschach Shirt"; "Henry the Ninth"; "The Lost City of Mars"; "Christus Apollo" (poem). The Avon expanded edition includes the first eleven stories from *Long after Midnight* (76-B).

69-C   *Six Masterpieces of Tomorrow*
Paperback boxed set. New York: Bantam, [autumn] 1969 (paperback). Contents: Boxed set of *MC* (50-A), *IM* (51-A), *GA* (53-A), *MM* (59-A), *SW* (62-B), and *MJ* (64-A). Boxed

set of six Bantam paperback titles issued for the Christmas book season. Later packages (1971–72) substitute *IS* for *SW*. See *The Best of Bradbury* (76-A) for other boxed marketing packages.

Stories

69–1 "Downwind from Gettysburg" (279)
Playboy June 1969. Collected *IS* (FBA, 1969), *BS* (2003). Anthologized *The Pocket Playboy 5* (1974). Anthologized in one textbook, *Composition Choice* (1981). Adapted (TV) by Bradbury for *Ray Bradbury Theater* (USA), Oct. 17, 1992.

69–2 "The Beautiful One Is Here" ("I Sing the Body Electric!") (280)
McCall's Aug. 1969. Collected *IS* (1969), *TS* (1979), *SRB* (1980), as "I Sing the Body Electric!" Anthologized *Neutron Stars* (1977), *The Twilight Zone: The Original Stories* (1985), *The Twilight Zone Omnibus* vol. 1 (1999), as "I Sing the Body Electric!" Anthologized in five textbooks, beginning with *Points of View in Writing* (1972), all as "I Sing the Body Electric!" Adapted (TV) for broadcast on *NBC Peacock Theater*, Jan. 17, 1982, as "The Electric Grandmother." The story evolved from Bradbury's original teleplay for *The Twilight Zone* (CBS), broadcast May 18, 1962, as "I Sing the Body Electric!"

69–3 "A Final Sceptre, a Lasting Crown" ("Henry the Ninth") (281)
Magazine of Fantasy and Science Fiction Oct. 1969. Collected *IS* (FBA, 1969), *BS* (2003), as "Henry the Ninth." Anthologized *Twenty Years of the Magazine of Fantasy and Science Fiction* (1970).

69–4 "The Haunting of the New" (282)
Vogue (U.K.) Oct. 1, 1969. Reprinted *Marriage and Divorce* June 1974, as "Hauntings." Revised and collected *IS* (FBA, 1969), *SRB* (1980). Anthologized *The Nightmare Reader* (1973). Adapted (TV) by Bradbury for *Ray Bradbury Theater* (USA), Sept. 15, 1989.

69–5 "The Terrible Conflagration up at the Place" (283)
IS (FBA, [Oct. 24], 1969). Collected *SRB* (1980). Adapted for radio and broadcast on NPR, July 2, 1976.

69–6 "Yes, We'll Gather at the River" (284)
IS (FBA, [Oct. 24], 1969). Reprinted *Coast* Jan. 1976. Collected *SRB* (1980).

69–7 "The Hour of Ghosts" (285)
Saturday Review Oct. 25, 1969. An "ad-story" for AT&T. Anthologized *Ghost Tour* (FBA, U.K., 1984).

69–8 "The Inspired Chicken Bungalow Court" (286)
(Los Angeles Times) West Nov. 2, 1969. Reprinted *Reader's Digest* Feb. 1982, as "The Inspired Chicken Motel" (condensed). Revised and collected *IS* (1969), *SRB* (1980), as "The Inspired Chicken Motel." Adapted (TV) for *A&E Short Stories*, 1986, as "The Inspired Chicken Motel" (did not air).

1970

Stories

70–1 "McGillahee's Brat" (287)
The Irish Press Mar. 21, 1970. Reprinted *Welcome Aboard* (U.K.) fall 1970, *Magazine of Fantasy and Science Fiction* Jan. 1972. Collected *SRB* (1980). Anthologized *Into the Unknown* (FBA, 1973).

Stories

71–1 "The Messiah" (288)

Welcome Aboard spring 1971. Collected *LAM* (FBA, 1976), *GF* (1981), *BS* (2003). Adapted (TV) and inserted into *MC* miniseries (NBC), Jan. 27–29, 1980. Nevertheless, it remains an "unchronicled" Martian tale.

71–2 "My Perfect Murder" ("The Utterly Perfect Murder") (289)

Playboy Aug. 1971. Reprinted *The Saint Detective Magazine* June 1984, *Scholastic Voice* Mar. 21, 1986, *Stories for Bedtime* 1987, as "The Utterly Perfect Murder." Collected *LAM* (FBA, 1976), *SRB* (1980), as "The Utterly Perfect Murder." Anthologized in two textbooks, beginning with *Flashpoint 2* (1987), both as "The Utterly Perfect Murder." Adapted (TV) by Bradbury for *Ray Bradbury Theater* (USA), Feb. 7, 1992, as "The Utterly Perfect Murder."

1972

Books

72-A *The Wonderful Ice Cream Suit and Other Plays*

Collection of plays adapted by Bradbury from his stories. New York: Bantam, [Apr.] 1972 (paperback); simultaneously issued in a book-club edition; London: Rupert Hart-Davis, MacGibbon, 1973. Contents: "Introduction"; *The Wonderful Ice Cream Suit; The Veldt; To the Chicago Abyss* (see 50–20, 58–3, 63–1, 86-C, 88-D, 88-E, 91-B).

72-B *The Halloween Tree*

Novel (juvenile). New York: Knopf, [Aug.] 1972 (trade and library bindings); London: Rupert Hart-Davis, MacGibbon, 1973; New York: Bantam, 1974 (paperback); [London]: Corgi, 1975 (paperback); New York: Bantam, 1994 (large-format trade paperback); New York: Knopf, 1999 (large-format trade paperback); London: Earthlight, 2000 (large-format trade paperback). Excerpts anthologized in one textbook, *Literature of the Americas,* vol. 1 (1980). Adapted (TV) by Bradbury as an animated Hanna-Barbera production, airing (TBS) Oct. 30, 1993, and on various subsequent dates in syndication.

Stories

72–1 "The Parrot Who Met Papa" (290)

Playboy Jan. 1972. Reprinted as a single-story book (90-E). Collected *LAM* (FBA, 1976); *SRB* (1980).

1973

Stories

73–1 "Have I Got a Chocolate Bar for You!" (291)

Penthouse Oct. 1973. Reprinted *Honey* (U.K.) Sept. 1977. Collected *LAM* (FBA, 1976), *SRB* (1980).

73–2 "The Wish" (292)

Woman's Day Dec. 1973. Collected *LAM* (FBA, 1976), *BS* (2003).

Books

75-A   *Ray Bradbury*
Story collection (textbook). Ed. Anthony Adams. London: Harrap, [autumn] 1975. Contents: "The Veldt"; "Let's Play 'Poison'"; "Fever Dream"; "Zero Hour"; "The Foghorn"; "A Sound of Thunder"; "The Wind"; "The Scythe"; "Marionettes, Inc."; "The Other Foot"; "The Pedestrian"; "The Trolley"; "The Smile"; "The Gift"; "The Last Night of the World."

75-B   *Pillar of Fire and Other Plays*
Collection of plays adapted by Bradbury from his stories. New York: Bantam, [Oct.] 1975 (paperback). Contents: "Introduction"; *Pillar of Fire; Kaleidoscope; The Fog Horn* (see 48–8, 49–14, 51–12, 86-D, 91-B).

Stories

75-1   "Invasion Eve" (293)
The Ray Bradbury Companion (FBA, 1975). A facsimile of a single-page story of the U.S. home front on the eve of the Normandy invasion of June, 6, 1944.

75-2   "The Ghosts" (294)
The Ray Bradbury Companion (FBA, 1975). A facsimile of a single-page typescript Martian story or bridge between stories similar to those developed for *MC*. The leaf dates to the late 1940s and may, in fact, be an early try at a bridge between stories of first contact. A more mature version may be "The Disease," which was deleted from *MC* during prepublication revisions.

75-3   "El Hombre Que Ardea" ("The Burning Man") (295)
Gente (Argentina) July 31, 1975. First printed in Spanish; reprinted (in English) *Ariel 2* Mar. 1977, as "The Burning Man." Collected (in English) *LAM* (FBA, 1976), *BS* (2003), as "The Burning Man." Anthologized (in English) *New Stories from the Twilight Zone* (1991; U. K. 1992), as "The Burning Man." Adapted (TV) for broadcast on *The Twilight Zone* (CBS), Nov. 15, 1985, as "The Burning Man."

Books

76-A   *The Best of Bradbury*
Paperback boxed set. New York: Bantam, [1976, 1978, 1979] (paperback). Contents (1976): Boxed set of *DW, IM, IS, MC,* and *RR.* Slipcase is papered with an *IM* cover illustration. Contents (1978): Boxed set of *IM, IS, LAM, MC,* and *RR.* Slipcase is papered with an *RR* cover illustration. *LAM* replaces *DW.* Contents (1979): Boxed set of *DW, GA, IM, LAM,* and *MC.* Slipcase is papered with a *GA* cover illustration. *DW* and *GA* replace *IS* and *RR.* See *Six Masterpieces of Tomorrow* (69-C) for an earlier boxed marketing package from Bantam. See *The Best of Ray Bradbury* (77-A) for the U.K. retail equivalent.

76-B   *Long after Midnight*
Story collection. New York: Knopf, [Aug. 31], 1976; New York: Knopf, [1976] (bookclub edition, reset); London: Rupert Hart-Davis, MacGibbon, [Apr.] 1977; New York: Bantam, 1978 (paperback); London: Granada, 1978 (paperback); London: Earthlight, 2000. Contents: "The Blue Bottle"; "One Timeless Spring"; "The Parrot Who Met Papa"; "The Burning Man"; "A Piece of Wood"; "The Messiah"; "G. B .S.—Mark V";

"The Utterly Perfect Murder"; "Punishment without Crime"; "Getting through Sunday Somehow"; "Drink Entire: Against the Madness of Crowds"; "Interval in Sunlight"; "A Story of Love"; "The Wish"; "Forever and the Earth"; "The Better Part of Wisdom"; "Darling Adolph"; "The Miracles of Jamie"; "The October Game"; "The Pumpernickel"; "Long after Midnight"; "Have I Got a Chocolate Bar for You!" The first eleven stories are included in Avon's 1998 conflated edition of *IS and Other Stories* (69-B, 98-B).

Stories

76–1 "Drink Entire: Against the Madness of Crowds" (296)
Gallery Apr. 1976. Collected *LAM* (FBA, 1976). Anthologized *Magic for Sale* (1983), *Murder on the Railways* (U.K., 1996).

76–2 "Darling Adolf" (297)
LAM (FBA, [Aug. 31], 1976). Collected *BS* (2003). Anthologized *Tales from the Rogues Gallery* (U.K., U.S., 1994).

76–3 "G. B. S.—Mark V" (298)
LAM (FBA, [Aug. 31], 1976). Collected *BS* (2003).

76–4 "The Better Part of Wisdom" (299)
Harper's Weekly Sept. 6, 1976. Reprinted *After Stonewall 4* 1977. Collected *LAM* (FBA, 1976), *SRB* (1980).

1977

Books

77-A *The Best of Ray Bradbury*
Paperback boxed set. London: Panther, [spring–summer] 1977 (paperback). Contents: Boxed set of *DW*, *F451*, *GA*, *IM*, and *SL*. (See 76-A for the U.S. retail equivalent.)

77-B *A Sound of Thunder*
Single story (52–8) in book format (educational). [London: Blackie and Sons, 1977].

Stories

77–1 "The Execution" (300)
Xenophile 36 [Nov.] 1977. Story fragment. Expanded and reprinted *Gallery* Mar. 1979 and *The Best of Gallery*, Winter–Spring 1980, as "The Beautiful Shave"; reprinted as revised *Telegraph Sunday Magazine* (U.K.) May 27, 1979, as "The Shave"; collected as revised *BS* (2003), as "The Beautiful Shave." Anthologized in one textbook, *GCSE English Literature* (FBA, 1989), as "The Shave."

1978

Books

78-A *The Mummies of Guanajuato*
Single story in illustrated book format. New York: Abrams, 1978. Contents: "The Next in Line" (47-11) with photo-illustrations from the location that inspired the story.

Stories

78–1 "Gotcha!" (301)
Redbook Aug. 1978. Reprinted *Over 21* (U.K.) Mar. 1979. Collected *SRB* (1980). Anthologized *The Year's Finest Fantasy Volume 2* (FBA, 1979), *A Century of Horror Stories* (1996).

Adapted (TV) by Bradbury for *Ray Bradbury Theater* (USA), Feb. 20, 1988. Adapted to comic-strip form for *The Ray Bradbury Chronicles* vol. 3 (Nov. 1992).

1979

Books

79-A *To Sing Strange Songs*

Story collection (textbook). [Exeter, U.K.]: Wheaton, [June 1979]. Contents: "If Only We Had Taller Been" (poem); "Fever Dream"; "A Sound of Thunder"; "The Fog-Horn"; "The April Witch"; "Illumination"; "Statues"; "All Summer in a Day"; "Icarus Montgolfier Wright"; "I Sing the Body Electric!"; "Uncle Einar"; "Boys! Raise Giant Mushrooms in *Your* Cellar"; "Why Viking Lander, Why the Planet Mars?" (poem).

79-B *The Aqueduct*

Single story (79-2) in book format. [Glendale, Calif.:] Roy A. Squires, [Sept. 11], 1979.

Stories

79-1 "A Summer Day" (302)

Redbook Aug. 1979.

79-2 "The Aqueduct" (303)

First printed as a single-title, limited-edition book (FBA, 79-B). Reprinted *(The Chicago Tribune) Tempo* Oct. 30, 1980. Collected *SRB* (1980). Adapted to comic-strip form for *The Ray Bradbury Chronicles* vol. 3 (Nov. 1992). Original composition: c. 1949.

1980

Books

80-A *The Last Circus and the Electrocution*

Story pair (80-1, 46-13) in book format. Limited edition. Northridge, Calif.: Lord John, [Aug. 22], 1980. Contents: "The Last Circus"; "The Electrocution." Concept developed by Donn Albright and publisher Herb Yellin of Lord John Press.

80-B *The Stories of Ray Bradbury*

Story collection (retrospective compilation). New York: Knopf, [Oct. 10], 1980; New York: Knopf, 1981 (Book-of-the-Month Club reissue); London: Granada, 1981; London: Granada, 1983 (paperback). Contents: "The Night"; "Homecoming"; "Uncle Einar"; "The Traveler"; "The Lake"; "The Coffin"; "The Crowd"; "The Scythe"; "There Was an Old Woman"; "There Will Come Soft Rains"; "Mars Is Heaven!"; "The Silent Towns"; "The Earth Men"; "The Off Season"; "The Million-Year Picnic"; "The Fox and the Forest"; "Kaleidoscope"; "The Rocket Man"; "Marionettes, Inc."; "No Particular Night or Morning"; "The City"; "The Fire Balloons"; "The Last Night of the World"; "The Veldt"; "The Long Rain"; "The Great Fire"; "The Wilderness"; "A Sound of Thunder"; "The Murderer"; "The April Witch"; "Invisible Boy"; "The Golden Kite, the Silver Wind"; "The Fog Horn"; "The Big Black and White Game"; "Embroidery"; "The Golden Apples of the Sun"; "Powerhouse"; "Hail and Farewell"; "The Great Wide World Over There"; "The Playground"; "Skeleton"; "The Man Upstairs"; "Touched with Fire"; "The Emissary"; "The Jar"; "The Small Assassin"; "The Next in Line"; "Jack-in-the-Box"; "The Leave-Taking"; "Exorcism"; "The Happiness Machine"; "Calling Mexico"; "The Wonderful Ice Cream Suit"; "Dark They Were, and Golden-Eyed"; "The Strawberry Window";

"A Scent of Sarsaparilla"; "The Picasso Summer"; "The Day It Rained Forever"; "A Medicine for Melancholy"; "The Shoreline at Sunset"; "Fever Dream"; "The Town Where No One Got Off"; "All Summer in a Day"; "Frost and Fire"; "The Anthem Sprinters"; "And So Died Riabouchinska"; "Boys! Raise Giant Mushrooms in *Your* Cellar"; "The Vacation"; "The Illustrated Woman"; "Some Live like Lazarus"; "The Best of All Possible Worlds"; "The One Who Waits"; "Tyrannosaurus Rex"; "The Screaming Woman"; "The Terrible Conflagration up at the Place"; "Night Call, Collect"; "The Tombling Day"; "The Haunting of the New"; "Tomorrow's Child"; "I Sing the Body Electric!"; "The Women"; "The Inspired Chicken Motel"; "Yes, We'll Gather at the River"; "Have I Got a Chocolate Bar for You!"; "A Story of Love"; "The Parrot Who Met Papa"; "The October Game"; "Punishment without Crime"; "A Piece of Wood"; "The Blue Bottle"; "Long after Midnight"; "The Utterly Perfect Murder"; "The Better Part of Wisdom"; "Interval in Sunlight"; "The Black Ferris"; "Farewell Summer"; "McGillahee's Brat"; "The Aqueduct"; "Gotcha!"; "The End of the Beginning."

Stories

80–1 "The Last Circus" (304)
The Last Circus and the Electrocution (FBA, [Aug. 22], 1980). Collected *TC* (1988). Original composition: c. 1950.

80–2 "A Touch of Petulance" (305)
Anthologized *Dark Forces*. New York: Viking, (FBA, [Sept.] 1980). Collected *TC* (1988). Anthologized again in *Time Machines* (1998). Adapted (TV)by Bradbury for *Ray Bradbury Theater* (USA), Oct. 12, 1990. Original composition: c. 1950.

80–3 "Farewell Summer" (306)
SRB (FBA, [Oct. 10], 1980). A Green Town story, though never added to *DW*.

1981

Books

81-A *The Ghosts of Forever*
Poems and a reprinted story. New York: Rizzoli, 1981. Contents: prologue; six poems; and the story "The Messiah" (71–1). Foreign edition (Buenos Aires, 1980) precedes U.S. edition.

Stories

81–1 "Heart Transplant" (307)
Playboy Jan. 1981. Collected *OM* (2002). Included in the page proofs of *SRB* (1980) but deleted prior to publication at the request of *Playboy* editors, who had already arranged for first publication.

81–2 "Colonel Stonesteel's Genuine Home-Made Truly Egyptian Mummy" (308)
Omni May 1981. Reprinted *Families* Nov. 1981 (condensed), *Literary Cavalcade* Oct. 1988. Collected *TC* (FBA, 1988), *BS* (2003). Anthologized *Omni Book of Science Fiction 2* (1985), *The Mummy* (1988), *Into the Mummy's Tomb* (2001). Adapted (TV) by Bradbury for *Ray Bradbury Theater* (USA), Jan. 24, 1992, as "Colonel Stonesteel and the 'Desperate Empties.'" Original composition: c. 1949.

Books

82-A *The Other Foot*

Single story (51–6) in book format (educational). [Logan, Iowa]: Perfection Form, [Sept.] 1982 (paperback).

82-B *The Veldt*

Single story (50–20) in book format (educational). [Logan, Iowa]: Perfection Form, [Sept.] 1982 (paperback).

82-C *The Love Affair*

Single story (82-1) in book format (limited edition). Northridge, Calif.: Lord John, [Dec.] 1982. Concept by William F. Nolan and Herb Yellin.

Stories

82-1 "The Love Affair" (309)

The Love Affair (FBA, 82-A). Collected *TC* (1988). Anthologized *The Planets* (1985) and *Mars Probes* (2002). Original composition: c. 1948.

Books

83-A *Dinosaur Tales*

Story collection (juvenile). New York: Bantam, [May 2], 1983 (large-format trade paperback); New York: Bantam, 1984 (mass-market paperback); New York: Barnes and Noble, 1996 (first hardbound edition). Contents: "Besides a Dinosaur, Whatta Ya Wanna Be When You Grow Up?"; "A Sound of Thunder"; "The Fog Horn"; "Tyranosaurus Rex"; forward by renowned animator Ray Harryhausen; introduction and two poems by Bradbury.

Stories

83-1 "Besides a Dinosaur, Whatta Ya Wanna Be When You Grow Up?" (310)

DT (illustrated, FBA, [May 2], 1983). Anthologized *The Ultimate Dinosaur* (1992). Adapted to comic-strip form for *Ray Bradbury Comics* 3 (June 1993).

Books

84-A *A Memory of Murder*

Story collection. [New York]: Dell, [Feb.] 1984 (paperback). Contents: "The Small Assassin"; "A Careful Man Dies"; "It Burns Me Up!"; "Half-Pint Homicide"; "Four-Way Funeral"; "The Long Night"; "Corpse Carnival"; "Hell's Half Hour"; "The Long Way Home"; "Wake for the Living"; "'I'm Not So Dumb!'"; "The Trunk Lady"; "Yesterday I Lived!"; "Dead Men Rise Up Never"; "The Candy Skull."

84-B *Forever and the Earth*

Radio adaptation by Bradbury from his story (50–7). [Athens, Ohio:] Croissant, [1984]. Includes an author's note.

84-C *The Novels of Ray Bradbury*

Novel omnibus. London: Granada, [June] 1984. Contents: contains *SW*, *F451*, and *DW*, complete in one binding.

Stories

84–1 "The Toynbee Convector" (311)

  Playboy Jan. 1984. Reprinted *Playboy* (Australia) Feb. 1984, *Scholastic Scope* Jan. 10, 1992. Collected *TC* (FBA, 1988), *BS* (2003). Anthologized in one textbook, *Travel and Tourism* (Canada, 1995). Adapted (TV) by Bradbury for *Ray Bradbury Theater* (USA), Oct. 26, 1990. Adapted to comic-strip form for *The Ray Bradbury Chronicles* vol. 1 (July 1992).

84–2 "By the Numbers!" (312)

  Playboy July 1984. Reprinted *Playboy* (Australia) Aug. 1984. Collected *TC* (FBA, 1988), *BS* (2003). Adapted (TV) by Bradbury for *Ray Bradbury Theater* (USA), Sept. 11, 1992.

84–3 "Banshee" (313)

  Gallery Sept. 1984. Reprinted *The Twilight Zone* Oct. 1984, *The Best of Gallery* winter–spring 1985, *Woman's Own* (U.K.) Mar. 15, 1986. Collected *TC* (FBA, 1988), *BS* (2003). Adapted (TV) by Bradbury for *Ray Bradbury Theater* (HBO), Feb. 22, 1986.

84–4 "I Suppose You Are Wondering Why We Are Here?" (314)

  Omni Oct. 1984. Collected *TC* (FBA, 1988).

84–5 "Bless Me, Father" (315)

  Woman's Day Dec. 11, 1984. Collected *TC* (FBA, 1988) and *BS* (2003), as "Bless Me Father, for I Have Sinned." Anthologized *A Literary Christmas* (1992), as "Bless Me Father, for I Have Sinned."

1985

Books

85-A *Death Is a Lonely Business*

  Novel. New York: Knopf, [Oct.] 1985; Franklin Center, Pa.: Franklin Library, 1985; London: Grafton, 1986; London: Guild, 1986; Thorndike, Maine: Thorndike, [1986]; London: Grafton, 1986 (overseas-edition paperback; reprinted for domestic distribution in U.K., 1987); New York: Bantam, 1987 (mass-market paperback); New York: Bantam, 1992 (large-format trade paperback).

85-B *The Wonderful Death of Dudley Stone*

  Single story (54–10) in book format, privately printed. Northampton, Mass.: Pyewacket, 1985.

Stories

85–1 "One for His Lordship, and One for the Road!" (316)

  Playboy Jan. 1985. Reprinted *The Irish Times* Apr. 26, 1987. Collected *TC* (FBA, 1988), *BS* (2003).

85–2 "Trapdoor" (317)

  Omni Apr. 1985. Reprinted (*Santa Barbara News*) *People/Today* May 13, June 14, 1992. Collected *TC* (FBA, 1988), *BS* (2003). Adapted to comic-strip form for *Ray Bradbury Comics* 5 (Oct. 1993).

1986

Books

86-A *The Martian Chronicles*

  Play adapted by Bradbury from *MC*. Woodstock, Ill.: Dramatic Publishing, [Feb. 1986].

86-B *The Flying Machine*
Play adapted by Bradbury from his story (53-4). Woodstock, Ill.: Dramatic Publishing, [1986].

86-C *The Wonderful Ice Cream Suit*
Play adapted by Bradbury from his story (58–3). Woodstock, Ill.: Dramatic Publishing, [1986]. First separate publication; see also 72-A.

86-D *Kaleidoscope*
Play adapted by Bradbury from his story (49–14). Woodstock, Ill.: Dramatic Publishing, [1986]. First separate publication; see also 75-B.

86-E *Fahrenheit 451*
Play adapted by Bradbury from *F451* (53-B). Woodstock, Ill.: Dramatic Publishing, [Mar. 1986].

86-F *A Device Out of Time*
Play adapted by Bradbury from his story "The Last, the Very Last" (55–2). Woodstock, Ill.: Dramatic Publishing, [Apr. 1986].

1987

Books

87-A *The April Witch*
Single story (52-2) in book format (educational). Mankato, Minn.: Creative Education, [Sept.] 1987.

87-B *The Fog Horn*
Single story (51–12) in book format (educational). Mankato, Minn.: Creative Education, [Sept.] 1987.

87-C *The Other Foot*
Single story (51–6) in book format (educational). Mankato, Minn.: Creative Education, [Sept.] 1987.

87-D *The Veldt*
Single story (50–20) in book format (educational). Mankato, Minn.: Creative Education, [Sept.] 1987.

87-E *Ray Bradbury*
Omnibus of novels and story collections. New York: Octopus/Heinemann, [Sept.] 1987. Contains *DW* (57-B), *F451* (53-B), *GA* (53-A), *IM* (51-A), and *MC* (50-A) complete.

87-F *Fever Dream*
Single story (48–11) in illustrated-book format. New York: St Martin's, [Oct.] 1987.

Stories

87–1 "The Laurel and Hardy Love Affair" (318)
Playboy Dec. 1987. Reprinted *Reader's Digest* Sept. 1988 and (Canada) May 1990 (condensed). Collected *TC* (FBA, 1988), *BS* (2003). Anthologized *American Film Stories* (1996).

1988

Books

88-A *The Dragon*
Single story (55–4) in book format, privately printed. [Round Top, N.Y.: Footsteps, 1988].

88-B   *The Toynbee Convector*
        Story collection. New York: Knopf, [May 24], 1988; New York: Knopf, [June] 1988 (Book-of-the-Month Club reissue); London: Grafton, 1989 (also reissued for Guild Book Club); New York; Bantam, 1989 (paperback); London: Grafton, 1989 (overseas edition paperback; reprinted for domestic distribution in U.K., 1990). Contents: "The Toynbee Convector"; "Trapdoor"; "On the Orient, North"; "One Night in Your Life"; "West of October"; "The Last Circus"; "The Laurel and Hardy Love Affair"; "I Suppose You Are Wondering Why We Are Here?"; "Lafayette, Farewell"; "Banshee"; "Promises, Promises"; "The Love Affair"; "One for His Lordship, and One for the Road!"; "At Midnight, in the Month of June"; "Bless Me, Father, for I Have Sinned"; "By the Numbers!"; "A Touch of Petulance"; "Long Division"; "Come, and Bring Constance!"; "Junior"; "The Tombstone"; "The Thing at the Top of the Stairs"; "Colonel Stonesteel's Genuine Homemade Truly Egyptian Mummy."

88-C   *Dandelion Wine*
        Play adapted by Bradbury from *DW* (57-B). Woodstock, Ill.: Dramatic Publishing, [Oct. 1988]. Includes Bradbury's introduction from the Knopf edition of the novel (1975), abridged.

88-D   *To the Chicago Abyss*
        Play adapted by Bradbury from his story (63–1). Woodstock, Ill.: Dramatic Publishing, [Apr. 1989]. First separate publication; see also 72-A.

88-E   *The Veldt*
        Play adapted by Bradbury from his story (50–20). Woodstock, Ill.: Dramatic Publishing, [Apr. 1989]. First separate publication; see also 72-A.

Stories

88–1   "Come, and Bring Constance!" (319)
        TC (FBA, [May 24,] 1988).

88–2   "Junior" (320)
        TC (FBA, [May 24,] 1988). Collected *BS* (2003).

88–3   "Lafayette, Farewell" (321)
        TC (FBA, [May 24,] 1988). Reprinted *Magazine of Fantasy and Science Fiction* Oct. 1988. Collected *BS* (2003).

88–4   "Long Division" (322)
        TC (FBA, [May 24,] 1988). Collected *BS* (2003).

88–5   "On the Orient, North" (323)
        TC (FBA, [May 24,] 1988). Collected *BS* (2003). Rewritten as a chapter in *FDR* (2001). Adapted (TV)by Bradbury for *Ray Bradbury Theater* (USA), Apr. 30, 1988.

88–6   "One Night in Your Life" (324)
        TC (FBA, [May 24,] 1988). Original composition: c. 1950.

88–7   "Promises, Promises" (325)
        TC (FBA, [May 24,] 1988).

88–8   "West of October" (326)
        TC (FBA, [May 24,] 1988). Rewritten as a chapter in *FDR* (2001). Anthologized *The Vampire Omnibus* (U.K., 1995; U.S., 1996). Original composition: c. 1946, as "Trip to Cranamockett"; pulled from galleys of *DC*. Subsequent manuscript title: "From the Dust Returned"; retitled for publication in *TC*. This story also becomes the title piece for the French edition of *TC*, published as *A l'Ouest d'Octobre*.

88–9　"The Thing at the Top of the Stairs" (327)

Magazine of Fantasy and Science Fiction July 1988. Collected TC (FBA, 1988).

1989

Books

89-A　*Falling Upward*

Play adapted by Bradbury from two of his stories. [Logan, Iowa]: Perfection Form, [Apr.] 1989 (paperback). Contents: Play adapted from the stories "The Great Collision of Monday Last" (58–4) and "The Cold Wind and the Warm" (64–2).

89-B　*There Will Come Soft Rains*

Single story (50-13) in book format (educational). [Logan, Iowa]: Perfection Form, [Sept.] 1989 (paperback).

1990

Books

90-A　*Classic Stories 1*

Remixed story collection. New York: Bantam, [May] 1990; New York: Avon, [Nov.] 1997 (large-format trade paperback), retitled *The Golden Apples of the Sun and Other Stories*. Contents: Combines GA (53-A) and RR (62-C) stories in original volume order but deletes seven stories to avoid overlap with each other and with CS2. GA here lacks "The Pedestrian," "Invisible Boy," "A Sound of Thunder," and "Hail and Farewell"; RR lacks "The Fog Horn," "The Golden Apples of the Sun," and "The Gift." The first two printings accidentally eliminate "The Golden Apples of the Sun" from the GA selections, leaving the volume without the title story of the first collection; it is restored in the 3d printing, and the volume is reset from that point; but the original Bradbury introduction from RR, which divides the two collections in the first two printings, is deleted, perhaps to save space, in the reset 3d (and subsequent) printings. The RR introduction is included in the Avon retitled edition (97-B).

90-B　*Classic Stories 2*

Remixed story collection. New York: Bantam, [May] 1990; New York: Avon, [Feb.] 1998 (large-format trade paperback), retitled *A Medicine for Melancholy and Other Stories*. Contents: Combines MM (59-A) and SS (66-C) stories in original volume order but deletes seven stories to avoid overlap with each other and with CS1. MM here lacks "The Dragon," "The End of the Beginning," "Icarus Montgolfier Wright," "Dark They Were, and Golden-Eyed," "The Smile," and "The Strawberry Window"; SS lacks "The Flying Machine."

90-C　*A Graveyard for Lunatics*

Novel; sequel to DLB (85-A). New York: Knopf, [July] 1990; London: Grafton, 1990; London: Grafton, 1991 (overseas edition paperback), reprinted for domestic distribution in U.K., 1991; New York: Bantam, 1991 (export edition paperback); New York: Bantam, 1992 (large-format trade paperback). Excerpt published in advance by Knopf in *The Borzoi Reader* 2, no. 1 ([Feb. 12], 1990).

90-D　*The Day It Rained Forever*

Play adapted by Bradbury from his story (57–4). Woodstock, Ill.: Dramatic Publishing, [1990].

90-E   *The Parrot Who Met Papa*
Single story (72–1) in book format, privately printed. Rochester, Mich.: Pretentious Press, 1990.

1991

Books

91-A   *Dark They Were, and Golden-Eyed*
Single story (49–11) in book format (educational). New York: Writer's Voices, [May 1991].

91-B   *Ray Bradbury on Stage*
Omnibus edition of Bradbury's play collections. New York: Donald I. Fine, [Nov.] 1991 (large-format trade paperback). Contents: Contains Bradbury's published stage adaptations of his stories (and one original play) previously collected in *AS* (63-A); *WICS* (72-A); and *PF* (75-B) complete.

91-C   *The Smile*
Single story (52–9) in book format (educational). [Mankato, Minn.]: Creative Education, [Dec. 1991] (paperback).

Stories

91–1   "Where's Lefty?" (328)
Playboy Mar. 1991.

91–2   "The Troll" (329)
Anthologized *The Bradbury Chronicles* (FBA, [Nov.] 1991). Anthologized again in *New Masterpieces of Horror* (1996), *The Little Big Book of Chills and Thrills* (2001). Original composition: c. 1950.

1992

Books

92-A   *Green Shadows, White Whale*
Autobiographical novel. New York: Knopf, [May] 1992; [Hastings-on-Hudson, N.Y.: Ultramarine, 1992] limited edition created from rebound copies of the first edition; London: HarperCollins, 1992; New York: Bantam, [Aug.] 1993 (paperback); London: HarperCollins, 1994 (paperback); New York: Avon, 1998 (large-format trade paperback). Excerpt published in advance by Knopf in *The Borzoi Reader* 4, no. 2 (1992). The excerpt began as the unpublished play "Stop, Think, Consider, Do" and became part of the larger play *Falling Upward* (1988) before Bradbury developed it into chap. 26 of *GS*. Contents: Eleven of Bradbury's "Irish" stories, based on events from the half year spent in Ireland writing the *Moby Dick* screenplay with director John Huston, are rewritten into untitled chapters: chap. [4], from "The Great Collision of Monday Last" (58–4); chap. [12], "The Terrible Conflagration up at the Place" (69-5); chap. [13], "The Beggar on the Dublin Bridge" (61–1); chap. [15], "The Haunting of the New" (69–4); chap. [18], "One for His Lordship, and One for the Road!" (85–1); chap. [21], "Getting through Sunday Somehow" (as revised from "Tread Lightly to the Music" (62–5); chap. [22], "The First Night of Lent" (56–2); chap. [23], "McGillahee's Brat" (70–1); chap. [27], "Banshee" (84–3); chap. [28], "The Cold Wind and the Warm" (64–2); chap. [29], "The Anthem Sprinters" (as revised from "The Queen's Own Evaders," 63–3). Chap. [9] was

fictionalized from an essay, "The Hunt Wedding," published in *The American Way* (American Airlines, May 1992).

92-B   *The Toynbee Convector*

Single story (84–1) in illustrated book format. Atlanta: Turner, 1992.

Stories

92–1   "Great Day in the Morning" (330)

American Way (American Airlines) May 15, 1992.

92–2   ["The Hunt Wedding"] (331)

American Way (American Airlines) May 15, 1992. An essay revised and fictionalized as chap. [9] in *GS* (FBA, 1992).

1993

Stories

93–1   "My Son, Max" (332)

American Way (American Airlines) June 15, 1993. Collected *OM* (FBA, 2002).

93–2   "Fee Fie Foe Fum" (333)

Anthologized *Monsters in Our Midst* (FBA, [Oct.] 1993). Collected *DB* (1997). Adapted (TV) by Bradbury for *Ray Bradbury Theater* (USA), Oct. 27, 1992. Original composition: c. 1948.

93–3   "Remembrance" (334)

American Way (American Airlines) Nov. 1, 1993.

1994

Stories

94–1   "Unterderseaboat Doktor" (335)

Playboy Jan. 1994. Collected *QE* (FBA, 1996). Anthologized *The Year's Best Fantasy and Horror: Eighth Annual Collection* (1995).

94–2   "The Very Gentle Murders" (336)

Ellery Queen's Mystery Magazine, May 1994. Collected *QE* (FBA, 1996). Original composition: c. 1947.

94–3   "The Enemy in the Wheat" (337)

New Rave Aug. 1994 (premier issue). Collected *OM* (FBA, 2002). Deleted from *OC* (1955) prior to publication. Original composition: c. 1949.

94–4   "From the Dust Returned" (338)

Magazine of Fantasy and Science Fiction Sept. 1994.

94–5   "No News or What Killed the Dog?" (339)

American Way (American Airlines) Oct. 1, 1994. Collected *QE* (FBA, 1996), *BS* (2003).

94–6   "Last Rites" (340)

Magazine of Fantasy and Science Fiction Dec. 1994. Reprinted *Rosebud* 25 [Dec.] 2002. Collected *QE* (FBA, 1996), *BS* (2003).

1995

Stories

95–1   "At the End of the Ninth Year" (341)

American Way (American Airlines) Jan. 1, 1995. Collected *QE* (FBA, 1996). Original composition: c. 1950.

95–2 "Another Fine Mess" (342)
Magazine of Fantasy and Science Fiction Apr. 1995. Collected *QE* (FBA, 1996), *BS* (2003). Anthologized *Best from* Fantasy and Science Fiction *50th Anniversary Anthology* (1999).

95–3 "Grand Theft" (343)
Ellery Queen's Mystery Magazine July 1995. Collected *DB* (FBA, 1997). Original composition: c. 1950.

95–4 "Dorian in Excelsis" (344)
Magazine of Fantasy and Science Fiction Sept. 1995. Collected *QE* (FBA, 1996). Original composition: c. 1959–62.

95–5 "Once More, Legato" (345)
Omni fall 1995. Collected *QE* (FBA, 1996) and *BS* (2003).

95–6 "Quicker Than the Eye" (346)
Anthologized *David Copperfield's Tales of the Impossible* (FBA, [Nov.] 1995). Collected *QE* (1996). Original composition: c. 1951. Manuscript title: "The Magic Trick."

95–7 "The Witch Door" (347)
Playboy Dec. 1995. Collected *QE* (FBA, 1996), *BS* (2003). Original composition: c. 1951.

1996

Books

96-A *Quicker Than the Eye*
Story collection. New York: Avon, [Nov.] 1996; New York: Avon, [Oct.] 1997 (paperback); Franklin Center, Pa.: Franklin Library, 1997 (collector's edition); Thorndike, Maine: Thorndike, 1997 (large-print edition); London: Earthlight (HarperCollins), [Mar.] 1998 (paperback); [Surrey]: Severn House, 1999. Manuscript titles: *Dorian in Excelsis* (1994), *The Same Only Different* (1995). Contents: "Unterderseaboat Doktor"; "Zaharoff/Richter Mark V"; "Remember Sascha?"; "Another Fine Mess"; "The Electrocution"; "Hopscotch"; "The Finnegan"; "That Woman on the Lawn"; "The Very Gentle Murders"; "Quicker Than the Eye"; "Dorian in Excelsis"; "No News, or What Killed the Dog?"; "The Witch Door"; "The Ghost in the Machine"; "At the End of the Ninth Year"; "Bug"; "Once More, Legato"; "Exchange"; "Free Dirt"; "Last Rites"; "The Other Highway." Includes "Make Haste to Live: An Afterward."

Stories

96–1 "That Woman on the Lawn" (348)
Magazine of Fantasy and Science Fiction Aug. 1996. Collected *QE* (FBA, 1996) and *BS* (2003).

96–2 "The Finnegan" (349)
Magazine of Fantasy and Science Fiction Oct.–Nov. 1996. Collected *QE* (FBA, 1996) and *BS* (2003). Original composition: c. 1950.

96–3 "Free Dirt" (350)
American Way (American Airlines) Oct. 1996. Collected *QE* (FBA, 1996). Anthologized *Dark Terrors 3* (U.K., 1997). Original composition: c. 1951.

96–4 "Bug" (351)
QE (FBA, [Nov.] 1996). Collected *BS* (2003). Original composition: c. 1948.

96–5 "Exchange" (352)
QE (FBA, [Nov.] 1996). Anthologized *In the Stacks* (2002). Original composition: c. 1948.

96–6   "The Ghost in the Machine" (353)
       QE (FBA, [Nov.] 1996).
96–7   "Hopscotch" (354)
       QE (FBA, [Nov.] 1996). Collected *BS* (2003). Original composition: c. 1950.
96–8   "The Other Highway" (355)
       QE (FBA, [Nov.] 1996). Original composition: c. 1950. Manuscript title: "Snakeskin."
96–9   "Remember Sascha?" (356)
       QE (FBA, [Nov.] 1996). Collected *BS* (2003). Original composition: c. 1949.
96–10 "Zaharoff/Richter Mark V" (357)
       QE (FBA, [Nov.] 1996).

1997

Books

97-A   *Driving Blind*
       Story collection. New York: Avon, [Sept.] 1997; New York: Avon, 1998 (paperback); London: Earthlight, [Aug.] 1998. Contents: "Night Train to Babylon"; "If MGM Is Killed, Who Gets the Lion?"; "Hello, I Must Be Going"; "House Divided"; "Grand Theft"; "Remember Me?"; "Fee Fie Foe Fum"; "Driving Blind"; "I Wonder What's become of Sally"; "Nothing Changes"; "That Old Dog Lying in the Dust"; "Someone in the Rain"; "Madame et Monsieur Shill"; "The Mirror"; "End of Summer"; "Thunder in the Morning"; "The Highest Branch of the Tree"; "A Woman Is a Fast-Moving Picnic"; "Virgin Resusitas"; "Mr. Pale"; "That Bird That Comes Out of the Clock." Includes "A Brief Afterward."

97-B   *The Golden Apples of the Sun and Other Stories*
       See 53-A, 90-A. New York: Avon, [Nov.] 1997 (large-format trade paperback). A trade-paperback edition of Bantam's *CS1* (90-A). Contents: See 90-A.

Stories

97–1   "The Offering" (358)
       Magazine of Fantasy and Science Fiction Mar. 1997. Deleted from *OM*.
97–2   "Driving Blind" (359)
       DB (FBA, [Sept.] 1997). Anthologized *The Year's Best Fantasy and Horror: Eleventh Annual Collection* (1998). Original composition: c. 1960.
97–3   "Hello, I Must Be Going" (360)
       DB (FBA, [Sept.] 1997).
97–4   "The Highest Branch on the Tree" (361)
       DB (FBA, [Sept.] 1997).
97–5   "House Divided" (362)
       DB (FBA, [Sept.] 1997). Original composition: c. 1948.
97–6   "I Wonder What's Become of Sally?" (363)
       DB (FBA, [Sept.] 1997). Original composition: c. 1945
97–7   "If MGM Is Killed, Who Gets the Lion?" (364)
       DB (FBA, [Sept.] 1997).
97–8   "Madame et Monsieur Shill" (365)
       DB (FBA, [Sept.] 1997).
97–9   "The Mirror" (366)
       DB (FBA, [Sept.] 1997). Original composition: c. 1950.

97–10 "Mr. Pale" (367)
  DB (FBA, [Sept.] 1997). Anthologized *Year's Best SF* 3 (1998). Deleted from *OC* (1955) prior to publication. Original composition: c. 1950. Manuscript title: "The Pale One."

97–11 "Night Train to Babylon" (368)
  DB (FBA, [Sept.] 1997). Reprinted *Ellery Queen's Mystery Magazine* Dec. 1997. Anthologized *The Cutting Edge* (1998).

97–12 "Nothing Changes" (369)
  DB (FBA, [Sept.] 1997).

97–13 "Remember Me?" (370)
  DB (FBA, [Sept.] 1997).

97–14 "Someone in the Rain" (371)
  DB (FBA, [Sept.] 1997). Original composition: c. 1950.

97–15 "That Bird That Comes Out of the Clock" (372)
  DB (FBA, [Sept.] 1997).

97–16 "That Old Dog Lying in the Dust" (373)
  DB (FBA, [Sept.] 1997). Developed from the essay "Mexicali Mirage," 1974.

97–17 "Thunder in the Morning" (374)
  DB (FBA, [Sept.] 1997). Original composition: c. 1947.

97–18 "Virgin Resusitas" (375)
  DB (FBA, [Sept.] 1997).

97–19 "A Woman Is a Fast-Moving Picnic" (376)
  DB (FBA, [Sept.] 1997).

1998

Books

98-A *A Medicine for Melancholy and Other Stories*
  See 59-A, 90-B. New York: Avon, [Feb.] 1998 (large-format trade paperback). A trade-paperback edition of Bantam's *CS2* (90-B). Contents: See 90-B.

98-B *I Sing the Body Electric! and Other Stories*
  See 69-B and 76-B. New York: Avon, [May] 1998 (large-format trade paperback). Contents: Contains *IS* (69-B), complete, and the first eleven stories from *LAM* (76-B).

98-C *Ahmed and the Oblivion Machines*
  Children's storybook. New York: Avon, [Dec.] 1998.

1999

Stories

99–1 "Pilgrimage" (377)
  Anthologized *California Sorcery* (FBA, [Aug.] 1999). Original composition: c. 1950. Deleted from *OM*.

2000

Stories

00–1 "The Laurel and Hardy Alpha Centauri Farewell Tour" (378)
  Amazing Stories (spring 2000). Collected *OM* (FBA, 2002).

00–2 "Quid Pro Quo" (379)
  Magazine of Fantasy and Science Fiction Oct.–Nov. 2000. Collected *OM* (FBA, 2002).

00–3   "The Haunted House" (with Elizabeth Albright) (380)

Anthologized *The Mammoth Book of Haunted House Stories*, (FBA, 2000). A child's short-short story.

00–4   "Overkill" (381)

Playboy Nov. 2000. Deleted from *OM*.

Books

01-A   *From the Dust Returned*

Novelized story cycle. New York: Morrow, [Oct.] 2001. Avon, Sept. 2002 (paperback), closing with "The World of Ray Bradbury," excerpts from the following Bradbury books: *DW* (opening chapter), *IM* (50–16; found only in the Avon edition), *MC* ("Ylla"), *OC* ("The Small Assassin"), *SW*, *DLB*, and *GL*. Excerpt of *FDR* anthologized in *A Celebration of Ray Bradbury* (2000). Contents: Prologue, "The Beautiful One Is Here"; "The Town and the Place"; "Anuba Arrives"; "The High Attic"; "The Sleeper and Her Dreams"; "The Wandering Witch"; "Whence Timothy?"; "The House, the Spider, and the Child"; "Mouse, Far Traveling"; "Homecoming"; "Many Returns"; "On the Orient, North"; "Nostrum Paracelsius Crook"; "The October People"; "Uncle Einar"; "The Whisperers"; "The Theban Voice"; "Make Haste to Live"; "The Chimney Sweeps"; "The Traveler"; "Return to the Dust"; "West of October"; "The One Who Remembers"; "The Gift."

Stories

01–1   "We the People, Inc." (382)

Hemispheres (United Air Lines), June 2001. Deleted from *OM*. Manuscript title: "Corpus Populi and So on and So Forth."

01–2   "Fore!" (383)

Fantasy and Science Fiction, Oct.–Nov. 2001. Collected *OM* (FBA, 2002).

Books

02-A   *One More for the Road*

Story collection. New York: Avon, [Apr.] 2002. Contents: "First Day"; "Heart Transplant"; "Quid Pro Quo"; "After the Ball"; "In Memoriam"; "Tête-à-Tête"; "The Dragon Danced at Midnight"; "The Nineteenth"; "Beasts"; "Autumn Afternoon"; "Where All Is Emptiness There Is Room to Move"; "One-Woman Show"; "The Laurel and Hardy Alpha Centauri Farewell Tour"; "Leftovers"; "One More for the Road"; "Tangerine"; "With Smiles as Wide as Summer"; "Time Intervening"; "The Enemy in the Wheat"; "Fore!"; "My Son, Max"; "The F. Scott / Tolstoy / Ahab Accumulator"; "Well, What Do You Have to Say for Yourself?"; "Diane De Forêt"; "The Cricket on the Hearth." Includes "Afterword: Metaphors, the Breakfast of Champions." Published stories deleted in manuscript are "The Offering" (97–1), "Pilgrimage" (99–1), "Overkill" (00–4), and "We the People, Inc." (01–1). Unpublished stories deleted in manuscript are "Arielle," "Come away with Me," "The Elevator," "Ghost," and "The Tarot Card Manana Nail Emporium."

02-B   *Let's All Kill Constance!*

Novella. New York: Avon, [Dec.] 2002. Excerpt published in *(Los Angeles Times) Book Review* Apr. 16, 2000.

Stories

02–1 "After the Ball" (384)
   OM (FBA, [Apr.] 2002).

02–2 "Autumn Afternoon" (385)
   OM (FBA, [Apr.] 2002). Original composition: 1947.

02–3 "Beasts" (386)
   OM (FBA, [Apr.] 2002).

02–4 "The Cricket on the Hearth" (387)
   OM (FBA, [Apr.] 2002). Original composition: c. 1950.

02–5 "Diane de Forêt" (388)
   OM (FBA, [Apr.] 2002).

02–6 "The F. Scott / Tolstoy / Ahab Accumulator" (389)
   OM (FBA, [Apr.] 2002).

02–7 "First Day" (390)
   OM (FBA, [Apr.] 2002).

02–8 "In Memoriam" (391)
   OM (FBA, [Apr.] 2002).

02–9 "Leftovers" (392)
   OM (FBA, [Apr.] 2002).

02–10 "The Nineteenth" (393)
   OM (FBA, [Apr.] 2002).

02–11 "One More for the Road" (394)
   OM (FBA, [Apr.] 2002).

02–12 "One-Woman Show" (395)
   OM (FBA, [Apr.] 2002). Original composition: c. 1950.

02–13 "Tangerine" (396)
   OM (FBA, [Apr.] 2002).

02–14 "Tête-à-Tête" (397)
   OM (FBA, [Apr.] 2002).

02–15 "Well, What Do You Have to Say for Yourself?" (398)
   OM (FBA, [Apr.] 2002).

02–16 "Where All Is Emptiness There Is Room to Move" (399)
   OM (FBA, [Apr.] 2002). Original composition: c. 1949. Manuscript title: "In Lonely Places."

02–17 "Austin and Justin: The Twins of Time" (400)
   The Strand Magazine 9 ([Fall–Winter 2002]).

2003

Books

03-A *Bradbury Stories*
   Story collection (retrospective compilation). New York: Morrow, [Aug.] 2003.
   Contents: Introduction (untitled); "The Whole Town's Sleeping"; "The Rocket"; "Season of Disbelief"; "And the Rock Cried Out"; "The Drummer Boy of Shiloh"; "The Beggar on O'Connell Bridge"; "The Flying Machine"; "Heavy-Set"; "The First Night of Lent"; "Lafayette, Farewell"; "Remember Sascha"; "Junior"; "That Woman on the Lawn"; "February 1999: Ylla"; "Banshee"; "One for His Lordship, and One for the Road!"; "The Laurel and Hardy Love Affair"; "Unterderseaboot Doktor"; "Another Fine

Mess"; "The Dwarf"; "A Wild Night in Galway"; "The Wind"; "No News, or What Killed the Dog?"; "A Little Journey"; "Any Friend of Nicholas Nickleby's Is a Friend of Mine"; "The Garbage Collector"; "The Visitor"; "The Man"; "Henry the Ninth"; "The Messiah"; "Bang! You're Dead!"; "Darling Adolf"; "The Beautiful Shave"; "Colonel Stonesteel's Genuine Home-Made Truly Egyptian Mummy"; "I See You Never"; "The Exiles"; "At Midnight, in the Month of June"; "The Witch Door"; "The Watchers"; "2004–05: The Naming of Names"; "Hopscotch"; "The Illustrated Man"; "The Dead Man"; "June 2001: And the Moon Be Still as Bright"; "The Burning Man"; "G.B.S.—Mark V"; "A Blade of Grass"; "The Sound of Summer Running"; "And the Sailor, Home from the Sea"; "The Lonely Ones"; "The Finnegan"; "On the Orient, North"; "The Smiling People"; "The Fruit at the Bottom of the Bowl"; "Bug"; "Downwind from Gettysburg"; "Time in Thy Flight"; "Changeling"; "The Dragon"; "Let's Play 'Poison'"; "The Cold Wind and the Warm"; "The Meadow"; "The Kilimanjaro Device"; "The Man in the Rorschach Shirt"; "Bless Me Father, for I Have Sinned"; "The Pedestrian"; "Trapdoor"; "The Swan"; "The Sea Shell"; "Once More, Legato"; "June 2003: Way in the Middle of the Air"; "The Wonderful Death of Dudley Stone"; "By the Numbers!"; "April 2005: Usher II"; "The Square Pegs"; "The Trolley"; "The Smile"; "The Miracles of Jamie"; "A Far-away Guitar"; "The Cistern"; "The Machineries of Joy"; "Bright Phoenix"; "The Wish"; "The Life Work of Juan Diaz"; "Time Intervening"; "Almost the End of the World"; "The Great Collision of Monday Last"; "The Poems"; "April 2026: The Long Years"; "Icarus Montgolfier Wright"; "Death and the Maiden"; "Zero Hour"; "The Toynbee Convector"; "Forever and the Earth"; "The Handler"; "Getting Through Sunday Somehow"; "The Pumpernickel"; "Last Rites"; "The Watchful Poker Chip of H. Matisse"; "All on a Summer's Night." Contents listing based on examination of un-corrected proofs (Spring 2003). "2004–05: The Naming of Names" is a bridge passage from *MC*, and should not be confused with "The Naming of Names" (49–11).

Stories

03-1   "Sixty-Six." (401)
        The Strand Magazine 12 ([Fall–Winter 2003])

APPENDIX B

Unpublished Fiction

This listing represents the most significant categories of Ray Bradbury's unpublished fiction. Unless otherwise noted, all are typescripts, for Bradbury composed and rewrote his drafts almost exclusively on the typewriter. Long fiction is listed first, including complete works as well as outlines and treatments for novels and novellas that never reached a stage of sustained composition. Short fiction follows, but only complete or nearly complete working typescripts are listed here. They total 236 distinct stories and include entries for four of the eleven discarded chapter-stories of *Summer Morning, Summer Night* that were also prepared as stand-alone tales. Three discarded and yet-unpublished chapters of *The Martian Chronicles* were also retyped as separates and are listed here. All such relationships to other works are so indicated in the individual story listings. Story fragments, as well as complete but unpublished projects intended solely for other media, are not listed.

To a large extent, the older layers of the long-fiction groupings remain in a disordered state. The boxes containing the last working drafts of *All on a Golden Afternoon* and *Farewell Summer* represent complete and continuous working materials, but the earlier drafts of these novels in progress will require a great deal of study before the original sequences of composition can be recovered or at least interpolated; some chapters were carried forward intact into later drafts, while some were moved into other fiction projects entirely. On a smaller scale, many of the unpublished stories will also require further study before various drafts (often retitled and completely rewritten) can be ordered with any degree of certainty. The listing that follows is based on a close but preliminary examination of these materials; further scholarship will no doubt lead to a fuller genealogical picture of the unpublished fiction.

Each work is listed alphabetically by category; those with multiple titles are listed under the title of the most mature form first, with earlier titles following in parenthesis. Dates given in brackets are editorial estimates based on paper and story content; all other dates are Bradbury's own annotations on the typescripts or their folders. We are grateful to William F. Nolan for pioneering the work of recovering these materials. By far, though, the greatest debt is owed to Donn Albright, who carried out the decades-long work of locating all these typescripts within Bradbury's nachlass and, in many cases, recovering the basic compositional order of multiple-draft stories. Most of these titles are no longer active projects, but readers should bear in mind that some of the more recent stories, as well as the novel *Farewell Summer*, remain works in progress. One may assume that such projects have been carried forward by Bradbury and may yet reach print.

Novels and Novellas

All on a Golden Afternoon (Somewhere a Band Is Playing), Mar. 1998. Complete 162-page TS novel, numbered 1–88, O1–O14, Q1–Q8, 120–48, 148A, Z1–Z10, 149–61. Includes a title page and thirty-two pages of discards. Several hundred pages of earlier draft materials date back as far as 1958 and document the development of this concept from its origins in the *Farewell Summer* materials through teleplay, screenplay, and novella forms.

Dial Double Zero (The Telephone, or "Night of the Jabberwock"), [c.1952–62]. Materials for a novella, consisting of 107 pages of short-story drafts and further episodes designed to extend the basic story into a novella. Dramatized excerpts were used in NBC's biographical special on Bradbury, *The Story of a Writer* (aired Nov. 20, 1963, and in subsequent syndication).

Farewell Summer (Summer Morning, Summer Night; The Blue Remembered Hills; The Wind of Time; The Small Assassins), 1946–98. Novel in progress consisting of a continuous 181-page TS and three unassigned inserts numbered A1–A2, B1–B5, and C1–C3; B1–B5 is a story-length episode. There are hundreds of pages of story drafts, chapter indexes, and fragments discarded from the *Summer Morning, Summer Night* phase (1947–57). A story index, two title pages, and sixty-one pages of expanded episodes remain from *The Blue Remembered Hills* phase (1946); nine pages, consisting of early versions of the two opening chapters, survive from *The Wind of Time* phase (c. 1946), a title that appeared in two biographical notes of this period as a work in progress; and five pages of working papers survive from *The Small Assassins* (c. 1945). There are eleven complete but unpublished story-chapters discarded from the first three phases of this novel: "Arrival and Departure," "The Beautiful Lady," "The Circus," "The Death of So-and-So," "(The Game of) Anna Anna Anna Anna Anna," "I Got Something You Ain't Got!" "Hallowe'en in July" ("The KKK Parade"), "The Love Potion," "Night Meeting," "Summer Nights," and "A Serious Conversation." Four of these were also prepared as standalone stories and are included in the listing of unpublished short stories below.

Interval in Sunlight [c. 1950–1953]. A complete draft of "Interval in Sunlight" (54 pages), three drafts of "The Next in Line" (32, 28, and 29 pages), and a total of thirty-three pages of bridges and opening narratives designed to weave these two novella-length stories into a short novel of Americans traveling through Mexico. One leaf in a twenty-page run of bridges intended to extend the stories is dated February 22, 1950; the remaining thirteen pages appear to be openings for the unwritten first third of the novel, which was tentatively titled "The Volcano." One of these opening leaves is a title page bearing the date January 26, 1953, and the subtitle "A short novel containing some 40,000 words." Bradbury's earliest attempt to develop this concept, consisting of twenty-seven pages written during and just after his extended tour of Mexico during the autumn of 1945 and titled *The Fear of Death Is Death*, is also part of the Mexican novel typescript. Among these leaves is a seventeen-chapter table of contents containing descriptive titles and length estimates totaling 27,000 words. Alternate titles within this 1945 grouping include *Quiet Under the Sun* and *Nothing But Night*.

The Mask beneath the Mask beneath the Mask (The Masks), [c. 1947–49]. An outline for a 50,000- to-70,000–word novel, consisting of thirty pages of sequential episodes and narrative highlights for the complete novel and forty pages of nonsequential fragments and episodes. There are also fragments of two related radio-play treatments and material for his unsuccessful 1949 Guggenheim grant proposal for this project.

Nemo! 1963. Bradbury's ten-page (paginated A-J) synopsis for a novel that brings Verne's most famous protagonist and his submarine into the twentieth century survives with eighty-nine additional pages from two distinct but incomplete drafts of a half-dozen short opening chapters. One of the title pages associated with these drafts bears the date 1963; two single-page chapter listings, containing eleven and fifteen chapter titles respectively, vary significantly from each other and are both incomplete. This project evolved as Bradbury researched and wrote "The Ardent Blasphemers," his influential introduction to the 1962 Bantam paperback edition of Verne's *Twenty Thousand Leagues Under the Sea.*

Where Ignorant Armies Clash by Night, 1947. Sixty-six pages. Early materials for a 50,000-word novel that projects the darker aspects of performance and entertainment culture into a nihilistic future world. This project was a rehearsal of the themes later developed in "The Fireman" and its expansion into *F451.* The surviving materials consist of an outline of chapters (one page), outline notes (three pages), several draft chapters with variant pages (forty pages), outlines and text for a dramatization (*They Clash by Night,* ten pages), and a standalone story, "Of All Things—Never to Have Been Born Is Best" (five pages, listed below), that compresses the essence of the novel into a single carnivalized act of nihilism. The title of this story also appears as the epigraph for the novel (one page); title pages and a dedication (four pages) include the title variation, *We Are the Hollow Men.* There is also a draft note to an unidentified editor (one page) and a personal reminder to keep chapters short (one page). The final chapter is an early form of "The Smile" (52–9).

Novel Concepts

Crusade (1945), a seven-page outline treatment survives for a projected novel chronicling a female astronaut's explorations in space.

The Diary of Melita Harris: A Novel in Seventeen Chapters (c. 1941), three opening pages describing her first meeting with a young man. Five diary dates (May 24–25, 27, 30–31, 1941) are written in Bradbury's hand at the beginning of the typed text.

The Long Way Home (1958). A series of outlines and episodes for a novel "about six priests and their search through space and time for further proofs of God." Alternate titles include *Perhaps We Are Going Away* and *Pius the Wanderer.*

Single-page outlines survive for these unpublished novel concepts: *The Appointed Round* (c. 1940s); *Earthport, Mars* (1944); *The Cistern* (c. 1947); *The Library* (c. late 1940s, with opening page of text); *The Space War* (1949); *There Will Come Soft Rains* (c. early 1950s); and *The Watchful Wakers* (1958).

Periodic listings of planned novels include single-line entries for these unpublished concepts: *The Green Rain* (Venus, projected 1960); *The Next in Line* (the Mexican novel, projected c. 1953 [*Ray Bradbury Review*] and 1968); *The Plaid Amoeba; These Are All Innocents; Third Person Singular; Weather and War* (1961).

"Able Seaman Albert Drummond," 1971. 16 pp.

"Ah, Juastaningo!" [article-story, 1950s]. 4 pp.

"Alba of Alnitak," 1937. 16 pp.

"Algy—Drunken Master at the Zoo!" 1938. 14 pp.

"All These People," 1947. 7 pp.

"All Things Living" ("Please, Not on the Grass," "Please Don't Step on the Grass"), 1952. 16 pp.

"Always around but Never In" ("And Liberty Is Green"), [late 1940s]. 7 pp.

"An Ugly Head or Two," 1940. 5 pp.

"And She Talked in Voices like the Sea" ("And She Spoke in Voices like the Sea"), [1960]. 11 pp.

"Animal, The: Here There Be Tygers," [date uncertain]. 3 pp.

"Anna Anna Anna Anna Anna," 1946. 3 pp. and 1 p. variant. A version of the story-chapter discarded from *Summer Morning, Summer Night* and designated as a standalone story.

"Ape-Ch-Nock, The," [late 1940s]. 3 pp.

"Anniversary Gifts, The" ("The Anniversary Presents"), 1952. 3 pp.

"Application to Ceos," [1942–44]. 41 pp. under a Julius Schwartz agent cover page. Original lost; photocopy held by Donn Albright.

"Appointment for Dinner," [1942–44]. 6 pp. under a Julius Schwartz agent cover page. Original lost; photocopy held by Donn Albright.

"Arielle," [c. 2000]. 11 pp. Deleted from *OM* prior to publication.

"Arrival and Departure," [late 1960s]. 16 pp. A version of the story-chapter discarded from *Summer Morning, Summer Night* and designated as a standalone story.

"As I Was Going up Green Hill," 1960. 9 pp. Revised from "The Meeting," 1952. 6 pp.

"Assassin Machine, The" ("The Long Guillotine"), 1969. 10 pp. with holograph revisions.

"Aunt Signe and Her Wild Rose Ear Trumpet," [late 1940s]. 15 pp. with holograph revisions.

"Automobile, The" ("Lovely as a Tiger," "The Gift"), 1953. 5 pp. and 6 pp. variants.

"Avant le Derrière!" 1965. 21 pp.

"Beautiful Child, The" ("The Murder," "The Rose Child," and variations), [late-1940s]. 23 pp. of various drafts.

"Best Hotel in the World, The," 1950. 7 pp.

"Bomb, The," [1950s]. 2 pp.

"Book, The," [1959]. 8 pp.

"Book of Fire, The," 1952. 9 pp.

"Boss, The" ("Top Man"), [mid-1940s]. 28 pp., including text on some versos. Holograph revisions. Unsubmitted detective fiction.

"Brave Man's Wife, The" ("The Wife of the Brave One"), 1952. 15 pp.

"Bullet Trick," 1950. 16 pp. with autograph revisions. The unpublished source of the Bradbury teleplay of the same title (*Jane Wyman Presents*, 1956).

"Bygone Murders, The," 1949. 27 pp. with autograph revisions. Original lost; photocopy held by Donn Albright.

"Castle, The," [1946]. 22 pp. A complete but abandoned forerunner of *MC*'s story-chapter "April 2005: Usher II" ("Carnival of Madness," 50–8).

"A Child Is Born" ("The Ocean Sea," "The Captain of the Ocean Sea," "In a Time Between"), 1953. 13 pp.

"Castle Deep," 1938. 15 pp.

"Christmas on Mars," [early 1950s]. Two versions: 8 pp. and 7 pp. Sold to *Esquire* but never published.

"Chrysalis," [1946]. 15 pp., including variants and a 13-page version. No relation to "Chrysalis" (46–11).

"Cinnamon Box, The," [mid-1940s]. 4 pp.

"City of Intangibles," 1941. 38 pp. Coauthored with Henry Hasse.

"City That Was Alive, The" ("The Awful City"), 1958. 11 pp. and contents listing for proposed novel, *The Watchful Wakers.*

"Clam, The," [c. 1950]. 4 pp.

"Clay Darriell, The," [late 1940s]. 13 pp.

"Clay in the Rain," 1945. 7 pp. Unsubmitted detective fiction.

"Clock, The," [c. 1950]. 9 pp. ("The Clock of the World," 12 pp.; "Exodus," 2 pp.)

"Come Away with Me," [c. 2000]. 13 pp. Deleted from *OM* prior to publication.

"Collector, The," 1959. 5 pp.

"Courtship of Timothy Wilkes, The," [late 1940s]. 14 pp.

"Cricket Cage, The," [1942–44]. 22 pp., under a Julius Schwartz agent cover page.

"Crickets, The," [early 1950s]. 11 pp.

"Cycle," [1943]. 4 pp.

"Dancer, The," [mid-1940s]. 3 pp.

"Dark Dies, If Evil Is," 1970–91. 22 pp.

"Day the Royal Grand Hotel Stood Open, The," 1950. 1 p.

"Death of a Son," [1940s], 12 pp. Related to "Interim *(Epoch)*."

"Death of So-and-So, The," [mid-1940s]. 9 pp. A version of the story-chapter discarded from *Summer Morning, Summer Night* and designated as a standalone story.

"Death's Racket," 1937. 5 pp. Written in response to a high school assignment.

"Disease (March 2001), The," [c. 1949]. 4 pp. A deleted *MC* chapter replaced by opening revisions to the story of the fourth expedition, "June 2001:—And the Moon Be Still as Bright" (48–7).

"Dragon Who Ate His Tail, The," [1950s]. Unpublished sequel to "The Fox and the Forest" ("To the Future," 50–14).

"Dream, The" ("The Dreaming Woman"), 1952. 7 pp.

"Drothldo, The," [late 1940s]. 6 pp., with the William Elliott pseudonym byline.

"Duel, The," [1942–44]. 11 pp., under a Julius Schwartz agent cover page. Original lost; photocopy held by Donn Albright.

"Elevator, The," 1951. Three versions with variant pages: 8 pp., 8 pp., 11 pp. (with carbon). Adapted for television and broadcast on *The Twilight Zone* (CBS), Jan. 31, 1986. Deleted from *OM* prior to publication.

"Emotionalists, The," [early 1940s]. 44 pp. Coauthored with Henry Hasse.

"Eye, The" ("The House That Lived"), [early 1950s]. 5 pp.

"Face of Natalie, The," [mid-1940s]. 10 pp.

"False Snow" ("The Night Before"), [early to middle 1950s]. 5 pp.

"Fat, The," 1950. 8 pp. Story about Fannie Florianna, a character in *DLB.*

"Family One, The," [mid-1940s]. Two versions: 6 pp. and 5 pp.

"Final Day," [1945]. 5 pp.

"First Machine, The," [1942–44]. 12 pp., under a Julius Schwartz agent cover page. Original lost; photocopy held by Donn Albright.

"Fisherman, The," [c. 1950]. Two versions, 5. pp. and 5 pp., with outline for expansion to short novel. A marionette/robot story.

"Fly Away Home," 1952. 15 pp., with holograph revisions.

"'Focus,'" 1948. 5 pp.

"For Sale: Tomorrow," 1941. 26 pp. Under a Julius Schwartz agent cover page.

"Frederich Bing Had a Wife," [1950]. 18 pp.

"From Now On—," [late 1940s]. 43 pp.

"Gallagher the Great" ("The Dancing Magician"), 1954. 21 pp., including variant text.

"Garbage Collector, The," [early 1950s]. 14 pp., with 2 variant pages.

"Gentleman Pays a Visit, The," [1944]. 2 pp.

"Ghost," [c. 2000]. 8 pp. An Irish story deleted from *OM* prior to publication.

"Ghosts, The," 1948. 8 pp. complete draft. An early single-page draft was published as facsimile in *The Ray Bradbury Companion* (75–2).

"Gift from the People, A" ("The Face"), 1950. 16 pp. and a variant opening page. Holograph revisions.

"God Is a Lady," [c. 1950], 11 pp.

"Golden Brain, The," [c. 1945]. 8 pp., conflated from two versions.

"The Golden Harp," [late 1940s], 10 pp., with 4 pp. of false starts.

"Golden Window, The," [early 1940s]. 3 pp.

"Good Way to Go, A" ("Mr. Smith and the Tintorettos"), 1954. 6 pp.

"Grand Tour, The," [late 1940s]. 10 pp. Closely related to "A Thousand Times Great Grandma" and *FDR*, but the adventure recounted here did not appears in the published novel.

"Grandma and the Gettysburg Address," [late 1940s]. 8 pp.

"Grendel" ("Sweetness and Light"), 1949–50. 6 pp.

"Gull, The," [early 1940s]. 10 pp., comprising two 5 pp. versions.

"Hallowe'en in July" ("Mr. Electrico Gives Douglas Faith," "The KKK Parade," "Waiting"), [late 1940s]. 11 pp., with holograph revisions. A version of the story-chapter discarded from *Summer Morning, Summer Night* and designated as a standalone story. "Mr. Electrico" may have been intended as a lead-in or a follow-on to the story, but it eventually became a retrospective narrative and was never merged with this tale.

"Harvest" ("Marijuana"), [1943]. 9 pp.

"High Tension," [late 1940s]. 10 pp., with 2 pp. of variants.

"House, The" ("Spoil Fun"), 1947. 11 pp.

"House Party" ("House Warming"), 1952. 9 pp.

"Hunchback and the Child, The," 1938. 10 pp.

"I'm Not the Only One," 1953. 4 pp.

"Idol, The," 1942. 16 pp., with periodic revisions through 1952.

"If at First You Don't Succeed, Try Again," [mid-1940s]. 5. pp.

"If Dark Does, if Evil Is-," 1991. 15 pp.

"If Paths Must Cross Again," [1942–44]. Two versions: 7 pp. and 5 pp., under a Julius Schwartz agent cover page.

"In Durance Vile" ("Hand in Glove," "The Jail"), 1962. Story developed from Bradbury's ABC *Alcoa Premiere* teleplay "The Jail" (aired Feb. 6, 1962).

"In the Eye of the Beholder," 1953. 44 pp., including 2 pp. outline.

"In Search of a Son," 1952. 5 pp., with holograph revisions.

"In the Forest," 1950. 4 pp.

"In the Shade of the Old Apple Tree," 1953. 6 pp.

"Insinkerator, The" ("Lion in the House"), 1955. 9 pp.

"Interference," 1941. 16 pp. Pagination indicates first two leaves are missing.

"Island, The," 1952. Two versions: 17 pp. and 18 pp.

"It Can Happen to Anyone," 1944. 4 pp. The fictitious publication of this story in *Dime Detective* is described by the narrator of *DLB* (99–100).

" . . . It Too Returned to the Night," 1937–38. 9 pp.

"Jimmy and the Long Gone Smile,"1955. 4 pp.

"Joke, The" ("Life-Death"), [1950]. 6 pp.

"Juju Bones," [1942–44]. 14 pp., under a Julius Schwartz agent cover page. Submitted to *Short Story* but never sold.

"Just in Case," [mid-1940s]. 4 pp.

"Karpwell's Pyramid," 1947. Two versions: 10 pp. and 8 pp.

"Ladies at the Service, The," [1955]. 4 pp.

"Lady Up Ahead, The," [1942–44]. 9 pp., under Julius Schwartz agent cover page.

"Lamplight," [1946]. 3 pp.

"Last of a Species, The," 1950. 8 pp.

"Literary Encounter, A," 1947. 6 pp.

["Little Babe"], [late 1940s]. 7 pp.

"Little Boy Ran, The," [late 1940s]. 12 pp.

["Lizzurius!"] [mid-1940s]. 6 pp.

"Long Live the Douser!" [1942–44]. 14 pp., under Julius Schwartz agent cover page. The third (and only unpublished) "Douser" detective story.

"Lorelei," 1938. 39 pp., with an illustration by Hannes Bok.

"Lots of Time" ("Ming Toy Was Her Name"), [late 1940s]. 9 pp., with holograph revisions.

"Love Affair," 1951. 5. pp. An unchronicled Martian love story, very different from the published (and also unchronicled) Martian story of the same title (82–1).

"Machine, The," [c. 1950]. 3 pp.

"Ma Perkins Comes to Stay," [late 1940s]. 21 pp., with holograph revisions.

"Marie Koppee Tielliggo Skee!" ("Camouflage," "The Emigrants"), [late 1940s to early 1950s]. 18 pp.

"Marriage, The," [c. late 1940s]. 8 pp. An unchronicled Martian story.

"Martian Bulwark," [1942–44]. 19 pp., under a Julius Schwartz agent cover page. Original lost; photocopy held by Donn Albright.

"Martian Ghosts, The," [mid-1950s]. 6 pp. An expansion of the single-page "Ghosts" (75–2), published as facsimile in *The Ray Bradbury Companion.*

"A Matter of Taste," 1952. 18 pp. Offered to *The Magazine of Fantasy and Science Fiction.*[1]

["Mechanical Man, The"], [mid-1940s]. 3 pp. and a variant page. A forerunner to "The Night Sets" (47–12).

"Mesa, The," [1942–44]. Two versions, each 13 pp., under a Julius Schwartz agent cover page. Bradbury's only western.

"Meteors, The," [1942–44]. 21 pp. and a 4 pp. revised opening, under a Julius Schwartz agent cover page.

"Minor Masterpiece, A" ("Something Short and Snappy"), 1954. Two versions: 6 pp. and 4 pp. ("Yakkity-Yak," "The Scriptwriter for the FBI").

"Minority Problem," 1942. 11 pp., under a Julius Schwartz agent cover page.

"Mirage, The," [late 1940s]. 9 pp. and a variant first page.

"Miss Remembrance," 1969. 7 pp.

"Modern Moral Tales: No. 1 'Paul's Neighbors,'" [1945]. 2 pp.

"Moment of Spring," [1942–44]. 7 pp., under a Julius Schwartz agent cover page.

"Mr. Bacteria" ("Mr. B."), [c. late 1940s]. 10 pp.; 8 pp. are holograph.

"Mr. Electrico," [early 1950s]. 7 pp., with holograph revisions.

"Mr. Saturday" ("Every Saturday Night"), [mid-1940s]. 12 pp. William Elliott byline indicated.

"Murder, The," [c. 1950]. 8 pp.

"Murderer, The," [c. late 1940s]. 10 pp., with 4 pp. of notes.

"Murderee, The" ("Before the Tiger Arrives"), [late 1940s]. 11 pp. A forerunner to "Touched with Fire" ("Shopping for Death," 54–8).

"No Hiding Place," 1943. Two versions: 28 pp. and 29 pp., under a Julius Schwartz agent cover page. The longer version contains holograph revisions; there are also 8 more pages of rewrites.

["No Snow Allowed"], [c. 1950]. 5 pp.

"Noise Like Love, A," [1942–44]. 4 pp., under a Julius Schwartz agent cover page.

"Noon Conversation," [mid-1950s]. Two versions: 12 pp., with holograph revisions; 15 pp. rewrite, dated 1957.

"Nor Iron Bars a Cage," [c. mid-1940s]. 3 pp., with variant opening titled "The Penitent" and 10 other variant pages.

"Number One," 1950. 15 pp., with holograph revisions.

"Of All Things—Never to Have Been Born Is Best," 1947. 5 pp.

"Old Mr. Young, The" ("The Young Mr. Old"), 1951. Possibly three versions: 10 pp., 10 pp., 9 pp., with holograph revisions.

"Once upon a Time," [mid-late 1940s]. Planned collection of children's stories containing "The Magical Chimney,"6 pp.; "The Golden Window," 4 pp.; "Once upon a Time," 6 pp.; and other fragments, including a thirteen-story contents page.

"One in the Dark," 1944. 19 pp. and a single-page outline. Crime story.

"Only a Matter of Time," [mid-1940s]. 2 pp.

"Onward, Christian Mama!" ("Mama and the Church People"), [late 1940s]. 11 pp.

"Parallel, The," 1941. 10 pp., under a Julius Schwartz agent cover page.

"Parrot Who Met Papa, The," ("Papa from Finca"), 1953. 6 pp. Unrelated to "The Parrot Who Met Papa" (72–1).

"Patch McPumpkin," 1970. 19 pp. Children's book.

"People Upstairs, The," [1949]. 9 pp.

"Phonograph, The," [1950]. 5 pp.

"Poe—Lodging for the Night," 1948. Three versions: 4 pp.; 15 pp. ("The Old Man"); and 8 pp. ("The Roomer").

"Poor Bob Terle, Did You Hear?," [mid-1940s]. 1 p.

"Prisoner, The," [1948]. 4 pp.

"Probability Zero," [1941]. 5 pp.

"Pterodactyls, The," 1962. 11 pp., and a variant opening page. Annotated as a revision of an unlocated 1954 draft.

"R Is for Rocket," [mid-1940s]. 7 pp. Unrelated to the published story "R Is for Rocket" ("King of the Gray Spaces," 43–11).

["Rain"], [c. mid-1940s], 11 pp.

"Rain before Morning," 1953. 8 pp.

"Rapunzel," [late 1940s]. Three versions: 10 pp., 11 pp., and 19 pp.

"Reincarnate, The," [1942–44]. 23 pp., under a Julius Schwartz agent cover page. Original lost; photocopy held by Donn Albright.

"Remember Helen Charles . . . ?," 1942. Two versions: 7 pp., under a Julius Schwartz agent cover page, and a subsequent undated 17-page version.

"Remembrance, Ohio," 1946–50. Two versions: 4 pp. and 8 pp. ("Quiet under the Sun").

"Revolt of the Pedestrians, The," [late 1940s]. 18 pp., with holograph revisions.

"Road to Autumn's House, The" 1938. 12 pp.

"Rocket for the Reverend, A," [1941]. 5 pp. Written, under the Leonard Spaulding byline, for the "Probability Zero" column of *Astounding Science Fiction.*

"Sauce Diable," 1957. 2 pp.

"Search for a Stranger" ("In Search of a Stranger"), 1956. 8 pp., with holograph revisions, and 8 pp. conflated from other versions.

"Seizure of Thomas Wayne, The," 1954. 4 pp.

"Several Kinds of Murder," [early 1950s]. 26 pp. Unsubmitted detective fiction.

"Shadow of Junius C.——, The" ("The Terrible Shadow of Junius D——"), 1959. 8 pp.

"Shop of the Mechanical Insects, The," [early 1950s]. 4 pp.

"Sirens, The," 1952. 17 pp., with typed and holograph revisions.

"Snow" ("The Snow Man," "The Snow Maiden"), [c. 1950]. 12 pp.

"Solution from a Bottle," [1942–44]. 14 pp., under a Julius Schwartz agent cover page. Original lost; photocopy held by Donn Albright.

"Some of My Best Friends Are Martians," [1947]. 4 pp.

"Some Time before Dawn," 1950. Two versions: 12 pp., with holograph revisions, and 13 pp. Thematically related to "The Fox and the Forest" ("To the Future," 50–14).

"Something Suspended," [1947–48]. 12 pp.

"Spring Day, The," 1950. 14 pp.

"Study in Bronze" ("Bronze Image"), [late 1940s]. 17 pp. and an outline. Indications of a William Elliott byline.

"Summer on SII," [1950s]. 2 pp.

"Surprise, The," [c. 1950]. 16 pp., with holograph revisions.

"Ta-Ta, Toddle-oo, Goodbye," [mid-1950s]. 11 pp.

"Tapestry, The," [1949]. 5 pp.

"Tarot Card Manana Nail Emporium, The," [c. 2000]. Deleted from *OM* prior to publication.

"Tar-Pit Murders, The," [mid-1940s]. 8 pp. Unsubmitted detective fiction.

"That's Me . . . Third from the Left," [1941]. 4 pp. Written for the "Probability Zero" column of *Astounding Science Fiction.*

"Theatre, The," 1953. Three versions: 3 pp. and two much earlier versions combined in 10 pp. ("Bobbie and the Tenement" or "And Look through All the Windows"), [1944].

"These Are the Innocents," ("These All Are Innocents," "All These Are Innocents"), [1947]. 26 pp. interleaved drafts.

"They All had Grandfathers [September 2001]," 1947. 13 pp. A deleted chapter of *MC;* a carbon of the chapter, pulled from the submitted copy prior to setting, survives in Bradbury's copy of the Doubleday submission.

"They Never Got Mad," 1946. 5 pp.

"Things, The," [1942–44]. 18 pp., under a Julius Schwartz agent cover page. Original lost; photocopy held by Donn Albright. An unpublished sequel to "Doodad" (43–7).

"This Time for Keeps," [mid-late 1940s]. Two versions: 33 pp. and 29 pp. (lacking conclusion).

"Thousand Time Great Grandma, A," [late 1940s]. Three related episodes: 4 pp., 5 pp. ("Grandma a Thousand Times Great"), and 1 p. ("The Death of Ten Thousand Greats Grandma"). Contains early concept of the plot elements that would open and conclude the novel *FDR.* See also the unpublished story, "The Grand Tour."

"Time and Time Again," [mid 1940s]. 30 pp. Various drafts.

"To Be or Not to Be" ("The Baby That Would Not Be Born"), [late 1940s]. 6 pp.

"Tonight Is Now," [c. 1950]. 20 pp., with holograph revisions.

"Transformation, The" ("The Negroid Transformation"), [late 1940s]. Two versions: 8 pp. and earlier 9-page version (titled "White Man Tattooed Black").

"Triangle," 1951. 13 pp.

"Unaccustomed as I Am—," [1942–44]. 9 pp.

[Untitled], 1938. 29 pp.

"Very Special Occasion, A," 1953. Two versions: 5 pp. and 8 pp. (as "Rain before Morning").

"The Visit,"1984. 6 pp.

"Voice in the Sky," [1950]. 2 pp.

"Waiting for Something to Happen," [1948]. 4 pp.

"Walker in the Night, The," [early 1950s]. 7 pp.

"Walls, The," 1949–50. 42 pp., with internal variant leaves and holograph revisions throughout.

"'The Way It All Happened,' Psychiatrist Shoots Himself," 1948. 4 pp., with holograph revisions.

"Welcome Home Our Hero!" [mid-1940s], 16 pp.

"We'll Just Act Natural," 1948–49. 9 pp.

"What to Do on a Rainy Day," 1954. 10 pp. Children's book.

"Wheat Field, The," 1947, 1971. 16 pp., possibly unfinished.

"Wheel, The [July 2003]," 1 pp. A deleted bridge passage from *MC.* A carbon of this bridge, pulled from the submitted copy prior to setting, survives in Bradbury's copy of the Doubleday submission.

"Where Everything Ends," [1942–44]. 23 pp., under a Julius Schwartz agent cover page. Original lost; photocopy held by Donn Albright. Submitted to *Flynn's Detective Fiction.*² The source of the canal murders in the detective novel *DLB* (85-A).

"Whose Little Corpse Are You?" [1942–44]. 36 pp. Detective fiction submitted to Standard Publications but never sold.

"Windowpane and the Leaflet, The," [early 1940s]. 6 pp.

"Woman in the Car Ahead" ("Woman on the Train Ahead"), [mid-1940s]. 6 pp. and one variant opening page.

"Yakkity-Yak" ("Conversation Piece"), 1953. 6 pp. Distinct from "Yakkity-Yak," 4 pp. version of "A Minor Masterpiece."

"You Wouldn't Think It to Look at Him," [late 1940s]. 5 pp.

"Young Man in His 20s," 1951–52. Two versions: 7 pp. and 8 pp. (as "The Golden Lad").

Notes

Location information for unpublished materials is limited to the following designations for the major repositories of Bradbury's papers: Lilly (Lilly Rare Book and Manuscript Library, Indiana University, Bloomington), Ransom (Alfred A. Knopf Publisher's Deposit, Harry Ransom Humanities Research Center, University of Texas, Austin), Madison (August Derleth Papers, State Historical Society of Wisconsin, Madison), Butler (Congdon and Matson Agency Deposits, Butler Library, Columbia University, New York), and Albright Collection (personal archive of Donn Albright, Westfield, New Jersey). Those items held by Bradbury himself are designated by "personal papers." Nearly all of Bradbury's letters are typed. Occasional misstrikes are silently corrected; errors and omissions are allowed to stand as indicated ([*sic*]) or are corrected within editorial brackets. His consistent representation of story and book titles in capitals is retained.

Preface

1. For a recent appraisal of Bradbury as primarily a writer of short stories, see David Mogen, "Ray Bradbury," in *The Columbia Companion to the Twentieth-Century American Short Story*, ed. Blanche H. Gelfant (New York: Columbia Univ. Press, 2000), 162–66.

Introduction. Metaphors, Myths, and Masks

1. Aljean Harmetz, "Filming a Ray Bradbury Fantasy," *New York Times*, April 24, 1983, 17.

2. Robert Scholes and Eric S. Rabkin, *Science Fiction: History, Science, Vision* (Oxford: Oxford Univ. Press, 1977), 65.

3. On genre study and works of science fiction and fantasy, see the discussion in William F. Touponce, *Ray Bradbury and the Poetics of Reverie: Fantasy, Science Fiction, and the Reader* (Ann Arbor: UMI Research Press, 1984); rev. 2d ed., I. O. Evans Studies, vol. 32 (San Bernardino, Calif.: Borgo, 1998). Our views on the relationship of authorship and textuality are aptly expressed in Jerome J. McGann, "The Socialization of Texts," *Documentary Editing* 12, no. 3 (1990): 58:

Nevertheless, the literary work by its very nature sets in motion many kinds of creative intentionalities. These orbit the universe of the creative work—but not around some imaginary and absolute center. Rather, they turn through many different kinds of motion, many structural scales, and in various formal relationships. The universe of *poiesis* no more has an absolute center than does the stellar universe we have revealed through our astronomy. What it has are many relative centers which are brought to our attention by our own acts of observation. The universe of literature is socially generated and does not exist in a steady state. Authors themselves do not have, *as authors*, singular identities; an author is a plural identity and more resembles what William James like to call the human world at large—a multiverse.

McGann is here working on a variant of the "decentering" of the author so prevalent in postmodern theory and drawing out its implications for literary editing. We, of course, are not editing Bradbury in any formal sense. But we hope to give our readers a sense of this "multiverse" of Bradbury's texts and to uncover some of the poetic laws governing their "gravitation" (to pursue the astronomical metaphor) to each other. Modern astronomy has also revealed the presence of asteroid belts in the solar system, the remains of planets that did not form. We too have discovered vast belts of textual remains left over from the formation of Bradbury's " planets" (i.e., his published works), and these are very important to an understanding of his authorship in this literary solar system.

4. Ray Bradbury, "Day after Tomorrow: Why Science Fiction?" *The Nation*, May 2, 1953, 365. This important essay has been reprinted in Bradbury, *Yestermorrow: Obvious Answers to Impossible Futures* (Santa Barbara, Calif.: Joshua Odell Editions/Capra, 1991), 93–104. Here Bradbury talks about science fiction as "great serious fun" and relates it to a long tradition of fiction that criticizes society, from Plato through François Rabelais (whose work was deeply influenced by carnival) to Poe and George Orwell. One of Bradbury's early insights as a science fiction author has to do with this relating of the genre to the "great time" of the Western tradition. A decade or so later, Gilbert Highet would situate Bradbury's writings even more firmly in that tradition (see his introduction to *VB)*. For Bradbury, the genre is a literature of ideas, but it is not dogmatic or narrowly ideological. Rather, it is a question of an "open" seriousness that allows one to construct ideas and then tear them apart again. Bradbury was producing carnivalized introductions to the "grotesque realism" of other fantasy and science fiction writers as well. For instance, his mock-jealous introduction to Theodore Sturgeon's *Without Sorcery* (1948) claims that Sturgeon's writing is "a giant carnival distorted but all the more real for its unreality. We see ourselves caught in grotesque gesture, in mid-act." Ray Bradbury, "About Theodore Sturgeon," foreword to *The Ultimate Egoist. Volume I: The Complete Stories of Theodore Sturgeon,* by Theodore Sturgeon, ed. Paul Williams (Berkeley, Calif.: North Atlantic, 1994), xi.

5. Henry Kuttner, "Ray Bradbury's Themes," in *Ray Bradbury Review,* ed. William F. Nolan (1952; reprint, Los Angeles: Graham, 1988), 21. Decades later Nolan himself surveyed the intervening published criticism about Bradbury's fiction for mention of carnival themes, finding the work of Richard Steven Dimeo ("The Mind and Fantasies of Ray Bradbury" [Ph.D. diss., University of Utah, 1970], which catalogs various carnival-related words in Bradbury's texts on pages 122–23) and Anita Sullivan significant in this respect, and added his own observations about two previously uncollected stories by Bradbury with carnival or circus settings: "The circus represents lost innocence, the carnival corruption and evil." William F. Nolan, introduction to *The Last Circus and the Electrocution,* by Ray Bradbury (Northridge, Calif.: Lord John, 1980), xvi. Bradbury wrote an afterword to this volume, in which he indicates the

continuing relevance of carnival experiences (and he broadens this category to include the films of Lon Chaney as well) to his writings.

6. See, for instance, the definition given by J. A. Cuddon's *Dictionary of Literary Terms and Literary Theory*, 3d ed. (New York: Penguin, 1991), 119–20. The various forms that the carnivalization of literature took in different historical periods are discussed in Mikhail Bakhtin, *Problems of Dostoevsky's Poetics*, ed. and trans. Caryl Emerson, *Theory and History of Literature*, no. 8 (Minneapolis: Univ. of Minnesota Press, 1984), 122–37. In his book on François Rabelais, Bakhtin was intent on showing that the medieval culture of folk humor actually belonged to all the people: "The truth of laugher embraced and carried away everyone; nobody could resist it." *Rabelais and His World,* trans. Hélène Iswolsky (Bloomington: Indiana Univ. Press, 1984), 82. There are no "footlights" in carnival, no spectators. Everyone participates. But Bakhtin also presents in that book a kind of Marxist literary history of laughter's fate in literature, which shows its diminishing power and shrinking gifts after Rabelais. Ibid., 101–36. We can see something of his negative feelings toward the literary carnivals of class culture in his critique of the Romantic use of masks (discussed below). But later in his career, when Bakhtin revisited his Dostoevsky book to include a discussion of "reduced" forms of laughter (such as parody) in that author's texts, he was more optimistic about "carnivalization," which he defines as "the transposition of carnival into the language of literature." Ibid., 122. It now seems possible for some authors to find a way to restore the footlights while maintaining something of the carnival spirit—despite the fact that we as readers can never fully be participants—and to make us feel that carnival has *only just* been transposed into literature. We argue in chapter 4 that Bradbury has achieved this remarkable feat with *SW.*

7. Bakhtin, *Problems of Dostoevsky's Poetics,* 125, 127.

8. Strictly speaking, Bakhtin does not use the term "carnivalization of genre(s)" in *Problems of Dostoevsky's Poetics* or anywhere else insofar as we know, but his insistence that the life of a genre consists in its constant "rebirths and renewals in *original* works" and that there exists a "carnivalistic generic tradition in literature" would seem to imply such a notion. *Problems of Dostoevsky's Poetics,* 141, 157. For him, carnival itself was a kind of quasi-genre that, when transposed into literature, could become a fully realized literary genre. Bakhtin does not discuss the modern fantastic per se but does suggest that carnivalization is a process that extends throughout Western literature and includes the "fantastic story" and the "philosophical fairy tale," forms characteristic of Romanticism. Ibid., 137. We argue that some of Bradbury's works are more fully carnivalized than others depending on how much they transpose carnival forms of language to renew the genre.

9. Boris Tomashevsky, "Thematics," in *Russian Formalist Criticism: Four Essays,* trans. Lee T. Lemon and Marion J. Reis (Lincoln: Univ. of Nebraska Press, 1965), 63; Tzvetan Todorov, *The Fantastic: A Structural Approach to a Literary Genre,* trans. Richard Howard (Ithaca, N.Y.: Cornell Univ. Press, 1975), 93. Tomashevsky's study of thematics includes the study of narrative themes.

10. Ray Bradbury, "Journey to a Far Metaphor," *Book World (The Washington Post),* September 11, 1994, 10.

11. Dorothea Brande, *Becoming a Writer* (1934; reprint, Los Angeles: J. P. Tarcher, 1981), 69–74. For Brande, the artistic temperament discovers itself in daydreaming. Further, reverie produces the very stuff of fiction, its *materia prima.* But these "wordless" daydreams need to be linked to the structure of writing, and this requires work and discipline. And there is no guarantee that the finished product will actually be a literary reverie, such as we have identified for Bradbury's work. See the introduction to Touponce, *Ray Bradbury and the Poetics of Reverie,* which distinguishes object reverie, cosmic reverie (those based on the material imagination), and reveries toward childhood, all categories developed by Gaston Bachelard.

12. Ray Bradbury, introduction to *DW*, vii; Ray Bradbury, introduction to *SRB*, xiii; Bradbury, "Journey," 11.

13. Ray Bradbury, *Zen and the Art of Writing* (Santa Barbara, Calif.: Capra, 1973), 17.

14. *DLB*, 66.

15. *Observer*, Sept. 16, 1951; *Time*, Mar. 23, 1953. For Bradbury tributes to Hemingway and Wolfe, see "The Kilimanjaro Device," *SRB*; and "Forever and the Earth," *LAM*.

16. "April 2026: The Long Years," *MC*.

17. "February 2002: The Locusts," *MC*, 78.

18. Roman Jakobson, "Two Aspects of Language," in *Language in Literature* (Cambridge, Mass.: Harvard Univ. Press, 1987), 95–114.

19. See also Todorov, *The Fantastic*, 107–39.

20. Ray Bradbury, "Death Warmed Over," in *The Hollywood Nightmare*, ed. Peter Haining (London: Macdonald, 1970), 267–76. The scene is "The Exiles" (*IM*, not *MC*).

21. For a recent discussion of Nietzsche's importance to American culture, see Allan Bloom, *The Closing of the American Mind* (New York: Simon and Schuster, 1987). Bloom traces the (mis)appropriation of Nietzsche's ideas both in American popular culture and in academia. For him, Nietzsche is the godfather of cultural relativism, which asserts that culture is a war not only against chaos but also against other cultures. According to Bloom, a cultural relativist must "care for culture more than truth, and fight for culture while knowing it is not true." Ibid., 202. This leads to the untenable situation in which cultural relativism teaches the need to believe while undermining belief. Bloom does not ask how popular poets and mythmakers such as Bradbury might help students survive and affirm their lives after the decline of the Enlightenment belief in scientific and absolute reason. See also discussion of *Fahrenheit 451* in chap. 3.

22. *Zen in the Art of Writing*, 157–58; Bradbury's commentary is cited in James L. Christian, *Philosophy: An Introduction to the Art of Wondering*, 4th ed. (New York: Holt, Rinehart, and Winston, 1986), 426. Bradbury adds: "Life has *always* been lying to ourselves! As boys, young men, old men. As girls, maidens, women, to gently lie and prove the lie true. To weave dreams and put brains and ideas and flesh and the truly real beneath the dreams. Everything, finally, is a promise. What seems a lie is a ramshackle need, wishing to be born." This Nietzschean phrase first appeared in "Federico Fellini," *Los Angeles Times Book Review*, Nov. 27, 1977 (and collected in *Yestermorrow*.) The phrase, translated as "We possess *art* lest we *perish of the truth*," occurs in Friedrich Nietzsche, *The Will to Power*, ed. Walter Kaufmann, trans. Walter Kaufmann and R. J. Hollingdale (New York: Vintage, 1968), sec. 822.

23. "Death Warmed Over" was published in 1968. Not long after (1975), Bradbury stressed in an extended interview that his authorship was tied to carnival, which deconstructs the opposition of high and low culture: "We must be entertainers—carnival people, circus people, playwrights, poets, tellers of tales in the streets of Baghdad, we're all of the same family that exists throughout history to explain ourselves to one another." Ray Bradbury interview, "The Skull behind the Flesh," in *Endangered Species* (Cambridge, Mass.: Da Capo, 2001), 86.

24. For discussion of the role of masks in Nietzsche's philosophy, see W. D. Williams, "Nietzsche's Masks," in *Nietzsche: Imagery and Thought*, ed. Malcom Pasley (Berkeley: Univ. of California Press, 1978), 83–103, and Walter Kaufman, *Nietzsche, Heidegger, and Buber* (New Brunswick, N.J.: Transaction Publishers, 1992), 137–64.

25. Friedrich Nietzsche. "Attempt at Self-Criticism," *The Birth of Tragedy*, in *Basic Writings of Nietzsche*, trans. and ed. Walter Kaufman (New York: Modern Library, 1968), 19.

26. For a discussion of Bradbury's children in a broad and comparative literary context, see Sabine Büssing, *Aliens in the Home: The Child in Horror Fiction* (Westport, Conn.: Greenwood, 1987).

27. Ray Bradbury, *They Have Not Seen the Stars: The Collected Poetry of Ray Bradbury* (Lancaster, Pa.: Stealth Press, 2002), 1–3.

28. Wayne L. Johnson, *Ray Bradbury* (New York: Frederick Ungar, 1980), 145.

29. "Christus Apollo," *IS*, 300–1.

30. Ibid., 301, 302.

31. Ray Bradbury, "The God in Science Fiction" (*Saturday Review*, Dec. 10, 1977, 38, 43). Among the stories Bradbury discusses here are "The Fire Balloons," "The Man," and "The Messiah" as well as his "new" ending for the film *King of Kings*, which stages a "supper after the last supper." His ending for the film is also fictionalized as an episode in his autobiographical work *GL*. An earlier statement concerning Bradbury's views on the nature of God's immanence in creation can be found in an interview with Oriana Fallaci in *If the Sun Dies*, trans. Pamela Swinglehurst (New York: Atheneum, 1966), 9–26. Bradbury indicates to Fallaci that his religious thinking had gone far beyond the Nietzschean notion of the death of God (that man created God) to embrace a another notion: "I say *we* are God . . . , God is this flesh, this voice. That's what I mean when I say that God has grown curious, when I speak of matter that can reproduce itself." Ibid., 24. Bradbury rejects the notion of an immortal transcendent God far removed from his creation for one immanent in his creation and who wants to be mortal in order to die and be born again. There is much to learn here about Bradbury's notion of authorship, for the relation of God to his creation mirrors that of author to his hero/work. See also our discussion of "The Fire Balloons" in chap. 7.

32. Ray Bradbury, "Christ, Old Student in a New School," in *Again, Dangerous Visions*, vol. 1, ed., Harlan Ellison (New York: Signet, 1972), 192–93. See Bakhtin, *Problems of Dostoevsky's Poetics*, 150.

33. Bradbury, "Christ, Old Student in a New School," 194–95.

34. The clearest statement of Bradbury's conception of technology as the embodiment of ideas is "Cry the Cosmos," *Life*, September 14, 1962.

35. *F451*, pt. 1 (New York: Ballantine/Del Rey, 1988), 14. For further analysis, see Touponce, *Bradbury and the Poetics of Reverie*.

36. Ray Bradbury, "The Ardent Blasphemers," introduction to *20,000 Leagues under the Sea*, by Jules Verne (New York: Bantam, 1962).

37. Bradbury, *They Have Not Seen the Stars*, 38–41.

38. Arnold Hauser, *The Philosophy of Art History* (New York: Knopf, 1963), 59, 63.

39. One of the radio plays is described in the title line as "a play for the World Security Workshop"; the other is titled "The Masks and the Man Within." Albright Collection.

40. "Plans for Work," first leap of unnumbered forty-page typescript of discontinuous working papers. Albright Collection.

41. John Huston biographer Lawrence Grobel maintains that, early in Bradbury's working relationship with Huston on the *Moby Dick* screenplay (1953), Bradbury asked the director: "What kind of script do you want? Are you a Freudian? A Jungian?" *The Hustons* (New York: Avon, 1989), 417. Grobel's alleged source is Evelyn Keyes, but he offers no documentation.

42. "The Earthmen," *MC*, 21.

43. Bakhtin, *Rabelais*, 39, 40.

44. Mikhail Bakhtin, *The Dialogic Imagination: Four Essays*, ed. Michael Holquist, trans. Caryl Emerson and Michael Holquist (Austin: Univ. of Texas Press, 1981), 163.

45. Ibid., 171, 159.

46. Ibid., 36.

47. Bakhtin, *Rabelais*, 49.

48. For example, see *GL*, chapter 68, 256.

49. Perhaps we have not declined the role of but simply the name "psychobiography," which has acquired such a bad reputation among scholars. For a recent attempt to revive this field in a more scholarly and responsible fashion, see Alan C. Elms, *Uncovering Lives: The Uneasy Alliance of Biography and Psychology* (Oxford: Oxford Univ. Press, 1994). While admitting that psychobiography will probably not cure the "endemic reductionism" of psychological approaches to literature, he provides four short essays of his own on science fiction authors: John W. Campbell, Cordwainer Smith, Jack Williamson, and Isaac Asimov. These essays, while interesting and insightful, still seem principally reductive, finding the key to thematic structures in the author's work by reducing them to circumstances in his personal life. We doubt not so much the validity of this approach as the necessity for it in Bradbury's case. Bradbury has always talked openly about the personal sources of his stories, and thus there is no longer much of a mystery about what incidents in his life inspired most of them (see the recent Gauntlet edition of *Dark Carnival* or any of Bradbury's numerous prefaces to his works). We argue in this study that Bradbury's fantasies are deeply rooted in his personal experiences of carnival, but however personal they may be, we seek to understand them at the level of the text, where they are transformed by the social process of carnivalization. We locate the origins of his authorship in his encounter with Mr. Electrico when he was twelve years old (see afterword) but otherwise we have not sought to read beneath that level and into his family history. For a recent attempt to write a psychobiography of Bradbury along Jungian lines, see Marvin E. Mengeling, *Red Planet, Flaming Phoenix, Green Town: Some Early Bradbury Revisited* (Bloomington, Ind. First Books Library, 2002).

50. Brian Aldiss, *Trillion Year Spree: The True History of Science Fiction* (New York: Avon, 1986), 248.

51. Ray Bradbury, "Marvels and Miracles—Pass It On," *New York Times Magazine*, March 20, 1955, 56, 27.

52. "The Other Me," *Zen in the Art of Writing* (New York: Bantam, 1992), 148–49.

53. "We Have Our Arts So We Won't Die of Truth," ibid., 157–58.

54. "Maundered Melville" may mean that he was impoverished by his dedication to novel writing; Melville's career fell into oblivion after the publication of *Moby Dick.* "Maunder" is an obsolete term for a beggar, hence its primary meaning today of wandering aimlessly or talking incoherently.

55. Although Victor Hugo thought that the grotesque—a primary feature of carnival according to Bakhtin—was always present in Shakespeare's plays "even when it is silent," he lists the meeting between Romeo and the apothecary, Macbeth and the witches, King Lear and his fool, and Hamlet and the gravediggers as overt examples of its presence. See Jonathan Bate, ed., *The Romantics on Shakespeare* (New York: Penguin, 1992), 226–27. To romantic thinkers, the grotesque is not just an aspect of Shakespeare, it is the very sign of his creative genius, which can mingle, without a discordant note, the monstrous and the sublime, thereby encompassing many sides of life. Bradbury's sense of Shakespeare, especially in *SW*, is deeply rooted in this tradition of interpretation.

56. Ray Bradbury, *They Have Not Seen the Stars*, 195–96.

57. Friedrich Nietzsche, *The Birth of Tragedy*, sec. 7, in *Basic Writings*, 60. Nietzsche's own views on the poet's need for masks can be found in "The Song of Melancholy," pt. 4 of *Thus Spoke Zarathustra*, in *The Portable Nietzsche*, ed. and trans. Walter Kaufmann (New York: Penguin, 1968), 408–12. The magician sings of poetry's melancholy "banishment" from the truth by philosophy, which accuses the poet of using "fools' masks." Of course, Zarathustra the philosopher masks himself and his truth, so his rival the magician is attempting to discredit, through poetry, Zarathustra's own claim to truth, a situation that would delight a deconstructionist but that we mention here only by way of contrasting it with Bradbury's aesthetic use of masks,

which are knowingly intended to hide the truth. Incidentally, part 4 of *Zarathustra* is often seen by Nietzsche scholars as a carnivalization of his ideas. See discussion in Lawrence Lampert, *Nietzsche's Teaching: An Interpretation of* Thus Spoke Zarathustra (New Haven: Yale Univ. Press, 1986), 289.

58. Aldiss, *Trillion Year Spree*, 247.

59. This is a key Nietzschean concept whose complex meaning is presented mostly in *Thus Spoke Zarathustra*. Basically, it opposes everything that would set men's desires on another world—especially heaven or the Platonic realm of ideas—as somehow more "true" than the life of the body and the senses, the life of this world. The meaning of the Earth is to be won back from all those who disparage it with otherworldly dreams, dreams that eventually give rise to nihilism in Nietzsche's view.

60. Tom Shippey, ed., *The Oxford Book of Fantasy Stories* (Oxford: Oxford Univ. Press, 1994), xx. For an account of the internalized Gothic, see Mark Edmundson, *Nightmare on Main Street: Angels, Sadomasochism, and the Culture of Gothic* (Cambridge: Harvard Univ. Press, 1997). Edmundson argues that most Gothic writers are haunted not so much by precursors as by specters of their own creation embodied in the hero-villains they create. We are arguing that Bradbury explored Gothic literature but passed beyond the limiting "sadomasochistic cycle" contained in it toward a kind of post-Gothic affirmation. Edmundson is also very insightful about Freud's undeniable influence on popular Gothic forms (he discusses contemporary popular culture alongside the literary) as well as the influence of the Gothic mode on Nietzsche's concern to overcome the spirit of revenge. The necessity to overcome this spirit, which binds us to a dark past, is also evident in Bradbury's thematics and is explored in later chapters.

61. *DLB*, 271. Our sense of the fantastic after Freud derives in part from Harold Bloom, "Wrestling Sigmund," in *The Breaking of the Vessels* (Chicago: Univ. of Chicago Press, 1982), 43–70. For Bloom, Freud is *the* inescapable mythologist of our age: "our literary culture speaks to us in the language of Freud, even when the writer, like Nabokov or Borges, is violently anti-Freudian. . . . We come after, and we must say that psychoanalysis itself is the culture of which it purports to be the description. If psychoanalysis and our literary culture no longer can be distinguished, then criticism is Freudian whether it wants to be or not," Ibid., 63. Bradbury vehemently denies learning anything from Freud, always claiming that *literary* precursors of Freud such as Shakespeare and Melville are the fathers and Freud the son. See Bradbury's poem "Shakespeare the Father, Freud the Son" in *They Have Not Seen the Stars*, 240–41. At issue here is Freud's enormous influence on fantasy literature. See Todorov, *The Fantastic*, 160–61.

62. Nietzsche, *Will to Power*, bk. 1, 32.

63. Harold Bloom, "The Life of the Author," in *Modern Fantasy Writers* (New York: Chelsea House, 1995), x.

64. Although neither the editor nor the publisher for these two stories have been identified, the language of the unsent letter Bradbury composed for his novel project reveals his serious intent: "Here I have written a long short story of values in the coming century. I believe that by a complete reversal I have made the values of our time stand forth in relief. The story is one of anarchy and disillusion, of death and destruction and the art and value of death in a world set to valueing [*sic*] it. The final breakdown of the faith of the world's peoples in themselves, their works, their religions. I hope that you will be impressed with the thought and work I have put upon this story."

65. Ray Bradbury, ed., *The Circus of Dr. Lao and Other Improbable Stories* (New York: Bantam, 1956), viii. In the last quote, Bradbury is citing Henry James as cited by Trilling.

66. Ibid., x.

67. Ibid., viii. The question of the extent of Nietzsche's influence on Bakhtin is still being debated among scholars, but there is no doubt that they share many affinities of thought. In

particular, there is a great deal of overlap between the Dionysian aspects of Nietzsche's culture criticism and Bakhtin's carnival. Robert Stam writes:

> Both Bakhtin and Nietzsche contrast a stifling official culture with a vital unofficial one. Nietzsche's recuperation of the Dionysian parallels Bakhtin's recuperation of the forbidden, the repressed, the grotesque, the noncanonical. Both celebrate the body not as a self-contained system delineated by the ego but rather as the site of dispersion and multiplicity. . . . Similarly, the implicit cognitive thrust of "gay relativity" and carnival as a popular mode of knowledge evokes Nietzsche's "fröhliche wissenschaft" as a joyful descent into contradiction. Both thinkers share a belief in *homo ridens,* in the profundity and cognitive value of laughter. . . . Nietzsche's polemic against monism, finally, recalls Bakhtin's arguments against monologism, just as the Bakhtinian trope of "nonfinalizability" of human character and meaning recalls Nietzsche's Dionysus as the embodiment of the eternally creative principle, forever exulting in the transformation of appearances.

Robert Stam, *Subversive Pleasures: Bakhtin, Cultural Criticism, and Film* (Baltimore: Johns Hopkins Univ. Press, 1989), 89. We have assumed this kind of general conceptual overlap in our use of Nietzschean and Bakhtinian terminology. We find a particularly significant overlap between: (1) the bodily life revealed by carnival and Nietzsche's meaning of the Earth as an inexhaustible source of new values, (2) overcoming the spirit of gravity and one-sided seriousness with laughter, and (3) redeeming mankind from the spirit of revenge (in the form of guilt and sin posed by the Gothic past). There are important differences between the two thinkers, however, and especially in their preferences for different social classes. These issues are discussed in our reading of *MC,* where Bradbury seems to prefer an aristocratic definition of culture. See chap. 2.

68. Julia Kristeva, who coined the term "intertextuality," gives a textual and semiotic redefinition to the process of authorship we are here investigating.

> A carnival participant is both actor and spectator; he loses his sense of individuality, passes through a zero point of carnivalesque activity, and splits into a subject of the spectacle and an object of the game. Within the carnival, the subject is reduced to nothingness, while the structure of *the author* emerges as anonymity that creates itself and sees itself created as self and other, as man and mask. The cynicism of this carnivalesque scene, which destroys a god in order to impose its own dialogical laws, calls to mind Nietzsche's Dionysianism. The carnival first exteriorizes the structure of reflective literary productivity, then inevitably brings to light this structure's underlying unconscious: sexuality and death. Out of the dialogue that is established between them, the structural dyads of carnival appear: high and low, birth and agony, food and excrement, praise and curses, laughter and tears.

Julia Kristeva, "Word, Dialogue, and Novel," in *Desire in Language, A Semiotic Approach to Literature and Art,* ed. Leon S. Roudiez (New York: Columbia Univ. Press, 1980), 78.

1. Out of the House of Arkham

1. Bradbury to Derleth, Nov. 23, 1939, Madison.
2. Peter Ruber, *Arkham's Masters of Horror* (Sauk City, Wis.: Arkham House, 2000), 262.

Bradbury's initial fan letter gives an account of his friendship with de Castro, who had coauthored stories with Ambrose Bierce and later corresponded with Lovecraft. According to Ruber, de Castro gave a score of his Lovecraft letters to Bradbury, who made copies for the Arkham project. Derleth's work did not appear in any issue of *Futuria Fantasia*.

3. Ray Bradbury, interview by Don Congdon, "I Have All the Answers, Now What Are the Questions?" (June 1970; corrected, 1998), 1B. 15 [hereafter cited as Bradbury interview (Congdon)]. In an undated letter to Derleth (probably written in January 1940), Bradbury tells of sending two stories, "The Ravine" and "The Sculptor," to Farnsworth Wright at *Weird Tales*. These were rejected and only fragments of "The Ravine" have ever been located (Albright Collection).

4. Ray Bradbury, interview by Craig Cunningham, Los Angeles, Jan. 12–Apr. 11, 1961, UCLA Oral History Program Transcript, 127–28 [hereafter cited as Bradbury interview (Cunningham)].

5. Ray Bradbury, "Magic, Magicians, Carnival and Fantasy" in Nolan, *Bradbury Review*, 8–9; Bradbury interview (Cunningham), 128.

6. Bradbury to Derleth, Sept. 21, 1944, Madison. Bradbury's New York agent, Julius Schwartz, had relayed the *Weird Tales* position to him earlier. Schwartz to Bradbury, Sept. 9, 1944, personal papers.

7. Ruber, *Arkham's Masters of Horror*, 263. Ruber's knowledge of Derleth's offer may be based solely on references in Bradbury's reply, but he offers no documentation of sources. Donn Albright, Bradbury's principal bibliographer, noted that Derleth initially wanted a concept for the collection. Donn Albright, interview by Jonathan R. Eller, Muncie, Ind., June 2000.

8. Bradbury to Derleth, Jan. 29, 1945, Madison. (Ruber misdates the letter January 27.) The developing concepts described in the following paragraphs are found in Bradbury to Derleth, Jan. 29, 31, and Mar. 8, 1945, Madison. (Bradbury's personal papers contain a draft of the March 8 letter.)

9. Jack Snow to Ray Bradbury, Nov. 10, 1944, personal papers.

10. The content of Derleth's letters prior to 1946 is inferred from Bradbury's responses in the Derleth Papers, the State Historical Society of Wisconsin, Madison.

11. Bradbury to Derleth, Mar. 8, 1945, Madison.

12. The jacket description, which has a great deal to do with the development of *SW*, is discussed in chap. 5.

13. Bradbury to Derleth, Mar. 8, 1945, Madison.

14. Bradbury interview (Cunningham), 164–67. The sales were "One Timeless Spring" *(Collier's)*, "The Miracles of Jamie" *(Charm)*, and "Invisible Boy" *(Mademoiselle)*.

15. The ongoing discussion between author and agent is found in Schwartz to Bradbury, Feb. 4, 24; Sept. 8, 1945, personal papers.

16. Bradbury to Derleth, Dec. 10, 1945 (undated draft), personal papers.

17. Derleth to Bradbury, Dec. 12, 1945, Madison (copy). Derleth's response is the earliest carbon copy preserved from the correspondence; Bradbury's personal file of received originals begins with a letter dated April 30, 1946. The influence of Derleth's own experiences as an author is described in Ruber, *Arkham's Masters of Horror*, 13–14. Other houses the publisher used as models include Coward-McCann, Duell, and Sloan and Pearce.

18. Progress on the dust-jacket design and approval is documented in Bradbury to Derleth, Dec. 19, 1945, Feb. 2, Mar. 8, 1946, Madison. Bradbury mentioned Robinson's *The Perfect Round* in his December 19 letter; the novel concerns a wounded World War II veteran's attempt to rebuild his life by rebuilding a merry-go-round. Robinson later wrote a bestseller, *The Cardinal*.

19. Derleth's spring 1946 catalog listing garnered immediate interest: "Advance orders for DARK CARNIVAL are beginning to come in; we must have at least 50 so far, which is encouraging, indeed." Derleth to Bradbury, Apr. 30, 1946, personal papers.

20. Bradbury to Derleth, June 2, 1946, Madison. Bradbury describes his negotiations with the major magazines during this period in Bradbury interview (Cunningham), 144–50.

21. The discussion of the copyright statement and its ramifications is found in a sequence of four letters: Bradbury to Derleth, June 7, 15, 1946, Madison; and Derleth to Bradbury, June 11, 18, 1946, personal papers.

22. Congdon had read "Invisible Boy" in the fall of 1945 and wrote to Bradbury to see if he had a novel in the works that Simon and Schuster might consider. Ray Bradbury, interview by Donn Albright, "Story Origins," Los Angeles, October 2001.

23. Bradbury to Derleth, Mar. 12, 1947, Madison. The late changes in galleys are documented in Bradbury to Derleth, Nov. 26, 1946, Madison. The revisions in page proofs are discussed in Bradbury to Derleth, Mar. 12, 17, [c. 20], 1947, Madison.

24. Bradbury interview (Cunningham), 146–48. "The story did not fit the magazine; and, after months of debate, they finally decided to change the magazine to fit the story. . . . They then put together an entire issue around my story and called in Charles Addams. . . . He did a two-page spread in *Mademoiselle*, a lovely thing, of this old house and all these wonderful creatures flying through the air and loping along the ground, coming to it. As I remember, they got Katherine Anne Porter to do an article on ghosts, and they printed various weird photographs. Then they covered all their mannequins with cobwebs and owls and what have you, and had an entire ghost issue of *Mademoiselle*." Bradbury's recollection is wrong on one point—the ghost article was actually the work of Kay Boyle.

25. Ibid., 144–45. "I would like to have cut two pages out of THE MAN UPSTAIRS. Compare the *DC* version with the Harper's version. The Harper's is shorter, cleaner, neater, four of the scenes are combined into two scenes." Bradbury to Derleth, [late Mar. 1947], Madison.

26. Bradbury interview (Congdon), 56–57; William F. Nolan, *The Ray Bradbury Companion* (Detroit: Gale, 1975), 56; Derleth to Bradbury, May 8, 1947, personal papers. Derleth's letter implies that both Arkham House and Hamish Hamilton (Bradbury's first British publisher) were initially interested in the *Summer Morning, Summer Night* manuscript, but Bradbury did not complete this project during his years with these publishers. After *Dandelion Wine* appeared (1957), unpublished parts of this manuscript were retitled "Farewell Summer." For a fuller discussion of Bradbury and Congdon's relationship, see Bradbury interview (Congdon), 2.51–80.

27. Derleth to Bradbury, May 12, 1947, Madison (carbon).

28. Ian Norrie, *Mumby's Publishing and Bookselling in the Twentieth Century*, 6th ed. (London: Bell and Hyman, 1982), 58, 65–66.

29. Ibid., 91; Hamish Hamilton to Bradbury, Aug. 15, 1949, personal papers.

30. Bradbury to Derleth, Jan. 13, 1949, Madison.

31. Norrie, *Mumby's Publishing and Bookselling*, 131; Hamilton to Bradbury, Aug. 15, 1949, personal papers; Hart-Davis to Bradbury, Nov. 25, 1954, ibid. Bradbury's *October Country* correspondence with Rupert Hart-Davis indicates that *Dark Carnival* had sold out in England by 1954.

32. The colophon gives a print run of 3,000 copies, but in *Thirty Years of Arkham House*, Derleth gives the figure as 3,112. Trade editions of the hardcover *October Country* are nearly as rare, followed by the clothbound *MC* and *F451*. The stock figures for 1951 are from Derleth to Bradbury, Feb. 10, Mar. 17, 1951, personal papers.

33. Ruber, *Arkham's Masters of Horror*, 18. Contemporary reviews of *Dark Carnival* include Anthony Boucher, "Dark Carnival," *San Francisco Chronicle*, June 22, 1947, 17; Will Cuppy,

"Mystery and Adventure," *New York Herald Tribune*, May 25, 1947, 30; and N. O., "Tales for the Library of a Haunted House," *Chicago Sun*, June 29,1947, 3.

34. For Derleth's side of the reprint issue, see Derleth to Bradbury, Oct. 12, 18, 23, 1950, May 9, 1953, personal papers. Selections from other unexamined letters, used by Ruber to restate Derleth's view, are quoted from Ruber, *Arkham's Masters of Horror.*

35. Derleth to Bradbury, April 7 1948, Madison (Carbon); quoted in Ruber, *Arkham's Masters of Horror,* 267–68. Ruber does not give the date of the letter.

36. Bradbury to Derleth, May 6, 13, 1953, Madison; Derleth to Bradbury, May 9, 1953, June 26, 1954, personal papers; Derleth to Nelson Bond, n.d., cited in Ruber, *Arkham's Masters of Horror,* 268.

37. "The Crowd," *Weird Tales,* May 1943, 93.

38. Compared texts from "The Crowd," *Weird Tales,* 92; and "The Crowd," *DC,* 124.

39. Compared texts from "The Smiling People," *Weird Tales,* May 1946, 53; and "The Smiling People," *DC,* 69.

40. Bradbury, "The Inherited Wish," introduction to Nolan, *Bradbury Companion,* 13.

41. W. Bradbury to R. Bradbury, May 6, 1953, personal papers.

42. Ibid. An excellent account of this period in Ian Ballantine's career is found in Kenneth C. Davis, *Two-Bit Culture: The Paperbacking of America* (Boston: Houghton-Mifflin, 1984), 101–9, 158–69.

43. The initial contract and developmental details for *The October Country* are found in Ballantine to Bradbury, June 18, 1953, personal papers; Kauffmann to Bradbury, Aug. 12, 1953, ibid.; and Kauffmann to Congdon, Mar. 19, 1954, personal papers (copy); original, Butler.

44. Kauffmann to Bradbury, Dec. 14, 1954, personal papers.

45. Ray Bradbury, interview by Jonathan R. Eller, Palm Springs, Mar. 14, 2002.

46. His own records show that "Uncle Einar" (sent January 9) and "Jack-in-the-Box" (sent January 24) were two of the last stories sent. "The Emissary" is not even included on the list and was probably sent even later. Bradbury submission list, personal papers.

47. Baker to Stanley Kauffmann, Dec. 30, 1955, transcribed copy attachment, Ballantine to Bradbury, Jan. 5, 1956, personal papers. Contemporary reviews of *The October Country* include Carlos Baker, *New York Times,* Dec. 11, 1955, 30; William Hogan, "Ray Bradbury's World of Reasonable Bogeymen," *San Francisco Chronicle,* Nov. 16, 1955, 31; and Richard Sullivan, *Chicago Tribune,* Jan. 1, 1956, 4.

48. Ian Ballantine to Bradbury, Jan. 31, 1956, personal papers.

49. Bradbury to Boucher, Jan. 10, 1952, Lilly.

50. Anthony Boucher, "Ray Bradbury, Beginner," in Nolan, *Bradbury Review,* 16.

51. Ray Bradbury, "Where Do You Get Your Ideas?" in Nolan, *Bradbury Review,* 43.

52. Ray Bradbury, "Magic, Magicians, Carnival, and Fantasy," in Nolan, *Bradbury Review,* 1952, 10; Bradbury to Boucher, July 10, 1947, Lilly.

53. Bakhtin, *Rabelais,* 25–26; *Dark Carnival,* Gauntlet ed., 2001, 203.

54. Bradbury, "Magic, Magicians, Carnival, and Fantasy," 10.

55. Ibid., 9; Bradbury interview (Cunningham), 137.

56. Compared texts from *DC,* 54; and *OC,* 97.

57. Interestingly, Bradbury thought enough of the story potential of "Cistern" to work up a contents outline for a "short novel of suspense" in which sexual frustration and suicide are replaced by murder. The outline has some suggestive water imagery and other characters—tramps—who live in the cisterns beneath Los Angeles.

58. Compared texts from *DC,* 276–77; and *OC,* 246.

59. *DC,* 277.

60. *OC,* 68.

61. Todorov, *The Fantastic,* 161.

62. Sigmund Freud, "The Relation of the Poet to Day-Dreaming," in *On Creativity and the Unconscious,* comp. Benjamin Nelson, trans. I. F. Grant Duff (New York: Harper and Row, 1958), 51.

63. *OC,* 4.

64. Ibid., 10.

65. Ibid., 8.

66. Ibid., 15.

67. Ibid., 266.

68. Ibid., 274, 275.

2. Martian Carnivals

1. Gary K. Wolfe, "Ray Bradbury," in *Twentieth-Century American Science Fiction Writers,* Part 1 (Detroit: Gale Research, 1981), 66. For an informative account of Bradbury and *The Martian Chronicles* in the context of American science fiction, see Thomas D. Clareson, *Understanding Contemporary American Science Fiction: The Formative Period, 1926–1970* (Columbia: Univ. of South Carolina Press, 1992), 41, 50–58.

2. Bradbury to William F. Touponce, Aug. 18, 1981, in author's possession.

3. Ray Bradbury, "Day after Tomorrow: Why Science Fiction?" *Nation,* May 2, 1953. This essay was reprinted in *Yestermorrow* (quote, 97).

4. Bradbury interview (Congdon), 2.22.

5. Bradbury's interaction with major presses during this period is documented in Bradbury interview (Congdon), 2.57–61; Bradbury interview (Cunningham), 195–96; and Bradbury to Derleth, Apr. 21, 1949, Madison.

6. Bradbury interview (Cunningham), 197. Congdon remembers that Doubleday wanted the novel manuscript *Summer Morning, Summer Night* for the second contract, but Ray Bradbury eventually persuaded Walter Bradbury to take the second story collection. Doubleday would eventually publish versions of both projects under different titles.

7. Ibid., 200–201.

8. Ibid., 197.

9. Bradbury to Touponce, Aug. 18, 1981. "When I got back to Los Angeles, I did additional outlining and sent the manuscript to Walter Bradbury midsummer. At the time it had more stories in it . . . , which we took out, for the book was already long enough." Bradbury eventually considered and eliminated "The One Who Waits," "The Naming of Names," "The Blue Bottle," and in December 1949 "Payment in Full." Only "The Naming of Names" appears in the known outlines prepared after June 1949.

10. In his 1979 teleplay, Richard Matheson (another of the so-called California School) titled the major sections of his adaptation "Expeditions," "Settlers," and "Martians."

11. Bradbury annotated the box containing the carbon copy of the surviving typescript as being completed on October 8, 1949 (Albright Collection). In a letter to Walt Bradbury dated two days later, he notes that he has just posted the typescript to Congdon. R. Bradbury to W. Bradbury, Oct. 10, 1949, Lilly.

12. R. Bradbury to Walter Bradbury, Feb. 17, 1950, Lilly.

13. Bradbury interview (Cunningham), 197.

14. Bradbury, introduction to *MC* (1950; reprint, New York: Avon, 1997), viii–ix.

15. "Rocket Summer," *Planet Stories* (Spring 1947): 50.

16. There are several unpublished accounts of this moment in Chicago. It is also discussed in Bradbury, "The Long Road to Mars," introduction to *MC*, 40th anniv. ed. (New York: Doubleday, 1990), x.

17. Contemporary American reviews of *The Martian Chronicles* include Anon., *Kirkus* 18 (Mar. 1950): 144; E. F. Walbridge, *Library Journal*, May 1, 1950, 774; Rex Lardner, *New York Times*, May 7, 1950, 21; Don Fabun, in "This World," *San Francisco Chronicle*, May 14, 1950, 18; August Derleth, *Chicago Sunday Tribune*, May 21, 1950, 3; Anthony Boucher, *Chicago Sun*, June 4, 1950, 6; Fletcher Pratt, *Saturday Review of Literature*, June 17, 1950, 32; and Christopher Isherwood, "Christopher Isherwood Reviews *The Martian Chronicles*," *Tomorrow* 10:2 (1950): 56–57.

18. R. Bradbury to Walter Bradbury, July 22, 1950, Lilly.

19. R. Bradbury to Walter Bradbury, Jan. 13, 1950, Lilly.

20. Hart-Davis to Bradbury, Nov. 10, 1950, personal papers. B. A. Y[oung], "L'Invitation au Voyage," *Punch*, Sept. 19, 1951, 338; Christopher Isherwood, "Migration to Mars," *Observer* (London), Sept. 16, 1951, 7. Other contemporary British reviews of *The Silver Locusts/The Martian Chronicles* include Angus Wilson, "Angus Wilson Writes [about] *The Martian Chronicles*," *Science Fiction News* (U.K.), May–June 1953; and [J. B. Priestly], "They Came from Inner Space," *New Statesman and Nation* (U.K.), Dec. 5, 1953, 712.

21. Hart-Davis offered to send page proofs to Bradbury for correction, but the two men decided to go with the British copyediting, which was closely supervised by Hart-Davis himself. Hart-Davis to Bradbury, Nov. 21, 1950, Feb. 18, 1952, personal papers.

22. Hart-Davis to Bradbury, Nov. 23, 1951, Feb. 18, 1952, personal papers; R. Bradbury to Walter Bradbury, July 30, 1950, Lilly.

23. Of the stories pulled from the Doubleday edition, Bradbury has said: "They didn't go into the book, but with one of them, I realize now, it was a mistake. In the English edition, I've put back a story called 'Fire Balloons.'" Bradbury interview (Cunningham), 197.

24. Bradbury's original letter to Boucher has not been located, but is quoted back in Boucher to Bradbury, Nov. 8, 1957, Carbon, Lilly. An excellent account of Bantam under Ian Ballantine is found in Davis, *Two-Bit Culture*, 101–9. Bradbury's negotiations with Bantam for *MC* is detailed in correspondence with Walter Bradbury; see R. Bradbury to W. Bradbury, July 22, 1950, Lilly; and W. Bradbury to R. Bradbury, July 25, 1950. personal papers.

25. Bradbury to Anthony Boucher, Aug. 7, 1958, Lilly. In his letter announcing that Isherwood would review *MC*, Bradbury went on to say, "Now if we could only get one from Edmund Wilson or Fadiman." R. Bradbury to Walter Bradbury, July 22, 1950.

26. It was still available in hardback at this time as *The Silver Locusts* in England, but Rupert Hart-Davis saw little chance to capitalize on *Sputnik*, which generated far less competitive interest in the British Isles. Hart-Davis to Bradbury, Nov. 28, 1957, personal papers.

27. R. Bradbury to W. Bradbury, Oct. 30, 1957, Lilly.

28. Boucher to Bradbury, Nov 8, 1957, personal papers; R. Bradbury to Walter Bradbury, Nov. 9, 1957, Lilly. "The Strawberry Window" would be collected in *MM* (1959) but never appeared in any edition of *MC*.

29. Bradbury to Boucher, Aug. 7, 1958.

30. An earlier U.S. SFBC edition appeared in 1952 and was reprinted (with a different dust jacket) in 1978. Both are identical to the Doubleday first American edition text and originate with the sixth printing (1952).

31. For Bradbury's account of his difficulties in publishing this story, see Bradbury interview (Congdon), 2.76.

32. Perhaps the best-known brief definition of the story cycle is found in Malcolm Cowley's introduction to the revised edition of *Winesburg, Ohio* (New York: Viking, 1960). Forrest L. Ingram, *Representative Short Story Cycles of the Twentieth Century* (The Hague: Mouton, 1971), provides a more comprehensive study of this genre. Bradbury himself uses Steinbeck to illustrate the underlying primacy of the story itself: "Think of *The Long Valley* and the *Pastures of Heaven*, and, in a way, *Tortilla Flat*—even though it's billed as a novel, it's really a series of short stories. You even think of *Grapes of Wrath*. Again, it's supposed to be a novel, but it is really a loose series of chronicles of a family moving west, and you can tell it's the work of a short story writer because of its construction." Bradbury interview (Cunningham), 183.

33. Roland Barthes, "Theory of the Text," in *Untying the Text*, ed. Robert Young (London: Routledge, 1981), 31–47,

34. See the several articles on this subject collected in *Ray Bradbury*, ed. Joseph D. Olander and Martin Harry Greenberg, Writers of the Twenty-First Century Series (New York: Taplinger, 1980); and the discussion in David Mogen, *Ray Bradbury*, Twayne U.S. Authors Series (Boston: G. K. Hall, 1986), 82–93. See also Mogen's reading of the Martian material in the context of the American frontier myth, in the same volume.

35. Northrop Frye, *Fables of Identity* (New York: Harcourt, Brace, and World, 1963), 54. We are following the poetics of the historical work according to Hayden White, *Metahistory: The Historical Imagination in Nineteenth Century Europe* (Baltimore: Johns Hopkins Univ. Press, 1973), 1–42.

36. We are indebted to Christopher Isherwood for some of the incidental phrasing of what follows in this discussion.

37. *MC*, 79. Related, unpublished pages on a more sinister Martian carnival are located in the Albright Collection.

38. "The Third Expedition" was originally published as "Mars Is Heaven!" (*Planet Stories* [Fall 1948]) and has been extensively reprinted (see app. A, 48–14). This is the one story by which Bradbury is recognized as a science fiction writer, and the original pulp version appears in the first volume of *The Science Fiction Hall of Fame* series as chosen by the Science Fiction Writers of America.

39. Bradbury to Touponce, Aug. 18, 1981.

40. *MC*, 66–67.

41. Friedrich Nietzsche, *Untimely Meditations*, trans. R. J. Hollingdale (Cambridge: Cambridge Univ. Press, 1983), 59–123. See also Hayden White's discussion of Nietzsche in *Metahistory*, 349–51.

42. Friedrich Nietzsche, *The Genealogy of Morals*, in *Basic Writings*, trans. Kaufmann, 503, 521.

43. See David Ketterer, *New Worlds for Old: The Apocalyptic Imagination, Science Fiction, and American Literature* (New York: Anchor, 1974), 33–34.

44. *MC*, 96.

45. Robert Crossley, in an introduction to Octavia Butler's science fiction novel *Kindred*, cites this story (which Butler encountered as a youthful reader of *MC*) as an exception to the patronizing liberal attitudes of the early postwar era. Crossley, introduction to *Kindred*, by Octavia Butler (Boston: Beacon, 1988), xv.

46. Bradbury has used the metaphor of the hammer before in describing how he used the science fiction genre in *MC*. Here he possibly was thinking of Nietzsche, whose subtitle to *Twilight of the Idols* was "How one philosophizes with a hammer." This phrase passed into the body of common knowledge about Nietzsche, but the hammer he had in mind was actually closer to a tuning fork. The notion was to sound the ideas of other philosophers and listen for the "hollow" tone they might give back.

47. *MC,* 107.

48. Bakhtin, *Dialogic Imagination,* 199–200.

49. Among Bradbury's unpublished fiction is an earlier version of "Usher II" called "The Castle," in which the house—not on Mars but on Earth, where censorship of the fantastic has prevailed—itself takes revenge on the main character, Beddoes, who has constructed it under the guise of a scientific experiment to test whether or not the supernatural still exists and can be lured into the open. This version evokes Poe's "The Masque of the Red Death" and "The Telltale Heart" to construct its version of the return of the repressed. The house eventually kills Beddoes and his laughing and mocking guests in ways described by Poe's stories. But Bradbury's piece hesitates between a rational and a supernatural explanation of the events that occur in the house (the mysterious beating of a heart not designed by its owner) and therefore constitutes the evanescent genre of the fantastic according to Tzvetan Todorov.

50. Throughout this study we have assumed a very close overlap of Nietzsche and Bakhtin in our terminology, but it is also important to note some of the main differences between them in terms of social classes. As Robert Stam points out, Bakhtin prefers to talk of carnival in terms of the lower classes and the "lower bodily stratum," whereas Nietzsche has an affection for "higher souls" and "finer sensibilities." Furthermore, Nietzsche associates Dionysianism with "high tragic" myth, while Bakhtin associates carnival with the "low" and "vulgar" comic genres, with wordplay and parody. Nietzsche felt an aversion to the masses that Bakhtin does not (he may even romanticize "the folk" in his writings): "Bakhtin does not share, in short, Nietzsche's thoroughgoing elitism. While Nietzsche praised a glorious state of solitude in which the philosophical soul renewed contact with the spirit of Nature, Bakhtin was more interested in the sentiment of community and *gemeinshaft* fostered by the promiscuous interminglings of carnival." Stam, *Subversive Pleasures,* 90.

At first glance the Bradbury of *MC* may seem to prefer the aristocratic in culture as represented by such figures as the artist, the nobleman, and the sovereign individual, but actually his general position on authorship is much more "democratic" in arguing that there are no "elites" in science fiction. "We Americans have been science-fiction writers from the beginning of our revolution. We came here and settled on an isolated 'planet'—the United States. Through this isolation we were able to experiment with a science fictional concept which is 'democracy': a thing which has not yet birthed itself completely, and never will! It's a continuing process, and its uprooting everything continually. It doesn't allow an elitist group to remain in charge too long. That's fine, because I hate elitist groups. I'm an elitist myself, but when the time comes for me to be shoved out of the way, I'll be shoved, and rightfully so. Maybe I will have gained too much power by then." Robert Jacobs, "The *Writer's Digest* Interview: Ray Bradbury," *Writer's Digest,* Feb. 1976, 20. Bradbury here presents his authorship as a continuing process of carnivalization in which he himself is willing to be decrowned.

51. Bakhtin, *Problems of Dostoevsky's Poetics,* 179; *MC,* 108.

52. The term "carnivalesque" refers here to a literary mode that subverts and liberates the assumptions of the traditional literary canon through "popular-festive" forms of ambivalent humor. Bakhtin likens the carnivalesque in literature to the types of activities and speech genres that occur in medieval and Renaissance carnivals, particularly the lampooning and overturning of traditional hierarchies and values, by mingling high or official culture with the profane. *Rabelais,* 217–18. Elsewhere, he demonstrates how forms like the novel provide a space for such carnivalization though the use of focal characters derived from "popular masks" such as the fool, the clown, and the rogue and, as a result, allow for alternative voices to he heard. See *Dialogic Imagination,* 36, 158–63.

53. "The Martian," *MC,* 129.

54. Jorge Luis Borges, *Selected Non-Fictions*, ed. Eliot Weinberger (New York: Viking, 1999), 419.

55. "There Will Come Soft Rains," *MC,* 167.

56. Ibid., 171.

57. Ibid.

58. "The Disease," carbon of submitted typescript, Oct. 8, 1949, 69 (Albright Collection).

59. Nolan, *Bradbury Companion,* 94.

60. Bradbury to Touponce, Aug. 18, 1981.

61. R. Bradbury to Walter Bradbury [c. Dec.10, 1949], personal papers.

62. "—And the Moon Be Still as Bright," *MC,* 54; "Payment in Full," *Thrilling Wonder Stories,* Feb. 1950, 137.

63. Wayne L. Johnson gives a brief account of most of them; see *Ray Bradbury,* 118–19.

64. "The Million-Year Picnic," *Planet Stories* (Summer 1946): 97.

65. "Mars Is Heaven!" *Planet Stories* (Fall 1948): 47.

66. Bradbury to Touponce, Aug. 18, 1981.

3. *Simulacrum of Carnival*

1. Ballantine to Bradbury, Apr. 7, 1954, personal papers.

2. For a similar use of carnival themes, images, and language by an earlier master, see Bakhtin, *Rabelais,* 269.

3. Robert Stam, a critic who has applied Bakhtin to popular culture, cautions that real-life carnivals can be politically ambivalent. He argues that one, therefore, always ought to ask who is carnivalizing whom, for what reasons, by which means, and in what circumstances. He distinguishes between carnivals whose function is to regenerate the status quo and those that hold out the promise of liberation from fear: "it is useful to distinguish between 'bottom up' carnival as communitarian festivity and adversary culture, on the one hand, and top-down 'ersatz' or 'degraded' carnivals, on the other." Stam's model for the latter is a Nazi rally, but the notion of false carnival could be applied to the McCarthy hearings (as done in our narrative). Montag's experiences among the book people would then be an example of the former, "true" carnival being rediscovered. This leaves open the notion of the mass media as a "simulacrum of carnival," which Stam goes on to argue should be understood in a dialogic and even progressive sense. Stam, *Subversive Pleasures,* 224–27.

Not everyone is persuaded, however, that the carnivalization of American culture that began in the 1950s can be understood in an unambiguously progressive sense. For a critique of carnivalization, see James B. Twitchell, *Carnival Culture: The Trashing of Taste in America* (New York: Columbia Univ. Press, 1992). Twitchell discusses the difficulties of Ian Ballantine, one of the cultural "gatekeepers" in Bradbury's career, who was fired from American Penguin because of his use of "vulgar" book covers that did not suggest the "literary" qualities Penguin wanted to maintain. Ibid., 89–90. In his own publishing ventures, Ballantine had to struggle with a market dominated by magazines in order to make his paperbacks sell; at that time Americans primarily read magazines. This cultural situation is reflected in part 2 of *F451* where Captain Beatty tells Montag about how books finally lost the battle against mass-market periodicals: "Today, thanks to them [technology, mass exploitation, and minority pressure], you can stay happy all of the time, you are allowed to read comics, the good old confessions, or trade journals." It is important to remember that not all forms of reading are banned in this dystopian society, only literary reading (see note 26 below). Bradbury's feelings about the rise of mass media in the 1950s is probably closer to Twitchell's feelings about the rise of vulgarity (or the decline of any real sense of taste) than Stam's notion of mass media as a progressive force. Bradbury argues, however, that the mass media *could* be presenting "texture" but are not, for political reasons—support of the status quo (we must all be the same is Captain Beatty's constant admonition to Montag). For further discussion of *F451* in the political context of paperback publishing during the McCarthy era, see Davis, *Two-Bit Culture*, 169.

4. For a survey of this line of development through the earlier stories (missing only "Pillar of Fire"), see Bradbury, introduction to *F451*, 40th anniv. ed. (New York: Simon and Schuster, 1993). He also describes the real-life pedestrian encounter with police that triggered first "The Pedestrian" and then "The Fireman"; a more recent (2001) version of this story is preserved as *RayBradbury.com* http://www.raybradbury.com/at_home_clips.html. The actual incident occurred at Wilshire Boulevard and Western Avenue in 1949 (Bradbury, interview by Jonathan Eller, Oct. 12, 1998). An earlier run-in with police over an after-midnight walk through Pershing Square in 1941 included his friend and early collaborator, Henry Hasse (Bradbury to Hasse [Dec. 1942], Albright Collection). His public concern with the plight of the pedestrian actually goes back to his high school days; Donn Albright has confirmed this uncredited editorial as Bradbury's: "Pedestrian becomes Freak among Modern Inventions," *(Los Angeles High School) Blue and White Daily*, Feb. 22, 1938.

5. Bradbury, introduction to *F451* (1953; reprint, New York: Simon and Schuster, 1967), 12–13; Willis E. McNelly, "Ray Bradbury: Past, Present, and Future," *CEA Critic*, Mar. 1969 (rewritten for *Voices for the Future*, vol. 1, ed. Thomas D. Clareson [Bowling Green, Ohio: Bowling Green State Univ. Popular Press, 1976], 167–74; and reprinted as "Two Views, Part I," in *Ray Bradbury*, ed. Joseph D. Olander and Martin Harry Greenberg [New York: Taplinger, 1980]).

6. Manuscript submission dates for Bradbury's first two Doubleday books are confirmed by R. Bradbury to Walter Bradbury, Oct. 10, 1949, Aug. 19, 1950, Lilly. Bradbury drafted "The Pedestrian" late in the winter of 1950 and submitted it to Congdon during March; Congdon notes his first reading of the manuscript in Congdon to Bradbury, Mar. 31, 1950, personal papers. For the sale of "The Fireman" to *Galaxy*, see Congdon to Bradbury, Nov. 7, 1950, personal papers.

7. For Gold's general policies, see "Yardstick for Science Fiction," *Galaxy* (Feb. 1951). This editorial opened the issue that also included "The Fireman." The contractual and editorial details surrounding publication of the novella are found in Gold to Bradbury, Oct. 30, [c. Nov.], and Dec. 21, 1950; and Congdon to Bradbury, Nov. 7, 17, 1950, personal papers.

8. The adaptations were *It Came from Outer Space* (Universal, 1953), based on (but not shot from) Bradbury's several unpublished screen treatments and scripts, and *The Beast from 20,000 Fathoms* (Warner Brothers, 1953), loosely based on Bradbury's story of that title (often reprinted and collected as "The Fog Horn").

9. Congdon to Bradbury, Aug. 22, 1952, personal papers.

10. The first collection, *Star Science Fiction Stories* (1953), actually included "A Scent of Sarsaparilla." Eventually, Pohl would contract an "unchronicled" Martian tale, "The Strawberry Window," for *Star Science Fiction Stories 3* (1954).

11. Congdon to Bradbury, Aug. 22, 1952.

12. Congdon to Bradbury, Dec. 19, 1952, Jan. 7, 1953, personal papers.

13. Congdon to Bradbury, Feb. 10, 16, 1953, Feb. 1, 1952, personal papers.

14. Congdon to Bradbury, Sept. 17, Dec. 19, 1952.

15. Ballantine to Bradbury, Mar. 19, Apr. 3, 1953, personal papers.

16. Bradbury, introduction to *F451* (1967), 13. Bradbury confirms his return to the UCLA library in his "Burning Bright," foreword to *F451*, 40th anniv. ed. (Simon and Schuster, 1993).

17. Congdon to Bradbury, July 24, 29, 1953, personal papers.

18. Congdon to Bradbury, July 24, 1953.

19. The three quotes are "No one is such a liar as an indignant man" (*Beyond Good and Evil*, 2:26); "History is nothing more than the belief in the senses, the belief in falsehood" ("Reason," in Philosophy, *Twilight of the Idols*, 1); and "After coming into contact with a religious man, I always feel I must wash my hands" *(Ecce Homo)*. All three represent various attacks on other thinkers that in the process justify Nietzsche's own position. Given the personal nature of these attacks, they would have provided evidence for Captain Beatty's assertion that philosophy is just a matter of "one philosopher shouting down another's gullet."

20. John Huntington, "Utopian and Anti-Utopian Logic: H. G. Wells and his Successors," *Science-Fiction Studies* 27, pt. 2 (July 1982): 122–46. Huntington does not consider the text of "The Fireman" or the role that contradictions might play in stimulating reader interaction with the text. See Touponce, *Bradbury and the Poetics of Reverie*, chap. 6.

21. "The Fireman," *Galaxy*, Aug. 1951, 56.

22. Ibid., 55.

23. Nietzsche did not live long enough to see the global simulacrum of carnival produced by the mass media, but most probably he would have seen it too as an opponent of the meaning of the earth, as Bradbury does. Just how Nietzsche proposed that meaning is to be won back from those who disparage the life of this world with "afterwordly" dreams is a matter of debate among scholars. It encompasses more, however, than just respect for nature and our place in it (which technology and modern science have caused us to forget), though that is certainly part of it. In the last meaning given to life by Zarathustra, it is the table on which the gods play dice, the object of their creative new words. For Nietzsche, the meaning of the earth had a poetic and creative function as the source of new values. Bradbury explores these new values with his earthly reveries.

24. For Bradbury's recollection of these events, see "Burning Bright," 19–20.

25. George Guffey, "*Fahrenheit 451* and the 'Cubby-Hole' Editors of Ballantine Books," in *Coordinates: Placing Science Fiction and Fantasy*, ed. George E. Slusser, et al. (Carbondale: Southern Illinois Univ. Press, 1983), 101, 103. Guffey's findings are retold in Noel Perrin, *Dr. Bowdler's Legacy: A History of Unexpurgated Books in England and America*, 2d ed. (Boston: Godine, 1992), 268–70.

26. Theodor W. Adorno and Max Horkheimer, "The Culture Industry: Enlightenment as Mass Deception," in *Dialectic of Enlightenment*, trans. John Cumming (New York: Seabury, 1972), 120–67. Adorno and Horkheimer are concerned in their analyses with the notion of domination, which not only affects society but also extends to nature. They argue that this was one of the results of the Enlightenment and has become nearly total in our modern technological civilization. According to them, Nietzsche saw both aspects of the Enlightenment, "both the universal movement of sovereign Spirit (whose executor he felt himself to be), and a 'nihilistic' anti-life force in the enlightenment." Ibid., 44. We are indebted to their discussions in our understanding of Bradbury's development of these ideas. They too link the culture industry to a simulacrum of carnival (ibid., 143) and see laugher as perverted by it: "In the false society laughter is a disease which has attacked happiness and is drawing it into its worthless totality." Ibid., 141. They help us understand how Bradbury can be at the same time critical of myths created by modern mass culture and a writer of myths himself. His myths in *F451*, such as the myth of the wilderness and the myth of Antaeus, are not about domination and exploitation, but about the need to rediscover the meaning of the earth, which lies outside of any notion of progress.

27. *F451*, pt. 1, 41.

28. Ibid, 62.

29. See Nietzsche, "Zarathustra's Prologue," *Thus Spoke Zarathustra,* in *Portable Nietzsche,* 129–30.

30. The various stages of nihilism are presented in Nietzsche, *Will to Power,* bk. 1, 7–82. They are schematized by Michel Haar, "Nietzsche and Metaphysical Language," in *The New Nietzsche: Contemporary Styles of Interpretation,* ed. David B. Allison (New York: Delta, 1977), 12–16. Our discussion here is indebted to Haar's schematization, but Nietzsche too describes nihilism as a psychological state of exhaustion in which the soul, which longs to admire and revere, finds itself wallowing in "the idea of some supreme from of domination and administration." Nietzsche, *Will to Power,* bk. 1, 12. This, in part, explains Beatty's worshipful attitude toward fire, in which he rejects what science reveals about it—he knows full well that science and reason cannot create values. Of course, his fascination with fire does not create life-affirming values for him but rather destroys them.

31. *F451,* pt. 2, 76–77.

32. "Enlightened by Hobbes and Locke to the fear of death as the fundamental fear, Zarathustra's audience [the last man] is in the process of surrendering all aspiration except for comfortable self preservation." Lampert, *Nietzsche's Teaching,* 25. Lampert's discussion of the figure of the last man in Nietzsche's text has guided our own discussion here. He points out that the last men are those "of technological mastery" among whom uniformity and sameness have prevailed. But although the last men have won out in the struggle against the forces of inequality and scarcity in nature, their happiness is fragile, for it requires recognition and reassurance from others like themselves. Most devastating is the global effect of their reign, for the universal domination of the last men prevents the Earth from having any meaning. We have taken Beatty to be one of the last men, a representative of that final and most dangerous form of nihilism (per Lampert) brought about, in Nietzsche's view, by universal claims of the democratic enlightenment that abolishes all differences or diverts them into the madhouse (what the authorities intend to do with people like Clarisse, whose name ironically means light and illumination). Beatty celebrates the pleasures of the last man, which Nietzsche mocked as "wretched contentment," and derides any attempt to pursue higher spiritual values as doomed to failure from the outset.

33. Nietzsche to Carl Fuchs, Aug. 26, 1888, as quoted in Michael Haar, "Nietzsche and Metaphysical Language," in *The New Nietzsche,* ed. David B. Allison (New York: Dell, 1977), 7.

34. Gaston Bachelard, *L'Air et les songes* (Paris: Corti, 1943), 146–85. Bachelard, in fact, wrote two studies of reveries of the earth, which serves to indicate the importance of this element to the poetic imagination. The forge, which Montag discovers in the third part of the book, is discussed by Bachelard as one of the reveries of the will. In his other book Bachelard studies the earth in relation to reveries of rest and repose, which also can be found in this section of the book when Montag enters the hay barn. Selections from his writings about literary reveries of the material imagination can be found in *On Poetic Imagination and Reverie,* trans. with an introduction by Colette Gaudin (New York: Bobbs-Merrill, 1971). These studies broaden and deepen our understanding of the meaning of the Earth in *Fahrenheit 451.*

35. Donald Watt, "Burning Bright: *Fahrenheit 451* as Symbolic Dystopia," in Olander and Greenberg, *Ray Bradbury,* 195–213.

36. Gilbert Durand, "Psychanalyse de la neige," *Mercure de France* 1, no. 8 (1953): 615–39.

37. *F451,* pt. 2, 83.

38. See "On Redemption," pt. 2 of *Thus Spoke Zarathustra,* in *Portable Nietzsche.* For willing backward, see "On Immaculate Perception," in ibid.

39. *F451,* pt. 3, 141.

40. Ibid., pt. 3, 162.

41. See Nietzsche, "On the Afterworldly," pt. 1 of *Thus Spoke Zarathustra*, in *Portable Nietzsche*.

42. Nietzsche, "On the Higher Man," pt. 4 ibid.

43. Bakhtin, *Rabelais*, 249.

4. The Carnival Blaze of Summer

1. Bradbury, headnote to "The Night," *Starwind* (Spring 1976): [31]; notes from *The Small Assassins*, [1] (Albright Collection).

2. Notes from *The Small Assassins*, [2] (Albright Collection).

3. Bradbury's notes for *The Small Assassins* end with these observations: "CHAPTER FIFTEEN: TIMELESS SPRING . . . how to grow up? fall in love. SIXTEEN: HOW TO GROW OLDER, ANCIENT? Why, have children, of course. Love solves both problems for both sides, for the old man getting ancient, and for the young boy growing older." Ibid, [3].

4. Bradbury to August Derleth, May 12, 1946, Madison, notes Bradbury's work on a full draft of the novel.

5. ["The Three Streets"], c. Feb. 1951, typescript, [1–2], Albright Collection. These four unnumbered pages include variant paragraphs.

6. Ibid, [3].

7. W. Bradbury to R. Bradbury, July 12, 1951, Mar. 10, 17, 1952, personal papers; Congdon to R. Bradbury, June 4, 1952, personal papers. For a discussion of the early circulation of the novel, see Bradbury interview (Congdon), 2.56–57.

8. R. Bradbury to W. Bradbury, June 10, 1952, Lilly.

9. Bradbury's relationship as an editor for Bantam anthologies during this period is discussed in chapter 5.

10. Walter Bradbury alludes to at least thirty-three chapters in the manuscript that had evolved since the 1951 submission. Memorandum by W. Bradbury, June 3, 1954, personal papers.

11. W. Bradbury to R. Bradbury, June 25, 1954, personal papers.

12. The *Summer Morning, Summer Night* outline survives within the two boxes of draft discards in the Albright Collection. The boxes are labeled in sequence as containing pre- and post-1951 materials, but in reality the contents are mixed across the entire 1946–1955 period. There are 167 pages in box 1 and 293 in box 2. The boxes' contents range from complete draft chapters to fragments and working outlines. The following quotes describing the chapters of this unpublished work come from Bradbury's descriptive outline.

13. Dannay to Bradbury, Aug. 26, 1952, personal papers; Congdon to Bradbury, Aug. 6, Sept. 9 (postscript), Nov. 28, Dec. 4, 1952, personal papers.

14. Bradbury to the Writers Guild of America (West), Mary Dorfman, Credit Arbitration Secretary, June 1, 1955, carbon copy, personal papers; Dorfman to Bradbury, June 1, 1955, personal papers. These letters contain the initial favorable ruling. Bradbury's unaddressed carbon of his three-page rebuttal to the arbitration reversal is dated November 16, 1955 (personal papers).

15. This picture book received an unusual amount of review space in major venues, including the *New York Herald Tribune*, the *New York Times*, the *Saturday Review of Literature*, *Commonweal*, and *Kirkus*.

16. The details of the Bradbury-Laughton-Gregory collaboration are recorded in Gregory to Congdon, May 4, 1955, Butler; Congdon to Bradbury, May 26, June 28, Aug. 17, 29, Sept.

12, 14, 1955, Jan. 12, 1956, personal papers. The record of Bradbury's television and radio work during this period is documented in the unpublished bibliography by Jim Welsh and Don Albright, "October's Friend."

17. Congdon to Bradbury, Sept. 9, 1952.

18. R. Bradbury to W. Bradbury, Jan. 27, 1955, Lilly.

19. R. Bradbury to W. Bradbury, Aug. 28, 1955, Lilly.

20. W. Bradbury to R. Bradbury, Feb. 9, 1955, personal papers.

21. On December 15, 1955, Walt Bradbury followed up on a suggestion made during his late-November trip out to Los Angeles: "I hope you are giving continued thought to the suggestion I made that we do a 'mark-time' book using some of the Illinois stories that can be spared from the plot of the novel, as a kind of an 'introduction' to the novel which will come later. I think we could do this without the necessity of your spending more time on it, and thus ease up the pressure to get the novel done." Follow-up letters document the author's enthusiasm as well as the development of the *Dandelion Wine* title. W. Bradbury to R. Bradbury, Dec. 15, 22, 1955, Feb. 3, 1956, personal papers.

22. W. Bradbury to R. Bradbury, Apr. 18, 1956, personal papers.

23. R. Bradbury to W. Bradbury, Aug. 14, 1956, Lilly. The Albright Collection contains all the *Dandelion Wine* publishing materials, which are annotated by Bradbury as returned to him in early February 1958. These include the 356-page (originally 347-page) submitted typescript with the first January 1957 revision of "The Happiness Machine" tipped in to replace the original section, Bradbury's corrected and revised galleys, and his set of page proofs.

24. R. Bradbury to W. Bradbury, Aug. 28, 1955, Lilly.

25. W. Bradbury to R. Bradbury, Dec. 4, 1956, personal papers.

26. R. Bradbury to W. Bradbury, Aug. 14, 1956, Lilly.

27. Details of these and subsequent revisions are documented in W. Bradbury to R. Bradbury, Jan. 11, 24, Feb. 8, 26, 1957, personal papers; and R. Bradbury to W. Bradbury, Feb. 27, 1957, Lilly. The latter covered the transmittal of the corrected proof back to Doubleday.

28. R. Bradbury to W. Bradbury, Aug. 14, 1956, Lilly.

29. Doubleday (Betty Shapian) to Bradbury, Mar. 26, 1957, personal papers. The discussion on reactions to proof copy at home and abroad is found in W. Bradbury to R. Bradbury, Apr. 17, 1957, personal papers; and Don Congdon to Bradbury, Apr. 30, 1957, personal papers.

30. Congdon to Bradbury, Apr. 30, 1957, personal papers.

31. Details of the *Post* situation are found in Congdon to Bradbury, Apr. 30, May 15, June 12, 1957, personal papers.

32. *Kirkus 25* (Aug. 1957): 314.

33. *Saturday Review of Literature*, Sept. 7, 1957, 18.

34. Mary Ross, review of *DW*, *Herald Tribune Book Review*, Sept. 8, 1957, 4.

35. V. P. Hass, review of *DW*, *Chicago Tribune*, Sept. 8, 1957, 1; Marc Rivette, review of *DW*, *San Francisco Chronicle*, Nov. 10, 1957, 25; Bradley to Bradbury, May 24, 1958, personal papers.

36. Anon., review of *DW*, *Times* (London) *Literary Supplement*, Nov. 8, 1957, 669; Hart-Davis to Bradbury, Nov. 19, 1957, personal papers.

37. The sales figures, and Doubleday's paperback negotiations with Bantam, are described in W. Bradbury to Congdon, Nov. 1, 1957, Butler; and W. Bradbury to R. Bradbury Dec. 2, 1957, personal papers. The advertising campaign is discussed in W. Bradbury to Congdon, Nov. 1, 1957 (in response to a missing Congdon letter dated Oct. 21, 1957). Congdon's reaction is summarized in Congdon to R. Bradbury, Nov. 6, 1957, personal papers.

38. Congdon to Bradbury, Mar. 8, May 3, 1957, personal papers. The agent made his recommendation in the March 8 letter.

39. Bradbury, introduction to *DW* (New York: Knopf, 1975), ix–x.

40. *DW*, 9–10.

41. This consciousness astonished at the presence of the world, which appears fantastic, not only is central to our understanding of the thematics of *Dandelion Wine* but also finds expression elsewhere in Bradbury's writings. For instance, in his introduction to his own collection of fantastic fiction, *Timeless Stories for Today and Tomorrow* (1951), Bradbury writes that "Life itself is more than fantastic." Although he admits here that life can indeed be terrible (one of the stories collected is Kafka's "The Penal Colony"), Bradbury opines that most people, if given the chance, would cling to their dirty and mired existence with a ferocity bordering on madness. This intense awareness of life—enunciated by Douglas's "I'm alive"—represents for Bradbury a sense of the mystery of existence that he finds at the heart of all true fantasy.

42. *DW*, 64–67.

43. Gilles Deleuze and Felix Guattari, *Anti-Oedipus, Capitalism, and Schizophrenia*, trans. Robert Hurley, Mark Seem, and Helen R. Lane (New York: Viking, 1977), 47. Deleuze and Guattari use the concept of the desiring machine (based on the notion of part objects in Melanie Klein) to explode the notion of the unconscious as a theater of representations. A desiring machine does not represent but connects organs to part objects (the baby's mouth to the breast) in relations of desiring production: "Ray Bradbury demonstrates this very well when he describes the nursery [in "The Veldt," *IM*]as a place where desiring-production and group fantasy occur, as a place where the only connection is that between partial objects and agents."

44. Bakhtin, *Rabelais*, 394.

45. Nietzsche, *Birth of Tragedy*, sec. 10 in *Basic Writings*.

46. There are only two episodes in the novel in which characters are represented as wearing masks. One centers on seventy-two-year-old Mrs. Helen Bently, whom the children see as wearing a "yellow mask face" that indicates to them that she has never been young. The other concerns the romance of young William Forrester, the town reporter, and ninety-five-year-old Miss Helen Loomis. As the oldest old maid of the novel, Loomis remarks to him that until the age of thirty, she was "a crazy creature with a headful of carnival spangles" and that any wisdom she may seem to have now is just "an act and a mask." In one episode the character becomes identified with her mask and admits to never having been young. In the other the mask is unmasked.

47. *DW*, 239.

48. Nietzsche, *Birth of Tragedy*, sec. 9 in *Basic Writings*.

49. This psychoanalytic/symbolic term for the erect male member does not, in fact, appear in Bradbury's text, though its semiotic function as the "signifier of desire" is clearly indicated. See J. Laplanche and J.-B. Pontalis, *The Language of Psychoanalysis*, trans. Donald Nicholson-Smith (New York: W. W. Norton, 1973), 312–14. To say that the story is "phallocentric," however, would be to overstate things because the phallus presents itself to Douglas in fairly carnivalized (i.e., ambivalent) terms.

50. *Farewell Summer*, 44.

51. *Farewell Summer*, 165–66.

52. *Farewell Summer*, 178–79.

5. Fathering the Carnival

1. Stephen King, *Danse Macabre* (New York: Berkley, 1983), 324. "But I believe that *Something Wicked This Way Comes*, a darkly poetic tall tale set in the half-real, half-mythical community of Green Town, Illinois, is probably Bradbury's best work—a shadowy descendant

from that tradition that has brought us stories about Paul Bunyan and his blue ox, Babe, Pecos Bill, and Davy Crockett."

2. Darrell Schweitzer, "Ray Bradbury's Horror Fiction," in *Fantasy Review* 10, no. 2 (1987): 18, 16; William F. Nolan, interview by Jonathan R. Eller, Los Angeles, Mar. 13, 2002; Clive Barker, afterword to *Dark Carnival*, by Ray Bradbury (Springfield, Penn.: Gauntlet, 2001); King, *Danse Macabre*, 326. The California Group is listed by Schweitzer and described in detail in Christopher Conlon, "California Sorcerers," introduction to *California Sorcery*, ed. William F. Nolan and William Schafer (New York: Ace, 2001). Nolan attributes the group's name to critic Robert Kirsch; see "Remembering 'The Group,'" preface to *California Sorcery*.

3. Bradbury to Derleth, Mar. 8, 1945, Madison; a variant draft also survives in Bradbury's personal papers.

4. Bradbury also left a blurred area in the jacket's center to suggest the motion of the carousel. He would later recall this strategy in a letter to his film and television agent, Ben Benjamin, written in late 1960.

5. This folder of materials, containing thirty-one pages of text and a title page indicating that Don Congdon read the selections while at Simon and Schuster, has been published as bonus material in a special collector's print run of Gauntlet's 2001 limited-edition *DC*.

6. *Outré*'s 1997 reprint of "The Black Ferris" includes an excellent introduction by William F. Nolan that summarizes the history of this story and its germinal relationship to *SW*.

7. Bradbury to Ben Benjamin, n.d. [Dec. 1960], carbon copy, personal papers. The original oil painting is included in Jerry Weist's tribute to Bradbury's book, magazine, and comic illustrators; see *Ray Bradbury: An Illustrated Life* (New York: William Morrow, 2002), 76.

8. Bradbury related portions of these events as they were unfolding in a letter to his Doubleday editor, Walter Bradbury; R. Bradbury to W. Bradbury, Jan. 27, 1955, Lilly. A more retrospective summary is contained in Bradbury to Benjamin, n.d. [Dec. 1960].

9. The following account of the Bradbury-Kelly relationship and the screen treatment that resulted is derived from Bradbury, interviews by Jonathan R. Eller, Los Angeles, Mar. 11–12, 14, 2002; and Gene Kelly to Bradbury, telegrams, Aug. 8 and 10, 1955, personal papers; a draft of Bradbury's response to the August 8 telegram also survives in his personal papers. King's *Danse Macabre* includes an account of these events from an undocumented letter by Bradbury, but the excerpt misstates the year as 1958. Both the 1998 Avon paperback and the 1999 Avon hardbound editions of *SW* contain afterwords by Bradbury that recount variations of these events.

10. Walt Disney to Bradbury, Dec. 2, 1955; Bernard Smith (Hecht-Hill-Lancaster) to Bradbury, May 20, 1957; David Brown (Twentieth Century Fox) to Bradbury, Aug. 11, 1958; and John Montgomery (Peters Agency) to Bradbury, Aug. 6, Dec. 12, 1958, personal papers. A number of letters to Bradbury during 1957 relate to the Reed-Bradbury collaboration; reasons for the collapse of this project are best summarized in Bradbury to August Derleth, July 8, 1958, Madison. The filming of Nevil Shute's novel *On the Beach* (1958), which focuses on themes central to "And the Rock Cried Out," also worked against the Bradbury–Reed venture. Bradbury to Congdon, Sept. 27, 1960 (Butler).

11. The initial teleplay, "The Bullet Trick," was turned down by the producers of both the *GE* and *Star Stage Shows*. Revue Productions to Bradbury, Dec. 28, 1955, personal papers. Bradbury's fascination with the bullet trick dates from his reading about Ching Ling Soo, the Oriental magician killed while performing the trick in 1910.

12. The dates of all four major drafts, as well as the surviving preliminary draft runs and discard sheets of the first draft, are dated from Bradbury's notes on the boxes containing these drafts of the novel. All four drafts are in the Albright Collection.

13. Congdon to Walter Bradbury (copy to Ray Bradbury), May 15, 1958, Congdon to R. Bradbury, May 28, 1958, personal papers.

14. Congdon to Bradbury, Apr. 15, Oct. 22, 1959, personal papers.

15. Bradbury to Congdon, Apr. 4, 1960, Butler. Bradbury wrote a five-page discussion of concerns in a letter intended for Seldes, Sept. 29, 1959. Instead, he forwarded it to Congdon, who persuaded Bradbury to withhold it (Butler). Congdon's three-page letter of October 22, 1959, contains a detailed rationale for postponing a confrontation with Doubleday. The publisher's parallel view regarding reprints with the release of a new book is reported in Congdon to Bradbury, Nov. 6, 1959, personal papers.

16. The break with Doubleday is documented in the follow sequence of letters: Congdon to Bradbury, May 23, 1960, personal papers; Bradbury to Seldes, June 2, 1960, Lilly; Seldes to Bradbury, June 7, 24, 1960, personal papers; Seldes to Congdon (copy to Bradbury), July 1, 1960, personal papers; Bradbury to Seldes, July 8, 1960, Lilly (asking for release); and Congdon to Seldes, July 13, 1960, Lilly (transmitting Bradbury's release request). Five letters finalize the release: Congdon to Bradbury, July 21, 1960, personal papers; Seldes to Bradbury, July 27, 1960, personal papers; Congdon to Bradbury, July 28, 1960, personal papers; Bradbury to Congdon, July 29, 1960, Butler; and Seldes to Bradbury, Sept. 26, 1960, personal papers (correcting the terms of the release).

17. Bradbury to Congdon, July 12, 24, 1960 (Butler); Congdon to Bradbury, July 28, Sept. 8, 13, 16, 1960, personal papers.

18. Gottlieb to Congdon, Sept. 9, 1960, Butler.

19. The discussions with Goldwyn are described in a detailed five-page letter, Congdon to Bradbury, Nov. 23, 1960, personal papers. Bradbury's position is summarized in a letter to his film agent, Bradbury to Ben Benjamin, n.d. [Dec. 1960], copy in personal papers.

20. Bradbury to Congdon, Apr. 4, 1960, Butler.

21. Bradbury's most detailed account of his encounter with Mr. Electrico and the Dill Brothers Show is in "Mr. Electrico," *Guideposts Magazine* (1991), rpt. *Wonder: The Children's Magazine for Grown-Ups,* 8 (Spring 1994): 8–9.

22. Congdon's three-page typed review of the second submission is dated Aug. 24, 1960. He returned the first two submissions so that Bradbury could make revisions with a cover letter dated June 6, 1961.

23. Compared texts from first draft discards (Albright Collection) and *SW* (New York: Bantam, 1963), 168–69, reset without variation from the first edition (1962).

24. Bradbury to Gottlieb, Nov. 28, 1961, copy, personal papers. The subsequent delays in submission and scheduled release are discussed in Gottlieb to Bradbury, Nov. 30, 1961, Jan. 3, Feb. 8, 28, 1962, personal papers; Congdon to Bradbury, Feb. 6, 1962, personal papers; and Bradbury to Gottlieb (copies), Feb. 17, Mar. 6, 1962. Further details of the final revision process are annotated on the box containing the final submission.

25. Editor-author discussions about postsubmission revisions, design issues, and promotion of the novel are found in Gottlieb to Bradbury, Mar. 8, 23, Apr. 24, May 14, June 12, July 5, 13, 1962, personal papers; Bradbury to Gottlieb (copy), Apr. 21, 1962, personal papers.

26. Gilbert Highet to Bradbury, June 13, 1962, personal papers; *Life* (Graves) to Congdon, Feb. 9, 1961, Butler.

27. Responses to the second set of excerpts include Congdon (by Rina Shulman) to Bradbury (re: *Good Housekeeping*), Nov. 23, 1960, personal papers; *Harper's* (Joyce Bermel) to Congdon, Oct. 19, 1961, Butler; *Saturday Evening Post* (Stuart Rose) to Congdon, Apr. 16, July 9, 1962, Butler; and *Life* (Ralph Graves) to Bradbury, Sept. 25, 1962, personal papers. For Simon and Schuster's advertising campaign for Heller's novel, see Jonathan Eller, "Catching a Market: The Publishing History of *Catch-22*," *Prospects* 17 (1992).

28. For correspondence regarding promotion and advertising, see Bradbury to Gottlieb (copy), July 16, 1962, personal papers; Gottlieb to Bradbury, July 20, Aug. 21, Sept. 11, 17, 1962, personal papers; and Congdon to Bradbury, Sept. 11, 1962, personal papers.

29. Orville Prescott, "Books of the Times," *New York Times*, Sept. 19, 1962, 37. Prescott mistakenly assumed that Bradbury had written Dinelli's "Merry-Go-Round" teleplay, which predisposed him to think of the novel in terms of that uneven production. Bradbury sent Prescott a tactful correction and a copy of *The Martian Chronicles*. See Prescott to Bradbury, Sept. 26, 1962, personal papers.

30. Beaumont to Bradbury, Oct. 3, 1962, personal papers; Nolan to Bradbury, July 6, 1962, personal papers.

31. H. H. Holmes [Anthony Boucher], review of *SW*, *New York Herald Tribune Books*, Sept. 16, 1962, 3; Baldwin to Bradbury, Oct. 30, 1962, personal papers.

32. An untitled review in the "Briefly Noted" section of "Books," *The New Yorker*, Oct. 27, 1962, 216.

33. The details of the negotiation are contained in Gottlieb to Bradbury, Sept. 11, 1962; and Congdon to Bradbury, Sept. 11, 1962.

34. The plagiarized adaptation of *Fahrenheit* is discussed in Bradbury to Congdon, Oct. 14, 1957, May 30, June 25, July 18, 1959 (Butler). Gottlieb's letter of transmittal for the unlocated Finney letter is dated Oct. 30, 1962 (personal papers). For Bradbury's detailed response summarizing how the *Fahrenheit*-CBS case helped define the guidelines for film and television adaptations of literature, see Bradbury to Gottlieb (copy), Oct. 31, 1962, personal papers.

35. Bloch to Bradbury, n.d. [Spring/Summer 1947], personal papers. The letters concerning the long-delayed *Dr. Lao* anthology are Saul David to Bradbury, Mar. 27, June 8, 1953, June 29, Sept. 1, 28, 1954, Dec. 13, 1955, Jan. 17, 1956, personal papers. David was clearly not aware that Bradbury's parallel work on "The Dark Carnival" screenplay was keeping him from reading *Dr. Lao*. Bradbury's criticisms of *Dr. Lao* in the anthology introduction are discussed in David to Bradbury, Jan. 17, Feb. 9, 1956, personal papers.

36. Finney's letter to Simon and Schuster has not been located, but his frustration with Bradbury's success may have originated with the lukewarm introduction and Bantam's cover design for the 1956 anthology, which fails to link Finney's name to the title story at all.

37. Bradbury to Gottlieb (copy), Oct. 31, 1962.

38. Harold Bloom writes: "Personality, in our sense, is a Shakespearean invention, and it is not only Shakespeare's greatest originality but also the authentic cause of his perpetual pervasiveness. Insofar as we ourselves value, and deplore, our own personalities, we are the heirs of Falstaff and of Hamlet, and all the other persons who throng Shakespeare's theater of what might be called the colors of the spirit." Harold Bloom, *Shakespeare: The Invention of the Human* (New York: Riverhead, 1998), 4. Bloom also asserts of Shakespeare's characters that they were the first in literature who overhear themselves speaking, interpret what they have said, and so garner the power to change. These dialogic aspects of character are exhibited prominently by Charles Halloway in the book's central interpretive chapters, which, incidentally, Bradbury claims are his favorite chapters.

39. The three-way negotiations between Bradbury-Congdon, the London-based A. D. Peters Agency, and Rupert Hart-Davis appear in Hart-Davis to Bradbury, Apr. 24, May 22, June 5, 1962, personal papers; Bradbury to Hart-Davis, May 27, 1962, copy, personal papers; Margaret Stephens (of Peters) to Congdon, Apr. 25, Sept. 7, 1962, Butler; A. D. Peters to Congdon, May 25, June 20, 1962, Butler; Congdon to Stephens, May 9, June 19, 1962, copies, personal papers; and Congdon to Bradbury, May 4, 1962, personal papers.

40. Bradbury to Hart-Davis, May 27, 1962.

41. A last-minute misunderstanding over the advance delayed the contract signing until

September 1962. Both Peters and Hart-Davis felt that Bradbury's May 27 assertion that promotion meant more than money upfront superseded Congdon's request for the advance increase to £500. Bradbury and Congdon pursued the higher amount as a pledge of better promotion. Since Margaret Stephens of Peters had already negotiated a paperback deal on the novel with Corgi for Hart-Davis, the publisher agreed to increase the advance. Congdon to Stephens (copies), Aug. 17, 23, 1962, Butler; Stephens to Congdon (copy), Aug. 21, 1962, personal papers; Congdon to Bradbury, Aug. 22, 1962, personal papers; Bradbury to Congdon (copy), Aug. 26, 1962, personal papers.

42. The British *Argosy* publication negotiations are recorded in Fleetway Publications (Peggy Sutherland) to Bradbury, Mar. 16, 1962; (Joan Stevenson), May 2, 14, 1962, personal papers.

43. Robert Taubman, review of *SW*, *New Statesman*, Mar. 1, 1963, 312; London *Times Literary Supplement*, Mar. 15, 1963, 189.

44. Harold Prince to Don Congdon, May 25, June 19, 1962, Butler. Copies also went to West Coast studios, including MGM. Milton Beecher to Bradbury, Sept. 17, 1962, personal papers. For an extensive discussion of the film and the evolution of the successive Bradbury screenplays, see "Ray Bradbury's Something Wicked This Way Comes," in *Cinefantastique* (June–July 1983): 28–49.

45. King, *Danse Macabre*, 324–38. King claims that his first experience with real horror came when he heard a radio broadcast of Bradbury's "Mars Is Heaven!" ("The Third Expedition," *MC*) in 1951. Although he now finds Bradbury's style, so attractive to him as an adolescent because of its rhetorical excesses, to be a bit oversweet, he still finds *SW* to be a powerful book of childhood remembered in myth. Interestingly, King tries to understand this myth in terms of a thematics of Apollonian norm and Dionysian invasion. On a personal level, Bradbury has indicated to King that the book was an unconscious tribute to his father, who died in 1957. In terms of the life of fiction we are here investigating, we can only repeat Bradbury's own words in that same letter to King: "[In *SW*] I said all and everything, just about, that I would ever want to say about my younger self and how I felt about that terrifying thing: Life, and that other terror: Death, and the exhilaration of both." King, *Danse Macabre*, 327.

46. Mikhail Bakhtin, "Forms of Time and Chronotope in the Novel," in *Dialogic Imagination*, 162–63. Our analysis acknowledges that *SW* is structured by fathers, living and dead, literary and real, in all of its versions. Bradbury makes Shakespeare the center of his interpretive clock in chapter 37, and the title of the book comes from *Macbeth*. For many romantic thinkers, and certainly for Bradbury too, Shakespeare was the greatest of artists because he overcame the limitations of classical aesthetics and embraced the grotesque realism of carnival as a necessary part of life. For Bradbury, Shakespeare embodies the totality of life, culture both high and low.

47. King, *Danse Macabre*, 329.

48. See ibid., 330–31.

49. *SW*, chap. 18, 52.

50. Ibid., chap. 12, 38.

51. Todorov, *The Fantastic*, 160.

52. Deleuze and Guattari, *Anti-Oedipus*, 298. In a programmatic sense, Deleuze and Guattari are carrying out a carnivalization of Freud's theories and their dogmatic seriousness. They even use one of Bradbury's story, "The Nursery" *(IM)*, in arguing that some forms of fantasy are nonfamilial and that psychoanalysis has failed utterly to take them into account. Ibid., 47.

53. Bakhtin, *Dialogic Imagination*, 161–612.

54. *SW*, 54, 55.

55. Ibid., 14.

56. Ibid., 20–21.

57. Ibid., throughout chap.15, 89.

58. Ibid., chap. 51. Compared texts from first draft discards and SW, 62.

59. Bakhtin, *Rabelais*, 316.

60. *SW*, chap. 35 and throughout

61. Ibid., 156.

62. Michel Foucault, *Language, Counter-Memory, Practice*, ed. and trans. Donald F. Bouchard and Sherry Simon (Ithaca, N.Y.: Cornell Univ. Press, 1977), 161. The following discussion of carnivalized history is based on that of Foucault.

63. *SW*, 147–48.

64. Foucault, *Language, Counter-Memory, Practice*, 149.

65. Ibid., 147.

66. *SW*, chap. 24, 80.

67. Ibid., 158–59.

68. Ibid., 127.

69. See introduction, note 57, above.

70. *SW*, 156.

71. Bakhtin, *Rabelais*, 91; *SW*, 212.

72. *SW*, 192.

73. Nietzsche, "On Reading and Writing," pt. 1 of *Thus Spoke Zarathustra*, in *Portable Nietzsche*, 153.

6. Corpse Carnivals

1. Julius Schwartz to Ray Bradbury, Sept. 2, 1942, personal papers.

2. Peter Haining, *The Classic Era of American Pulp Magazines* (Chicago: Chicago Review Press, 2001), 61–64, 131–33.

3. An undated story-status sheet, prepared by Bradbury and returned with updates by Schwartz, reveals that Schwartz was still waiting to offer a Bradbury story to *Ellery Queen;* it probably dates from late 1943. By the spring of 1944, he was willing to offer to *Black Mask.* Schwartz to Bradbury, May 4, 1944, personal papers.

4. Ray Bradbury, "Henry Kuttner: A Neglected Master," introduction to *The Best of Henry Kuttner* (Garden City, N.Y.: Nelson Doubleday, 1975), ix. The detective work of Kuttner and Moore is found in Sam Moskowitz, *Seekers of Tomorrow* (New York: Ballantine, 1967), chaps. 17–18.

5. Schwartz to Bradbury, Aug. 20, 1944, personal papers; Haining, *Classic Era of American Pulp*, 152.

6. Schwartz to Bradbury, Aug. 20, 1944.

7. Mogen, *Ray Bradbury*, 150.

8. William F. Nolan, *Hammett: A Life on the Edge* (New York: Congdon and Weed, 1983); Schwartz to Bradbury, Mar. 18, 25, 1944, personal papers. Nolan had already published a well-received chapbook on Hammett, and in 2002 he completed another study based on previously unexamined source materials.

9. Compared texts from "Where Everything Ends," 1943–1944, Albright Collection, 1–2; *DLB*, 3.

10. *DLB*, 7.

11. Bradbury to Jim McKimmey, Oct. 24, 1963, William Anthony Parker White (Anthony Boucher) Papers, Lilly.

12. The initial Knopf responses are consolidated in Nicholas to Bradbury, Oct. 9, 1984, personal papers. Additional details are found in Nicholas to Eller, Apr. 22, 2003, in the author's possession.

13. Nolan interview, Mar. 13, 2002. The following discussion of Sid Stebel's significant recommendations for the final draft of the novel are from Stebel to Bradbury, Dec. 30, 1984, personal papers.

14. In 1962 CBS aired Bradbury's *Twilight Zone* episode, "I Sing the Body Electric!" (based on "The Beautiful One Is Here" [1969]). In 1985–1986, the new CBS *Twilight Zone* series aired "The Burning Man" (based on "El Hombre Que Ardea" [1975]) and "The Elevator," which has never been published as a story.

15. Bradbury interview (Eller), Mar. 14, 2002.

16. "Yesterday I Lived," *MEM*, 155.

17. Bradbury interview (Eller), Mar. 14, 2002.

18. Kathy Hourigan, interview by Jonathan R. Eller, telephone, May 29, 2001. Her letter discussing revisions with Bradbury is dated Mar. 22, 1989 (personal collection); it has not been examined.

19. For how the Avon production staff worked with Bradbury to replace a clichéd Hollywood image of Rita Hayworth (who does not appear in the novel at all) in the original design with Bradbury's carnivalized design of the Hollywood graveyard, see Bradbury to Jennifer Brehl (Avon), Oct. 10, 2000, personal papers; and Brehl to Bradbury, Oct. 19, 2000, personal papers.

20. Bradbury interview (Eller), Mar. 14, 2002.

21. Bradbury, introduction to *MEM*, 8; Geoffrey Hartman, "Literature High and Low, the Case of the Mystery Story," in *The Fate of Reading and Other Essays* (Chicago: Univ. of Chicago Press, 1975), 216. It is a fairly well-known fact that Freud was aware of the analogies between psychoanalytic investigation and detective work. For instance, he admired Arthur Conan Doyle and his creation, Sherlock Holmes.

22. "Killer Come Back to Me!" *Detective Tales*, July 1944, 43.

23. "It Burns Me Up!" *MEM*, 43.

24. Laplanche and Pontalis, *Language of Psychoanalysis*, 111. The usual translation is either "deferred action" or "deferred revision."

25. Among Bradbury's unpublished manuscripts dating from 1942–44 are seven detective stories. One, "Long Live the Douser!" has Bradbury's diminutive detective staging his own mock funeral in such a way (using hidden microphones and voices) as to trick the attending criminals into incriminating themselves in his "murder" and causing them to attack each other. Another, already mentioned, is "Where Everything Ends," which foreshadows the themes of role and identity in *DLB*. A circus has dumped its wagons into the canals, where the murderer swims by night to reach his victims. In order to solve the murder, the detective must recreate the killer's actions by swimming in the canals in search of him. The theme of trapping or caging a criminal is present in both stories, but it is developed into the much larger issue of authorial creative freedom in the novel, where the author wants to avoid being trapped in a clownish identity.

26. Todorov, *The Fantastic*, 139.

27. "Killer Come Back to Me!" 37.

28. Bradbury to McKimmey, Oct. 24, 1963; Hartman, "Literature High and Low," 203.

29. Hartman, "Literature High and Low," 216, 218.

30. One must distinguish carefully here between the mask of the clown and that of the fool. The former is something sinister that Bradbury would never wear. Writing of his experience with carnivals and circuses, Bradbury tells us: "Clowns were never funny to me. I probably guessed there was something of the grinning skull to them." He finds them to be "inadvertent

metaphors for mortality" instead of figures of life. Despite their origins in carnival culture (according to Bakhtin, the clown is a "synthetic form for the parodied exposure of others"), Bradbury almost never adopts the mask of the clown. We can see clown figures, however, in the drawing Bradbury drew for *The Masks*, his abandoned novel. Concerning clowns and the carnivalesque, he goes on to add: "I have found myself curious about the grotesques of existence, of which clowns are high on the list, having come down off Notre Dame, given up their marble aspects and put on zinc oxide. Humor is not a part of them." Ray Bradbury, "Under the Circus Tent," afterword to *The Last Circus and the Electrocution* (Northridge, Calif.: Lord John, 1980), 26.

31. For the intertextual connection between Bradbury's Mars and Baum's Oz, see the discussion in Brian Attebery, *The Fantasy Tradition in American Literature, from Irving to LeGuin* (Bloomington: Indiana Univ. Press, 1980), 133–41.

32. For examples of "dread" Nietzsche, see *DLB*, 66, 182, 259, 278.

33. Ibid., 213–14.

34. Jean-Paul Sartre, *The Psychology of the Imagination*, trans. Bernard Frechtman (New York: Washington Square, 1966), 207–29.

35. Nietzsche, "On Redemption," pt. 2 of *Thus Spoke Zarathustra*, in *Portable Nietzsche*, 249–54.

36. Bakhtin, *Problems of Dostoevsky's Poetics*, 150–51.

37. The two-faced god Janus is the very symbol of the grotesque body and carnival ambivalence. See Bakhtin, *Rabelais*, 165.

38. Bradbury to William F. Touponce, Aug 18, 1981, in author's possession.

39. They Have Not Seen the Stars, 240–41. Harold Bloom has pretty much the same thing to say about the relationship of psychoanalysis to literature: "It was Shakespeare . . . who was there before Freud arrived at his depth psychology, and it is Shakespeare who is there still, well out ahead of psychoanalysis. We see what Freud would not see, that psychoanalysis is Shakespeare prosified and systematized. Freud is part of literature, not of 'science.'" Bloom, "Life of the Author," x.

40. A large network of carnivalized religious themes and metaphors is woven through the novel, creating the notion that Bradbury is also playing on a variation of the theme of the "holy fool." "Bradbury" tries to "save" the actor J.C. from killing himself. The accident that disfigured Arbuthnot happened in front of a church, and a priest, Father Kelly, was involved; Arbuthnot still goes to the church for confession. In real life Bradbury wrote some of the narration for *King of Kings* and suggested another ending for that film, which in the novel he calls the "second Ascension following The Supper After the Last Supper." Bradbury, searching for clues about the beast, discusses his patching of the film script with Father Kelly, who remarks that the New Testament itself is a "patchwork," pointing up the nature of its textuality.

41. *The Phantom of the Opera* is cited several times in the novel: e.g., 97, 204, 262.

42. Ibid., 204.

43. Bradbury interview (Eller), Mar. 14, 2002.

44. *LAKC*, 50.

45. Ibid., 170–71.

7. *Carnival Sideshows*

1. Bradbury's contract with Doubleday for these two books is dated June 22, 1949 (personal papers).

2. R. Bradbury to W. Bradbury, July 22, 1950, Lilly. Walt Bradbury's approval of the

contract change from novel to story collection can be inferred from R. Bradbury to W. Bradbury, June 16, 1950, Lilly.

3. Correspondence detailing the development and submission of *IM* includes Ray Bradbury to Walt Bradbury, July 22, 25, 30, Aug. 19, 1950, Lilly.

4. During the 1950s, as fantasy for Bradbury took on a political dimension, he began to be concerned with censorship issues. Both of these stories are about the censorship of fantasy by an increasingly rationalized culture in the United States. *The Wizard of Oz* was, in fact, removed from public libraries during this period, scapegoated as escapist literature that children ought not to be reading when America was trying to catch up with Russian advances in space science. He was especially concerned about the role that American ego psychology was playing in "normalizing" or adjusting the ego to society. Conformity was the order of the day. "The Exiles" explicitly addresses a politics of fantasy in relation to psychoanalysis. Originally published in Canada as "The Mad Wizards of Mars" in *Macleans* (Sept. 15, 1949), the story explores the desperate situation of the fantastic from the point of view of dead authors who pretty much defined the field in the nineteenth century. Indeed, the plot of "The Exiles" makes Tzvetan Todorov's assertion about psychoanalysis taking over the themes of the fantastic into a literal happening, as rocket men from Earth, among whom there are psychoanalysts, destroy the ghosts of Poe and other authors of the fantastic by burning the last remaining copies of their books. No less than five versions of this story exist. There were many variations in the character-authors—for instance, a substitution of Dickens for Hawthorne and new passages depicting H. P. Lovecraft were instigated by Anthony Boucher for the story's republication in the second issue of *The Magazine of Fantasy and Science Fiction* (Winter/Spring 1950). There were also some significant changes in setting: for instance, in all versions, the story is set on Mars, and Bradbury once had the story in mind for inclusion in *MC*, but for the first book appearance in *IM*, he changed the House of Usher to the Emerald City of Oz. No doubt these changes were motivated by the politics of the times. Perhaps the most significant sign of changing cultural climates, however, is that the most recent revision, first published in 1962 (*RR*) and now collected in *CS1*, deletes any direct mention of psychoanalysis, which the four earlier versions contain. We discuss the thematics of "Pillar of Fire" below.

5. Correspondence on the science fiction colophon and the reprint rights includes R. Bradbury to W. Bradbury, Sept. 29, 1950, Lilly.

6. W. Bradbury to R. Bradbury, June 6, 1952, personal papers.

7. R. Bradbury to W. Bradbury, Feb. 12, 1952, Lilly.

8. W. Bradbury to R. Bradbury, Feb. 18, 1952, personal papers.

9. Bradbury, *IM*, 79.

10. Nolan, *Bradbury Review*, 61; W. Bradbury to R. Bradbury, July 12, 1951, personal papers.

11. For Congdon's recommendation on the Mexican novel concept, see Congdon to R. Bradbury, Nov. 17, 1950, personal papers. The problems with *Summer Morning, Summer Night* and the plan for a new story collection are documented in W. Bradbury to R. Bradbury, Mar. 10, 17, June 6, 1952, personal papers. The two outlines listing *Fahrenheit 451* are discussed in chap. 3. Bradbury's earliest outline for the new collection, dated January 1952, is titled "The Witch Door, a new anthology of stories by Ray Bradbury." This thirteen-story concept indicates that he was planning the collection well before he approached Doubleday with his intentions. "The Witch Door," subsequently published as "The April Witch," found its way into the final table of contents. For the ongoing discussion of contents and volume title for what became *GA*, see W. Bradbury to R. Bradbury, June 13, 26, 30, 1952, personal papers; and R. Bradbury to W. Bradbury, June 10, 17, July 1, and Aug. 5, 1952, Lilly.

12. R. Bradbury to W. Bradbury, June 17, 1952, Lilly.

13. Ibid. The developing jacket design and line art for *GA* is discussed in R. Bradbury to W. Bradbury, Aug. 6, 1952, Lilly; W. Bradbury to R. Bradbury, Sept. 8, Oct. 1, 1952, personal papers; Joe Mugnaini to W. Bradbury, Oct. 7, 1952, copy forwarded with a note from Mugnaini, personal papers; W. Bradbury to Mugnaini, Oct. 10, Nov. 7, 1952, carbon copy, personal papers.

14. For Walt Bradbury's responses to his author's jacket-copy requests, see W. Bradbury to R. Bradbury, Feb. 4, 5 (telegrams), Feb. 6, 1953, personal papers. Ray Bradbury's file copies of his original jacket liner notes also survive in his papers. The marketing issues, including Bradbury's offer to bear illustration expenses, are discussed in W. Bradbury to R. Bradbury, Oct. 1, 1952, Mar. 31, 1953, personal papers; and Don Congdon to R. Bradbury, Oct. 2, 16, 1952, Feb. 16, 1953, personal papers.

15. W. Bradbury to R. Bradbury, Mar. 31, 1953.

16. The contract discussions and terms are documented in Don Congdon to R. Bradbury, May 2, 22, 28, 1958, personal papers; and Congdon to W. Bradbury (copy), May 15, 1958, Butler.

17. The title discussion and the evolving contents are contained in R. Bradbury to Donn Congdon, June 22, 1958 (Butler), and W. Bradbury to R. Bradbury, June 11, 17, July 18, 23, 1958, personal papers.

18. Bradbury no longer remembers the Albertus Magnus text, but it was most likely *The Book of Secrets* (c. 1250). Bradbury interviews (Eller), Oct. 21–25, 2002. Casanova is known to his modern biographers, and especially to those who have written psychobiographies of him, as someone deeply imbued with the spirit of carnival and sexual masquerade. His favorite repertory of masks belongs to the tradition of commedia dell'arte, in which story was not as important as the actors' improvised performance: "Casanova makes a perpetual carnival of his life. Like his incestuous utopia, the carnival suspends time and derives from a will to create one's own laws." Lydia Flem, *Casanova: The Man Who Really Loved Women* (New York: Farrar, Straus, Giroux, 1997), 163. We do not know which part of Casanova's memoirs may have influenced "A Medicine for Melancholy," but perhaps it is just the general spirit of sexual masquerade to be found in his writings. At any rate, it is interesting to note that later on in his career, Bradbury would be prompted to give a negative review to director Frederico Fellini's film of Casanova because of its deliberate exposure of the more mechanical and "lifeless" aspects of seduction (Fellini has Casanova interact with marionettes). It is in this review (actually of a book on Fellini's career) that he first uses the Nietzschean phrase "We have our Arts so we won't die of Truth." The review is collected in *Yestermorrow*. The influence of Casanova on "A Medicine for Melancholy" was first noted by Ray Russell (Congdon to Bradbury, July 30, 1958).

19. Bradbury's fears about the potential of the democratic crowd (or "mob"' as the text has it) to destroy high culture culminates in a scene in *Where Ignorant Armies Clash by Night* (1947) in which the Mona Lisa is ritually debased (this society destroys not only books but all signs of high culture). It is clear that the painting is being destroyed because of its enigmatic smile, which is not easily understandable by the masses (or even by art critics—it provoked John Ruskin to call her a vampire, while Red Skelton said on his comedy show during the heyday of live television that she was smiling because she was having her picture painted, so maybe the masses are not so dumb after all). In this "democratic" rite in which people are allowed to identify with themselves by spitting on the Mona Lisa—but not to destroy it, for that has to be done ritually for them by the assassin—Bradbury builds up a disturbing sense of how true carnival can be perverted. This incident, which was to have been the last chapter of the novel, was reworked and published as "The Smile" (1952).

20. The evolving changes in content and title for the U.K. edition are documented in Hart-Davis to Bradbury, May 16, 30, July 11, 21, 31, 1958, personal papers.

21. Title choices for the British collection are discussed in Hart-Davis to Bradbury, May 8, 16, 19,30, July 18, 1958, personal papers.

22. Walt Bradbury expressed concern with the support of other Doubleday departments in W. Bradbury to R. Bradbury, Mar. 12, 1959, personal papers.

23. Doubleday interoffice memorandum, Cochran to Shapian (copy to Bradbury), July 19, 1973, personal papers.

24. Seldes's reaction to the idea was passed along to Bradbury in Congdon to Bradbury, Nov. 6, 1959, personal papers.

25. Gottlieb to Congdon (copy to Bradbury), Mar. 16, 1961, personal papers.

26. Doubleday (Blanche Van Buren) to Bradbury, May 4, 1962, personal papers; Doubleday (Betsy Beilenson) to Bradbury, May 22, 1962, personal papers.

27. Bradbury would encounter a reprint problem with the original serial publisher, Fiction House, for "The Creatures That Time Forgot." Malcolm Reiss had released film and television rights to a number of Bradbury stories years earlier but still had rights to this novella and demanded 25 percent of the royalties the story would earn as "Frost and Fire." Bradbury's strong counterproposal noted that Fiction House had received "superb stories at starvation wages" from Bradbury in the 1940s and should not in good conscience pursue the claim. Bradbury to Reiss (copy), May 26, 1962, personal papers. Reiss apparently relented, but Bradbury would have to take a different approach over the Popular Publications rights to his pulp detective tales.

28. Doubleday (Claiborne Watkins) to Bradbury, June 14, 1962, personal papers. The censorship of *F451* is discussed in chap. 3.

29. These marketing and sales discussions are preserved in managing editor for Doubleday's Books for Young Readers (Blanche Van Buren) to Bradbury, Oct. 5, 17, 1962, personal papers; Advertising Manager Robert Carter to Bradbury, Oct. 22, 1962, personal papers; and Publicist Betsy Beilenson to Bradbury, Oct. 23, Dec. 3, 19, 1962, personal papers. Two letters from Young Readers editor Margaret Lesser downplayed Doubleday's central role in the poorly played debut of *RR*, prompting a detailed recounting of the publisher's miscues from Bradbury: "In sum, I am being treated as if I were an unreasonable child, when it is Doubleday that has been unthinking and unbusinesslike." Lesser to Bradbury, Dec. 19, 1962, personal papers; Lesser to Congdon, Dec. 19, 1962, Butler; Bradbury to Lesser (copy), Dec. 22, 1962, personal papers.

30. Doubleday internal sales memorandum, Cochran to Shapian (copy to Bradbury), July 19, 1973, personal papers.

31. Bradbury to Gottlieb, (copy), June 3, 1962, personal papers.

32. During the late 1950s, Bradbury had developed an outline and story episodes for a novel on this theme, but the idea went no further except as self-contained stories (see app. B).

33. In August 1963 Bradbury had offered a design for a white cover and an inset print from Giovanne Battista Brachielli's *Bizarie* (1624), a book of "fifty small etchings depicting robot forms and semi-geometric nudes." Bradbury to Gottlieb (copy), Aug. 30, 1963, personal papers. It is not known why this design was discarded.

34. "The Tombling Day" appears on an undated list of stories in progress (c. 1948) with a progress date of September 1947.

35. William F. Nolan to Jonathan R. Eller, Aug. 5, 2002, in author's possession; Bradbury interview (Eller), Oct. 21–25, 2002.

36. Johnson, *Ray Bradbury*, 78.

37. Nolan used a similar title, *Things beyond Midnight*, for one of his own story collections in 1984.

38. Nancy Nicholas, interview by Jonathan R. Eller, telephone, May 22, 2001. The marketing of *IS* is discussed at length in Bob Gottlieb to Bradbury, Nov. 6, 1969, Feb. 18, 1970, personal papers; Bradbury to Don Congdon, Dec. 22, 1969, Butler; and Gottlieb to Congdon, Jan. 9, 1970, Butler. Marketing of *The Halloween Tree* is discussed in the conclusion.

39. The transition between editors at Knopf is described in Hourigan interview; Nicholas interview; Gottlieb to Bradbury, Feb. 10, 1987, personal papers; and Hourigan to Bradbury, Apr. 5, 1987, personal papers.

40. Hourigan to Bradbury, Apr. 5, 1987.

41. Gottlieb to Bradbury, Feb. 10, 1987; Hourigan interview. The Bantam honorific appeared on Bradbury's paperback covers during the 1960s and 1970s.

42. Nicholas interview; Hourigan interview.

43. Bradbury to Mike Tilden (draft), c. 1944, personal papers. Tilden was one of Bradbury's detective fiction editors at Popular Publications, which also published *Argosy* at that time.

44. For many years, "Masinello Pietro" (1964), which is based on Bradbury's Mexican tenement experiences of the early 1940s, was the only significant uncollected story. It was also passed over for the 2003 compilation, *BS*, which included "The Execution" (1977). "From the Dust Returned" (1994) evolved into the closing episodes of the novel of that title.

45. Nicholas interview.

46. Saul David's recommendation to Congdon for a major Bradbury collection was relayed in Congdon to Bradbury, Oct. 22, 1959, personal papers.

47. Gilbert Highet, "Introduction," *VB*, viii-ix.

48. Thomas M. Disch, "Tops in Brand-Name Recognition," *New York Times Book Review*, Oct. 26, 1980.

49. Bradbury, introduction to *PF*; Nietzsche, "On the Tarantulas," pt. 2 of *Thus Spoke Zarathustra*, in *Portable Nietzsche*, 211–14.

50. Deleuze and Guattari, *Anti-Oedipus*, 273–382. Deleuze and Guattari's polemical purpose is both to demolish Freud's representation of the unconscious as a private theater of dire family secrets and to replace it with what they call "the delirium of desiring-machines" as the general matrix of all social investments. (Bradbury's Green Town and the ravine are full of such machines.) Whether in the field of psychoanalysis or of literature, for them, delirium is always a political matter because the unconscious always directly invests the social field, bypassing the familial structures (of castration, of the father) on which psychoanalysis is founded. In discussing their project of "schizoanalysis," which is heavily influenced by Nietzsche, they attack psychoanalysis and its dependence on Oedipal, or familial, structures because it cannot think beyond them to the ways in which fantasy is political. They distinguish between two poles of social libidinal investment: the paranoiac, reactionary, and fascisizing *(fascisant)* pole, and the schizoid revolutionary pole. The former invests the formation of a central sovereignty, or state, the latter breaches the walls set up by the state, causes flows of desire to move, and follows lines of escape (their version of the Bakhtinian carnival). Paranoia territorializes and enslaves, schizophrenia decodes and deterritorializes. The former is molecular, the latter molar. They oppose social segregation with "nomadism" as a social goal. One should recall here the book people at the end of Bradbury's *F451* as an example of nomads and compare psychoanalysis in general to the machines of the dark carnival that invades Green Town in *SW*.

51. "Pillar of Fire," *SS*, 44.

52. Bradbury, introduction to *PF*, x.

53. Deleuze and Guattari, *Anti-Oedipus*, 329.

54. "Pillar of Fire," *SS*, 65–66

55. "I am every name in history," proclaimed Nietzsche in a letter written just before his collapse into madness. *Portable Nietzsche*, 686.

56. "Pillar of Fire," *SS*, 30.

57. There are clear echoes of "Pillar of Fire" in one of Bradbury's unpublished novel manuscript s dating from 1947, *Where Ignorant Armies Clash by Night*, which also deals with a crisis of values. Lantry's name appears on one fragmentary page, probably as an alternative name for the assassin of that novel, whose job it is to kill people ritually. In a short scene he murders an unsuspecting victim with a knife but complains that the act, however artistically performed, no longer has any value for him. He has done it so many times that it has been drained of any meaning: "It's like all values when they have been mined too long, valueless." The great assassin of that novel often reflects negatively on the meaninglessness of his exalted calling in passages that are similar in tone to Montag's unhappiness about his job as a fireman.

Conclusion. A Carnival Sense of Life

1. Bakhtin, *Rabelais*, 439. For a presentation of Bradbury's book-related art, see Weist, *Ray Bradbury*, 167–76. Weist also shows one of Bradbury's letters illustrated with carnival figures. Ibid., 78.

2. Grobel, "Skull behind the Flesh," 86. This interview, originally published in a shorter form in 1975, is one of the most revealing Bradbury has ever given about his notion of authorship.

3. Anthony Boucher, "The Publishing of Science Fiction," in *Modern Science Fiction, Its Meaning and Its Future*, ed. Reginald Bretnor (New York: Coward-McGann, 1953), 25. This same volume contains an article by Gerald Heard linking the process of ideas in modern science fiction to laughter: "laughter is not merely frankness; it is a necessary force for insight" (256). Heard's ideas had a major impact on Bradbury's understanding of his authorship, as he tells us in the afterword.

4. Bakhtin, *Rabelais*, 122–23, 66.

5. Harold Bloom, introduction to *Ray Bradbury, Modern Critical Views* (New York: Chelsea House, 2001), 1. For Bloom, Bradbury is "an admirable entertainer, and deserves appreciation precisely as such."

6. For a recent Freudian account of the romantic gothic in American culture, both popular and literary, see Edmundson, *Nightmare on Main Street*. His idea of the "internalized Gothic" binds the writer to his guilty past and has much in common with Freud's later view of the psyche as structured by id, ego, and superego. The latter, largely unconscious, agency is the repository of punishing figures of the imagination: "The sadistic superego is Freud's hero-villain, and I believe the most brilliantly drawn exemplar of that archetype in the Gothic tradition." Ibid., 34. Edmundson points out the disdain for carnival forms of the Gothic entertainment among members of high romantic culture (e.g., William Wordsworth) but points out how close their own writings were to it. Ibid., 158–59.

7. Bradbury to Jonathan R. Eller, Mar. 14, 2002, in author's possession. Bradbury makes clear his disdain for "authors": "I'm a writer who has a hell [of] a lot of fun, and as a result of it, you have fun. But these people [self-styled authors] are high-falluting."

8. Bradbury to William F. Touponce, Aug. 18, 1981, in author's possession.

9. Bakhtin, *Problems of Dostoevsky's Poetics*, 143.

10. Bakhtin, *Rabelais*, 66, 122.

11. Bakhtin, *Dialogic Imagination*, 159–61; Bakhtin, *Rabelais*, 454.

12. Bakhtin argues that an individual cannot be completely incarnated in the flesh of existing sociohistorical categories: "All existing clothes are always too tight, and thus comical, on a man. But this surplus of un-fleshed out humanness may be realized not only in the hero, but also in the author's point of view (as, for example, in Gogol)." Bakhtin, *Dialogic Imagination*, 37.

13. For a discussion of the paradoxes of temporality in the novel along Bakhtinian lines, see Gary Saul Morson, *Narrative and Freedom: The Shadows of Time* (New Haven: Yale Univ. Press, 1994). Morson argues that true creative authorship must be understood as a genuine process of unpredetermined becoming, not the unfolding of an already determined sequence: "So conceived, the creative process typically traces not a straight line to a goal but a series of false leads, missed opportunities, new possibilities, improvisations, visions, and revisions. It is constituted by an intention that evolves over time. To be sure, authors typically remove the traces of this process and present their work as if it were the product of a clear plan, known from the outset. By convention, works are usually offered as the expression of an intention that is essentially instantaneous even if it took time to execute and time to appreciate. After the work is complete, the authors remove the 'scaffolding' as Bakhtin liked to say. But the process of creation is anything but regular." Ibid., 25.

Throughout, we have tried to restore the many textual "scaffoldings" Bradbury used in the construction of his works, but such a detailed analysis of his detective fiction is beyond the scope of this study. There is certainly ample evidence to suggest, however, that he always thought of his works less as completed items than as ongoing events. For him, the work was never over even when it was over. And after a half century of writing, Bradbury's authorial intentions are now deeply embedded in a kind of "great time" that begins with the detective fiction.

14. The genesis of *HT* described here is quoted and summarized from Ray Bradbury, interview by Jonathan R. Eller, Los Angeles, Oct. 12, 1998.

15. Dissatisfaction with Knopf's advertising and marketing strategies for *The Halloween Tree* is outlined in Congdon to Gottlieb (copy to Bradbury), June 20, 1973, personal papers. The full discussion of these issues, as well as the underlying dispute over Knopf's decision to market the book as a juvenile title, is preserved in the Knopf archives (Ransom). Substantial letters include Bradbury to Congdon, June 6, 1973 (copy); Congdon to Gottlieb, June 11, 20; Gottlieb to Congdon (copy), June 21 (copy); Bradbury to Gottlieb, July 14; Gottlieb to Bradbury (copy), July 20.

16. When asked about the origins of *HT*, Bradbury responded with a statement about his authorship in general:

> It started as a painting I did in 1960, of a tree full of pumpkins, the metaphor for the root system of death. All of my work is like that. I only find out, when I am finished, who or what I am. . . . No, I have never read Nietzsche, save for that one quote about art saving us from dying of the truth, a great quote. Intellect should never dominate. Accusing someone of not being intellectual is, to me, a compliment. I want people to eat my apples and oranges and notice later that the skin containing them was mind, was intellect. Intellect is the skin around a living thing, to keep its blood and fluids going, and in place. But if we are all skin, as some intellectuals are, how dreadful. You wouldn't be able to hear their hearts beat inside their parched armour.

Bradbury to William F. Touponce, Oct. 10, 1986, in author's possession.

To Bradbury, the intellect is a kind of defensive armor, part of the ego's defense mechanisms, as indeed it is in Freud (see Bradbury, "Defense Mech," *Planet Stories* [Spring 1946], for an early, humorous treatment of this notion). Bradbury is giving us here some broad indications about his authorship and about how he wishes to be read. He asks primarily to be understood as an artist—as one who gives life ("I want people to eat my apples and oranges")—and not as an intellectual. Moreover, it is through the force of his art, his deployment of metaphors, myths, and masks, that meaning, even unintended unconscious meanings, can be discovered in his texts, usually to the surprise of the author himself.

17. *HT*, 179.

18. Ibid., 13.

19. This is the basis of Hegelian dialectics, which expounds human history as the struggle against the negativity of death. See Alexandre Kojève, *Introduction to the Reading of Hegel*, ed. Allan Bloom, trans. James H. Nichols Jr. (Ithaca: Cornell Univ. Press, 1980), 3–30.

20. The difference between sovereignty and authority (or the Hegelian *Herrschaft*, lordship) is that sovereignty does not seek to grasp or master concepts but rigorously looks to explode them with laughter. See Jacques Derrida, *Writing and Difference*, trans. Alan Bass (Chicago: Univ. of Chicago Press, 1978), 251–77. This philosophical use of laughter is, of course, at the heart of carnival as well.

21. *HT*, 36.

22. Gaston Bachelard, *The Psychoanalysis of Fire*, trans. Alan C. M. Ross (Boston: Beacon, 1964), 14–16.

23. *HT*, 170–71.

24. Ibid., 79.

25. Bradbury interview (Eller), Mar. 14, 2002.

26. *GS*, 258.

27. Ibid., 192.

28. Bradbury's imitation of Shaw's voice has not convinced some of his critics. See John R. Pfeiffer, "Ray Bradbury's Bernard Shaw," in *Shaw and Science Fiction*, vol. 17 of *SHAW: The Annual of Bernard Shaw Studies*, ed. Milton T. Wolf (University Park: Pennsylvania State Univ. Press, 1997), 123. Bradbury has also expressed his literary relationship to Shaw, Gilbert Chesterton, Poe, and Oscar Wilde, among others, in the long fantasy poem *The R. B., G. K. C. and G. B. S. Forever Orient Express* (Santa Barbara: Joshua Odell Editions, 1994).

29. *FDR*, 63.

30. Problems of this sort arise whenever texts are assembled to form larger patterns of meaning, which is quite often in Bradbury. For instance, in all of its versions *The Martian Chronicles* refers to Father Peregrine in one its bridges. Peregrine is a character in "The Fire Balloons," a story that is sometimes included in expanded versions of the text but most often not. *Dandelion Wine*, which textually was torn away from the massive Ur-text of *Summer Morning, Summer Night*, makes it clear *who* is hit by the Green Machine in that novel (the victim Colonel Quartermain, is the principle antagonist of *Farewell Summer*, another offshoot). Such problems also occur in stories that undergo thematic development, such as *Fahrenheit 451*. In "The Fireman" Montag reads exclusively in the Bible from the Book of Job. Bradbury later changed this to Ecclesiastes and Revelations for a more hopeful ending but forgot to rewrite some of the earlier scenes. There are others. We are only interested in such "continuity" mistakes insofar as they affect thematic structures of meaning.

31. Ibid., 136–37.

32. Ibid., 145.

33. Mikhail Bakhtin, "Towards a Methodology for the Human Sciences," in *Speech Genres and Other Essays*, trans. Vern W. McGee, ed. Caryl Emerson and Michael Holquist (Austin: Univ. of Texas Press, 1986), 168.

34. Bakhtin, *Rabelais*, 8–9.

35. For the notion of great time and how it affects literary meaning, see Bakhtin, "Response to a Question from *Novy Mir*," in *Speech Genres*, 5: "A work of literature . . . is revealed primarily in the differentiated unity of the culture of the epoch in which it was created, but it cannot be closed off in this epoch: its fullness is revealed only in *great time*."

36. But see Touponce, "Our Harvest Is Fear: Aspects of Carnival in Ray Bradbury's Screen Treatment for *It Came from Outer Space*" in *It Came from Outer Space* (Springfield, Penn.: Gauntlet Publications, 2003). Forthcoming.

37. Bakhtin writes about the "dialogue" with past meanings in literary history that " at certain moments of the dialogue's subsequent development along the way they [past meanings] are recalled and invigorated in renewed form (in a new context). Nothing is absolutely dead: every meaning will have its homecoming festival." Bakhtin, "Towards a Methodology for the Human Sciences," 170.

Appendix A.

1. Listed as "Flight of the Good Ship Clarissa" in William F. Nolan, *The Ray Bradbury Companion* (Detroit: Gale, 1975), 180, 184.

2. Nolan, *The Ray Bradbury Companion*, 53, 186.

3. William F. Nolan, "Leigh Brackett and Ray Bradbury," in *The Human Equation*, ed. William F. Nolan (Los Angeles: Sherbourne, 1971), 63.

4. Ibid., 63.

5. On the genesis of "The Beast from 20,000 Fathoms," see William F. Nolan, "Bradbury: Prose Poet in the Age of Space," *Magazine of Science Fiction and Fantasy*, May 1963.

6. For an account of the origin of "Sun and Shadow," see Ray Bradbury, "The Joy of Writing," *Writer* (Oct. 1956) (collected in Bradbury, *Zen and the Art of Writing* and *Zen in the Art of Writing*).

7. On the motivations behind "The Trolley," see ibid.

8. Bradbury discusses the origins and significance of "Summer in the Air," ibid.

9. Nolan, *The Ray Bradbury Companion*, 137, 206.

10. Bradbury, "Make Haste to Live: An Afterword," *QE*.

Appendix B

1. J. Francis McComas to Bradbury, June 28, 1952, personal papers. This story was the thematic catalyst for the Bradbury screen treatment, *It Came from Outer Space* (Fall 1952). The film was made by Universal in 1953.

2. Julius Schwartz to Bradbury, Mar. 18, 25, 1944, personal papers.

Selected Bibliography

Appendix A, "Bradbury's Fiction Year-by-Year," represents a comprehensive bibliography of his fiction, so those listings are not duplicated here. The following selected bibliography provides a reference to Bradbury's writings and interviews on the subject of fiction writing as well as writings by others on his works. The secondary bibliographical entries are listed by categories and, within each category, alphabetically by author. Book reviews are not included here; each title's principal reviews are listed in the notes of the chapter devoted to that title. In addition, we have included a bibliography of collateral readings on literary criticism, textual theory, and cultural studies that have informed our discussion of Bradbury's fiction.

Bradbury on Fiction

Books

Yestermorrow: Obvious Answers to Impossible Futures. Santa Barbara, Calif.: Joshua Odell Editions/Capra, 1991.

Zen and the Art of Writing. Santa Barbara, Calif.: Capra, 1973.

Zen in the Art of Writing. Santa Barbara: Joshua Odell Editions/Capra, 1989; rpt. Bantam, 1992.

Articles

"About Theodore Sturgeon." Foreword to Theodore Sturgeon, *The Ultimate Egoist. Volume I: The Complete Stories of Theodore Sturgeon*, edited by Paul Williams (Berkeley: North Atlantic, 1994).

"Afterword: Fifty Years, Fifty Friends." In *The Bradbury Chronicles*, edited by William F. Nolan and Martin H. Greenberg (New York: Roc, 1991).

"The Ardent Blasphemers." Introduction to Jules Verne, *20,000 Leagues under the Sea* (New York: Bantam, 1962).

"At What Temperature Do Books Burn?" *New York Times*, November 13, 1966. Reprinted as introduction to *Fahrenheit 451* (New York: Simon and Schuster, 1967).

"Beyond 1984." *Playboy*, January 1979. Collected in Bradbury, *Beyond 1984: Remembrance of Things Future* (New York: Targ, 1979).

"Book Burning without Striking a Match." *Book Review (Los Angeles Times)*, May 27, 1979.

"Cry the Cosmos." *Life,* September 14, 1962.

"Day after Tomorrow: Why Science Fiction?" *Nation,* May 2, 1953.

"Death Warmed Over." In *The Hollywood Nightmare: Tales of Fantasy and Horror from the Film World,* edited by Peter Haining (New York: Taplinger, 1972). First published in *Playboy,* January 1968.

"Dusk in the Robot Museums, the Rebirth of Imagination." *Mosaic* (Canada) 13:3–4 (double issue; Spring–Summer 1980). Collected as "On the Shoulders of Giants," in Bradbury, *Zen in the Art of Writing.* Reprinted in Harold Bloom, *Ray Bradbury* (Philadelphia, Penn.: Chelsea House, 2001).

"G. B. S. Refurbishing the Tin Woodman: Science Fiction with a Heart, a Brain, and the Nerve!" In *Shaw and Science Fiction,* vol. 17, edited by Milton T. Wolf (University Park: Pennsylvania State Univ. Press, 1997).

"The God in Science Fiction." *Saturday Review of Literature,* December 10, 1977.

"How Did I Get Here from There?" *The Journal* (Writers Guild of America, West) (February 1995).

"How I Write" (commentary). *Writer's Digest,* December 1995.

"How to Be Madder Than Captain Ahab or, Writing Explained." *Literary Cavalcade,* October 1973.

"How to Keep and Feed a Muse." *Writer,* July 1961. Collected in Bradbury, *Zen in the Art of Writing.*

"Journey to a Far Metaphor." *Book World (Washington Post),* September 11, 1994.

"The Joy of Writing." *Writer,* October 1956. Collected in Bradbury, *Zen and the Art of Writing* and *Zen in the Art of Writing.*

"Literature in the Space Age." *California Librarian,* July 1960.

"Marvels and Miracles—Pass It On." *New York Times Magazine,* March 20, 1955.

"Magic, Magicians, Carnivals, and Fantasy." In *Ray Bradbury Review,* edited by William F. Nolan (San Diego: Nolan, 1952).

"Moby Dick, John Huston, and I." *Waukegan Sun-News,* February 9, 1955.

"On the Shoulders of Giants." In Bradbury, *Zen in the Art of Writing.*

"Novelist Appraises Himself, His Craft." *Los Angeles Times,* December 11, 1960.

"Ray Bradbury: Views of a Grand Master." *Locus,* August 1996.

"Remembrances of Things Future." *Playboy,* January 1965. Collected in Bradbury, *Beyond 1984.*

"Run Fast, Stand Still, or the Thing at the Top of the Stairs, or New Ghosts from Old Minds." In *How to Write Tales of Horror, Fantasy and Science Fiction,* edited by J. N. Williamson (Cincinnati: *Writer's Digest,* 1987). Collected in Bradbury, *Zen in the Art of Writing.*

"Science and Science Fiction." In *Ray Bradbury Review,* edited by William F. Nolan.

"The Secret Mind." *Writer,* November 1965. Collected in Bradbury, *Zen in the Art of Writing.*

"We Are Aristotle's Children." *New York Times,* February 9, 1977.

"Where Do I Get My Ideas?" *Book News,* Summer 1950.

"Where Do You Get Your Ideas?" In *Ray Bradbury Review,* edited by William F. Nolan. Originally published in *Etaoin Shrdlu,* April 1950.

"Zen and the Art of Writing." *Writer,* October 1958. Collected in Bradbury, *Zen and the Art of Writing* and as "Zen in the Art of Writing," in *Zen in the Art of Writing.*

Selected Interviews with Bradbury

Albright, Donn. "Interview with Ray Bradbury." *Gauntlet* 2 (March 1991).

Banker, Stephen. "An Earthbound Time Traveler." *Book World (Washington Post),* September 23, 1979.

Elliot, Jeffrey. "An Interview with Ray Bradbury." *San Francisco Review of Books*, June 1977.

———. "The Bradbury Chronicles." *Future* 5 (October 1978).

———. "Ray Bradbury: Poet of Fantastic Fiction." In *Science Fiction Voices 2*, edited by Jeffrey Elliot (San Bernardino, Calif.: Borgo, 1979).

Etchison, Dennis. "Bradbury in Hollywood." *The Spook*, December 2001. metropolemag.com/backissues.html. Accessed March 2002.

Fallaci, Oriana. *If the Sun Dies* Trans. Pamela Swinglehurst. New York: Atheneum, 1966.

Frank, Jeffrey A. "Ray Bradbury's Timeless Terrain." *Style (Washington Post)*, July 7, 1989.

Golden, Chris. "Ray Bradbury: King of All Media." In *1994 Science Fiction Annual*, June 1994.

Grabowski, William. "Whales, Libraries, and Dreams." *The Horror Show*, Winter 1985. Reprinted in *Fantasy Review*, July–August 1986.

Grobel, Larry. "Ray Bradbury: Visitor from Outer Space." *Los Angeles Free Press*, December 4, 1975.

———. "The Skull behind the Flesh." In *Endangered Species, Writers Talk about Their Craft, Their Visions, Their Lives*. Cambridge, Mass.: Da Capo, 2001.

Herndon, Ben. "The Ray Bradbury Theatre." *Cinefantastique*, May 1986.

Hibberd, James. "Ray Bradbury Is on Fire!" *Salon*, August 29, 2001. salon.com/people/feature/2001/08/29/bradbury/index.html. Accessed September 2001.

Jacobs, Robert. "The *Writer's Digest* Interview: Ray Bradbury." *Writer's Digest*, February 1976. Reprinted as "Bradbury on Bradbury—and Beyond," in *Fiction Writer's Market*, edited by John Brady and Jean M. Fredette (Cincinnati: *Writer's Digest*, 1981).

Kelley, Ken. "Playboy Interview—Ray Bradbury." *Playboy*, May 1996.

Miller, Walter James. "Ray Bradbury's Life, Time, and Work." In *Ray Bradbury's* The Martian Chronicles: *A Critical Commentary*, edited by Walter James Miller (New York: Monarch Notes, 1988).

Moore, Everett T. "A Rationale for Bookburners: A Further Word from Ray Bradbury." *American Library Association Bulletin* 55 (May 1961).

O'Conner, Norman. "Interview . . . Ray Bradbury." *Literary Guild*, November 1976.

Otterburn-Hall, William. "Ray Bradbury Isn't Afraid of the Future." *St. Louis Post Dispatch*, January 19, 1970.

———. "The Supremo of Science Fiction Writers." *Chicago Tribune*, August 26, 1971.

Perrin, Timothy. "Ray Bradbury's Nostalgia for the Future." *Writer's Digest*, February 1986.

Roberts, Frank. "An Exclusive Interview with Ray Bradbury." Parts 1 and 2. *Writer's Digest*, February 1967; March 1967. Reprinted (with the interviewer identified as Frank Filosa) in *On Being a Writer*, edited by Bill Strickland (Cincinnati: *Writer's Digest*, 1989).

Shapiro, Mark. "An Interview with Ray Bradbury." *Los Angeles Free Press*, September 15, 1972.

Shreffler, Philip A. "Follow Your Wildest Dreams." *St Louis Post-Dispatch*, December 7, 1976.

Soucek, Carol. "The Truth in Fantasy." *Los Angeles Herald-Examiner*, March 10, 1974.

Spring, Mike. "L C Interviews Ray Bradbury." Parts 1 and 2. *Literary Cavalcade*, March 1980; November 1980.

Tibbetts, John. "The Martian Chronicler Reflects." *Christian Science Monitor*, March 20, 1991.

Unger, Arthur. "Ray Bradbury: The Science of Science Fiction." *Christian Science Monitor*, November 25, 1980.

Warfield, Polly. "Ray Bradbury: The Martians Are Here." *Los Angeles Free Press*, February 16, 1978.

Unpublished Interviews with Bradbury

Albright, Donn, interviewer. The *Dark Carnival* interview, Los Angeles, March 2001.

———, interviewer. Story origins interviews, Los Angeles, October 2001 and March 2002.

Congdon, Don, interviewer. "I Have All the Answers, Now What Are the Questions?" (An exchange between Bradbury and his agent, Don Congdon.) June 1970. Corrected, 1998 (Albright Collection).

Cunningham, Craig, interviewer. Los Angeles, January 12–April 11, 1961. UCLA Oral History Program Transcript.

Eller, Jonathan R., interviewer. Palm Springs, October 12, 1998; Los Angeles, March 11–12, 2002; Palm Springs, March 14, 2002; Los Angeles, October 21–25, 2002.

Secondary Works

Books

Aldiss, Brian. *Trillion Year Spree: The True History of Science Fiction.* New York: Avon, 1986.

Attebery, Brian. *The Fantasy Tradition in American Literature, from Irving to LeGuin.* Bloomington: Indiana Univ. Press, 1980.

Bloom, Harold, ed. *Ray Bradbury.* Modern Critical Views. Philadelphia, Pa.: Chelsea House, 2001.

———, ed. *Ray Bradbury's* Fahrenheit 451. Modern Critical Interpretations. Philadelphia, Penn.: Chelsea House, 2001.

Borges, Jorge Luis. *Selected Non-Fictions.* Ed. Eliot Weinberger. New York: Viking, 1999.

Büssing, Sabine. *Aliens in the Home: The Child in Horror Fiction.* Westport, Conn.: Greenwood, 1987.

Clareson, Tom. *Understanding Contemporary American Science Fiction: The Formative Period, 1926–1970.* Columbia: Univ. of South Carolina Press, 1992.

Cochran, David. *American Noir: Underground Writers and Filmmakers of the Postwar Era.* Washington, D.C.: Smithsonian Institution Press, 2000.

Ellison, Harlan, ed. *Again, Dangerous Visions.* Vol. 1. New York: Signet, 1972.

Indick, Ben. *Ray Bradbury, Dramatist.* Essays on Fantastic Literature, Number Three. San Bernardino, Calif.: Borgo, 1992.

Johnson, Wayne L. *Ray Bradbury.* New York: Ungar, 1980.

Ketterer, David. *New Worlds for Old: The Apocalyptic Imagination, Science Fiction, and American Literature.* Bloomington: Indiana Univ. Press, 1974.

King, Stephen. *Danse Macabre.* New York: Everest House, 1981.

de Koster, Katie, ed. *Readings on Fahrenheit 451.* San Diego: Greenhaven, 2000.

Mengling, Marvin E. *Red Planet, Flaming Phoenix, Green Town: Some Early Bradbury Revisited.* Bloomington, Ind.: First Books Library, 2002.

Mogen, David. *Ray Bradbury.* Twayne U.S. Authors Series. Boston: G. K. Hall, 1986.

Nolan, William F. *The Ray Bradbury Companion.* Detroit: Gale, 1975.

———, ed. *Ray Bradbury Review.*

———, comp. *The Ray Bradbury Index.* San Diego: Nolan, 1954.

Nolan, William F., and Martin H. Greenberg, eds. *The Bradbury Chronicles.* New York: Roc, 1991.

Olander, Joseph D., and Martin Harry Greenberg, eds. *Ray Bradbury.* Writers of the Twenty-First Century Series. New York: Taplinger, 1980.

Reid, Robin. *Ray Bradbury.* Westport, Conn.: Greenwood, 2000.

Scholes, Robert, and Eric S. Rabkin. *Science Fiction: History, Science, Vision.* Oxford: Oxford Univ. Press, 1977.

Slusser, George Edgar. *The Bradbury Chronicles.* San Bernardino, Calif.: Borgo, 1977.

Touponce, William F. *Ray Bradbury and the Poetics of Reverie: Fantasy, Science Fiction, and the*

Reader. Ann Arbor: UMI Research Press, 1984. (Rev. 2d ed., vol. 32, I. O. Evans Studies [San Bernardino, Calif.: Borgo, 1998].)

———. *Ray Bradbury*. Starmont Reader's Guide 31. Mercer Island, Wash.: Starmont, 1989.

Weist, Jerry. *Bradbury: An Illustrated Life*. New York: William Morrow, 2002.

Articles

Anderson, Nelson. "The Next Generation." *Detour*, March 1996.

Anonymous. "Ray Bradbury: The Master of Science Fiction." *Rancho Magazine*, February 12, 1992.

Arana-Ward, Marie. "Ray Bradbury." *Book World (Washington Post)*, September 11, 1994.

Ash, Lee. "WLB Biography: Ray Bradbury." *Wilson Library Bulletin* (November 1964).

Bennett, Rod, and Brad Linaweaver. "I Sing the Image Electric!: Bradbury on Video." *Wonder* 8 (Ray Bradbury issue), April 1994.

Bloom, Harold, ed. "Ray Bradbury." In *Modern Fantasy Writers*. Philadelphia, Pa.: Chelsea House, 1995.

———, ed. "Ray Bradbury." In *Science Fiction Writers of the Golden Age*. Philadelphia, Pa.: Chelsea House, 1995.

Burleson, Donald R. "Connings: Bradbury/Oates." *Studies in Weird Fiction*, 11 (Spring 1992).

Carrouges, Michel. "Ray Bradbury, les martiens, et nous." *Monde Nouveau* 79 (May 1954).

Clarke, Arthur C. "About Ray Bradbury." *Science Fiction News* (U.K.), March–April 1953.

Conlon, Christopher. "Introduction." In *California Sorcery*, edited by William F. Nolan and William Schafer (Los Angeles: Cemetery Dance, 1999; New York: Ace, 2001).

D'Ammassa, Don. "Explore the Red Planet Mars with Tour Guide Ray Bradbury." *Science Fiction Age*, March 1996.

Daniel, Mark. "Ray Bradbury, The Master of Fantastic Fiction." *Upland Magazine*, February 1992.

Davis, Douglas M. "The Writers Who Revived America's Own Literary Form, the Short Story." *National Observer*, March 23, 1964.

Deutsch, Michel. "Ray Bradbury et la poésie du futur." *Critique*, 22 (July 1957).

Dimeo, Steve. "Man and Apollo: Religion in Bradbury's Science Fantasies." In *Ray Bradbury*, edited by Joseph D. Olander and Martin Harry Greenberg.

Diskin, Lahna. "Bradbury on Children." In *Ray Bradbury*, edited by Joseph D. Olander and Martin Harry Greenberg. Reprinted in *Ray Bradbury*, edited by Harold Bloom.

Dobzynski, Charles. "Ray Bradbury, fabuliste de notre temps." *Europe*, 139–40 (July–August 1957).

Forrester, Kent. "The Dangers of Being Earnest: Ray Bradbury and *The Martian Chronicles*." *Journal of General Education* (Spring 1976).

French, Braddon. "Lost at Sea." In *The Classic American Novel and the Movies*, edited by Gerald Peary and Roger Shatzkin (New York: Frederick Ungar, 1977).

Galbraith, Stuart, IV. "It Came from Outer Space." *Filmfax*, May–June 1995.

Gallagher, Edward J. "The Thematic Structure of *The Martian Chronicles*." In *Ray Bradbury*, edited by Joseph D. Olander and Martin Harry Greenberg.

Grimsley, Juliette. "'The Martian Chronicles': A Provocative Study." *English Journal* (December 1970).

Grobel, Larry. "Ray Bradbury: A Man for All Centuries." *Easy Living* (Winter 1976).

Guffey, George R. "The Unconscious, Fantasy, and Science Fiction: Transformations in Bradbury's *Martian Chronicles* and Lem's *Solaris*." In *Bridges to Fantasy*. Carbondale: Southern Illinois Univ. Press, 1982.

Hamblen, Charles F. "Bradbury's 'Fahrenheit 451' in the Classroom." *English Journal* (September 1968).

Hienger, Jörg. "The Uncanny and Science Fiction," translated by Elsa Schieder. *Science-Fiction Studies* 6.2 (July 1979).

Hoskinson, Kevin. "*The Martian Chronicles* and *Fahrenheit 451:* Ray Bradbury's Cold War Novels." *Extrapolation* 36:4 (Winter 1995). Reprinted as "Ray Bradbury's Cold War Novels" in *Ray Bradbury*, edited by Harold Bloom.

Huntington, John. "Utopian and Anti-Utopian Logic: H. G. Wells and his Successors." *Science-Fiction Studies*, 27, pt. 2 (July 1982).

Jancovich, Mark. "Fantasies of Mass Culture: The Fiction of Ray Bradbury." *Rational Freaks.* New York: Manchester Univ. Press, 1996.

Johnson, Wayne L. "The Invasion Stories of Ray Bradbury." *Critical Encounters: Writers and Themes in Science Fiction.* New York: Ungar, 1978. Reprinted in *Ray Bradbury*, edited by Harold Bloom.

Kagle, Steven E. "Homage to Melville: Ray Bradbury and the Nineteenth Century American Romance." In *Celebrations of the Fantastic*, edited by Donald E. Morse, Marshall B. Tymn, and Csilla Bertha (Detroit: Greenwood, [1992]).

Karolides, Nicholas; Margaret Bald; and Dawn B. Sova. *"Fahrenheit 451." 100 Banned Books: Censorship Histories of World Literature.* New York: Checkmarks, 1999.

Kirk, Russell. "The World of Ray Bradbury." In *Enemies of Permanent Things.* New Rochelle, N.Y.: Arlington House, 1969.

Knight, Damon. "When I Was in Kneepants: Ray Bradbury." *In Search of Wonder: Essays on Modern Science Fiction.* Chicago: Advent, 1956. Reprinted in *Ray Bradbury*, edited by Harold Bloom.

Lem, Stanislaw. "The Time-Travel Story and Related Matters of SF Structuring." *Science-Fiction Studies* 1.3 (Spring 1974).

Linaweaver, Brad. "Ray Bradbury This Way Comes!" *Wonder* 8 (Ray Bradbury Issue) (April 1994).

Logsdon, Loren. "Ray Bradbury's 'Kilimanjaro Device': The Need to Correct Errors of Time." *Midwestern Miscellany* 20 [1992].

McGiveron, Rafeeq O. "Bradbury's *Fahrenheit 451*." *The Explicator* 54:3 (Spring 1996).

———. "Do You Know the Legend of Hercules and Antaeus? The Wilderness in Ray Bradbury's *Fahrenheit 451*." *Extrapolation* 38:2 (Summer 1997).

———. "'To Build a Mirror Factory': The Mirror and Self-Examination of Ray Bradbury's *Fahrenheit 451*." *Critique: Studies in Contemporary Fiction* 39:3 (Spring 1998).

McMahon, Jeff. "Beneath 'Something Wicked.'" *New Times*, October 30–November 8, 1997.

McNelly, Willis E. "Ray Bradbury: Past, Present, and Future." *CEA Critic*, March 1969. Rewritten for *Voices for the Future*, vol. 1, edited by Thomas D. Clareson (Bowling Green, Ohio: Bowling Green State Univ. Popular Press, 1976). Reprinted as "Two Views, Part I," in *Ray Bradbury*, edited by Joseph D. Olander and Martin Harry Greenberg.

———. "Ray Bradbury." In *Science Fiction Writers*, 2d ed., edited by Richard Bleiler, Macmillan Library Reference (New York: Scribners, 1999).

Mengeling, Marvin E. "Ray Bradbury's 'Dandelion Wine': Themes, Sources, and Styles." *English Journal*, October 1971.

———. "The Machineries of Joy and Despair: Bradbury's Attitudes toward Science and Technology." In *Ray Bradbury*, edited by Joseph D. Olander and Martin Harry Greenberg.

Miller, Calvin. "Ray Bradbury: Hope in a Doubtful Age." In *Reality and the Vision*, edited by Philip Yancey (Dallas: Word Publishing, 1990). Reprinted in *The Classics We've Read, the Difference They've Made*, edited by Philip Yancey (New York: McCracken, 1993).

Mogen, David. "Ray Bradbury." In *The Columbia Companion to the Twentieth-Century American Short Story*, edited by Blanche H. Gelfant (New York: Columbia Univ. Press, 2000).

Moskowitz, Sam. "Ray Bradbury." *Seekers of Tomorrow: Masters of Modern Science Fiction.* Cleveland: World, 1966. Originally published as "What Makes Bradbury 'Burn'?" *Amazing Stories,* October 1961.

Nolan, William F. "The Bradbury Years." *Inside,* September 1953.

———. "Ray Bradbury" (profile). *Rogue,* October 1961.

———. "Bradbury: Prose Poet in the Age of Space." *Magazine of Fantasy and Science Fiction,* May 1963.

———. "Ray Bradbury: Space Age Storyteller." In *Sinners and Supermen.* North Hollywood, Calif.: All Star, 1965. Volume reprinted as *Legends and Lovers* (San Bernardino, Calif.: Borgo, 1997). Revision of "Bradbury: Prose Poet in the Age of Space."

———. "Ray Bradbury." In *3 to the Highest Power,* edited by William F. Nolan (New York: Avon, 1968).

——— [as F. E. Edwards]. "Bradbury on Screen." *Venture SF,* August 1969.

———. "Leigh Brackett and Ray Bradbury." In *The Human Equation,* edited by William F. Nolan (Los Angeles: Sherbourne, 1971).

———. "Ray Bradbury: A Biographical Sketch." In Bradbury, *The Martian Chronicles,* spec. ed. (New York: Doubleday, 1973).

———. "Bradbury in the Pulps." *Xenophile* (November 1977).

———. Introduction to Ray Bradbury, *"The Last Circus" and "The Electrocution"* (Northridge, Calif.: Lord John, 1980).

———. "Introduction: A Half-Century of Creativity." In *The Bradbury Chronicles,* edited by William F. Nolan and Martin H. Greenberg (New York: Roc, 1991).

———. "Behind the Illustrations: The Real Ray Bradbury." Special-edition profile for Ray Bradbury, *The Illustrated Man* (Springfield, Penn.: Gauntlet, 1996).

———. "Ray Bradbury: A Space Legend." *Firsts* (June 2001).

———. [untitled headnotes.] Brief introductions to the following Bradbury story reprintings: "Time in Thy Flight," *Gamma* 1 (1963); "Sombra y Sol," *Gamma* 2 (1963); "Payment in Full," in *Man against Tomorrow* (New York: Avon, 1965); "Changeling," in *The Pseudo-People* (Los Angeles: Sherbourne, 1965); "I. Mars," in *A Wilderness of Stars* (Los Angeles: Sherbourne, 1969); "The Blue Bottle," in *A Sea of Space* (New York: Bantam, 1970); "A Careful Man Dies," *Urban Horrors* (Los Angeles: Dark Harvest, 1990); "The Black Ferris," *Outré* (October 1997). Also the original publication headnotes for "The Troll," in *The Bradbury Chronicles* (New York: Tor, 1992) and "Pilgrimmage," in *California Sorcery,* with William Schafer (Los Angeles: Cemetery Dance, 1999).

Pell, Sarah-Warner J. "Style Is the Man: Imagery in Bradbury's Fiction." In *Ray Bradbury,* edited by Joseph D. Olander and Martin Harry Greenberg.

Pfeiffer, John. "Ray Bradbury's Bernard Shaw." In *Shaw and Science Fiction,* vol. 17 of *Shaw: The Annual of Bernard Shaw Studies,* edited by Milton T. Wolf (University Park: Pennsylvania State Univ. Press, 1997).

Pierce, Hazel. "Ray Bradbury and the Gothic Tradition." In *Ray Bradbury,* edited by Joseph D. Olander and Martin Harry Greenberg. Reprinted in *Ray Bradbury,* edited by Harold Bloom.

Platt, Charles. "Ray Bradbury" (profile based on an interview). *Dream Makers: SF&F Writers at Work.* London: Xanadu, 1987.

Rabkin, Eric S. "To Fairyland by Rocket: Bradbury's *The Martian Chronicles.*" In *Ray Bradbury,* edited by Joseph D. Olander and Martin Harry Greenberg.

Reed, Jim. "H. G. Wells and Ray Bradbury: The First and Final Time Travelers." *The H. G. Wells Newsletter,* Spring 1998.

Reilly, Robert. "The Artistry of Ray Bradbury." *Extrapolation* (December 1971).

Ruber, Peter. "Ray Douglas Bradbury." In *Arkham's Masters of Horror,* edited by Peter Ruber (Sauk City, Wis.: Arkham House, 2000).

Schwartz, Julius, and Elliot S. Maggio. "Quoth Bradbury: Thank God for Julie." *Amazing Stories,* September 1993.

Sisario, Peter. "A Study of Allusions in Bradbury's 'Fahrenheit 451.'" *English Journal* (February 1970).

Smiley, Robin H. "Books into Film: *Fahrenheit 451.*" *Firsts* (June 2001).

Steed, David. "The Flight from the Good Life: *Fahrenheit 451* in the Context of Post-War American Dystopias." *The Journal of American Studies* 28:2 (August 1994).

Stupple, A. James. "The Past, The Future, and Ray Bradbury." In *Ray Bradbury,* edited by Joseph D. Olander and Martin Harry Greenberg.

Sullivan, Anita T. "Ray Bradbury and Fantasy." *English Journal* (December 1972).

Teitelbaum, Sheldon. "Ray's World." *Sci-Fi Universe,* February 1996.

Tibbetts, John C. "Ray Bradbury: An Appreciation." *Archon* 20 (October 4–6, 1996).

———. *"Fahrenheit 451."* In John C. Tibbetts and James M. Welsh, *Novels into Film: The Encyclopedia of Movies Adapted from Books* (New York: Checkmark, 1999).

———. *"Something Wicked This Way Comes."* In *Novels into Film.*

Touponce, William F. "The Existential Fabulous: A Reading of Ray Bradbury's 'The Golden Apples of the Sun.'" *Mosaic* 13:3–4 (Spring–Summer 1980). Reprinted in *Ray Bradbury,* edited by Harold Bloom.

———. "Some Aspects of Surrealism in the Work of Ray Bradbury." *Extrapolation* 25.3 (Fall 1984).

———. "Laughter and Freedom in Ray Bradbury's *Something Wicked This Way Comes.*" *Children's Literature Association Quarterly* (Spring 1988).

———. "Ray Bradbury." In *American Writers,* sup. 4, pt. 1, edited by Walton Litz (New York: Scribner's, 1996).

Valis, Noël M. *"The Martian Chronicles* and Jorge Luis Borges." *Extrapolation,* 20:1 (Spring 79).

Wagner, Rob L. "The Compleat Bradbury: When Script Discovered Ray Bradbury's Vision." *Scene (The Daily Bulletin),* April 14, 1993.

Watt, Donald. "Burning Bright: *Fahrenheit 451* as Symbolic Dystopia." In *Ray Bradbury,* edited by Joseph D. Olander and Martin Harry Greenberg.

Wolfe, Gary K. "The Frontier Myth in Ray Bradbury." In *Ray Bradbury,* edited by Joseph D. Olander and Martin Harry Greenberg. Reprinted in *Ray Bradbury,* edited by Harold Bloom.

———. "Ray Bradbury." In *Twentieth-Century American Science-Fiction Writers,* edited by David Cowart and Thomas Wymer (Detroit: Gale Research, 1981).

Wood, Diane S. "Bradbury and Atwood: Exiles as Rational Decision." In *The Literature of Emigration and Exile,* edited by James Whitlark and Wendell Aycock ([Lubbock]: Texas Tech Univ. Press, [1992]).

Bibliographies and Checklists

Albright, Donn. "Ray Bradbury: An Index." *Xenophile* (May 1975; September 1976; November 1977).

———. "Ray Bradbury: A Checklist of Selected First Editions." *Firsts* (June 2001).

Anonymous. "The Essential Bradbury." *Wonder* 8 (Ray Bradbury issue), April 1994.

Eller, Jonathan R. "The Stories of Ray Bradbury: An Annotated Checklist (1938–1991)." *Bulletin of Bibliography* 49 (March 1992).

———. "The Body Eclectic: Sources of Bradbury's *The Martian Chronicles.*" *University of*

Mississippi Studies in English, n.s., 11–12 (1993–95). Includes three bibliographical appendices (A–C).

Nolan, William F. "The Ray Bradbury Index." In *Ray Bradbury Review,* edited by William Nolan.

———. "The Ray Bradbury Index." *Shangri-LA* (Fall–Winter 1953). A supplement to "The Ray Bradbury Index" in *Ray Bradbury Review,* edited by William Nolan.

———. "A Ray Bradbury SF/Fantasy Index." In *3 to the Highest Power,* edited by William F. Nolan.

———. "The Crime/Suspense Fiction of Ray Bradbury: A Listing." *Armchair Detective* (April 1971).

———. "The Books and Short Stories of Ray Bradbury." In *The Martian Chronicles,* by Ray Bradbury. Spec. ed. New York: Doubleday, 1973.

———. "Bibliography of Books by Ray Bradbury." In *The Best from Fantasy and Science Fiction.* New York: Doubleday, 1974.

———. "Ray Bradbury's Textbook Appearances: 1955–1972." *Presenting Moonshine,* August 1974.

———. "Writings about Ray Bradbury." *The Ray Bradbury Companion.* Detroit: Gale, 1975.

———. "The Writings of Ray Bradbury: A Comprehensive Checklist." *The Ray Bradbury Companion.*

———. "Bradbury's First Book Appearances." *Xenophile* (November 1977).

———. "Bradbury's Textbook Appearances, 1955–1972." *Xenophile* (November 1977).

———. "About Ray Bradbury." *Firsts* 11.6 (June 2001).

Smiley, Robin H. "A Ray Bradbury Core Collection." *Firsts* (June 2001).

Tymn, Marshall B. "Ray Bradbury: A Bibliography." In *Ray Bradbury,* edited by Joseph D. Olander and Martin Harry Greenberg.

Welsh, Jim, and Donn Albright. "October's Friend." Unpublished bibliography.

Unpublished Works

Dimeo, Richard Stephen. "The Mind and Fantasies of Ray Bradbury." Ph.D. diss., University of Utah, 1970.

Nolan, William F. "A Descriptive Catalog: The William F. Nolan Collection of Works by and about Ray Bradbury." Bowling Green State University, Bowling Green, Ohio, 1981.

Schroeder, Yvonne. "Register of Manuscripts, Books, and Ephemera: Ray Bradbury." Unpublished finding aid, Collection 471, UCLA Special Collections, July 7, 1960.

Unpublished Secondary Interviews

Ackerman, Forrest J. Interview by Jonathan R. Eller. Los Angeles, March 15, 2002.

Albright, Donn. Interviews by Jonathan R. Eller. Muncie, Ind., June 1995, June 2000.

Hourigan, Kathy. Interview by Jonathan R. Eller. Telephone, May 29, 2001.

Nicholas, Nancy. Interview by Jonathan R. Eller. Telephone, May 22, 2001.

Nolan, William F. Interviews by Jonathan R. Eller. Los Angeles, October 13, 1998; Woodland Hills, Calif., October 15, 1998; Los Angeles, March 13, 2002.

Collateral Readings

Books

Adorno, Theodor W., and Max Horkheimer. *Dialectic of Enlightenment.* Trans. John Cumming. New York: Seabury, 1972.

Allison, David B., ed. *The New Nietzsche: Contemporary Styles of Interpretation.* New York: Delta, 1977.

Bachelard, Gaston. *The Psychoanalysis of Fire.* Trans. Alan C. M. Ross. Boston: Beacon Hill, 1964.

———. *On Poetic Imagination and Reverie.* Trans. and with an introd. Colette Gaudin. New York: Bobbs-Merrill, 1971.

Bakhtin, Mikhail. *The Dialogic Imagination: Four Essays.* Ed. Michael Holquist. Trans. Caryl Emerson and Michael Holquist. Austin: Univ. of Texas Press, 1981.

———. *Problems of Dostoevsky's Poetics.* Ed. and Trans. by Caryl Emerson. Theory and History of Literature, no. 8. Minneapolis: Univ. of Minnesota Press, 1984.

———. *Rabelais and His World.* Trans. Hélène Iswolsky. Bloomington: Indiana Univ. Press, 1984.

———. *Speech Genres and Other Essays.* Trans. Vern W. McGee. Ed. Caryl Emerson and Michael Holquist. Austin: Univ. of Texas Press, 1986.

Barthes, Roland. *S/Z.* Trans. Richard Miller. New York: Hill and Wang, 1974.

Bate, Jonathan, ed. *The Romantics on Shakespeare.* New York: Penguin, 1992.

Bernstein, Michael A. *Bitter Carnival: Ressentiment and the Abject Hero.* Princeton: Princeton Univ. Press, 1992.

Bloom, Allan. *The Closing of the American Mind.* New York: Simon and Schuster, 1987.

Bloom, Harold. *Shakespeare: The Invention of the Human.* New York: Riverhead, 1998.

Brande, Dorothea. *Becoming a Writer.* 1934. Reprint, Los Angeles: J. Tarcher, 1981.

Deleuze, Gilles, and Felix Guattari. *Anti-Oedipus, Capitalism, and Schizophrenia.* Trans. Robert Hurley, Mark Seem, and Helen R. Lane. New York: Viking, 1977.

Derrida, Jacques. *Writing and Difference.* Trans. Alan Bass. Chicago: Univ. of Chicago Press, 1978.

Edmundson, Mark. *Nightmare on Main Street: Angels, Sadomasochism, and the Culture of Gothic.* Cambridge: Harvard Univ. Press, 1997.

Elms, Alan C. *Uncovering Lives: The Uneasy Alliance of Biography and Psychology.* Oxford: Oxford Univ. Press, 1994.

Flem, Lydia. *Casanova, The Man Who Really Loved Women.* Trans. Catherine Temerson. New York: Farrar, Straus, and Giroux, 1997.

Foucault, Michel. *Language, Counter-Memory, Practice.* Ed. Donald F. Bouchard. Trans. Donald F. Bouchard and Sherry Simon. Ithaca, N.Y.: Cornell Univ. Press, 1977.

Freud, Sigmund. *Delusion and Dream and Other Essays.* Ed. Philip Rieff. Boston: Beacon, 1956.

Hauser, Arnold. *The Philosophy of Art History.* New York: Knopf, 1959.

Hyman, Timothy, et al. *Carnivalesque.* London: Hayward Gallery, 2000.

Ingram, Forrest L. *Representative Short Story Cycles of the Twentieth Century, Studies in a Literary Genre* (in French). Paris: Mouton, 1971.

Jakobson, Roman. *Language in Literature.* Cambridge: Harvard Univ. Press, 1987.

Kaufmann, Walter. *Nietzsche, Heidegger, and Buber.* New Brunswick, N.J.: Transaction Publishers, 1992.

Kojève, Alexandre. *Introduction to the Readings of Hegel.* Ed. Allan Bloom. Trans. James H. Nichols Jr. Ithaca, N.Y.: Cornell Univ. Press, 1980.

Kristeva, Julia. *Desire in Language: A Semiotic Approach to Literature and Art.* Ed. Leon Roudiez. New York: Columbia Univ. Press, 1980.

Lacan, Jacques. *Ecrits: A Selection.* Trans. Alan Sheridan. New York: W. W. Norton, 1977.

Lampert, Laurence. *Nietzsche's Teaching: An Interpretation of* Thus Spoke Zarathustra. New Haven: Yale Univ. Press, 1986.

Laplanche, J., and J.-B. Pontalis. *The Language of Psychoanalysis.* Trans. Donald Nicholson-Smith. New York: W. W. Norton, 1973.

Morson, Gary Saul. *Narrative and Freedom: The Shadows of Time.* New Haven: Yale Univ. Press, 1994.

Morson, Gary Saul, and Caryl Emerson. *Mikhail Bakhtin, Creation of a Prosaics.* Stanford, Calif.: Stanford Univ. Press, 1990.

Nietzsche, Friedrich. *Basic Writings of Nietzsche.* Trans. and ed. Walter Kaufmann. New York: Modern Library, 1968.

———. *The Portable Nietzsche.* Trans. and ed. Walter Kaufmann. New York: Viking Penguin, 1968.

———. *The Will to Power.* Ed. Walter Kaufmann. Trans. Walter Kaufmann and R. J. Hollingdale. New York: Vintage, 1968.

———. *Untimely Meditations.* Trans. R. J. Hollingdale. Cambridge: Cambridge Univ. Press, 1983.

Sartre, Jean-Paul. *The Psychology of the Imagination.* Trans. Bernard Frechtman. New York: Washington Square, 1966.

Stam, Robert. *Subversive Pleasures: Bakhtin, Cultural Criticism, and Film.* Baltimore: Johns Hopkins Univ. Press, 1989.

Todorov, Tzvetan. *The Fantastic: A Structural Approach to a Literary Genre.* Trans. Richard Howard. Ithaca: Cornell Univ. Press, 1975.

Twitchell, James B. *Carnival Culture: The Trashing of Taste in America.* New York: Columbia Univ. Press, 1992.

White, Hayden. *Metahistory: The Historical Imagination in Nineteenth Century Europe.* Baltimore: Johns Hopkins Univ. Press, 1973.

Articles

Bloom, Harold. "Wrestling Sigmund." *The Breaking of the Vessels.* Chicago: Univ. of Chicago Press, 1982.

Boucher, Anthony. "The Life of the Author." *Modern Fantasy Writers.* New York: Chelsea House, 1995.

———. "The Publishing of Science Fiction." In *Modern Science Fiction, Its Meaning and Future,* edited by Reginald Bretnor (New York: Coward-McGann, 1953).

Durand, Gilbert. "Psychanalyse de la neige." *Mercure de France* 1:8 (1953).

Hartman, Geoffrey. "Literature High and Low: The Case of the Mystery Story." *The Fate of Reading and Other Essays.* Chicago: Univ. of Chicago Press, 1975.

McGann, Jerome J. "The Socialization of Texts." *Documentary Editing* 12:3 (September 1990).

Nagel, James. "The American Short Story Cycle." *The Columbia Companion to the Twentieth-Century American Short Story.* New York: Columbia Univ. Press, 2000.

Shippey, Tom. "Introduction." *The Oxford Book of Fantasy Stories.* Oxford: Oxford Univ. Press, 1994.

Tomashevsky, Boris. "Thematics." In *Russian Formalist Criticism: Four Essays,* translated by Lee T. Lemon and Marion Reis (Lincoln: Univ. of Nebraska Press, 1965).

Trilling, Lionel. "Art and Fortune." *The Liberal Imagination.* New York: Anchor, 1953.

Williams, W. D. "Nietzsche's Masks." In *Nietzsche: Imagery and Thought,* edited by Malcom Pasley (Berkeley: Univ. of California Press, 1978).

Index

Nietzsche, Friedrich, 145–46, 152, 194–95, 294, 302, 307, 343, 518n21; RB's affinities with, 14, 16, 38; differences from, 39; use of, 176

nihilism: cycles of, 41; description, 14; in *Fahrenheit 451*, 186, 189–93, 413; in *The Martian Chronicles*, 144, 146, 153; and Nietzsche, 20, 189–93; problems of, 23; RB's use of 27, 41–43, 144, 167, 387; and Shakespeare, 411

Nolan, William F. (author), 49, 157, 383; biography on Dashiell Hammett, 318–20; Bradbury archive, 167; ideas about fantasy genre, 284; introduction to The Martian Chronicles, 131; *Ray Bradbury Review*, 49, 91, 365–66, RB's influence on, 256–67; reviews, 323

Norton, Alden, 312, 313, 316, 317, 318

Phantom of the Opera, The (1925 silent), 11, 24, 326, 404

Playboy, 180, 382

Poe, Edgar A., 36, 150–51, 312, 343, 406–7

Popular Publications, 311, 313, 316, 317

Prescott, Orville, 2, 180, 283–84, 539n29

Rabelais, Francois, 106, 241, 313

Ray Bradbury Companion, 385, 386

Ray Bradbury Review (Nolan), 49, 91, 365, 366

Ray Bradbury Theater (teleplays), 51, 324–25, 329, 387

Reed, Sir Carol, 236, 264, 374

reverie, literary, 421–22; in Dandelion Wine, 248–49; definition, 8; and the deformation of images, 155; in *Fahrenheit 451*, 180, 194–97, 203, 205, 207; in "Interim," 92–93; in "The Lake," 94–98; in *Something Wicked*, 297; and wine and drinking, 232

Sartre, Jean-Paul, 344–45

Saturday Evening Post, 236, 283, 373, 381

Schwartz, Julius, 47, 59, 209, 311–13, 316–8, 541n3

scene of instruction, 341

scene of suffering (detective fiction), 322, 333–34, 339, 340, 349

Science Fiction Book Club: British, 126, 130; American, 130, 372, 527n30

Science Fiction WorldCon (1939), 53, 311

Seldes, Tim, 266, 267, 268, 375

Shakespeare, William, 38, 247, 287–88, 346–47, 405, 430

Shaw, George Bernard, 425–26

Shippey, Tom, 40

Simon and Shuster (publisher), 62, 269, 389; collections of RB's, 379, 381–82; negotiations with RB, 286; publisher to RB, 181, 256, 281–83, 288, 291; RB's move to, 48, 130, 240, 375–76

Smith, Thorne, 312–13, 318

Stebel, Sid, 49, 323, 324, 328, 329

Steinbeck, John, 131, 528n32

thematics, definition of, 5

themes: religious, 6, 18, 21, 38, 178, 198–99, 201–2, 206–7, 248, 294, 298, 304–6, 348, 350, 353, 364–65, 383, 415, 519n31, 543n40; Byronic hero, 147; dandelion wine (as restorative), 232, 248–50; death of the author, 40, 42, 84, 321, 347; desiring machines, 152, 230, 232, 246–47, 404, 536n43; horror and weird (Freudian) reversal, 90, 98; jokes, 93, 157, 151–52, 162, 166, 254–55, 305, 308, 341–42; meaning of the earth, 42, 92, 178, 180, 186–87, 196–97, 201–5, 249, 254, 302, 403, 404, 407, 413, 521n59; 532n23, 532n34; mirror maze, 3–4, 102–3, 273, 294, 303, 307, 355; Oedipus complex, 33, 34, 334; phallus, 254–55; pregnant death, 92–93, 305, 430; *ressentiment* (resentment/revenge), 148, 150–51, 153, 159, 195, 253, 302, 345, 401, 404; revaluation of values, 10, 14, 145, 186–87, 195, 201, 203, 206, 250, 284, 293, 298, 305, 306; science fictional, 1, 412

Tilden, Mike, 311–13

Todorov, Tzvetan, 5, 100, 295, 406

Tomashevsky, Boris, 5

Truffaut, Francois, 48, 181, 389

Trilling, Lionel, 49, 50

Twain, Mark (Samuel Clemens), 215, 229, 237, 272, 344

Twilight Zone, The, 270, 325, 383

Verne, Jules, 22, 36

Weird Tales, 44, 53–55, 61, 259, 310, 311, 313, 317, 398

William Morrow (publisher), 49, 107, 240, 398

Yeats, William Butler, 367, 369